VAN GOGH: A Self-Portrait

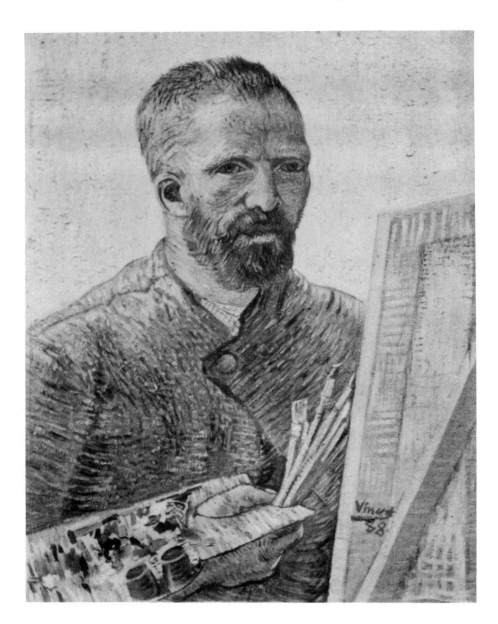

Portrait of the Artist at his Easel, oil, 1888.

VAN GOGH
A Self-Portrait

Letters revealing his life

as a painter, selected by

W. H. AUDEN

Marlowe & Company
NEW YORK

First paperback edition, 1994

Published in the United States by
Marlowe & Company
632 Broadway, Seventh Floor
New York, New York 10012

Distributed to the trade by Publishers Group West.

Manufactured in the United States of America

ISBN 1-56924-862-1

FOREWORD

In most cases, to go through a man's correspondence and make the proper selection for publication would be easy. One would merely have to pick out the few letters which were interesting and discard the many which were dull or unintelligible to the general reader without elaborate editorial notes. But there is scarcely one letter by Van Gogh which I, who am certainly no expert, do not find fascinating. Anyone who can afford them will want to possess and ought to buy the magnificent three volumes edited by Vincent W. van Gogh.

"What," I asked myself, "is the single most important fact about Van Gogh?" To that there seemed only one answer – "That he painted pictures."

I have, therefore, confined my selection to those of his letters which contain reflections upon the art of painting and the problems of being a painter, and have only included letters concerned with his personal relations, to his father and his brother, for example, in so far as these throw direct light upon his career as a painter.

Van Gogh was such an extraordinary character, however, that I have also generously selected from the descriptions given of him by acquaintances at various times in his life, which are printed in the complete edition.

W. H. AUDEN

GENEALOGICAL NOTES

The family name van Gogh occurs as early as the fifteenth century, in connection with religious institutions in The Netherlands. The earliest ancestor who can be traced directly to Vincent the painter was also called Vincent van Gogh. He was born in September, 1674, at The Hague; he was a Protestant and his godfather bore the same name.

From father to son the family went as follows:

Vincent van Gogh	1674–1746
David van Gogh	1697– ?
Jan van Gogh	1722–1796
Johannes van Gogh	1763–1840
Vincent van Gogh	1789–1874
Theodorus van Gogh	1822–1885
Vincent van Gogh	1853–1890

Up to the painter's grandfather, these forefathers were tradespeople and citizens of The Hague. They all married in their own circle; one of the wives came from Belgium.

Jan van Gogh (1722–1796) had a brother Vincent (1720–1802), who was childless. He had acquired some wealth, which Vincent, the painter's grandfather, inherited and used to study theology at the University of Leiden and to become a clergyman. He married Elisabeth Huberto Vrijdag, whose grandfather had come from Switzerland; her family belonged to the same class as the Van Goghs.

This couple had eleven children, of whom Theodorus (1822–1885), the painter's father, was the eldest. He studied theology at the University of Utrecht and became a clergyman at Zundert (in the province of North Brabant, near the Belgian border) where Vincent and Theo were born. Their mother was Anna Cornelia Carbentus (1819–1905). Her family name seems to indicate a French origin (Charpentier), but in 1672 her direct forefather already lived in The Netherlands. Her family were also townspeople, and since the beginning of the eighteenth century they had lived in The Hague.

INTRODUCTION

On March 30, 1852, a son was born in the rectory at Zundert; he lived only a few weeks. A year later, on the same date, a healthy son was born who received the names of his two grandfathers, Vincent Willem. Two years later a daughter was born, and on May 7, 1859, another son, Theodorus, named after his father; he was to play a great role in Vincent's life. These children were followed by two more daughters and another son. In later years the youngest sister was the only one with whom Vincent corresponded.[1]

The grave of the little brother who was born a year before Vincent is situated near the chapel where his father preached. Even in his earliest childhood Vincent had seen it often, and this may have caused an unconscious inner guilt. This may have been partly relieved by the coming of another brother (Theo), who was there as long as Vincent could consciously remember. Most likely this constitutes a basic factor in the two brothers' lifelong friendship and their mutual support.

Zundert was a village in the middle of a poor country worked by small farmers who were predominantly Roman Catholic. For a short while Vincent was enrolled in the public school, but as his parents thought he had become too rough through his contact with the boys, they took him home and engaged a governess to teach the children.

According to two of his sisters, the children loved the country life, in which they were isolated among their own little group. Contrary to older opinions, *recent* investigations have brought out the fact that Vincent started drawing early. Four sketches of 1862 (when he was nine years old) have been preserved;[2] two of them are from nature, the others, copies. Some known landscapes date from 1863 to 1873; in them his great power of observation is already apparent.

When he was twelve years old, he was sent to a small private boarding school at Zevenbergen, a town some fifteen miles away from Zundert. According to the principal, who was interviewed around 1930, there was nothing special about the boy, as he did not remember him. Vincent himself wrote later on in a letter to Theo that he learned very little there. After that he seems to have been at another boarding school at Tilburg (a larger town), but nothing is known of that period.

At Goupil's

Vincent's paternal grandfather (also named Vincent) was a clergyman in the town of Breda, where he was also attached to the Military Academy. He had eleven children, the oldest of whom was Theodorus, Vincent and Theo's father. One son entered the navy and eventually became a rear admiral, then the highest rank

[1] Vincent's letters to his youngest sister Willemien (Will) are published in THE COMPLETE LETTERS OF VINCENT VAN GOGH, an English translation published in 1958 by New York Graphic Society, Greenwich, Connecticut, 3 vols., with 200 facsimile reproductions of sketches in the letters.

[2] See "The beginnings of Vincent's art," by Professor J. G. van Gelder, Utrecht, in the DETAILED CATALOGUE WITH FULL DOCUMENTATION OF 272 WORKS BY VINCENT VAN GOGH, BELONGING TO THE STATE MUSEUM KROLLER-MULLER (at Otterlo, The Netherlands), published in English, July, 1960, illustrated.

(Vincent later lived for a while at his house in Amsterdam). Another son became a civil servant. Two of the daughters married high-ranking military men; three remained unmarried. But for Vincent and Theo, the most important fact was that three of their uncles (Cornelius, Hendrik, and Vincent) chose the art-dealing business as their profession.

College education being rather rare in those days, these uncles made their own way. Uncle Vincent started as an apprentice in a paint store in The Hague, which he later transformed into an establishment dealing in paintings. He then became affiliated with the Goupil firm of Paris. With the social changes in the first half of the nineteenth century, the nobility were no longer the only ones who were interested in paintings. Among the new commercial and industrial classes, some very rich people became buyers. Furthermore, there was a growing demand for reproductions. As photography was still unknown, the procedure was to make a drawing on stone after an oil painting or a woodcut, and print therefrom. The demand for these reproductions became international. Goupil's of Paris was a leader in this field, and it was also among the great dealers in paintings. It had branches in Brussels, Berlin, London, The Hague, and New York.[3]

Uncle Vincent married a sister of the painter's mother. He became very rich, and after retiring from business, lived on an estate at Prinsenhage (near Breda), not far from Zundert. Hence a rather close contact developed with his namesake, who, at sixteen, became an apprentice at Goupil's in The Hague (July 30, 1869). Uncle Hendrik (Hein) was then head of Goupil's at Brussels, where Theo went in January, 1873, when he was fifteen years old. Uncle Cornelius established himself independently at Amsterdam, where Vincent later visited him frequently.

In 1873 Vincent was transferred to Goupil's in London, which jobbed reproductions only, and no paintings. Then the difficulties began. So far he had enjoyed life like any young man who enters the world and has an interesting job and few cares. He was attracted by all the new things he saw and got pleasure from the feeling of learning and of developing himself. The people for whom he worked were satisfied with him, and much later he himself mentioned in a letter that up to that time he was a good salesman.

In London he fell in love with the daughter of his landlady, a clergyman's widow, but the girl refused him. Thereupon he left his boardinghouse and went to live in furnished rooms; he kept his own council more and more, lost his joy of life, and became more and more religious. At his parents' request his uncle got him transferred to Paris for a short while (from October to December, 1874), a gesture which made him angry. In May, 1875, he went to Paris permanently. He felt displaced, and when not at work, he stayed in his room, reading the Bible. At Christmastime, the busiest season, he went home for a holiday; after his return this led to his dismissal as of April 1, 1876. It should be noted that during his association with Goupil Vincent saw many paintings, which he absorbed in minute detail. He read a lot and learned English and French to perfection.

---

[3] For the American activities of the Goupil firm see the Columbia Historical Portrait of New York, p. 197; the Goupils were active in founding the American Art Union.

Vincent liked England and returned there in April, 1876, as a teacher in a boarding school in Ramsgate; the establishment was soon moved to Isleworth, near London. He received board and lodging only, no salary, so that he soon accepted a position at another boarding school in the same locality. His religious zeal continued. At the end of the year, seeing no possibility for advancement, he gave up England altogether. His uncle Vincent helped him find employment in a bookstore in Dordrecht. However, he had no interest whatsoever in the work, and finally formulated his wish to devote himself to religion by becoming a minister of the gospel, like his father. That required studying for the university's entrance examination, but his family helped him. He lived with the uncle who was then commander of the naval establishment at Amsterdam. His uncle Stricker, a clergyman married to one of his mother's sisters, found him a good teacher of Latin and Greek, and he could go on seeing paintings at his uncle Cornelius' art gallery.

It was not much use, though Vincent studied the classical languages for over a year. He would punish himself for not advancing sufficiently, for example, by sleeping on the floor, but soon he began to realize that it was not the study of grammar he was after, but doing something beneficial for other people. He gave up his studies and, soon after, discovered a chance of getting to the colliery district in the south of Belgium, the Borinage, as an evangelist. The requirement would be a three-month course at a missionary school in Brussels where one had to pay for board and lodging only. Though he was the most intelligent of the very few pupils, his behavior did not quite fit in; furthermore, he had difficulty speaking in public from memory. At the end of the course he failed to get the coveted appointment.

He then went to the Borinage on his own, giving Bible lessons, visiting the sick, and, in the evenings, teaching the children of the house where he boarded. When the evangelical committee met again in January, he received a six-month trial appointment. He devoted himself thoroughly to the work, but, as before, he exaggerated enormously. He gave away his own clothes and his bed to others whom he thought needed them more and lived in a shack, sleeping on the floor. His superiors considered him overzealous and warned him about his activities. When his contract expired, it was not renewed. During this time there was a great accident in one of the mines, and it made an enormous impression on him.

The first years as a draftsman

Vincent stayed on in the Borinage the whole winter 1879–1880, without any fixed employment, and living on the little his parents and Theo could provide him. Then, in the summer, he realized that he could not do anything for others any more. He compared himself with a bird in a cage, living without care, like a gentleman at large (a queer kind at that!); to get to freedom he had to change his plumes. And then he started to draw anew—the beginning of his becoming a professional—with Theo helping him financially. Having found a permanent occupation which liberated his spirit, he grew constantly, despite his difficulties.

During the next winter he lived in Brussels, where he became acquainted with the Dutch painter Van Rappard, a friendship which lasted five years.[4] He worked hard, but the expenses were too high and he wanted to leave and get into the country once more. Therefore, he moved to his parents' at Etten, where he stayed for eight months. During the summer he fell in love with his cousin, a young widow with a baby son who had come for a short visit with his parents. She didn't want him, and that was another blow. He reproached his parents for not having helped him in this matter, became increasingly nervous, and finally left for The Hague at the end of 1881.

The stay in this city marks the first great period of Vincent's work; there he made a number of magnificent drawings and his first paintings. As before, his relations helped him. After he had left Goupil, his uncles had helped him in Amsterdam; in the Borinage his father had stood behind him; in The Hague his cousin Anton Mauve and other painters took an interest in him, as well as H. C. Tersteeg, then head of the Goupil firm. But, as always, Vincent's friendships (with the exception of the one with Theo) soon came to an end, as he was too critically outspoken.

The gulf between Vincent and those who meant him well widened when Vincent began to live with a woman he had picked up in the street. She already had one child and was soon to have another. Theo was the only one who continued to support him; his father was not in a position to do more than give some clothes. Vincent worked hard and made beautiful drawings, but the household deteriorated and soon became unbearable; the illusion of having a home and family of his own could not last.

First years as a painter

In November, 1883, the household was broken up and Vincent left for the province of Drenthe (in the northeastern Netherlands), a sparsely populated region where peat digging was the only occupation. The poverty and bleakness appealed to Vincent, and he made a lot of sketches and some small paintings. However, when the winter came, with its early darkness, he felt very forlorn and did what many people have done in similar circumstances: he returned to his parental home.

His father was now a clergyman at Nuenen (in the eastern part of the province of North Brabant), a village as small as those where he had lived before. Vincent's stay at the parsonage was not a pleasant arrangement for any of the parties concerned. His not being understood and his work not being appreciated was a great hardship for Vincent. On the other side, the presence of an unsocial intruder (which was what the inmates considered him) created a strain. Very little remained of the old admiration for his father. His bond with the spiritual world of his mother was as slight as ever, though he cared for her with great devotion when

4 Vincent's letters to Van Rappard are also published in the COMPLETE LETTERS OF VINCENT VAN GOGH (see note 1).

she broke her leg and was in bed for a few months. Next door to his parents lived the only woman who ever cared for Vincent; she was older than he; through the influence of the families nothing came of this attachment.

In Nuenen Vincent became a full-fledged painter. He made a great number of portraits of farm laborers and peasant women, but also scenes on the land, still lifes, etc. His large drawings of people at work rank among his most celebrated ones. The paintings were all very dark, though he experimented with color from the beginning. Their texture is already the same as that of the later colorful pictures. His work's peak at Nuenen is the splendid canvas "The Potato Eaters," which shows the result of his efforts in portrait painting. He made it shortly after the sudden death of his father, which made a great impression on him; it meant also that once more his home was broken up.

With Theo helping financially, Vincent moved to Antwerp to become a pupil at the Academy. Notwithstanding the large series of paintings which he had made with so great an effort, he wanted to learn from others and to work after models, which he could seldom pay for himself. The professor in drawing considered his work inadequate and had him put back into the preparatory class! Vincent carried on, however, and also joined drawing clubs with his comrades so he could work evenings. After so much of the rather dull country life, he enjoyed the big city. Of great importance to him was the museum, where he studied especially the works of Peter Paul Rubens, the great Flemish painter of the seventeenth century. From him he learned how to paint brighter colored faces; this was the beginning of the lightening of his whole palette.

Vincent spent most of the money Theo sent him on models and paint, neglecting his food completely. Together with the hard work, this brought him to exhaustion and longing for another change.

Experimenting at Paris

One morning a small note was brought to Theo in the Goupil gallery on the Boulevard Montmartre, where he was in charge; it was written by Vincent, and said that he was waiting for Theo in the *salon carré* of the Louvre museum. Vincent then went to live with Theo in his apartment on the Rue Laval; because he needed a studio, they moved after a couple of months to the Rue Lepic, also on the Montmartre hill. Vincent started work in Cormon's studio, where he met Toulouse-Lautrec, Emile Bernard, and others. Theo had been one of the advocates of the impressionists in his gallery, and Vincent was influenced by them. The work of these painters was a revelation to him. He made a number of experiments, and his palette became lighter, but he did not follow their technical methods of representation. He considered that they depicted the superficial aspect of things only, and he wanted to do more. Having found his own way, his paintings at the end of his stay in Paris are almost as full in color and expression as the famous ones done in the South.

Vincent stayed in Paris for two years; then the strain of city life became too much for him and he longed again for the country. For Theo it was a difficult time because of Vincent's endless discussions, which few of his friends could bear. Theo was at that time very close to Andries Bonger, who was his age and was employed commercially; he later married the latter's sister Johanna.

The glorious South

In February, 1888, Vincent moved to Arles, in the South of France, on the Rhone River. When he arrived, the orchards were just in bloom, an engaging sight anywhere, and especially for someone from the big city. He painted them eleven times. When the summer advanced, he was struck by the bright sunshine and the glowing colors. He worked extremely hard, in the full sun and in the wind. In Paris he had already influenced those around him; here in the South, with no painters or other direct influences from the past, even Theo, his creativity was stimulated to the utmost. His friends were mostly plain people, and therefore violent discussions on artistic matters did not occur. In the subjects he painted, reminiscences from Holland often come to the fore (roads in the landscape, the bridges, etc.). The same subjects recur throughout his paintings. During the hot months he produced some of his best-known works: "The Sunflowers," "The Yellow House," "The Harvest," "The Drawbridge," "The Boats on the Beach," etc., the last of which was painted at nearby Saintes-Maries de la Mer.

Theo continued to send him an allowance as well as colors and canvas; Vincent spent most of his money on paint and brushes and completely neglected his bodily needs. He was very proud of having a little abode of his own and dreamed of establishing a co-operative society of painters for mutual artistic and material support. With Theo's help, the first and last one to try the experiment was Paul Gauguin. At that time he was living in Brittany, and he also had financial difficulties. Two months of these powerful characters working under the same roof ended in a quarrel, and Gauguin left immediately after Van Gogh suffered the first of his crises. This happened at the time Theo became engaged to be married. Vincent might have worried about this ending his material support, but Theo did not even consider withdrawing. However, Vincent was overworked and got into difficulties with the neighbors and the authorities because of his alleged queer conduct.

He himself decided it would be wise to be cared for permanently, and he entered the Asylum St. Paul at St. Rémy-en-Provence, not far from Arles. This institution was splendidly located, but its inmates must have made Vincent's life extremely difficult.

Around the time of Theo's marriage, after the announcement of the coming of a baby, and after its birth, Vincent passed through serious crises; however, he recovered each time. He may unconsciously have feared losing his support, but actually there never was any question on this matter. Vincent's creativity continued to grow to the end; only during the crises did the old passivity seem to recur.

In January, 1890, the important French monthly *Mercure de France* published an enthusiastic article on Vincent's work by a well-known art critic, Albert Aurier, who had seen his paintings at Theo's. With the coming of the spring Vincent felt better and longed to leave the depressing asylum. He came to Paris, staying a few days with Theo, who lived with his wife and baby at no. 8 Cité Pigalle. He met some of his old acquaintances, but soon he wanted to be in more quiet surroundings, where he could go on with his painting.

Theo had heard from Camille Pissarro, whose works he handled at Goupil's gallery on the Boulevard Montmartre, about Auvers-sur-Oise, at one time a painters' colony where famous men like Daubigny (of the Barbizon school), Cézanne, and Pissarro himself had worked. A friend of all these men, Dr. Gachet, himself an amateur painter, still lived there, and Vincent was recommended to him. Dr. Gachet was reputed to be familiar with mental healing as practiced in those times, and Pissarro and Theo supposed he could help Vincent if it were necessary. The two men met frequently; Vincent painted his portrait and that of his daughter, as well as some other famous canvases. Though Vincent was most industrious, the number of paintings and drawings that he could make in the ten weeks he lived at Auvers at best falls below the number that current literature ascribes to him.

The physician failed to exert a steadying influence; perhaps it was the opposite. On July 27 Vincent attempted to end his life; he died on the twenty-ninth. Half a year later, on January 21, 1890, Theo also passed away. They rest next to each other in the cemetery of Auvers-sur-Oise.

Vincent W. van Gogh

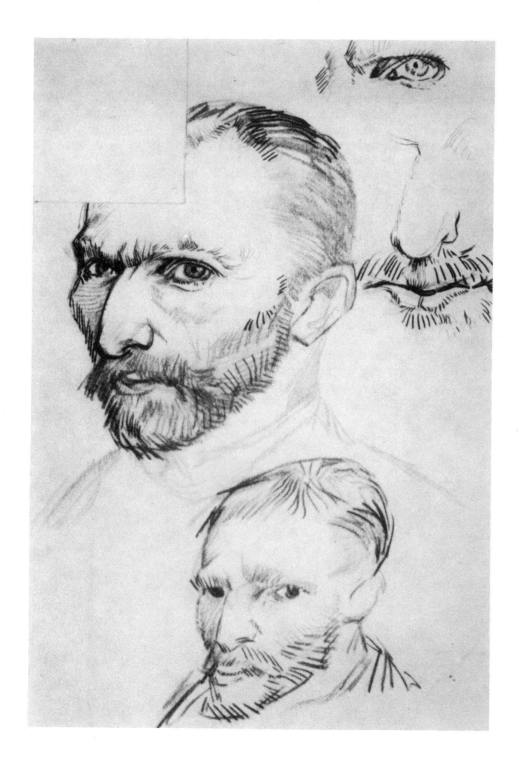

NOTES ON THE ILLUSTRATIONS

Immediately following are twenty-seven representative drawings by Vincent van Gogh, reproduced from both the letters and those in the collection of the Stedelijk Museum in Amsterdam. A number of color plates of his major paintings are scattered throughout the text. The numbered annotations below refer to the drawings:

1. One of Vincent's first attempts, done from a copybook when he was a boy of ten, probably after an illustration in a magazine.

2. View from Vincent's window in the school where he taught at Ramsgate, England. April 21, 1876, (Letter 62.)

3. A saloon in Laeken, a suburb of Brussels, from letter 126, November 15, 1878, in which Vincent writes: "The little drawing 'Au Charbonnage' is not particularly remarkable, but I made it because one sees here so many people who work in the coal mines, and they are a rather distinctive type; it is a small inn which adjoins the big coal shed, and the workmen come to eat their bread and drink their glass of beer during the lunch hour."

4. Drawn in The Hague , June–July 1882. From letter 217, showing one of Sien's children while Vincent was living with her: "What I want to save is Sien's life and that of her two children. I do not want her to fall back into that terrible state of illness and misery in which I found her."

5. One of the very few drawings in the correspondence given a title, *Sorrow*. From The Hague period, October–November 1882. It was a sketch for a lithograph. (Letter 244.)

6. Nuenen, December 1885, probably the parsonage where the elder Van Goghs lived. Drawn shortly after Vincent's return home from Drenthe. His studio was in a shed behind the house. (Letter 344.)

7 and 8. "Scratches of studies of heads—perhaps you would find something in them, perhaps not, I can't help it. I repeat, I know no other way." From letters 393–94, Nuenen, January–February 1885. In drawing these studies of peasant women Vincent was preparing himself for his first great painting, *The Potato Eaters*,

done during this period and of which drawing 9 was a descriptive sketch.

9. Sketch of *The Potato Eaters* from letter 399, April 1885.

10. Nuenen, spring 1885, another of Vincent's deeply sympathetic studies of the peasants of the region, letter 409, of which he writes: "peint avec de la terre."

11. Nuenen, June–July 1885. In letter 425 Vincent writes: "I am now busy painting still lifes of my birds' nests ... I think some people who are good observers of nature might like them because of the colors of the moss, the dry leaves and the grasses."

12. A sketch of one of Vincent's most important still lifes, *The Breakfast Table*, mentioned in letter 489, written in Arles, May 20, 1888.

13 and 14. These two magnificent drawings were both sent to his painter friend, Bernard, from Arles, letter B 6 [6], the second half of June 1888.

15. In letter 554, October 15–20, 1888, to Theo, Vincent begins: "At last I can send you a little sketch to give you at least an idea of the way the work is shaping up. For today I am all right again. My eyes are still tired, but then I have a new idea in my head and here is a sketch of it. ... This time it's just simply my bedroom, only here color is to do everything, and giving by its simplification a grander style to things, it is to be suggestive here of *rest* or of sleep in general. In a word, looking at the picture ought to rest the brain, or rather the imagination. ... It is going to be a contrast to, for instance, the Tarascon diligence and the night café."

16. "This is a sketch of the latest canvas I am working on, another *Sower*. An immense citron-yellow disk for the sun. A green yellow sky with pink clouds. The field violet, the sower and the tree Prussian

blue." So wrote Vincent at the end of October 1888 from Arles, letter 558a.

17. A sketch sent to his sister Wilhelmina, letter W 9 of November 1888, in which he describes the scene as an imaginary garden in which his mother and sister are walking, as in a poem or in a dream.

18. In March 1889 Vincent had seen his friend, the painter Paul Signac (letter 581), to whom he wrote in April, letter 583b, "I have just come back with two studies of orchards. Here is a crude sketch of them."

19. In an unfinished letter (643) to Gauguin, which was found among his papers, written at Auvers-sur-Oise, June 1890, Vincent writes: "I still have a cypress with a star from down there, a last attempt . . . a night sky with a moon without radiance, the slender crescent barely emerging from the opaque shadow cast by the earth . . . one star with an exaggerated brilliance, if you like, a soft brilliance of pink and green in the ultramarine sky, across which some clouds are hurrying. Below, a road bordered with tall yellow canes, behind these the blue *Basses Alpes* [Alpilles], an old inn with yellow lighted windows, and a very tall cypress, very straight, very somber."

The following eight drawings, 20–27, not from the correspondence, are in the large and important collection of Van Gogh material in the Stedelijk Museum.

20. Old man grieving, pencil, 1882, The Hague.

21. Old man with top hat, black crayon and ink, 1882, The Hague.

22. The weaver at his loom, pen heightened with white, 1884, Nuenen.

23. The garden of the parsonage, pen and pencil, 1884, Nuenen.

24. Digging peasant, black crayon, 1885, Nuenen.

25. Peasant woman digging, black crayon, 1885, Nuenen.

26. The fountain in the hospital garden, pen and ink, 1889, St. Rémy.

27. Cottage with cabbage patch and cypresses, black crayon, 1889, St. Rémy.

ACKNOWLEDGMENTS

Van Gogh, A Self-Portrait is a selected condensation by W. H. Auden of The Complete Letters of Vincent van Gogh, published in 1958 by the New York Graphic Society in three volumes, with more than 200 tipped-on, facsimile reproductions of all the drawings and water colors from the correspondence. Any letters referred to above by number, not published in A Self-Portrait, will be found in the three-volume edition of The Complete Letters.

The editors of this one-volume selection wish to express their thanks and appreciation to Vincent W. van Gogh for his constant and devoted help throughout its preparation and particularly for his contribution of the *Introduction* and *Genealogical Notes* on his uncle, the painter. Dr. Jan Hulsker, of the Ministry of Education, Arts and Sciences at The Hague, has earned our special thanks for permitting his recent revisions in the dating of the correspondence to be used throughout. Full credit is hereby given and thanks warmly extended to the Stedelijk Museum in Amsterdam for the use of its printing blocks and the permission to reproduce all the color plates and eight of the drawings that follow and are scattered throughout the text. Finally, New York Graphic Society is also most grateful to W. H. Auden for his thoughtful selection of the material for this book from among some 750 entries of the entire correspondence.

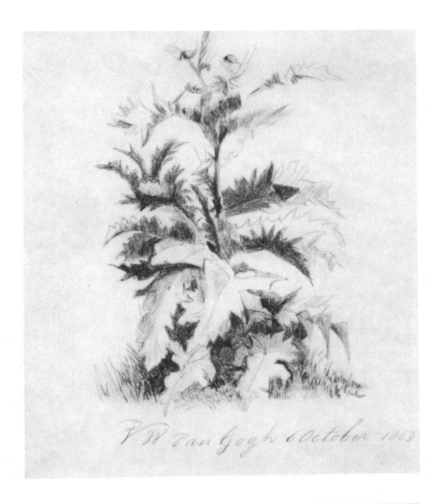

P B van Gogh 6 October 1863

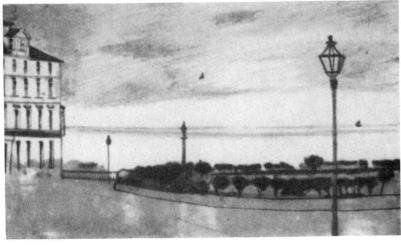

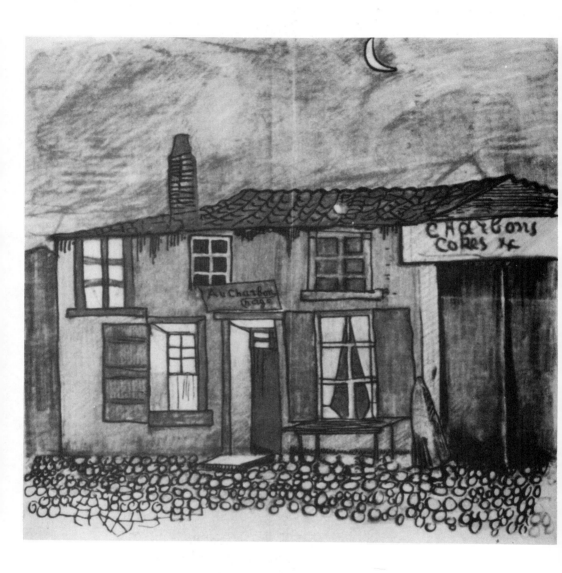

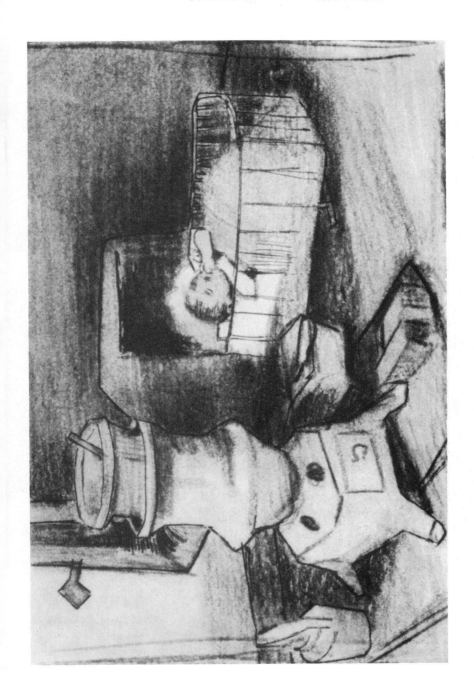

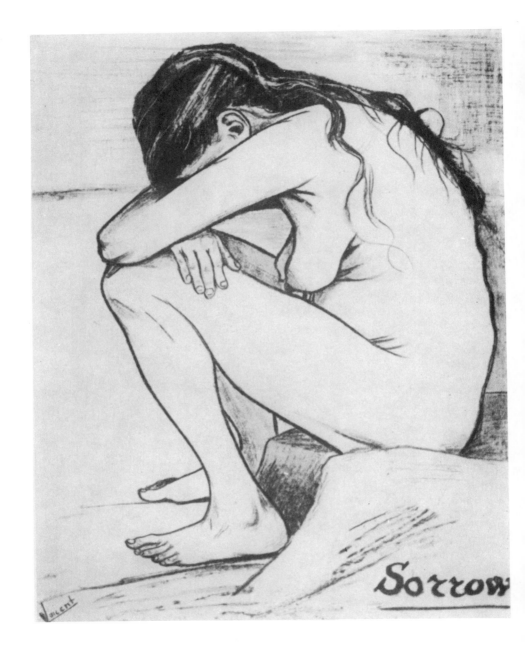

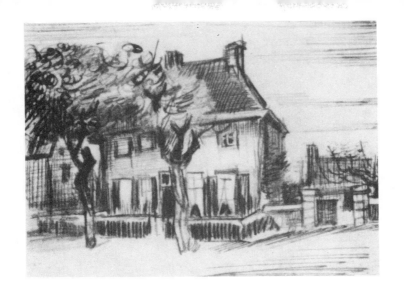

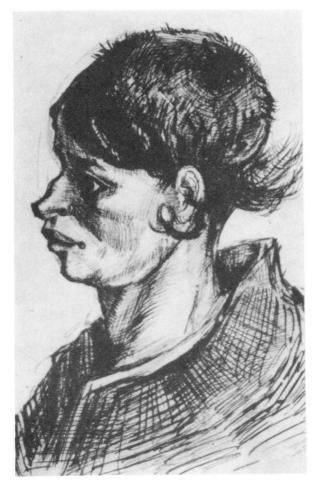

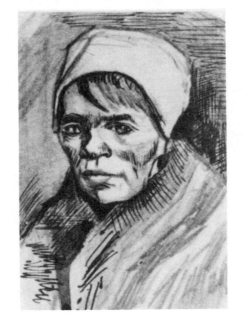

paar studies die ik maakte terwyl ik tevens
bezig ben op nieuw aan die boeren om
een schotel aardappels.
Ik kom er daarnet van thuis — en heb by het
lamplicht nog gewerkt en aan — afschoon
ik het by dag ditmaal heb aangezet.

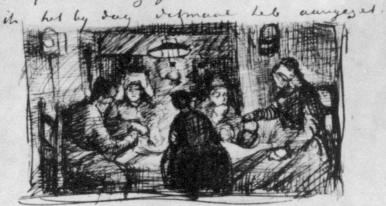

Ziehier hoe de compositie nu geworden is
Ik heb het op een vrij groot doek geschilderd ~~~~
~~~~ en zooals de Schets nu is zit geloof ik er wel
leven in —

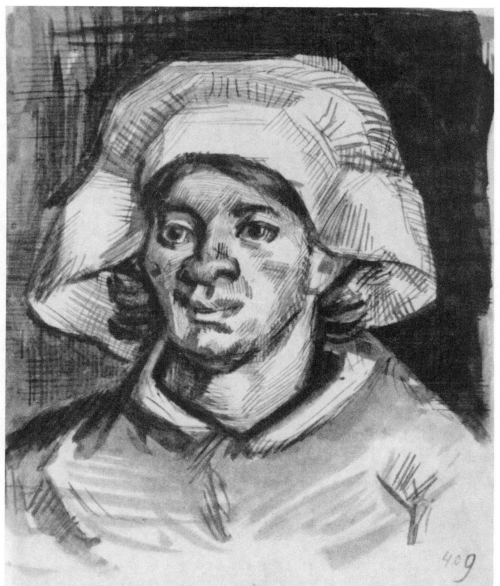

409

Waarde Theo, Zoover heb ik Germinal ontvangen waar
ik onmiddelijk aan begonnen ben. er het er een 50
pagina van gelezen — die ik prachtig vind.
ik het er ook eens gelezen.

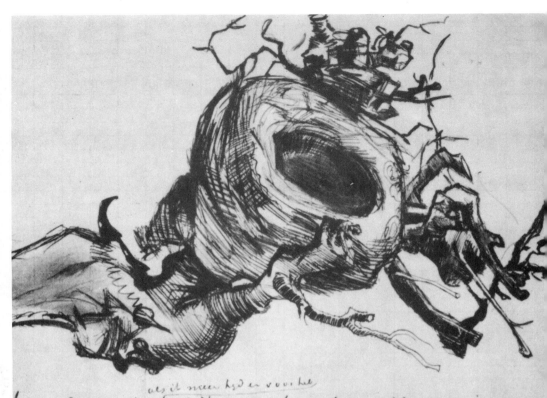

als il meer tijd en vooile

tegen den winter zal ik van dit soort gevallen eenige
tekeningen maken
la nichée et les nids voilà ce ch hark voue — vooral die menschen
die hutten op de hei en hunne bewoners —

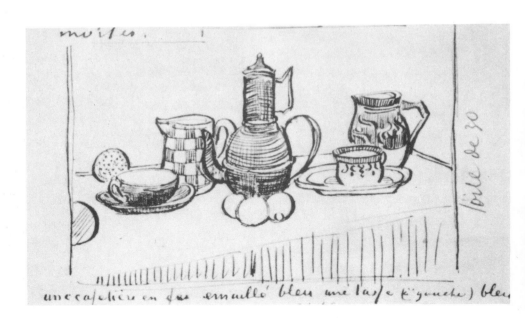

une cafetière en fer émaillé bleu une tasse (à gauche) bleu

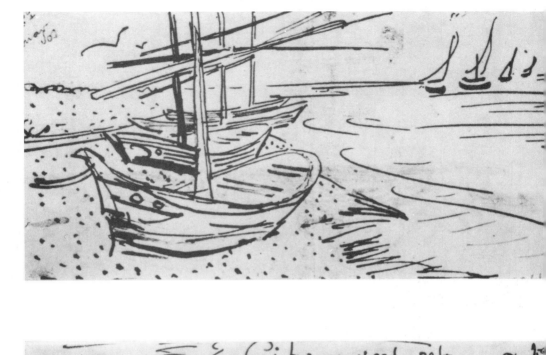

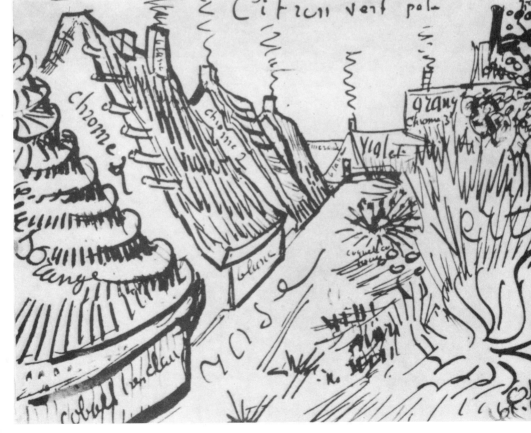

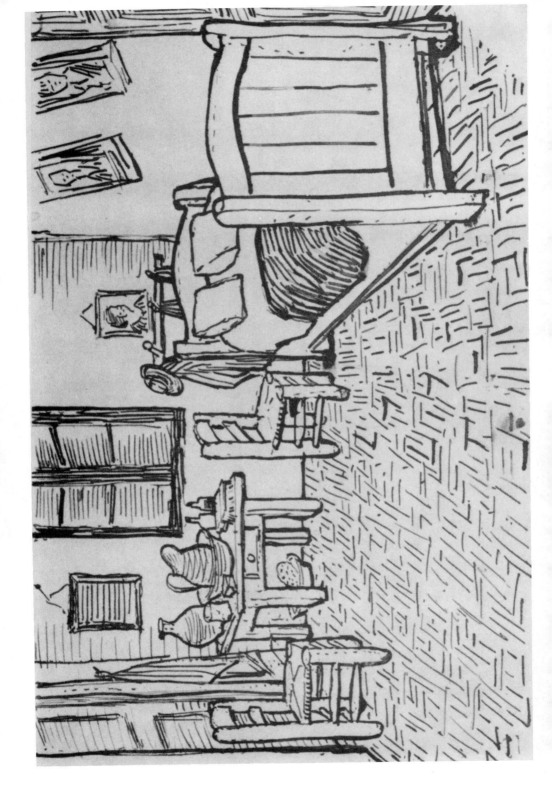

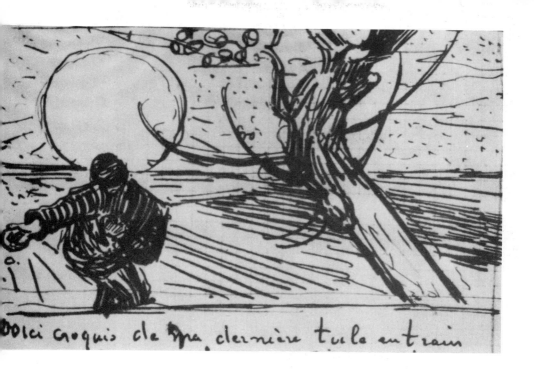

Voici croquis de ma dernière toile en train

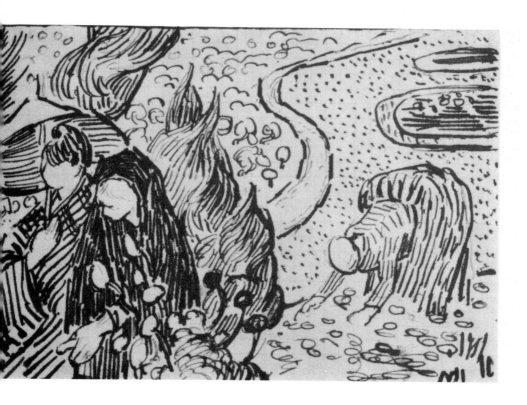

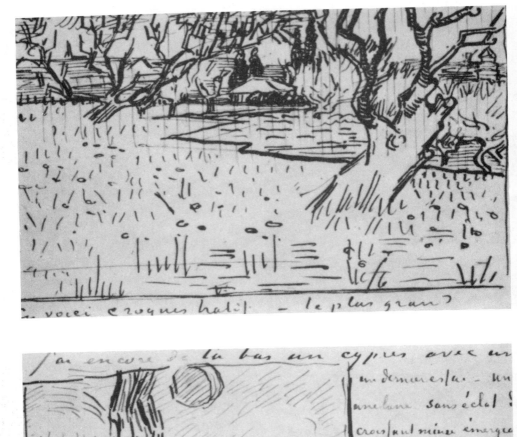

voici croquis hatif — le plus grand

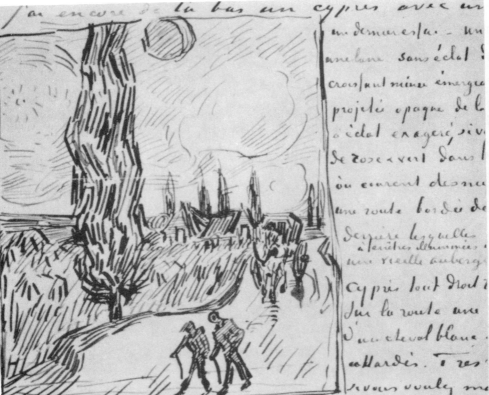

de la Provence. Probablement je graverai à l'eau

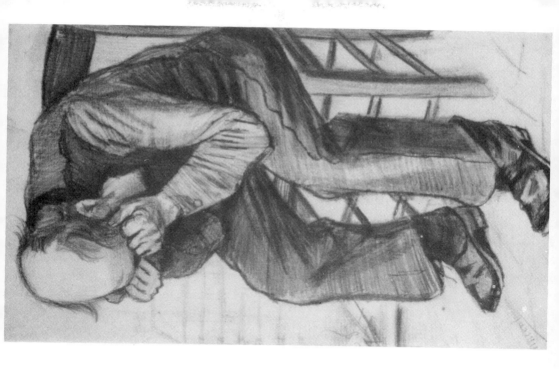

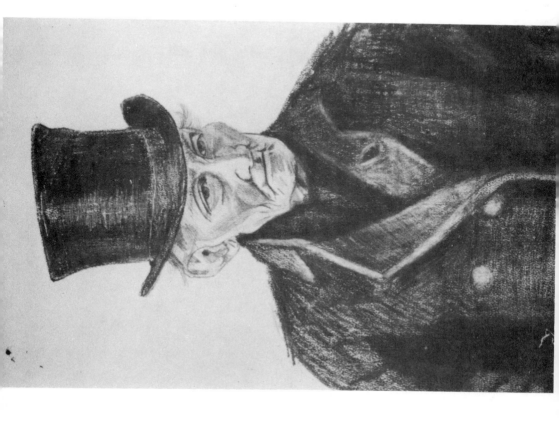

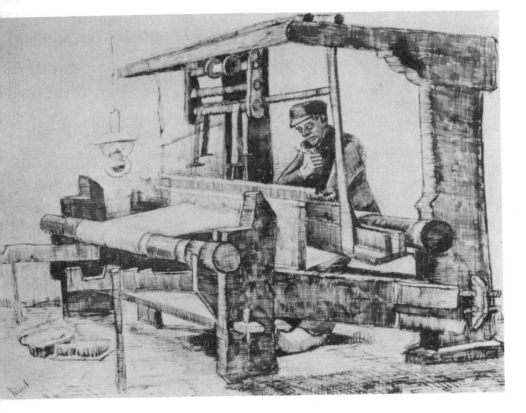

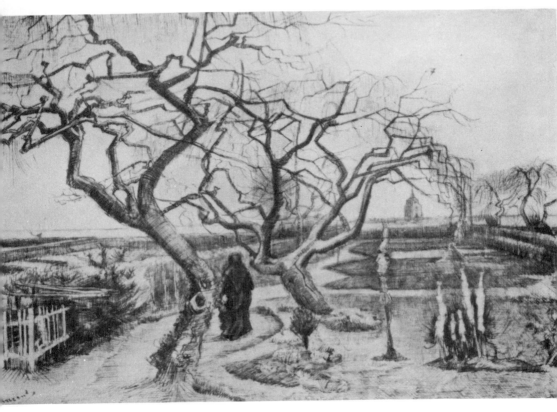

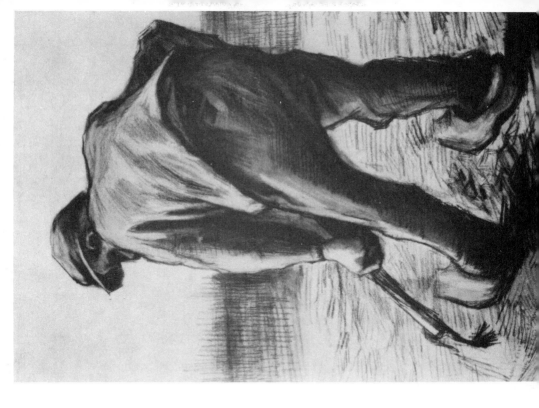

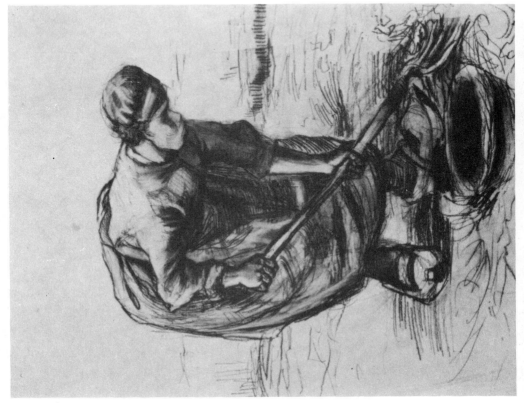

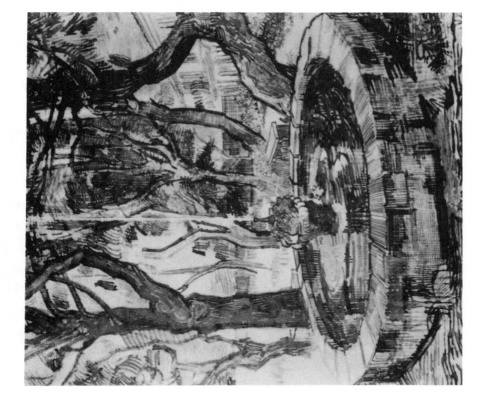

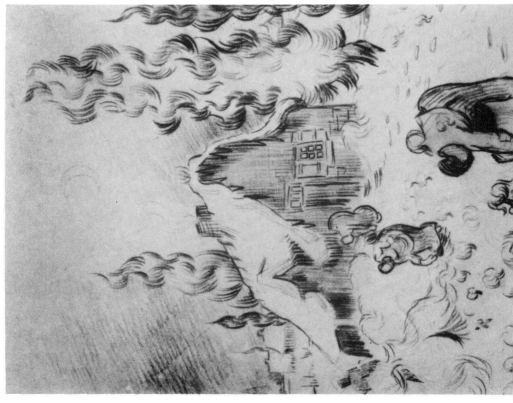

From London, Ramsgate, and Amsterdam, and the
personal reminiscence of a contemporary

11*a*
[Letter to the Van Stockum–Haanebeek family]

Dear Carolien and Willem,   London, October 1873

Many thanks for your letter of this morning, it was a delightful surprise. I am
glad you are doing so well.

Our Anna has passed her English and her needlework examinations; you can
imagine how delighted she is, as are we all. Pa and Mother have proposed that she
stay at school until next April, and then try French; but she doesn't have to
if she doesn't want to. I should like so much to find something for her here; you
know we have occasionally spoken about it.

You have already heard that Theo is going to The Hague. I believe it will be a
change for the better, though he will find it hard to leave that beautiful, pleasant
Brussels.

Some time ago I received a letter from your pa, also, to which I have replied, and
so you will probably have heard that all is still going well with me here, and some
particulars about my new lodgings.

What you say about winter is quite right; I completely agree. For myself, I can
hardly decide which season I like best; I believe I like them all equally. It is worth
noting that the old painters hardly ever painted autumn, and that the modern
ones have a predilection for it.

Enclosed are a few small photographs, which I hope you will like. Here you see
hardly any albums like those in Holland, but so-called scrapbooks into which you
put photographs like the ones in this letter (that is why we have the photographs
unmounted here). The advantage is that you can arrange your photographs on
the same page any way you like. I advise you to get a sort of copybook with white
paper, and begin by putting these in it.

"A Baptism" is after Anker, a Swiss who has painted a variety of subjects, all
equally intimate and delicate of feeling. "Puritans Going to Church" is after
Boughton, one of the best painters here. An American, he likes Longfellow very
much, and rightly so; I know three pictures by him inspired by *The Courtship of
Miles Standish*. Seeing these pictures has induced me to read *Miles Standish* and
Evangeline again; I don't know why, but I never realized these poems were *so* fine
as I think them now.

"Le bon frère" is after Van Muyden, a Swiss painter, "encore plus de modestie

33

que de talent" [as yet more modesty than talent]. Mr. Post in The Hague has this picture. If you should ever come to our shop, ask them to show you his (Van Muyden's) "Réfectoire." There are no more than four or five copies of this photograph in existence, as the negative is broken. Show it to Mr. Tersteeg some time.

The "Lune de Miel" [Honeymoon] is after Eugène Feyen, one of the few painters who pictures intimate modern life as it really is, and does not turn it into fashion plates.

I know the photograph "Der Wirthin Töchterlein" [The Landlady's Little Daughter], and I admire it very much. It is a good thing you appreciate Bourguereau. Not everybody is capable of perceiving the good and the beautiful as keenly as you do.

And now I am going to stop; I enclose another picture of autumn, this one by Michelet.

I hope you will be able to read this; I have written on without considering that one must take care a letter is intelligible. à Dieu; the best of luck to you all; many kind regards to all at the Poten, and any other friends you may meet.

Vincent

12

Dear Theo,   London, 19 Nov. 1873

I want to be sure you hear from me soon after your arrival at The Hague. I am eager to hear what your first impressions were of your new position and home. I heard that Mr. Schmidt gave you such a beautiful souvenir. That proves you have been very satisfactory in every respect. I am glad that we now work in the same house of Goupil. Lately we have had many pictures and drawings here; we sold a great many, but not enough yet—it must become something more established and solid. I think there is still much work to do in England, but it will not be successful at once. Of course, the first thing necessary is to have good pictures, and that will be very difficult. Well, we must take things as they are and make the best of it.

How is business in Holland? Here the ordinary engravings after Brochart do not sell at all, the good burin engravings sell pretty well. From the "Venus Anadyomene" after Ingres we have already sold twenty épreuves d'artiste. It is a pleasure to see how well the photographs sell, especially the colored ones, and there is a big profit in them. We sell the Musée Goupil & Co. photographs only en papillottes, on an average of a hundred a day.

I think you will like the work in the house at The Hague as soon as you have got used to it. I am sure you will like your home with the Roos family. Walk as much as your time will allow. Give my best love to everybody at Roos's.

You must write me sometime whom you like best among the older painters as well as among the moderns. Don't forget, as I am curious to know. Go to the museum as often as you can; it is a good thing to know the old painters also. If you have the chance, read about art, especially the art magazines, *Gazette des Beaux-Arts*, etc. As soon as I have the opportunity, I will send you a book by

Burger about the museums at The Hague and Amsterdam. Please send it back when you have read it.

Ask Iterson to write me when he has time, and especially to send me a list of the painters who have won awards at the Paris exhibition. Is Somerwill still in the office or did he leave when you arrived?

I am all right. I have a pleasant home, and although the house here is not so interesting as the one in The Hague, it is perhaps well that I am here. Later on, especially when the sale of pictures grows more important, I shall perhaps be of use. And then, I cannot tell you how interesting it is to see London and English business and the way of life, which differs so much from ours.

You must have had pleasant days at home; how I should like to see them all again. Give my compliments to everybody who inquires after me, especially at Tersteeg's, Haanebeek, Aunt Fie, Stockum and Roos; and tell Betsy Tersteeg something about me when you see her. And now, boy, good luck to you, write to me soon.

Vincent

Do you have my room at Roos's or the one you slept in last summer?

13

Dear Theo,   London, Jan. 1874

Thanks for your letter. I wish you a happy New Year with all my heart. I know that you are doing well at The Hague, for I heard it from Mr. Tersteeg. From your letter I see that you take a great interest in art; that is a good thing, boy. I am glad you like Millet, Jacque, Schreyer, Lambinet, Frans Hals, etc., for as Mauve says, "That is *it*."

Yes, that picture by Millet, "The Angelus," that is *it*—that is beauty, that is poetry. How I should like to talk with you about art; instead, we must write about it often. *Admire as much as you can; most people do not admire enough.* The following are some of the painters whom I like especially: Scheffer, Delaroche, Hébert, Hamon, Leys, Tissot, Lagye, Boughton, Millais, Thijs [Matthijs] Maris, De Groux, De Braekeleer, Jr., Millet, Jules Breton, Feyen-Perrin, Eugène Feyen, Brion, Jundt, Georg Saal, Israëls, Anker, Knaus, Vautier, Jourdan, Compte-Calix, Rochussen, Meissonier, Madrazo, Ziem, Boudin, Gérôme, Fromentin, Decamps, Bonington, Diaz, Th. Rousseau, Troyon, Dupré, Corot, Paul Huet, Jacque, Otto Weber, Daubigny, Bernier, Émile Breton, Chenu, César de Cock, Mlle. Collart, Bodmer, Koekkoek, Schelfhout, Weissenbruch, and last but not least, Maris and Mauve. But I might go on like that for I don't know how long. Then there are the old masters, and I am sure I have forgotten some of the best modern ones.

Try to take as many walks as you can and keep your love of nature, for that is the true way to learn to understand art more and more. Painters understand nature and love her and *teach us to see her*. Then there are painters who can only make good things, who cannot make anything bad, just as there are ordinary people who cannot do anything that doesn't turn out well.

I am doing very well here. I have a delightful home, and it is a great pleasure to me to study London, the English way of life and the English people themselves. Then I have nature and art and poetry. If that is not enough, what is? Still, I do not forget Holland—especially The Hague and Brabant. We are very busy in the office just now, taking inventory. However, it lasts only five days, so it is much easier for us than for you at The Hague.

I hope you had as happy a Christmas as I had.

Well, boy, I wish you all happiness, and write to me soon. In this letter I have just written what came into my mind, and I hope it is not too confused. à Dieu, my regards to everybody, especially at Aunt Fie's and Haanebeek's.

Vincent

67

Dear Theo, Ramsgate, 31 May 1876

Bravo on going to Etten May 21, so four of the six children were at home. Father wrote me in detail how the day was spent.

Thanks also for your last letter.

Did I tell you about the storm I watched recently? The sea was yellowish, especially near the shore; on the horizon a strip of light, and above it immense dark gray clouds from which the rain poured down in slanting streaks. The wind blew the dust from the little white path on the rocks into the sea and bent the blooming hawthorn bushes and wallflowers that grow on the rocks. To the right were fields of young green corn, and in the distance the town looked like the towns that Albrecht Dürer used to etch. A town with its turrets, mills, slate roofs and houses built in Gothic style, and below, the harbor between two jetties which project far into the sea.

I also saw the sea last Sunday night. Everything was dark and gray, but in the horizon the day began to dawn. It was still very early, but a lark was already singing. So were the nightingales in the gardens near the sea. In the distance shone the light from the lighthouse, the guard ship, etc.

From the window of my room that same night I looked on the roofs of the houses that can be seen from there and on the tops of the elm trees, dark against the night sky. Over those roofs one single star, but a beautiful, large, friendly one. And I thought of you all and of my own past years and of our home, and in me arose the words and the emotion: "Keep me from being a son that maketh ashamed; give me Thy blessing, not because I deserve it, but for my mother's sake. Thou art love, cover all things. Without Thy continued blessings we succeed in nothing."

Enclosed is a little drawing of the view from the school window through which the boys wave good-by to their parents when they are going back to the station after a visit. None of us will ever forget the view from the window. *You ought to have seen* it this week when it rained, especially in the twilight when the lamps were lit and their light was reflected in the wet street.

On such days Mr. Stokes is sometimes in a bad temper, and when the boys make more noise than he likes, they occasionally have to go without their supper. I wish you could see them looking from the window then, it is rather melancholy:

they have so little else except their meals to look forward to and to help them pass their days.

I should also like you to see them going from the dark stairs and passage to the dining room, where the bright sun is shining. Another curious place is the room with the rotten floor. It has six washbasins in which they have to wash themselves; a dim light filters onto the washstand through a window with broken panes. It is a rather melancholy sight.

I should like to spend a winter with them or to have spent a winter with them in the past to know what it is like. The boys made an oil stain on your drawing, please excuse them.

Enclosed is a little note for Uncle Jan. And now good night; if anybody should ask after me, give them my kind regards. Do you visit Borchers now and then? If you see him say hello to him for me, also Willem Valkis and all at Roos's. A handshake from

Your loving brother, Vincent

A 7

Dordrecht

[Letter written by P. C. Görlitz to Frederik van Eeden.[1]]

Your article in *De Nieuwe Gids* about the painter Vincent van Gogh induces me to give you some information about this man. I held regular intercourse with him for a year, now approximately fifteen years ago, at Dordrecht, where both he and I were employed, and where we boarded in the very same house.

I was an assistant teacher at Dordrecht, and fifteen years ago was living in Tolbrugstraatje there, a neighborhood of no high standing, when one day my landlord told me that a young man, a clergyman's son from Etten and Leur, had applied for board and lodging in his house. Seeing that he had already taken in three young people, he begged me to do him the favor of sharing my room with the newcomer, as otherwise he could not take him in. I agreed to this; the newly arrived young man was Mr. Vincent van Gogh, who had got the position of bookkeeper in Blussé & Van Braam's bookshop.

He was a man totally different from the usual type of the children of man. His face was ugly, his mouth more or less awry, moreover his face was densely covered with freckles, and he had hair of a reddish hue. As I said, his face was ugly, but as soon as he spoke about religion or art, and then became excited, which was sure to happen very soon, his eyes would sparkle, and his features would make a deep impression on me; it wasn't his own face any longer: it had become beautiful.

As we lived in one room, hardly any of his doings could escape my attention. When he came back from his office at nine o'clock in the evening, he would immediately light a little wooden pipe; he would take down a big Bible, and sit down to read assiduously, to copy texts and to learn them by heart; he would

---

[1] Frederik van Eeden wrote an appreciative article on Vincent in *De Nieuwe Gids* (the literary monthly *The New Guide*) of December 1, 1890. In connection with this Mr. Görlitz wrote him the following letter.

also write all kinds of religious compositions. When I said to him on such occasions, "Van Gogh, my boy, you're working yourself too hard, you had better go rest for a while," he would answer with a peculiar smile, half melancholy, half humorous, which made his sharp ugly features so attractive, so beautiful, "Oh dear, G., the Bible is my comfort, the staff of my life. It is the most delicious book I know, and to follow what Jesus taught mankind will be the purpose of my life."

Thus, evening after evening, he would sit reading his big folio volume or a small English New Testament, or the *Juweeltjes* [Little Jewels] by the Rev. Mr. Spurgeon (the only three books he used to read, as long as I knew him), and when he went to bed about one o'clock, he would go on reading the Bible until he fell asleep. And early in the morning I would find him lying on his bed with his beloved book on his pillow, and then I would wake him up so that he might go where his humdrum little job as a bookkeeper called him.

He was so modest, so timid in some respects. One day—we had known each other about a month—he asked me, again with his irresistibly charming smile, "G., you could do me such an enormously great favor if you wanted to."

I replied, "Well, by doing what? Say the word."

"Oh, you see, this room is really your room, and now I should so very much like to have your permission to paste some little Biblical pictures on the wallpaper." Of course I immediately acceded to this request, and he went to work with feverish haste. And within half an hour the whole room was decorated with Biblical scenes and ecce-homos, and Van Gogh had written under each Head of Christ, "Ever sorrowful, but always rejoicing."

This scriptural expression reflected the state of his own mind as clearly as anything could. On one of the Christian holy days, I think it was Easter, he framed every picture of Jesus in palm branches. I am not a religious man, but I thought *his* religious devoutness touching to contemplate.

When Sunday came Van Gogh would go to church three times, either to the Roman Catholic church, or to the Protestant or Old Episcopal church, which was commonly called the Jansenist church. When once we made the remark, "But, my dear Van Gogh, how is it possible that you can go to three churches of such divergent creeds?" he said, "Well, in every church I see God, and it's all the same to me whether a Protestant pastor or a Roman Catholic priest preaches; it is not really a matter of dogma, but of the spirit of the Gospel, and I find this spirit in all churches."

To the present day I have a clear memory of the pleased, intensely satisfied expression on his face when he succeeded at last in inducing us to accompany him to church. When we went home he asked, "Didn't you feel finer beneath those beautiful vaults, with that stately organ, than if you had been sitting in your room smoking cigars? Are you going to come with me next week? You will, won't you," he wheedled, and I could not refuse him; I went with him again.

He would often ask us if he might read something to us; and this he would do, not at all to the satisfaction of the youngest one among us, who would try to set us laughing by offering absurd observations or making faces. On one occasion I drew Van Gogh's attention to this, and told him, "Don't do such useless work, my dear fellow; the simple fact is that he thinks it ridiculous; he is laughing at it."

But the man answered, "Never mind, G., let him laugh, I shan't lose my temper because of that; he doesn't know better yet, someday he will learn to see it; if I succeed in inspiring his mind to seriousness, if only for a quarter of an hour, I shall think my trouble rewarded."

Van Gogh out of temper! Never, not once did I observe in his character the least little bit of an indication of an evil quality or inclination. He lived like a saint, and was as frugal as a hermit. In the afternoon, at the table, the three of us would eat with the appetite of famished wolves; not he, he would not eat meat, only a little morsel on Sundays, and then only after being urged by our landlady for a long time. Four potatoes with a suspicion of gravy and a mouthful of vegetables constituted his whole dinner. To our insistence that he make a hearty dinner and eat meat, he would answer, "To a human being physical life ought to be a paltry detail; vegetable food is sufficient, all the rest is luxury."

How sensitive a man he was will become evident to you from the two incidents I am now going to relate.

One Saturday afternoon we went out for a walk; suddenly he saw an emaciated, miserable, deserted street dog, a poor hungry beggar of a dog. He searched his purse and in it found a "dubbeltje" [twopence]—it was all the money he had, for it was the last days of the month. Then he bought two rolls for a penny to give to the dog, and stood looking at the animal full of complacency as it devoured the bread in a few swallows. Going back to his companions, Van Gogh said, "What do you think this animal told me just now? That he would like to have another couple of rolls like that," and following his impulse, he bought two more and gave them to the yearning dog. Now he didn't even have the money to buy a pack of tobacco, the only luxury he permitted himself.

The second incident was of a more serious nature.

It was again on a Saturday that he came to me with his own smile and said, "G., I need you, perhaps you can help me, I'm in a bad fix. I just got word from home that an old peasant I've known for years, and who has always been a faithful follower of my father, is dying. I'm so fond of that man, and I should like so much to see him once more; I want to close his eyes, but I can't pay for the journey to Breda, I haven't got any money left. Should you think it queer, G., to advance me the money for such a purpose?—and I don't dare ask our landlord for it."

"I think it queer, Van Gogh?—not on your life, but I shall not be able to manage the whole; here is something; the 'boss' will lend you the rest; I'll ask him to put it down on my bill, then we'll settle our account in due time, for instance on the Day of Atonement."

He went, and on Sunday night came home again, and when I asked him, "Well, Van Gogh, how did it go?" he answered, "When I came to that peasant's house it was too late; he had died a few hours earlier."

"God bless me, Vincent, that was a rotten thing for you!" But he replied, his smile a little more melancholy than at other times, "You use the wrong expression,

G., it wasn't a rotten thing; it was certainly a disappointment, but these things are there to strengthen man on his way through life; yet I'm glad I was there, for I did not go there in vain; I sat down with the members of the old man's family and prayed with them. I'll tell you what my words to them were: Let Jesus and his teachings be unto you the light on your path and the lamp for your feet, then you will learn to be resigned."

But although this man tried to do his job with an iron zeal and as cheerfully as was possible for him, this job weighed upon him like a leaden burden; the poor fellow was unfit for his profession. While bookkeeping he would write sermons or read them, and psalms or texts from the Bible; he struggled against it, but it was too much for him. Besides, it was as clear as daylight that his were not the qualities of a businessman. It was his job not only to keep the books but also to attend to the sale of the artistic prints in the shop. For instance he advised some ladies to buy a cheaper engraving, whose artistic value he explained, rather than a more expensive one, which was less beautiful according to him, but for which the ladies showed a preference. He drew unpleasant comments on his method of working and doing business, and this was painful to him; for a time he managed to hide his pent-up feelings—why? The why became clear to me when during a conversation I had with him he told me that he thought it so nice that he was no longer a burden to his parents—that he now earned his own bread, and that in the past he had found this difficult, in London and in Paris, where (if I am not mistaken) he had tried to qualify for the art-dealing business.

During the same conversation he remarked with great satisfaction, "Yes, G., I earn as much as my predecessor here." This was an illusion on his part, for he received 120 guilders[1] less than his predecessor, who had had experience; but fortunately for him his employer was considerate enough to let him keep his illusion.

He used to speak rather often about London and his stay there. Many a time on our rambles he would point out to me a picturesque back yard with a lean-to near the waterside, or something like that, and would then say, "Look how exquisitely beautiful this is; it reminds me of London; there I used to wander around a lot in the slum districts, and many a time I found a spot just as beautiful as here in Dordrecht." He also deeply enjoyed the fine river views in the neighborhood of Dordrecht; then his face would brighten wonderfully, his melancholy expression was gone, and it seemed as though he was breathing in this beauty. But on the whole during this period he was not dominated by his art but by his mystical religious feelings.

One evening he asked me, "What kind of school do you teach in?" I replied, "A charity school."

"Then you have a splendid job. Don't you think it delightful to teach those poor creatures something good, and to lift them out of their misery and evil ways? When I was in London I taught a class a few times a week, at night, in a school for the down-and-out, for pleasure. That time is unforgettable for me; a

[1] Or 20 guilders; this cannot be deciphered with any certainty [H. van Eeden].

40

venerable old man with a big gray beard was the headmaster; he had a special knack of fascinating those boys from the London slums with his stories. In the evening, in the poor light of that schoolroom, all those different faces, and the picturesque figure of that old man, all made a deep impression on me; those were delightful, unforgettable days."

It was a mild summer's evening; in the little street where we had our lodgings upstairs there was now and then a lack of fresh air; we sat talking together on the zinc leads of a roof, where we had a view of a number of gardens.

"What's the matter, G., you sit pondering so much, are you in some kind of trouble?"

"Trouble?—no," I replied, "but I shall make a clean breast of it; I'm about to take a leap in the dark. I'm thinking of getting married, and that makes me silent; there is much to be said for it and much against it."

At this moment the seriousness of his conception of life, his religious feelings took possession of him in good earnest. For more than an hour and a half he tried to dissuade me from the step I had in mind. I still remember one of his reasons clearly; this motive was characteristic of the whole man, therefore I will write it down.

"Do not marry, G., you are far too young, twenty-five years old. A man ought not to marry before his fortieth year or thereabouts; first the passions ought to be curbed before one may think of entering upon such a serious matter; one can only be a man in real earnest after the passions are conquered, for only then can one seek to be a spiritual being with good results; the animal must get out, then the angel can enter." Thus he spoke on until night began to fall and we went inside.

Once I found him engaged in darning a hole in his stocking with the greatest patience in the world. I thought this pathetic, and I said, "Vincent, don't do that, let the landlady do it, she does it for us all the time."

"Oh well," he answered, "the landlady doesn't have a servant girl; she has to look after her housekeeping and the shop and the three of us into the bargain, and it isn't the first time I've done this: in Paris I had to live quite a bit differently from this!"

At last his love of religion became too powerful for him; he wanted to be a clergyman at all costs. In those days I stayed for a night at his father's, the clergyman at Etten and Leur. His mama asked me, "Mr. G., how are things going with Vincent, please tell me everything you know about him—is he happy?—do tell me the absolute truth."

To this I replied, "Madam, to tell you the absolute truth, Vincent is unfit for his job; his ideal calls him elsewhere: it is religion."

Not long afterward, and probably as a result of this conversation, Vincent confessed to his parents that he could not stand it any longer; he longed ardently to teach the Gospel, and he might have added with a clear conscience: to the poor and oppressed in society—at least this was the essence of what he had often told me.

He left Dordrecht, and went to live in the house of his uncle, the Rear-Admiral

Van Gogh, at Amsterdam, if I am rightly informed; at his age he had to learn Latin, etc. I never saw him again; but later on I heard that he had chucked Latin, etc. (that a person should have to learn Latin and Greek in order to preach the teachings of the Gospel was something wholly out of keeping with his convictions), and that he had become an evangelist in Belgium, in the mining districts. I was not at all surprised at this; I think he may have comforted many a poor devil by the power of his rich mind.

I am afraid, most respected Mr. Van Eeden, that I have bored you with this lengthy story; should this be the case, please do not take it ill of me, for I felt it would be wrong for me to refrain from telling you all I know about this good man.

P. C. Görlitz

100

Dear Theo,   Amsterdam, 4 June 1877
You remember that night at Dordrecht when we walked together through the town, around the Great Church and through so many streets, and along the canals—in which the old houses and the lights from the windows were reflected? You spoke then about the description of a day in London by Théophile Gautier, the coachman for a wedding party in front of the door of a church on a stormy foggy day: I saw it all before me. If that struck you, you will also appreciate the pages[1] I enclose. I read them on a very stormy day last week: it was in the evening, and the sunset threw a ruddy glow on the gray evening clouds, against which the masts of the ships and the row of old houses and trees stood out; and everything was reflected in the water, and the sky threw a strange light on the black earth, on the green grass with daisies and buttercups, and on the bushes of white and purple lilacs, and on the elderberry bushes of the garden in the yard.

In London I had read that book of Lamartine's, and I was very much struck by it; the last pages especially made a deep impression on me again. Tell me what you think of it. These places mentioned in it—Hampton Court with its avenues of linden trees full of rookeries; Whitehall overgrown with ivy at the back; and the square bordering St. James's Park where one can see Westminster Abbey—they are all before me, and the weather and the gloomy atmosphere: cela m'empêche de dormir [it keeps me from sleeping].

Were you in Etten Sunday? I certainly hope so, and that you had a pleasant day. I gathered this from a sentence in the last letter from Etten, "We expect Theo probably next Sunday."

This evening I have to go to Uncle Stricker's. Went to early service yesterday morning, heard a sermon on the text: "Do you want to be healthy?"—how they that be whole need not a physician, but they that are sick. After that I heard Uncle Stricker in the well-known Amstel Church on II Cor. 4 : 18 : For the things which are seen are temporal; but the things which are not seen are eternal.

Toward the end there was a passage in which he spoke with much rapture and exclaimed, "But love remains"; how we are tied together by God with

[1] Lamartine's *Cromwell*. Vincent copied three full pages, part of which is added to this letter.

bonds that are in His hand, and in them lies our strength, for they are old and do not easily break.

I am very busy, so à Dieu; perhaps I will continue this letter tonight, a handshake from

Your loving brother, Vincent

Today when I passed the flower market on the Singel, I saw something very pretty. A peasant was standing selling a whole bunch of pots with all kinds of flowers and plants; ivy was behind it, and his little girl was sitting between it all, such a child as Maris would have painted, so simple in her little black bonnet, and with a pair of bright, smiling eyes. She was knitting; the man praised his ware—and if I could have spared the money I should have liked only too well to buy some—and he said, pointing unintentionally at his little daughter also, "Doesn't it look pretty?"

119

Dear Theo,   Amsterdam, 18 February 1878

Thanks for your letter of February 17; it made me very happy, as I had been looking forward to it so much. And I am answering it at once, boy, for I think of you and long for you so often, and every morning the prints on the wall of my little study remind me of you—"Christus Consolator"; the woodcut after Van Goyen, "Dordrecht"; "Le Four" by Rousseau, etc.—for I received them all from you. So the pot was calling the kettle black when you wrote me that I ought not to send you a print for your room sometimes when I find one that I think you will like. In my turn I say, Enough of that; but tell me if you have got some new acquisitions for your collection lately.

Last evening at Uncle Cor's I saw a whole volume of that magazine, *L'Art*; you have the issue with the wood engravings after Corot. I was especially struck by wood engravings after drawings by Millet, including "Falling Leaves," "The Ravens' Wedding," "Donkeys in a Marsh," "The Woodcutters," "Housewife Sweeping Her Room," "A Farm Courtyard" (night effect), etc. Also by an etching after Corot, "The Dune"; and "St. John's Eve" after Breton; and others by Chauvin; and another after Millet, "The Beans."

Last Sunday Uncle Jan and I spent the whole afternoon and evening at Uncle Cor's. It was a very pleasant day for me. I got up very early and went to the French church in the morning. A clergyman from the neighborhood of Lyons preached here—he had come to collect money for an evangelical mission. His sermon was mainly stories from the lives of the working people in the factories, and though he was not particularly eloquent and one could even hear that he spoke with some difficulty and effort, his words were still effective because they came from the heart—only such are powerful enough to touch other hearts.

At one o'clock I had to be at the Sunday school of an English clergyman, Adler, in the Barndesteeg; he has a small but very neat old church there. However, the school was held in a little room where even at that hour, in the middle of the day, the gaslight had to be turned on. There were perhaps twenty children from that poor section. Though he is a foreigner, he preaches in Dutch (but the service is in English) ; he teaches his Bible class in Dutch too, and does it very well. I had brought with me a sketch of the map of the Holy Land which I made for Father's birthday, in red crayon and on strong brown paper, and I gave it to him; I thought that little room would be a nice place for it, and I am glad it hangs on the wall there now. I had met him at Mr. McFarlane's, the incumbent of the English church in the Beguinage whom I had ventured to call on ; he received me kindly and I hope to repeat my visit someday.

Besides this English clergyman, I also ventured to call on the Reverend Mr. Gagnebin. He took it in good part and told me to come again some evening ; as he suggested tonight, I must go there in a little while. I hope to write you all about it. Father had also advised me to try and make some acquaintances. I was so glad to speak French and English again—it is a peculiar sensation when one hasn't for a long time.

The last two mornings I got up very early to work on a sketch of the map of Paul's travels which I had begun and have now finished; it looks well now (with the names in French), even better than those I made for Father and for my own room. I plan to give it to the Reverend Mr. Gagnebin, as I want to emphasize that visit if possible : he is a learned man who can perhaps give me some good advice later on if he realizes that my intentions are serious....

I have just been to Gagnebin's, but I was told that he was too busy to receive me (yet he had fixed this hour and this day for my visit). I heard music in the house, so probably there was something going on. I left what I had made for Gagnebin with the servant, requesting that it be given to him. I want to do such things now and then, for it certainly is very doubtful that I shall ever succeed, I mean, shall ever pass all the examinations. Five years at the least is a very long time ; if one begins earlier, it is so much easier. It is true I can work longer and concentrate better, and things that many others care about have no attraction for me ; but, after all, the work costs me greater effort. Even if I fail, I want to leave my mark here and there behind me.

There are so many, many things one has to know, and though they try to reassure me, it constantly gives me a terribly anxious feeling. There is no remedy but to set to work again, since it is clearly my *duty* to do this, whatever it costs. So I must push on, for standing still or going back is out of the question : it would make things even more difficult and cause confusion—and the end would mean the necessity of beginning all over again.

I had a nice letter from home ; the journey seems not to have done Father any harm. It is pretty late, and I am not a little tired, for I have walked quite a distance today. Have a good time, and blessings on your work and on all you undertake; write soon if you can. My regards to all at the Rooses', and a warm handshake in thought. Good night and sleep well, believe me,

Your loving brother, Vincent

Tuesday morning. It is beautiful weather this morning, I have to go to Mendes's in a few minutes.

Vincent's mission to the miners

127   Petites Wasmes, 26 December 1878

Dear Theo,   Borinage, Hainaut

It is time for me to write you again, first, to send you my very best wishes at the beginning of the New Year. May your share be everything that's good, and may God's blessing rest on your work in the year we now begin.

I am eager to receive a letter from you, to hear how you are and what you are doing, and also to hear perhaps if you have seen any beautiful and remarkable things lately.

As for me, I am sure you realize that here in the Borinage there are no pictures; generally speaking, they do not even know what a picture is. So of course I have not seen anything in the way of art since I left Brussels. Notwithstanding, the country is very picturesque and very unique here: everything *speaks*, as it were, and is full of character. Lately, during the dark days before Christmas, the ground was covered with snow; then everything reminded one of the medieval pictures by Peasant Brueghel, for instance, and of those by the many who have known how to express so remarkably well that peculiar effect of red and green, black and white. At every moment I am reminded here of the work of Thijs Maris or of Albrecht Dürer. There are sunken roads, overgrown with thornbushes, and old, gnarled trees with their fantastic roots, which perfectly resemble that road on the etching by Dürer, "Death and the Knight." So, a few days ago, it was an intriguing sight to see the miners going home in the white snow in the evening at twilight. Those people are quite black. When they come out of the dark mines into daylight, they look exactly like chimney sweeps. Their houses are very small, and might better be called huts; they are scattered along the sunken roads, and in the wood, and on the slopes of the hills. Here and there one can see moss-covered roofs, and in the evening the light shines kindly through the small-paned windows.

In our Brabant we have the underbrush of oak and in Holland, the pollard willows; here blackthorn hedges surround the gardens, fields and meadows. Now, with the snow, the effect is like black characters on white paper—like pages of the Gospel.

I have already spoken in public here several times, in a rather large room especially arranged for religious meetings, as well as at the meetings they hold in the evenings in the miners' cottages, which may best be called Bible classes. Among other things, I spoke about the parable of the mustard seed, the barren fig tree, the man born blind. On Christmas, of course, about the stable in Bethlehem and peace on earth. If with God's blessing I get a permanent appointment here, I shall be very, very happy.

Everywhere around one sees the big chimneys and the immense heaps of coal at the entrances to the mines, the so-called charbonnages. You know that large drawing by Bosboom, "Chaudfontaine"—it expresses the character of the country well, only here it is all coal; the stone quarries are in the north of Hainaut, and in Chaudfontaine it is iron.

I still think so often of the day you spent in Brussels and of our visit to the museum. And I often wish that you were nearer so we could be together more often. Write again soon. I look at that etching of "A Young Citizen" over and over again.

The language of the miners is not so very easy to understand, but they understand ordinary French well, provided it is spoken quickly and fluently; then, of course, it resembles their patois, which is spoken with great rapidity.

At a meeting this week my text was Acts 16 : 9, "And a vision appeared to Paul in the night; There stood a man of Macedonia, and prayed him, saying, Come over into Macedonia, and help us." And they listened attentively when I tried to describe what the Macedonian who needed and longed for the comfort of the Gospel and for knowledge of the only true God was like. How we must think of him as a laborer with lines of sorrow and suffering and fatigue in his face—without splendor or glamour, but with an immortal soul—who needed the food that does not perish, God's word. How Jesus Christ is the Master who can comfort and strengthen a man like the Macedonian—a laborer and working man whose life is hard—because He is the Great Man of Sorrows Who knows our ills, Who was called a carpenter's son though He was the Son of God, Who worked for thirty years in a humble carpenter's shop to fulfill God's will. And God wills that in imitation of Christ man should live humbly and go through life not reaching for the sky, but adapting himself to the earth below, learning from the Gospel to be meek and simple of heart.

I have already had occasion to visit some patients, as there are many sick people here.

I wrote today to the President of the Committee of Evangelization, asking him if my case could be brought up at the next meeting of the committee.

It has been thawing tonight; I cannot tell you how picturesque the hilly country is in the thaw, now that the snow is melting and the black fields with the green winter wheat are visible again.

For a foreigner the village here is a real labyrinth with innumerable narrow streets and alleys of small miners' huts, situated at the foot of the hills as well as on the slopes and on the top. You can best compare it to a village like Scheveningen, especially the back streets, or to those villages in Brittany which we know from pictures. But you have traveled through this part of the country on your way to Paris, and perhaps you remember it somewhat. The Protestant churches are small—like the one at De Hoeve, only a little larger—but the place where I spoke is only a large bare room which can accommodate a hundred people at the most. I also assisted at a religious service in a stable or shed, so you see it is quite simple and original.

Write soon if you have time, and know that you are again and again, aye constantly, in my thoughts. May God's blessing be yours in the New Year. Believe me, with a handshake, always,

Your so loving brother, Vincent

My regards to everyone at Roos's, and also to everyone who inquires after me.

When you write, please address your letter: M. van der Haegen, colporteur à Pâturages, près de Mons, Borinage, Hainaut.

I have just visited a little old woman in a charcoal-burner's family. She is very ill, but patient and full of faith. I read a chapter with her and prayed with them all. People here have a characteristic simplicity and good nature, like the Brabant people at Zundert and Etten.

129

Dear Theo, Wasmes, April 1879

It is time that you heard from me again. From home I heard that you had been in Etten for a few days and that you were on a business trip. I certainly hope you had a good journey. I suppose you will be in the dunes some of these days and occasionally in Scheveningen. It is lovely here in spring, too; there are spots where one could almost fancy oneself in the dunes, because of the hills.

Not long ago I made a very interesting expedition, spending six hours in a mine. It was Marcasse, one of the oldest and most dangerous mines in the neighborhood. It has a bad reputation because many perish in it, either going down or coming up, or through poisoned air, firedamp explosion, water seepage, cave-ins, etc. It is a gloomy spot, and at first everything around looks dreary and desolate.

Most of the miners are thin and pale from fever; they look tired and emaciated, weather-beaten and aged before their time. On the whole the women are faded and worn. Around the mine are poor miners' huts, a few dead trees black from smoke, thorn hedges, dunghills, ash dumps, heaps of useless coal, etc. Maris could make a wonderful picture of it.

I will try to make a little sketch of it presently to give you an idea of how it looks.

I had a good guide, a man who has already worked there for thirty-three years; kind and patient, he explained everything well and tried to make it clear to me.

So together we went down 700 meters and explored the most hidden corners of that underworld. The maintenages or gredins [cells where the miners work] which are situated farthest from the exit are called *des caches* [hiding places, places where men search].

This mine has five levels, but the three upper ones have been exhausted and abandoned; they are no longer worked because there is no more coal. A picture of the maintenages would be something new and unheard of—or rather, never before seen. Imagine a row of cells in a rather narrow, low passage, shored up with rough timber. In each of those cells a miner in a coarse linen suit, filthy and black as a chimney sweep, is busy hewing coal by the pale light of a small lamp. The miner can stand erect in some cells; in others, he lies on the ground (☐☐☐☐☐ tailles à droit, ☐☐☐ tailles à plat). The arrangement is more or less like the cells in a beehive, or like a dark, gloomy passage in an underground prison, or like a row of small weaving looms, or rather more like a row of baking ovens such as the peasants have, or like the partitions in a crypt. The tunnels themselves are like the big chimneys of the Brabant farms.

The water leaks through in some, and the light of the miner's lamp makes a curious effect, reflected as in a stalactite cave. Some of the miners work in the maintenages, others load the cut coal into small carts that run on rails, like a street-car. This is mostly done by children, boys as well as girls. There is also a stable yard down there, 700 meters underground, with about seven old horses which pull a great many of those carts to the so-called accrochage, the place from which they are pulled up to the surface. Other miners repair the old galleries to prevent their collapse or make new galleries in the coal vein. As the mariners ashore are homesick for the sea, notwithstanding all the dangers and hardships which threaten them, so the miner would rather be under the ground than above it. The villages here look desolate and dead and forsaken; life goes on underground instead of above. One might live here for years and never know the real state of things unless one went down in the mines.

People here are very ignorant and untaught—most of them cannot read—but at the same time they are intelligent and quick at their difficult work; brave and frank, they are short but square-shouldered, with melancholy deep-set eyes. They are skill-ful at many things, and work terribly hard. They have a nervous temperament—I do not mean weak, but very sensitive. They have an innate, deep-rooted hatred and a strong mistrust of anyone who is domineering. With miners one must have a miner's character and temperament, and no pretentious pride or mastery, or one will never get along with them or gain their confidence.

Did I tell you at the time about the miner who was so badly hurt by a firedamp explosion? Thank God, he has recovered and is going out again, and is beginning to walk some distance just for exercise; his hands are still weak and it will be some time before he can use them for his work, but he is out of danger. Since that time there have been many cases of typhoid and malignant fever, of what they call la sotte fièvre, which gives them bad dreams like nightmares and makes them delirious. So again there are many sickly and bedridden people—emaciated, weak, and miserable.

In one house they are all ill with fever and have little or no help, so that the patients have to nurse the patients. "Ici c'est les malades qui soignent les malades" [here the sick tend the sick], said a woman, like, "Le pauvre est l'ami du pauvre" [the poor man is the poor man's friend].

Have you seen any beautiful pictures lately? I am eager for a letter from you. Has Israëls done much lately and Maris and Mauve?

A few days ago a colt was born here in the stable, a pretty little animal that soon stood firm on his legs. The miners keep many goats here, and there are kids in every house; rabbits are also very common here in the miners' houses.

48

I must go out to visit some patients, so I must finish. When you have time, let me have a word from you soon, as a sign of life. My compliments to the Roos family, and to Mauve when you meet him. Many good wishes, and believe me always, with a handshake in thought,

Your loving brother, Vincent

130

Dear Theo,   Wasmes, June 1879

It is already relatively late, almost twelve o'clock, but I want to write to you before the day is over. In the first place, it is so long since I wrote you—but, my dear fellow, what shall I write? I am up to my ears in work here, so that the days pass without my having time to think of or keep up an interest in many things that used to attract me.

What prompts me to write is that I heard from home that you have had an offer to go to Paris for six weeks. If you go there, you will pass the Borinage. I wanted you to consider spending a day, or more if possible, here. I should so much like to have you know this country, too, because it has so many peculiarities for one who knows how to look at things attentively. To one who had never seen a village by the sea, would it not be interesting to see Scheveningen or Katwijk, or any other such village? Well, there is no sea here, but the character of everything is interesting and worthy of notice. So if you feel inclined and have an opportunity, stay here, but do write beforehand when you are coming and where, at which station I shall find you, and on what train.

I shall give this letter to Mother when she comes, for in all probability I shall meet her when she comes back from Paris.[1] I am looking forward to seeing her. Happily for Uncle, the danger seems past for the present.

The news of Frans Soek's death touched me deeply; if you know any particulars, I should like to hear them. Poor fellow, his life was not easy, for he had many struggles.

A few days ago we had a very heavy thunderstorm at about eleven o'clock in the evening. Quite near our house there is a spot from which one can see, far below, a large part of the Borinage, with the chimneys, the mounds of coal, the little miners' cottages, the scurrying little black figures by day, like ants in a nest; and farther on, dark pine woods with little white cottages silhouetted against them, a few church spires a way off, an old mill, etc. Generally there is a kind of haze hanging over it all, or a fantastic chiaroscuro effect formed by the shadows of the clouds, reminding one of pictures by Rembrandt or Michel or Ruysdael.

But during that thunderstorm in the pitch-dark night the flashes of lightning made a curious effect: now and then everything became visible for a moment. Near by the large, gloomy buildings of the Marcasse mine stood alone, isolated in the open field, that night conjuring up the huge bulk of Noah's Ark as it must have looked in the terrible pouring rain and the darkness of the Flood, illuminated by a flash of lightning. Tonight in a Bible class I described a shipwreck, still under the influence of that thunderstorm.

[1] Their mother had been called to Paris; on his way to the South, Uncle Vincent had fallen dangerously ill there.

I often read in *Uncle Tom's Cabin* these days. There is still so much slavery in the world, and in this remarkably wonderful book that important question is treated with so much wisdom, so much love, and such zeal and interest in the true welfare of the poor oppressed that one comes back to it again and again, always finding something new.

I still can find no better definition of the word art than this, "L'art c'est l'homme ajouté à la nature" [art is man added to nature]—nature, reality, truth, but with a significance, a conception, a character, which the artist brings out in it, and to which he gives expression, "qu'il dégage," which he disentangles, sets free and interprets. A picture by Mauve or Maris or Israëls says more, and says it more clearly, than nature herself. It is the same with books, and in *Uncle Tom's Cabin* especially, the artist has put things in a new light; in this book, though it is becoming an old book already—that is, written years ago—all things have become new. The sentiment in it is so fine, so elaborate, so masterly. It is written with so much love, so much seriousness, so faithfully. It is humble and simple, but at the same time so truly sublime, so noble and refined.

Recently I read a book about the English coal district, but it did not give many particulars. Enclosed is a wood engraving for your collection.

The other day I made the acquaintance of somebody who has been a foreman over the miners for many years. Of humble origin, he is a self-made man. Now he has a lung disease, serious enough, and can no longer stand the terribly fatiguing work down in the mine. It is very interesting to hear him speak about all those things relating to the mines. He has always remained a friend of the miner (unlike so many others who have also got on, but more for the sake of money than real distinction, and prompted by less noble and very often mean motives). He has the heart of a laborer—faithful and honest and brave—but he is far superior to most of them in intellectual development. More than once during a strike he has been the only person with any influence on the miners. They would listen to nobody, they would follow nobody's advice but his; and he alone was obeyed in the critical moment. When I met him for the first time, I thought of the etching by Meissonier which we know so well, "The Reader." One of the Denis boys is about to become engaged to his daughter, that is why he visits the house here now and then, though rarely, and so I made his acquaintance. Since then I visited him a few times. Have you ever read Legouvé, *Les Pères et les Enfants*? It is a remarkable book. I found it at his house and read it with interest.

A few days ago I received a letter from the Reverend Mr. Jones of Isleworth in which he writes about building little wooden churches here in the Borinage. Is that practicable, is it desirable? He is ready to work for that end, that is, for the erection of the first of such little buildings. He even speaks of coming here in the autumn to talk it over; I certainly hope it happens. If you have time, write me a line, and if you can, stop here when you go to Paris. At all events let me know, if possible, on what train you will be passing the station nearest to Wasmes, for then I will try to be there. Blessings on your work, believe me always,

Your loving brother, Vincent

50

133

My Dear Theo,   Cuesmes, July 1880

I am writing you with some reluctance, not having done so in such a long time, for many reasons.

To a certain degree you have become a stranger to me, and I have become the same to you, more than you may think; perhaps it would be better for us not to continue in this way. Probably I would not have written you even now if I were not under the obligation and necessity of doing so, if you yourself had not given me cause. At Etten I learned that you had sent 50 francs for me; well, I have accepted them. Certainly with reluctance, certainly with a rather melancholy feeling, but I am up against a stone wall and in a sort of mess. How can I do otherwise? So I am writing you to thank you.

Perhaps you know I am back in the Borinage. Father would rather I stay in the neighborhood of Etten; I refused, and in this I think I acted for the best. Involuntarily, I have become more or less a kind of impossible and suspect personage in the family, at least somebody whom they do not trust, so how could I in any way be of any use to anybody? Therefore, above all, I think the best and most reasonable thing for me to do is to go away and keep at a convenient distance, so that I cease to exist for you all.

As molting time—when they change their feathers—is for birds, so adversity or misfortune is the difficult time for us human beings. One can stay in it—in that time of molting—one can also emerge renewed; but anyhow it must not be done in public and it is not at all amusing, therefore the only thing to do is to hide oneself. Well, so be it.

Now, though it is very difficult, almost impossible, to regain the confidence of a whole family, which is not quite free from prejudices and other qualities as fashionable and honorable, I do not quite despair that by and by, slowly but surely, a cordial understanding may be renewed between some of us. And in the very first place, I should like to see that entente cordiale, not to put it stronger, re-established between Father and me; and I desire no less to see it re-established between us two. An entente cordiale is infinitely better than misunderstandings.

Now I must bore you with certain abstract things, but I hope you will listen to them patiently. I am a man of passions, capable of and subject to doing more or less foolish things, which I happen to repent, more or less, afterward. Now and then I speak and act too hastily, when it would have been better to wait patiently. I think other people sometimes make the same mistakes. Well, this being the case, what's to be done? Must I consider myself a dangerous man, incapable of anything? I don't think so. But the problem is to try every means to put those selfsame passions to good use. For instance, to name one of the passions, I have a more or less irresistible passion for books, and I continually want to instruct myself, to study if you like, just as much as I want to eat my bread. *You* certainly will be able to understand this. When I was in other surroundings, in the surroundings of pictures and works of art, you know how I had a violent passion for them, reaching the highest pitch of enthusiasm. And I am not sorry about it, for even now, *far from that land, I am often homesick for the land of pictures.*

You remember perhaps that I knew well (and perhaps I know still) who Rembrandt was, or Millet, or Jules Dupré or Delacroix or Millais or M. Maris. Well, now I do not have those surroundings any more—yet that thing called soul, they say it never dies, but lives on and continues to search forever and ever and ever. So instead of giving way to this homesickness, I said to myself: That land, or the fatherland, is everywhere. So instead of giving in to despair, I chose the part of active melancholy—in so far as I possessed the power of activity—in other words, I preferred the melancholy which hopes and aspires and seeks to that which despairs in stagnation and woe. So I studied somewhat seriously the books within my reach like the Bible, and the *French Revolution* by Michelet, and last winter, Shakespeare and a few by Victor Hugo and Dickens, and Beecher Stowe, and lately *Eschylus*, and then several others, less classical, several great "little masters." You know, those "little masters" include people like Fabritius or Bida.

Now he who is absorbed in all this is sometimes choquant, shocking, to others, and sometimes unwittingly sins against certain forms and customs and social conventions. It is a pity, however, when this is taken in bad part. For instance, you know that I have often neglected my appearance; I admit it, and I admit that it is shocking. But look here, poverty and want have their share in the cause, and also profound discouragement; and then, it is sometimes a good way to assure the solitude necessary for concentrating on whatever study preoccupies one. A very necessary study is that of medicine; there is scarcely anybody who does not try to know a little of it, who does not try to understand what it is about, and you see I do not yet know one word about it. All this absorbs and preoccupies one—all this gives one something to dream about, to reflect on and to think about.

Now for more than five years—I do not know exactly how long—I have been more or less without employment, wandering here and there. You say, Since a certain time you have gone down, you have deteriorated, you have not done anything. Is this quite true?

It is true that occasionally I have earned my crust of bread, occasionally a friend has given it to me in charity. I have lived as I could, as luck would have it, haphazardly. It is true that I have lost the confidence of many; it is true that my financial affairs are in a sad state; it is true that the future is only too gloomy; it is true that I might have done better; it is true that I've lost time in terms of earning my bread; it is true that even my studies are in a rather sad and hopeless condition, and that my needs are greater—infinitely greater—than my possessions. But is this what you call "going down," is this what you call "doing nothing"?

You will perhaps say, But why didn't you continue as they wanted you to—they wanted you to go through the university?

My only answer is, the expenses were too heavy, and besides, that future was not much better than the one on the road now before me.

But I must continue on the path I have taken now. If I don't do anything, if I don't study, if I don't go on seeking any longer, I am lost. Then woe is me. That is how I look at it: to continue, to continue, that is what is necessary.

But you will ask, What is your definite aim?

That aim becomes more definite, will stand out slowly and surely, as the rough draft becomes a sketch, and the sketch becomes a picture—little by little, by working seriously on it, by pondering over the idea, vague at first, over the thought that was fleeting and passing, till it gets fixed.

I must tell you that with evangelists it is the same as with artists. There is an old academic school, often detestable, tyrannical, the accumulation of horrors, men who wear a cuirass, a steel armor, of prejudices and conventions; when these people are in charge of affairs, they dispose of positions, and by a system of red tape they try to keep their protégés in their places and to exclude the other man. Their God is like the God of Shakespeare's drunken Falstaff, *le dedans d'une église* [the inside of a church]; indeed, by a curious chance some of these evangelical (???) gentlemen find themselves with the same point of view on spiritual things as that drunken character (perhaps they would be somewhat surprised to discover this if they were capable of human emotions). But there is little fear of their blindness ever changing to clear-sightedness in such matters.

This state of affairs has its bad side for him who does not agree, but protests against it with all his soul and all his heart and all the indignation of which he is capable. For my part I respect academicians who are not like these, but the respectable ones are rarer than one would first believe. One of the reasons why I am unemployed now, why I have been unemployed for years, is simply that I have different ideas than the gentlemen who give the places to men who think as they do. It is not merely the question of dress which they have hypocritically reproached me with; it is a much more serious question, I assure you.

Why do I tell you all this?—not to complain, not to excuse myself for things in which I may or may not have been wrong, but simply to answer you. During your visit last summer, when we walked together near the abandoned pit which they call *La Sorcière*, you reminded me that there had been another time when we two had walked together—near the old canal and mill of Rijswijk. "And then," you said, "we agreed in many things." But you added, "Since then you have changed so much, you are not the same any longer."

Well, that is not quite true. What has changed is that my life then was less difficult and my future seemed less dark; but the inner state, my way of looking at things and my way of thinking, has not changed. If there has been any change at all, it is that I think and believe and love more seriously now what I already thought and believed and loved then.

So you would be wrong in persisting in the belief that, for instance, I should now be less enthusiastic for Rembrandt, or Millet, or Delacroix, or whoever it may be; the contrary is true. But, you see, there are many things which one must believe and love. There is something of Rembrandt in Shakespeare, and of Correggio in Michelet, and of Delacroix in Victor Hugo; and then there is something of Rembrandt in the Gospel, or something of the Gospel in Rembrandt—whichever, it comes to the same if only one understands it properly, without misinterpreting it and considering the equivalence of the comparisons, which do not pretend to lessen the merits of the original personalities. And in Bunyan there is something of Maris or of Millet, and in Beecher Stowe there is something of Ary Scheffer.

If now you can forgive a man for making a thorough study of pictures, admit also that the love of books is as sacred as the love of Rembrandt—I even think the two complement each other. I am very fond of the portrait of a man by Fabritius which, one day when we were walking together, we stood looking at for a long while in Haarlem Museum. Yes, but I am as fond of Sydney Carton in Dickens's *Tale of Two Cities*, and I could show you other figures as curiously striking in other books, with a more or less remarkable resemblance. And I think that Kent, a character in Shakespeare's *King Lear*, is as noble and distinguished a personage as a figure by Th. de Keyser, though Kent and King Lear lived in a much earlier period. Not to say more. My God, how beautiful Shakespeare is! Who is mysterious like him? His language and style can indeed be compared to an artist's brush, quivering with fever and emotion. But one must learn to read, just as one must learn to see and learn to live.

So you must not think that I disavow things—I am rather faithful in my unfaithfulness and, though changed, I am the same; my only anxiety is, How can I be of use in the world? Can't I serve some purpose and be of any good? How can I learn more and study certain subjects profoundly? You see, that is what preoccupies me constantly; and then I feel imprisoned by poverty, excluded from participating in certain work, and certain necessities are beyond my reach. That is one reason for being somewhat melancholy. And then one feels an emptiness where there might be friendship and strong and serious affections, and one feels a terrible discouragement gnawing at one's very moral energy, and fate seems to put a barrier to the instincts of affection, and a choking flood of disgust envelops one. And one exclaims, "How long, my God!"

Well, what shall I say? Do our inner thoughts ever show outwardly? There may be a great fire in our soul, yet no one ever comes to warm himself at it, and the passers-by see only a wisp of smoke coming through the chimney, and go along their way. Look here, now, what must be done? Must one tend that inner fire, have salt in oneself, wait patiently yet with how much impatience for the hour when somebody will come and sit down near it—maybe to stay? Let him who believes in God wait for the hour that will come sooner or later.

For the moment it seems that things are going very badly with me, and it has already been so for a considerable time and may continue awhile in the future; but after everything has seemed to go wrong, perhaps a time will come when things will go right. I don't count on it, perhaps it will never happen; but if there is a change for the better, I should consider it so much gain, I should be contented, I should say, At last! you see *there was something after all!*

But you will say, Yet you are an intolerable being because you have impossible ideas about religion and childish scruples of conscience.

If my ideas are impossible or childish, I hope to get rid of them—I ask no better. But this is approximately what I think on the subject. In *Un Philosophe sous les toits*, by Souvestre, you will find how a man of the people, a simple miserable laborer, imagines his own country. "Perhaps you have never thought what your own country really is," he said, putting his hand on my shoulder. "It is everything around you, everything that has brought you up and nourished you, everything you have loved; those fields that you see, those houses, those trees, those young girls laughing as they pass—that is your country! The laws that protect you, the bread which rewards your labor, the words you speak, the joy and the sorrow that come to you from the people and the things among which you live—that is your country! The little room where you used to see your mother, the memories which she has left you, the earth in which she reposes— that is your country! You see it, you breathe it, everywhere! Figure to yourself the rights and the duties, the affections and the needs, the memories and the gratitude; gather it all under one name, and that name will be your country."

In the same way I think that everything which is really good and beautiful— of inner moral, spiritual and sublime beauty in men and their works—comes from God, and that all which is bad and wrong in men and in their works is not of God, and God does not approve of it.

But I always think that the best way to know God is to love many things. Love a friend, a wife, something—whatever you like—you will be on the way to knowing more about Him; that is what I say to myself. But one must love with a lofty and serious intimate sympathy, with strength, with intelligence; and one must always try to know deeper, better and more. That leads to God, that leads to unwavering faith.

To give you an example: someone loves Rembrandt, but seriously—that man will know there is a God, he will surely believe it. Someone studies the history of the French Revolution—he will not be unbelieving, he will see that in great things also there is a sovereign power manifesting itself. Maybe for a short time somebody takes a free course at the great university of misery, and pays attention to the things he sees with his eyes and hears with his ears, and thinks them over; he, too, will end in believing, and he will perhaps have learned more than he can tell. To try to understand the real significance of what the great artists, the serious masters, tell us in their masterpieces, *that* leads to God; one man wrote or told it in a book; another, in a picture. Then simply read the Gospel and the Bible: it makes you think, and think much, and think all the time. Well, think much and think all the time, it raises your thoughts above the ordinary level without your knowing it. We know how to read—well then, let us read!

It is true that there may be moments when one becomes somewhat absent-minded, somewhat visionary; some become too absent-minded, too visionary. This is perhaps the case with me, but it is my own fault; maybe there is some excuse after all—I was absorbed, preoccupied, troubled, for some reason—but one overcomes this. The dreamer sometimes falls into a well, but is said to get out of it afterward. And the absent-minded man also has his lucid intervals in compensation. He is sometimes a person who has his reasons for being as he is, but they are not always understood at first, or are unconsciously forgotten most of the time, from lack of interest. A man who has been tossed back and forth for a long time, as if on a stormy sea, at last reaches his destination; a man who has seemed good-for-nothing and incapable of any employment, any function, ends in finding one and becoming active and capable of action—he shows himself quite different from what he seemed at first.

I write somewhat at random whatever comes to my pen. I should be very glad if you could see in me something more than an idle fellow. Because there are two kinds of idleness, which are a great contrast to each other. There is the man who is idle from laziness and from lack of character, from the baseness of his nature. If you like, you may take me for such a one.

On the other hand, there is the idle man who is idle in spite of himself, who is inwardly consumed by a great longing for action but does nothing, because it is impossible for him to do anything, because he seems to be imprisoned in some cage, because he does not possess what he needs to become productive, because circumstances bring him inevitably to that point. Such a man does not always know what he could do, but he instinctively feels, I am good for something, my life has a purpose after all, I know that I could be quite a different man! How can I be useful, of what service can I be? There is something inside of me, what can it be? This is quite a different kind of idle man; if you like, you may take me for such a one!

A caged bird in spring knows quite well that he might serve some end; he is well aware that there is something for him to do, but he cannot do it. What is it? He does not quite remember. Then some vague ideas occur to him, and he says to himself, "The others build their nests and lay their eggs and bring up their little ones"; and he knocks his head against the bars of the cage. But the cage remains, and the bird is maddened by anguish.

"Look at that lazy animal," says another bird in passing, "he seems to be living at ease."

Yes, the prisoner lives, he does not die; there are no outward signs of what passes within him—his health is good, he is more or less gay when the sun shines. But then the season of migration comes, and attacks of melancholia—"But he has everything he wants," say the children that tend him in his cage. He looks through the bars at the overcast sky where a thunderstorm is gathering, and inwardly he rebels against his fate. "I am caged, I am caged, and you tell me I do not want anything, fools! You think I have everything I need! Oh! I beseech you liberty, that I may be a bird like other birds!"

A certain idle man resembles this idle bird.

And circumstances often prevent men from doing things, prisoners in I do not know what horrible, horrible, most horrible cage. There is also—I know it— the deliverance, the tardy deliverance. A justly or unjustly ruined reputation, poverty, unavoidable circumstances, adversity—that is what makes men prisoners.

One cannot always tell what it is that keeps us shut in, confines us, seems to bury us; nevertheless, one feels certain barriers, certain gates, certain walls. Is all this imagination, fantasy? I don't think so. And one asks, "My God! is it for long, is it forever, is it for all eternity?"

Do you know what frees one from this captivity? It is every deep, serious affection. Being friends, being brothers, love, that is what opens the prison by some supreme power, by some magic force. Without this, one remains in prison. Where sympathy is renewed, life is restored.

And the prison is also called prejudice, misunderstanding, fatal ignorance of one thing or another, distrust, false shame.

But to speak of other things, if I have come down in the world, you, on the contrary, have risen. If I have lost the sympathy of some, you, on the contrary, have gained it. That makes me very happy—I say it in all sincerity—and always will. If you hadn't much seriousness or depth, I would fear that it would not last; but as I think you are very serious and of great depth, I believe that it will. But I should be very glad if it were possible for you to see me as something more than an idle man of the worst type.

If ever I can do anything for you, be of some use to you, know that I am at your disposal. As I have accepted what you have given me, you might, in case I could render you some service, ask me to; it would make me happy, and I should consider it a proof of confidence. We are rather far apart, and perhaps we have different views on some things, but nevertheless there may come an hour, there may come a day, when we may be of service to one another.

For the present I shake hands with you, thanking you again for the help you have given me.

If you wish to write me one of these days, my address is, c/o Ch. Decrucq, Rue du Pavillon 3, Cuesmes, near Mons. And know that a letter from you will do me good.

Ever yours, Vincent

136

Dear Theo, Cuesmes, 24 Sept. 1880

Your letter has done me good—I thank you for having written the way you did. The roll containing a new collection of etchings and various prints has just arrived. Especially the splendid etching, "Le Buisson" by Daubigny and Ruysdael, *that is it.* I intend to make two drawings, either in sepia or in something else: one after that etching, the other after "Le Four dans les Landes" by Th. Rousseau. It is true that I have already done a sepia of the latter, but you know it lacks power compared with the etching by Daubigny, though the sepia itself may have some tone and sentiment. I must take it up again, and work on it.

I work regularly on the *Cours de Dessin Bargue*, and intend to finish it before I undertake anything else, for each day it makes my hand as well as my mind more supple and strong; I cannot be grateful enough to Mr. Tersteeg for having lent it to me so generously. The studies are excellent. Between times I am reading a book on anatomy and another on perspective which Mr. Tersteeg also sent me. The style is very dry, and at times those books are terribly irritating, but still I think I do well to study them.

So you see that I am in a rage of work, though for the moment it does not produce very brilliant results. But I hope these thorns will bear their white blossoms in due time, and that this apparently sterile struggle is no other than the labor of childbirth. First the pain, then the joy.

You speak about Lessore. I think I remember very elegant water-color landscapes by him, in a blond tone, of an apparently easy and light execution, yet correct and distinguée, with a somewhat decorative effect (*decorative* used here in a favorable sense). So I know something of his work, and you speak of someone who is not quite unknown to me. I love the portrait of Victor Hugo; it is very conscientiously done, with the evident intention of portraying the truth without any straining after effect.

This winter I have studied certain works by Hugo, including *Le Dernier Jour d'un Condamné*, and a very beautiful book on Shakespeare. I started studying that author long ago; he is as beautiful as Rembrandt. Shakespeare is to Charles Dickens or Victor Hugo what Ruysdael is to Daubigny, and Rembrandt, to Millet.

What you say in your letter about Barbizon is quite true, and I will tell you a few things which will prove I share the opinion. I have not seen Barbizon, but though I have not seen it, last winter I saw Courrières. I had undertaken a walking tour mostly in Pas-de-Calais, not La Manche [The Channel], but the department or province. I had undertaken the trip hoping to find some kind of work there if possible. I would have accepted anything. But after all, perhaps I went involuntarily, I can't exactly say why.

I had said to myself, You must see Courrières. I had only 10 fr. in my pocket, and having started by taking the train, I was soon out of money; I was on the road for a week, I had a long, weary walk of it. Anyhow, I saw Courrières, and the outside of M. Jules Breton's studio. The outside of the studio was rather disappointing: it was quite newly built of brick, with a Methodist regularity, an inhospitable, chilly and irritating aspect. If I could only have seen the interior, I would certainly not have given a thought to the exterior, I am sure of that. But what shall I say of the interior? I was not able to catch a glimpse, for I lacked the courage to enter and introduce myself.

I looked elsewhere in Courrières for traces of Jules Breton or some other artist; the only thing I was able to discover was his picture at a photographer's, and in a dark corner of the old church a copy of Titian's "Burial of Christ," which in the shadow seemed to me to be very beautiful and of wonderful tone. Was it by him? I do not know, as I was unable to discern any signature.

But no trace of any living artist; there was only a café called Café des Beaux Arts, also built of new bricks, equally inhospitable, chilly and repellent; the said café was decorated with a kind of fresco or mural painting representing episodes in the life of the famous knight, Don Quixote. Confidentially, those frescoes seemed to me a poor consolation, as they were of a rather inferior quality. I do not know who painted them.

But I have at least seen the country around Courrières, the haystacks, the brown earth or almost coffee-colored clay, with whitish spots here and there where the marl appears, which seems very unusual to those of us who are accustomed to black earth. And the French sky seemed to me very much clearer and more limpid than the smoky, foggy sky of the Borinage. Besides, there were farms and sheds which, the Lord be praised, still retained their moss-covered thatched roofs. I also saw flocks of crows made famous by the pictures of Daubigny and Millet. Not to mention, as I ought to have in the first place, the characteristic and picturesque figures of the different travelers, diggers, woodcutters, peasants driving horses, and here and there the silhouette of a woman in a white cap. Even in Courrières there was a charbonnage or mine. I saw the day shift coming up in the twilight: there were no women in men's clothes as in the Borinage, only miners with tired and miserable faces, blackened by the coal dust, clad in tattered miners' clothes, and one of them in an old soldier's cape.

Though this trip was almost too much for me and I came back overcome by fatigue, with sore feet, and quite melancholy, I do not regret it, for I have seen interesting things, and one learns to take a different but correct view of the hardships of real misery. Occasionally I earned some crusts of bread along the road in exchange for some drawings which I had in my valise. But when the 10 fr. were all gone, I had to spend the last nights in the open air, once in an abandoned wagon, which was white with frost the next morning—rather a bad resting place; once in a pile of fagots; and one time that was a little better, in a haystack, where I succeeded in making a rather more comfortable berth—but then a drizzling rain did not exactly further my well-being.

Well, even in that deep misery I felt my energy revive, and I said to myself, In spite of everything I shall rise again: I will take up my pencil, which I have forsaken in my great discouragement, and I will go on with my drawing. From that moment everything has seemed transformed for me; and now I have started and my pencil has become somewhat docile, becoming more so every day. The too long and too great poverty had discouraged me so much that I could not do anything.

Another thing which I saw during that excursion was the villages of the weavers.

The miners and the weavers still constitute a race apart from other laborers and artisans, and I feel a great sympathy for them. I should be very happy if someday I could draw them, so that those unknown or little-known types would be brought before the eyes of the people. The man from the depth of the abyss, *de profundis*—that is the miner; the other, with his dreamy air, somewhat absent-minded, almost a somnambulist—that is the weaver. I have been living among them for two years, and have learned a little of their unique character, at least that of the miners especially. And increasingly I find something touching and almost sad in these poor, obscure laborers—of the lowest order, so to speak, and the most despised—who are generally represented as a race of criminals and thieves by a perhaps vivid but very false and unjust imagination. Of course one can find criminals, drunkards, and thieves here, just as anywhere else, but none of them are the true type.

In your letter you mentioned vaguely my coming eventually to Paris, or in the neighborhood, if it were possible and if I wanted to. It would certainly be my great and ardent wish to go to Paris or to Barbizon, or elsewhere. But how could I, when I do not earn a cent? Though I work hard, it will be some time before I reach the point where I can consider such a thing as coming to Paris, for indeed to be able to work as is necessary, I should need at least 100 fr. a month—one can live on less, but then it is hardship, even want.

"Poverty keeps the good spirits from arriving" is an old Palissy proverb which has some truth in it, and which is perfectly true if one understands its real meaning and depth.

For the moment I do not see how the thing would be practicable; it is better for me to stay here, working as much as I can—and, after all, it is cheaper. But it is certain that I cannot remain very much longer in the little room where I am now. It is a small room anyway, and then there are two beds, one for the children and one for me. And now that I draw those rather large-sized Bargues, I cannot tell you how inconvenient it is. I don't want to upset the people's household arrangements, and they have already told me that I could by no means have the other room in the house, even if I paid more, for the woman needs it for her washing, which has to be done almost every day in a miner's house. So I should just like to take a small worker's house; it costs about 9 fr. a month.

Though every day difficulties crop up and new ones will present themselves, I cannot tell you how happy I am to have taken up drawing again. I had been thinking of it for a long time, but I always considered the thing impossible and beyond my reach. But now, though I feel my weakness and my painful dependence in many things, I have recovered my mental balance, and day by day my energy increases.

Now I will tell you my opinion about coming to Paris. If I had an opportunity to develop a friendship with some good and worthy artist, it would be of great advantage to me. But abruptly going there would only be a large-scale repetition of my trip to Courrières, where I had hoped to meet some living specimen of an artist, but found none. The thing for me is to learn to draw well, to be master of my pencil or my crayon or my brush; this gained, I shall make good things anywhere, and the Borinage is just as picturesque as old Venice, Arabia, Brittany, Normandy, Picardy or Brie.

If my work is bad, it is my own fault. But certainly at Barbizon one would have more chance than anywhere else of meeting some more advanced artist, who would be as one of God's angels to me. I say this in all seriousness and without exaggeration. So, if you eventually find the means or opportunity for it, think of me. In the meantime I'll stay here quietly in some little miner's hut, where I shall work as well as I can.

You wrote about Méryon, and what you say about him is quite true. I know his etchings a little. Would you like to see a curious thing? Put one of his correct and masterly drawings alongside some print by Viollet-le-Duc or some other architect. Then you will see Méryon in his full strength, because the other etching will serve to set off his work, to form a contrast. Well, what do you see? This Méryon, even when he draws bricks, or granite, or iron bars, or a railing of a bridge, puts into his etchings something of the human soul, moved by I do not know what inner sorrow. I have seen drawings of Gothic architecture by Victor Hugo. Well, without having Méryon's force and masterly technique, there was something of the same sentiment. What is that sentiment? It has some relation to what Albrecht Dürer expressed in his "Melancholia," and, in our day, James Tissot and M. Maris (different as these two may be); some profound critic rightly said of James Tissot, "He is a soul in anguish." However this may be, there is something of the human soul in his work; for that reason alone it is grand, immense, infinite: put Viollet-le-Duc alongside and it is Stone, while Méryon is Spirit. Méryon is said to have had such a capacity for love that, like Dickens's Sydney Carton, he loved even the stones of certain places. In Millet, in Jules Breton, in Jozef Israëls too, this precious pearl, the human soul, is even more in evidence—expressed in a nobler, worthier tone, more evangelically, if I can say it that way.

But to return to Méryon, he also has a distant relationship with Jongkind, I think, and perhaps with Seymour Haden, for at certain times these two artists have been very strong. Wait, perhaps someday you will see that I too am an artist; I do not now know what I can do, but I hope I shall be able to make some drawings with something human in them. But first I must draw the Bargues and do other more or less difficult things. The path is narrow, the door is narrow, and there are few who find it.

Thanking you for your kindness, especially for "Le Buisson," I shake hands with you in thought,

Vincent

Now I have taken your whole collection, but you will have another one, I hope; besides, for your collection of wood engravings I have some very good things from the two volumes of the *Musée Universel*, which I intend for you.

143*a*

[Reprinted from Louis Piérard, *La vie tragique de Vincent van Gogh*, Édition revue. Paris, Éditions Correa & Cie, 1939].

Reading an article by M. Pierre Godet in *L'Art Décoratif* and the comments it prompted from a certain Protestant publication, *Foi et Vie*, induced me one day to start investigating in my native country this disturbing period of Vincent van Gogh's life. I knew that Vincent had once been sent as a missionary to the Borinage; nothing more. I have patiently interrogated the pastors of numerous villages and a certain number of their congregations. And at last I had the information I sought.

It was during a strike. Before the Village Hall an old miner, squatting with his knees drawn up to his chin, a pipe between his teeth—in the favorite resting position of "*tapeurs à la veine*"—said in his rude patois, "*L'pasteur Vincent? Si j'mein souviés? Je l'crois bé!*" [Pastor Vincent? Do I remember him? I should think so!] ... I did my best to make him specify his memories more precisely. In his mind's eye he saw Van Gogh again, sitting on a campstool in the yard at the mine (at pit No. 10, Grisoeul), making sketches of the cage and "*la belle fleur*," the iron framework, and then of the emerging miners, black with coal dust, their eyes blinking at the sudden daylight, their lamps in their fists....

At last I learned that Van Gogh had boarded at the house of a certain Jean-Baptiste Denis, a baker, and had preached in the old "Salon de Bébé" (in the

Borinage, a hall for dancing and meetings is always called a *salon*). The old house, which at the time was something between a farm and a *salon*, has been much altered during the last thirty years. But when I found the vast kitchen intact, with its mighty beams covered with white stucco, the big open hearth, and in a corner the stone table at which Vincent liked to eat, I was moved.... The *Salon*, or as some said, *L'timpe* [the temple] of Bébé, was situated at the edge of the Colfontaine forest. The whitewashed walls of the meeting hall were bluish-white. Behind the preacher one could see the sloping gardens, the square vegetable plots, through the window....

So here Van Gogh lived after November 1878 in the Borinage, vast mining district in the neighborhood of Mons.... The Reformed religion has always possessed, and does to this day, important nuclei here. In every mining village, or in nearly every one, there is a Protestant church, and in some, two (one of the National Church, and the other of the Free Church, which refuses State subsidies)....

At last, after a long search, I found in the Tournaisis district an old pastor, M. Bonte, who was installed in Warquignies, a village in the neighborhood of Wasmes, in 1878, and received Vincent van Gogh with the greatest kindness. Here are the notes he was good enough to send me:

I should like to satisfy you as much as possible by putting together some reminiscences of Vincent van Gogh. In fact, I knew him some forty-five years ago in the Borinage, where he was an evangelist (not a pastor, as he had no theological degree). He worked at Wasmes about one year.

He was the son of a Dutch minister. I remember well his arrival at Pâturages : he was a blond young man of medium stature and with a pleasant face ; he was well dressed, had excellent manners, and showed in his personal appearance all the characteristics of Dutch cleanliness.

He expressed himself in French correctly, and was able to preach quite satisfactorily at the religious gatherings of the little Protestant group in Wasmes which they had entrusted to his care. Another community in Wasmes had a pastor. He worked near the edge of the forest, in the direction of Warquignies ; he led divine service in a former dance hall.

Our young man took lodgings in an old farm at Petit-Wasmes. The house was relatively pretty—it differed considerably from the dwellings in the neighborhood, where one saw only little miners' cottages.

The family which had taken Vincent in had simple habits, and lived like working people.

But our evangelist very soon showed toward his lodgings the peculiar feelings which dominated him : he considered the accommodation far too luxurious ; it shocked his Christian humility, he could not bear being lodged comfortably, in a way so different from that of the miners. Therefore he left these people who had surrounded him with sympathy and went to live in a little hovel. There he was all alone ; he had no furniture, and people said he slept crouched down in a corner of the hearth.

Besides this, the clothes he wore outdoors revealed the originality of his aspirations; people saw him issue forth clad in an old soldier's tunic and a shabby cap, and he went about the village in this attire. The fine suits he had arrived in never reappeared; nor did he buy any new ones. It is true he had only a modest salary, but it was sufficient to permit him to dress in accordance with his social position. Why had the boy changed this way?

Faced with the destitution he encountered on his visits, his pity had induced him to give away nearly all his clothes; his money had found its way into the hands of the poor, and one might say that he had kept nothing for himself. His religious sentiments were very ardent, and he wanted to obey the words of Jesus Christ to the letter.

He felt obliged to imitate the early Christians, to sacrifice all he could live without, and he wanted to be even more destitute than the majority of the miners to whom he preached the Gospel.

I must add that also his Dutch cleanliness was singularly abandoned; soap was banished as a wicked luxury; and when our evangelist was not wholly covered with a layer of coal dust, his face was usually dirtier than that of the miners. Exterior details did not trouble him; he was absorbed in his ideal of self-denial, but for the rest he showed that his attitude was not the consequence of *laisser-aller*, but a consistent practicing of the ideas governing his conscience.

He no longer felt any inducement to take care of his own well-being—his heart had been aroused by the sight of others' want.

He preferred to go to the unfortunate, the wounded, the sick, and always stayed with them a long time; he was willing to make any sacrifice to relieve their sufferings.

In addition, his profound sensitivity was not limited to the human race. Vincent van Gogh respected every creature's life, even of those most despised.

A repulsive caterpillar did not provoke his disgust; it was a living creature, and as such, deserved protection.

The family with whom he had boarded told me that every time he found a caterpillar on the ground in the garden, he carefully picked it up and took it to a tree. Apart from this trait, which perhaps will be considered insignificant or even foolish, I have retained the impression that Vincent van Gogh was actuated by a high ideal: self-forgetfulness and devotion to all other beings was the guiding principle which he accepted wholeheartedly.

It will not revile the memory of the man to confess that in my opinion he retained one weakness: he was an incorrigible smoker. At times I teased him about it; a loather of tobacco myself, I told him that he did wrong not to give it up, but he ignored me—Painters cannot do without a little spot of shade in the picture.

As far as his painting is concerned, I cannot speak as a connoisseur; besides, he was not taken seriously.

He would squat in the mine fields and draw the women picking up pieces of coal and going away laden with heavy sacks.

It was observed that he did not reproduce the pretty things to which we are wont to attribute beauty.

He made some portraits of old women, but for the rest, nobody attached any importance to an activity that was considered a mere hobby.

63

But it would seem that as an artist, also, our young man had a predilection for all that seemed miserable to him.

These, sir, are a few reminiscences which my aged memory has tried to collect....

Here is another letter. I did not have the heart to make any alteration in it. The good baker who wrote it and who had lived on intimate terms with Vincent van Gogh will not take it amiss if I reproduce it completely and faithfully.

Monsieur Piérard,

One fine spring day, when I saw our young friend Vincent van Gogh arrive, richly dressed, I could not stop looking at him, next day he paid a visit to the pastor, M. Bonte. Immediately putting himself on a level with the working class, our friend sank away into the greatest humiliations, and it was not long before he had disposed of all his clothes.

Having arrived at the stage where he had no shirt and no socks on his feet, we have seen him make shirts out of sacking. I myself was too young then.

My kind-hearted mother said to him : Monsieur Vincent, why do you deprive yourself of all your clothes like this—you who are descended from such a noble family of Dutch pastors? He answered : I am a friend of the poor like Jesus was. She answered : You're no longer in a normal condition.

The same year there was a firedamp explosion in Pit No. I of the Charbonnage Belge, and many miners were burned. Our friend Vincent did not give himself a moment's rest day and night cutting up the last remnants of his linen to make bandages with wax and olive oil on them, and then ran to the wounded to dress their burns.

The humanity of our friend continued to grow day by day, and yet the persecutions he suffered grew, too. And still the reproaches and insults and stoning by the members of the Consistory, though he always remained in the deepest abasement ! One day when he came to our house he started vomiting on the basement floor. It had been too great a luxury for him, he ought to have stayed in a thatched hovel. His food consisted of rice and treacle, no butter on his bread.

Yet he was always at his studies ; in a single night he read a volume of 100 pages ; during the week he taught a school he had founded for the children teaching them to fear God, and at the same time he was busy making drawings of photography and the mines.

On a very hot day a violent thunderstorm burst over our region. What did our friend do ? He went out to stand in the open field to look at the great marvels of God, and so he came back wet to the skin. So it came about that our friend was turned out of his ministry, he went away to Paris and we have not heard from him since. And when he walked [it was always] on the edge of the road, dear friend, Monsieur Piérard, I could not tell you more, I was only fourteen years at the time.

Some of his characteristics have been remembered vividly. When the miners of Wasmes went to the pits, they put old vests made of sacking over their linen work clothes, using them like pea jackets to protect themselves in the cages, from water spurting from the walls of the shafts. This miserable raggedness kindled Vincent van Gogh's pity most deeply. One day he saw the word *fragile* printed on the sackcloth on one miner's back. He did not laugh. On the contrary, for many days he spoke about it compassionately at mealtimes. People did not understand. This and the thunderstorm episode were enough to convince Madame Denis "that the young gentleman was not like all the others." Her motherly heart bled for him.... She wrote a letter to Van Gogh's mother, describing the miserable life Vincent led in his cabin.

An epidemic of typhoid fever had broken out in the district. Vincent had given everything, his money and his clothes, to the poor sick miners. An inspector of the Evangelization Council had come to the conclusion that the missionary's *"excès de zèle"* bordered on the scandalous, and he did not hide his opinion from the consistory of Wasmes. Van Gogh's father went from Nuenen [*sic*] to Wasmes. He found his son lying on a sack filled with straw, horribly worn out and emaciated. In the room, dimly lit by a lamp hanging from the ceiling, some miners with faces pinched with starvation and suffering crowded round Vincent. Large, fantastic shadows danced all over the walls plastered with green.

The missionary allowed himself to be led away like a child, and returned to the home of Madame Denis.

Van Gogh made many sensational conversions among the Protestants of Wasmes. People still talk of the miner whom he went to see after the accident in the Marcasse mine. The man was a habitual drinker, "an unbeliever and a blasphemer," according to the people who told me the story. When Vincent entered his house to help and comfort him, he was received with a volley of abuse. He was called especially a *mâcheux d'chapelets* [rosary chewer], as if he had been a Roman Catholic priest. But Van Gogh's evangelical tenderness converted the man.

People still tell how, at the time of the *tirage au sort*, the drawing of lots for conscription, women begged the holy man to show them a passage in the Holy Scripture which would serve as a talisman for their sons and ensure their drawing a good number and being exempted from service in the barracks !...

Traces of Van Gogh's sojourn in the Borinage are to be found in the records of the Protestant communities. One is a report of the "Église du Bois à Wasmes," drawn up under the *"hauspices (sic) du synode."* I have copied this report and this is how it reads :

Monsieur le pasteur Peron, of Dour, has come to Wasmes. Considering the number [of members, doubtless] and the works they could do, Messieurs Neven, Jean Andry and Peron aforenamed, all three pastors of the governing body of the Sté Synodale, agreed to send our situation (*sic*) to the Synodal Board in order to learn whether it can come to our aid.

After being commissioned, Mr. Peron came to Wasmes, and reaching an agreement, they thought it proper to take turns holding the service in a hall which Mr. Peron had visited together with the members of the consistory.

After a lapse of about a year and a half the Société Synodale was good enough to send us M. Vincent; after him came M. Huton, both of them evangelists during four years or thereabouts.

We have been powerfully assisted in the work of evangelization.

And here is the 1879–80 report of the Union of ¡Protestant Churches in Belgium, chapter "Wasmes" [twenty-third report of the Synodal Board of Evangelization (1879–80)]:

The experiment of accepting the services of a young Dutchman, Mr. Vincent van Gogh, who felt himself called to be an evangelist in the Borinage, has not produced the anticipated results. If a talent for speaking, indispensable to anyone placed at the head of a congregation, had been added to the admirable qualities he displayed in aiding the sick and wounded, to his devotion to the spirit of self-sacrifice, of which he gave many proofs by consecrating his night's rest to them, and by stripping himself of most of his clothes and linen in their behalf, Mr. Van Gogh would certainly have been an accomplished evangelist.

Undoubtedly it would be unreasonable to demand extraordinary talents. But it is evident that the absence of certain qualities may render the exercise of an evangelist's principal function wholly impossible.

Unfortunately this is the case with Mr. Van Gogh. Therefore, the probationary period—some months—having expired, it has been necessary to abandon the idea of retaining him any longer.

The evangelist, M. Hutton (sic), who is now installed, took over his charge on October 1, 1879.

1879, the tragic year: epidemics of typhoid fever, "the mad fever," broke out, and then a great catastrophe cast a pall of grief over the country (the firedamp explosion in the Agrappe at Frameries). Without a thought for himself, Vincent devoted himself to nursing the sick and the men suffering from burns, with their faces black and swollen.

A strike broke out; the mutinous miners would no longer listen to anyone except "l'pasteur Vincent," whom they trusted.

In the meantime Van Gogh was increasingly busy with his drawings. One day he started for Brussels on foot. He arrived at Pastor Pietersen's house in rags, his feet bleeding, but carrying with him some of his drawings (Pietersen was an amateur water-colorist). The reception was cordial and soothing. It was decided that Van Gogh would go back to the Borinage, but this time to another parish, Cuesmes.

One of my Protestant fellow citizens, M. G. Delsaut, who knew him at Cuesmes in 1880, sent me some notes which I reproduce without a word changed:

He was an intelligent young man, speaking little—always pensive. He lived very soberly: when he got up in the morning, he breakfasted off two slices of dry bread and drank a cold cup of black coffee.

Apart from his meals, he drank only water. He always had his meals alone, and took pains to avoid eating in company. While eating, he made drawings in his lap or he read. All his spare time was given to drawing. He often went to Ghlin Wood, to the cemetery of Mons, or into the country.

He drew chiefly landscapes, castles, a shepherd with his flock, cows in the meadows.

The most striking picture, which my sister-in-law, with whom he boarded, still remembers, was a drawing showing the family gathering in the crop of potatoes, some digging, others (the women) picking up the potatoes.

He left his drawings and his books behind, but now they have all disappeared because the family was scattered.

His board was paid by his father, who sent him money. He spent much money on Bibles and New Testaments, which he gave away when he went out to draw.

Once his father had to come to Cuesmes to put a stop to his spending money on books.

He would set out to draw, a campstool under his arm and his box of drawing materials on his back, like a peddler.

When he was annoyed he rubbed his hands as if he could not stop.

[In the *Groene Amsterdammer* (Amsterdam weekly) of September 19, 1925, Piérard added the following to his account.]

I thought I had collected all the particulars, until old Mr. Denis, whom I met some days ago, told me that one fine morning, when, as he put it, "the dew had, as it were, strewn the trees and flowers in the garden with pearls of silver," he was on the point of crushing a caterpillar underfoot when Van Gogh stopped him with the exclamation, "Why do you want to kill that little animal? God created it...."

Louis Piérard used to be the socialist senator for Hainaut, the province to which the Borinage belongs; after the liberation (1918) he was sometimes called the cultural ambassador of Belgium. To my question as to what grounds he had for his statements about Vincent's alleged endeavors to calm the strikers, he wrote the following letter a few weeks before his death.

Club des écrivains belges de langue française.

Pen Club
Président : Louis Piérard
47, av. Victor Rousseau, Forest (Brux.)
téléphone 44.39.17.

Dear Mr. Van Gogh,   Brussels, October 8, 1951
I hasten to answer your letter of October 4. I am happy to hear that you are preparing a new edition of *The Letters of Vincent*. Thank you for kindly conferring importance on the particulars I gave in my book on Van Gogh's sojourn in the Borinage.

The catastrophe to which I referred, and in the course of which Vincent exerted himself with the utmost unselfishness (which is confirmed by Pastor Bonte's letter), was one of those firedamp explosions that occurred again and again in the Agrappe Pit at Frameries, near Wasmes. There were hundreds of victims. Most of them were miners, killed on the spot by the explosion. But others, the wounded, were possibly burned by ignition of the coal dust.

Vincent tried to relieve the atrocious sufferings of these unfortunate wretches, applying compresses drenched in olive oil to their burns.

These frequent mining disasters (there had been three, one after the other, at the Agrappe and at the Boule) at last prompted an outbreak of anger and mutiny among the mining population. They believed that the inspection of the mines was not conducted in such a way as to protect the miner and guarantee his safety. So there were strikes which were in fact strikes of despair. Because of this, the strikers were tempted to commit acts of violence and destruction. The gendarmes and even the army were mobilized to maintain order. It is highly probable that, in order to prevent bloodshed, Vincent intervened and used his great moral authority to restore the miners' self-control.

I would also allude to the depth at which people have to work in the mines. Do you know that there is a pit at Quaregnon in which *at this very hour* people are working at a depth of *1400 meters* (about 4,700 ft.)?

Will you please give my kind regards to Mrs. Van Gogh.

Bien à vous

Louis Piérard,
47, av. V. Rousseau, Bruxelles

1881 BRUSSELS AND ETTEN

Vincent's career as an artist begins in earnest

140

My dear Theo,   72 Boulevard du Midi, Brussels, Jan. '81

You will quite forgive me when you know that I wrote my last letter in a moment of spleen. My drawings went all wrong, and not knowing what to do, I began to write. I certainly ought to have waited for a better moment, and this will show you that I myself undoubtedly belong to that class of people of which I spoke in my last letter, namely, that class of people who do not always reflect on what they say or do. This being so, let us drop it.

I can tell you one thing; during these last days there has been a change for the better. I have finished at least a dozen drawings, or rather sketches in pencil and in pen and ink, which seem to me to be somewhat better. They vaguely resemble certain drawings by Lançon, or certain English wood engravings, but as yet they are more clumsy and awkward. They represent a porter, a miner, a snow shoveler, a walk in the snow, old women, a type of old man ("Ferragus" from Balzac's *L'histoire des treize*), etc. I am sending you two small ones, "En Route" and "Devant les Tisons" [in front of the wood fire]. I see perfectly well that they are not good, but they are beginning to look like something.

I have a model almost every day, an old porter, or some working man, or some boy, who poses for me. Next Sunday perhaps one or two soldiers will sit for me. And because now I am no longer in a bad humor, I have quite a different and better opinion of you, and of the world in general. Also I have again drawn a landscape—a heath—a thing I had not done for a long time.

I love landscape very much, but I love ten times more those studies from life, sometimes of startling realism, which have been drawn so masterfully by Gavarni, Henri Monnier, Daumier, De Lemud, Henri Pille, Th. Schuler, Ed. Morin, G. Doré (*e.g.* in his "London"), A. Lançon, De Groux, Félicien Rops, etc., etc. Now without in the least pretending to compare myself to those artists, still, by continuing to draw those types of working people, etc., I hope to arrive at the point of being able to illustrate papers and books. Especially when I am able to take more models, also female models, I shall make more progress—I feel it, and know it. And I shall also probably learn to make portraits. But the condition is to work hard, "Not a day without a line," as Gavarni said.

So it is understood that for the present I shall stay here, till you perhaps find something better for me. Only write me now and then. I am for the moment busy drawing for the third time all the *Exercices au Fusain* by Bargue.

You told me of a change in the staff of the house Goupil & Co., and also of another change in your own position. I congratulate you, and as to those gentlemen Goupil & Co., I am inclined to believe that they are to be congratulated on having got rid of some of the staff. I have always thought that those gentlemen themselves were animated by a superior and nobler spirit than that of those who have now left. Perhaps the position the latter have occupied so long in the firm, the influence and domination, which Messrs. Goupil & Co. put up with, were repugnant to some of the other employees, whom the company would perhaps have done better to retain, but who were so driven to extremes that they resigned.

As you vaguely spoke to me some time ago about coming to Paris, I must tell you that I wish no better than to go someday soon, provided I were sure of finding some work there which would give me a salary of at least 100 fr. a month. I must also tell you that as I have begun to draw, I do not intend to drop it, so I will try chiefly to get on in that line. Not only does drawing figures and scenes from life demand a knowledge of the technique of drawing, but it also demands profound studies of literature, physiognomy, etc., which are difficult to acquire.

Enough for today; write me when you have a moment to spare, and believe me, with a handshake,

Yours sincerely, Vincent
72 Bd. du Midi

Someday I hope to go to see Mr. Horta.

142

Dear Theo,   72 Bd. du Midi, Brussels, 2/4, '81

In reply to your two good letters, and as a result of Father's visit, for which I had been longing for some time, I have a few things to tell you.

In the first place this. I hear from Father that without my knowing it you have been sending me money for a long time, in this way effectively helping me to get on. Accept my heartfelt thanks, I firmly believe that you will not regret it. In this way I am learning a handicraft, and though it certainly will not make me rich, I will at any rate earn my 100 fr. a month, which is the least one needs to live on, as soon as I become a better draftsman and get some regular work.

What you told us about the painter Heyerdahl[1] has greatly interested Van Rappard, as well as me.

As the former undoubtedly will write you about it himself, I speak about this question only in so far as it concerns me personally, more or less.

I find much truth in your remarks about the Dutch artists, that it is very doubtful if one could get from them any clear counsel on the difficulties of perspective, etc., with which I am struggling. At least I quite agree with you that someone like Heyerdahl would be far preferable (as he seems to be such a versatile man) to many others who do not possess the ability to explain their method and to provide the necessary guidance and teaching. You speak of Heyerdahl as one who takes great pains to seek "proportions for drawing"; that is just what I need. Many a good painter has not the slightest, or hardly any, idea of what proportions

[1] Norwegian painter, temporarily in Paris at Bonnat's studio.

for drawing are, or beautiful lines, or characteristic composition, and thought and poetry. Yet these are important questions which Feyen-Perrin, and Ulysse Butin, and Alphonse Legros—not to mention Breton and Millet and Israëls— take extremely seriously, and never lose sight of.

Many a Dutch painter would understand nothing, absolutely nothing, of the beautiful work of Boughton, Millais, Pinwell, du Maurier, Herkomer, and Walker, to name only a few artists who are real masters as draftsmen, not to mention their talent in other directions.

I say many of them look with contempt on such work, as many do on the work of De Groux, even among the painters here in Belgium who ought to know better. This week I saw some things by De Groux which I did not know, namely, a picture, "Departure of the Conscript," and a full-length drawing, "The Drunkard"—two compositions which resemble Boughton so much that I was struck by the resemblance, as of two brothers who had never met and who were yet of one mind.

So you see, I quite agree with your opinion on Heyerdahl, and I shall be very happy if later on you could put me in touch with that man; further, I will not insist on carrying out my plan of going to Holland, at least not if I have the prospect of going to Paris later and can more or less count on it.

But in the meantime what must I do? What do you think would be best? I can continue to work with Rappard for a few weeks, but then he will probably leave here. My bedroom is too small, and the light is not good, and the people would object to my partly shutting out the light from the window; I am not even allowed to put my etchings or my drawings up on the wall. So when Rappard leaves in May, I shall have to move; I should like to work awhile in the country— at Heyst, Calmphout, Etten, Scheveningen, Katwijk, anyplace, even nearer here, as Schaerbeek, Haeren, Groenendael. But preferably a place where there is a chance of coming into contact with other painters, and if possible of living and working together, because it is cheaper and better.

Wherever it may be, living expenses are always at least 100 fr. a month; if one has less, it means want, either physical or of the necessary material and tools. This winter I have spent, let us say, 100 fr. a month, though in reality it has scarcely been as much. And I spent a great deal of that on drawing materials and also got myself some clothes. I bought two workmen's suits of rough black velvet, of that material known as veloutine. It looks well, and one can wear it everywhere; besides, the suits will be of use to me later, because I shall want a great many workmen's clothes—as I do already—for my models, which of course I need like everybody else. Gradually I must make such a collection, of all kinds of garments, secondhand if necessary, men's as well as women's; but of course I need not do it all at once, though I have started, and am going on with it.

What you say is true, financial questions have either advanced or handicapped many people in the world. It is so, and Bernard Palissy's saying remains true, "Poverty prevents the good spirits from arriving." But when I think it over, I cannot help wondering, Isn't it right that in a family like ours—in which two Messrs. Van Gogh are very rich, and both in the art field, Uncle Cor and our uncle of Prinsenhage, and in which you and I of the younger generation have chosen the same line, though in different spheres—isn't it right, I wonder, that, this being so, I should be able to count in some way on 100 fr. a month during the time which must necessarily elapse before I can get regular work as a draftsman? Now three years ago I quarreled with C. M. about quite a different question, but is that any reason for C. M. to remain my enemy forever? I would much rather think that he had never been my enemy and consider it a misunderstanding, for which I gladly take all the blame, rather than argue about how much was really my fault, for I have no time for such things. Uncle Cor so often helps other draftsmen—would it be so unnatural now if someday, when I needed it, he showed me his good will? However, I do not say this to get financial help from him. He could help me in quite another way than by giving money : for instance, if it were possible, he might bring me into contact with persons from whom I could learn many things, or help me get regular work from some magazine.

This is the way I expressed myself to Father. I noticed that people talked about the strange and unaccountable fact that I was so hard up, although I belonged to such and such a family. I replied that I thought it was only temporary, and would come right after a time. Still, I thought it better to talk it over with Father and you, and I wrote something about it to Mr. Tersteeg. But he seems to have misunderstood my intention, as he got the impression that I planned to live on the bounty of my uncles ; this being his opinion, he wrote me a very discouraging letter, and said I had no right to do such a thing. I certainly do not pretend to have the right, but I want to prevent this affair from ever becoming the subject of gossip in the studios ; therefore I think that it is necessary for good relations between myself and the family to be re-established, at any rate provisionally and outwardly, in expectation of their changing their minds about me. If they are unwilling, que soit, but then I should not be able to prevent gossip here and there. Were I immediately to write C. M. or go to see his Honor, it is to be feared he would not read my letter, or would receive me too uncordially. That's why I am talking it over with Pa and yourself, as you might possibly drop a word occasionally, so that he will not misunderstand my intentions. I was not hoping to get money from his Honor, as Mr. Tersteeg seemed to think, but only hoping that if he gained faith and confidence in my future after a talk with me, he might see me with new eyes. And if he did, it stands to reason that I most certainly would not scorn his help ; and in that case he might smooth the way for me by means other than by giving me money, for instance, in the interval between now and my going to Paris.

I wrote back that I was not at all astonished at his misconstruing my letter in this way because you yourself had spoken one time of "living on my rents." And as I now gather from the tone of your letter that you no longer see my difficult position in that miserable light and as I infer it from your strong assistance, so I hope that Mr. Tersteeg's opinion will also change eventually. The more so because he was the first to help me with those Bargues, for which I shall always be grateful to him.

You write me about a manikin. I am not in a special hurry for it, but it would be of great service to me in composing and finding the right positions, you understand that. But I would rather wait awhile and have a better one than take one now that is too defective.

But please look out for all possible prints or books on proportion, and gather as much information about them as you can. It is of the greatest value to me, for without it, one cannot make a composition of figures quickly. Furthermore, I want something about the anatomy of the horse, and sheep, and cow—not from the veterinary point of view, but rather in relation to drawing those animals. If I ask you for these things, it is because you may occasionally find such prints cheaply, as I have. For instance, if you ever have the opportunity to ask Bargue or Viollet-le-Duc about those papers on proportion, they would perhaps be the best source of information.

Of course, I should be delighted to live with you later, but we haven't come to that yet. If C. M. would help me to find some job for the time being, I certainly would not refuse it.

Even from relatively bad artists one can learn much indirectly, for instance, as Mauve learned much from Verschuur about the perspective of a stable and a wagon, and the anatomy of a horse, and yet how far Mauve is above Verschuur.

If you can recommend a picture by Madiol for the Salon, do so, for there is much that is beautiful in his work; the man is hard up and has a great many little children. He is now painting a forge; it is very good. Not long ago he painted a little old woman in which the drawing and especially the coloring are superb. But the quality of his work is uneven. His charcoal drawings are often excellent.

This letter is rather long, but I cannot make it shorter. I speak about the possibility that C. M. and others should change their opinion of me at least outwardly, but I would much rather it were truly so. For example, somebody like Roelofs doesn't know what to make of such a false position—either there must be something wrong with me, or with the others; but what he is sure of is: anyhow, there is something wrong somewhere. So he is overprudent and will have nothing to do with me just at the moment when I most need advice or help.

Such experiences are not pleasant. The main question is, Am I making progress by working on with patient energy? I think I am. "Where there is a will, there is a way." And should I be to blame later if I took my revenge? An artist does not draw for the sake of revenge, but for the love of drawing; it urges you on more than any other motive. So perhaps some things that are now amiss will come right after all.

This winter I collected many wood engravings. Your Millets have increased in number, and you will see that I did not keep your capital of wood engravings, etc., without their bringing interest. I now have twenty-four wood engravings, by and after Millet, counting "Les Travaux des Champs."

But the main thing for me is to draw, and everything must contribute to that end. The cheapest way would perhaps be for me to spend this summer at Etten —I can find subjects enough there. If you think this right, you may write to Father about it. I am willing to give in about dress or anything else to suit them, and perhaps would meet C. M. there some day this summer. There are no real objections to it, as far as I know. Either inside or outside the family, they will always judge me or talk about me from different points of view, and you will always hear the most divergent opinions about me. And I blame no one for it, because relatively few people know why an artist acts as he does. But in general, he who searches all kinds of places to find picturesque spots or figures—holes and corners which another passes by—is accused of many bad intentions and villainies which have never entered his head. A peasant who sees me draw an old tree trunk, and sees me sitting there for an hour, thinks that I have gone mad and, of course, laughs at me. A young lady who turns up her nose at a laborer in his patched, filthy dirty clothes, of course cannot understand why anyone visits the Borinage or Heyst and goes down the shaft of a coal mine; she also comes to the conclusion that I am mad.

Naturally, I do not care at all what they think if only you and Mr. Tersteeg, and C. M. and Father, and others with whom I come into contact, know better, and instead of making remarks about it, say, Your work demands it, and we understand why it is so.

So I repeat, under the circumstances there is after all no urgent reason why I should not go, for instance, to Etten or to The Hague, if that were preferable, even though it may be criticized by some fops and silly girls. As Father said when he was here, "Just write to Theo, and arrange with him what is best, and what will be the cheapest way." I hope you will let me know your opinion soon.

Heyst and Calmphout are very picturesque. In Etten I could also find subjects enough, even here if necessary, though then I would move to Schaerbeek.

Scheveningen or Katwijk would perhaps be possible if C. M. changed his opinion of me, and then I could profit directly or indirectly by the Dutch artists. As to the expenses, I suppose they would amount to at least 100 fr. a month; to do with less is impossible: "Thou shalt not muzzle the ox when he treadeth out the corn."

So I wait for your reply about these things, and in the meantime I am working with Rappard.

Rappard has painted some good studies, among others a few after the models at the academy, which are well done. A little more fire and passion would not hurt him, a little more self-confidence and more courage. Somebody once said to me, "Nous devons faire des efforts de perdus, de désespérés" [We must make the same efforts as lost, desperate beings]. He does not do that as yet. His pen-and-ink drawings of landscape are very witty and charming, but in these, also, a little more passion, please.

And now I take my leave, with a handshake, and am always

Yours sincerely, Vincent

150

Dear Theo,   Etten, September '81

Though it is only a short time since I wrote you, I already have some news to tell you.

That is to say, my drawing has changed, the technique as well as the results. Also, as a result of some things Mauve told me, I have begun to work from a live model again. Fortunately, I have been able to persuade several persons here to sit for me, Piet Kaufman, the gardener, for instance. Studying the *Exercices au Fusain* by Bargue carefully and copying them over and over again have given me a better insight into drawing the figure. I have learned to measure and to observe and to seek for broad lines. So what seemed to be impossible before is gradually becoming possible now, thank God.

I have drawn five times over a man with a spade, a Digger [un Bêcheur], in different positions, a sower twice, a girl with a broom twice. Then a woman in a white cap, peeling potatoes; a shepherd leaning on his staff; and, finally, an old, sick farmer sitting on a chair near the hearth, his head in his hands and his elbows on his knees. And of course I shall not stop here—when a few sheep have crossed the bridge, the whole flock follows. Diggers, sowers, plowers, male and female, they are what I must draw continually. I have to observe and draw everything that belongs to country life—like many others have done before, and are doing now. I no longer stand helpless before nature, as I used to.

I brought some crayon in wood (like pencil) from The Hague, and that is what I use most often right now. I have also begun to touch up my work with a brush and a stump with a little sepia and India ink, and now and then with a little color. It is a fact that the drawings I have done lately have little resemblance to those I used to do. The size of the figures is about that of the *Exercices au Fusain*.

As to landscape, I think it will in no way lose by this; on the contrary, it will gain.

Enclosed are a few little sketches to give you an idea. Of course, I must pay the people who pose for me. It is not much, but as it recurs daily, it is that much more of an expense as long as I do not succeed in selling any drawings.

But as it seldom happens that a figure is a total failure, I think the expense of the models will pretty soon be repaid. For at the present time there is some demand for anyone who has learned to attack a figure and put it on paper well.

I need not tell you that I'm only sending you these sketches to give you an idea of the pose. I scribbled them in no time, and I see there is much to be said against the proportions, at least more than in the real drawings.

I had a nice letter from Rappard, who seems to be hard at work; he sent me some very good landscape sketches. I wish he would come back here for a few days.

This is a field of stubble, where they are plowing and sowing. I made a rather large sketch of it, with a thunderstorm overhead.

The two other sketches are poses of diggers.

I hope to make several more of them.

The other sower has a basket.

Above all, I should like to have a woman pose with a seed basket, to draw that little figure which I showed you last spring and which you see in the foreground of the last sketch.

Well, as Mauve says, "The factory is in full swing."

Please do not forget the Ingres paper the color of unbleached linen. Write soon and receive a handshake in thought,

Yours sincerely, Vincent

R 2

Amice Rappard,   Etten, 15 October 1881

In my opinion your letter must be answered on the spot. In the first place I want you to know that it interests me very much—more than any other letter I have received from you—I learned more from it than you yourself meant to write down.

I learned from it that my friend Rappard has taken a great step forward, or will do so shortly. Why? Oh, it doesn't matter right now, but I have my reasons for believing that you have reached a point of revolution and reform. Ça ira! Within a short time there will be fire and enthusiasm in you. Ça ira! But for the moment not another word about it in this letter.

But if by chance you should be surprised at what I have told you, I hope to be able to tell you more soon, in person. For in any case I expect to see you soon, whether you come by way of Breda or Rozendaal.

In the first place, on my parents' behalf I invite you to come and stay with us one of these days, for a longer or shorter time. So it is not necessary for you to ask if it is convenient, you will only have to write: I shall come on this or that day by this or that train.

If it is impossible for you to come and stay a few days, then I count on your skipping a train, either at the station at Breda or at Rozendaal, and on your letting me know by letter or postcard the hour and place of your arrival. Then I shall be on the spot according to your information. And then I shall bring along a number of drawings, the large one, "Worn Out," and several others that you do not know at all. I need not tell you that I hope that on the same occasion you on your part will show me some of your water colors, as I am anxious to see them.

Look, we really must arrange to meet somehow one of these days. There is only one thing which might prevent me from coming to the station on the day of your passing through, but it is most unlikely that it should happen just on that very day. It is like this: Mauve is going to Prinsenhage for a day, and after that he will come and spend a day here. We hope it will happen soon, but we don't yet know which day it will be. And when Mauve is here, I go where Mauve goes. Suppose you were staying here when Mauve came, would you think that so unpleasant? I don't think you would; I don't know whether you know Mauve personally, but I think meeting him or meeting him again would be a good thing indeed. Mauve gave me courage when I needed it not long ago. He is a man of genius.

Now you are thinking seriously of going to Brussels until Christmas to paint from the nude.

Well, in your case I can well understand it, and especially in your present mood I shall see you go with an easy mind. Ce que doit arriver arrivera—what must happen will happen.

Whether you go to Brussels or not, some new flame will be kindled in you. Ça ira, and your going to Brussels or not will make little difference, but the caterpillar will become a butterfly; in this I am speaking like a fellow adventurer.

I feel sure you need not think that a few days' stay at Etten would mean a neglect of duty; on the contrary, you may take it for granted that it will be devoting yourself to duty, for neither you nor I should be idle here.

You can do some figure drawing here too if you want to. I am not sure whether I told you that my uncle at Prinsenhage saw the little sketches in your letter and thought them very good, and noticed with pleasure that you are making progress in figure drawing as well as in landscape.

I am of the opinion, Rappard, that in the beginning you should work from the *clothed* model. Most certainly one must have a sound knowledge of the nude, but in reality we have to do with figures with clothes on. Unless you intend to go the way of Baudry, Lefebvre, Henner, and so many others who specialize in the nude. Of course in that case you should study the nude almost exclusively; in that case the more you confine yourself to it and concentrate on it, the better. But in point of fact, I do not think you will take this road. You have too much feeling for other things. You think a poor woman gathering potatoes in a field, a digger, a sower, a little lady in the street or at home, too beautiful not to feel the impulse to attack them in quite a different manner than you have done up to now. You have too much feeling for color, too keen a perception of tone, you are too much of a landscapist to follow in Baudry's footsteps. The more so because I believe that you, Rappard, will ultimately decide to settle down in Holland too. You are too much of a *Dutchman* to become a Baudry. But I certainly think it excellent that you paint such beautiful studies from the nude as the two big ones I know—the reclining pose and the brown seated figure—and I wish I had done them myself. I am telling you my thoughts unreservedly, and you on your part must always tell me yours unreservedly too.

Your remark about the figure of the Sower—that he is not a man who is sowing, but one who is posing as a sower—is very true.

However, I look upon my present studies purely as studies after the model, they have no pretension to being anything else.

Only after a year or a couple of years shall I have gained the ability to do a sower who is sowing; there I agree with you.

You tell me, Rappard, that you have done hardly anything for a fortnight. Surely I know these "fortnights"; I had them myself last summer. I did not work at drawing directly—but indirectly I did; what I did was go through one of those periods of metamorphosis.

77

I saw Mesdag's "Panorama." I was there with the painter De Bock, who collaborated on it, and he told me of an incident that happened after the Panorama was finished and that I thought quite funny.

Perhaps you know the painter Destrée. Between you and me and the lamppost : the incarnation of mealy-mouthed arrogance. Well, one day this gentleman came up to De Bock and said to him, very haughtily, very blandly, very condescendingly, "De Bock, I was invited to paint that Panorama too, but because it was so inartistic, I refused."

To which De Bock answered, "Mr. Destrée, what is easier, to paint a Panorama or to refuse to paint a Panorama? What is more artistic, to do a thing or not to do it?" I thought this answer very much to the point.

I have good news from my brother Theo—he sends his kind regards. Do not neglect to keep up your acquaintance with him by writing him once in a while. He is a clever, energetic fellow, and I am very sorry he isn't a painter, although it is a good thing for the painters that there are such persons as he. This you will find out if you keep up your acquaintance with him.

And now I shall say, "See you soon." Shall I? And believe me, with a handshake in thought,

Ever yours, Vincent

I am looking for a poem, I think by Tom Hood, "The Song of the Shirt"; do you happen to know it, or do you see your way to hunting it up for me? If you know it, I should like to ask you to write it out for me.

After I had closed this letter I opened it again to tell you that, although I quite understand your having made your plans, yet I want you to consider whether you will positively carry them out after all.

Speaking my mind unreservedly, I say to you, Rappard, stay here. But of course there may be reasons of which I am ignorant but which are weighty enough to make you decide on that plan.

Therefore, speaking only from an artistic point of view, I tell you that in my opinion you as a Dutchman will feel most at home in the Dutch intellectual climate, and will get more satisfaction from working after the character of this country (whether it be figure or landscape) than by concentrating on and specializing in the nude.

Although I like Baudry and others, such as Lefebvre and Henner, too—I greatly prefer Jules Breton, Feyen-Perrin, Millet, Ulysse Butin, Mauve, Artz, Israëls, etc., etc.

And I am speaking in this way because I am positive that fundamentally this is your opinion too. And though you have seen a lot, it is certain that I at least have not seen less than you of different kinds of art. Particularly seeing that I, though loosely speaking only a beginner in the art of drawing, am a pretty good judge of art in general, you should not take my opinion too lightly the few times I give it. And as I see it, both you and I cannot do better than work after nature in Holland (figure and landscape). Then we are ourselves, then we feel at home, then we are in our element. The more we know of what is happening abroad, the better, but we must never forget that we have our roots in the Dutch soil.

If I am not mistaken, you have made good progress with your work for Mr. Lantsheer; at least I am pleased to hear that he spoke that way about your picture at Arti. He has a clear eye for art, and there are not many who have so much knowledge and good taste.

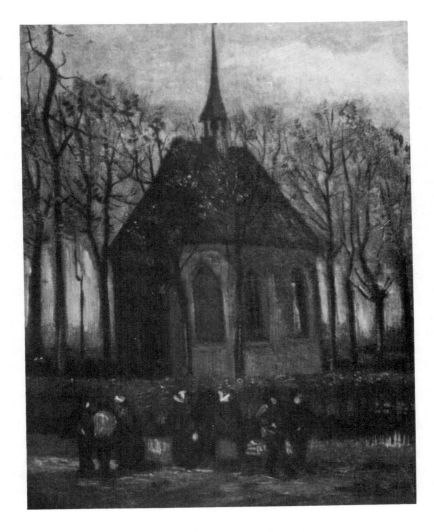

The Chapel at Nuenen, oil, 1884

R 3

Dear Rappard, Etten, 2 November 1881

Thanks for your quick reply—so you soon succeeded in finding rooms, and are now living near the academy.

With reference to a certain question, which I descried at the bottom of your postcard, I want to tell you that, far from thinking it "stupid" of you to go to the aforesaid sanctuary, I think it very wise, even so wise that—yes, that I am *almost* tempted to say, a little bit *too* wise and righteous.

In my opinion if you had not gone, if your expedition had not taken place, it would have been all the better, but since you have undertaken it, I wish you success from the bottom of my heart, and notwithstanding everything, I have no doubt about the good results.

You—and others too—even if you really and truly attend the lessons at the academy, you will of course never be in my eyes an "academician" in the despicable sense of the word. Of course I do not take you for one of those arrogant fellows whom one might call the Pharisees of art, and the prototype of whom is, I think, "good old" Stallaert. And yet even this man may have something good in him, and if I knew him better, I might think differently of his Honor. But it will be difficult to hammer it into my head that his Honor does not have something damned bad in him too, which eclipses his possible good qualities. Nothing pleases me more than discovering good qualities even in such fellows. It always hurts me, it always makes me nervous, when I meet a man of whose principles I am obliged to say, "But this is really too bad, this doesn't hold water," and I go on having this choking feeling until someday I discover something good in him.

Never think it gives me pleasure to notice something wrong; it grieves me and gives me so much pain that at times I cannot keep it to myself. Ça m'agace [it exasperates me].

I do not like catching myself at "having a beam in mine eye," and yet—yet I have happened to catch myself at it, but then I didn't let it go at that, and I tried to remedy it.

And exactly because I know from my own experience how terrible such a "beam in one's eye" is, I sympathize with others suffering from the same complaint.

Please, please do not take me for a fanatic or a partisan. Certainly I have the courage to take sides, like any other man; at times one is compelled to do so in life, one is *compelled* to speak one's mind and to give one's opinion candidly, and stick to it.

But seeing that I do my utmost to look at the undeniably good side of things in the first place, and only afterward, most unwillingly, look at the bad side too, I make bold to believe that, even if I have not quite succeeded in it, I shall eventually arrive at what I may call in general a mild and broad and unprejudiced judgment. And therefore it is to me a petite misère de la vie humaine to meet a man who thinks he is always right, and who demands to be taken for someone who is always right; and this is because I am so convinced of my own fallibility and, at the same time, of the fallibility of all the children of men.

Now as to you, I believe that you too are striving after a mild and broad and

80

unprejudiced judgment of things, in life but more especially in art. And therefore nothing is further from my mind than looking upon you as a Pharisee, either in the moral or in the artistic sense.

But for all that, such people as you and I, who decidedly have honest intentions, are not perfect after all, and often make very bad mistakes, and besides, are influenced by their environment and by circumstances. And we should be deceiving ourselves if we thought we stood so firm in our shoes that we had no need to take heed lest we fall.

You and I "think we stand," but malheur à nous if we should become foolhardy and careless because we feel sure—and rightly so—that we possess some more or less good qualities. Attaching too much importance to the good that is in us, even if it is really and truly there, may lead us to Phariseeism.

When you are making vigorous studies after the nude like the ones you showed me, whether at the academy or somewhere else, when I am drawing potato diggers in a field—then we are doing good things by which we shall make progress. But, as I see it, for all that we must be especially distrustful of ourselves and be on our guard against ourselves as soon as we perceive that we are on the right road. Then we must say : *Let me be very careful, for I am just the kind of man to spoil things for myself when they seem good*—unless I am careful. How must we be careful ? ? ? ... this I cannot define, but I am most decidedly of the opinion that in the case I mentioned, being careful is necessary, for from my own bitter experience, through my own sufferings and shame, I have become conscious of what I underlined just now. The fact that my being conscious of my own fallibility will keep me from making many mistakes will certainly not prevent my making a great many mistakes after all. But after we fall, we stand up again...!

So I think it a very good thing that you are painting from the nude at the academy, just because I am confident that you will not consider yourself righteous like the Pharisees on account of it, nor think those whose views differ from yours insignificant. Your work, far more than your words and expressions, has given me this conviction, and it has grown stronger and stronger.

Today I drew another digger. And also since your visit, a boy cutting grass with a sickle.

And a man and a woman sitting by the fire besides.

We all enjoyed your visit very much; I am so glad to have seen your water colors, you have made progress indeed.

Yet I should like to see you draw or paint ordinary people with their clothes on. I shouldn't be surprised if you made a success of it; I often think of that clerk whose portrait you drew during the sermon of the Very Reverend and Learned Dr. Kam. But since then I have not seen any more drawings by you like that one, which I regret—have you been reclaimed, by any chance, and are you listening more to the sermon nowadays instead of paying attention to the speaker and his audience ? In some cases the speaker can carry us with him to such an extent that we forget everything around us, but this often happens in church, and I should wish it were always like that in church.

Well, I hope that you will write soon, and that you will have a good time and good luck in Brussels. And don't forget to drop in on your return journey, if it is possible; let's agree on that as a matter of principle.

Kind regards from my parents and a handshake in thought from me. And believe me

Ever yours, Vincent

158

Dear brother,   Etten, Friday 18 November 1881

If I couldn't give vent to my feelings now and then, I think the boiler would burst. I must tell you something which would perhaps upset me if I had to keep it to myself; but if I can make a clean breast of it, perhaps it will not be so bad.

As you know, Father and Mother on one side and I on the other do not agree about what must be done or not done in regard to a certain "no, never never." Well, after hearing the rather strong expressions, "indelicate" and "untimely" for some time (just imagine that you were in love and they called your love indelicate, would you not have proudly resented it, and said, Stop!), I emphatically requested that these expressions not be used any more. This ceased, but another phrase appeared. Now they say that I am "breaking family ties."

Well, many a time I have told them earnestly, patiently and with feeling that such was not at all the case. It helped for a time, and then they began anew.

The fact that I "wrote letters" was the real grievance against me. But when they persisted in using so rashly and recklessly that miserable expression "breaking family ties," I did the following.

For a few days I did not speak a word or take any notice of Father and Mother. Against my wish, but I wanted to make them feel how it would be if those family ties were really severed. Of course they were astonished at my behavior, and when they asked me about it, I answered, See, *that is how it would be* if there were no tie of affection between us; but fortunately it does exist and will not be broken so easily. But I beg you, consider now how miserable that expression, "breaking ties," is, and do not use it any more.

But the result was that Father grew very angry, ordered me out of the room with a curse, at least it sounded exactly like one! Father is used to having everyone give in to him when he's in a passion, even I, but this time I was quite determined to let him rage for once. In anger Father also said something like I had better leave the house and go elsewhere; but because it was said in a passion, I do not attach much importance to it.

I have my models and my studio here; elsewhere living would be more expensive, and my work more difficult, and the models would cost more. But if Father and Mother said *go* in earnest to me, of course I should go. There are things which a man cannot put up with.

If one has to hear continually, "You are crazy," or, "You are a person who breaks family ties," or, "You are indelicate," any man with a heart in his body would protest with all his energy. Of course I have also told Father and Mother a thing or two, for instance that they were very much in error on the subject of this love affair and that their hearts were hardened, and that they were completely closed to a more gentle and humane way of thinking. In short, that their way of thinking seemed narrow-minded to me—neither tolerant nor generous enough; and also that to me *God* would merely be an empty sound if one were forced to hide one's love and were not allowed to obey the heart's dictates.

Well, I am quite willing to believe that at times I have not been able to curb my indignation when I heard "indelicate" and "breaking ties," but who could remain calm under it if there were no end to it?

Quoiqu'il en soit, in his fit of passion Pa muttered nothing less than a curse. However, I already heard something of the sort last year, and, thank God, far from being really damned, I developed new life and new energy within myself. So I am fully convinced it will be the same now, or more so, and more strongly than last year.

Theo, I love her—her, and no other—her, forever. And ... and ... and ... Theo, although as yet it never "seems" to be in full activity, there is a feeling of deliverance within me and it is as if she and I had stopped being two, and were united forever and ever.

Did you receive my drawings? Yesterday I made another, of a peasant boy lighting a fire early in the morning on the hearth over which a kettle is hanging; and another, of an old man putting kindling wood on the hearth. I am sorry to say there is still something harsh and severe in my drawings, and I think that *she*, her influence, must come to soften this.

Well, boy, I suppose there is no reason to take that curse of Father's so very seriously; perhaps I used too harsh a method to make Father and Mother *feel* what they would not *hear*. Well, I shake hands with you. Believe me,

Ever yours, Vincent

R 5

Dear Rappard,   Etten, 21 November 1881

To talk less abstractly this time, I am going to discuss some facts with you. You say that Ten Cate spoke to you about similar matters as I did. All right, but if this Mr. Ten Cate is the same person whom on a certain day I saw in your studio for a moment, I very much doubt whether he and I have exactly the same ideas fundamentally. Is he a man of small stature with black or at least dark hair, who on that occasion had a very pale complexion, or at any rate was very neatly dressed in a suit of black cloth? You should know that I am in the habit of observing very accurately the physical exteriors of people in order to get at their real mental make-up. However, I saw this Mr. Ten C. only once, and that very fleetingly—at least if I saw him at all—and so I cannot make up my mind about him. All the same, it is possible that in some respects he spoke to you as I did, and I don't object to that—all the better, I say. Actually your answer to my letter is no more than half an answer, thanks all the same. I think you will tell me the other half some time, but not in the near future. The other half, still to come, will be longer than the one I received, *and much more satisfactory*.

Suppose at some time you leave the academy for good, then I think that you will eventually have to struggle against a very peculiar difficulty, which is not quite unknown to you even now. A man who, like you, is working at the academy regularly cannot help feeling more or less out of his element when, instead of knowing, This or that is my task for today, he is forced to improvise, or rather *create*, his task every day anew. Especially in the long run this looking for and finding your work will not prove such an easy job by any means. At least it would not surprise me if, after having broken away from the academy for good, you did not occasionally feel that the ground was giving way under your feet. But I think you are not the kind of man to be thrown into a panic by such a natural phenomenon, and you will soon regain your balance.

However, when you have thrown yourself once and for all, headlong and without reservation, into reality (for after you have thrown yourself into it, you will never go back), you will speak to others who are still clinging to the academy, exactly as Ten Cate does and exactly as I do. For from what you have told me of Mr. Ten Cate I infer that his reasoning can be reduced to the following words: Rappard, give up your reservations, and throw yourself headlong into reality.

The Open Sea is your true element and even at the academy you do not belie your true character and nature; that is why the worthy gentlemen there will not recognize you in fact, and put you off with idle talk.

Mr. Ten Cate is not yet an able seaman, and I myself much less, and we cannot steer and maneuver yet as we would like to; but if we do not get drowned or smashed on the rocks in the seething breakers, we shall become good sailors. There is no help for it, everyone has to go through a period of worrying and fumbling after he has risked himself on the open sea. At first we catch little or no fish, but we get acquainted with our course and learn to steer our little vessel, and this is indispensable to begin with. And after a while we shall catch a lot of fish, and big ones too, be sure of that!

But I think Mr. Ten Cate is casting his nets for another kind of fish than I am, because to my mind our temperaments diverge; for every fisherman has a right to his own specialty, but now and then a fish of one kind will swim into the net meant for another kind, and vice versa, and so it may happen that at times there is a similarity between his catch and mine.

Now from time to time you dislike sowers and seamstresses and diggers. Well, what of it? So do I. However, with me this "disliking from time to time" is far outweighed by a certain enthusiasm, but with you the two things seem to have equal weight.

Have you kept my epistles? If you have a little time to spare, and they have not perished in the flames, then I say: read them again, although it may seem pretentious to ask such a thing of you. But I did not write them without serious intentions, though I was not afraid to speak my mind freely and to give free rein to my imagination. Now you say that l am a fanatic at heart, and that most certainly I am preaching a doctrine.

Well, if you want to take it that way, so be it; when it comes to the point I don't object to it, I am not ashamed of my feelings, I do not blush to own that I am a man with principles and a creed. But where does my fanaticism seek to drive people, especially myself? To the open sea! And what is the doctrine I preach? My friends, let us give our souls to our cause, let us work with our heart, and truly love what we love.

Love what we love, how superfluous a warning this seems to be, and yet it is justified to an enormous extent! For how many there are who waste their best efforts on something that is not worth their best efforts, whereas they treat what they love in a stepmotherly way instead of yielding wholly to the irresistible urge of their hearts. And yet we venture to call this conduct "firmness of character" and "strength of mind," and we waste our energy on an unworthy creature, all the while neglecting our true sweetheart. And all this "with the most sacred intentions," thinking "we are compelled to do it," out of "moral conviction" and a "sense of duty." And so we have the "beam in our own eye," confusing a pseudo- or would-be conscience with our true conscience. The person who at this moment is writing to his dear friend Rappard has been marching around on this earth with one, or even more than one, such object—but then of a monstrous size—in his eye for a long time.

Has this beam been got rid of? you ask. Well, what can the present writer answer to this? Of *one* thing he is sure, namely that one very big beam is got rid of, provisionally; but, for the very reason that he did not notice it when he was laboring under it, he does not deem it impossible that there are others of whose existence or nonexistence he is not fully aware. However, the person in question has learned to be on his guard against diseases of and beams in the eyes. The excessively big beam in question was of a more or less inartistic character. I won't tell you just now what kind of beam it was. For there are all kinds of eye beams, artistic, theological, moral eye beams (quite a multitude of them), practical eye beams and theoretical eye beams (sometimes the two are combined —*very ruinous indeed!*), and ... oh well, a lot more.

We must not let ourselves be thrown into too much of a panic if we are not without them, provided this "not being in a panic" does not lead us into carelessness or indifference in this respect, or even into stubbornness.

A few days ago I had a nice letter from my brother Theo, who also inquired after you; I had sent him some drawings, and he strongly advised me to go on with those Brabant types. What he says about art is always to the point and purpose, and he often gives hints that are practical and practicable.

Today I have again been attacking a certain "bête noire" of mine, to wit, the system of resignation; I believe this "bête noire" is of the race of the hydra—that is to say the more serpent's heads you cut off, the more spring up again. And yet there have been men who have succeeded in killing off such a "bête noir."

It is always my favorite occupation, as soon as I can find a spare half hour, to resume the fight against this old "bête noir". But perhaps you do not know that in theology there exists a system of resignation with mortification as a side branch. And if this were a thing that existed only in the imagination and the writings or sermons of the theologians, I should not take notice of it; but alas, it is one of those insufferable burdens which certain theologians lay on the shoulders of men, without touching them themselves with their little finger.

And so—more's the pity—this resignation belongs to the domain of reality, and causes many great and petites misères de la vie humaine. But when they wanted to put this yoke upon my shoulders, I said, "Go to hell!" And this they thought very disrespectful. Well, so be it. Whatever may be the raison d'être of this resignation, it—the resignation, I mean—is only for those who *can* be resigned, and religious belief is for those who *can* believe. And what can I do if I am not cut out by nature for the former, *i.e.* resignation, but on the contrary for the latter, *i.e.* religious belief, with all its consequences?

Well, if you have a little time to spare, write me again, and in the meantime believe me, with a handshake,

Ever yours, Vincent

R 6

Dear Rappard,   Etten, 23 November 1881

On rereading your letters, my dear fellow, I find such lively and funny sallies in them that I feel stimulated, particularly by the latter, to continue our correspondence.

Well, well! So after all I am a fanatic! All right, for your words have gone home, right through my skin! So be it—thanks for your revelation, yes, thank God, at first I dared not believe it, but you have made it clear to me—so I have a *will*, a *conviction*, I am going *in a definite direction*, and what is more, not being contented with this, I want others to go along with me! Thank God, so I am a fanatic! Well, from now on I won't be anything else. And now I should like to have my friend Rappard as a fellow traveler—it is not a matter of indifference to me to lose sight of him—do you think I am wrong in this?

Now I said in my hurry that I wanted to drive people "to the open sea" (see my previous letter). If I did nothing but this, I should be a sorry barbarian. But there is something else which renders the thing more reasonable. In the long run a man cannot stick it out in the open sea—he must have a little cottage on the shore with a bit of fire on the hearth—with a wife and children around that hearth.

Look, Rappard, whither I am trying to drive myself, and whither I am trying to drive others too, is to be fishermen on the sea that we call the Ocean of Reality, but on the other hand I want—for myself and for the fellow creatures whom I importune now and then—that "little cottage," most decidedly I do! And in that cottage, all those things! So the open sea and that resting place, or that resting place *and* the open sea. And as regards the doctrine I preach, this doctrine of mine—"My friends, let us love what we love"—is based on an axiom. I thought it superfluous to mention this axiom, but for clarity's sake I will add it. That axiom is: "My friends, we love."

From this I deduce that first thesis.

My friends, let us love what we love, let us be *ourselves*, "do not let us think we know better than God." This "do not let us think we know better than God" is not my expression, it belongs to Mauve. And this thesis I prove by *negative demonstration*, *i.e.* in the following way to begin with.

86

Suppose a man did not love what he loves, what a lot of misery he would cause himself and others, and how much turbulence he would create in God's world. In short, if all men were like the person who, as we suppose—at least if this is possible—for the moment, does not love what he loves, how the world (which, I think, our Lord put squarely on its feet, which is kept in that position by Him, and which will stay that way as long as you and I are alive—which will serve our time, you know!) ... if, I say, all men were like this imaginary one, willfully turned inside out and upside down— (and how fortunate it is that he can only exist in our imagination as an abstraction, just like our proof by negative demonstration of an *un*mathematical thesis)—how much the world, correctly created by God, would gradually seem to become a radically wrong world. Methinks, by continuing to work with this abstraction in our imagination—and this only for a short, even a very short while—I mean, with the above actually nonexistent man, willfully turned inside out and upside down—we cannot help feeling it goes so much "against the grain" that we are entitled to think we have proved definitely the correctness and reasonableness of our thesis : "My friends, let us love what we love." (Besides, if I have not demonstrated clearly enough that the incorrectness of the said thesis would be an enormous *absurdity*, you, who are much further advanced in mathematics than I, would easily succeed—if you would give your mind to it—in finding more conclusive proofs for my thesis.)

We now come to some remarkable conclusions or "deductions" from our primary thesis, as for instance :

1. The man who damn well refuses to love what he loves dooms himself.
2. He must have quite a lot of *o(a)bstinatie*[1] to stick it out in the long run.
3. If he changed, wouldn't his conversion be a great thing!

Yes, and whether I add it or not, I think you will understand that I am suggesting more or less, Rappard, by sticking so close to the academy you are clinging to a reservation as to a rope that has "strangled" many a one—I mean, who could not cut himself loose when he wanted to put to sea.

Are there still other "reservations" besides the academic ones? See the chapter "eye beams" in my previous letter. There are, if you will allow me to say so, as many kinds of reservations as there are kinds of eye beams.

How many? *Legions, I tell you, legions!*

This "being strangled" by a reservation is a much slower and more agonizing death than stoutly hanging oneself by means of a halter. Are there also moral reservations? Why shouldn't there be, just as there are moral "eye beams"? But you and I, have we labored under them, are we laboring under them, shall we labor under them?

Goodness gracious—I am far from sure, and if I were speaking for myself instead of for the two of us, I should say, I have labored, am laboring and shall labor under moral eye beams and moral reservations, but this has not altered,

[1] The *o* and the *a* happen both to be appropriate, eh? [This pun is untranslatable. The Dutch word *obstinatie* means "obstinacy," and the (incidentally incorrect) word *abstinatie* (correct : *abstinentie*) means "abstinence."]

does not alter and will not alter the fact that I have cast, am casting and shall go on casting moral beams out of my eyes, and that I have chucked away, am chucking away and shall go on chucking away moral reservations.

Until in the end I shall stand with a clear eye and a free neck.

When?

If I persevere until the end—in the end.

But I feel sure you will see that by continuing our correspondence we get *so much* profit out of it that gradually this correspondence is getting more serious.

For though, as I said, I give my imagination a free rein, yet I swear that I write in *dead earnest*, and not the reverse. Nothing is further from my thoughts than writing you out of a lust for argument, but my intention is "to wake Rappard up," and I doubt whether I shall drop off myself when "waking Rappard up." God forbid that this should be the case—far be it from me!

Now I told you on a former occasion that in general, and more especially with artists, I pay as much attention to the man who does the work as to the work itself. If the man is not there, I am now and then forced to draw conclusions from the work only (we cannot know all artists personally), or if the work is not there, to form an opinion of the man by himself. Now I know something of the work of a certain Mr. Van Rappard, and secondly something of the gentleman himself.

His work is always saying to me, Better is to come; his person is saying the same thing to me.

Better and better.

Do you think this a very merciless judgment? And (to jump from one subject to another) as regards my special "bête noire," today I had little opportunity to occupy myself with hunting it; but for all that I have not been able to refrain from attacking it a little.

And we shall have a bone to pick with it by and by. But it is beginning to be a little on its guard; the fact is that resignation is accustomed to resignation, and I thought it would give up the struggle. But lo! I am not yet in a mood for it. Oh well, later on I shall probably tell you something more about the said bête noire. Damned bête noire! And yet it amuses me.

Meanwhile believe me, with a handshake,

Ever yours, Vincent

I am writing you pretty often now, as shortly I shall have a lot of other correspondence to attend to.

1882—1886 THE HAGUE, DRENTHE, NUENEN, ANTWERP

A period of intense study and work

167

Dear brother, The Hague, 1 or 2 January 1882

I just send you my best wishes for the New Year. May it be a good year for you in every respect, and egoistically I add, for me too. Well, as for me it will perhaps please you to hear that I am installed in a studio of my own—a room with an alcove. The light is bright enough, for the window is large, twice as large as an ordinary window, but it faces the south.

The furniture I have taken is in the real "village-policeman style," as you call it; but I think mine is more so than yours, although you invented the word. (I have, for instance, real kitchen chairs, and a real strong kitchen table.)

Mauve has lent me 100 guilders for rent and furniture, and to have the window and light adjusted. You can imagine that this is a load on my mind, but, well, it was the only possible way, because in the long run it is much cheaper to have things of your own than always to spend money for a so-called furnished room.

Well, I had a lot of trouble getting everything, and before I could arrange the furniture so as to make it do.

But now, boy, I have a real studio of my own, and I am so glad.

I did not dare hope that it would happen so soon, but now I am very glad, and I hope you also approve of it.

Listen, you know that my expenses will be greater than in Etten, but I shall try to struggle along. Mauve gives me great hope that I shall soon begin to earn something. And now that I am in a studio of my own, this will not make an unfavorable impression on the persons who until now suspected me of amateurism, of idleness, of sponging on others. I hope you will be able to send me something these days. If I were greatly in need and asked Mauve, he would not refuse me, but I really think he has already done enough.

It happens that once in his life every man has to set up housekeeping, and though at first I greatly dreaded the feeling of being in debt, I feel after all it is better so.

We arranged that I shall work regularly from the model; it is the most expensive and yet the cheapest way in the end.

De Bock does not improve on further acquaintance: he rather lacks backbone, and he gets angry when one says some things which are only the ABC. He has some feeling for landscape, he knows how to put some charm into it (for instance, in a large picture which he is making now), but one gets no hold on him. It is too vague and insubstantial—du coton filé trop fin. His pictures are the shadow of an impression, and in my opinion that impression is hardly worth repeating so often.

I do not wish to associate much with other painters. Each day I find Mauve cleverer and more trustworthy, and what more can I want? However, Theo, I shall have to dress a little better now. I know now the direction in which I have to go, and need not hide myself, so I shall not avoid meeting other people— neither shall I seek them. Mauve and Jet send you their compliments.

Adieu, I still have a lot to do, believe me,

Yours sincerely, Vincent

192

Dear Theo,   The Hague, 3–9 May 1882

Today I met Mauve and had a very painful conversation with him, which made it clear to me that Mauve and I are separated forever. Mauve has gone so far that he cannot retract, at least he certainly wouldn't want to. I had asked him to come and see my work and then talk things over. Mauve refused point-blank: "I will certainly not come to see you, that's all over."

At last he said, "You have a vicious character." At this I turned around—it was in the dunes—and walked home alone.

Mauve takes offense at my having said, "I am an artist"—which I won't take back, because, of course, these words connote, "Always seeking without absolutely finding." It is just the opposite of saying, "I know, I have found it."

As far as I know, that word means, "I am seeking, I am striving, I am in it with all my heart."

I have ears, Theo. If somebody says, "You have a vicious character," what should I do next?

I turned around and went back alone, but with a heavy heart because Mauve had dared to say this to me. I shall not ask him to explain it, nor shall I excuse myself. And still—and still—and still—! I wish Mauve were sorry for it.

They suspect me of something—it is in the air—I am keeping something back. Vincent is hiding something that cannot stand the light.

Well, gentlemen, I will tell you, you who prize good manners and culture, and rightly so if only it be the true kind: Which is the more delicate, refined, manly —to desert a woman or to stand by a forsaken woman?

Last winter I met a pregnant woman, deserted by the man whose child she carried.

A pregnant woman who had to walk the streets in winter, had to earn her bread, you understand how.

I took this woman for a model, and have worked with her all winter. I could not pay her the full wages of a model, but that did not prevent my paying her rent, and, thank God, so far I have been able to protect her and her child from hunger and cold by sharing my own bread with her. When I met this woman, she attracted my attention because she looked ill. I made her take baths and as much nourishing food as I could afford, and she has become much stronger. I went with her to Leyden, to the maternity hospital where she will be confined. (No wonder she was ill, the child was not in the right position, and she had to have an operation—the child had to be turned with forceps. However, there is a good chance of her pulling through. She will be confined in June.)

It seems to me that every man worth a straw would have done the same in such a case.

What I did was so simple and natural that I thought I could keep it to myself. Posing was very difficult for her, but she has learned; I have made progress in my drawing because I had a good model. The woman is now attached to me like a tame dove. For my part, I can only marry once, and how can I do better than marry her? It is the only way to help her; otherwise misery would force her back into her old ways, which end in a precipice. She has no money, but she helps me earn money in my profession.

I am full of ambition and love for my work and profession; I gave up painting and water colors for a time only because I was so shocked by Mauve's deserting me, and if he came back, I would begin again with new courage. I cannot look at a brush now, it makes me nervous.

I have written: Theo, can you give me some information about Mauve's behavior? Perhaps this letter can give you light. You are my brother, it is natural that I speak to you about private things; but for the time being I cannot speak to anyone who says to me, "You have a vicious character."

I couldn't do otherwise, I did what my hand found to do, I worked. I thought I would be understood without words. I had not forgotten another woman for whom my heart was beating, but she was far away and refused to see me; and this one walked the streets in winter, sick, pregnant, hungry—I couldn't do otherwise. Mauve, Theo, Tersteeg, you have my bread in your hands, will you take it from me, or turn your back on me? Now I have spoken, and await whatever will be said to me next.

Vincent

I send you a few studies because you can see from them that she helps me a great deal by posing.

My drawings are done "by my model and me." The woman in a white bonnet is her mother.

But I should like these three back, as in a year—when I probably shall draw quite differently—my work will be based on these studies which I now make as conscientiously as I can. You can see they are carefully done. Later on when I make an interior or a waiting room or the like, these will be useful to me because I can consult them for the details. But I thought perhaps it would be good for you to see how I spend my time.

These studies require a rather dry technique; if I had tried for effect, they would be of less use to me later. But I think you will understand this yourself. The paper I should like best is that on which the bent figure of a woman is drawn, but the color of unbleached linen if possible. I have none of it left *in that thickness*, I think they call it double Ingres, I can't get it here. When you see how that drawing is done, you'll understand that it couldn't be done on thin paper. I wanted to send with it a small figure in black merino, but I can't roll it. The chair near the large figure is not finished because what I want there is an old oak chair.

207

Dear Theo,   The Hague, 8–10 June 1882

Few things have given me so much pleasure recently as hearing things from home which to a certain extent set my mind at ease about their feelings toward me. Sien came to tell me that a parcel had been delivered to the studio, and I told her to go and open it and see what was in it, and in case there was a letter, to bring it with her; so I learned that they had sent a whole package of things, underwear and outer clothing and cigars, and there was also 10 guilders enclosed in the letter. I cannot tell you how it touched me, it is much more than I expected; but they do not know everything yet.

I am just weak and feeble, Theo, and I need absolute, absolute rest to recover, so everything that makes for peace is welcome. But I felt much worse than now before I was lying here, and please bear in mind that it is not at all serious, and only a short period of treatment will make me well again. I wanted to tell you the news about Father and Mother immediately, because I thought it would please you, too.

Sien will probably go next Monday, for I think she is better off in the hospital now; she will be admitted about the middle of June. She wanted to stay here for me, but I wouldn't allow it.

I have my books on perspective here, and a few volumes of Dickens, including *Edwin Drood*; there is perspective in Dickens, too. Good God, what an artist! There's no one like him.

I hope my having to take a rest will have a good effect on my drawings; sometimes one gets a better view of things when one does not work on them for a while—then when one sees them again, they seem fresh and new.

The view from the window of the ward is splendid: yards on the canal, with the barges loaded with potatoes, rear view of houses that are being pulled down by workmen, part of a garden; and on the next, more distant, plane the Quay with its rows of trees and street lamps, a very complicated little almshouse with little gardens connected to it; and finally, all the roofs. The whole is a bird's-eye view which, especially in the evenings and in the mornings, is mysterious because of the light's effect, for instance, like a Ruysdael or Van der Meer. But I may not and cannot draw it as long as I am so weak. But though I'm forbidden to get out of bed, I cannot refrain from getting up to look at it every evening.

Write me soon; wasn't that parcel from home a surprise?—and especially coming at a time like this, it made me more than happy.

The rest cure does me good and makes me so much calmer, and takes away that nervousness which has troubled me so much recently. And the ward here is no less interesting to me than the third-class waiting room. But I may not and cannot draw yet. Adieu, I hope you will find time to write to me, believe me,

Yours sincerely, Vincent

I thought it so nice that this came from home, I wanted to let you know at once. Of course I do not need any more clothes now. I wrote home to thank them, and to tell them I was here. You know the address is—City Hospital—4 Class—Ward 6—No. 9. Brouwersgracht.

218

Dear brother,   The Hague, 19–23 July 1882

It is already late, but I want to write you once more. You are not here, but I wish you were, and sometimes it seems to me we are not far away from each other.

Today I promised myself something, that is, to consider my illness, or rather the remains of it, as nonexistent. Enough time has been lost, the work must continue. So, well or not well, I shall start drawing again, regularly from morning until night. I do not want someone to say to me again, "Oh! these are just old drawings."

Today I made a drawing of the baby's cradle with a few touches of color in it.

I am also working on a drawing like the one of the meadows I sent you recently. My hands have become too white, but is this my fault?

I will go out and work in the open air, even if it should cause my illness to return. I cannot keep from working any longer.

Art is jealous, she does not want us to choose illness in preference to her, so I do what she wishes.

Therefore I hope that within a short time you will receive a few pretty good new drawings again. People like me *must* not be ill, so to speak.

I want you to understand clearly my conception of art. One must work long and hard to grasp the essence. What I want and aim at is confoundedly difficult, and yet I do not think I aim too high.

I want to do drawings which *touch* some people. "Sorrow" is a small beginning, perhaps such little landscapes as "Laan van Meerdervoort," "Rijswijk Meadows," and "Fish Drying Barn" are also a small beginning. In those there is at least something straight from my own heart.

In either figure or landscape I should wish to express, not sentimental melancholy, but serious sorrow.

In short, I want to progress so far that people will say of my work, He feels deeply, he feels tenderly—notwithstanding my so-called roughness, perhaps even because of it.

It seems pretentious to talk this way now, but this is the reason why I want to push on with all my strength.

What am I in most people's eyes? A nonentity, or an eccentric and disagreeable man—somebody who has no position in society and never will have, in short, the lowest of the low. Very well, even if this were true, then I should want my work to show what is in the heart of such an eccentric, of such a nobody.

This is my ambition, which is, in spite of everything, founded less on anger than on love, more on serenity than on passion. It is true that I am often in the greatest misery, but still there is a calm pure harmony and music inside me.

I see drawings and pictures in the poorest huts, in the dirtiest corner. And my mind is drawn toward these things by an irresistible force.

More and more other things lose their interest, and the more I get rid of them, the quicker my eye grasps the picturesque things. Art demands persistent work, work in spite of everything, and continuous observation. By persistent, I mean not only continuous work, but also not giving up your opinion at the bidding of such and such a person.

I do hope, brother, that within a few years, perhaps even now, little by little, you will see things by me which will give you some satisfaction for your sacrifices.

I have had very little intercourse with other painters lately. I have not been the worse for it. It is not the language of painters but the language of nature which one should listen to. Now I understand better than I did six months ago why Mauve said, "Don't talk to me about Dupré; but talk about the bank of that ditch, or something like it." It sounds rather crude, but it is perfectly true. The feeling for the things themselves, for reality, is more important than the feeling for pictures—at least, it is more fertile and more enlivening.

Because I now have such a broad, ample feeling for art and for life itself, of which art is the essence, it sounds so shrill and false to me when people try to compel me.

Personally, I find in many modern pictures a peculiar charm which the old masters do not have.

For me one of the highest and noblest expressions of art is always that of the English, for instance, Millais and Herkomer and Frank Holl. What I mean about the difference between the old masters and the modern ones is this—perhaps the modern ones are deeper thinkers.

There is a great difference in sentiment between "Chill October" by Millais and "Bleaching Ground at Overveen" by Ruysdael; and also between "Irish Emigrants" by Holl and "The Bible Reading" by Rembrandt. Rembrandt and Ruysdael are sublime, for us as well as for their contemporaries; but there is something in the modern painters that appeals to us more personally and intimately.

It is the same with the wood engravings by Swain and those of the old German masters.

So, I think it was a mistake a few years ago when the modern painters went through a period of imitating the old masters.

Therefore I think father Millet is right in saying, "Il me semble absurde que les hommes veuillent paraître autre chose que ce qu'ils sont" [I think it absurd when people want to seem something different from what they are]. It seems like a commonplace saying, yet it is fathomless, as deep as the ocean, and personally I think one would do well to take it to heart.

I just wanted to tell you that I shall set to work regularly again in spite of everything; and I want to add that I am longing for a letter from you so very much, and now I wish you good night. Adieu, with a handshake,

Yours sincerely, Vincent

94

Please do not forget the *thick* Ingres if you can get it—a sample is enclosed. I still have enough of the thin kind. I can wash with water colors on the thick Ingres; on the other it always blurs through no fault of mine.

I hope I shall be able to draw that little cradle *persistently* a hundred times more, not counting what I did today.

221

Dear Theo,   The Hague, 31 July 1882

Just a line to welcome you in anticipation of your arrival. Also to acknowledge the receipt of your letter and the enclosed, for which I send my warmest thanks. It was very welcome, for I am hard at work and need a few more things.

As I understand it, we of course agree completely about black in nature. Absolute black does not really exist. But like white, it is present in almost every color, and forms the endless variety of grays—different in tone and strength. So that in nature one really sees nothing but those tones or shades.

There are only three fundamental colors—red, yellow and blue; "composites" are orange, green and purple. By adding black and some white one gets the endless varieties of grays—*red*-gray, *yellow*-gray, *blue*-gray, *green*-gray, *orange*-gray, *violet*-gray.

It is impossible to say, for instance, how many green-grays there are; there is an endless variety. But the whole chemistry of colors is no more complicated than those few simple rules. And having a clear notion of this is worth more than seventy different colors of paint—because with those three principal colors and black and white, one can make more than seventy tones and varieties. The colorist is the man who knows at once how to analyze a color, when he sees it in nature, and can say, for instance: That green-gray is yellow with black and blue, etc. In other words, the man who knows how to find nature's grays on his palette.

In order to take notes from nature, or to make little sketches, a strongly developed feeling for outline is absolutely necessary as well as for intensifying the drawing later. I believe one does not acquire this without effort, but first by observation, and particularly by strenuous work and research; and special study of anatomy and perspective is necessary too. A landscape study by Roelofs is hanging beside me—a pen drawing, but I cannot tell you how expressive its simple outline is; everything is in it.

Another even more striking example is the large woodcut "The Shepherdess" by Millet, which you showed me last year and which I have remembered ever since. And then, for instance, the pen-and-ink sketches by Ostade and Peasant Breughel.

When I see such results I feel the great importance of the outline even more strongly. And you know from "Sorrow," for instance, that I take a great deal of trouble to make progress in that respect.

But you will see when you come to the studio that apart from seeking the outline, I have, just like everybody else, a feeling for the power of color. And that I do not object to doing water colors; but their foundation is the drawing, and then many other branches sprout from the drawing besides the water color. This will develop in me in time, as in everybody who loves his work.

I have attacked that old giant of a pollard willow, and I think it is the best of the water colors. A gloomy landscape—that dead tree near a stagnant pool covered with reeds, in the distance a car shed of the Rhine Railway Company, where the tracks cross each other; dingy black buildings, then green meadows, a cinder path, and a sky with scudding clouds, gray with a single bright white border, and a depth of blue where the clouds are momentarily rent apart. In short, I wanted to make it the way the signal man in his smock and with his little red flag must see and feel it when he thinks, "It is gloomy weather today."

I have worked with great pleasure these last days, though now and then I still feel the effects of my illness.

Of the drawings which I shall show you now, I think only this: I hope they will prove to you that my work does not remain stationary, but progresses in a reasonable direction. As to the money value of my work, I do not pretend to anything less than that it would greatly astonish me if in time my work did not become just as salable as that of others. Of course I cannot tell whether that will happen *now* or *later*, but I think the surest way, which *cannot* fail, is to work from nature faithfully and energetically. Sooner or later feeling and love for nature meet a response from people who are interested in art. It is the painter's duty to be entirely absorbed by nature and to use all his intelligence to express sentiment in his work so that it becomes intelligible to other people. In my opinion working for the market is not exactly the right way; on the contrary, it means fooling art lovers. The true painters have not done this; the sympathy they eventually received was the result of their sincerity. That's all I know about it, and I don't think I need to know more. Of course it is a different thing to try to find people who like your work, and who will love it—of course this is permitted. But it must not become speculation; it would perhaps turn out wrong and would certainly cause one to lose time that ought to be spent on the work itself.

Of course you will find things that are not correct in my water colors, but this will improve in time.

But know it well, I am far from clinging to a system or being bound by one. Such a thing exists more in Tersteeg's imagination, for instance, than in reality. As to Tersteeg, you understand that my opinion of him is quite personal, and that I do not want to thrust on *you* the opinion I am forced to have. As long as he thinks and says the things about me you know of, I cannot regard him as a friend, nor as being of any use to me; on the contrary. And I am afraid that his opinion of me is too deeply rooted ever to be changed, especially because, as you say yourself, he will never take the trouble to reconsider some things and to change.

When I see how several painters I know here have *so* much trouble with their water colors and pictures, so that they cannot pull it off, I often think, Friend, the fault is in your drawing. I do not regret for a single moment that I did not go on with water color and oil painting in the beginning. I am sure I shall make up for that if I only work hard, so that my hand does not falter in drawing and in the perspective. But when I see young painters compose and draw *from memory*—and then haphazardly smear on whatever they like, *also from memory*—then look at it from a distance and pull a very mysterious, gloomy face while trying to find out what in heaven's name it looks like, and finally make something of it, always *from memory*—it sometimes disgusts me, and makes me think it all very tedious and dull.

The whole thing makes me sick!

But those gentlemen go on asking me, not without a certain solicitous air, "if I am not painting yet?"

Now sometimes I too sit and improvise, so to speak, at random on a piece of paper, but I do not attach any more value to this than to a rag or a cabbage leaf.

And I hope you will understand that I continue to stick to drawing for two reasons: because first of all I want to get a firm hand for drawing, and second, because painting and water coloring create a great many expenses on which there is no immediate return, and those expenses double and redouble ten times over when one works on a drawing which is not correct enough. And if I got into debt or surrounded myself with canvases and papers all daubed with paint without being sure of my drawing, then my studio would soon become a sort of hell, as I have seen some studios look. Now I always enter it with pleasure and work there with animation. But I do not believe that you suspect me of *unwillingness*.

It just seems to me that the painters here argue in the following way. They say, You must do this or that. If one doesn't do it, or not exactly so, or if one says something in reply, there follows a "So you know better than I?" So that immediately, sometimes in less than five minutes, one gets into a fierce quarrel and into such a position that neither party can go forward or backward. The least hateful result of this is that one of the parties has the presence of mind to keep quiet, and in some way or other makes a quick exit through some hole in the wall.

And one is almost inclined to say, Confound it, the painters are almost like a family, a fatal combination of persons with contrary interests, each of whom is opposed to the rest; and two or more are of the same opinion only when it's a question of combining together to annoy another member.

This definition of the word *family*, my dear brother, is, I hope, not always correct, especially not when it concerns painters or our own family. With all my heart I wish peace may reign in our own family, and I remain with a handshake,

Yours sincerely, Vincent

This is approximately the effect of the pollard willow, only in the water color itself there is no black other than in a broken tone. In the water color the strongest effects—dark green, brown and gray—are where the black is darkest in this little sketch.

Well, adieu, and believe me, sometimes I laugh heartily, because people suspect me of all kinds of malignity and absurdities which I shouldn't dream of. (I who am really nothing but a friend of nature, of study, of work, and especially of people.) Well, hoping to see you soon, with a handshake,

Yours sincerely, Vincent

Dear Theo,   The Hague, 5 August 1882

In my last letter you will have found a little sketch of that perspective frame
I mentioned. I just came back from the blacksmith, who made iron points for

[Handwritten Dutch draft of the letter, with a sketch of the perspective frame:]

Waarde Theo,

In mijn vorigen brief zult ge een krabbeltje gevonden hebben van
dat bewuste perspectiefraam. Daar net kom ik van den smid
vandaan die ijzeren punten aan de stokken heeft gemaakt
en ijzeren hoeken aan het raam.
Het bestaat uit twee lange palen.

met sterke houten pennen ⬤ gaat het raam
daarraan vast. 1 zij in de hoogte 1 zij in de breedte

Dit maakt dat men op 't strand of op 't weiland of
op een akker een kijkje heeft als door 1 venster
De loodlijnen & waterpas lijnen van 't raam verder
de diagonalen & het kruis —— of anders een verdeeling
in kwadraten geven vast & zeker eenige hoofdpunten
waardoor men met vastheid een teekening kan
maken die de groote lijnen & proporties aangeeft.

the sticks and iron corners for the frame. It consists of two long stakes; the
frame can be attached to them either way with strong wooden pegs.

So on the shore or in the meadows or in the fields one can look through it
like a window. The vertical lines and the horizontal line of the frame and the

diagonal lines and the intersection, or else the division in squares, certainly give a few fundamental pointers which help one make a solid drawing and which indicate the main lines and proportions—at least for those who have some instinct for perspective and some understanding of why and how the perspective causes an apparent change of direction in the lines and change of size in the planes and in the whole mass. Without this, the instrument is of little or no use, and looking through it makes one *dizzy*. I think you can imagine how delightful it is to turn this "spy-hole" frame on the sea, on the green meadows, or on the snowy fields in winter, or on the fantastic network of thin and thick branches and trunks in autumn or on a stormy sky.

Long and continuous practice with it enables one to draw quick as lightning —and, once the drawing is done firmly, to paint quick as lightning, too.

In fact, *for painting* it is absolutely the thing; for one needs a brush to express sky-earth-sea—or rather, in order to express all that in drawing, it is necessary to know and understand the treatment of the brush. I certainly believe that if I paint for some time, it will have great influence on my *drawing*. I already tried it in January, but then I had to stop, and what decided me, apart from a few other things, was that my drawing was too hesitant. Now six months have passed which have been entirely devoted to drawing. Well, it is with new courage that I start painting again.

The perspective frame is really a fine piece of workmanship; I'm sorry you didn't see it before you left. It cost me quite a lot, but I have had it made so solidly that it will last a long time. So next Monday I shall begin to make large fusains with it, and begin to *paint* small studies. If I succeed in these two things, then I hope that better painted things will follow soon.

I want my studio to be a real painter's studio by the time you come again. You know there were several reasons for my stopping in January, but after all, it may be considered like a defect in the machine, a screw or a bar which was not strong enough and had to be replaced by a stronger one.

I bought a pair of strong, warm trousers, and as I had bought a pair of strong shoes just before you came, I am now prepared to weather storm and rain. It is my definite intention to learn from this landscape painting a few things about the *technique* which I feel I need for the *figure*, namely, to express different *materials*, and the *tone* and the *color*. In one word, to express the body—the mass—of things. Your coming made it possible for me, but before you came not a day passed that I did not think about it this way, only I should have had to keep exclusively to black and white and to the outline a little longer.—But now I have *launched my boat*. Adieu, boy, once more, a warm handshake and believe me,

Yours sincerely, Vincent

224

Dear Theo,   The Hague, 8–12 August 1882

During the few days since you left, I have made some experiments with painting. And I thought you might be curious to know how it turned out. I wish you could spend an hour with me in the studio again, that would be the best way to tell you how it went. But as this is of course impossible, I shall only tell you that I now have three painted studies. One of a row of pollard willows in a meadow (behind the Geest bridge); then a study of the cinder path near here; and today I was at the vegetable gardens on Laan van Meerdervoort again, and saw a potato field with a ditch; a man in a blue smock and a woman were picking up potatoes, and I put their figures in.

It was a white, sandy field, partly dug up, partly still covered with rows of dried stalks, with green weeds in between. In the distance, dark green trees and a few roofs.

I did this last study with special pleasure. I must tell you that painting does not seem so strange to me as you would perhaps suppose; on the contrary, I like it very much, as it is a very strong means of expression. And at the same time one can express tender things with it too, let a soft gray or green speak amid all the ruggedness.

I am very glad I have the necessary materials, for already I had often suppressed the desire to paint. It opens a much broader horizon.

Now I should prefer to go on making quite a number of painted studies, and hang them in my studio without speaking to anybody about the change. And in case someone wonders at seeing things painted by me, I should say, Did you think that I had no sentiment for it, or was unable to do it?

But I have attached great value to drawing and will continue to, because it is the backbone of painting, the skeleton that supports all the rest. I like it so much, Theo, that it is only because of the expenses that I shall have to restrain myself rather than urge myself on. These studies are of medium size, a little larger than the cover of an ordinary paintbox, because I do not work inside the cover, but thumbtack the paper for the study onto a frame which has canvas stretched on it, and which I can carry easily in my hand. I will *draw* larger things before I paint them, or I will make grisailles of them if I can discover the technique—I will try to find it.

It becomes too expensive if one is not economical with the paint; but, boy, it is so delightful to have so many new and good materials; once more, many, many thanks. I will certainly try and take care that you never regret it, but have the satisfaction of seeing progress. I write you just this little word to tell you I have made a beginning. Of course the studies must get even better. I know they have many faults, but I believe that in these first ones you will already see something of the open air, which proves that I love nature and that I have a painter's heart. Enclosed, a small scratch of the Laan van Meerdervoort. Those vegetable gardens there have a kind of Old Dutch character which always appeals to me greatly.

Well, good night, it is already late, with a handshake,

Yours sincerely, Vincent

I am reading Zola's *La Curée.*

When I finished this letter, it seemed to me something was missing.

I thought, I ought to be able to write him that I have started to paint a scene of sand, sea and sky like the one we saw together at Scheveningen. So I kept my letter, and this morning I marched to the beach and have just returned from there with a rather large-size painted study of sand, sea and sky, a few fishing smacks, and two men on the beach. There is some dune sand in it, and I assure you that this will not be the last one. I thought you would like to hear that I had started it.

I repeat, I shall see to it that when you come back in half a year or in a few months or a year, the studio will have become a painter's studio. These pen-and-ink sketches have been made in a great hurry, as you can see. Now that I am making some progress, I will try and strike while the iron is hot—that means I shall go on painting. If you can send the usual amount about the twentieth, I can certainly go on painting for some time. I think that after a month of steady painting, the studio will have quite a different aspect. Hoping this will please you, I shake hands with you again and warmly wish you prosperity in everything.

225

Dear Theo,   The Hague, 14 August '82

You must not take it amiss if I write you again—it is only to tell you that painting is such a joy to me.

Last Saturday night I attacked a thing I had been dreaming of for a long time. It is a view of the flat green meadows, with haycocks. It is crossed by a cinder path running along a ditch. And on the horizon in the middle of the picture the sun is setting, fiery red. I cannot possibly draw the effect in such a hurry, but this is the composition.

But it was purely a question of color and tone, the variety of the sky's color scheme—first a violet haze, with the red sun half covered by a dark purple cloud which had a brilliant fine red border; near the sun reflections of vermilion, but above it a streak of yellow, turning into green and then into blue, the so-called *cerulean blue;* and then here and there violet and gray clouds, catching reflections from the sun.

The ground was a kind of carpetlike texture of green, gray and brown, but variegated and full of vibration—in this colorful soil the water in the ditch sparkles.

It is something that Émile Breton, for instance, might paint.

Then I have painted a huge mass of dune ground—thickly painted and sticky.

And as for these two, the small marine and the potato field, *I am sure no one could tell that they are my first painted studies.*

To tell you the truth, it surprises me a little. I had expected the first things to be a failure, though I supposed they would improve later on; but though I say so myself, they are not bad at all, and I repeat, it surprises me a little.

I think the reason is that before I began to paint, I had been drawing so much and had studied perspective in order to build up the composition of the thing I saw.

Now, since I have bought my paint and brushes, I have drudged and worked so hard on seven painted studies that right now I'm beat. One of them has a figure in it, a mother with her child, in the shadow of a large tree, in tone against the dune, on which the summer sun is shining—almost an Italian effect. I simply couldn't restrain myself or keep my hands off it or allow myself any rest.

As you perhaps know, there is an exhibition of the Black and White Society. There is a drawing by Mauve—a woman at a weaving loom, probably in Drenthe —which I think superb.

No doubt you saw some of them at Tersteeg's. There are splendid things by Israëls—including a portrait of Weissenbruch, with a pipe in his mouth and his palette in his hand. By Weissenbruch himself, beautiful things—landscapes and also a marine.

There is a very large drawing by J. Maris, a splendid town view. A beautiful W. Maris, among other things, a sow with a litter of pigs, and cows. Neuhuys, Duchâtel, Mesdag. By the last, besides a fine large marine, two Swiss landscapes which I think rather stupid and dull. But the large marine is splendid.

Israëls has four large drawings, a girl at the window, children near a pigsty— the sketch for the little picture at the Salon—a little old woman kindling the fire in the twilight, at the time engraved for the *Art Chronicle*.

It is very inspiring to see such things, for then I perceive how much I still have to learn.

But this much I want to tell you—while painting, I feel a power of color in me that I did not possess before, things of broadness and strength.

Now I am not going to send you things *at once*—let it ripen a little first—but know that I am full of ambition and believe that for the present I am making progress. (In three months, however, I will send something to give you an idea of how I'm getting on.) But that is just the reason for me to persevere and to acquire what I need.

So do not think that I am satisfied with myself from what I say about my work—the contrary is true; but I think this much is gained: in the future when something strikes me in nature, I shall have more means than before with which to give it new vigor.

And I am not displeased that what I shall make in the future will look more attractive.

Neither do I believe that it will hinder me if my health should give way a little from time to time. As far as I can see, the painters who occasionally cannot work for a week or two are not the worst ones. It may be because they are the ones "qui y mettent leur peau," as father Millet says. That doesn't matter, and in my opinion one must not spare oneself when there is something important to do. If a short period of exhaustion follows, it will soon pass, and so much is gained that one harvests one's studies just the way a farmer harvests his crops. Now for myself, I have not yet thought of taking a rest. Only yesterday, Sunday, I did not do so much—at least I did not go out to paint. I will see to it that even if you come this winter, you will find the studio full of painted studies.

I had a letter from Rappard yesterday; he has been to Drenthe, and judging from the two little sketches he sent me, he has not been idle. He seems to work very hard and well, too—figures as well as landscape.

Well, adieu, I must set off to work again; with a handshake,

Yours sincerely, Vincent

It is now just *two* years since I began to draw in the Borinage.

226

Dear Theo,   The Hague, 19 August 1882, Saturday evening
My sincere thanks for your letter and the enclosed. As soon as I received your letter I bought 7 guilders' worth of colors immediately, so as to have some provisions and to replenish my box. All during the week we have had a great deal of wind, storm and rain, and I went to Scheveningen several times to see it.

I brought two small marines home from there.

One of them is slightly sprinkled with sand—but the second, made during a real storm, during which the sea came quite close to the dunes, was so covered with a thick layer of sand that I was obliged to scrape it off twice. The wind blew so hard that I could scarcely stay on my feet, and could hardly see for the sand that was flying around. However, I tried to get it fixed by going to a little inn behind the dunes, and there scraped it off and immediately painted it in again, returning to the beach now and then for a fresh impression. So I brought a few souvenirs home after all.

But another souvenir is that I caught cold again, with all the consequences you know of, which now forces me to stay home for a few days.

In the meantime, I have painted a few studies of the figure—I'm sending you two sketches.

Painting the figure appeals to me very much, but it must ripen—I must get to know the technique better—what is sometimes called "la cuisine de l'art." In the beginning I shall have to do much scraping, and shall often have to begin anew, but I feel that I learn from it and that it gives me a new, fresh view of things.

The next time you send money, I shall buy some good marten brushes, which are the real *drawing* brushes, as I have discovered, for *drawing* a hand or a profile in color. Also, I see they are absolutely necessary for very delicate branches, etc. No matter how fine, the Lyon brushes make too broad stripes or strokes. My painting paper is also almost used up—toward the first of September I shall have to buy a few more supplies, but I shall not need more than the usual allowance.

Then I want to tell you that I quite agree with several points in your letter. Especially, I fully agree that, with all their good and bad qualities, Father and Mother are the kind of people who are becoming rare in the present time—more and more rare—and perhaps the new type is not at all better—and so one must appreciate them that much more.

Personally, I do indeed appreciate them. I am only afraid that the feeling about which you reassured them for the time being would come back, especially if they saw me again. They will never be able to understand what painting is. They cannot understand that the figure of a laborer—some furrows in a plowed field—a bit of sand, sea and sky—are serious subjects, so difficult, but at the same time so beautiful, that it is indeed worth while to devote one's life to expressing the poetry hidden in them.

In the future, whenever they saw me toiling and pegging away at my work—scraping it out and changing it—now severely comparing it to nature—then changing it a little so they can no longer exactly recognize the spot or the figure—it would always be a disappointment to them. They will not be able to understand that painting cannot succeed at once, and over and over again they will think, "He doesn't really know anything about it," and that real painters would work in quite a different way.

Well, I dare not allow myself any illusions, and I am afraid that Father and Mother may never really appreciate my art. This is not surprising, and it is not their fault; they have not learned to look at things as you and I have learned to look at them. They look at different things than we do; we do not see the same things with the same eyes, nor do the same thoughts occur to us. It is permissible to wish this were otherwise, but in my opinion it is not wise to expect it.

They will hardly be able to understand my frame of mind, and they will not know what urges me on. When they see me doing things which they think strange and eccentric, they will ascribe them to discontent, indifference, or carelessness, whereas in reality there is something quite different at the bottom of it, namely, the wish to pursue, coûte que coûte, what I need for my work. Now they are perhaps looking forward to the "painting in oil." Now at last it will come—and oh! how disappointed they would be, I am afraid, if they could see it; they would notice nothing but daubs of paint—besides, they consider drawing a *"preparatory study,"* an expression which many years ago I learned to hate inexpressibly, and think as incorrect as it can be. As you well know. And when they see me still at it, the way I was before, they will think I am going to be doing that preparatory study forever.

Well, let us hope for the best and try to reassure them.

What you tell me about their new surroundings is very interesting. I should certainly love to paint such a little old church, and the churchyard with its sandy grave-mounds and old wooden crosses. I hope I shall have the chance sometime.

Then you write about the stretch of heath and the pine wood close by. I can tell you, I feel an everlasting homesickness for heath and pine trees, with the characteristic figures—a poor woman gathering wood, a poor peasant carrying sand—in short, those simple things that have something of the grandeur of the sea. I have always had a wish to go and live somewhere quite in the country, if I had an opportunity and circumstances would permit. But I have plenty of subjects here—the woods, the beach, the Rijswijk meadows near by, and so, literally, a new subject at every footstep.

But it would also be to live more cheaply.

But for the moment, as far as I can see, there is no immediate reason, and so I am in no hurry.

I only tell you so you'll realize how sympathetic I am to scenery like that which you describe as Father and Mother's new surroundings.

104

It is the painting that makes me so happy these days. I restrained myself up to now, and stuck to drawing just because I know so many sad stories of people who threw themselves headlong into painting—who sought the solution of their problems in technique and awoke disillusioned, without having made any progress, but having become up to their ears in debt because of the expensive things they had spoiled.

I had feared and dreaded this from the start: I have considered drawing, and still do, the only way to avoid such a fate, and I have grown to love drawing instead of considering it a nuisance. Now, however, painting has unexpectedly given me much scope: it enables me to see effects that were unattainable before —just the ones which, after all, appeal to me most—and it enlightens me so much more on many questions and gives me new means by which to express effects. All together, these things make me very happy.

It has been so beautiful in Scheveningen lately. The sea was even more impressive before the gale, than while it raged. During the gale, one could not see the waves so well, and the effect was less of a furrowed field. The waves followed each other so quickly that one overlapped the other, and the clash of the masses of water raised a spray which, like drifting sand, wrapped the foreground in a sort of haze. It was a fierce storm, and if one looked at it long, even more fierce, even more impressive, because it made so little noise. The sea was the color of dirty soapsuds. There was one fishing smack on that spot, the last of the row, and a few dark little figures.

There is something infinite in painting—I cannot explain it to you so well— but it is so delightful just for expressing one's feelings. There are hidden harmonies or contrasts in colors which involuntarily combine to work together and which could not possibly be used in another way.

Tomorrow I hope to go and work in the open air again.

I have read most of Zola's *La Faute de l'Abbé Mouret* and *Son Excellence Eugène Rougon*, both beautiful. I think Pascal Rougon, the doctor who appears in his series of books, but always in the background, a noble figure. He really proves that no matter how degenerate a race may be, it is always possible for energy and will power to conquer fate. In his profession he found a force stronger than the temperament he had inherited from his family; instead of surrendering to his natural instincts, he followed a clear, straight path, and did not slide into the wretched muddle in which all the other Rougons perished. He and Madame François of *Le Ventre de Paris* are to me the most sympathetic figures.

Well, adieu, I often think of you, and how I should love to see you now and then. A handshake in thought and believe me,

Yours sincerely, Vincent

While writing this I have done another study, of a boy—gray, charcoal, oil, and very little color, just for the tone.

227

Dear Theo, The Hague, 20 August 1882, Sunday afternoon
I have just received a nice letter from home which pleased me very much, and showed clearly that your visit and the things you told them about me and my work have had a reassuring effect on them. I think the results can only be good. I particularly thank you for the way you spoke, though it seems to me you said more good about me than I yet deserve. At home they seem very much pleased with their new surroundings, and are still full of your visit.

For that matter, so am I, for several things you told me make me think of you more often than before, and certainly not with less affection. Especially what you told me about your health makes me think of you often. I am pretty well; my not sparing myself and acting as if I had never been ill works all right. But you realize that I have not entirely recovered. I feel it at times, especially in the evening when I'm tired; but fortunately it never got bad enough to prevent my working.

This week I have painted some rather large studies in the wood, which I tried to carry out more thoroughly and vigorously than the first ones.

The one which I believe succeeded best is of nothing but a piece of dug-up earth—white, black and brown sand after a pouring rain. Here and there the lumps of earth caught the light, and stood out in strong relief. After I had been sitting drawing that piece of ground for some time, there was another violent thunderstorm with a terrific cloudburst, which lasted for at least an hour. I was so eager to continue that I remained at my post and sheltered myself as well as I could behind a big tree. When it was over at last, and the crows flying again, I was not sorry I had waited, because of the beautiful deep tone which the rain had given to the soil. As I had begun before the rain, with a low horizon, on my knees, I now had to work kneeling in the mud, and it is because of such adventures, which often present themselves in different forms, that I think it is not superfluous to wear an ordinary workman's suit, which is less easily spoiled. The result of this was that I could bring that piece of ground home to the studio —though Mauve once rightly said, while speaking about a study of his, It is a hard job to draw those lumps of earth and get perspective into them.

The other study in the wood is of some large green beech trunks on a stretch of ground covered with dry sticks, and the little figure of a girl in white. There was the great difficulty of keeping it clear, and of getting space between the trunks standing at different distances—and the place and relative bulk of those trunks change with the perspective—to make it so that one can breathe and walk around in it, and to make you smell the fragrance of the wood.

It was with extreme pleasure that I made these two studies.

The same with a thing I saw at Scheveningen, a stretch in the dunes in the morning after the rain. The grass was comparatively green, and the black nets were spread over it in enormous circles, giving the soil deep reddish-black and greenish-gray tones. On this somber ground, women in white caps and men spreading or repairing the nets were sitting or standing, or walking around like dark fantastic ghosts. In nature it was as strikingly gloomy and serious as the most beautiful Millet, Israëls or De Groux one can imagine—over the landscape a simple gray sky with a light streak on the horizon.

Notwithstanding showers of rain, I made a study of it on a sheet of oiled Torchon.

Much will have to happen before I shall be able to make it as vigorous as I should like, but these are the things in nature that strike me most.

How beautiful it is outside when everything is wet from the rain—before—in—and after the rain. I oughtn't to let a single shower pass.

This morning I have put all the painted studies up in the studio. I wish I could talk them over with you.

As I had already expected and counted on, while I was busy, I had to buy a great many things, and the money is nearly all spent on them.

For two weeks I have painted from early in the morning until late at night, so to speak; if I continued this way, it would be too expensive as long as I do not sell.

I think it possible that if you saw the paintings, you would say that I ought to go on with it, not just at times when I feel particularly inclined, but regularly, as absolutely the most important thing, though it might cause more expenses. But though I myself love doing it, and for the present shall probably not paint as much as my ambition and desire demand because of the heavy expenses, I think I shall not lose by giving a great deal of my time to drawing, and I do this with no less pleasure. However, I am in doubt—painting comes easier to me than I expected—perhaps it would be better to throw myself into it with all my strength, first pegging away with the brush. I must say I cannot tell.

At all events, drawing in charcoal is something I am sure I must study now more than ever—at all events, I have enough to do and can go on. Even when I restrain myself a little in painting, I can work just as hard.

If I have now painted so many studies in a short time, it is because I work hard, literally working all day, scarcely taking time even to eat or drink.

There are little figures in several of the studies. I also worked on a large one and have scraped it off twice, which you would perhaps have thought too rash if you had seen the effect; but it was not impatience, it was because I feel I can do even better by grinding and trying, and I absolutely want to succeed in doing better, however much time, however much trouble it may cost.

Landscape, as I have taken it up now, decidedly requires the figure too. They are studies for backgrounds which one must do so thoroughly because the tone of the figure and the effect of the whole depend on it.

What I like so much about painting is that with the same amount of trouble which one takes over a drawing, one brings home something that conveys the impression much better and is much more pleasant to look at—and at the same time, more correct too. In a word, it is more gratifying than drawing. But it is absolutely necessary to be able to draw the right proportion and the position of the object pretty correctly before one begins. If one makes mistakes in this, the whole thing comes to nothing.

I am longing for autumn. I must be sure to have a stock of colors and other things against that time. I love so much, so very much, the effect of the yellow leaves; the green beech trunks stand out so well against them, and figures, too.

Lately I read part of a rather melancholy book, *Letters and Diary of Gerard Bilders*.[1]

He died at the age when I began. When I read that, I was not sorry that I started late. He certainly was unhappy and was often misunderstood, but at the same time I find a great weakness in him, something morbid in his character. It is like the story of a plant which shoots up too soon, and cannot stand the frost, and gets stricken to the roots by it on a certain night and then withers. At first everything goes all right—he is with a teacher (as in a hothouse)—he makes quick progress; but in Amsterdam he is almost alone, and with all his cleverness, he cannot stand it there, and comes back home to his father quite discouraged, dissatisfied, listless—he paints a little there, and then dies of consumption or of some other disease in his twenty-eighth year.

What I don't like about him is that *while he paints*, he complains of terrible dullness and idleness, as though it were something he couldn't do anything about; and he continues to run around with a, to him, too oppressive circle of friends, and persisting in the amusements and way of life which bore him to death. In short, he is a sympathetic figure; but I would rather read the life of father Millet or of Th. Rousseau or of Daubigny.

Reading Sensier's book on Millet gives one courage, and Bilders's makes one feel terrible.

I often find an enumeration of difficulties in Millet's letters, but still, "j'ai tout de même fait ceci ou cela" [I have done this or that after all], and then he always has other things in mind which he absolutely must do and which he will carry out.

And too often G. Bilders says, "I've been blue this week and have been making a mess of things—I went to this or that concert or theater, but came home even more miserable than when I went."

What strikes me in Millet is this simple, "I must do this or that *after all*."

Bilders is very witty, and can lament in a most ludicrous way about "Manila cigars"—which he likes and which he cannot afford—about tailors' bills which he cannot figure out how to pay. He describes his anxiety about money affairs so wittily that he himself and the reader have to laugh. But no matter how wittily these things may be told, I dislike it, and have more respect for Millet's private difficulties, "il faut tout de même de la soupe pour les enfants" [after all, there must be soup for the children]; he does not talk about "Manila cigars" or about amusements.

What I want to say is, Gerard Bilders's view of life was romantic, and he never got over the illusions perdues; for my part I think it a certain advantage that I started only when I had left romantic illusions behind me. I must make up for lost time now. I must work hard, but just when one has left the lost illusions behind, work becomes a necessity and one of the few pleasures left. And this gives a great quiet and tranquillity.

I regret that it will be a year perhaps before you will see all my paintings (even though I might send you something now and then) and before we can

[1] A Dutch painter who died young.

talk things over. I assure you that the things I have painted now will prove useful to me. Perhaps I shall succeed now where I did not succeed in January. The reason I enjoy painting so much is not its agreeable aspect, but its throwing light on various questions of tone and form and material. I used to be helpless before them, but now by means of painting I can attempt them. Now I also see a better chance of getting results with charcoal.

Please do not suspect me of being indifferent to earning money; I am trying to find the shortest way to that end. If only those means of earning money be real and lasting, which I personally can only see in the future if there is some real good in my work, not if I aim exclusively at salability—one has to suffer for that later—but if I study nature carefully.

If you saw that my painting would have the best chance, of course I should not refuse to paint more. But if it would be a long time before it became salable, I would be the first to say, Meanwhile we must practice the greatest economy, and, by drawing, many expenses are avoided and one makes solid though slow progress. I see a change in these painted things, and I am writing you about it because you can tell better than I how it may affect the eventual salability. At all events it seems to me that the painted studies have a *more pleasant aspect* than my drawings.

Personally, I attach less value to the more pleasant, less meager effect; my goal is the expression of more severe and virile things, for which I still have to drudge a great deal.

But if you said, Work on those landscapes or woods scenes or marines, I would have nothing against it, as it would not prevent my attempting larger or more serious things. I should only want the assurance that they are worth the brushes, the paint and the canvas, and that it is not throwing money away to do them, but that they are worth what they cost. In that case I should even work on them with great ambition. I will begin by letting them ripen a little more, by putting some more vigor into them. Then in a few months, for instance, I will send you something again, and we can see.

I believe most painters have eventually succeeded in reaching a higher level this way.

I should not want to make things that were intrinsically bad, untrue, and of false conception, because I love nature too much. But this is the problem: I must still make many studies to reach something higher and better. What will be most profitable, drawing those studies or painting them?

If the painted ones are unsalable, then certainly it will be more advantageous to draw with charcoal or something. But if it were possible to make good the expense of painted studies, then I want to tell you that in principle I have nothing against it, now that I see that they turn out rather well and may perhaps turn out to be a source of good fortune. In principle I am only against wasting paint on things which one can learn just as well another way, when there is no chance of selling them at present.

I should not want to cause either myself or you unnecessary expense, but I see clearly that the painted things have a more pleasant aspect. This makes me uncertain what to do. My money is not quite gone, but there is not much left. If I am not mistaken, today is the twentieth; I have spent less rather than more than usual on the household this month. It is true I have had to spend a good deal on painting materials, but much of this will last quite a while. But it is true that everything is very expensive. I hope you will be able to send something soon. Receive a warm handshake in thought and believe me,

Yours sincerely, Vincent

I certainly hope that you will not infer from this letter that I am pretentious enough to think these first studies salable. Formerly I could tell better than now what things were worth, whether they were salable or not; now I notice daily that I do not know any more, and studying nature is more important to me than studying the prices of pictures.

But I think I see that the painted studies have a much more pleasing aspect than either those drawn in black and white or the water colors you saw recently. And therefore I am uncertain as to whether it might possibly be more profitable after all to make painting absolutely the principal thing, notwithstanding the greater expense. I would rather you decided this than I, because I think you are more competent to judge financial success, and I absolutely trust your judgment.

You told me to try to finish a little drawing in water color. I believe that by painting I shall actually be able to make better water colors than before, if I start them again. But if it does not turn out well, you must not get discouraged, neither must I, and you must not be afraid to criticize me. I do not systematically ignore criticism, but it generally takes more time to change a thing than to indicate a change. Thus I have only just put into practice things that Mauve told me in January. And, for instance, I painted that piece of ground according to a conversation I had with him about a study of his.

228

Dear Theo,   The Hague, 3 September 1882, Sunday morning
I just received your very welcome letter, and as I want to take some rest today, I'm answering it at once. Many thanks for it and for the enclosure, and for the things you tell me.

And many thanks for your description of that scene with the workmen in Montmartre, which I found very interesting, as you describe the colors too, so that I can see it. I am glad you are reading the book about Gavarni. I thought it very interesting, and it made me love him twice as much.

Paris and its surroundings may be beautiful, but we have nothing to complain of here either.

This week I painted something which I think would give you the impression of Scheveningen as we saw it when we walked there together: a large study of sand, sea and sky—a big sky of delicate gray and warm white, with a single little spot of soft blue gleaming through—the sand and the sea, light—so that the whole becomes blond, but animated by the characteristically and strikingly colorful figures and fishing smacks, which are full of tone. The subject of the sketch is a fishing smack with its anchor being weighed. The horses are ready to be hitched to the boat and then to draw it into the water. Enclosed is a little sketch of it.

It was a hard job. I wish I had painted it on a panel or on canvas. I tried to get more color into it, namely depth and firmness of color. How curious it is that you and I often seem to have the same thoughts. Last night, for instance, I came home from the wood with a study, and I had been deeply absorbed in that question of depth of color for the whole week, and especially then. And I should have liked to have talked it over with you, especially with reference to the study I made; and look here, in this morning's letter you accidentally speak of having been struck in Montmartre by the strong, vivid colors, which were nevertheless harmonious.

I do not know if it was exactly the same thing that struck us both, but I know well that you would certainly have felt what struck me so particularly, and probably you would have seen it in the same way too. I begin by sending you a little sketch of the subject and will tell you what it was about.

The wood is becoming quite autumnal—there are effects of color which I very rarely find painted in Dutch pictures.

In the woods, yesterday toward evening, I was busy painting a rather sloping ground covered with dry, moldered beech leaves. This ground was light and dark reddish-brown, made more so by the shadows of trees casting more or less dark streaks over it, sometimes half blotted out. The problem was—and I found it very difficult—to get the depth of color, the enormous force and solidity of that ground—and while painting it I perceived for the very first time how much light there still was in that dusk—to keep that light and at the same time the glow and depth of that rich color.

For you cannot imagine any carpet as splendid as that deep brownish-red in the glow of an autumn evening sun, tempered by the trees.

From that ground young beech trees spring up which catch light on one side and are brilliant green there; the shadowy sides of those stems are a warm, deep black-green.

Behind those saplings, behind that brownish-red soil, is a sky very delicate, bluish-gray, warm, hardly blue, all aglow—and against it all is a hazy border of green and a network of little stems and yellowish leaves. A few figures of wood gatherers are wandering around like dark masses of mysterious shadows. The white cap of a woman bending to reach a dry branch stands out suddenly against the deep red-brown of the ground. A skirt catches the light—a shadow is cast— a dark silhouette of a man appears above the underbrush. A white bonnet, a cap, a shoulder, the bust of a woman molds itself against the sky. Those figures are large and full of poetry—in the twilight of that deep shadowy tone they appear as enormous terracottas being modeled in a studio.

I describe nature to you; how far I rendered the effect in my sketch, I do not know myself; but I do know that I was struck by the harmony of green, red, black, yellow, blue, brown, gray. It was very like De Groux, an effect like that sketch of "Le départ du conscrit," for instance, formerly in the Ducal Palace.

It was hard to paint. I used for the ground one and a half large tubes of white
—yet that ground is very dark—more red, yellow, brown ocher, black, sienna,
bister, and the result is a reddish-brown, but one that varies from bister to deep
wine-red, and even a pale blond ruddiness. Then there is still the moss on the
ground, and a border of fresh grass, which catches light and sparkles brightly,
and is very difficult to get. There you have at last a sketch which I maintain has
some significance, and which expresses something, no matter what may be said
about it.

While painting it, I said to myself, I must not go away before there is something
of an autumn evening in it, something mysterious, something serious. But as this
effect does not last, I had to paint quickly. The figures were put in at once with
a few strong strokes of a firm brush.

It struck me how sturdily those little stems were rooted in the ground. I began
painting them with a brush, but because the surface was already so heavily covered,
a brush stroke was lost in it—then I squeezed the roots and trunks in from the
tube, and modeled it a little with the brush. Yes—now they stand there rising
from the ground, strongly rooted in it.

In a certain way I am glad I have not *learned* painting, because then I might
have *learned* to pass by such effects as this. Now I say, No, this is just what I
want—if it is impossible, it is impossible; I will try it, though I do not know
how it ought to be done. *I do not know myself* how I paint it. I sit down with a
white board before the spot that strikes me, I look at what is before my eyes,
I say to myself, That white board must become something; I come back dissatisfied—I put it away, and when I have rested a little, I go and look at it with
a kind of fear. Then I am still dissatisfied, because I still have that splendid scene
too clearly in my mind to be satisfied with what I made of it. But I find in my
work an echo of what struck me, after all. I see that nature has told me something,
has spoken to me, and that I have put it down in shorthand. In my shorthand
there may be words that cannot be deciphered, there may be mistakes or gaps;
but there is something of what wood or beach or figure has told me in it, and it is
not the tame or conventional language derived from a studied manner or a system rather than from nature itself.

Enclosed another little sketch made in the dunes. Small bushes are standing
there, the leaves of which are white on one side and dark green on the other,
and are constantly rustling and glittering. In the background, dark trees.

You see I am absorbed in painting with all my strength; I am absorbed in
color—until now I have restrained myself, and I am not sorry for it. If I had
not drawn so much, I should not be able to catch the feeling of and get hold of
a figure that looks like an unfinished terracotta. But now I feel myself on the
open sea—the painting must be continued with all the strength I can give it.

When I paint on panel or canvas, the expenses increase again. Everything is
so expensive, the colors are also expensive and are so soon gone. Well, all
painters have those difficulties. We must see what can be done. I know for sure
that I have an instinct for color, and that it will come to me more and more,
that painting is in the very marrow of my bones. Doubly and twice doubly

I appreciate your helping me so faithfully and substantially. I think of you so often. I want my work to become firm, serious, manly, and for you also to get satisfaction from it as soon as possible.

One thing I want to call your attention to, as being of importance. Would it be possible to get colors, panels, brushes, etc., *wholesale?* Now I have to pay the retail price. Have you any connection with Paillard or some such person? If so, I think it would be very much cheaper to buy white, ocher, sienna, for instance, wholesale, and then we could arrange about the money. It would of course be much cheaper. Think it over. Good painting does not depend on using much color, but in order to paint a ground forcefully, or to keep a sky clear, one must sometimes not spare the tube.

Sometimes the subject requires delicate painting, sometimes the material, the nature of the things themselves requires thick painting. Mauve, who paints very soberly in comparison to J. Maris, and even more so in comparison to Millet or Jules Dupré, has cigar boxes full of empty tubes in the corners of his studio; they are as numerous as the empty bottles in the corners of rooms after a dinner or soirée, as Zola describes it for instance.

Well, if there can be a little extra this month, it will be delightful. If not, that will be all right, too. I shall work as hard as I can. You inquire about my health, but how is yours? I am inclined to believe that my remedy would be yours also —to be in the open air, to paint. I am well, but I still feel it when I am tired. However, it is getting better instead of worse. I think it a good thing that I live as frugally as possible, but painting is my special remedy. I sincerely hope that you are having good luck and that you will find even more. A warm handshake in thought and believe me,

Yours sincerely, Vincent

You see there is a blond, tender effect in the sketch of the dunes, and in the wood there is a more gloomy, serious tone. I am glad both exist in life.

R 16

Amice Rappard,　　　　　　　　　　The Hague, September-October 1882

I received your letter, and I want to thank you very much for it. How eager I am sometimes to see something of your work. As regards "Arti," I think that these gentlemen are up to their usual tricks again—one of those things that won't change, which used to be and will always be what they are now. I congratulate you on their refusal. I cannot tell you anything about a similar experience of my own, for the simple reason that I don't even dream of exhibiting my work. The idea leaves me absolutely cold. Now and then I wish some friend could have a look at what I have in my studio—which happens very seldom; but I have never felt the wish and I think I never shall—to invite the general public to look at my work. I am not indifferent to appreciation of my work, but this too must be something silent—and I think a certain popularity the least desirable thing of all.

A short while ago I collected all the studies I have done since the time of your visit or thereabouts. I found about a hundred figure drawings of men, women and children, not counting what I have drawn in my sketchbook. Although the number does not matter so much, I just mention it to show you that I am trying to push on energetically, and yet I am looked down upon, and considered a nonentity, by fellows who are certainly working less hard than I am—which by the way leaves me pretty cold—and nobody here pays the slightest attention to my work.

And from this you will see that, though what is happening to me is not exactly the same as your experience, it is after all tweedledum and tweedledee.

On the other hand I am of the opinion that whoever wants to do figures must first have what is printed on the Christmas number of *Punch*: "*Good Will to All*" —and this to a high degree. One must have a warm sympathy with human beings,

and go on having it, or the drawings will remain cold and insipid. I consider it very necessary for us to watch ourselves, and to take care that we do not become disenchanted in this respect, and I therefore think it of little importance to meddle in what I will call "painters' intrigues" and to assume any attitude toward them other than defensive. I always think of the old proverb, "One does not gather figs from thorns," as soon as I realize that some people believe they will be stimulated by their intercourse with artists. I believe Thomas a Kempis says somewhere, "I never mingled with human beings without feeling less human." In the same way I think one feels weaker as an artist (and rightly too) the more one associates with artists. Only when artists seriously combine to co-operate on a task that is too much for only one man (for instance Erckmann-Chatrian in their works—or the artists of the *Graphic* for the *Graphic*) do I think it an excellent thing. But in most cases it turns out to be much ado about nothing.

If I said just now that at times I wish I could see your work, on the other hand I often wish you could see mine too. The reason is that I think I could profit by your opinion, and also that you would see that the separate drawings are gradually beginning to form a whole, and also that we might talk things over and try to find a way of making some money out of them.

Not without some trouble I have at last discovered how the miners' wives in the Borinage carry their sacks. You may remember that when I was there I did some drawings of it—but they were not yet the real thing. Now I have made twelve studies of the same subject. Look, the opening of the sack is tied up and hangs down. The points at the bottom are joined together, and in this way you get a very funny-looking sort of monk's hood. (At the points 1 and 2 the hands grasp it.) I often made a woman with such a sack pose for me, but it never turned out right. Now a man who was loading coal at the Rhine railway junction has shown me.

This week I came across a volume of *Punch* for 1855 and also one for 1862. In the former there is a cartoon by old Swains which is indescribably noble in character. The Czar of Russia of that time had, I think, in a "speech from the throne" referring to the Crimean War that was then going on, declared that Russia had two generals on whom she could depend, namely the winter months January and February. Now it happened that in the month of February of that same year his Majesty the Emperor fell ill, having caught a cold, and died.

Now you see in this cartoon, probably drawn by Tenniel, the old emperor on his deathbed, and *General February turned a traitor* is standing near this deathbed —in the shape of a skeleton dressed in general's uniform; the deathbed as well as the phantom near it are covered with snow and glazed frost. It is glorious, and, if such a thing is possible, I think its sentiment even more profound and serious than that of Holbein's "Death Dance."

C. R. [Robinson], whose beautiful cartoon I sent you, is rather uneven in his work, by which I mean that his figures, though they are always well drawn, do not always move one. But now I have found another cartoon that is nearly as beautiful as Caldecott's "Afternoon in Kingsroad"—a long row of figures looking over a low fence at a collapsed bridge.

Do you have the Dagnan and the Montbard about which I wrote you—"Charmeur au Jardin des Tuileries" and "Arab Beggars"—you know they are at your disposal. I have found another beautiful sheet by Emslie, "The Rising of the Waters," a peasant woman with two children on a half-flooded meadow with pollard willows.

I assure you, every time I feel a little out of sorts, I find in my collection of wood engravings a stimulus to set to work with renewed zest. In all these fellows I see an energy, a determination and a free, healthy, cheerful spirit that animate me. And in their work there is something lofty and dignified—even when they draw a dunghill. When you read in that book about Gavarni, with reference to his drawings, that "il sabra jusqu'à 6 par jour" [he dispatched up to six a day], and you think of the enormous productivity of most of those men who make these "little illustrations"—"those things you find on the reading table of the South Holland Café," you know—you can't help thinking that there must be an extraordinary amount of ardor and fire in them. And I think, having this fire within oneself and stirring it up continually is better than having the arrogance of those artists who disdain looking at it. I think that bit of reasoning of your friend, or rather your critically critical (how can one express it?) visitor, about the *"impermissible* line" highly curious and characteristic. Will you be so kind as to convey to him, at the first opportunity, my profound respect for his wisdom and competence, although I have neither the privilege nor the pleasure of knowing his Honor, for I am not wholly unacquainted with men of that ilk, and so ...

Just ask your friend of the impermissible line whether he wants to object to the "Bénédicité" by De Groux or the "Last Supper" by Leonardo da Vinci—in which compositions the heads are also placed in a nearly straight line.

Do you know "A Midsummer Night's Dream" by Harry Furniss, showing some people—an old man, a street urchin, a drunk—spending the night on a bench under a chestnut tree in the park? This sheet is as beautiful as the most beautiful Daumier.

Don't you think Andersen's *Fairy Tales* are glorious?—he is surely an illustrator too!

231

Dear Theo,   The Hague, 17 September 1882

The weeks pass quickly and it is Sunday again.

I have often been to Scheveningen these last few days, and one evening I just hit that curious moment when a fishing smack was coming in. Near the monument is a little wooden shed in which a man sits on the lookout. As soon as the boat came in sight, the fellow appeared with a large blue flag, followed by a crowd of little children who just reached his knees. It was apparently a great pleasure for them to stand near the man with the flag, and I suppose they fancied they were helping the fishing smack come in. A few minutes after the man had waved his flag, a fellow on an old horse arrived who had to go and get the anchor.

Then the group was joined by several men and women—including mothers with children—to welcome the crew. When the boat was near enough, the man on horseback went into the water and came back with the anchor.

Then the men were carried ashore on the backs of men wearing high wading boots, and there was a great cheer of welcome at each new arrival. When they were all ashore, the whole troop marched home like a flock of sheep or like a caravan, with the man on the camel—I mean the man on the horse—towering over them like a tall spectre.

Of course I tried to sketch the various incidents most carefully. I have also painted part of it, namely, the group of which I enclose a little sketch.

Then I painted another study of a marine, nothing but a bit of sand, sea, sky—gray and lonely. I sometimes long for that quiet, where there is nothing but the gray sea—with a solitary sea bird—except for that, no voice other than the roaring of the waves. It is a refreshing change from the noisy bustle of the Geest or the potato market.

For the rest, this week I have been working on sketches for water colors.

I also carried the large one of the bench out further, and then I made a sketch of women in the hospital garden, and part of the Geest.

You can see from the enclosed sketch what I want to make—groups of people who are in action some way or another.

But how difficult it is to bring life and movement into it and to put the figures in their places, yet separate from each other. It is that great problem, *moutonner*: groups of figures form one whole, but in it the head or shoulders of one rise above those of another; in the foreground the legs of the first figures stand out strongly, and somewhat higher the skirts and trousers form a kind of confusion in which the lines are still quite visible. Then to the right or the left, according to the point of view, the greater or lesser extension or shortening of the sides. As to composition, all possible scenes with figures—either a market or the arrival of a boat, a group of people in line at the soup kitchen, in the waiting room of the station, the hospital, the pawnshop ... groups talking in the street or walking around—are based on that same principle of the flock of sheep, from which the word *moutonner* is surely derived, and it all depends on the same problems of light and brown and perspective. There is the same effect of the chestnut trees here as you describe in your last letter, as you will have seen from the drawing of the little bench; only here very little of the new green leaves is still visible, though some time ago I also noticed it, but here they are withered by the many gales.

Soon the leaves will really start to fall here, and then especially I hope to paint many studies of the wood and also of the beach, for though there are no effects of autumn leaves there, the peculiar light of autumn evenings has its own effect, and it is twice as beautiful there during this time of the year, as it is everywhere.

Am rather short of colors and other things, but you know how it is—I can vary my work in different ways, and there are always so many things to draw. For the group of figures in the enclosed sketch varies infinitely and requires innumerable separate studies and sketches of each figure, which one must catch quickly in the street. In this way it gradually gets character and vigor. Recently I made a study of ladies and gentlemen on the beach, a bustling crowd of people.

Sooner or later, after some more study, I should love to do drawings for illustrations. Perhaps one thing will result from the other. The main thing is to continue working.

I certainly hope you are well, and that you will write me about yourself and the things which strike you in your surroundings. Adieu, with a handshake,

Yours sincerely, Vincent

I am so afraid that you are in great embarrassment because of the occurrence you wrote me about, and I hope things will settle themselves.

You see from the little sketch that I have started the thing I mentioned in my last letter, namely, regularly sketching the scenes of working people, of fishermen, which strike me—either drawing or painting them; and these are the very things which, with some practice, might serve as illustrations, I think.

Of course the characters must be much more vigorously executed for that purpose.

I made about ten different sketches of the fishing smack's arrival, also of the weighing of the anchor which I sent you in my last letter.

237

Dear Theo,   The Hague, 22 October 1882, Sunday afternoon

Your letter and the enclosure were very welcome. I need hardly tell you it comes just in time and is of great help to me.

It is real autumn weather here, rainy and chilly, but full of sentiment, especially splendid for figures that stand out in tone against the wet streets and the roads in which the sky is reflected. It is what Mauve does so often and so beautifully. So I have again been able to work on the large water color of the crowd of people in front of the lottery office, and I also started another of the beach, of which this is the composition.

I completely agree with what you said about there being times in our lives when we seem deaf to nature or when nature doesn't seem to speak to us any more. I often have that feeling, too, and sometimes it helps to undertake quite a different thing. When I have had enough of landscape or light effects, I attack figures, and vice versa. Sometimes one can do nothing but wait until it passes, but many a time I succeed in chasing that feeling of impassiveness away by changing subjects. More and more, however, I become interested in the figure.

I remember there was a time when the feeling for landscape was very strong in me, and I was more impressed by a picture or drawing which rendered a light effect or the atmosphere of a landscape well, than by the figure.

Painters of the figure in general inspired me more with a kind of cool respect than with a warm sympathy.

However, I remember quite well having been very much impressed at that time by a drawing by Daumier, an old man under the chestnut trees in the Champs Elysées (an illustration for Balzac), though that drawing was not so very important. But I remember being so very much impressed at the time by something so strong and manly in Daumier's conception that I thought, It must be a good thing to think and feel that way, and to overlook or to pass up many things in order to concentrate on things which provide food for thought, and which touch us as human beings more directly and personally than meadows or clouds.

And so I always feel greatly attracted by the figures either of the English draftsmen or of the English authors because of their Monday-morning-like soberness and studied simplicity and solemnity and keen analysis, as something solid and strong which can give us strength in the days when we feel weak. So, among the French authors, the same is true of Balzac and Zola.

I do not know the books by Murger which you mention, but I hope to become acquainted with them soon.

Did I tell you that I was reading Daudet's *Les Rois en Exil*? I rather like it.

The titles of those books are very interesting to me, for instance, *La Bohème*. How far we have strayed nowadays from the Bohème of Gavarni's days. In my opinion, at that time there was a more hearty and cheerful and lively feeling than now. I do not know for certain. There is much good in our time too, or there might be more than is actually the case if there were more good fellowship.

Right now I see a beautiful effect from the window of my studio. The city, with its towers and roofs and smoking chimneys, stands out as a dark, somber silhouette against the horizon of light. This light is, however, merely a broad streak, over which hangs a dark cloud more concentrated at the bottom, but torn apart at the top by the autumn wind; large tufts are being driven away. That streak of light, however, makes the wet roofs glisten here and there in the dark mass of the city (in a drawing one would indicate it by a streak of body color), and enables one to distinguish between red tiles and slates, though the whole mass has but one tone. The Schenkweg runs through the foreground like a shining streak through the water; the poplars have yellow leaves; the banks of the ditches and the meadows are a deep green; the little figures are black.

I would draw it, or rather try to draw it, if I hadn't been busy all afternoon drawing figures of men carrying peat; my mind is still too full of them to have room for anything new.

I long for you so much and think of you so often. What you tell me about the character of some artists in Paris, who live with women and are less narrow-minded than others, perhaps trying desperately to retain a youthful air, I think perfectly observed. Such people exist there as well as here. There it is perhaps even more difficult than here to keep some freshness in one's domestic life: it means even more rowing against the current there. How many have become desperate in Paris—calmly, rationally, logically and justly desperate. I read something of the kind about Tassaert, whom I like very much, and it pains me that such was the case with him.

For this very reason I think that every effort in that direction is worthy of respect. I also believe that it may happen that one succeeds after all, and one must not begin to despair, even though one is defeated occasionally, and even though one sometimes feels a kind of exhaustion; it is necessary to take heart again and new courage, even though things go differently than one at first expected. You must not think that I look with disdain on persons like those you describe because their lives are not founded on serious and well-thought-out principles. My opinion about this is: the result must be an *action*, not an abstract idea.

I approve of principles and think them worth while only when they develop into actions, and I think it well to reflect and to try to be conscientious, because this strengthens a man's energy and unites his different activities into a whole. Those people whom you describe would, I think, be more stable if they thought more about what they were going to do, but for the rest I greatly prefer them to those people who air their principles without taking the slightest trouble or even thinking of putting them into practice. For the latter have no use for their most beautiful principles, and the former are just the people who, if they begin to live with energy and reflection, might achieve something great. For great things are not done just by impulse, but are a series of small things put together.

What is drawing? How does one learn it? It is working through an invisible iron wall that seems to stand between what one *feels* and what one *can do*. How is one to get through that wall—since pounding against it is of no use? One must undermine the wall and drill through it slowly and patiently, in my opinion. And, look here, how can one continue such a work assiduously without being disturbed or distracted from it—unless one reflects and regulates one's life according to principles? And it is the same with other things as it is with art. Great things are not accidental, but they certainly must be *willed*. Whether a man's principles originate in actions or the actions in principles is something which seems to me insoluble, and as little worth decision as the question of which came first, the chicken or the egg. But I consider it of very positive and great value that one must try to develop one's power of reflection and will.

I am very curious to know whether you will find something in the figures I am making now when you eventually see them. That is also a question like the one about the chicken and the egg—must one make figures after a composition is found, or must one combine the separate figures into a composition which follows from them? I think that the result would be pretty much the same provided one *works*.

I conclude the same way you ended your letter: that we have in common a liking for looking behind the scenes in a theater; or, in other words, we both are inclined to analyze things. It is, I believe, exactly the quality one needs for painting—in painting or drawing one must exert that power. It may be that to some extent nature has endowed us with a gift (but you certainly have it, and so do I—for that perhaps we are indebted to our childhood in Brabant and to surroundings which contributed more than is usually the case to our learning to think) but it is especially later on that the artistic feeling develops and ripens through work. I do not know *how* you might become a very good painter, but I certainly believe that it is in you and might be developed.

Adieu, boy, thanks for what you sent me and a warm handshake,

Yours sincerely, Vincent

My little stove is already burning. Oh, boy, how I wish we could sit together some evening, looking at drawings and sketches and wood engravings. I have a splendid new one.

This week I hope to get some boys from the orphanage to pose for me, then I should perhaps be able to save that drawing of the group of orphans.

238

Dear Theo,   The Hague, 10 October 1882

Your letter and its contents, literary as well as financial, were very welcome, and I thank you warmly for it. In the first place, I was especially glad to hear that perhaps it will not be so very long before you come to Holland again. I should like very much to know as soon as it is possible for you to decide whether it will be before or after New Year's. Am very glad that you sent off the studies. These days, when I am making many new ones, I feel so strongly that I must try to keep my studies after the model together. How delightful it would be if I could consult with you about the work more, but we are too far away from each other.

Recently I saw, and I also have it in my collection, a large wood engraving after a picture by Roll, "Une Grève de Charbonniers" [Miners' Strike]. Perhaps you know that painter, and if so, what have you seen of his work? This one represents the entrance to a mine, before which there are groups of men and women and children who have evidently stormed the building. They are standing or sitting around an overturned cart, and are kept in order by mounted police. One fellow is about to throw a stone, but a woman is trying to seize his arm. The characters are excellent, and it is drawn roughly and vigorously; I am certainly sure it is painted quite in accordance with the nature of the subject. It is not like Knaus or Vautier, but done with more passion, as it were—hardly any details, everything massed and simplified—but there is much style in it. There is much expression and atmosphere and feeling, and the movements of the figures —the different actions—are masterfully expressed. I was greatly impressed by it, and so was Rappard, to whom I also sent one. It was in *L'Illustration*, but in an old number.

By chance I have another one by an English draftsman, Emslie, whose subject is men going down into a mine to assist, if possible, the injured, while women stand waiting. One seldom comes across such subjects.

As to the one by Roll, I myself was once present at such a scene, complete in every detail, and I think the beauty of his picture is that it expresses such a situation so accurately, though one finds but very few of the details in it. I thought of a saying by Corot, "Il y a des tableaux où il n'y a rien et *pourtant tout y est*" [There are pictures in which there is nothing and *yet everything is in them*]. There is something grand and classic in the whole, in the composition and in the lines, as in a beautiful historical painting; and that is a quality which is as rare nowadays as it always has been and always will be. It reminds me a little of Géricault, namely, "Le Radeau de la Méduse" [Medusa's Raft], and at the same time of Numkaczy, for instance.

This week I have drawn a few heads and also some children's figures and a few old men from the almshouse.

I agree with you in what you say about those small drawings, namely, that the one of the little bench is done in more of an old-fashioned manner. But I did it more or less on purpose, and will perhaps do it again sometime. However greatly I may admire many pictures and drawings that are made especially with a view to the delicate gray harmonious color, and the local tone, yet I believe that many artists, who aimed less at this, and are called old-fashioned now, will always remain green and fresh because their manner *had, and will keep*, its own raison d'être.

To tell you the truth, I couldn't spare either the old- or the new-fashioned manner. Too many beautiful things have been done too unusually well for me to prefer one to the other systematically. And the changes which the moderns have made in art are not always for the better; not everything means progress— neither in the works nor in the artists themselves—and often it seems to me that many lose sight of the origin and the goal, or in other words, they do not stick to the point.

Your description of that night effect again struck me as very beautiful. It looks very different here today, but beautiful in its own way, for instance, the grounds near the Rhine railway station: in the foreground, the cinder path with the poplars, which are beginning to lose their leaves; then the ditch full of duck-weed, with a high bank covered with faded grass and rushes; then the gray or brown-gray soil of spaded potato fields, or plots planted with greenish purple-red cabbage, here and there the very fresh green of newly sprouted autumn weeds, above which rise bean stalks with faded stems and the reddish or green or black bean pods; behind this stretch of ground, the red-rusted or black rails in yellow sand; here and there stacks of old timber—heaps of coal—discarded railway carriages; higher up to the right, a few roofs and the freight depot—to the left, a far-reaching view of the damp green meadows, shut off far away at the horizon by a grayish streak, in which one can still distinguish trees, red roofs and black factory chimneys. Above it, a somewhat yellowish yet gray sky, very chilly and wintry, hanging low; there are occasional bursts of rain, and many hungry crows are flying around. Still, a great deal of light falls on everything; it shows even more when a few little figures in blue or white smocks move over the ground, so that shoulders and heads catch the light.

I think, however, that in Paris everything probably looks much cleaner and less chilly. For the chilliness even penetrates the house, and when one lights a pipe, it seems damp from the drizzling rain. But it is very beautiful.

But it's on days like this that one would like to go and see some friend or would like a friend to come to the house; and it's on days like this that one has an empty feeling when one can go nowhere and nobody comes. But it's then that I feel how much the work means to me, how it gives tone to life, apart from approval or disapproval; and on days which would otherwise make one melancholy, one is glad to have a will.

I had a model for a few hours today, a boy with a spade, hod-carrier by trade, a very intriguing type—flat nose, thick lips and very coarse, straight hair—yet whenever he does something, there is grace in the figure, at least style and character. I think I shall have some good models this winter; the owner of the yard has promised to send me the ones who come to ask for work, which often happens in the slack season. I am always glad to give them a few sixpences for an afternoon or morning, for that is just what I want. I see no other way than to work from the model. Of course one must not extinguish one's power of imagination, but the imagination is made sharper and more correct by contin-ually studying nature and wrestling with it. Next Sunday I hope to have the same boy again. Then I should like to draw him as if he were towing one of the boats filled with stones, which one often sees in the canal here.

Working out-of-doors is over now—I mean, sitting quietly, for it is getting too chilly—so we shall have to take up our winter quarters.

I look forward to the winter with pleasure; it is a delightful season, when one can work regularly. I have some hope I shall get on well. I need not tell you that I sincerely hope you will get back the money in question. As you know, I carried painting and water colors further than I originally intended, and now I have to pay for it by being hard up. But we shall get over that, and it must not be a reason for slacking off. I now vary my work by drawing a great deal from the model, though that is also rather expensive, but it fills my portfolios in proportion to its emptying my purse.

If you do not have the whole sum by the twentieth of the month, send me part of it; but I would rather receive it a day sooner than later, as I have to pay the week's rent on that day.

The house continues to please me, except that one wall is very damp. I can work here with a model much better than at the other studio. I can even work with several people at the same time, for instance, two children under an umbrella, two women standing talking, a man and woman arm-in-arm, etc.

But how short a spring and summer we have really had. Sometimes it seems to me as if there had been nothing between last autumn and this one, but perhaps it is because of my illness lying between. I feel quite normal now, except when I am very tired; then I sometimes have a day or half a day when I feel indescribably weak and faint, much more so now than before. However, I do not pay attention to it any more, for I'm getting sick of it, and I can't afford to be ill, as I have too much work to do. At such times taking a long walk to Scheveningen or somewhere often helps me.

Well, be sure to write by the twentieth, I have had to buy some Whatman paper and brushes. You cannot believe how many things one sometimes needs. Well, it's the same with every painter.

A handshake in thought, and believe me,

Yours sincerely, Vincent

248

Dear Theo, The Hague, 26 and 27 November 1882

Yesterday I happened to read a book by Murger, namely *Les Buveurs d'Eau* [The Water Drinkers]. I find something of the same charm in it as, for instance, in drawings by Nanteuil, Baron, Roqueplan, Tony Johannot—something witty, something bright.

Still, it is very conventional, at least this book is, I think. I haven't read any of his other books yet, and I think there is the same difference between him and, for instance, Alphonse Karr and Souvestre as there is between a Henri Monnier and a Comte-Calix and the above-mentioned artists. I try to choose all the persons I compare from the same period. It has a fragrance of the Bohemian period (though the reality of that period is obscured in the book), and for that reason it interests me, but in my opinion it lacks originality and sincerity of sentiment. However, perhaps his books in which no painter types occur are better than this one; authors always seem to be unlucky with their types of painters. Balzac, among others (his painters are rather uninteresting), Zola, even though his Claude Lantier is real—there certainly are Claude Lantiers, but after all, one would like to see Zola depict a different kind of painter than Lantier, who seems

123

to be drawn from life after somebody who certainly was not the worst representative of that school, which I think is called impressionistic. And they are not the nucleus of the artistic group.

On the other hand, I know very few well-drawn or well-painted author types; on that score painters generally lapse into the conventional and make an author nothing more than a man sitting at a table full of papers, or they do not even go that far, and the result is a gentleman with a collar and an expressionless face.

There is a painting by Meissonier which I think beautiful: it is a figure viewed from behind, stooping over, with his feet on the rung of the easel, I think; one sees nothing but a pair of drawn-up knees, a back, a neck, and the back of a head, and just a glimpse of a fist with a pencil or something like it in it. But the fellow is there, and one feels the action of strained attention just as in a certain figure by Rembrandt, a little fellow reading, also bent over with his head leaning on his fist, and one feels at once that he is absolutely lost in his book.

Take Bonnat's Victor Hugo—fine, very fine—but I still prefer the Victor Hugo described in words by Victor Hugo himself, nothing but, "Et moi je me taisais, tel que l'on voit se taire un coq sur la bruyère" [And I kept silent, just as one sees a cock keeping silent on a heather bush]. Isn't that little figure on the heath splendid? Isn't it just as vivid as a little general of '93 by Meissonier—about one centimeter in size?

There is a portrait of Millet by Millet himself which I love, nothing but a head with a kind of shepherd's cap, but the look out of half-closed eyes, the intense look of a painter—how beautiful it is—also that piercing gleam like in a cock's eye, if I may call it so.

It is Sunday again. This morning I took a walk on the Rijswijk road. The meadows are partly flooded, so that there was an effect of toneful green and silver with the rough black and gray and green trunks and branches of the old trees distorted by the wind in the foreground, a silhouette of the little village with its pointed spire against the clear sky in the background, and here and there a gate or a dungheap on which a flock of crows sat pecking. How you would like such a thing, how well you would paint it if you tried.

It was extraordinarily beautiful this morning, and it did me good to take a long walk, for what with drawing and the lithography, I had hardly been outdoors this week.

As to the lithography, tomorrow I hope to get the proof of a little old man. I hope it will turn out well. I made it with a kind of crayon especially designed for this process, but I am afraid that the common lithographic crayon will prove to be best after all, and that I shall be sorry I did not use it.

Well, we'll see how it turns out.

Tomorrow I hope I shall learn several things about printing which the printer will show me. I should love to learn the art of printing itself. I think it quite possible that this new method will bring new life into the art of lithography. I think there might be a way of combining the advantages of the new way with the old; one cannot tell for certain, but perhaps it may bring about the publishing of new magazines.

I wrote this far last night. This morning I had to go to the printing office with my little old man, now I have watched everything—transferring to the stone, preparing the stone and the printing itself. And I have a better idea now of what changes I can still make by retouching. Enclosed you will find the first print, not counting one spoiled proof. After a time I hope to do better, this doesn't satisfy me at all, but, well, the progress must come by working and trying.

It seems to me it's a painter's duty to try to put an idea into his work. In this print I have tried to express (but I cannot do it well or so strikingly as it is in reality; this is merely a weak reflection in a dark mirror) what seems to me one of the strongest proofs of the existence of "quelque chose là-haut" [something on high] in which Millet believed, namely the existence of God and eternity—certainly in the infinitely touching expression of such a little old man, which he himself is perhaps unconscious of, when he is sitting quietly in his corner by the fire. At the same time there is something noble, something great, which cannot be destined for the worms. Israëls has painted it so beautifully. In *Uncle Tom's Cabin*, the most beautiful passage is perhaps the one where the poor slave, sitting with his wife for the last time, and knowing he must die, remembers the words,

> "Let cares like a wild deluge come,
> And storms of sorrow fall,
> May I but safely reach my home,
> My God, my Heaven, my all."

This is far from theology, simply the fact that the poorest little woodcutter or peasant on the heath or miner can have moments of emotion and inspiration which give him a feeling of an eternal home, and of being close to it.

On my return from the printing office, I found your letter. I think your Montmartre splendid, and I certainly would have shared your emotion; in fact, I think that Jules Dupré and Daubigny have often tried to evoke these thoughts in their work. At times there is something indescribable in those aspects—all nature seems to speak; and going home, one has the same feeling as when one has finished a book by Victor Hugo, for instance. As for me, I cannot understand why everybody does not see it and feel it; nature or God does it for everyone who has eyes and ears and a heart to understand. For this reason I think a painter is happy because he is in harmony with nature as soon as he can express a little of what he sees. And that's a great thing—one knows what one has to do, there is an abundance of subjects, and as Carlyle rightly says, "Blessed is he who has found his work."

If work like that of Millet, Dupré, Israëls, etc., strives to bring peace, sursum corda, lift up your heart to heaven, then it is doubly stimulating—one is then also less lonely, because one thinks, It's true I'm sitting here alone, but while I am sitting here silently, my work perhaps speaks to my friend, and whoever sees it will not suspect me of being heartless.

But I tell you that dissatisfaction with bad work, the failure of things, the difficulties of technique, can make one dreadfully melancholy. I can assure you that I am sometimes terribly discouraged when I think of Millet, Israëls, Breton, De Groux, so many others, Herkomer, for instance; one only knows what these fellows really are when one is at work oneself. And then to swallow this despair and melancholy, to be patient with oneself as one is—not in order to sit down and rest, but to struggle on notwithstanding thousands of shortcomings and faults and the uncertainty of conquering them—all these things are the reason why a painter is unhappy too.

The struggle with oneself, the trying to improve oneself, the renewal of one's energy—all this is complicated by material difficulties.

That picture by Daumier must be beautiful. It is a mystery why a thing which speaks as clearly as that picture, for instance, is not understood—at least that the situation is such that you are not sure of finding a buyer for it even at a low price.

This also is something unbearable for many a painter, or at least almost unbearable. One wants to be an honest man, one is that, one works as hard as a slave, but still one cannot make both ends meet; one must give up the work, there is no chance of carrying it out without spending more on it than one can get back, one gets a feeling of guilt, of shortcoming, of not keeping one's promises, one is not honest, which one would be if the work were paid for at its natural, reasonable price. One is afraid of making friends, one is afraid of moving; like one of the old lepers, one would like to call from afar to the people: Don't come too near me, for intercourse with me brings you sorrow and loss. With all that huge burden of care on one's heart, one must set to work with a calm everyday face, without moving a muscle, live one's ordinary life, get along with the models, with the man who comes for the rent—in fact, with everybody. With a cool head, one must keep one hand on the helm in order to continue the work, and with the other hand try not to harm others.

And then storms arise, things one has not foreseen; one doesn't know what to do, and one has a feeling that one may strike a rock at any moment.

One cannot present oneself as somebody who comes to propose an advantageous deal or who has a plan which will bring great profit; on the contrary, it is clear that it will end in a deficit. And yet one feels a power surging within—one has work to do and it must be done.

One would like to talk like the people of 1793, this and that must be done, first these have to be killed, then those, then the last ones; it is duty, so it is inevitable, and nothing more need be said.

But is this the time to combine and to speak out? Or is it better, since so many have fallen asleep and do not like to be awakened, to try to stick to things one can do alone, for which one is alone liable and responsible, so that those who sleep may go on sleeping and resting.

Well, you see that for this once I express more intimate thoughts than usual; you yourself are responsible for it, as you did the same.

I think this of you, you are certainly one of the watchers, not one of the sleepers—wouldn't you rather watch while painting than while selling pictures?

I say this in all coolness, without adding what I think would be preferable, and with full confidence in your own insight into things. That there is a great chance of going under in the struggle, that a painter is something like a sentinelle perdue, these and other things, of course. You must not think me so easily frightened —for instance, to paint the Borinage would be something so difficult, so comparatively dangerous as to make life a thing far removed from any tranquillity or pleasure. Yet I would undertake it if I could—that is, if I didn't know for sure, as I do now, that the expenses would exceed my means. If I could find people who would interest themselves in such a project, I would risk it. But just because for the moment you are really the only one who is interested in what I do, the thing must be shelved for the present, and remain so, and meanwhile I shall find other things to do. But I would not give it up to spare myself.

I hope you will be able to send the money not later than December 1. Well, boy, hearty thanks for your letter and a warm handshake in thought, believe me,

Yours sincerely, Vincent

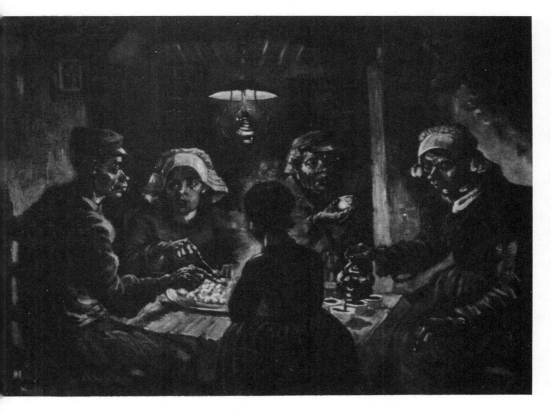

The Potato Eaters, oil, 1885

Dear Theo,   The Hague, 31 December 1882 and 2 January 1883
It is New Year's Eve and I want another chat with you.

When I wrote my last letter, I spoke of some large heads I was working on. At that time I was busy making an experiment of which I can tell you the initial outcome, as I had models for two drawings the day before yesterday, yesterday and today.

When I made the lithographs, it struck me that the lithographic crayon was very pleasant material, and I thought, I'll make drawings with it.

However, there is one drawback which you will understand—as it is greasy, it cannot be erased in the usual way; working with it on paper, one even loses the only thing with which one can erase on the stone itself, namely the scraper—which cannot be used strongly enough on the paper because it cuts through it.

But it occurred to me to make a drawing first with carpenter's pencil and then to work in and over it with lithographic crayon, which (because of the greasiness of the material) fixes the pencil, a thing ordinary crayon does not do, or, at least, does very badly. After doing a sketch in this way, one can, with a firm hand, use the lithographic crayon where it is necessary, without much hesitation or erasing. So I finished my drawings pretty well in pencil, indeed, as much as possible. Then I fixed them, and dulled them with milk. And then I worked it up again with lithographic crayon where the deepest tones were, retouched them here and there with a brush or pen, with lampblack, and worked in the lighter parts with white body color.

In this way I made a drawing of an old man sitting reading, with the light falling on his bald head, on his hand and the book. And the second one, the bandaged head of a injured man. The model who sat for this really had a head injury and a bandage over his left eye. Just like a head, for instance, of a soldier, of the old guard in the retreat from Russia.

Now when I compare these two heads with the others I have done, there is a great difference in the power of effect. So I hope that the drawings done this way will lend themselves to reproduction by the process which you described to me. Especially if the paper you sent is not absolutely necessary for the reproduction.

And if it is, I should be more apt to get a better than a worse effect on this gray paper with the same ingredients. When I looked at what Buhot had scratched on one of the samples, I saw at once that the black was of a very deep tone, and I can understand that this is a real necessity for the reproduction where photography and galvanography are used. So I at once began to try to find what kind of black to use and still stick to my usual way of sketching.

First I tried it with ink, but that didn't satisfy me; however, I think that with the lithographic-crayon method the results will be better.

Well, I am not writing about it to worry you during your busy days; I am in no hurry for it, and am even very glad to have a little time for additional experiments.

But I am writing you about it so that you may know I am working heart and soul on it to get a good and useful result. What is called Black and White is in fact *painting in black*, meaning that one gives the same depth of effect, the same richness of tone value in a drawing that ought to be in a painting.

Some time ago you rightly said that every colorist has his own characteristic scale of colors.

This is also the case with Black and White, it is the same after all—one must be able to go from the highest light to the deepest shadow, and this with only a few simple ingredients. Some artists have a nervous hand at drawing, which gives their technique something of the sound peculiar to a violin, for instance, Lemud, Daumier, Lançon—others, for example, Gavarni and Bodmer, remind one more of piano playing. Do you feel this too ?—Millet is perhaps a stately organ.

2 January

This is as far as I got on New Year's Eve, I had hoped your letter would come. If you haven't written already, do so now, for I haven't a cent left. But you are very busy, I suppose.

Since then I have again done a few sketches with the lithographic crayon—it makes drawing almost as delightful as painting, and it gives a great vigor and depth of tone.

I long very much indeed to see you again. I have so many plans—not all of which will be realized, I suppose, nor will they all be failures—and I want so badly to talk them over with you because I have so little time to think them over and I am so little in touch with what is in demand that I cannot judge what is practicable. Please do not let my having done nothing salable this year worry you ; you once said the same thing to me, and if I say so now, it is because I see a few things within my reach in the future which I didn't see before.

I sometimes think of the time, a year ago, when I came here to The Hague. I had imagined that the painters formed a kind of circle or society in which warmth and cordiality and a certain kind of harmony reigned. This seemed to me quite natural, and I didn't suppose it *could* be different.

Nor should I want to lose the ideas I had about it then, though I must modify them and distinguish between what is and what might be. I cannot believe so much coolness and disharmony is natural.

What's the reason ? ? ? I don't know and it's not my business to find out, but it's a matter of principle with me that I personally must avoid two things. First, one must not quarrel but, instead of that, try to promote peace—for others as well as for oneself. And second, my opinion is that if one is a painter, one must not try to be something other than a painter in society ; as a painter, one must avoid other social ambitions and not try to keep up with the people who live in the Voorhout, Willemspark, etc.[1] For in the old dark, smoky studios there was a good fellowship and genuineness which was infinitely better than what threatens to replace it.

If you should find some progress in my work when you come here again, should have no other desire than to go on in the same way I have—that is, to

[1] Aristocratic neighborhoods in The Hague and Amsterdam respectively.

continue my work quietly without mixing with anybody else. When there is bread in the house and I have some money in my pocket to pay the models, what more can I want? My pleasure lies in the progress of my work, and that absorbs me more and more.

Well, boy, if you haven't written already, do so soon, for I am rather hard up. Once more, my best wishes for the New Year. I had a nice letter from home. Adieu. With a handshake,

Yours sincerely, Vincent

257

Dear Theo,   The Hague, 3 January 1883

I wrote you yesterday, but I am doing so again today to acknowledge receipt of your letter and to thank you for it and to tell you that it cheered me. I was rather worried that you might think I had begun to slacken because you had seen so little of my work recently.

On the contrary, I have been working very hard lately, and am still absorbed in all kinds of things in which I am beginning to see a light, but which I do not quite have within my grasp yet. In my last letter I told you I was making experiments in Black and White with lithographic crayon.

You speak too well of me in your letter, but your thinking well of me is all the more reason for me to try not to be quite unworthy of it. And as to what I said about having made some progress by the experiments in question, perhaps I do not see my own work clearly. Perhaps it is a step forward, perhaps not—will you tell me your opinion of it in reference to the two studies I sent you, which I did recently along with a few others?

In seeking a more vigorous process than the one I have used up to now, I am trying to follow somewhat the English reproductions made by the process you described; and as to the value of black, I am also guided by the black sketches which Buhot made on the sample paper. And if you have an opportunity, please talk it over with an expert and ask him if reproduction of drawings like these, for instance, would be possible (aside from the secondary question of whether these or similar ones would be to their particular taste).

As to the sentiment of the drawings, I should like to know *your* opinion because, as I have already said, I myself cannot judge what is or isn't in them.

Or rather, it is because I myself prefer studies like these—even though they are not quite finished and many things in them have been neglected—to drawings with a definite subject: they remind me more vividly of nature itself. You will understand what I mean: there is something of life itself in the real studies, and the person who makes them will not think of himself, but of nature, and so prefer the study to what he may perhaps make of it later—unless something quite different should finally result from the many studies, namely the *type* distilled from many *individuals*.

That's the highest thing in art, and *there* art sometimes rises above nature—in Millet's "Sower," for instance, there is more *soul* than in an ordinary sower in the field.

But what I want you to tell me is whether you think that this process would eliminate some of your objections to pencil. They are a few "Heads of the People."

And I intend to try to form a collection of many such things, which wouldn't be quite unworthy of the title "Heads of the People."

By working hard, boy, I hope to succeed in making something good. It isn't there yet, but I aim at it and struggle for it. I want something serious—something fresh—something with soul in it! Forward—forward——

From what I have just said you will see clearly enough that I want to do some serious work for reproduction rather than be contented with having one little drawing printed.

But all information and hints about processes are very welcome to me.

In Goupil & Co.'s show window I saw a large etching by Fortuny, "Un Anachorète," as well as his two beautiful etchings, "Kabyle Mort" and "La Garde du Mort." I was very sorry then that I had told you some time ago that I didn't like Fortuny—I like *this* very much. But of course you understand this, too.

It's the same with Boldini.

But Fortuny's seriousness in those three etchings, for instance, is just the thing many of his imitators lack : they settle down into the style for which Fortuny set the fashion, for instance, in "Le Choix d'un Modèle," etc.

And *that* is diametrically opposed to the somber, noble art of Brion, De Groux, Israëls, etc.

If possible, please send me a recent issue of the *Vie Moderne*, choosing one with reproductions such as those which you wrote about. The magazine is nowhere to be found here (and the few numbers I have are years old).

When you come sooner or later, I can show you more, and then we can talk about the future. You know well enough how unfit I am to cope with either dealers or art lovers, and how contrary it is to my nature. I should like it so much if we could always continue as we are now, but it often makes me sad to think that I must always be a burden to you. But who knows, in time you may be able to find someone who takes an interest in my work, who will take from your shoulders the burden which you took upon yourself at the most difficult time. This can only happen when it is quite evident that my work is serious, when it speaks more clearly for itself than it does now.

I myself am too fond of a very simple life to wish to change it, but later on, in order to do greater things, I shall have greater expenses, too. I think I shall always work with a model—always and always. And I must try to arrange matters so that the whole burden doesn't always fall on you.

This is only a beginning—later you will get better things from me, my boy. In the meantime, let me know whether you think that some of the objections to the use of pencil alone may have been taken care of somewhat by this crayon. Don't you also think that by making such drawings, I perhaps indirectly learn things useful for the actual lithographing ?

Adieu. Once more many thanks for your letter.

With a handshake,

Yours sincerely, Vincent

Dear Theo,   The Hague, January 1883

The more I think of it, the deeper the impression your last letter made on me is.

Generally speaking (apart from the difference between the two persons in question), to you and to me there appeared on the cold, cruel pavement a sad, pitiful woman's figure, and neither you nor I passed it by—we both stopped and followed the human impulse of our hearts.

Such an encounter has the quality of an apparition about it, at least when one recalls it; one sees a pale face, a sorrowful look like an Ecce Homo on a dark background—all the rest disappears. That is the sentiment of an Ecce Homo, and there is the same expression in reality, but in this case it is on a woman's face. Later it certainly becomes different—but one never forgets that first expression.

I think it probable that your meeting this woman will take your thoughts back to the period some ten or even twenty years ago, and even further back. Anyway, what I mean is that you will rediscover yourself in her, a phase of your own life you had nearly forgotten—that is to say, the past—and I do not know whether, after having been with her for a year, you will view the present with the same eyes as, for instance, before you knew her.

Underneath a figure of an English woman (by Paterson) is written the name Dolorosa; that expresses it well.

I was thinking of the two women now, and at the same time I thought of a drawing by Pinwell, "The Sisters," in which I find that Dolorosa expression. That drawing represents two women in black, in a dark room; one has just come home and is hanging her coat on the rack. The other is smelling a primrose on the table while picking up some white sewing.

That Pinwell reminds one a little of Feyen-Perrin—in his early work; it also reminds one of Thijs Maris, but with an even purer sentiment.

He was such a poet that he saw the sublime in the most ordinary, commonplace things. His work is rare—I saw very little of it, but that little was so beautiful that now, at least ten years later, I see it as clearly as I did the first time.

At the time they used to say of that club of draftsmen, "It is too good to last." Alas, Herkomer's words show that it was true; but it is not dead yet, and in literature as well as in art, it will be difficult to find a better conception of that time than theirs.

I often disliked many things in England, but that Black and White and Dickens are things which make up for it all. I speak from my own experience. It's not that I disapprove of everything in the present, far from it, but still it seems to me that something of the fine spirit of that time which ought to have been preserved is disappearing—in art especially. But also in life itself. Perhaps I express myself too vaguely, but I cannot say it differently—I don't know exactly what it is, but it is not just the Black and White which changed its course and deviated from its healthy, noble beginning. Rather, there is in general a kind of skepticism and indifference and coolness, notwithstanding all the activity. But all this is too vague, too indefinite. I do not think too much about it, because I think of my drawings and have no time to spare.

I am still busy making heads this week, especially women's heads and women with bags, among other things.

Did you ever see anything by Boyd Houghton—he is one of the *Graphic's* early contributors who, though little known, nevertheless has his own niche (he died young)? I thought of him once when you wrote about Daumier's "Barricade." At the time he drew the Parisian pétroleuses and barricades too, but later he went to America, and I know drawings of his of Quakers, and a Mormon church and Indian women, etc., and immigrants.

In such a barricade scene, for instance, he had something ghostly, or rather mysterious, like Goya. He also treated the American subjects in that same way, quite Goya-like; but then all at once there are some with a wonderful soberness which reminds one of Méryon. His wood engravings might almost pass for etchings.

The world says, "*Too good to last,*" but for that very reason, because it is rare, the *good lasts*. It is not produced every day, it will never be achieved mechanically, but what is, is; it is not lost, but lasts. And if another good thing turns up later on, the first retains its value, so I think one must not regret that such and such doesn't become more common; even though they are uncommon, the good and beautiful things that exist remain.

What about the etchings which Cadart started at that time? Did they also prove to be something "too good to last"?

I know quite well that many beautiful etchings are published nowadays. But I mean the old series, "société des aquafortistes" [etchers' club], in which appeared "Les Deux Frères" by Feyen-Perrin and the "Park à Moutons" by Daubigny and work by Bracquemond and so many others—did they keep their full power or did they slacken?

Even if they slackened, aren't the things they did important enough to endure forever, so that the expression "too good to last" loses its meaning? Daubigny, Millet, Feyen-Perrin, so many others, showed what the etching needle can do, just as the *Graphic*, etc., showed what black and white can do.

And this is a lasting truth, which can give energy to whomever wants it.

The truth is that whenever different people love the same thing and work at it together, their union makes strength; combined, they can do more than if their separate energies were each striving in a different direction. By working together one becomes stronger and a whole is formed, though the personality of each need not be blotted out by working together. And therefore I wish that Rappard were entirely better; we do not really work together, but we have the same thoughts about many things. He is recovering, though, and we are already fussing over our wood engravings again.

But it is my constant hope that we shall become even better friends than we are now, and that perhaps later we shall go and visit the miners together, for instance. But for the moment, I think we must both apply ourselves to a thorough study of the figure; the better we master that, the easier it will become to carry out such plans. He writes that he had a fever, that's all, that he is still very weak; but he writes little about his illness.

We've had snow again, which is thawing just now. That thaw weather is very beautiful. Today, while the snow is melting, one feels spring approaching, as it were, from afar.

I think when you come, sooner or later, we'll have a really good time together.

I long for the spring breezes to blow away the weariness from working indoors so long.

I am very glad to have my sou'wester; I wonder if you will find some good in those fishermen's heads. The last one I made this week was of a fellow with white throat whiskers.

I know a drawing by Boyd Houghton which he calls "My Models"; it represents a passage where a few invalids, one with crutches, a blind man, a street urchin, etc., come to visit the painter on Christmas Day.

There is something very pleasant in the intercourse with the models, one learns much from them. This winter I have had some people whom I shall not easily forget. It is a charming saying of Edouard Frère's that he kept the same models so long that "celles qui posaient dans le temps pour les bébés, posent maintenant pour les mères" [those who used to pose for the babies, are now posing for the mothers].

Well, adieu, Theo, write soon, my best wishes, believe me, with a handshake,

Yours sincerely, Vincent

265

Dear Theo,   The Hague, 8 February 1883

My hearty congratulations on Father's birthday, and thanks for your letter, which I was very glad to receive just now. I congratulate you especially on the operation's being over. Such things as you describe make one shudder! May the worst be over now, at least the crisis past! Poor woman! If women do not always show the same energy and elasticity of thought as those men who are inclined to reflection and analysis, we cannot blame them, at least in my opinion, because in general they have to expend so much more energy than we in suffering pain. They suffer more and are more sensitive.

And though they do not always understand our thoughts, they are sometimes quite capable of understanding that one is good to them. Not always, though, but "the spirit is willing," and sometimes there is a curious kind of goodness in women.

It must be a great load off your mind that the operation is over.

What a mystery life is, and love is a mystery within a mystery. It certainly never remains the same in a literal sense, but the changes are like the ebb and flow of the tide, which leave the sea unchanged.

Since I last wrote you, I have given my eyes some rest and it has done me good, though they still ache now and then.

Do you know what occurred to me? That in the first period of a painter's life one unconsciously makes it very hard for oneself—by a feeling of not being able to master the work—by an uncertainty as to whether one will ever master it—by a great desire to make progress, by a lack of self-confidence—one cannot banish a certain feeling of agitation, and one hurries oneself though one doesn't like to be hurried.

This can't be helped, and it is a period which one must go through, and which in my opinion cannot and must not be changed.

In the studies, too, one is conscious of a nervousness and a certain dryness which is the very opposite of the calm, broad touch one is striving for, and yet it doesn't work well if one tries too hard to acquire that broadness of touch.

This gives one a feeling of nervous unrest and agitation, and one feels an oppression, as on summer days before a thunderstorm. I had that feeling again just now, and when I have it, I change my work, just to start something fresh.

This trouble which one has in the beginning sometimes gives an awkwardness to the studies.

But I am not discouraged by this, because I have noticed it in myself as well as in others, who later simply got rid of it gradually.

And I believe that *sometimes* one keeps this *painful* way of working one's whole life, but not always with so little a result as in the beginning. What you write about Lhermitte is quite in keeping with the review of the exhibition of Black and White. They, too, mention the bold touch which can almost be compared only to Rembrandt's. I should like to know such an artist's conception of Judas —you write of his drawing Judas before the scribes. I think that Victor Hugo could describe that in detail, *so that one would see it*, but to paint those expressions would be even more difficult.

I found a page by Daumier, "ceux qui ont vu un drame" and "ceux qui ont vu une vaudeville" [those who have seen a drama *and* those who have seen a vaudeville]; I am increasingly eager to see more Daumiers. He has pith and a staid profundity, he is witty and yet full of sentimental passion; sometimes, for instance in "The Drunkards"—and possibly also in "The Barricade," which I do not know—I find a passion which can be compared to the white heat of iron.

Some heads by Frans Hals, for instance, have the same quality; it is so sober that it seems cold, but when one looks at it for a short while, one is astonished to see how a man who apparently worked with so much emotion, and so completely wrapped up in nature, had at the same time the presence of mind to put it down with such a firm hand. I found the same thing in studies and drawings by De Groux; perhaps Lhermitte glows with the same white heat. And Menzel, too.

There are sometimes passages in Balzac or Zola, for instance in *Père Goriot*, where words reach a white heat of passion.

Sometimes I think I will make an experiment, and try to work in quite a different way, that is, to dare more and to risk more, but I don't know whether I first ought to study the figure directly from the model more.

I am also looking for a way to shut off the light in the studio, or to let it in, at will. It doesn't fall sufficiently from overhead, I think, and there is too much of it. At present I occasionally shut it off with cardboard, but I must try to get the landlord to put up some shutters.

What was in the letter I told you I tore up was quite in keeping with what you say.

But though finding increasingly that one is not perfect oneself, and makes mistakes, and that other people do too, so that difficulties continually arise which are the opposite of illusions, I think that those who do not lose courage and who do not grow indifferent ripen through it; one must bear hardships in order to ripen.

Sometimes I cannot believe that I am only thirty years old, I feel so much older.

I feel older *only* when I think that most people who know me consider me a failure, and that it might really be so if some things do not change for the better; and when I think *it might be so*, I feel it so intensely that it quite depresses me and makes me as downhearted as if it were really so. In a calmer and more normal mood I am sometimes glad that thirty years have passed, and not without teaching me something for the future, and I feel strength and energy for the next thirty years, if I live that long.

And in my imagination I see years of serious work ahead of me, and happier than the first thirty.

How it will be in reality doesn't depend *only* on myself, the world and circumstances must also contribute to it.

What concerns me and what I am responsible for is making the most of the circumstances and trying my best to make progress.

For the working man, the age of thirty is just the beginning of a period of some stability, and as such, one feels young and full of energy.

But at the same time a chapter of life is closed; it makes one melancholy, thinking some things will never come back. And it is no silly sentimentalism to feel a certain regret. Well, many things really begin at the age of thirty, and certainly all is not over then. But one doesn't expect to get from life what one has already learned it cannot give; rather one begins to see more and more clearly that life is only a kind of sowing time, and the harvest is not here.

Perhaps that's the reason why one is sometimes indifferent to the world's opinion, and if that opinion depresses us all too strongly, we may shake it off.

Perhaps I had better tear up this letter again.

I understand perfectly that you are quite absorbed in the woman's condition, this is one of the things necessary for her safety, and also for her recovery. For one must throw oneself into it headlong, and the English saying is true, "If you want it well done, you must do it yourself, you mustn't leave it to others." It means that one must keep the general care and the management of the whole in one's own hands.

We had a few real spring days, last Monday, for instance, which I enjoyed very much.

The people are very sensitive to the changing seasons. For instance, in a neighborhood like the Geest and in those courts of the almshouses or those "charitable homes," the winter is always a difficult, anxious and oppressive time, and spring, a deliverance. If one pays attention, one sees that such a first spring day is something like a Divine Message.

And it is pathetic to see so many gray, withered faces come out-of-doors on such a day, not to do anything special, but as if to convince themselves that spring is there. So, for instance, all kinds of people whom one wouldn't expect it of throng the market at the spot where a man is selling crocuses, snowdrops, bluebells and other bulbs. Sometimes a dried-up government clerk, apparently a kind of Jusserand in a threadbare black coat with a greasy collar—to see *him* next to the snowdrops is a fine sight!

I think the poor people and the painters have that feeling for the weather and the changing seasons in common. Of course everybody feels it, but it is not so important to the well-to-do middle class, and it doesn't influence their general frame of mind very much. I thought something a navvy said typical, "In winter I suffer as much from the cold as the winter corn does."

Now spring will be welcome to your patient too—may it do her good! How terrible that operation was—at least the description frightened me.

Rappard is recovering—did I tell you he had brain fever? It will be some time before he can go to work again, but he is beginning to take a walk now and then.

If my eyes do not improve, I'll take your advice and bathe them with tea. As it is, they are getting better, so for the present I'll leave them alone. For they have never troubled me before, except once this winter when I had a toothache, so I believe it is nothing but strain and overwork.

On the contrary, recently my eyes have been better able to stand the fatigue of drawing than at first.

Write soon again if you can, and believe me, with a handshake,

Yours sincerely, Vincent

I do not know whether you know those little "charitable homes" on the Brouwersgracht opposite the hospital. I should like to draw there when the weather permits. I already made a few scratches there this week. They are a few rows of small houses with little gardens, which I think belong to the charity board.

270

Dear Theo,   The Hague, 2 March 1883

Thanks for your letter and the enclosure. I think the news about your patient is very favorable. Congratulations, the recovery from that anemia is decidedly a result of renewed hope and vitality, brought about by sympathy and kindness.

> The heart that is fainting
> May grow full to o'erflowing
> And they who behold it
> Shall wonder and know not
> That God at its fountains
> Far off has been raining.

Now you will already have received—at least I sent it yesterday afternoon—a very rough sketch of a water color.

This, in answer to your question about that.

It was not done recently, however. I started it a few months ago, and have occasionally given it a few touches since then. But it is still crude. Since then, I have made a large number of studies—that is, drawings of the figure, and especially of heads—with just such a scene in mind as this sketch represents; it must be finished by adding character and relief, especially to the heads, hands and feet. I am sending them to you because you will see in them more clearly than in many other water colors I have done till now that I have a keen eye for striking colors—that I see them fresh, through a gray haze. However unfinished and imperfect it may be, this is part of a street chosen at random and done in the way in which I want to represent the Geest or the Jewish quarter. This sketch was no accident: I can take all kinds of scenes I see this far, getting the same relatively strong effects of color and tone. Now if you compare this drawing with the *lithographs* and *drawings of heads* I sent you this winter, you can see my intentions clearly from those various *failures*.

The large studies of heads, for instance, of which I have still many others—for instance, with sou'westers, with shawls and white bonnets and top hats and caps —must serve for compositions such as the one I am sending you this time.

But I shall have to put up with many more failures, for I believe that in water color much depends on a great dexterity and quickness of touch. One must work in it before it is dry to get harmony, and one hasn't much time for reflection then. So the principal thing is not finishing each one separately, no, one must put down those twenty or thirty heads rapidly, one after the other. Here follow a few curious sayings about water colors: "L'aquarelle est quelque chose de diabolique"; and the other is by Whistler, who said, "Yes, I did that in two hours, but I studied for years to be able to accomplish this in two hours."

Enough of this; I love water color too much ever to give it up entirely, I come back to it again and again. But the foundation of everything is the knowledge of the figure, so that one can readily draw men and women and children whatever they are doing. So this is my chief aim, which cannot be realized in any other way, I think.

And I try to work myself up to a higher level of knowledge and ability in general, rather than to care very much about finishing off some particular sketch. After having drawn for a month, I now and then make a few water colors, for instance, by way of casting the plummet to fathom my depth. Each time I see that I have overcome some obstacles, but that new difficulties have arisen. Then I start drudging again to conquer those.

As for the colors, they are really all used up—and not only that, but because of some relatively heavy expenses, I am not only hard up, but absolutely penniless.

Spring is coming, and I should like to take up painting again, too. So that is partly the reason why I am not working in water color right now.

But indirectly I am always working at it, and now that I can study the effects of chiaroscuro better because of the alterations in the studio, I shall work more and more with the brush, even in Black and White drawings, and wash the shadows in with neutral tint, sepia, India ink, Cassel earth, and accentuate the lights with Chinese white.

Do you remember that last summer you brought me pieces of mountain crayon? I tried to work with it at the time, but it didn't work well. So a few pieces were left, which I picked up the other day; enclosed you'll find a scratch done with it; you see it is a peculiar, warm black. You would greatly oblige me by bringing some more of it this summer. It has a great advantage—the big pieces are much easier to handle while sketching than a thin stick of conté, which is hard to hold and which breaks all the time. So for sketching outdoors, it is delightful.

Well, boy—it is difficult to write it all, and I wanted to answer your question about water color in more than words. I should not want anybody to see just this one sketch of mine, because I myself think nothing is right in this sketch except the general aspect, and I will wrestle with the figures till I get in water color what they are beginning to get in lithography—that is, more character and effect.

It is not pleasant to make sketches like the one I sent you, and then not to be able to finish them; I hate this so much that I rarely make them, except as a trial to see if I have made any progress. But now I have new courage and interest, just because I have been making a great many studies again.

I think the change in the studio will help me on, not the first day, but after a few months' struggling.

I can now do part of my work perfectly well at home, studying with models, such effects as the water color I sent you.

Here the windows are closed at the bottom so that the light on the group of figures falls from above. In this way I can group them in the studio, and then I get, for instance, the high lights on the heads of the figures.

Like in this water color.

I have tried it already with the old man, the woman and the children—it gives *splendid* effects. The desire to make them is not wanting, but I expect new failures—which I hope, however, will have *something* in them to encourage rather than to make one lose courage, though they are failures.

I had to pay for so many things at once out of the money you sent that I wish you could send some more; but arrange it as best you can—I have so much work now that I can vary it just as I like. I long very much for your coming, just to show you the studies and to talk about the work.

Adieu, thanks again. With a handshake,   Ever yours, Vincent

165*b*

[Reprinted from Benno J. Stokvis, LL.D., *Nasporingen omtrent* (Investigations concerning) *Vincent van Gogh in Brabant* (Amsterdam, S. L. van Looy, 1926).]

Etten

Etten-Leur, a small village between Breda and Roozendaal, makes a far less prosperous impression than Zundert. However, it appears that there are no fewer Protestants here than in the latter village.

After having been stationed at Helvoirt for some years, the Rev. Mr. Van Gogh came to Etten in 1875 as successor to the Rev. Mr. Peaux (father of the poetess Augusta Peaux). He remained there until 1882. Here his intercourse seems to have been limited to the members of his own parish more than it was in Zundert. However, here too non-Catholics and Catholics remember him with equal sympathy.

If anyone failed to appear in church on a Sunday, he could be sure that the Rev. Mr. Van Gogh would look him up that very week to lecture him, however far in the "interior," however remote from the village, his farm might be situated. He even visited the people living on the most distant farms regularly.

The Rev. Mr. Van Gogh was charitable: at times he distributed more among the poor than the consistory could approve of. But at the same time he was described as a severe and forceful personality. This observation may help to dispel the notion advanced in some writings on Vincent that the father behaved in a spineless, powerless fashion toward his son (in support of which, I refer to letter 158).

Although the people of Zundert were in general fully aware of Vincent's fame as a painter, in Etten I was struck by an almost complete ignorance on the subject. Neither old villagers who had known him personally, nor even his one-time models whom I met, knew that he had made a name for himself; and when I told them so, they looked amazed—they would never have expected such a thing of "that Vincent"!

I asked an old Protestant woman whether she had known the Rev. Mr. Van Gogh's son, "who had drawn." "Drawn?" was the counter-question. "You mean to say he was drawn into the East Indian army?" Though such intellectual agility on the old lady's part may provoke laughter, from a psychological point of view such an answer proves, after all, how little Vincent's activities were actually taken seriously.

The painter returned repeatedly to Etten; the last time he stayed there for about one year. So he was present at the wedding of his sister Anna at Etten, at which the Rev. Mr. Van Gogh himself officiated.

The following persons were interviewed by me:

J. A. Oosteryck's father was an elder of the church under the Rev. Mr. Van Gogh. Vincent often used to drop in upon the Oosterycks and would then make drawings indoors and in the granary. Once he made a portrait of my informant's mother which was a very good likeness. His father was also immortalized by Vincent in a large picture of him plowing his field.

According to the son the picture of his father's figure did not look like him, but for the rest, "a photograph could not have been more perfect." When the painting was finished, old Mr. Oosteryck happened to remark that Vincent had forgotten to put in the dog. Vincent obligingly took up his brushes and added the dog. Those for whom Vincent had a liking [literally, "who had a good odor in his nostrils"] were given a drawing by him more than once. Vincent worked a great deal in the vicinity of the village; he was highly respected by the farmers. When he set off for work, he generally wore a sort of raincoat and a sou'wester. In general his attire was rough ["raw"]. Every day he might be seen walking with a small campstool under one arm and a square frame (??) under the other, always staring straight in front of him, and he took little notice of people. Without doing strikingly eccentric things, he yet seemed a queer sort of man.

When Vincent was busy painting, he did not like to be watched; if anyone stood watching him longer than he liked, he unreservedly begged the importunate person to clear off. At times he was anything but meek.

Toward the poor he always showed himself exceedingly open-handed; he once gave a beggar his own velvet suit, which was as good as new. Now and then he would hand over a number of drawings to his father for distribution among the members of the consistory. If a drawing did not come off "choicely" enough to his taste, he immediately tore it up.

Opinion on the work of the painter was briefly formulated in the words, "All that he made was as accurate as a photograph."

C. Kerstens has for many years been the occupant of an outlying farm. He used to know Vincent well, though the latter did not come his way very often. It was intimated with emphasis that Vincent made his drawings and paintings almost exclusively among the Protestants. The artist had "peculiar" ways. As a rule he walked all alone. He was of "sturdy build."

A. de Graaf. Informant is now seventy-six years old. In the time of the Rev. Mr. Van Gogh he was the verger at the Protestant church.

A carpenter by profession, in this capacity he made the above-mentioned folding stool for Vincent, who thenceforth took it with him when he went out painting. Vincent had drawn a rough model of the stool on a board, and De Graaf put it together accordingly.

Vincent was "a good boy," who would go all over the place to make his little sketches. This occupied him continually and was all he spoke of. He wasn't the least bit proud, and was a regular visitor in the houses of poor people. He was a serious man, who never made jokes.

Now and then the Rev. Mr. Van Gogh would confide to De Graaf that "there was such an extraordinary spirit in Vincent," and that he would have liked so much to make a preacher of him.

Piet Kauffmann, a still strong and active man of sixty. He often served as Vincent's model, and Vincent repeatedly mentioned him in his letters (*e.g.* in letter 148: "I think I shall find a good model here in Piet Kaufman, the gardener, but I think it will be better to let him pose with a spade or plow or something like that—not here at home, but either in the yard or in his own home or in the field." Note the wrong spelling: Piet Kaufman!)

Put on the trail by finding this reference, I set out to find him. According to some whom I questioned he had been dead a long time, and had not left any children; but I know that to err is human, and in some respects I had come to know something of the "southerly" imagination of the North-Brabant people, and consequently I decided not to take the man's death for granted before I had beheld his tombstone with my own eyes. So I refused to be discouraged, and in a pub at Leur, about an hour's walk from Etten, I had the satisfaction of meeting him, very much alive.

He could remember the painter quite clearly. At the time when Kauffmann posed for Vincent, he was the Rev. Mr. Van Gogh's gardener and seventeen years old. Vincent often made drawings of him at the parsonage, especially on Saturdays: as a rule Kauffmann posed standing, holding a rake or spade. Vincent also drew pictures of him a number of times as a sower, with a piece of cloth hanging from his shoulders.

At times Vincent would work on a drawing for hours: he worked on until he had caught the expression he was aiming at. The Rev. T. van Gogh's servant girl at that time used to tell how Vincent would occasionally continue to paint all through the night: many a time it happened that his mother found him still at work when she came down in the morning. Often Vincent would not take time for lunch: at such times his mother would call him repeatedly, and he would keep answering, "Yes, I'm coming," but all the same he would either not make an appearance at all, or come more than an hour later.

Generally Vincent went about with a portfolio under one arm and a camp-stool under the other, and he used to hold his head a little to one side—"he always walked lost in thought"; he never recognized anybody in the street, "he was a queer little fellow."

A few times Kauffmann received some drawings by way of a present, but they had been lost when he moved from one house to another. Informant estimates that he posed for Vincent some forty or fifty times.

The Rev. Mr. Dijkman showed me a map of the Holy Land which Vincent had drawn by hand; for years it hung on the vestry wall (until 1916).

At Etten Vincent was not registered as a member of the Reformed Church.

Data furnished by the registrar's office [often inaccurate—*Ed.*]:

October 22, 1875. Arrival of the Van Gogh family in the municipality from Helvoirt.

Departure of the family for Nuenen: August 4, 1882.

Arrival of Vincent Willem (*i.e.* the painter) at Etten from Brussels: August 18, 1881.

Departure of Vincent Willem for The Hague: July 20, 1882.

In the Register his profession is stated to be "painter."

Some birth dates, accidentally found, may be mentioned here as a matter of curiosity:

The Rev. T. Van Gogh: February 8, 1822.

Mrs. Van Gogh-Carbentus: September 10, 1819.

Cornelis Vincent (the painter's younger brother Cor): May 17, 1867.

Elisabeth Huberta (the painter's well-known sister Lies): May 16, 1859.

291

Dear Theo,   The Hague, 5 or 6 June 1883

Today I received a letter from home, and though Father does not mention you in it, I want to speak to you about it because just now you would perhaps like to know something more about their frame of mind than what they write to you directly. And it is my impression that for the present you need not worry about it.

The said letter is Father's first since his visit here, and it is very kind and cordial, and was accompanied by a parcel containing a woman's coat, a hat, a packet of cigars, a cake, a money order. In the letter was a draft of a sermon, of which I liked the text by far the best, and which touched me less than a simple word about a funeral from a farmhand did afterward.

I tell you this in such detail so that you may see there is nothing abnormal or any definite overexcitement; but I did get the impression that Father was in a rather passive or submissive mood, more inclined toward a friendly, melancholy view of things than might be supposed from the expressions of disapproval you passed on to me.

I suppose those words were intended more as advice or warning—but not as a sign of direct opposition to your firm decision.

Because in my previous letter I disapproved so strongly of what Father had said—and I still disapprove of it, as I am most decidedly of the opposite opinion, and consider it irrelevant to raise difficulties and financial and religious objections in this case—I should like to soften my words to this extent that I think we are concerned with an error (at least number one[1] is an error) which exists more in his words than in his heart or his frame of mind. And I cannot help reminding you that Father is an old man, and so fondly attached to you, and I am sure you will find that he will give in to you if it must be so, even though it be contrary to his own opinion, but that it would be impossible for him to live estranged from you or on less friendly terms. Well, I suppose I know Father somewhat, and I think I notice signs of a little melancholy.

And looking at it from a human point of view I withdraw my opinion that "by talking the way they did, they have shown themselves unworthy of your confidence, and therefore I think you need not consult them any longer" or something of the kind, for I do not remember exactly what I wrote. But please understand what I mean: not because I disapprove less of what they said, but because I have the impression that in this case you need not resent it so much, and that there is no urgent need to start hostilities as long as they confine themselves to words. Better forestall unpleasantness by saying, for instance: "You take rather a somber view of the future," or, "But you cannot demand of me that I act as if the clock were going to strike the hour of the world's end," which I think would be more sensible than attaching too much weight to their words.

I have the impression Father is somewhat melancholy, and that perhaps he is worrying over you, and imagining gloomy things—but I repeat, Father did not write one syllable about the matter itself, and did not say a word about it on the occasion of his visit, though this avoidance of mentioning it is somewhat abnormal too.

If you want to remedy this, write somewhat cheerfully and lightly, and write about your visit this summer as if it were certain that you would see them soon (even if you do not know yourself how you can fix the time of your coming).

For perhaps, perhaps Father himself is conscious of having gone a little too

[1] I.e. the financial objections.

far, or perhaps he is anxious about how you will take it, and is afraid you will not come.

Of course I do not know it for sure and can only guess; but what I think is, Father is an old man and deserves to be cheered up if possible.

That it is my opinion that you ought to be faithful to the woman, you know well enough; there is no question of saying anything less about it than I did; you must act as you think right, but don't be angry with Father if he is mistaken.

That is what I wanted to say. Don't even mention that he is mistaken unless he continues to press the point; perhaps he will change his mind of his own accord.

Now again about the work: today I asked permission to make sketches in the old people's asylum, that is, of the men's ward, of the women's ward and of the garden.

I was there today. From the window I sketched an old gardener near a twisted apple tree, and the carpenter's shop of the asylum, where I had tea with two old almshouse men. In the men's ward I can come as a visitor: it was very striking, indescribably striking.

One little fellow, for instance, with a long thin neck, in a wheel chair, was splendid. That carpenter's shop with those two old men and a view of the cool green garden was just the thing, like Bingham's photograph of that little picture by Meissonier, those two priests sitting at the table drinking. Perhaps you know what I mean.

But it is not quite certain that I shall get the permission, and the application must be made to the deacon in charge. I have done so, and must come back for the answer.

Meanwhile, I am making sketches for the drawing of the refuse dump. I wrote you, I hoped to get a Scheveningen cape; well, I have got it, and an old bonnet into the bargain; the latter is not very good, but the cape is superb, and I set to work on it at once. I am just as delighted with it as I was with the sou'wester before.

And the sketch of the refuse dump is so far advanced that I have caught the sheepfold-like effect of the interior in contrast with the open air and the light under the gloomy sheds: and a group of women emptying their dustbins is beginning to develop and take shape. But, the moving back and forth of the wheelbarrows, and the dustmen with the dung forks, that rummaging under the sheds, must still be expressed without losing the effect of light and brown of the whole: on the contrary, it must be strengthened by it.

I suppose you will take Father's words in the same way of your own accord, so that I'm not telling you anything new, but I should be glad if, with a little good will, peace might be preserved. Last winter Father was nearly as much opposed to my living with the woman as he is in your case now, yet he sent me a warm woman's coat "I might have some use for," not precisely indicating for what, but obviously with the thought, "Perhaps she is suffering from the cold." Well, you see that is the right thing, and for *one* such deed I would endure a whole shower of words with pleasure.

144

For neither do I myself belong among those people who always use the right words—such people would be perfect—and I haven't the slightest pretension to perfection.

But what I wanted to point out to you is this: At all events Father certainly objects to my living with the woman *much more* than in your case, and notwithstanding that, last winter he thought, "Confound the woman but she must not freeze." And perhaps in your case, "That poor Catholic girl must not be forsaken," or something like that; so don't worry, keep good courage and try to reassure them. Adieu, lad, with a handshake,

Yours sincerely, Vincent

292

Dear Theo,   The Hague, 10 June 1883

Your letter and the enclosure were very welcome, many thanks. And I was glad to see that you take things calmly, though I did not expect anything else.

Since I wrote you last I have been drudging very hard on that drawing of the refuse dump: it is a splendid scene.

The first drawing of it has already undergone so many corrections; first it was white, then black in all kinds of patches, so that I copied it on a second sheet, because the first one was too overworked. And I am working on it anew. I must get up early in the morning for it, for then I get the effects I need. If I could only get it the way I have it in my mind!

Well, the second one is of the same size as the two former ones of the peat cutting and the sand digging, and it fits in the frame. For the moment it is looking rather good, but I am afraid I'll spoil it. But one must not be afraid of that either, otherwise one never succeeds. And meanwhile I made a large study of a seamstress besides.

But the asylum has been a disappointment in that they refused me permission to draw there—they said there was no precedent for it, and besides, they were in the midst of spring-cleaning, and new floors were being laid in the wards. Well, never mind, there are more homes for the poor, but in this one I know a man who posed for me regularly, and that would have made it easy for me to make sketches. Last winter I saw the old almshouse in Voorburg. It is of course much smaller, but almost even more striking.

It was toward evening when I was there, the old people were sitting on benches and chairs round an old stove, very characteristic.

Perhaps I'll try that one at Voorburg, since I have no permission here. I also spent a day at Scheveningen, and saw a beautiful scene there of men with a cart full of nets which had been tarred and were being spread out on the dunes. Someday I must certainly make a large drawing of that or of *mending* the nets.

It is an improvement, Theo, having those stretchers and that frame for charcoal drawings, or whatever, for it is pleasant working with them. I think you are quite right in what you say about too much intercourse with painters *not* being good, but *some* intercourse, very much so. And for that reason I am glad Van der Weele is coming.

Indeed, one can have a deep longing sometimes to talk things over with people who know about one's craft. Especially if each works and seeks in the same spirit, it is possible greatly to strengthen and animate each other, and one is not so easily discouraged. One cannot always live away from one's native land, and one's native land is not nature alone—there must also be human hearts who search for and feel the same things. And only then is the native land perfect, only then does one feel at home.

This now is the composition of the refuse dump. I do not know how much you can make out. In the foreground, women are emptying dustbins; behind them are the sheds where the dung is kept, and the men at work with wheelbarrows, etc. The first one I made of it was a little different; there were two other men in the foreground with sou'westers, which they often wear in bad weather, and the group of women was darker.

But that light effect is really there because the light falls from overhead between the sheds on the figures in the pathways. It would be a splendid thing to paint. I think you will understand all about it. I wish I could talk it over with Mauve. But perhaps it's better as it is, for it does not always help to get advice from somebody else, clever though he may be, and those who are cleverest are not always clever in explaining things clearly. I repeat, I hardly know myself what is best. In the first place, painting is not my principal object, and perhaps I will be ready for illustrating sooner all by myself than if somebody, who wouldn't think of illustrations at all, advised me. I get on best of all with Rappard.

Adieu, boy. All best wishes and thank you for your timely help.

Yours sincerely, Vincent

R 37

Amice Rappard,   The Hague, May-June 1883

I was just writing you a letter when the postman brought me your very welcome letter; I am glad to hear that you have made progress with your drawing. I never doubted you would, for that matter, for you attacked it in a virile way.

Now, to begin with I want to tell you that I think what you say about the English black-and-white artists perfectly right and proper. I saw in your work exactly what you say. Well, I quite agree with you—particularly about the bold contour.

Take Millet's etching "The Diggers," take an engraving by Albrecht Dürer, above all take the large woodcut by Millet himself, "The Shepherdess"—then you see with full clarity what may be expressed by such a contour. And, as you say, you feel "that is how I have always wanted to do it, if I had always gone my own way, etc." That's well said, old fellow, and spoken like a man.

Now I think another example of characteristic, bold and vigorous drawing is Leys's pictures, and more especially that series of decorations for his dining room —"La Promenade dans la Neige," "Les Patineurs," "La Réception," "La Table," "La Servante." And De Groux has it too, and so has Daumier.

Even Israëls, and at times Mauve and Maris too, cannot refrain from drawing a vigorous contour, but they *don't* do it in the manner of Leys, or of Herkomer.

146

But when you hear them talk, they will have none of it, and more often they are talking about "tone" and "color." And yet, in certain charcoal drawings Israëls has also used lines that remind one of Millet. I want to state flatly that personally, however much I admire and respect these masters, I regret that, when they speak to others, they—and particularly Mauve and Maris—do not point out more emphatically what can be done with the contour, and advise them to draw cautiously and softly. And so it happens that water colors are the order of the day nowadays, and are considered the most expressive medium, whereas in my opinion too little attention is being paid to black and white, so much so that there is even a certain antipathy against it. There is no black, so to speak, in a water color, and that is what they base themselves on in order to say, "Those black things." It is not necessary, however, to devote my whole letter to this.

I wanted to tell you that I have four drawings on my easel at the moment—peat cutters—sand pit—dunghill—loading coal. I even did the dunghill twice; the first one was too overworked to be continued.

Besides I have not ventured to work too much in them with printer's ink and turpentine; instead I have used charcoal, lithographic crayon and autographic ink so far.... Except in the case of the dunghill that became too overworked; I attacked this one with it and not unsuccessfully; it became rather black, it's true, but for all that the freshness returned somewhat, and now I see my way again to working on it some more, although I thought it hopeless before I put on the printer's ink.

I have been working very hard since I visited you; I had not done any compositions for such a long time—only a lot of studies—that when I once started I went quite wild about it. I was pegging away at it many mornings as early as four o'clock. I am extremely eager for you to see them, for I can make neither head nor tail of what Van der Weele, the only one who has seen them, said.

Van der Weele's opinion was rather sympathetic, but he said about the *sand pit* that there were too many figures in it; the composition was not simple. He said, "Look here, just draw that one little fellow with his wheelbarrow on a little dike against the bright sky at sundown; how beautiful such a thing would be—now it is too turbulent."

Then I showed him Caldecott's drawing "Brighton Highroad," and said, "Do you mean to say that it is not permitted per se to introduce many figures into a composition? Never mind my drawing, just tell me what you think of this composition."

"Well," he said, "I don't like that one either. But," he added, "I am speaking personally, and I can't speak any other way than personally, and this is not the kind of thing I like and want to look at." Well, I thought this well said in a certain way, but you will understand that I did not find in him exactly that sound knowledge of things which I was looking for. But he is quite a sound fellow on the whole, and we took a very pleasant walk together, and he pointed out some damned fine things to me.

It was while taking a walk with him that I saw that sand pit too, but he hardly looked at it on that occasion, and next day I went back to it alone. I have drawn that sand pit with many figures because at times there really are very many fellows toiling there, because in winter and in autumn the town gives employment in this way to persons who are out of work. And then the scene is extremely busy.

I have had some beautiful models of late. A superb grass mower, a magnificent peasant boy, exactly like figures by Millet. A fellow with a wheelbarrow, the same whose head you may remember I drew, but then in his Sunday clothes and with a Sunday-clean bandage around his blind eye. Now I have him in his everyday clothes, and—as I see it—it is difficult to believe that this is the same man who posed for both studies.

The size of these four large drawings is 40 × 20 inches.

I am much pleased with using a brown passe-partout with a very deep black inner rim. Then many blacks seem to be gray, whereas they would show up too black in a white passe-partout, and the whole retains a clear effect.

Lord, how I wish you could see them, not because I think them good myself, but I should like to know what you think of them, although I am not yet satisfied with them. In my opinion they are not yet sufficiently pure figure drawings, though they are figure drawings all right, but I should like to accentuate the drawing of the actions and the structure more cleanly and boldly.

What you write about feeling that you are now on a *road*, and not on little bypaths and crossroads, is very true, in my opinion. I have a similar feeling myself, because during the past year I have been concentrating on figures even more than I used to.

If you believe that I have eyes to see with, then you may be sure that there most certainly is sentiment in your figures; what you are doing is healthy and virile—never doubt yourself in this respect, and for the very reason that you do not doubt, dash it on without hesitation.

I think the studies of the heads of those blind fellows are superb.

It must not surprise you that some of my figures are so entirely different from the ones that I sometimes make after the model. I very seldom work from memory—I hardly practice that method. But I am getting so used to being confronted immediately with nature that I am keeping my personal feelings unfettered to a far greater extent than in the beginning—and I get less dizzy—*and I am more myself just because I am confronted with nature.* If I have the good fortune to find a model who is quiet and collected, then I draw it repeatedly, and then at last a study turns up which is different from an ordinary *study*— I mean more characteristic, more deeply *felt*.

And yet it was made under the same circumstances as the more wooden, less deeply felt studies that preceded it. This manner of working is as good as any other—just a little more easily understood—like these "Little Winter Gardens." You said it yourself—they are *felt*; all right, but that was not accidental; I drew them over and over again before, and that feeling was *not* in them then. After that—after the iron-like ones—came these, and also that clumsiness and awkwardness. *How does it happen that I express something with that?*—because the thing has shaped itself in my mind before I start on it.

The first ones are absolutely repulsive to others. I say this to make you understand that, *when* there is something in it, this is not accidental but most certainly *reasoned out* and *willed*.

I am delighted to hear that you've noticed that I'm doing my best at present —and that I attach importance to it—to express the relation of the values of the masses against each other, and to show how in the dizzying tangle of every corner in nature things will show up separate.

Formerly the light and brown in my studies was rather fortuitous, at least not logically carried through, and that is why they were colder and flatter.

When once I *feel*—I *know*—a subject, I *usually* draw three or more *variations* of it —whether it is figure or landscape—but every time and for each one I consult nature. And I even *do my best not to give details*—for then the dreaminess goes out of it. And when Tersteeg and my brother, and others, say, "What is this, is it grass or cabbage?"—then I answer, "*Delighted* that *you* can't make it out."

And yet they are sufficiently true to nature for the honest natives of these parts to recognize certain details which I have hardly paid any attention to; they will say, for instance, "Yes, that's Mrs. Renesse's hedge," or, "Look, there are Van de Louw's beanpoles."

I want to tell you something besides about a kind of Faber lead pencil that I have discovered. Here is the diameter of the lead; they are soft and of a better quality than the carpenter's pencils; they give a glorious black, and are very pleasant to work with for large studies. I drew a seamstress with it on gray papier sans fin [*i.e.* cut from the roll], and got an effect like lithographic crayon. The lead is enclosed in soft wood painted dark green, and they cost 20 cents apiece.

Before I forget, I should like to borrow from you the issues of *Harper's* magazine you have, for I want to read the articles on Holland that are illustrated by Boughton and Abbey. I shall send you a package with the old loose numbers I have containing illustrations by Howard Pyle and others, so that you can look through them at your leisure, and I shall add Erckmann-Chatrian's *Histoire d'un Paysan*, illustrated by Schüler, as well as a few illustrations by Green, which you'll remember I promised you. If you have some more duplicates, please send them along with the *Harpers* (at least if you can spare the latter for some four days, so that I can read them), and also Zola's little book about Manet, at least if you have finished it.

I am distressed to hear that your health is not yet what it should be; all the same I think that making progress with your drawings will reanimate you more than those baths, or whatever other tricks they may perform at Soden. I think you will long to be back in your studio as soon as you have left it. I clearly remember how terribly melancholy Mauve was on his pilgrimage to a similar kind of works —speaking with all due respect.

As you know, I am rather an infidel about such things, and I sympathize with what Bräsig, in Fritz Reuter's *Dried Herbs*, had to say about what this authority called "*die Wasserkunst*,"[1] I think.

How beautiful Fritz Reuter's work is! I think you will admire that book by Erckmann-Chatrian.

[1] The literal translation is "water art," but what is meant is "hydropathic tricks."

Another thing I must tell you is that the other day I got hold of a marvelous old Scheveningen woman's cape as well as a cap, but the cap is not so beautiful. And I shall also get a fisherman's jacket with a high turned-up collar and short sleeves. I am immensely eager to see your charcoal drawing; perhaps when my brother comes here—I don't know exactly when—I shall go with him to Brabant, and then, as we are passing through Utrecht, and if I can manage it, I shall look in on you; but at any rate I shall try to come to you without that, for I am very curious to see it.

As for you, try to keep your promise to come to The Hague, for you will have to come here anyway for that wedding party, you know. If my recent luck with finding models holds out, I shall certainly make some more large drawings this summer.

I should like to go on working on those I have in hand, so as to raise them to a high standard against the time my brother comes here.

In *Harpers Weekly* I came across a very characteristic thing after Smedley, the black figure of a man on a white sandy road. He calls it "A Generation Ago"; the figure is some kind of clergyman, and perhaps I could describe my impression of it thus—Yes, that's what my grandfather looked like. I wish I had done it. In the same issues, after Abbey, two girls standing fishing on the side of a ditch with pollard willows. Both of these things in *Harpers* are only sketches in a review of an exhibition.

I should like to send you sketches of my drawings, but I don't have much time to spare.

I asked permission to make drawings in the old men's and old women's almshouse here, but they refused again. Oh well, there are more almshouses in the villages near by. But here I knew some fellows that I have used as models. But I went there to have a look, and among other things I saw a little old gardener near an old twisted apple tree, very characteristic.

Well, here comes my model. Adieu, send the *Harpers* if you can spare them, with a handshake,

Ever yours, Vincent

299

Dear Theo,   The Hague, 10 July 1883

I had already been on the lookout for your letter and was glad when it came. Many thanks.

What you write about the exhibition is very interesting. How was that old picture by Dupré which you liked so much? I should love to hear more about it. Your description of the Troyon and the Rousseau, for instance, is striking enough for me to get an idea of the manner in which they are done. About the time of Troyon's "Pré Communal" [Common] more pictures had a certain sentiment which I should like to call *Dramatic*, though there are no figures in them. Speaking of a Jules Dupré (the large one in the Mesdag collection), Is-raëls expressed it exactly, "It is like a figure-painting." It is this dramatic touch which causes one to find a je ne sais quoi which makes one feel what you say, "It expresses that moment and that spot in nature where one can go alone without company."

Ruysdael's "Buisson" also has it very strongly.

Don't you remember having seen old Jaques in which it was somewhat exaggerated, perhaps a little sensational—no, not that after all—which one admired for that very reason—though they were not ranked among the best Jaques by the general public?

Speaking of Rousseau, do you know the Rousseau in the Richard Wallace Collection, a "Lisière de Bois" [The edge of the forest] in autumn after the rain, with a glimpse of a wide stretch of swampy meadows—in which cows are grazing, the foreground quite in tone? To me it is one of his finest—very like the one with the red sun in the Luxembourg. The dramatic effect in those pictures is a thing which, more than anything else in art, makes one understand "un coin de la nature vu à travers d'un tempérament" [a nook of nature seen through (the medium of) a temperament], and "l'homme ajouté à la nature" [man added to nature]; and one finds the same thing, for instance, in portraits by Rembrandt. It is more than nature, it is a kind of revelation. And it seems to me that one must feel all respect for it, and not join those who often say that it is exaggerated or mere mannerism.

Oh, I must tell you, Theo, that De Bock has been to see me—it was a rather pleasant visit. Yesterday Breitner appeared—I hadn't in the least expected him because he seemed to have broken off relations entirely. I was very glad, because at the very beginning of my stay here he was very pleasant to go out with. I do not mean in the country, but in the city itself, to look for characters and intriguing models.

There isn't a single person in The Hague with whom I ever did this within the city. Most of the painters think the city ugly and won't look at anything. And yet the city is very beautiful too sometimes, isn't it? For instance, yesterday in the Noordeinde I saw workmen busy pulling down that part opposite the palace, men all white with lime dust, with carts and horses. It was cool windy weather, the sky was gray, and the spot was very characteristic.

Last year I met Van der Velden one evening at De Bock's, when we were there to see De Bock's etchings. I told you then that he made a very favorable impression on me, though he spoke very little and was not very sociable that evening. But my immediate impression of him was that he is a solid, serious painter. He has a square Gothic head, with a keen, sharp, and yet gentle look, strongly built, in fact quite the opposite of Breitner and De Bock. There is something manly and powerful in him, even though he doesn't say or do anything in particular.

I hope to come into closer contact with him someday—perhaps through Van der Weele.

Last Sunday I was at Van der Weele's; he was working on a picture of cows by a creek, for which he has some serious studies. He is now going to the country for some time.

For a change, this week I have done a few water colors out-of-doors, a little cornfield and a small part of a potato field, and I have also drawn a few landscapes as studies for the surroundings of a few figure drawings I am planning. These are very hasty sketches of those figure drawings. The topmost is the burning of weeds; the other one, the return from the potato field.

I seriously intend to paint a number of figure studies especially for the sake of working up the drawings more thoroughly.

What delightful news that you intend to come to Holland in the beginning of August, for, as I've told you often enough, I long very much for your coming.

I am rather anxious to hear from you to what extent your woman is versed in art matters. At any rate, I imagine a good many things will have to be done and cultivated in this respect. Tant mieux. At all events I hope she will get some sort of scrapbook, for which I expect you will have some items among the smaller drawings. Now and then there are pages in the sketchbook which, though rough, are nevertheless more or less striking. I am going to make a small collection of them against the time of her arrival.

Well, I talked it over with De Bock again, and I can leave my things at his house when I go to make studies in Scheveningen. I also hope to go and see Blommers someday soon. I spoke to De Bock about his picture at the Salon, "November," the reproduction of which I liked so much in the catalogue. He must still have a sketch of it, and I should like to see it.

As to my eventually going to London for a shorter or longer time, I quite agree with you that there would be more chance of selling my work, and I also think that I could learn a great deal if I came into contact with some artists there. And I can assure you, I should have no lack of subjects there. What beautiful things one could make at those dockyards on the Thames! Well, we must talk all these things over when you are here. I hope you won't be in too great a hurry: there are so many things we must discuss.

I wish I could go to Brabant again and make some studies in the autumn.

Above all, I should like to make studies of a Brabant plow, of a weaver, and of that village churchyard at Nuenen. But again, it will all cost money.

Well, good-by. Once more, thanks for your letter and the enclosure. Have a good time. Do you intend to bring the woman with you to Holland, or don't you think this advisable yet? I should like it if you did.

Adieu, boy. With a handshake,

Yours sincerely, Vincent

I add a few more lines to tell you some particulars about Breitner too, as I have just come home from his temporary studio (you know he is actually living in Rotterdam at present). Do you know Vierge or Urabiette, the draftsmen for *L'Illustration*? Well, at times Breitner reminds me of Vierge, but very seldom. When his work is good, it looks like something hasty by Vierge; but when his—that is, Breitner's—work is too hasty or unfinished, then it is hard to say what it looks like: it doesn't look like anything—except strips of faded old wall-paper of I don't know what period, but at all events a very strange kind and probably very ancient. Just imagine, I entered the small attic he has rented at

Siebenhaar's. It was furnished for the greater part with many matchboxes (empty ones), some razors, and a box with a bed in it. I saw something standing against the chimney—three endlessly long strips which I took for sun-blinds at first. But on closer inspection they proved to be canvases of the following size :

As you see from the above illustrations, they are covered with some mystical scene, which at first sight one would suppose to be taken from the Apocalypse. But I was told it represents artillery maneuvers in the dunes. According to my careful estimate, it was about 4 meters long to ¾ meter broad.

The second one is the story of a man leaning against a wall, in the extremest left corner of the picture ; in the right corner diverse specimens of ghastly women stand staring at him; care had been taken to leave sufficient space between these two groups. And I was told that the man in the left corner represents a drunkard, which doubtlessly may have been the painter's intention, but it might be anything else.

The third one is a little better, and is a sketch of the market place which he made last year but which has changed from a Dutch to a Spanish market since then, at least as far as one can make out. What kind of merchandise is sold in that market—in which country it may be—I for myself doubt that it is intended to be on this globe : to the naïve spectator it would seem rather that it must represent a scene on one of those planets visited by Jules Verne's imaginary travelers in a projectile. It is impossible to define what kind of merchandise is actually sold there, but from afar it looks like enormous masses of candied fruits or sweets. Try to imagine such a thing, but absurd and ponderous besides, and you have the work of friend Breitner.

Seen at a distance, they are patches of faded color on a bleached, dusty, and moldy wallpaper, and in this respect it has some qualities, which for me, however, are absolutely unsatisfactory.

I cannot understand how it is possible for a man to make such a thing. It is like things one sees in fever, or impossible and absurd, like the most fantastic dream.

I really think that Breitner has not quite recovered, and actually made these things while he was feverish.

Last year, when I had recovered but remained feverish and could not sleep, I too had moments when I wanted to force myself to work, and made some large things ; later I couldn't believe I had done them myself.

Therefore I believe Breitner will be all right again, but I find these things absurd.

Crumpled in a corner was a water color, a study of a few little birch trees in the dunes, which was much better. But those large things were trash.

At Van der Weele's I saw another bad one, and a head that was very good ; but again, the portrait of Van der Weele he had started was bad. At times I like the work of Hoffmann and Edgar Poe (the *Fantastic Tales, Raven*, etc.) but this work is impossible, because the imagination behind it is ponderous and meaningless, and has no contact with reality. I think it very repulsive. Van der Weele has two rather intriguing little water colors of his with a certain chic, a "je ne sais quoi," or what the English call "weird." Well, we must wait and see what comes of it. He is intelligent enough, but he obstinately tries to realize a predilection for eccentricity.

Well, I am starting in Scheveningen this week. If you could have sent a little extra, I might have bought some new painting material.

I am going to have a few drawings photographed in cabinet size or a little larger (to see how they will look on a smaller scale) by a photographer who has photographed drawings by Meulen, Duchâtel and Zilcken. He charges 75 cents, which isn't much, is it? I will begin with "The Sower" and "The Peat Cutters," the one with many small figures, the other with a single large one. If they turn out well, I could always send you photos of the drawings I have made, so that you could show them to Buhot, for instance, to see if he could find a buyer. They could reproduce those that were accepted from the original drawings, or I could copy them onto their paper.

Once more good-by, Theo. Good luck. Write again soon. I am having those photos taken because we must work Buhot for all he is worth. I must try to earn some money in order to be able to start new things, and to try my hand at painting too, for I am right in the mood for it.

After all, I don't think it nice of C. M. never to have answered a syllable to my letter, in which I took the trouble to enclose two sketches of the drawings in question. Nor is it nice of Tersteeg not to come to see me, since for my part I tried to make it up. It is nonsense to say he is too busy, for that isn't the reason; *once* a year he might find time to come.

Mauve has not only quarreled with me, but he has also quarreled with Zilcken, for instance. Not long ago I saw Zilcken's etchings, and just now at the photographer's I saw photos of Zilcken's drawings. Leaving myself out of the question, I declare I don't understand what Mauve has against Zilcken: his drawings are good—not at all bad—but Mauve is capricious.

I add another half-page to talk a little about Brabant. Among the studies of types from the people I've done there are several which have what many would call a decidedly old-fashioned character, also in the conception, for instance a digger who looks more like those one sees on the wooden bas-reliefs of the Gothic church pews than like a present-day drawing. Very often I think of the Brabant types, what a strong sympathy I feel for them.

The thing which I should immensely like to make, which I feel I can make, provided there is the inclination for patient posing, is the figure of Father on a path through the heath; the figure austerely drawn, with character, and I repeat, a stretch of brown heath with a narrow white sandy path running through it, and a sky just delicately tinged, yet brushed with some passion. Then Father and Mother arm in arm—in an autumn landscape or against a little row of beeches with withered leaves.

I should also like to draw Father's figure when I draw a peasant's funeral, which I certainly intend to do, though it would be very difficult. Leaving the difference of religious opinion out of the question, the figure of a poor country clergyman is to me, in type and character, one of the most sympathetic sights I know, and I should not be true to myself if I didn't try it someday.

When you come, I should like to consult you about how to arrange such a trip to Brabant. When you see my drawings of almshouse men, you will understand my intentions and what I want.

What I want to make is a drawing which will not be exactly understood by everyone : the figure essentially simplified with intentional neglect of those details which do not belong to the real character, and are only accidental. For it must not be a portrait of Father, but rather the type of a poor village clergyman on his way to visit the sick. In the same way, the couple arm in arm against the little row of beeches must be the types of a man and a woman who have grown old together in love and faith rather than the portraits of Father and Mother—though I hope they will pose for it. But they must know that it is a serious thing, which perhaps they would not see of their own accord if the likeness were not exact.

And they ought to be more or less prepared for it that in case they should have to pose, they should have to do so in the attitude I shall select, and not alter it. Well, that will come all right, and I do not work so slowly that it need be very troublesome to them. And I for my part would love to do it.

Simplifying the figures is something which greatly preoccupies me. Well, you will see it for ourself in the figures I show you. If I go to Brabant, it certainly must not be a kind of pleasure trip, but a short time of very hard and quick-as-lightning work. Speaking of the expression of a figure, more and more I come to the conclusion that it is not so much in the features as in the whole attitude. There are few things I hate more than most of the academical têtes d'expression. I prefer to look at "the night" by Michelangelo, or a drunkard by Daumier, or the diggers by Millet, and that well-known large woodcut of his, "The Shepherdess," or an old horse by Mauve, etc.

306

Dear Theo,   The Hague, 27 or 28 July 1883

To my surprise, I received another letter from you yesterday with a bank note enclosed. I needn't tell you how glad I was, and I thank you heartily for it. But they refused to change the bank note because it was too torn. However, they gave me 10 guilders on it, and it has been forwarded to Paris. If the bank refuses it, I'll have to pay back the 10 guilders—for which I had to sign a receipt—but if the bank changes it, I'll get the rest later.

In your letter you write about the conflict one sometimes has about whether one is responsible for the unfortunate results of a good action—if it wouldn't be better to act in a way one knows to be wrong, but which will keep one from getting hurt—I know that conflict too. If we follow our conscience—for me conscience is the highest reason—the reason within the reason—we are tempted to think we have acted wrongly or foolishly ; we are especially upset when more superficial people jeer at us, because they are so much wiser and are so much more successful. Yes, then it is sometimes difficult, and when circumstances occur which make the difficulties rise like a tidal wave, one is almost sorry to be the way one is, and would wish to have been less conscientious.

I hope you don't think of me as other than having that same inner conflict continually, and often very tired brains too, and in many cases not knowing how to decide questions of right and wrong.

When I am at work, I have an unlimited faith in art and the conviction that I shall succeed; but in days of physical prostration or when there are financial obstacles, I feel that faith diminishing, and a doubt overwhelms me, which I try to conquer by setting to work again at once. It's the same thing with the woman and the children; when I am with them and the little boy comes creeping toward me on all fours, crowing for joy, I haven't the slightest doubt that everything is right.

How often that child has comforted me.

When I'm home, he can't leave me alone for a moment; when I'm at work, he pulls at my coat or climbs up against my leg till I take him on my lap. In the studio, he crows at everything, plays quietly with a bit of paper, a bit of string, or an old brush; the child is always happy. If he keeps this disposition all his life, he will be cleverer than I.

Now what shall we say about the fact that at times one feels there is a certain fatality which makes the good turn out wrong and the bad turn out well.

I think one may consider these thoughts partly the consequence of over-wrought nerves, and if one has them, one must not think it one's duty to believe that things are really as gloomy as one supposes; if one did, it would make one mad. On the contrary, it is reasonable to strengthen one's physique then, and later set to work like a man; and even if that doesn't help, *one must still always continue to use those two means*, and consider such melancholy fatal. Then in the long run one will feel ones energy increase, and will bear up against the troubles.

Mysteries remain, and sorrow or melancholy, but that eternal negative is balanced by the positive work which is thus achieved after all. If life were as simple, and things as little complicated as a goody-goody's story or the hackneyed sermon of the average clergyman, it wouldn't be so very difficult to make one's way. But it isn't, and things are infinitely more complicated, and right and wrong do not exist separately, any more than black and white do in nature. One must be careful not to fall back on opaque black—on deliberate wrong—and even more, one has to avoid the white as of a whitewashed wall, which means hypocrisy and everlasting Pharisaism. He who courageously tries to follow his reason, and especially his conscience, the very highest reason—the sublime reason—and tries to stay honest, can hardly lose his way entirely, I think, though he will not get off without mistakes, rebuffs and moments of weakness, and will not achieve perfection.

And I think it will give him a deep feeling of pity and benevolence, broader than the narrow-mindedness which is the clergyman's specialty.

One may not be considered of the slightest importance by either of the parties, and one may be counted among the mediocrities and feel like a thoroughly ordinary man among ordinary people—for all that one will obtain a rather steady serenity in the end. One will succeed in developing one's conscience to such a point that it becomes the voice of a better and higher self, of which the ordinary self is the servant. And one will not return to skepticism or cynicism, and not belong among the foul scoffers. But not at once. I think it a beautiful saying of

156

Michelet's, and in those few words Michelet expresses all I mean, "Socrate naquit un vrai satyre, mais par le dévouement, le travail, le renoncement des choses frivoles, il se changea si complètement qu'au dernier jour devant ses juges et devant sa mort il y avait en lui je ne sais quoi d'un dieu, un rayon d'en haut dont s'illumina le Parthénon." [Socrates was born as a true satyr, but by devotion, work and renouncing frivolous things he changed so completely that on the last day before his judges and in the face of death, there was in him something, I do not know what, of a god, a ray of light from heaven that illuminated the Parthenon.]

One sees the same thing in Jesus too; first he was an ordinary carpenter, but raised himself to something else, whatever it may have been—a personality so full of pity, love, goodness, seriousness that one is still attracted by it. Generally, a carpenter's apprentice becomes a master carpenter, narrow-minded, dry, miserly, vain; and whatever may be said of Jesus, he had another conception of things than my friend the carpenter of the backyard, who has raised himself to the rank of house owner, and is much vainer and has a higher opinion of himself than Jesus had.

But I must not become too abstract. What I want to do first is renew my strength, and I think when it has risen again from below par, I shall get new ideas for my work, for trying to overcome that dryness.

When you come here, we shall talk it over. I don't think it's a question of a few days.

In a few days, when I shall have had some more nourishing food than recently, I think I shall get rid of my *worst depression*; but it is *more deeply rooted* than that, and I wish I could get to the point where I had plenty of health and strength, which is after all not impossible when one is out-of-doors a great deal and has a task one loves.

For it is a fact that now all my work is *too meager and too dry*.

Recently this has become as clear as daylight to me, and I haven't the slightest doubt that a general thorough change is necessary. I intend to talk over with you, *after you have seen this year's work*, whether you agree with me about some measures; and if you agree with me, I think we shall succeed in overcoming the difficulties. We must not hesitate, but "avoir la foi de charbonnier."

I hope they will change the bank note. I am so glad you have managed to send something, for I think it saves me from illness. I'll let you know how the story of the bank note ends. And it would be a good thing if you could send the usual again by the first of August. I always think that it is possible that we shall hit on another plan for the future when looking through the work together. I don't know what, as yet—but somewhere there must be work which I can do just as well as anybody else. If London were nearer, I should try there.

Know it well that I should be enormously pleased if I could make something that was salable. In that case I should have less scruples about the money I get from you, which after all you need as much as I. Once more many thanks, good-by.

Yours sincerely, Vincent

157

316

Dear brother,   The Hague, 21 August 1883

Your letter came today and comforted me in many ways. My thanks for speaking to C. M.—I will write to thank him myself, and send him a few studies, but for the rest—especially about the woman—*nothing*. One more thing, however. One of these days I shall write you a letter; I shall write it carefully and try to make it short, but say everything I think necessary. You might keep that letter then, so that in case you should meet somebody who might be induced to buy some of my studies, you could tell that man my own thoughts and intentions exactly. My thought in this being especially: one of my drawings taken separately will never give complete satisfaction in the long run, but a number of studies, however different in detail they may be, will nevertheless complement each other. In short, for the art lovers themselves it is in my opinion better to take a number of them than just a single one. As to the money, I would rather deal with an art lover who buys cheaply but regularly than with one who buys only once, even if he paid well then.

Perhaps you might, either in your own words or in mine, propose to C. M. what we discussed last year; the result might be that because of my expressing myself more clearly, he might like the idea better.

Well, more about this later on.

Now I still have to tell you of a visit from Rappard, who saw the large drawings and spoke warmly of them. When I told him that I felt rather weak, and that I thought making the drawings might have had something to do with it, he did not seem to doubt the probability.

We spoke about Drenthe. He is going there again one of these days, and he will go even farther, namely to the fishing villages on Terschelling. Personally I should love to go to Drenthe, especially after that visit from Rappard. So much so that I have already inquired if it would be easy or difficult to move the furniture there.

The furniture can be sent by Van Gend & Loos, even the stove and the bed, by taking half a van; then few or no packing cases are needed.

Of course I am thinking of it because, though those things of mine are of little or no value, it would be very expensive to buy them all over again.

My plan would be to go with the woman and the children.

Of course there will be the moving and traveling expenses.

Once there, I think I would remain permanently in that country of heath and moorland, where more and more painters are settling down, so that perhaps, after a time, a kind of colony of painters might spring up. Life is so much cheaper there that I think I should economize at least 150 or 200 guilders a year, especially on rent.

And having paid my debts with the money from C. M., I think it might be good to act quickly.

In fact, I think it would be superfluous for me to go there first to gather information.

I have a little map of Drenthe in front of me. On it I see a large white spot without any village names; it is crossed by the Hoogeveen canal, which ends suddenly, and I see the words "peat fields" on the map, written across the blank space. Around that blank space, a number of black dots with names of villages, a red one for the little town of Hoogeveen.

Near the border, a lake—the Black Lake—a name full of suggestions, I imagine all kinds of workmen dredging on its banks.

Some of the names of the villages—like Easthills, Erica—are also suggestive. Well, tell me your opinion about the possibility of a quick move to that region.

If it happened, I should begin by acting on Rappard's information based on his experiences there, then I would follow his advice to go more to that secluded part of which I told you how it looked on the map.

I am now trying to get a more detailed map of Drenthe, indicating the different terrains.

We should have an immediate cash outlay, but in the long run we should economize a lot, I think. But more important, I think, I should be staying in a country which would certainly stimulate me and make my mind receptive to all that is serious, so that my work can only improve by it.

What would the expenses be? I shall figure that out more exactly for you one of these days.

I suppose the whole family will be counted as $2\frac{1}{2}$ persons, but they can demand the fare for three.

The railway expenses are not given in the timetable, but I suppose it will be under 10 guilders a head.

According to Van Gend & Loos, half a van to Assen is 20 guilders. But one would have to spend a few days in an inn, which would cost a guilder per person per day.

Here the rent especially, and the high cost of living, too, are murder. And the heaviest expense, the one for models, would be different over there: either I should have more and better models for the same money, or just as many for less money.

I suppose if I settled down there, Rappard would visit that same neighborhood even more often than now, so that we could profit a little from each other's company. As I told you, it was especially since his visit and our talking about the work that my mind became fixed on Drenthe.

Of course if it must be, I can also look for a cheaper house here, and I think it beautiful here too, but yet—I should like to be alone with nature for a time—far away from the city.

I can hardly tell you how pleased I am with what you say about my work, I am glad you are of the opinion that it would be the wrong policy to undertake some outside job at the same time.

This leads to half measures, which make one half a man.

The most important thing is to get that "quelque chose de mâle" [something manly] *more and more* into my work.

I don't believe you will need to take back that you notice something of it already, especially if I regain my strength.

It is very troublesome that my stomach is upset by even the most ordinary food, and if I followed my inclination, I should only care to eat—sour apples. I don't indulge myself in this, but my stomach is weaker than it ought to be.

I expect another letter from Rappard about Drenthe. At all events I will write you again soon, also about another plan of staying quietly here, when I have had information from my landlord about the house at Voorburg, which he says I can perhaps get cheaply.

Adieu, again many thanks.

Yours sincerely, Vincent

319

Dear Theo,   The Hague, 4 September 1883

I received your letter just now, coming home from the dunes behind Loosduinen, wet through, for I had been sitting in the rain for about three hours on a spot where everything was reminiscent of Ruysdael, Daubigny or Jules Dupré. I came back with a study of twisted, gnarled little trees, and another one of a farm after the rain. Everything is already bronze-colored. Everything is what one can see in nature only during this time of the year, or when one looks at some pictures by Dupré, for instance; and it is so beautiful that one's imagination always falls short of it.

You write about your work that Sunday in Ville d'Avray; at the same moment on the same day, I too was walking alone, and I too want to tell you something about that walk, when our thoughts probably met again. As I wrote you, I had spoken to the woman—we felt that in the future it would be impossible for us to stay together, nay, that we should make each other unhappy, yet we both felt how strongly we are attached to each other—and then I went far out into the country to have a talk with nature. Well, I walked to Voorburg and from there to Leidendam. You know the scenery there, splendid trees, majestic and serene, right next to horrible green toy summerhouses and all the absurdities the heavy fancy of retired Dutchmen can invent in the form of flower plots, arbors and porches. Most of the houses very ugly; some, however, old and stately. Now at that very moment, high over the meadows, boundless as the desert, one mass of clouds after the other came sailing on, and the wind first struck the row of country houses with their clumps of trees on the other side of the canal, bordered by the black cinder path. Those trees were superb; there was drama in each *figure* I was going to say, but I mean in each tree. But the scene as a whole was even more beautiful than those scourged trees viewed apart, because at that moment even those absurd little summerhouses assumed a curious character, dripping with rain and disheveled.

It seemed to me an image of how even a man of absurd deportment and conventions, or another one full of eccentricities and caprice, may become a dramatic figure of a peculiar type, if only real sorrow strikes him—a calamity befalls him. And the thought crossed my mind, how at moments when today's deteriorating society is society seen against the light of a renewal, it stands out as a large, gloomy silhouette.

Yes, for me, the drama of storm in nature, the drama of sorrow in life, is the most impressive.

A "Paradou" is beautiful, but Gethsemane is even more beautiful.

Oh, there must be a little bit of light, a little bit of happiness, just enough to indicate the shape, to make the lines of the silhouette stand out, but let the whole be gloomy.

I must say that the woman is bearing up well. She is unhappy about it, as I am, but she is not disheartened and keeps busy. I had just bought a piece of material to make canvases for my studies, and have now given it to her to make underwear for the kids, and some of my things can be altered for them too, so that she will not leave me empty-handed. So she is very busy sewing these things.

When I say we part as friends, it is true—but the parting is final, and after all I am more resigned than I thought I'd be, because her faults were such that it would have been a fatal thing to be bound together, for me as well as for herself, because one is, so to speak, responsible for one another's faults.

But I ask myself anxiously—how will she be in a year?

I shall certainly *never* take her into my house again, but I do not want to lose sight of her, for I am too fond of her and the children.

And for the very reason that it was and is a feeling other than passion, this is possible too.

I hope the Drenthe project will be carried out.

You ask me what I should need.

I need not tell you that I intend to work hard. I must do that in order to renew myself. And no painting materials whatever are available down there, so as to stocking up on them, the more one has of the really useful things, the better. Good materials are never thrown away, and though they are expensive, one makes up for it later, and a lot of painting must be done in order to make progress. I hope to waste very little of the time I shall spend there, and hope to have models often, which probably will be much cheaper there.

And life is cheaper and I shall be able to do more with the 150 francs there than here.

But I can arrange all this according to the circumstances. I wish I could have a large amount to spend, because I need so many things that others have, and which one can hardly do without.

My intention is to make so much progress in painting in Drenthe that when I come back I might be admitted as a member of the Society of Draftsmen. This is again in reference to a second plan to go to England.

I don't think it wrong to speculate, if only one doesn't do it in thin air, or on too unsolid a basis. This in regard to England.

I certainly expect it will be easier for me to sell there than here, that's true, so I sometimes think of England; but I do not know to what extent my work will please the English art lovers, and as I do not know this, I will first make a small positive start in selling before I shall think it advisable to try it there. Once I have sold a few things here, then I shall hesitate no longer, but start sending things or go there myself.

But as long as I sell absolutely nothing here, I could easily be mistaken in the right moment if I were not wise enough to wait till I see an opening here. I hope you will approve of this idea; that would comfort me, for in England they are very serious once they start something: whoever catches the public's fancy in England finds faithful friends there. Take, for instance, Ed. Frère and Henriette Browne, who remain as interesting now as they were when their work was first shown there.

But to have success, one must give good work, and be sure of keeping up to the standard of what one has set.

I was glad to see from your letter that you approve of the Drenthe plan; that's enough for me, the advantages it will bring will be apparent later. For me, it is directly connected with my trying to become a member of the Society of Draftsmen, and then going to England—because I know for sure that if I succeed in putting some sentiment into the subjects out there, they will find sympathy in England.

Well, I must carry out the Drenthe plan, be it with more or less money. As soon as I can pay the fare, I shall go, even if I have only a small supply of painting materials.

Because the moment of the autumn effects is already there, and I must catch some of them.

But I hope I shall be able to leave something behind for the woman, to help her through the first weeks. But as soon as I *can* go, I *will*.

I tell you that I intend to help the woman a little at first; I *may* not do much, nor *can* I, but I mention this only to you.

And you may depend on it that whatever may happen to her, I neither can nor ever will live with her again, for she is incapable of doing what she ought to do.

I also dropped Father a line to tell him that I had parted company with her, but that for all that, my letter to Father about my continuing to be true to her and being willing to marry her remained a fact. And another fact is that Father avoided the issue at the time, and did not reply to the fundamental question. And I do not know how it will appear to me in later years—for instance, whether this might not have been better than leaving her; now we are too close to the facts to get the right view of the basic interrelation and consequences of all the things.

I do *hope* everything will come out right, but her future as well as my own looks gloomy. I am inclined to believe there is some latent good in her still, but the trouble is, it *ought to have been* roused already. Now, as she has nobody to rely on, it will be more difficult for her to follow her good impulses.

Now she never cared to listen; *then* she will long to speak with me, and I shall no longer be there. As long as she was with me, she had no other standard of comparison, and in other surroundings she will remember things which she does not care for and which she did not pay attention to. *Now* by contrast she will be reminded of them.

Sometimes it is an anguishing thought, that we both feel it is impossible for us to struggle along together in the future, and yet are *so* much attached to each other. Of late she has been more trustful with me than usual, and she has refused to play some ugly tricks which her mother had instigated. Things of the kind you mentioned when you were here, of starting a row and the like.

162

You see there is a seed of more seriousness in her, if that might only stay. I wish she could marry, and when I tell you I am keeping an eye on her, it is because I advised her to do *that*.

If she could only find a man who was not altogether bad, that would do; the foundation that was laid here would then develop, namely that of a more domestic, simpler disposition; and if she sticks to that, in the future I need not leave her quite to her fate, for then I at least remain her friend, and a true one too.

Write soon again and believe me,

Yours sincerely, Vincent

324

Dear Theo,   Drenthe, September-November 1883

Now that I have been here a few days, and have strolled about in different directions, I can tell you more about the neighborhood where I have taken up my quarters. I enclose a little scratch of my first painted study in these parts: a cottage on the heath. A cottage made only of sods of turf and sticks. I also saw the interior of about six of that kind, and more studies of them will follow.

I cannot express how their outside looks in the twilight, or just after sunset, more directly than by reminding you of a certain picture by Jules Dupré, which I think belongs to Mesdag—two cottages, their moss-covered roofs standing out very deep in tone against a hazy, dusky evening sky.

That's the way it is here. Inside those cottages, dark as a cave, it is very beautiful. I find what I observe here shown most realistically in drawings by certain English artists who worked on the moors in Ireland.

Alb. Neuhuys gives the same, but a little more poetically than it first strikes the eye in reality; but he never makes a thing that is not basically true.

I saw splendid figures out-of-doors—striking because of a sober quality. A woman's breast, for instance, has that heaving movement which is quite the opposite of voluptuousness, and sometimes, when the creature is old or sickly, arouses pity or respect. And the melancholy which things in general have here is of a healthy kind, like in Millet's drawings. Fortunately, the men here wear short breeches, which show the shape of the leg and make the movements more expressive.

In order to give you an idea of one of the many things which gave me new sensations and feelings on my excursions, I will tell you that here one may see peat barges in the *very middle of the heath*, drawn by men, women, children, white or black horses, just as in Holland, for instance, on the Rijswijk towpath.

The heath is splendid. I saw sheepfolds and shepherds more beautiful than those in Brabant.

The ovens are more or less like the one in Th. Rousseau's "Four Communal." They stand in the gardens under old apple trees or between cabbages and celery. In many places there are beehives too. In many faces one can see that the people are not in good health; it's not exactly healthy here, I believe; perhaps because of foul drinking water. I have seen a few seventeen-year-old girls, or even younger, who look very fresh and beautiful, but generally they look faded at a very early age. But this does not interfere with the great noble aspect of some figures, which, close up, are already very faded.

In the village there are four or five canals to Meppel, to Dedemsvaart, to Coevorden, to Hollands Veld.

As one goes down them, one occasionally sees a curious old mill, farmyard, wharf, or lock, and always the bustle of peat barges.

To give you an idea of the quaintness of these parts—while I was painting that cottage, two sheep and a goat came to browse *on the roof* of the house. The goat climbed onto the top and looked down the chimney. Hearing something on the roof, the woman rushed out and threw her broom at said goat, which jumped down like a chamois.

The two hamlets on the heath where I have been, and where this incident occurred, are called Driftsand and Blacksheep. I have been in several other places too, and now you can imagine the originality here, as after all Hoogeveen is a town, and yet quite near by there are already shepherds, those ovens, those peat huts, etc.

I often think with melancholy of the woman and the children, if only they were provided for; oh, it's the woman's own fault, one might say, and it would be true, but I am afraid her misfortunes will prove greater than her guilt. I knew from the beginning that her character was spoiled, but I hoped she would improve; and now that I do not see her any more and ponder some things I saw in her, it seems to me more and more that she was too far gone for improvement.

And this only increases my feeling of pity, and it becomes a melancholy feeling because it is not in my power to redress it.

Theo, when I meet on the heath such a poor woman with a child on her arm, or at her breast, my eyes get moist. It reminds me of her, her weakness; her untidiness, too, contributes to making the likeness stronger.

I know that she is not good, that I have an absolute right to act as I do, that *I could not* stay with her back there, that I really could not take her with me, that what I did was even sensible and wise, whatever you like; but, for all that, it cuts right through me when I see such a poor little figure feverish and miserable, and it makes my heart melt inside.

How much sadness there is in life, nevertheless one must not get melancholy, and one must seek distraction in other things, and the right thing is to work; but there are moments when one only finds rest in the conviction: "Misfortune will not spare me either." Adieu, write soon. Believe me,

Yours sincerely, Vincent

330

Dear Theo,   N. Amsterdam, September-November 1883

This once I write to you from the very remotest part of Drenthe, where I came after an endless expedition on a barge through the moors. I see no possibility of describing the country as it ought to be done; words fail me, but imagine the banks of the canal as miles and miles of Michels or Th. Rousseaus, Van Goyens or Ph. de Konincks.

Level planes or strips of different color, getting narrower and narrower as they approach the horizon. Accentuated here and there by a peat shed or small farm, or a few meager birches, poplars, oaks—heaps of peat everywhere, and one constantly meets barges with peat or bulrushes from the marshes. Here and there lean cows, delicate of color, often sheep—pigs. The figures which now and then appear on the plain are generally of an impressive character; sometimes they have an exquisite charm. I drew, for instance, a woman in the barge with crape around her golden head-plates[1] because she was in mourning, and afterward a mother with a baby; the latter had a purple shawl over her head. There are a lot of Ostade types among them: physiognomies reminding one of pigs or crows, but now and then a little figure that is like a lily among thorns.

Well, I am very pleased with this excursion, for I am full of what I have seen. This evening the heath was inexpressibly beautiful. In one of the Boetzel Albums there is a Daubigny which gives exactly that effect. The sky was of an indescribably delicate lilac white, no fleecy clouds, for they were more compact and covered the whole sky, but dashes of more or less vivid lilac, gray, white, a single rent which the blue gleamed through. Then a glaring red streak at the horizon, below which the very dark stretch of brown moor and standing out against the brilliant red streak, a number of low-roofed little sheds.

In the evening this moor often shows effects which the English call "weird" and "quaint." Fantastic silhouettes of Don Quixote–like mills or curious giants of drawbridges stand out against the vibrating evening sky. In the evening such a village, with the reflections of lighted windows in the water or in the mud puddles, sometimes looks extremely friendly.

Before I left Hoogeveen, I painted a few studies there, including one of a large moss-roofed farm. For I had had Furnée send colors, as I thought the same as you wrote in your letter, that by getting absorbed in my work, and quite losing myself in it, my mood would change, and it has greatly improved already.

But at times—like those moments when you think of going to America—I think of enlisting in the East Indian army; but those moments when one is overwhelmed by things are miserable and gloomy, and I could wish you might see those silent moors, which I see here from my window, for such a thing is soothing, and inspires more faith, resignation, steady work. I drew several studies in the barge, but I stayed here awhile to paint some more. I am quite near Zweeloo, where Liebermann, among others, has been; and besides, there is a place here where you still find large, very old sod huts which haven't even a partition between the stable and the living room. First of all I intend to visit that place one of these days.

But what tranquillity, what expanse, what calmness in this landscape—one feels it only when there are miles and miles of Michels between oneself and the ordinary world. I cannot give you a permanent address yet, as I do not know exactly where I shall be the next few days, but by October 12 *I shall be in Hoogeveen,*

[1] A kind of golden casque worn by Frisian women. It consists of two oval plates with ornamental spirals at the temples. Over these plates is worn a cap of stiff lace with wide frills. Often this (costly) headgear is very becoming.

and if you send your letter at the usual time *to the same address*, I shall find it there, on the 12th, in Hoogeveen.

The place where I am now is New Amsterdam.

Father sent me a money order for 10 guilders, which, along with the money from you, enables me to paint a little now.

I intend to settle at the inn where I am now for a long time, provided that from there I can easily reach the district with the large old sod huts, as I should have better light and more space there. As to that picture by that Englishman you mention, with the lean cat and the small coffin; though he got his first inspiration in that dark room, he would hardly have been able to paint it in that same spot, for if one works in too dark a room, the work usually becomes too light, so that when one brings it into the light, all the shadows are too weak. I just had that experience when I used the barn to paint an open door and a glimpse of the little garden. Well, what I wanted to say is that there will be a chance to remove that obstacle too, for here I can get a room with good light that can be heated in winter.

Well, boy, if you do not think any more about America, nor I of Harderwijk,[1] I hope things will take care of themselves. I admit your explanation for C. M.'s silence may be right, but sometimes one can purposely be careless. On the back of the page you will find a few scratches. I write in haste, it is already late.

How I wish we could walk here together, and paint together. I think the country would charm and convince you. Adieu, I hope you are well and are having some luck. I have been thinking of you continually during this excursion. With a handshake,   Yours sincerely, Vincent

Postscript to number 332, Drenthe, fall 1883
I am sending you the enclosed sketches to give you an idea of the many extremely different things this apparently monotonous country presents. You see, I am just sampling at random—I catch hold of one thing and another; later things will arrange themselves and settle into shape of their own accord. But here I will not begin with a prearranged plan; on the contrary, I want my plan to result from my studies. As yet I do not know the real character of the country; now I draw everything that presents itself, but later on, after some experience, I shall try to reproduce it in its real character.

One thing depends so much on another that one must catch hold of everything; however much one should like to concentrate on a single subject, not one thing can be left out.

So there is work enough. I now have a pretty large room (where a stove has been put), which happens to have a small balcony, from which I can see the heath with the huts. In the distance I see a very curious drawbridge.

Downstairs there is the inn, and a farmer's kitchen with a peat fire on the hearth, very cosy in the evening. Such a fireplace with a cradle beside it is an excellent place for meditation. When I am feeling melancholy or worried about something, I just run downstairs for a while.

[1] A garrison town where the volunteers for the East Indian army used to enlist.

I can tell you that in a roundabout way I have heard something about the woman. I could not imagine why she did not write me.

So I wrote the carpenter next door, if the woman had not been to ask my address. And the scoundrel answered: "Oh yes, sir, but I thought you wouldn't like her to know your address, so I pretended not to know it." The damned wretch.

So I wrote her at once, though it was not as good as the express arrangement I had made with him and with her; but I do not want to hide myself *now* or *ever*, and I would rather write her at her family's address than conceal myself in any way. That's my opinion about it. And I also sent her some money; if this should have bad consequences, I am not responsible for it. I *will not* act falsely. I found that scoundrel's letter at Hoogeveen on my last visit there.

Friend Rappard has written to me again from Terschelling, and now today from Utrecht—he is home again. He has brought studies from there, especially of the almshouse. I don't understand it exactly, he told me the doctor had prescribed sea air for him during the winter; besides, he longed to spend a winter in the country, but it seems to have turned out differently in the end.

You wrote to me about Liebermann: his palette consists of slate-gray tones, principally running from brown to yellowish-gray. I have never seen anything of his, but now that I have seen the landscape here, I can understand perfectly how logically he is led to it.

Often the color of things reminds me of Michel; you know, he also has a gray sky (slate-colored sometimes), a brown soil with yellowish-grays. It is absolutely true, and according to nature.

There are Jules Dupré effects, to be sure, but in this autumn season it is exactly that—as you describe Liebermann's palette. And if I may find what I seek—and why shouldn't I find it?—I shall certainly often do it in the same way, in that same chromatic gamut.

Mind you, to see it like that, one must not look at the local color by itself, but in conjunction with the color of the sky!

That sky is gray—but so iridescent that even our pure white would be unable to render *this* light and shimmer. Now, if one begins by painting this sky gray, thus remaining far below the intensity of nature, how much more necessary it is to tone down the browns and yellowish-grays of the soil to a lower key, in order to be consistent. I think if once one analyzes it thus, it is so logical, one can hardly understand not having always seen it so.

But it is the local color of a green field, or a ruddy brown heath, which, considered apart, easily leads one astray.

Write soon again, for your last letter was remarkably brief, too brief, but it was obviously written in the office.

What about that Triennial Exhibition? There will be many beautiful things. I long to hear about it, because these certainly are the characteristic things of the present, and not of past years. So if you have a moment, tell me about it.

There is a rumor that Liebermann is somewhere here in the neighborhood. I should like to meet him.

I must say I am very glad to have found a better place to work in, so that

167

I needn't sit idle at home now that there is so much rain and bad weather is expected. I wish you could see the country here. In the evening it is inexpressibly beautiful.

And I think, with snow, it will also be splendid.

I read a very beautiful little book of Carlyle's, *Heroes and Hero Worship*, nice sayings, as, for instance: we have the *duty* to be *brave*, though in general this is wrongly considered to be an exception. In life it is the same, goodness rises so high above everything that of course we cannot reach such a height. The most reasonable thing, and the thing that makes life less impossible, is to put our gamut in a lower key, and yet to try to be luminous, and not to subside into dullness.

One finds here the most wonderful types of Nonconformist clergymen, with pigs' faces and three-cornered hats. Also adorable Jews, who look uncommonly ugly amidst Millet-like types or on this naïve, desolate moor. But they are very characteristic. I traveled with a party of Jews who held theological discussions with some farmers. How is it possible for such absurdities to exist in a country like this? Why couldn't they look out of the window or smoke their pipes, or at least behave as reasonably as, for instance, their pigs, which make no disturbance whatever, though they are pigs, and are in place in these surroundings and in harmony with them. But before the clergymen of the type I saw here reach the cultural and rational level of ordinary pigs, they must improve considerably, and probably it will take ages before they arrive at this point. Now any pig is better, as far as I can see.

Well, I am off again for a walk, write me if you can spare a moment, and look out for something of Liebermann's at the exhibition.

Good-by, my address is here for the present. Best wishes, with a handshake,

Yours sincerely, Vincent

335

Dear brother,   Drenthe, September-November 1883

This morning I received your letter; in many respects the contents does not surprise me. It does surprise me a little that you should credit me with the slightest insight into business, as I am considered a dreamer in that respect, as you know, and I could not suppose that you thought differently about it. I think your idea of changing your situation is a very rational one. In the first place, one is not obliged to wait for the moment when the employers will arrive at a better insight; and in the second place, if one considered oneself obliged to do so, one might go on waiting forever and ever, and a young employee might doubt whether, when that moment came, he would not be too tired to redress things; how much more would this be the case with the old "pochards pleins" themselves. The latter will have lost their wits entirely by then; and decadence being decadence, a deserved ruin of a business will follow, the fatal consequence of certain mistakes. I don't mean to say it is if it happens through thoughtlessness, but if it happens through that odious, wanton, capricious, reckless way of outliving one's fame, and through supposing that everything is only a question of money, and

168

that anything is allowed; it may succeed many a time, but the end is a breakdown, and such a managing director is the only man who gets off safely for the moment.

Well—it's the old, old story—but of course all those departments, officious as well as official, all that bookkeeping, it's all nonsense, and *that's* not the way to do business. Doing business is surely also *action*, a measure of personal insight and energy. That does not count now—that is handicapped—thence your complaint, There are not enough pictures.

Suffit, in my opinion the house of G. & Co. is going in for gambling now, and who sows the wind shall reap the whirlwind. I—who was with them for six years—though I was one of the lowest employees—even now after at least ten years, I still feel that part of my heart is in it. I think it very, very sad. In Uncle Vincent's time they started with a few employees who were not treated nearly so arrogantly and as if they were machines. Then there was real co-operation, then one *could* be in it with all one's heart. Since then the number of employees has increased, but has consisted less and less of persons who really put their hearts into the business and whose knowledge is sound.

I myself witnessed some curious instances of this. In the meantime the gentlemen became more and more haughty, and I am of the opinion that now they are absolutely blind to reality. And if I may express my thoughts frankly, I believe that the best thing that could happen to them would be that their business go to the dogs. In their disenchantment, although they would be too old to redress things, it might be possible for them to be redressed themselves as human beings.

I note with pleasure that you don't mention the gentlemen personally; that is right—indeed, I didn't expect anything else from you. But for the rest, for you yourself it is indeed curiously difficult. Your heart is in it, and you are more faithful to them than any of the others. I think you would rather stay on if possible, even in case another situation were more advantageous, because the house is what it is. All that is counted for nothing, at least it seems so; though for instance old Mr. Goupil felt a certain affection for you, he would probably say nothing about it, because they themselves keep silent, and let things accumulate quietly.

Now from your letter I see that the situation in which you are placed at the moment is pretty well untenable. Perhaps it would be a good thing if, for instance, you went to see old Mr. Goupil privately, and told him that you had kept silent as long as you could, but that now you cannot wait any longer, so that you feel obliged to ask what the gentlemen really want, because if it goes on like this, you will no longer be a party to it. Something like this—for which you will hardly find an opportunity—there will hardly be a question of that—I realize that—but something to the effect that you might accept an equally good situation, not nearly so well-paid at first and still to be created, instead of your present one—which, as I see it, might act as an eye opener. I do not think that anything of the sort would lead to results or to an amelioration of things, but, whatever might happen, old Mr. Goupil would trust you, and there is the possibility that in any case you might still be of service to him.

But I must not lose myself in situations which I can only estimate quite in general, and now speak about what you say further about a project of your own.

Under the circumstances—always taking the necessity of a change for granted—excellent—a modern business, in which energy might achieve something—where one is not hampered by so much routine and so complicated an administration that everything, absolutely everything is paralyzed by it. You tell me there is capital : there is (and this means more than capital) a good apparatus for reproductions—and if in addition the directors of this concern are people who mean well, and who intend to sell good things, quand même to seek their success in honesty, then, as I said, it is excellent. But Wisselingh at Collier's collided too violently with his employer's character (although *he* never told me or anybody else so, but I have drawn this conclusion independently, which tallies with Wisselingh's saying, "I wasted my time at Collier's"). And I am disposed to think that the latter's character is the kind that will *talk* grandly rather than *act* grandly, so I say: Are *those* people at the head of the other concern *willing?*

The *being able* is rather more the result of these two items than people are ready to admit in most cases. After all, one should know one's own mind.

Now I come to what you write about myself.

Of course I should very much like to spend some time in Paris, because I think I should find there that intercourse with artists which I shall need someday or other.

Is that possible ? It would be if it did not get you into too much trouble. I should like it well enough.

I should love to talk with you about what you wrote, but what would be the use? It is better to lend a helping hand when there is a chance. "N'importe comment."

For I think that it would greatly help me in my work if I had an opportunity to see more of printing, for instance. I have had some years' practice in painting now, so I stick to that. But if I could get some work in a printer's office or something, that would be a help rather than a hindrance—but I should have to learn all that. I think, however, I should be able to draw reproductions myself, for instance. And I am willing to try my hand at *anything* of that kind, especially if a living may be earned in that way over there. Indeed, I believe that the time will come when I will not have to earn a living in any other way than by painting ; but be sure that I shall not have the slightest objection to going to Paris, whenever you think it would be useful or necessary for some reason or other.

My advising *you* in business matters would hardly be the thing. I have been out of it too long, but if I came into it again, we would be of the same opinion in a great many things. And I do know I have seen what I have seen, and in matters of reproduction or publication I daresay I know what is good. And I am willing to lend a helping hand as to carrying things out, no matter in what way.

But I need not tell you that here on this beautiful moor I haven't the slightest longing for Paris, and I wouldn't think about it at all if it hadn't been for your letter. And I simply say this, If it must be, all right, I shall go to Paris ; if it must be, all right, I shall stay on the moors.

I shall find things to paint everywhere. It is splendid here, and I think I learn to paint somewhat better while painting. And *my heart is in it*, I need not tell you that.

Besides, I believe that knowing a handicraft is the most solid profession after all, one reason more for me to stick to it.

But *if* it might happen for some reason or other—on account of its being more convenient to you, or because of urgent necessity—that we should be together in Paris—I dare predict that I shall tell you, start drawing, and I would give you a few hints in the beginning.

I know how much I still have to learn myself, yet I begin to see light, and in some way or other, by practice or by learning from others what can be of use to me, I will stick to my painting with all my heart. And if it might be that you came to a point where you saw *light*, well, so much the better.

You say your heart is in the art business, all right, but even more in art itself, I believe.

Well, boy, write soon again—if you kept silent about it now, I should imagine all kinds of worries. So if something is the matter, write that; if nothing is the matter, write that; but don't keep it all to yourself, for that's not worth while.

Oh, I have had a letter from the poor woman; she was glad that I wrote her, but she is worried about the children, and she goes out working as a charwoman. She is obliged to live with her mother. Poor things.

But we must keep courage notwithstanding everything.

I enclose a few scratches from here. The country is so beautiful that I cannot describe it. *As soon as* I can paint a little better—then! You can arrange things for me exactly as you think best, I shall learn here, and I should learn out there, too, I think.

However things may go, I don't suppose it will make you more unhappy, and perhaps you have already put up with things too long. The best thing would be, if it turned out so, that you were more appreciated by your directors, and that they left you more liberty to do business as you think best. But I should be surprised if things took this turn, seeing that Uncle Vincent himself was not treated very fairly when he left.

But leaving that out of it, it seems to me that the whole art business is rotten —to tell you the truth, I doubt if the present enormous prices, even for master-pieces, will last. A "je ne sais quoi" has passed over it which has chilled everything—and enthusiasm has been put to flight. Is this of great influence on the artists? Not at all, for generally the greatest of them personally profited but little from those enormous prices, except in their last period, when they were already famous, and they—Millet and others, particularly Corot—would not have painted less, or less beautifully, without that enormous rise. And whatever may be said of art business, for the present it will remain so that he who can make a thing worth seeing will always find certain persons interested in it, who will make it possible for him to earn a living.

I would rather have 150 francs a month as a painter than 1500 francs a month in another position, even as an art dealer.

I think one feels more a man among other men as a painter, than in a life which is founded on speculation, and in which one has to heed conventions. I wonder how it will all turn out, but it is all the same to me, one way or another.

And as to you, I don't consider it would be such bad luck if the consequences were that you became a painter in your thirtieth year. I should consider it great good fortune. One's real life begins at thirty, in fact, that is to say, its most active part.

Friends and family may consider you old, or I don't know what, but you can feel a renewal of energy for all that.

But then it is necessary to reflect well, and to have a will, and to be wide-awake. But in that period, a change is really necessary; one must wipe out the whole thing and start anew. *Just as one does when a boy*—but more maturely. Tom, Dick and Harry, who drowse away in the same old way, think this foolish, and say they don't see any good in it; all right, leave Tom, Dick and Harry alone, as long as they don't attack you; they are as little awake as a somnambulist. For oneself one must not doubt that it is the way of nature, and that one works against nature only by *not* changing. There is an old saying, They have ears but they hear not, they have eyes but they see not, they have a heart but feel not; their heart is hardened, and they have closed their ears and eyes because they *do not want to hear and do not want to see*. I think that in any case you and I are honest enough so that we need not be afraid to open our eyes and look at things as they are and as they occur. That little old saying means so much, expresses it all so exactly, that I cannot help thinking of it again and again.

This little scratch is of peat gatherers who were eating their lunch behind a mound of peat, with a fire in the foreground; the others are loading peat, but I am afraid the scratches are absolutely indecipherable.

These are two evening effects; I am still working on that weed burner, which is better than before in a painted study, so that it renders more strongly the immensity of the plain and the gathering twilight, the fire with a bit of smoke being the only spot of light. I went again and again to look at it in the evening, and I found this cottage on a muddy evening after the rain; seen on the spot, it is splendid.

I repeat, I think that there are things for me to learn in Paris as well as here on the moor; in the city, I should have an opportunity to learn from other people and to see what they are doing, and that is worth something; but working here, I think I can make progress even without seeing other painters. And for my own pleasure I would much rather stay here. But if a change in your position made it desirable for me to go to you, perhaps to earn something in the same business, it is all right, and I haven't the slightest objection.

Be sure to write me about all these things, which of course I shall not mention to anybody else. If my affairs might change somewhat for the better, if I could count on C. M.'s buying my studies for instance, then the best thing for me would be to stay here, as it is cheaper here; and after I had made some more progress, and if you decided to become a painter, it would be an excellent place for study here—excellent.

Has C. M. been to see you already? Once more, keep good courage, I will try to do the same; and if you ever decide to become a painter, do so with inner cheerfulness and all possible optimism. Then, taking a broad view of things, you would have to consider the time between now and your thirtieth year as a rather hard experimental time; but at the end of it you would find all things renewed, and a rich future before you. Think of what you told me when those Swedish painters were in Paris; one must have pluck, the more so because one sees how shaky and tottering everything is. "Efforts de perdu, que soit" [efforts of lost souls, so be it]—but they are our duty in the times which we live in, and very often one has to choose between that and dreaming one's time away.

Well, boy, good luck, write again soon, with a handshake,

Yours sincerely, Vincent

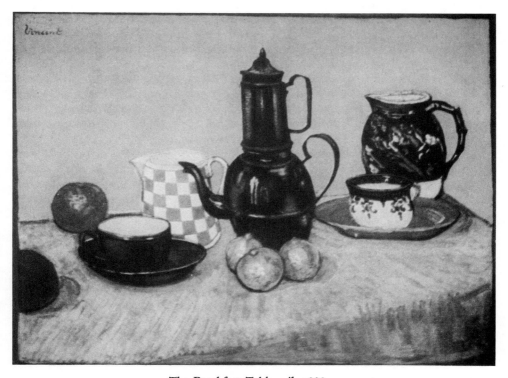

The Breakfast Table, oil, 1888

336
Dear brother,   Drenthe, September-November 1883
It is Sunday today and you are not out of my thoughts for a moment. I should think it quite appropriate to apply to business the words, "plus tu y resteras plus ça t'embêtera" [the more you stay in it the more it will bore you], and to painting, "plus ça t'amusera," using "amusera" in the more serious sense of energy, cheerfulness, vitality.

Oh, I said I should give Tom, Dick and Harry their due—by all means—let's do; but having done justice to those things, aren't they absurd, those formalities and conventions—in fact, aren't they really *bad*?

In order to maintain a certain rank, one is obliged to commit certain villainies, falsehoods—willingly and knowingly, premeditatedly. That's what I call the fatal side, even of the rayon noir, let alone when there is no rayon at all.

Now take, for instance, the painters of Barbizon: not only do I understand them as men, but in my opinion *everything*—the smallest, the most intimate details—sparkles with humor and life. The "painter's family life," with its great and small miseries, with its calamities, its sorrows and griefs, has the advantage of having a certain good will, a certain sincerity, a certain real human feeling. Just because of that *not* maintaining a certain standing, not even thinking about it.

If you take "amusera" in the highly serious sense of "thinking it interesting," then I say, it will amuse you.

And as to the safe position, there is "embêtera," "abrutira" [(will) stupefy].

Do I say this because I despise culture? On the contrary, I say it because I look upon the real human feelings, life in harmony with, not against, nature, as the true civilization, which I respect as such. I ask, What will make me more completely human?

Zola says, "Moi artiste, je veux vivre tout haut—*veux vivre*" [I, as an artist, want to live as vigorously as possible—(I) *want to live*], without mental reservation—naïve as a child, no, not as a child, as an artist—with good will, however life presents itself, I shall find something in it, I will try my best on it. Now look at all those studied little mannerisms, all that convention, how exceedingly conceited it really is, how absurd, a man thinking he knows everything and that things go according to his idea, as if there were not in all things of life a "je ne sais quoi" of great goodness, and also an element of evil, which we feel to be infinitely above us, infinitely greater, infinitely mightier than we are.

How fundamentally wrong is the man who doesn't feel himself small, who doesn't realize he is but an atom.

Is it a loss to drop some notions, impressed on us in childhood, that maintaining a certain rank or certain conventions is the most important thing? I myself do not even think about whether I lose by it or not. I know only by experience that those conventions and ideas do not hold true, and often are hopelessly, fatally wrong. I come to the conclusion that I do not know anything, but at the same time that this life is such a mystery that the system of "conventionality" is certainly too narrow. So that it has lost its credit with me.

What shall I do now? The common phrase is, "What is your aim, what are your aspirations?" Oh, I shall do as I think best—how? I can't say that before-hand—you who ask me that pretentious question, do you know what *your* aim is, what *your* intentions are?

Now they tell me, "You are unprincipled when you have no aim, no aspirations."

My answer is, I didn't tell you I had *no* aim, *no* aspirations, I said it is the height of conceit to try to force one to define what is indefinable. These are my thoughts about certain vital questions. All that arguing about it is one of the things of which I say "embêtera."

Live—do something—that is more amusing, that is more positive. In short—one must of course give Society its due, but at the same time feel absolutely free, believing not in one's own judgment, but in "reason" (my judgment is human, reason is divine, but there is a link between the one and the other), and that my own conscience is the compass which shows me the way, although I know that it does not work quite accurately.

I should like to refer to the fact that, whenever I recall the past generation of painters, I remember an expression of yours, "they were *surprisingly* gay." What I want to say is that, if you become a painter, you should do it with this same *surprising* gaiety. You will need this to offset the gloomy circumstances. It will be a greater help to you than anything else. What you want is a spark of genius; I know no other word for it, but what I mean is the exact opposite of "being ponderous," as people call it. Please don't tell me that neither you nor I could have this. I say this because I am of the opinion that we must do our best to become like that; I do not claim that either I myself or you have sufficiently captured it—but what I say is, Let's do our best to get it. And I say this to show you—writing these things down, although I think you will be able to understand what is in my mind anyway—that you are not mistaken in my ideas. I believe the whole plan would be enhanced immeasurably if your remaining with the woman you are with now were combined with it.

And if it is in your nature as well as hers to feel even a certain pleasure—a surprising gaiety—in the face of circumstances—a je ne sais quoi of surprising *youthfulness*—and I do not count this among the impossibilities, for you said she is intelligent—well then, you will be able to do more together than alone. And in this case, if persons of the same sentiment, persons who have the same pretty serious misery, combine to see things through, what I say is, the more the merrier.

And what I say is—if this had come about or should come about, this combining to carve your own way in the world means infinitely more than any standing on form, and rises above all gossip, all qu'en dira-t-on.

I know all these things have a perilous money side, but what I say is, let's weaken this perilous money side as much as possible, in the first place by not being under its sway too long, and then by feeling that if one will only set about things with love, with a certain understanding of each other and co-operation and mutual helpfulness, many things which would otherwise be insupportable would be softened—yes, even totally changed.

As for me, if I could find some people whom I could talk to about art, who felt for it and wanted to feel for it—I should gain an enormous advantage in my work—I should feel more myself, *be* more myself. If there is enough money to keep us going in the very first period, by the time it is gone I shall be earning money. The more I think it over, the more it appears to me in the way I felt it in the beginning.

Your heart is partly with the firm of Goupil & Co., but in their presumption

G. & Co. demand unreasonable things. In the first place, they are doing you a great wrong, which causes you much grief. This is not only a question of money, your heart is in it, for you it means heartache. You would start on a new career with the same heartache, and possibly with a similar result. Look, is this possible?

What I say is, I doubt it.

It seems to me that you, who are very young, do not act recklessly when you argue, I have had enough of the art-dealing business but not of art; I'll drop the business, and aim at the very heart of the profession.

That is what I ought to have done at the time. My making a mistake was perhaps a natural error of judgment, because then I did not know anything about teaching or about the Church—did not know anything about it, and cherished ideals about it.

You will say, Doesn't one sometimes have ideals about art that are incompatible with existing conditions?

Well, answer that question for yourself. I also answer it for myself by asking, Is Barbizon, is the Dutch school of painters a fact or not?

Whatever may be said of the art world, it is not rotten. On the contrary, it has improved and improved, and perhaps the summit has already been reached; but at all events we are still quite near it, and as long as you and I live, though we might reach the age of a hundred, there will be a certain real vitality. So he who wants to paint—must put his shoulder to the wheel. If the woman came, of course she would have to paint too.

Everybody would have to paint here—the wife of one of the Van Eycks also had to do it. And I tell you that the people don't seem disagreeable or intriguing. There is a kind of benevolence in this place, and I think you can do exactly what you think best. There is a suprisingly youthful atmosphere in existence here.

One should begin by saying with all possible courage, gaiety, enthusiasm, I know none of us can do a thing, but for all that, we are painters. Our *wanting* in itself means *action*. This is what I believe should be the main idea. We are alive—if we do not work "comme plusieurs nègres," we shall die of want, and we shall cut a most ridiculous figure. However, we happen to abhor this mightily —because of that same thing which I call surprising youthfulness—and in addition, a seriousness that is damned serious.

That ... y mettre sa peau.

Well, if this were mere speculation, I should not want to think of it—but in this case it means a fight to free ourselves from the world of conventions and speculation. It is something good, something peaceful, an honest enterprise. Most certainly it will be our intention to try to earn our bread, but only in the literal sense of the word. Money, as far as it is not used for the absolute necessaries of life, leaves us cold. We shall do nothing we need be ashamed of; with what Carlyle calls "quite a royal feeling," we shall be able to roam about in nature freely, and to work—we shall be able to work, because we are honest. We shall say, When we were children we made a mistake, or rather, We had to obey, and do certain things to earn our bread. Later such and such things happened, and then we thought it advisable to turn handicraftsmen. Because certain things were too puffed up. If you should talk this over with other people, they would advise against it unanimously, I think, except perhaps the woman you are with.

If you have come to a decision for yourself, avoid other people, because they can only weaken your energy. Just at the very moment when one has not yet lost one's outer clumsiness, when one is still green, a "ni fait, ni à faire" [neither done nor to be done] is enough to cause discouragement for half a year, after which one at last sees that one ought not to have let oneself be led astray.

I know the soul's struggle of two people : Am I a painter or not? Of Rappard and of myself—a struggle, hard sometimes, a struggle which accurately marks the difference between us and certain other people who take things less seriously ; as for us, we feel wretched at times ; but each fit of melancholy brings a little light, a little progress ; certain other people have less trouble, work more easily perhaps, but then their personal character develops less. You, too, would have that struggle, and I tell you, don't forget that you are in danger of being upset by people who undoubtedly have the very best intentions.

If you hear a voice within you saying, "You are not a painter," *then by all means paint*, boy, and that voice will be silenced, but only by working. He who goes to friends and tells his troubles when he feels like that loses part of his manliness, part of the best that's in him ; your friends can only be those who themselves struggle against it, who raise your activity by their own example of action. One must undertake it with confidence, with a certain assurance that one is doing a reasonable thing, like the farmer drives his plow, or like our friend in the scratch below, who is harrowing, and even drags the harrow himself. If one hasn't a horse, one is one's own horse—many people do so here.

There is a saying of Gustave Doré's which I have always admired, "J'ai la patience d'un bœuf," I find a certain goodness in it, a certain resolute honesty—in short, that saying has a deep meaning, it is the word of a real artist. When one thinks of the man from whose heart such a saying sprang, all those oft-repeated art dealer's arguments about "natural gifts" seem to become an abominably discordant raven's croaking. "J'ai la patience"—how quiet it sounds, how dignified; they wouldn't even say it except for that very raven's croaking. I am not an artist—how coarse it sounds—even to think so of oneself—oughtn't one to have patience, oughtn't one to learn patience from nature, learn patience from seeing the corn slowly ripen, seeing things grow—should one think oneself so absolutely dead as to imagine that one would not grow any more? Should one thwart one's own development on purpose? I say this to explain why I think it so foolish to speak about natural gifts and no natural gifts.

But in order to grow, one must be rooted in the earth. So I tell you, take root in the soil of Drenthe—you will germinate there—don't wither on the sidewalk. You will say there are plants that grow in the city—that may be, but you are corn, and your place is in the cornfield.

Well, I too suppose that for financial reasons now may not be the right moment, but at the same time I suppose that circumstances may just make it possible. If there were only half a possibility, I believe you would do well to risk the venture. I do not think you would ever regret it. You would be able to develop the best that is in you, and have a more peaceful life altogether. Neither of us would be alone, our work would merge. In the beginning we should have to live through anxious moments, we should have to prepare ourselves for them, and take measures to overcome them; we should not be able to go back, we should not look back nor be able to look back; on the contrary, we should force ourselves to look ahead. But it's in this period that we shall be far removed from all our friends and acquaintances, we shall fight this fight without anybody seeing us, and this will be the best thing that can happen, for then nobody will hinder us. We shall look forward to victory—we feel it in our very bones. We shall be so busy working that we shall be absolutely unable to think of anything else but our work.

I don't suppose I'm telling you anything at all new, I only ask, Don't thwart your own best thoughts. Think that idea over with a certain good-humored optimism instead of looking at things gloomily and pessimistically. I see that even Millet, just because he was so serious, couldn't help keeping good courage. This is something peculiar, not to all styles of painting, but to Millet, Israëls, Breton, Boughton, Herkomer and others.

Those who seek real simplicity are themselves so simple, and their view of life is so full of willingness and courage, even in hard times.

· Think these things over, write me about them. It must be "une révolution qui est, puisqu'il faut qu'elle soit" [a revolution that is, because it must be]. With a handshake,

Yours sincerely, Vincent

337

Dear brother,   Drenthe, September-November 1883

I cannot count the grains in a sack of corn just by smelling it—I cannot look through the planks of the barn door—but sometimes I can see by the lumps whether it is a sack of potatoes or of corn, or, though the barn door be closed, I can tell when the pig is killed from the squealing.

Only in this way can I and will I judge the circumstances in which you find yourself just now, from the indications I have, however vague they may be, and it is not a prophecy I am making.

But now to the point! Just consider coolly whether you are not faced by what they call fatality on the battlefield. Just consider the faces of your friends, your sham friends and your enemies, just consider the je ne sais quois—just consider whether a certain void is not developing around you, so that you are losing your hold on things, or at any rate so that it is less easy for you to put through business deals. In short, consider whether this fatality is in your favor or decidedly against you.

Tell me this one thing, am I mistaken when I conclude from some symptoms that there is a question of one of those malignant crises which at times arise in large businesses in the big cities? Do things have a desperate aspect? Do you feel this cannot be redressed? Or do you feel redress is possible, and that therefore this crisis is no reason to change your position?

Unless you write me, "No, it is not so bad as that," I personally think matters have a rather desperate aspect.

Think it over cool-headedly—I know you have your composure, your presence of mind, I know you try to analyze things, and for this reason I should like to know if you yourself see something which I *fear* is there.

You know, boy—as long as the position was tolerable—as long as business was possible, I have never dared to advise you openly, Give it up, especially out of respect for your position, which you kept, not for your own pleasure, but for the welfare of us all.

But your former duties, which, moreover, you have taken on yourself of your own free will, cease to be duties when business conditions become such that to continue would not only be a hopeless struggle, but at the same time would inevitably bring about your own ruin.

In short, there are limits, and my intuition tells me you have almost reached that point.

Look here—as regards now or never—making oneself scarce or disappearing, neither you nor I should *ever* do that, no more than commit suicide.

I too have my moments of deep melancholy, but I say again, both you and I ought to regard the idea of disappearing or making oneself scarce as becoming neither you nor me.

And notwithstanding all, one should take the risk of going on, even when one feels that it is *impossible*, of going on with the desperate feeling that it will end in disappearance—but on the other hand, in our consciences there is that *"beware!!!"*

Should I be mistaken—should my presentiment be at variance with the facts, about which I ask you the question, Have they a decidedly desperate aspect or not?—very well, then I am willing to believe your simple assurance, I expect things to come out right, or some such words, *as soon as you write me that.*

In the event of your being faced with a fait accompli in one of those venomous crises such as Paris and London produce—if this is so definitely to be expected that you feel it is a power that would crush you if they should try to force the worst to happen by resorting to a maneuver of opposition—well, under these circumstances leave the sinking ship, and concentrate your mind and energy, not on clinging to your present position, but on creating something wholly new. For a long time your *duty* has seemed too complicated to me; your duty ought to be something simple, and your present duty would grow more and more involved and doubtful, leaving the question of whether I think it is really and truly your duty out of it. By starting to paint, you will find a very clear duty and a very simple, straight path for your feet.

My idea is that going on in your present situation would prove to be not only more and more unbearable, but also less and less profitable. I do not say this only as far as Goupil & Co. is concerned, but also in general with regard to *you* as a *dealer.* I do not say that you and I will get rich together, but in any case we shall be able to preserve our aplomb and our balance, although—I cannot deny this—we shall have a very hard time of it during the first few years.

But I see not the *unfavorable* but the *favorable* fatality hovering over our painting enterprise, but you would crush not only yourself but me too, I am afraid, by carrying through something which in my opinion goes utterly against the grain. In the first place we shall not be able to assist each other, and we shall be too much cast upon ourselves, and in the second place we shall make each other waver by working in diametrically opposite directions, so that notwithstanding our friendship, at times we shall have to turn our backs on each other.

Well, my dear fellow, to me painting is too logical, too reasonable, too straightforward to allow me personally ever to change my course. Besides, you yourself helped me realize the idea of a handicraft, and I know that basically it is your idea too, so I think we ought to co-operate from now on.

My reason, my conscience, compel me to tell you what is partially your own view too; there is nothing to fall back on but a *radical* renewal.

I know that my words will be in strange contrast to those of others you might consult, who want to pass the matter off with, "It will come out all right," "The desired changes will occur." I do not wish to flatter you, all right, I do not flatter. As to rousing your courage, yes, I dare to, I dare rouse the very highest courage and serenity in you, but only as regards painting; and about Paris, I can only say this, Look well, and see if *fate* is not against you on that battlefield.

As far as I can see, going on in Paris, even if you were able to stick it out for many years, will not grant you peace, and there would not be so much opportunity for being as useful to others as if you were a painter.

I see that Paris will put you into what I would call a crooked position in regard to *your own duty.* Leaving your being useful to others out of it for the moment, seeing that I do not know if *in the long run* I myself should remain truly firm, because you are directing the simpler minds of others toward Paris, a thought which will disturb exactly *these* people because they *might* be intoxicated by it.

Understand clearly what I say: Until now everything has had its reason, but *now* the signs of the times suggest a change of direction, as I see it, in a way quite different from and far more decisive than anything in the past.

There is no question of slackening or giving in here; on the contrary, in this there is an attacking the calamity at the core: the same energetic principle as that of sowing superior plants in better soil.

The calamity leaves us our old courage and our old earnest energy. Let the world say venomously what it cannot refrain from saying; it will leave you and me cold. On the contrary, we are counting on the possibility of a hard life which will have a purpose other than earning as much money as possible.

Our purpose is in the first place self-reform by means of a handicraft and of intercourse with nature, believing as we do that this is our first duty in order to be honest with others and to be consistent—our aim is walking with God—the opposite of living in the midst of the doings of the big cities.

We shall not harm anybody by this.

Though some people may think it hypocritical to say so, our belief is that God will help those who help themselves, as long as they turn their energy and attention in this direction, and set to work *to this end.*

I see that Millet believed more and more firmly in "Something on High." He spoke of it in a way quite different than, for instance, Father does. He left it more vague, but for all that, I see more in Millet's vagueness than in what Father says. And I find that same quality of Millet's in Rembrandt, in Corot—in short, in the work of many, though I must not and cannot expatiate on this. The end of things need to be the power to explain them, but basing oneself effectively upon them.

In short, Theo, I have a vague but firm feeling that it is our first duty to fix the heart on high, and this feeling forces me to recommend to you, brother to brother, friend to friend, preparing yourself for a life based on simpler principles. Principles which I am unable to define for others, but which I feel; one can hardly imagine *duty* commanding one to *do business in Paris*; rather, it will induce one to retire from it.

Can you share these feelings to a certain extent? Think it over, deliberate on it; if you want time, search your heart, and take your time. All hesitation based on the objection "I am not an artist" seems reasonable to me only as long as you do *not* prevent yourself from *becoming one*. To what degree we *are* or are *not* artists, neither we ourselves nor others can definitely ascertain. However, the How-to-do-it system entails saying, *I shall do my best to do it*, without asking any such questions; on the other hand, it seems to me that it is the How-NOT-to-do-it system which says, "I know in advance I shall not be able to do it."

One is not sure of things all at once, one cannot foresee things except very vaguely, but there is something called conscience after all, a kind of compass by which one can distinguish between this direction and that—between North and South—between right and left—at least broadly speaking. Which means—notwithstanding fortuitous currents and certain deceptively inviting coasts—being able to say, This is not the right course for me after all. And look, earning money in Paris, even for others' sakes, would, considering your recent experiences, seem to me such a deceptive fata morgana: a coast that recedes more and more when you approach to make a landing *there*, at the same time causing you to be driven farther and farther off your course. I respect all hesitations and doubts, I respect your weighing all the pros and cons, I will not try to force an immediate decision upon you. But I only point out very, very seriously that in my opinion it is an incontrovertible fact that you are standing at a crossroads, and that you will have to look before you leap to the decision simply to continue in Paris. The signs of the times, not I, say: Wait a bit! What do you want? Do you choose Paris? All right, if *you have made up your mind* that it is to be so, then I should not want to interfere; but it will not be as easy as all that, and I am afraid you will be in for fatality. I am damned doubtful whether you will remain at peace with your lot.

I see *everything except* fatality against painting; *for* Paris I see everything *except* fatality!

Fatality, in which with an unutterable feeling I see God, Who is the White Ray of Light, and Who has the last word; what is not good through and through is not good at all, and will not last—He, in Whose eyes even the Black Ray will have no plausible meaning.

What is before you is something terrible, something "awful"—those things are so inexpressible that I can find no words for them; and if I were not your brother and your friend, who considers being silent ungrateful as well as inhuman, I should say nothing. But seeing that you say, First, inspire me with courage, and second, do not flatter me, I say now, Look, I see all these things here on the silent moor, where I feel God high above you and me. With a warm handshake,

Yours sincerely, Vincent

338

Theo,   Drenthe, September-November 1883

Some time ago you wrote me about a certain difference in our respective physiognomies. All right. And your conclusion was that I was more of a thinker. What can I say to that? I do feel in myself a faculty for thinking, but that faculty is not what I feel specially organized in me. I think myself to be something other than specially a thinker. When I think of you, I see very characteristic action, that is well and good, but also most decidedly not isolated but on the contrary accompanied by so much sentiment, and real *thought* too, that for me the conclusion is that there is more resemblance than difference between you and me. I do not say there is no difference—but having learned to know you better of late, the difference seems smaller to me than I used to think sometimes in former years.

When I consider our temperament and type of physiognomy, I find similarity, and a very pronounced resemblance between, for instance, the Puritans and ourselves besides. I mean the people in Cromwell's time or thereabouts, the little group of men and women who sailed from the Old World to America in the *Mayflower*, and settled there, firmly resolved to live simple lives.

Times are different—they cut down forests—we would turn to painting. I know that the initiative taken by a small group, called in history The Pilgrim Fathers, however small in itself, had great consequences; and as to ourselves, I think that in the first place we should philosophize but little about great consequences, and only try to find a path for ourselves to travel through life as straightforwardly as possible. To meditate on consequences is not our way, *neither yours nor mine*.

If I mention The Pilgrim Fathers, it is because of the physiognomy, to show you that certain reddish-haired people with square foreheads are neither only thinkers nor only men of action, but usually combine both elements. In one of Boughton's pictures I know a little figure of one of those Puritans, for which I should think *you* had posed if I didn't know better. It is exactly, exactly the same physiognomy—a small silhouette on a rock against a background of sea and fog; I can show you myself also, that is to say, that *variation* of the same physiognomy, but my profile is less characteristic.

Father used to ponder over the story of Jacob and Esau with regard to you and me—not quite wrongly—but fortunately there is less discord, to mention only *one* point of difference, and in the Bible itself there are plenty of examples of better relations between brothers than existed between the venerable patriarchs mentioned above.

I myself have sometimes thought about that being a thinker, but more and more it becomes clear to me that it was not my vocation, and because of the unfortunate prejudice that a man who feels the need to think things over is *not* practical, and belongs only among the dreamers, because this prejudice is greatly respected in Society, I often met with rebuffs because I didn't keep things to myself enough.

But since then that very history of the Puritans, and the history of Cromwell, as for instance Carlyle gives it, made me see that thinking and acting do not exclude each other, and that the sharp dividing lines which are drawn nowadays between thinking and acting—as if the one excluded the other—do not really exist. As to doubting whether one is an artist or not—that question is too much of an abstraction.

I confess, however, that I don't object to thinking it over, provided I can draw and paint at the same time.

And *my* aim in *my* life is to make pictures and drawings, as many and as well as I can; then, at the end of my life, I hope to pass away, looking back with love and tender regret, and thinking, "Oh, the pictures I might have made!" But this does not exclude making what is possible, mind you. Do you object to this, either for me or for yourself?

I wish painting would become such a fixed idea in your mind that the problem of "Am I an artist or am I not?" would be placed in the category of abstractions, and the more practical questions of how to put together a figure or a landscape, being more amusing, would come to the fore.

Theo, I declare I prefer to think how arms, legs, head are attached to the trunk, rather than whether I myself am more or less an artist or not.

I suppose that you prefer thinking of a sky with gray clouds, and their silver lining above a muddy field, to being engrossed in the question of your own personality. Oh, for all that, I know sometimes the mind is full of it, which is only natural. But look here, brother, even if our mind is now and then full of the problem, "*Is there a God* or *is there not?*" it is no reason for us to commit an ungodly act intentionally.

In the same way, in the matter of art, the problem, "Am I an artist or am I not?" must not induce us *not* to draw or *not* to paint. Many things defy definition, and I consider it wrong to fritter one's time away on them. Certainly when one's work does not go smoothly and one is checked by difficulties, one gets bogged in the morass of such thoughts and insoluble problems. And because one feels sorely troubled by it, the best thing to do is to conquer the cause of the distraction by acquiring a new insight into the practical part of the work.

Now I, for my part, seeing both in you and in myself something of the Puritan character, which so unites thinking and acting and is so far removed from wanting to be only a thinker or only a machine, which needs principles of simplicity *as well as* of sensible work, I do *not* admit a difference or divergence, much less a contrast between you and me.

In my opinion, it would be an error of judgment if you continued doing business in Paris.

So the conclusion is : both brothers painters.

Whether it fits your character? It might well be that you are fighting hard and futilely *against* your character, frustrating your own liberation just because you doubt whether you can do it.

Alas, I know all about this from experience. After all—however much we may be our own enemies—I am beginning to realize more and more that l'homme s'agite, Dieu le mène, that man proposes and God disposes. Above our doing the right thing and doing the wrong thing there is an infinitely powerful force. The same is true of your circumstances—act wisely in them—perhaps wisely enough to become a painter, to cut matters short. In the depth of my heart I should be so greatly reassured if I saw you taking up the paintbrush that I should consider the calamity and the shipwreck of the moment of less importance than the certainty of a future in a direction you would never regret.

But I wish that at the same time you may find rest for your heart in the matter of women. If this were possible, you would be *even stronger*, as being loved gives one certain wings, a certain surprising courage and energy. Then one is more of a *complete* man than otherwise. And the more one is this, the better.

At all events, I count it among the possibilities that you yourself may become conscious that painting is your vocation, and then, dear brother, Puritan "sans le savoir" [without knowing it], it might be that your days in Paris were numbered, that an old world closed itself to you, in a rather ungenerous way—but that at the same time a new world opened itself to you.

Well, think it over, a long or a short time. But it would be of little use if you said, Vincent, keep silent about it; for to that my answer is: Theo, it will not keep silent within *yourself*.

> On le contient plus malaisément
> Que la source des grands fleuves.
> [It is more difficult to repress
> Than the source of great rivers.]

Theo, I have heard from the poor woman a few times; she seems to be doing her best, working, washing for people, going out as a charwoman. Her writing is almost indecipherable and incoherent, she seems to regret some things in the past. The children are well and happy.

My pity and affection for her are certainly not dead, and I hope that a bond of affection may remain between us, though I do not see the possibility or the good of living together again—pity may not be love, but for all that it can be rooted deeply enough.

Well, brother, to change the subject, it is snowing here today, in the form of enormous hailstones. I call it snow because of the effect.

I don't speak about the beauty of the scenery here because I should have to say *too much* about it to you. As to the work, I am almost too preoccupied with the idea that you should take it up too, which quite absorbs me. I wish it were settled, then we could make definite plans for working together. Drenthe is so beautiful, it absorbs and satisfies me so absolutely that if I could not be here forever, I should wish I had never seen it. It is inexpressibly beautiful.

With a handshake,

Yours sincerely, Vincent

340

Dear brother,   Drenthe, September-November 1883

I must just tell you about a trip to Zweeloo, the village where Liebermann stayed a long while, and where he made studies for his picture at the last Salon, the one with the poor washerwomen. Where Ter Meulen and Jules Bakhuyzen have also been a long time. Imagine a trip across the heath at three o'clock in the morning, in an open cart (I went with the landlord, who had to go to the market in Assen), along a road, or "diek" as they call it here, which had been banked up with mud instead of sand. It was even more curious than going by barge. At the first glimpse of dawn, when everywhere the cocks began to crow near the cottages scattered all over the heath and the few cottages we passed—surrounded by thin poplars whose yellow leaves one could hear drop to earth—an old stumpy tower in a churchyard, with earthen wall and beech hedge—the level landscapes of heath or cornfields—it all, all, all became exactly like the most beautiful Corots. A quietness, a mystery, a peace, as only he has painted it.

But when we arrived at Zweeloo at six o'clock in the morning, it was still quite dark; I saw the real Corots even earlier in the morning.

The entrance to the village was splendid: Enormous mossy roofs of houses, stables, sheepfolds, barns.

The broad-fronted houses here stand between oak trees of a splendid bronze. In the moss are tones of gold green; in the ground, tones of reddish, or bluish or yellowish dark lilac gray; in the green of the cornfields, tones of inexpressible purity; on the wet trunks, tones of black, contrasting with the golden rain of whirling, clustering autumn leaves—hanging in loose tufts, as if they had been blown there, and with the sky glimmering through them—from the poplars, the birches, the lime and apple trees.

The sky smooth and clear, luminous, not white but a lilac which can hardly be deciphered, white shimmering with red, blue and yellow in which everything is reflected, and which one feels everywhere above one, which is vaporous and merges into the thin mist below—harmonizing everything in a gamut of delicate gray. I didn't find a single painter in Zweeloo, however, and people said *none* ever came *in winter*.

I, on the contrary, hope to be there *just* this winter.

As there were no painters, I decided not to wait for my landlord's return, but to walk back, and to make some drawings on the way. So I began a sketch of that little apple orchard, of which Liebermann made his large picture. And then I walked back along the road we had driven over early in the morning.

For the moment the whole country around Zweeloo is entirely covered—as far as the eye can see—with young corn, the very, very tenderest green I know.

With a sky over it of a delicate lilac-white, which gives an effect—I don't think it can be painted, but which is for me the keynote that one must know in order to understand the keynotes of other effects.

A black patch of earth—flat—infinite—a clear sky of delicate lilac-white. The young corn sprouts from that earth, it is almost moldy-looking with that corn. That's what the good fertile parts of Drenthe are basically; the whole in a hazy atmosphere. Think of *Brion's* "Le dernier jour de la création"; yesterday it seemed to me that I understood the meaning of that picture.

The poor soil of Drenthe is just the same—but the black earth is even blacker still—like soot—not lilac-black like the furrows, and drearily covered with ever-rotting heather and peat. I see that everywhere, the incidentals on the infinite background: on the moors, the peat sheds; in the fertile parts, the very primitive gigantic structures of farms and sheepfolds, with low, very low little walls and enormous mossy roofs. Oak trees all around them.

When one has walked through that country for hours and hours, one feels that there is really nothing but that infinite earth—that green mold of corn or heather, that infinite sky. Horses and men seem no larger than fleas. One is not aware of anything, be it ever so large in itself; one only knows that there is earth and sky. However, in one's quality of a little speck noticing other little specks—leaving the infinite apart—one finds every little speck to be a Millet.

I passed a little old church exactly, exactly "The Church at Gréville" in Millet's little picture in the Luxembourg; instead of the little peasant with his spade in that picture, there was here a shepherd with a flock of sheep walking along the hedge. There was not a glimpse of the true sea in the background, but only of the sea of young corn, the sea of furrows instead of the sea of waves.

The effect produced was the same. Then I saw plowers, very busy—a sandcart, a shepherd, road menders, dungcarts. In a little roadside inn I drew an old woman at the spinning wheel, a dark little silhouette out of a fairy tale—a dark little silhouette against a light window, through which one saw the clear sky, and a small path through the delicate green, and a few geese pecking at grass.

And then when twilight fell—imagine the quiet, the peace of it all! Imagine then a little avenue of high poplars with autumn leaves, imagine a wide muddy road, all black mud, with an infinite heath to the right and an endless heath to the left, a few black triangular silhouettes of sod-built huts, through the little windows of which shines the red light of the little fire, with a few pools of dirty yellowish water that reflect the sky, and in which trunks lie rotting; imagine that swamp in the evening twilight, with a white sky over it, everywhere the contrast of black and white. And in that swamp a rough figure—the shepherd—a heap of oval masses, half wool, half mud, jostling each other, pushing each other—the flock. You see them coming—you find yourself in the midst of them—you turn around and follow them. Slowly and reluctantly they trudge along the muddy road. However, the farm looms in the distance—a few mossy roofs and piles of straw and peat between the poplars.

The sheepfold is again like the silhouette of a triangle—dark. The door is wide open like the entrance to a dark cave. Through the chinks of the boards behind it gleams the light of the sky. The whole caravan of masses of wool and mud disappear into that cave—the shepherd and a woman with a lantern shut the doors behind them.

That coming home of the flock in the twilight was the finale of the symphony I heard yesterday.

That day passed like a dream, all day I was so absorbed in that poignant music that I literally forgot even food and drink—I had taken a piece of brown bread and a cup of coffee in the little inn where I drew the spinning wheel. The day was over, and from dawn till twilight, or rather from one night till the other, I had lost myself in that symphony.

I came home, and sitting by the fire, I felt I was hungry, yes, very hungry. But now you see how it is here. One is feeling exactly as if one had been to an exhibition of the Cent chef-d'œuvres, for instance; what does one bring home from such a day? Only a number of rough sketches. Yet there is another thing one brings home—a calm ardor for work.

Do write soon, today it is Friday, but your letter has not yet arrived; I am longing to get it. It also takes some time to get it changed, as I have to go to Hoogeveen for it, and then return here. We do not know how things will go, otherwise I should say, *now* the simplest thing would be perhaps to send the money *once* a month. At all events, write soon. With a handshake,

Yours sincerely, Vincent

345

Dear Theo,   Nuenen, 3-5 December 1883

I was lying awake half the night, Theo, after I wrote you last night.

I am sick at heart about the fact that, coming back after two years' absence, the welcome home was kind and cordial in every respect, but basically there has been no change whatever, not the slightest, in what I must call the most extreme blindness and ignorance as to the insight into our mutual position. And I again feel almost unbearably disturbed and perplexed.

The fact is that things were going extremely well until the moment when Father—not just in the heat of passion, but also because he was "tired of it" —banished me from the house. It ought to have been understood then that this was supremely important to my success or failure—that things were made ten times more difficult for me by this—almost insupportable.

If I had not had the same feeling at the time which I now have again, namely that notwithstanding all good intentions, notwithstanding all the kindness of the reception, notwithstanding anything you like, there is a certain hardness in Father, like iron, an icy coldness—something that gives the impression of dry sand or glass or tinplate—for all his outward gentleness—if, as I said, I had not had this feeling already, I should not have resented it so much.

[Written in the margin] I am not so much interested in a kind or an unkind reception—it grieves me that they do not regret what they did at the time.

Now I am again in an almost unbearable state of wavering and inner struggle.

You understand that I should not write as I do—having undertaken the journey hither of my own free will, having been the first to swallow my pride —if I did not find real obstacles in my way.

If I had now noticed some eagerness to do as the Rappards did, with the best results, and as we began here with good results too—if I had noticed that Father had also realized that he ought *not* to have shut his house to me, then I should have felt some confidence in the future.

Nothing, nothing of all that.

In Father's mind there was not then, there is not now, the faintest shadow of a doubt that what he did was the right thing.

Father does not know remorse like you and me and any man who is human.

Father believes in his own righteousness, whereas you and I and other human creatures are imbued with the feeling that we *consist* of errors and efforts of the lost souls. I commiserate with people like Father—*in my heart of hearts I cannot be angry with him*—because I think they are more unhappy than I. Why do I think them unhappy?—because the good within them is wrongly applied, so that it acts like evil—because the *light* within them is black and spreads darkness, obscurity around them.

Their cordial reception grieves me—their *indulgence* without acknowledging their error is, for me, perhaps worse than the error itself. Instead of a ready understanding and a certain eager contribution to my, and indirectly their own, well-being, I feel in everything a hesitation and delay which paralyze my own ardor and energy like a leaden atmosphere.

My masculine intellect tells me that I must consider it an irrevocable, fatal fact that in the depth of our souls Father and I are irreconcilable. My compassion for Father as well as for myself says to me, "Irreconcilable?"—"Never!"—indefinitely, for ever and ever, there is the possibility of, and one should have faith in the possibility of, a decisive reconciliation. But this—ah, why is it probable, alas, that it will turn out "an illusion"?

Do you call this moroseness on my part?

Our life is an appalling reality, and we ourselves are infinitely driven, things are—as they are—and whether we take them more or less gloomily does not in any way alter the nature of things. I think about it this way, for instance at night when I lie awake, or I think about it this way in the storm on the heath, in the evening, in the dreary twilight.

In the daytime, in ordinary life, I may sometimes look as thick-skinned as a wild boar, and I can understand perfectly well that people think me *coarse*. When I was younger I thought, much more than now, that things depended on chance, on small things or misunderstandings that had no reason. But getting older, I feel it more and more differently, and see deeper motives. Life is "a queer thing" too, brother.

You see how agitated my letters are, one moment I think that *it can be done*, the next, that *it cannot*. One thing is clear to me, "that things don't go readily, that there is no eagerness."

I have decided to go and see Rappard, and tell him that I myself should be agreeable to staying at home, but that notwithstanding all the advantages this would have, there is a je ne sais quoi in Father which I am beginning to look upon as incurable and which makes me listless and powerless. Last night it was decided that I shall stay here for a time—and notwithstanding this, next morning I again hear, Let's think it over some more—oh yes, sleep on it a night or so, and think it over!!!—*when they have been able to think it over for two years—ought* to have thought it over of their own accord, as a matter of course.

Two years, every day of which was a day of distress to me; for them—everyday life, as if nothing had happened, as if nothing could happen—the burden did not weigh on them. You say they do not express it, but they feel it—*I do not believe it.* I have thought so myself, but it is *all wrong.* One *acts* as one *feels*—our acts, our ready compliance or our hesitation, they are what people may know us by—not by what we say with our lips, kindly or unkindly. Good intentions, opinions, in reality all this is *less than nothing.* I see now what I saw *then*—then I spoke *flatly against Father*—now I speak, and in all respects I speak, however it may turn out, flatly *against* Father again, because he is *unwilling,* because he makes it *impossible.*

[Written in the margin] They think *they did no harm at the time,* this is *too* bad.

Damn it, brother, the Rappards acted intelligently, but here!!!!! And everything you did for it, and do still, becomes three-quarters useless through their fault. It's stupid, brother. With a handshake,

Yours, Vincent

346

Dear brother,   Nuenen, 15 December 1883

I feel what Father and Mother think of me *instinctively* (I do not say *intelligently*).

They feel the same dread of taking me in the house as they would about taking a big rough dog. He would run into the room with wet paws—and he is so rough. He will be in everybody's way. *And he barks so loud.* In short, he is a foul beast.

All right—but the beast has a human history, and though only a dog, he has a human soul, and even a very sensitive one, that makes him feel what people think of him, which an ordinary dog cannot do.

And I, admitting that I am a kind of dog, leave them alone.

Also this house is too good for me, and Father and Mother and the family are so terribly genteel (not sensitive underneath, however), and—and—and they are clergymen—a lot of clergymen.

The dog feels that if they keep him, it will only mean putting up with him and tolerating him *"in this house,"* so he will try to find another kennel. The dog is in fact Father's son, and has been left rather too much in the streets, where he could not but become rougher and rougher; but as Father already forgot this years ago, and in reality has never meditated *deeply* on the meaning of the tie between father and son, one need not mention that.

And then—the dog might bite—he might become rabid, and the constable would have to come to shoot him.

Yes, all this is very true.

On the other hand, dogs are guardians.

But that is superfluous, there is peace, and there is no question of any danger, they say. So I keep silent about it.

The dog is only sorry that he did not stay away, for it was less lonely on the heath than in this house, notwithstanding all the kindness. The dog's visit was a weakness, which I hope will be forgotten, and which he will avoid committing in the future.

As I have had no expenses since I have been here, and as I have twice received money from you, I have paid the journey myself, and also paid for the clothes Father bought because mine were not good enough, and at the same time I returned the 25 guilders to friend Rappard.

I think you will be glad of this, it seemed so careless.

Dear Theo, enclosed you will find the letter I was writing when I received yours, which I will now answer after reading what you say carefully.

I begin by saying, I think it noble of you that, thinking I *hurt* Father, you take his part, and give me a good scolding.

I appreciate this in you, though you are fighting against one who is neither Father's nor your own enemy, but who most decidedly wants to submit a number of serious problems to Father's and your consideration, telling you what I tell you because I feel that way, and asking, Why is this so?... In many respects your remarks in answer to various passages in my letter are not foreign to my own thoughts. Your objections are partly my own objections, but they are not conclusive. Once again I see your good will in it, and at the same time your longing for reconciliation and peace—which for that matter I do not doubt. But, brother, on the other hand I could raise a lot of objections to your remarks, only I think this would be tedious, and I think there is a shorter way. There is a desire for peace and reconciliation in Father and in you and in me. And yet we do not seem able to bring about peace.

Now, I believe that I am the stumbling block, and so I must try to find a way not to "*bother*" you or Father any longer. So you also think that I hurt Father's feelings and that I am a *coward. Really?* Well, in the future I shall try to keep everything to myself, I shall not visit Father again, and shall stick to my proposal to put a stop to our arrangement about the money toward March, if you agree, in order to keep our mutual freedom of thought, in order not to *bother you* any longer (which I fear is going to be your unintentional conclusion too). I ask for a little time for the sake of order, and to allow myself some time to take a few measures which, though they have very little chance of success, for conscience's sake I may not put off. You must take this calmly and in kindness, brother—it is not an ultimatum I am sending you. But if our feelings differ too widely, we must not force ourselves to avoid calling things by their names. Isn't that your opinion too?

But you know, don't you, that I consider you *to have saved my life.* I shall *never*

190

forget that; *though we put an end* to relations which I am afraid would bring us into a false position, I am not only your brother, your friend, but at the same time, I have *infinite* obligations of gratitude to you for the fact that you lent me a helping hand at the time, and have continued to help me. Money can be repaid, not kindness such as yours.

Let me go my own way—it is a disappointment to me that there has not been a thorough reconciliation now; I wish it could happen still, but you people do not understand me, and I am afraid you *never* will.

Send me the usual amount by return of mail if possible, then I need not ask Father for anything when I go away, which I must do as soon as possible. I gave all the 23.80 guilders of December 1 to Father, for 14 guilders borrowed, and shoes and trousers.

I gave all the 25 guilders of December 10 to Rappard.

I have just a quarter and a few cents in my pocket. That is the account, which you will understand, if you know besides that I paid my expenses in Drenthe for a long time out of the money of November 20, which arrived December 1, because there had been some delay then that was set right later, and that I paid for my journey, etc., out of the 14 guilders (which I borrowed from Father and have since given back).

I shall go from here to Rappard.

And from Rappard, perhaps to Mauve.

So my intention is to try to arrange everything in calmness and order.

There is much in my frankly stated opinion about Father which I cannot take back under the circumstances. I appreciate your objections, but many of them I cannot consider conclusive; of others I have already thought myself, though what I have written I have written. I expressed my feelings in strong terms, and it stands to reason that they are modified by the appreciation of much that is good in Father—of course this modification is considerable.

Permit me to tell you that I did not know a man of thirty was *a boy*, especially not if he has gone through more experiences than most during those thirty years. But if you like—consider my words the words of a boy. I am not responsible for your interpretation of my words, am I? That is your own business.

Also as to Father—I shall venture not to take to heart what he thinks of me, as soon as we part.

It may be politic to be silent about one's feelings—but on the other hand it has always appeared to me that serenity is a duty, particularly for a painter. Whether they understand me or not, whether I am judged rightly or wrongly, leaves me unchanged, as you once pointed out to me yourself.

And brother, even if there is a separation or whatever else, I am your friend— perhaps *much more than you know or guess*. With a handshake,

Yours sincerely, Vincent

In any case I am neither Father's enemy nor yours, and I *never* shall be.

347

Dear Theo,   Nuenen, 16 December 1883

Mauve once said to me, "You will find yourself if you go on painting, if you penetrate more deeply into art than you have up to now"; he said that two years ago.

Of late I often think about these words of his.

I have found myself—I am that dog.

This idea may be a little exaggerated—reality may be less pronounced in its contrasts, less starkly dramatic, but I believe the rough character outline is true after all. The shaggy shepherd dog which I tried to describe to you in yesterday's letter is my character, and the life of that animal is my life, that is to say, omitting the details and only stating the essentials.

This may seem exaggerated to you—but I will not take it back. Without being personal, just for the sake of an impartial character study, as if I did not speak about you and me but about strangers, for the sake of analysis, I point out to you once more how it was last summer. I see two brothers walking about in The Hague (*see them as strangers*, do not think of yourself and me).

One says, "I must maintain a certain standing, I must stay in business, I don't think I shall become a painter."

The other says, "I am getting to be like a dog, I feel that the future will probably make me more ugly and rough, and I foresee that 'a certain *poverty*' will be my fate, but, but *I shall be a painter*."

So the one—a certain standing as an art dealer.

The other—poverty and painter.

And I see those same brothers in former years, when you had just entered the world of pictures, when you just began to read, etc., etc.—I see them near the mill at Rijswijk or, for instance, on a walk to Chaam in winter across the snowy heath early in the morning! *Feeling, thinking* and *believing* so exactly alike that I ask myself, Are those the same??? The question is, How will things turn out—will they separate forever, or will they forever follow the same path?

I tell you, I consciously choose *the dog's path through life*; I will remain a *dog*, I shall be *poor*, I shall be a *painter*, I want to *remain human*—going *into* nature. In my opinion the man who goes *out of* nature, whose head is always stuffed with thoughts of maintaining this and maintaining that, even if this causes him to go out of nature to such an extent that he cannot but acknowledge it—oh—in this way one is apt to arrive at a point where one can no longer distinguish white from black—and—and one becomes the exact opposite of what one is considered and of what one thinks oneself to be. For instance—at present you have a manly fear of mediocrity in the unfavorable sense of the word—why then are you going to kill, to extinguish, what is best in your soul? Then, aye, *in that case* your fear might come true. How does one become mediocre? By compromising and making concessions, today in this matter, tomorrow in another, according to the dictates of the world—by never contradicting the world, and by always following public opinion! Please do not misunderstand me—on the contrary, I mean to say that basically you are better than that—I see it in you when, for instance, you stand up for Father, when you think I am bothering Father. You apply your opposition in the wrong way in this matter, at least as I see it, with your kind permission, but that is exactly what I appreciate, and I say, Now add wisdom to this, and apply your anger somewhere else, and use the same vigor to fight against other influences than precisely mine—and—and—you will probably be less troubled in your mind.

I do not speak against Father when I consider his character separately, but I speak against Father as soon as I compare him with the great father Millet, for instance.

Millet's doctrine is so great that Father's views appear wretchedly petty by comparison. You think this judgment awful in me—I can't help it—it is my deep conviction, and I make no secret of it, because *you* confuse Father's character with Corot's character, for instance. How do I look upon Father?—as a person with a character similar to Corot's father's—but Father has nothing in common with Corot himself. For all that, Corot loved his father, *but he did not follow him.* I also love Father, as long as my way in life is not made difficult by differences of opinion. I *do not* love Father at the moment when a certain narrow-minded pride prevents a complete, decisive and so desirable reconciliation from being brought about generously and efficaciously. I did not in the least intend to put Father or you to great expense by the measures I have in mind, and for the sake of which I came home; on the contrary, what I wanted was to use the money to better advantage, in such a way that we should lose less, namely less time, less money and less energy. Am I therefore to be blamed when I point to the Rappards, who, although they are richer than Father or you or me, act more sensibly and get better results by being in harmony, though probably it is not always very easy for them either? Am I to be blamed for wanting to put a stop to the discord in the family by saying hitherto but no further? In what respect am I wrong if I want this completely and decisively, not being contented with *appearances* or a *half-hearted* reconciliation? A reconciliation with mental reservations, conditions, etc., bah!—this I decline to put up with. *Readily*—or *not at all*; with true zeal, otherwise it is utterly useless, and worse is to be expected.

You say you think it *cowardly* of me to rebel against Father—in the first place it is a rebellion in words—there is no question of violence. On the other hand, however, the view may be taken that I am all the sadder and more disappointed, that I speak all the more seriously and resolutely, because of the very fact that Father's gray hairs make it clear to me that, forsooth, perhaps we have not so much time left for a reconciliation. I do not attach much value to deathbed reconciliations, I prefer to see them *during life.* I am quite willing to concede that Father means well, but I should think it infinitely better if it did not remain restricted to meaning well and might lead to understanding each other at least some time, though it be very late. I am afraid it will never happen! If only you knew how sad I think this is, if you knew how I mourn over it....

You say, Father has other things to think of—really? all right—but I know how unimportant the said things which prevent Father, year after year, from thinking matters out appear to me. This is the core of the problem—Father does not feel there is anything to be reconciled about, anything that ought to be redressed—all right—leave him to his "other things." Father says, "But we have always been good to you, etc.," and I say, Really? Are you contented? I am not.

Something better than the time of the Rijswijk mill—namely the same thing for ever and ever: two poor brothers—artists—absorbed in the same feeling for the same nature—will it ever end in this? The secure social position, the secure wealth, will they be victorious? Oh, let them be victorious—but let it only be for a time, which will surely lead you to disappointment in them; this is what I expect will happen before you are thirty years old. And if not—well, if not, then—then—then—*so much the worse.*

With a handshake,

Yours sincerely, Vincent

[Enclosed in this letter] Dear brother, these are certainly ticklish questions to discuss, but do not take offense at my being unable to find better words for what is in my mind, and look upon my attempts to speak to you confidentially and unreservedly as a brother toward a brother, as a friend toward a friend.

Theo, in the past I often quarreled with Father, because Father said dictatorially: "It is like this," and I told him, "Pa, you are contradicting yourself, what you say militates absolutely against what you vaguely feel at your heart's core, even if you do not want to feel it." Theo, I stopped quarreling with Father wholly and completely long ago, because it is now clear to me that Father has never reflected upon certain very important things, and never will reflect upon them, and that he clings to a system and does not reason, nor did he ever, nor will he ever reason on the basis of the naked facts. There are too *many* who do as he does, so that he always finds certain support and strength in the thought, Everyone thinks this about it (namely primarily all the well-regulated, respectable clergymen). But he has no other strength, and it is all built on convention and a system, otherwise it would collapse like any other vanity. Father does not wrestle with the plain truth. But now I am of the opinion that one is one's own enemy if one does not want to think things out, if one does not say (especially in one's youth): Look here, for myself I do not want to be sustained by a system, I want to attack things according to reason and conscience. I take less notice of my own father, though he is not a bad man, and though I do not speak about him, than I do of people in whom I find more truth.

You see, dear brother, I feel a deep, deep, deep respect for Millet, Corot, Daubigny, Breton, Herkomer, Boughton, Jules Dupré, etc., etc., Israëls—I am far from confusing *myself* with *them*—I do not consider myself their equal—no—yet I say, however conceited or whatever else people may think me—for all that I say, *You* will show me the way, and I am ready to follow your example rather than Father's, or some schoolmaster's, or whoever else's.

I myself find in Father and Tersteeg something of the school of Delaroche, Muller, Dabuffe, and so on—I may think it clever, I may be silent about it,

I may take it at its face value, I may even have a certain respect for it—but all this does not prevent my saying, The least painter or man who wrestles directly with the naked truths of nature is more than you are.

In short, my dear fellow, neither Father nor Tersteeg has given other than a spurious tranquillity to my conscience, and they have not given me freedom, nor have they ever approved of my desire for freedom and plain truth and of my feeling of ignorance and darkness.

Now, left to myself, I have not attained the light or what I wanted to do yet, never mind; but by resolutely rejecting their systems I think I have gained a certain hope that my exertions will not be unavailing.

And that, before I close my eyes forever, I shall see the rayon blank. However fierce the struggle in my mind may have been because of my not having found it, I have never regretted saying that I considered the rayon noir the rayon noir, and having definitely avoided it—except that one should not quarrel over it, and if I ever quarreled over it, it was a mistake.

Now for myself, knowing what I know, I look at you and ask the question, "What shall he do with it?" Theo, when we quarreled a little some time ago in The Hague, and you said, I feel more and more drawn to Father, I told you, Boy, this is a difficult question, follow your own conscience. But since then I have tried to explain to you too that for myself I cannot find tranquillity in Father's and H. C. Tersteeg's way of thinking, the latter's being about the same, I think—and that I have become increasingly aware of the fact that there is a rayon noir and a rayon blanc and that I have found their light to be black and a mere convention compared to the cool honesty of Millet and Corot, for instance.

Now I have been thinking all this over four years longer than you have, as I am four years older and calmer—in any case time and experience have induced me to reject and avoid certain things. And I do not want to influence you, but on the other hand I do not want to conceal myself from you, or to do otherwise than speak openly.

I come to the following conclusion:

What Father and Tersteeg tried to force on me as a *duty* was the *specter* of a duty. What they *really* said was (though not in so many words): "Earn money, and your life will become straight." Millet says to me: *Make your life straight* (at least try to do so and to wrestle with the naked truth), *and even earning money can be managed, and in this too you will not be dishonest.*

And I felt then, and I feel more and more strongly now, that Father and Tersteeg, and for instance C. M. and I don't know who else (although they thought their intentions straight, and I do not suspect them of dishonesty—but as I said, I take them at their face value—and leave them alone), that they and all the influences of the past dragged me more and more *out of* nature. Now, whatever may be said of Millet, at least it was he who took me back *into* nature, more than any other might have been able to do in my desperate state of mind.

My youth was gloomy and cold and sterile under the influence of the rayon noir. And, brother, essentially your youth too. My dear fellow, this time I will not flatter you. After all, I will reproach nobody but myself with it—yet the rayon noir is unutterably cruel—unutterably—— And at this moment I feel within myself as many repressed tears as there are in a figure by Monteyne!

But, brother, my very grief over so much proves to me that I myself have definitely *done* with the systems in question. I have suffered from them, but in my heart of hearts I no longer belong to that side of life. And now I say to you, as brother to brother and as friend to friend, Though your youth was gloomy and frustrated, *in the future* let us seek that soft light for which I know no better name than the white ray of light or the good.

Not looking upon ourselves as having obtained it, of course, but as seeking it, believing in it with the foi de charbonnier. Whatever may be true of my losing patience with Father as well as with Tersteeg, etc., etc., do not think of me as being in the least influenced by hate or spitefulness toward them. I do not envy them, in my opinion they are not happy themselves, and in my heart of hearts I am certainly not their enemy nor do I bear them malice, neither do I look upon them as my enemies, although it is a fact that I do not recall their influence with much pleasure. I do not suspect them of wicked intentions. I think they do follow their conscience, but that it is haunted by ghosts. And I *do not* see in Millet or Corot that there were ghosts haunting *their* consciences. There I see greater calm and serenity of a higher quality. Once again: I am far removed from this myself. However, every study I make, every attempt in the direction of painting, every new love for or struggle with nature, successful or unsuccessful, gets me one little unsteady step nearer. As far as religion is concerned, I find less of it in Father than in Uncle Jan, for instance, though it stands to reason that many would say the reverse. I think Father the opposite of a man of faith. Well, look here, going in for painting requires a certain foi de charbonnier because one *cannot* prove at the outset that it will succeed and everyone takes a gloomy view of it. But, Theo, though it be true that you as well as I begin with as many repressed tears as the figures by Monteyne and Grollo, at the same time we have a little quiet hope mixed with all our sadness. In the first years of hard struggling it may even be a sowing of tears, so be it, but we shall check them, and in the far distance we may have a little quiet hope of the harvest.

With a handshake,

Yours sincerely, Vincent

Since I wrote the enclosed letter, I have again thought over your remarks, and have again spoken with Father. My decision not to stay here was almost taken, no matter what they might think of it, or what the consequences might be; but then the conversation took another turn, by my saying, "I have been here two weeks, and do not feel a bit more advanced than the first half hour; now if we had understood each other better, we should have things arranged by now— I have no time to lose, and I must make a decision. A door must be either open or closed. I do not understand anything between the two, and it does not really exist in fact."

So the result is that the little room at home where the mangle stands will be at my disposal to put away my things—to use as a studio too, in case this might be necessary. And they have now begun to clear out the room, which had been put off while things were still undecided.

I can tell you one thing, which I see better now than when I wrote you about Father. I am softened in my opinion, also because I seem to detect in Father proofs (and one of your hints fits in with this to a certain extent) of his really being unable to follow me when I try to explain something to him. He clings to a *part* of what I say, which becomes incorrect when one tears it from its context. This may have more than one cause, but assuredly it is largely the fault of old age. I respect old age and its weakness as *you* do, though it may not seem so to you, though you do not believe this of me. What I mean is that I shall tolerate certain things in Father which I should resent in a man with unimpaired mental powers —for the reasons mentioned.

I also thought of Michelet's saying (he learned it from a scientist), "Le mâle est très sauvage." And as I know myself to have strong passions at this period of my life—which I think it is right to have—I look upon myself as being indeed "a savage." And yet my passion abates when I stand before one who is weaker, and then I do not fight.

Although for that matter, engaging in a *verbal* dispute with a man who, mark well, occupies the position in society of a director of men's inner life is most decidedly not only permitted, but cannot possibly be cowardly. For in truth, they are each other's equals in arms. Think this over some time or other, if you will, particularly as I say that for many reasons I want to give up engaging in verbal disputes because now and then I think Father no longer possesses the full mental strength to concentrate his thoughts on one single point.

Surely in certain cases a man's age is an additional force. Getting to the heart of the matter, I now tell you that it's just because of Father's influence that you have concentrated more on commerce than was in your nature. And I believe that, however sure you may be of yourself in the matter of being and remaining a businessman, a certain something in your original nature will continue to be active, and may well react more strongly than you bargained for.

Since I know that our thoughts coincided when we were first at G. & Co.'s —that is to say, that both you and I then thought of becoming painters, but so secretly that we did not dare tell even each other—it might happen that now, in later years, we should become more united. The more so because of the circumstances and situations in the trade itself, which has already undergone a change since our early years, and which, as I see it, will change more and more.

At that time I forced myself so hard and was so much oppressed by a prejudice that I was certainly no painter that, *even* when I left Goupil, I did not settle on art, but turned to another thing (which was a second mistake added to the first), being then discouraged about its possibility because the timid, very timid advances made to a few painters were not even noticed.

What I tell you is not because I want *to force* you to think as I do—I do not want to force anybody—I only tell you in brotherly, in friendly confidence.

My views may sometimes be out of proportion, that may be, but I believe there *must* be some truth in their character, and action, and direction.

My trying to get Father to take me in again, even to have a studio here, was not done primarily out of egoism. I see in it that, though we do not understand each other in many things, there will be, either always or by fits and starts, good will between you, Father and myself. As the estrangement between us has already lasted so long, it can do no harm to try to put some weight on the other side, so that in the eyes of the world we shall not appear more divided than we really are, so that in the eyes of the world we shall not lapse into extremes.

Rappard said to me, "A man is not a lump of peat, that is to say, he cannot bear to be flung away in a loft, and to be forgotten there"—and he insisted that he thought it a great misfortune for me not to be able to live at home. Just think this over, please.

I think it has been taken rather too much for granted that I acted willfully or recklessly, well, you know it better than I do; whereas in reality I was forced to some things, and could not act differently. And the very method used to accuse me of base intentions made me very cool and rather indifferent to many people.

Brother, I repeat—reflect deeply at this time of your life, I think you will have to verify the perspective of your life all over again, and that *then your life will have a better aspect.* I do not say so as if I know it, nor do you; I say it because I begin to see more and more how terribly difficult it is to know where one is right or where one is wrong.

348

Dear Theo,   Nuenen, 20 December 1883

I received your letter today, and also one from friend Rappard in the same mail.

Let me begin by thanking you for the money.

And let me add at once that I appreciate it that both you and Rappard approve of my coming here. This gave me courage at a moment when I myself was hopelessly discouraged about my coming here, and bitterly regretted it, because on my part I perceived deep in the background of all the discussions I had with Father a je ne sais quoi of cold reticence over reconciliation, a cold evasiveness, which made me desperate because I saw that there would remain a cancerous root which would later make everything as impossible as in the past.

But your letter and a very intelligent, very kind, very cordial letter from friend Rappard, and both your opinions that my journey hither might bring about some good, have induced me not to consider the case as lost yet, but to practice patience and wisdom.

Have patience with me, brother, and do not suspect me of ill will.

As for me, in many respects I know Father very intimately and thoroughly, and in the matter we are faced with it is impossible for me to leave things as they are. I had to get Father's opinion about this and that in order to compare it with certain precedents. For instance, I directed the conversation to subjects that had nothing to do with the matter in question, and then I got enough troubles.

Do you know, your advice "do not speak to them about certain things" makes me think you refer to one particular thing, of which you take a correct view.

But in reality that question of long ago was of the utmost importance (at least to me personally, I mean)—entering upon a new future with Father is once again a highly important thing, which nobody can ask me to engage upon, leaving things as they are.

At the moment, particularly after the receipt of your letter, Father and I are on the best possible terms, and Father is not even disinclined to make certain arrangements.

Besides, I want you to know I quite agree with you that they mean well—I do not suspect them of consciously *wishing* any adversity to befall me, although at times they bring it on me, or of *intentionally* putting obstructions in my way, although occasionally I am thwarted by them ("not without good intentions," as Mauve would express it). But Father's character is highly variable and at the same time highly obstinate—(I know, most people do not know this)—Father's character is dark (rayon noir, I once reminded you), Father has a very narrow-minded or rather icy cold quality. I cannot express this, I can only feel it. I have often thought this problem over, I have paid a great deal of attention to Father, I know Father from various angles, very often I have tried to come to an agreement with Father, yet I *do not* think Father *good*. I *cannot* declare that I think Father straightforward or simple or clear-headed enough.

And now there is, and there will remain, a je ne sais quoi that worries me, and at the back of it all I am aware of the same fatal atmosphere as in the past.

I was struck by the fact, Theo, that friend Rappard *now* writes that he had perceived that during the summer of the year I stayed at Etten I changed so much (it was then that I met her). And at the same time he hints that he understands *something* happened then, *though he does not know what*. As I see it, Father and Mother and some others acted with very little delicacy at the time.

If you should be able to agree with me on that, Theo, I should like to say to you, They show the same lack of delicacy now, and you should know something of it.

So, although you need not attach much importance to some conversations with Father in the beginning, by which I only attempted to discover what Father thought of things, although all this means nothing, and at the present moment some arrangement might be made, which in many respects would make my work easier for me and give me the inner quiet to work, yet I see at the outset a je ne sais quoi, especially in Father, which fills me with anxiety, a heavy, still anxiety about the future.

Keeping the peace with Father is a hard job. Once again I understand my own rebellious attitude in the previous period. I do not say it will lead to nothing, but I point out—it will be difficult. You will point out to me what I know full well myself, that in many respects I personally am very difficult to deal with. Yes, that is true, and I must take it into account, too. There is an excuse for me, and that is the passion and the frequent absorption which everyone who paints, writes, or composes must needs have.

Does the same apply to Father? No—it is something else. If you should say, But Father is also a thinker and a writer—then I answer, I wish he were this in another way, for now I cannot call him happy. I say this more sadly than you may think; what I say is *serious*. Is it impossible for you to enter into my feelings?

I wrote you my last letter in a moment's desperation, of which the real purport was, "I *cannot* do it after all." And I thought a decisive separation from Father, irrevocable and with *éclat*, the only thing I could do. "If I do not do this, I should seem to be of one mind with a person whose principles I do not even respect, and I cannot stand the least appearance of being in agreement with him, for I am dead against him, absolutely in opposition to him."

But now today I received your letter, and at the same time a letter from Rappard, written in a tone which I can understand and appreciate. And after another discussion with Father, we have arrived at a provisional arrangement and calmness.

A calmness which perhaps is "It," but which to a far greater extent is not "It." Que faire?

I hereby declare that, for myself, I agree with Rappard when he says, "Stay at home for a *long* time"—he stresses this.

There are a lot of reasons for this, Theo. Oh, if only you could see all that I see in it—how much security it might grant us for the future!—I hope it will prove to be possible.

In Father's case there is an eternal contrast between what he says and what he does, but it took me a long time to discover it and to understand that usually Father is *not* conscious of it, so that one is often unable to decide whether he really wanted to do what he actually did. I shall tell you frankly, brother, what I think of it. Father does not always know what he *does*—though he chooses his words awfully systematically, his actions are most haphazard.

In short, *it will be a hard job* to get good results from my stay here.

However, the circumstances are such as to make it urgently necessary that an arrangement is brought about that will really be carried through.

I have proposed that the room that can most easily be spared shall be used to keep my things in, and if necessary as a studio, in case not only *I* but *you and I* think it necessary and suitable that I work at home for a time, especially when there are financial reasons to force us to it. Business is business, and it is clear enough to you as well as to me that this is a good arrangement.

I have been too long without this resting place, and I think that it must be settled in this way if we want to succeed in our enterprise.

I believe it is possible, and I shall have the courage to start it when you and I agree that we must carry it through and settle that you will not be vexed with me if, in case of some disagreement with Father, I do not take it as seriously as I did two years ago.

I will go my own way quietly and follow your advice *not* to speak with Father about several things provided only that I find in you the person to whom I *can* speak about them, and to whom I can say, I should like to do this or that, for this or that reason.

Then I *can* leave Father out of it, and *not* discuss the problems with Father. But it was necessary to break the ice, and this I did by going to Nuenen, and on that occasion I *had to* have an explanation with Father; however, *I am going to leave it at that.*

I can tell you now that I have succeeded in getting Father's permission to fix up a room here.

If you approve of it, *this will become my regular storeroom and my studio in times when we have no money to be elsewhere.* And about further arrangements and business, I will not speak first with Father but with you—and you and I together will get Father so far that things will steadily improve in the long run too.

I think you will approve of my having insisted on getting some fixed arrangement. I think it *decidedly a good thing* that I shall have a studio here (though I shall not always be in that studio).

So let's stick to that, and let this letter, and not the last one, be our starting point. Well, brother, I am only writing you on this one subject, but your letting me know what you think of the Paris trade is very important to me. *I shall let you do whatever you want to do, even in case you should turn to painting, for in the latter case I am convinced you would land on your feet.*

With a handshake,

Yours, Vincent

Yes—que faire? I tell you I do not choose to go through the same experiences as two years ago. *It does not depend on me alone* (no more than it depended *on me alone* at the time) to keep the peace. *Can, must* one keep the peace with Father?

Perhaps you do not understand this—my even saying "must," my going so far as to say that. I shall give you an example: if they should reproach you, Rappard, or me with something—*suppose undeservedly*—we should never budge, we should answer back, and we should make them feel our nails a little. But because we are what we are, we should *never* say, You must not reproach me with anything. We should say, *Reproach me as much as you like, I am a match for you.* Father sees sacrilege in observations *that are not reproaches at all,* observations that are unavoidable when discussing things. Observations that one should never avoid if they refer to things about which an understanding must be arrived at before one engages in an enterprise. Proudhon says, "La femme est la désolation du juste"—I think one can feel and understand this pronouncement, although one does not claim to be "un juste" oneself, or to be looked upon as such. Although in general a clergyman, and in particular Father, is certainly not a *woman,* there is something equally unutterably hopeless in his way of speaking and acting.

A phenomenon I have often tried to analyze, but which remains a mystery to me, for which I can give no other and no more correct definition than Hugo's words: "Il a le rayon noir," or the words of somebody else, "The gentlest of all cruel men."

I say this to explain what I think, and in order to throw light on the problem which we face. *You* will gradually have begun to understand that usually my mind is calm.

But now, what is to be done? If it were possible, it would be an excellent thing if I could get a studio at home. In Rappard's case things went marvelously well, and Rappard writes me, "I considered it *your greatest misfortune* that you could not live at home." And this is true, and I felt it terribly, not only afterward, but also at the moment, two years ago now, when I had to face it. Father did not do this intentionally—I say Father has little delicacy of feeling, and even now, although I at last told him so for the first time, Father does not yet know that it was a great difficulty for me. Father still says—and this is something so icy cold that I shudder when I think of it—Father says after two years *that in the past he acted according to his conviction and principles*. An ordinary person, you or I, if we had done something like that, we should, I believe—I hope—I trust—have already regretted it for a long, long time, whether it was our fault or not. If you say Father did not mean to do so much harm, it may be true, but what one means to do is one thing, and the result of what one does is another. However, Father's convictions are undoubtedly well-intentioned and all that—but as for myself I hope his Honor is not going to acquire new convictions of the same kind.

[Enclosed in letter 348] What Father is like you may see from what he went on to say, for instance, after stating that he could not take back anything of what he did in the past and so on, which in fact embodies a basic implacability. He immediately followed up with, "But we do not lack indulgence."

Indulgence combined with implacability.

This too is in reality a "désolation du juste."

In short, *this* is what Father is—he is "*a stupid one.*" To speak with whom is unutterably hopeless for me.

If Father were not Father, I should not worry, but can one always act as if one's father did not exist? This is impossible for me too.

But the fact is that I am not the man to swallow "indulgence" when basically I see implacability.

Every once in a while C. M. also used to trot out the word "unpardonable." And people like Father and C. M. stick to it—and act upon it year after year—save for "indulgence."

Bah, I think it's utterly disgusting. Approving of it, and entering into it—no! Then I prefer a refreshing row, and I personally will not mince words. You see what I am, brother, and think whatever you like, but never suppose that I will have anything to do with that sophism of indulgence together with implacability.

I want to be reconciled "*efficaciously*"—*effectively*, thoroughly, else I prefer an open disagreement, a conflict, in such a way that the world can perceive it—ah well....

Vivre tout haut is simply one's duty—one should not act like the Jesuits and their kind.

Vincent

358

Dear Theo,   Nuenen, 18-24 February 1884

Thanks for your letter—Mother is getting on well; at first the doctor said it would take half a year before the leg would be cured—*now* he speaks of three months—and he told Mother: "But we have your daughter to thank for this, for it is very seldom that I find such good nursing." What Wil does is exemplary, exemplary, I shall not easily forget it.

From the beginning nearly everything fell on her shoulders, and Mother was spared a lot of misery by what she did.

To mention only one thing by way of example, it is *most decidedly* owing to her that Mother is so little troubled with bedsores (which began to look very serious at first, and were really in an advanced state). And I assure you the jobs she has to do are not always pleasant.

Just listen—after having read your letter about the drawings, I at once sent you a new water color of a weaver, and five pen drawings. For my part I will also tell you frankly that I think it true what you say, that my work must become much better still, but at the same time, that your energy to sell them for me may become somewhat stronger too.

You have *never sold a single one for me*—neither for much nor for little—and in fact *you have not even tried*.

You see, I am not *angry* about it, but—we must call things by their names. In the long run, I would certainly not put up with that.

You, on your part, can also continue to speak out frankly.

As to being salable or unsalable, that is an old file, on which I do not intend to blunt my teeth. Well, you see my answer is that I send you some new ones, and I will go on doing so very willingly—I ask no better.

But I insist on your speaking out quite frankly—that is what I like best— whether you intend to interest yourself in them henceforth, or whether your dignity does not allow it. Leaving the past for what it was, I must face the future, and apart from what you think of it, I decidedly intend to try and sell them.

Not so long ago you told me yourself you are a *merchant*—all right—with a merchant one does not lapse into sentimentality, one says, Sir, if I give you a number of drawings on commission, may I then count on your showing them? The merchant should know for himself whether he would say "yes"—or "no"— to this, or something in between. But the painter would be crazy to send them on commission if he observed that the merchant considered his work something which could not bear the light of day.

Well, old fellow—we are both living in a real world, and as we do not want to put a spoke in each other's wheel, we must speak frankly. If you say, I cannot occupy myself with it—excellent—I shall not get angry—but on the other hand I am not obliged to believe you are an infallible oracle, am I? You say the public will take offense at this or that little spot, etc., etc. Now listen, this may be true, but *you* in your capacity as merchant take *even more* offense at it than the public in question—I have observed this so often—and you *start* it.

I must make my own way, Theo, and with you I am exactly as far as I was a few years ago; what you say about my work now, "it is almost salable, *but*"—*is literally the same as what you wrote me when I sent you my first Brabant sketches from Etten.*

So I repeat, that is an old file, and my conclusion is that I suppose you will always say the same thing—and that I, who was systematically wary of trying my luck with dealers up to now, will change my tactics now, and try hard to get my work sold.

By this time I understand that my doings are indifferent to you, but if *you* are indifferent, I for my part always think it rather rotten, and I look forward with pain to certain things that will hardly fail to present themselves—for instance, when they ask me, How queer, don't you do business with your brother or with Goupil? Well, in that case I shall say, "It is beneath the dignity of *ces Messieurs* G. & Co.—Van Gogh & Co." That will probably make a bad impression as far as I am concerned—something I am prepared for by this time—yet I foresee I shall get colder and colder in my feelings toward you too.

I have now painted the little old church and another weaver. Are those studies from Drenthe so very bad then? I do not feel greatly inclined to send you the painted studies from here, no, we shall just leave them where they are—you can see them when you perhaps come here in spring.

What you write about Marie is quite comprehensible—if a woman is not very milk-and-watery, I can well understand she does not feel much inclined to sit and mope in the company of an ill-natured father and of spiritual sisters besides; then at all events the temptation, for a man *as well as* for a woman, to shatter the stagnation at all cost is fairly pressing—the stagnation that begins with what may be beautiful resignation, but which one will be forced to regret in the long run, as soon as one feels one would freeze to death if it went on. Once I read something by Daudet about spiritual women—"The two faces looked at each other—they exchanged an evil, cold, secretive glance—what is the matter with her? Always the same thing." There you have that particular look of the Pharisees and devout ladies. Yes, as for *us*—what is the matter with us too is always ... *"la même chose."*

Yes—what must I conclude from what you say about my work? Let me take the studies from Drenthe, for instance—there are some that are very superficial, I said that myself; but what do you reproach me with about those that are painted simply and quietly from nature, trying *to express nothing but what I saw?* You say, "Aren't you too preoccupied with Michel?" (I am speaking now of that study of the cottage in the twilight, and of the largest of the sod huts, that is to say the one with the green plot in the foreground.) You would certainly say exactly the same of the old churchyard.

And yet neither before the churchyard nor before the sod huts did I think of Michel, I thought only of the subject I had before me. A subject which, I think, would have stopped Michel if he had passed, and would have struck him.

I do not put myself at all on the same line with Master Michel, but *imitate* Michel is what I decidedly do not do.

Well, perhaps I will try to sell something in Antwerp, and I am going to put a few of those very studies from Drenthe in a black wooden frame, which the carpenter here is making for me. I prefer to see my work in a deep black frame, and he makes them cheaply enough.

You must not take offense at my speaking about it, brother. I want something sober and characteristic in my work; I approve as little of its being neglected as I want to see my work in fluted frames, in first-class galleries.

Now my opinion is that we should start steering a middle course, and I want to know somewhat definitely what I may expect of you, or rather I tell you once again, though you are still beating about the bush, I believe that as a matter of fact you are *not* going to show it, and I do not even believe that you are going to change your mind in the near future.

I do not want to discuss whether you are right in this.

You will answer me that other dealers will treat me exactly as you do, except that you, though you cannot occupy yourself with my work, pay me money, and that other dealers certainly will not do so. And that I cannot yet live without money.

My answer is that in reality things are not so cut and dried, and I shall try to manage living from hand to mouth. I told you before that I wanted to come to some decision this month, and so I must. Because you already intend to come this spring, I do not insist on your taking a decision *immediately*, but I tell you I cannot be satisfied with things as they are now; wherever I go, especially at home, I am always watched, to see what I do with my work, if I get paid for it, etc.; in our society almost everybody is always looking out for that, and wants to know all about it.

And that is very natural. But it is very awkward for me to always be in a false position.

Allons—things cannot remain as they are now; why not?—because they can't. If my attitude toward Father—toward C. M.—is utterly cold, why should I pretend to be different where you are concerned if I should oberve the same tactics of never speaking out frankly in you? Do I count myself better than Father or you? Quite possibly not—it is quite possible that I make less and less mental distinction between good and bad, but I do know that these tactics are unacceptable to a painter, and that as a painter one must speak out frankly and cut some Gordian knots.

Well—I believe a door must be either open or shut. I think you will understand that a dealer *cannot* be neutral toward the painters; that it makes *exactly* the same impression whether you say No with or without compliments, and it is perhaps even more irritating if it is said in too complimentary a way.

This is something you will perhaps understand better later than you do now— I pity the dealers when they get old—they may have made their fortunes, but that isn't a remedy for everything—at least not then. "Tout se paye," and it very often becomes an icy cold desert for them *then*.

Well—but perhaps you think differently about this.

And then you will say that it is also rather tragic when a painter breathes his last in a hospital and is buried along with the whores in a common grave where, after all, many lie—especially if one considers that dying is perhaps not so difficult as living.

A dealer cannot be blamed for not always having money to help others, but I think he is certainly to blame when one sees that he speaks very kindly, but is ashamed of me at heart, and utterly neglects my work.

So, frankly, I shall not take it ill of you if you tell me without reserve that you do not think my work good enough, or that there are other reasons besides this for your not wanting to busy yourself with it, but it is not kind if my work is stowed away in a dark corner and you do not show it, accompanying this with the assurance—*which cannot be considered true*—that you yourself see something in it. I do not believe it—your sincerity in saying it is about nil. And from the very fact that you say you know my work better than anybody else, I can justly conclude that your opinion of it must be very low indeed if you will not soil your hands with it. Why should I obtrude myself upon you?

Now, if I only saw that, thinking me not far enough advanced, you did something to help me to make progress, for instance, now that Mauve is out of the question, to bring me into contact with some other sound painter, in short *anything*, some sign that proved to me that you really believed in my progress, or wanted to further it. But instead there is—the money, yes, but for the rest, nothing except that "just keep on working," "have patience!"

I cannot live on that, it is getting too lonesome, too cold, too empty and too dull for me.

I am no better than anybody else, and I have my needs and wishes as everybody else, and obviously one must protest when one *feels clearly* that one is kept on too tight a rein and is underrated.

If one goes from bad to worse—in my case, this would not be impossible—what does it matter after all? If one is badly off, one has to take a chance to better oneself.

Brother—I must remind you once more how I was when we first worked together. From the very first I have also drawn your attention to the question of women, I still remember seeing you off at the station at Rozendaal in the first year, and that I told you then that I hated being alone so much that I preferred being with a bad whore to being alone. Perhaps you remember that?

Except for the few years which I can hardly understand myself, when I was confused by religious ideas—a kind of mysticism—leaving that period out of it, I have always lived with a certain warmth.

Now it is getting grimmer and colder and duller around me. And when I tell you that, in the first place, I *will* not stand it, leaving the question of whether I *can* out of it, I refer to what I said at the very beginning of our relation.

What I have objected to in you during the past year is your kind of relapsing into a cold respectability, which I think sterile and useless—diametrically opposed to what is action and, in particular, what is artistic.

I tell you so because I mean it, and not in order to make you wretched, but I want you to see and if possible to feel what is wrong, what makes me no longer able to think with the same pleasure of you as a brother and a friend.

My life must become more stimulating if I want to get more *brio* into my work; I do not advance a hair's breadth by practicing patience. If on your part you relapse into the above-mentioned condition, you cannot take offense at my not being the same toward you as I was during the first year, for instance. Well, good-by.

Yours sincerely, Vincent

As to my drawings—at this moment it seems to me that the water colors, the pen-and-ink drawings of weavers, the last pen-and-ink drawings, on which I am working now, are not altogether so dull that they are quite worthless. But *if* I myself come to the conclusion that they are no good, and Theo is right not to show them to anybody—then—then it will be additional proof to me that I have reason for disapproving of our present false position, and I shall try all the more to change it—for better or worse, but not let it stay the way it is. If you write, "You remind me of the old people who say that things were better in their youth than they are now, forgetting that they themselves have changed," it would not put me out. And if you ask me in your letter how it is that you never hear me say "I wish I were like this or like that"—it is because I think that those who cry "I wish I were like this or like that" loudest, try least to reform themselves. Those who talk so much about it generally don't do it.

At first the idea that our relation would cease seemed almost unbearable to me, and I wished so ardently that we might have found some way out—but on the other hand I am not always able to make myself believe without rhyme or reason that it is possible.

The depression about it was one of the causes of my writing so positively from Drenthe, urging you to become a painter.

Which calmed down at once when I saw your dissatisfaction with business disappear when you were on a better footing with Goupil once more. At first I only half approved of it: then afterward, and even now, I find it quite natural, and consider it more a mistake on my part to have written you, Become a painter, than a mistake on your part to have resumed your business activities with gusto at the moment when they were fit for resumption and the machinations intended to make things impossible for you had ended.

But for all that I remain quite dejected by the falseness of our position. For the moment, it is of much more importance to me to earn 5 guilders than to get 10 guilders by way of protection.

Now, most decidedly it is a fact that you repeatedly wrote that, in the first place as a dealer (I leave this aside and do not take it ill of you), but in the second place also privately (which I do take ill of you a little), you did not, you do not, and in the near future you will not, exert yourself in behalf of my work.

In this I must not be spineless or an impotent dullard so, to put it bluntly, *if you do not do anything with my work, I do not cherish your protection.* I state the reason for this without reserve; and so I shall too, when I can hardly avoid giving a reason for it.

So the fact is not that I ignore the help you have given since the beginning, or wish to belittle it. Here the fact is that I expect more good from the most miserable drudgery and poverty than from protection, into which it is deteriorating.

At the very first one cannot do without it, but now in Heaven's name I must try to wriggle through—God knows how—rather than accede to something that after all would *not* get us any further.

Brotherly or not brotherly, if you can give me nothing more than financial help, you may keep that too. As things have been during this last *year*, I almost venture to say, it has been limited exclusively to money.

And it has become evident to me that—although you say you leave me absolutely free—as a matter of fact, when for instance I have some affair with a woman which you and others do not approve of, perhaps rightly so, a thing that *once in a while* I do not give a damn about, there comes such a little tug at the financial bridle in order to make me feel that it is "in my own interest" to conform to your opinion.

In the matter of that woman you also got what you wanted, but ... but I am damned if I care to receive a little bit of money if I have to practice morality in exchange.

After all, in itself I do not think it absurd of you not to approve of my insisting on going through with it last summer. But in time to come I foresee the following: Suppose I should again enter into relations with one belonging to what you call a lower station in life—then I shall meet with the same opposition if I am still involved with you.

An opposition that you might all persevere in with a semblance of fairness only if I received so much from you that I could live differently—which you do not give, cannot give, and as a matter of fact will not give, neither you, nor Father, nor C. M., nor any others who are the very first to disapprove of this or that—and which, when it comes to the point, I do not want from you, seeing that I do not give much thought to higher or lower station in life.

Do you see why it would not be a reckless act on my part if I tried it again?

Although in the first place I have no pretensions to maintain a sort of station in society, as you call it, and *do not in the least* feel the call to do so, and because in the second place I do not receive the means from anyone nor do I earn them, I count myself absolutely free to enter into relations with a so-called inferior if it should come my way.

We should be faced with the same problem forever.

Now ask yourself the question whether I am the only one among those of the same profession who most decidedly declines protection if it entails obligations to maintain a sort of social station, whereas the money obtained is below the level of making it possible, so that instead of making progress one has to run into debt. Were it possible on the money, perhaps I should no more refuse to resign myself to it than others. But we certainly have not got that far yet—you say yourself that I have a number of years to look forward to in which my work will have wretchedly little commercial value. *All right—then I would rather toil and live from hand to mouth* and *manger de la vache enragée*—which I have done before now—than fall into the hands of Messrs. Van Gogh.

I regret that I quarreled with Father at the time only to the extent that I did not do so ten years before. If you continue following in the footsteps of Father, etc., you will live to see how much you will gradually be bored—and—how you will become a bore to certain persons. But this is ill-tempered grumbling, and you will say, This carries no weight.

Just because we began as friends and with a mutual feeling of respect, I know that for myself I will not suffer it to degenerate into *protection*—I definitely refuse to become your protégé, Theo.

Why? Because I won't. And more and more it threatens to degenerate into this.

You do absolutely nothing to procure me some distraction, which I need so badly now and then—of meeting people, and seeing things.

Think it over, boy, I do not hide my deepest thoughts from you. I weigh the pros and cons on both sides.

A *wife* you cannot give me, a *child* you cannot give me, work you cannot give me. Money, yes.

But what good is it to me if I must do without the rest? Your money remains sterile because it is not used in the way I always wanted—a laborer's home if need be, but if one does not see that one gets a home of one's own, it fares badly with art.

And I for my part—I told you already plainly enough when I was younger, if I cannot get a good wife, I shall take a bad one, better a bad one than none at all.

I know enough people who assert flatly the contrary, and who are just as afraid of having "children" as I am of having "no children."

And for my part, though a thing may turn out wrong many a time, I do not easily give up a principle.

And the reason why I am little afraid of the future is that I know how and why I acted as I did.

And because I know there are more people who feel the same way I do.

You are suspicious, you say, but why, of what? And what good will it do you or me? Do you grow wiser by being suspicious?—you know the contrary is true, I hope. But then again, it is loyal of you to tell me yourself that you are suspicious, that is why I reply to it, which would otherwise have been beneath me. And my reply is very short—either toward you or toward Father or toward anybody else, I am contemplating no harm, but it is my very serious intention to consider separating from you, and looking for a new relation, precisely to prevent harm in the future.... We might collide later, as Father and I collided, and *then I could not allow myself to give in.* That is all; on the one hand my duty commands me to love my father and brother—*which I do*—but on the other hand we are living in a time of renovation and reform, and many things have totally changed, and consequently I see, I feel, I believe otherwise than Father, otherwise than you. And seeing that I try to make a distinction between the abstract ideal of good and my own imperfect ego notwithstanding, I do not come out with big words, but I simply say, The way to remain good friends is to part company. It is a hard thing for me to say—but I am at peace with it.

No doubt you understand that, although I do not see the future clearly, I am not afraid; and that I am even in a tranquil frame of mind. But for all that there is a good deal going on in my thoughts—and this is caused on the one hand by a deep feeling of obligation, which will persist; on the other hand by a feeling of disappointment, because truly I consider the reason for my career being broken in the direction in which it began—that is, with your assistance and support—so *absurd*.

But I should do wrong to go on—because *if* we went on like this, it is highly probable that in a few years' time we should most probably have a violent quarrel, which might end in hatred.

Now there is still time for me to try and find a hold elsewhere—and if I should be forced to fight it out elsewhere, at least it will not be with my brother. And this—isn't it thought out and calculated well and coolly?

I shall not get melancholy over it, believe me, but at the same time I do not act recklessly. I have found calm now that I am firmly resolved upon a separation, and I have gained the conviction that *afterward, if* we went on, we should be more of a hindrance than a help to each other.

Rappard said, Don't go to Antwerp unless you are sure you will find something there—but how can one know what one will find in advance? And if I keep my studio here as a refuge, then now is the time to start. However, this will always be possible, and therefore it is certainly not my intention to leave this region for good and all. I think you understand, Theo, that on my long rambles I have thought things over often and at length: I do not want to be mixed up in a second series of quarrels (such as I had with *Father No. I*) with *Father No. II*. *And Father No. II would be you. One is enough*—the expression is unvarnished and the center of my ideas; draw your own conclusions. Moreover, you should know that I was never aggressive in my actions toward Father, nor do I want to become aggressive toward you, my brother. I have often restrained myself, whereas if I had been dealing with other people, I should have fought in quite a different way and much more violently. But this is exactly what renders me powerless under the circumstances. I shall find a new field abroad, one where I can do whatever I take it into my head to do, as a stranger among strangers; abroad I shall have neither rights nor obligations. And I shall be able to make shorter work of people—bonne volonté d'être inoffensif, certitude de résister [good will to be inoffensive, certainty to resist] —that is my ideal, and I am seeking it with all that is in me. But taking everything lying down is something you smart for afterward—consequently action is necessary. Working here and at the same time looking for a new connection is the way to get on. Unfortunately for both of us, money is indispensable, and prospects for being able to break loose are bad. And—time is also money—and—going on in the way I do—I do not get richer. However, you know my motives—if I should go on, you would become Father No. II in my life, and although I know you mean well, you do not understand me at all, and so it is impossible to make headway.

R 43

Amice Rappard,   Nuenen, April 1884

Thanks for your letter; it gave me much pleasure. I was delighted to hear that you saw something in my drawings.

I am not going to discuss generalities about technique, but I most decidedly expect that, as I gain in what I will call expressive force, people will not say *less* frequently, but on the contrary *even more* frequently, that I have *no* technique.

Consequently, well, you see—I quite agree with you that what I am expressing in my present work will have to be expressed more *vigorously*—and I am working hard to try to gain strength in this respect—but that, *when I have gained it*, the general public will understand me better . . . no . . .

But this does not alter the fact that in my opinion the reasoning of that virtuous fellow who asked with reference to your work, "Does he paint for money?" is the reasoning of a f—— fool—as this intelligent creature evidently reckons among the axioms the maxim that originality prevents one from making money.

Passing this off as an axiom—*because* it can most decidedly *not* be proved as a *thesis*—is, as I said, one of the usual tricks of such f—— fools—those *lazy* little Jesuits.

Do you think that I do not care about technique, that I do not seek it? Most certainly I do—but only insofar as I want to say what I have to say—and if I cannot do it or cannot do it sufficiently well, I am doing my best to correct and improve myself—but I don't care a damn whether my language is in conformity with that of the grammarians. (You know that you yourself used this simile—if somebody had something useful, something true, something necessary to say, and he did it in terms that were hard to understand, would this be of any great advantage to either the speaker or to his listeners?)

I want to stick to this point for a while, especially as I have found a rather curious phenomenon in history over and over again.

Let this be distinctly understood, that it is obvious one must speak in the native language of the audience—if this audience knows only one language—and it would be absurd not to accept this as a matter of course.

But now the second part of the problem. Suppose a man has something to say, and that he speaks a language which his audience knows instinctively—then every now and then there will be the phenomenon that the *speaker of truth* has little *oratorical elegance*, and that what he says is not to the liking of the majority of his audience—nay, that he will be called a man "of slow speech and of a slow tongue," and be *despised* as such.

He may consider himself fortunate if there is *one*, or at the most a very few, who are edified by his words, because what these listeners were looking for was—not oratorical tirades—but most decidedly the true, the useful, the necessary content of his words, which enlightened them and broadened their minds, made them freer and more intelligent.

And now as regards painters—is it the purpose, the non plus ultra, of art to produce those peculiar spots of color—that capriciousness of drawing—that are called the distinction of technique? Most certainly not. Take a Corot, a Daubigny, a Dupré, a Millet or an Israëls—fellows who are undoubtedly the great leaders—well, their work is *outside the paint*; it is as different from that of the elegant fellows as an oratorical tirade by Numa Roumestan, for instance, is different from a prayer—or a good poem.

So it is *necessary* to work at the technique, as it is one's duty to express better, more accurately, more earnestly what one feels—and the less verboseness, the better. As for the rest—one need not bother about that. Why do I say this?—because I think I've noticed that you sometimes disapprove of things in your own work which are in my opinion decidedly good. In my eyes *your* technique is better than Haverman's, for instance—because already the stroke of your brush often has something personal, characteristic, accounted for and *willed*, while in Haverman's work it is an everlasting convention, reminding one always of the studio and never of nature.

For instance those sketches of yours which I saw—"The Poor Little Weaver" and the "Females of Terschelling"—they hit the core of things. Haverman makes me feel uncomfortable and bored, and little else.

I am rather afraid that you—and I congratulate you on the fact—are going to hear the same old remarks about your technique too in the future, apart from remarks on your subjects and in short everything else—even when that stroke of your brush, which already has so much character, acquires even more of it.

Nevertheless there are art lovers who sincerely appreciate things that are painted with emotion—although we are no longer living in the days of Thoré and Théophile Gautier, alas——

Just think over whether it is particularly wise to speak about technique much nowadays—but you will say that's what I am doing myself—as a matter of fact I regret it.

As for me, what I intend to do—even when I have a much more thorough command of my brush than I have now—is to tell those fellows systematically *that I cannot paint.* Do you hear?—*even when* I have achieved a manner of my own, more complete and concise than the one I have now. I thought what Herkomer said when he opened his own art school—for a number of fellows *who could already paint*—was excellent; he urgently begged his pupils to be so kind as *not* to paint the way he did himself, but according to their own selves. "What I want to do," he said, "is to set originalities free, not to recruit disciples for Herkomer's *theory*."

Entre lions on ne se singe pas (Lions don't ape each other).

Well, I have been painting quite a lot recently—a girl sitting winding bobbins for the weavers, and the separate figure of a weaver.

I am rather eager for you to see my painted studies one of these days, not because I am satisfied with them, but because I believe they will convince you that I am most certainly training my hand, and that, when I say I attach comparatively little importance to technique, I don't say it because I want to avoid taking pains or grappling with difficulties—for this is hardly my method.

Moreover, I want very much for you to get acquainted someday with this corner of Brabant—in my opinion much more beautiful than the Breda district. Right now it is really marvelous.

There is a village here called "Zon en Breugel" which is amazingly like Courrières, where the Bretons live—but the figures are even more beautiful over there. As one's love for the form increases, one may happen to come to hate "the Dutch Costumes," as they are called on the books of photographs which are sold to foreigners.

Rappard, I dislike writing or speaking about *technique* in general—although I may be eager to discuss the manner of executing some idea of mine either with you or with somebody else, and I never make light of the practical usefulness of such discussions. But the latter does not invalidate my first thought—which perhaps I did not formulate accurately. This thought—I cannot find the correct words for it—is based, not on something negative, but on something positive... the positive consciousness of the fact that art is something greater and higher than our own adroitness or accomplishments or knowledge; that art is something which, although produced by human hands, is not created by these hands alone, but something which wells up from a deeper source in our souls; and that with regard to adroitness and technical skill in art I see something that reminds me of what in religion may be called self-righteousness.

My sympathies in the literary as well as in the artistic fields are most strongly attracted to those artists in whom I see the working of the soul predominating. For instance, Israëls is clever as a technician, but so is Vollon; I prefer Israëls to Vollon, however, because I see something more in Israëls's work, something quite different from the masterly reproduction of the materials, something quite different from the light and brown, something quite different from the color—and yet this "something quite different" is brought about by the exact rendering of the light effects, the materials, the color. Eliot has this particular "something different," which I see so much more in Israëls's work than in Vollon's, to a high degree, and so does Dickens.

Is this because of the choice of subjects? *No!* for this too is only a *result*.

And what I want to say, among other things, is this—that Eliot is masterly in her execution, but quite apart from this there is a genius-like quality about which I should like to say, Perhaps one improves when one reads those books—or, These books possess an awakening power.

Without meaning to I am writing a lot about exhibitions; in reality I pay blessed little attention to them. Now that I find myself thinking about them quite accidentally, I observe my own thoughts with a certain astonishment. I should not express them completely enough if I did not add that there is something so thoroughly honest and good in some pictures that something good is bound to emanate from them, whatever is done with them—whether they fall into good or bad, into honest or dishonest hands. "Let your light shine before men" is something that I think is the duty of every painter; but it is not an inevitable conclusion, I should say, that this letting one's light shine before men *must* be brought about by means of exhibitions. Let me tell you that I desire *more* and *better* opportunities than exhibitions to bring art to the people, seeing that instead of hiding my candle under a bed I want to put it in a candlestick. Well, enough of this.

The other day I reread *Felix Holt, the Radical* by Eliot. This book has been very well translated into Dutch. I hope you know it; but if you don't, try to get it somewhere. There are certain conceptions of life in it that I think are excellent —deep things, said in a guilelessly humorous way; the book is written with great vigor, and various scenes are described in the same way Frank Hol or someone like him would draw them. The conception and the outlook are similar. There aren't many writers who are as thoroughly sincere and good as Eliot. This book *The Radical* is not so well known in Holland as het *Adam Bede*, for instance, and her *Scenes of Clerical Life* are not so well known either—which is regrettable in the same way that it is regrettable that not everybody knows Israëls's work.

I am sending you a little booklet about Corot. I think that if you don't know it you will read it with great pleasure; it contains some accurate biographical details. I have seen the exhibition for which this little book is the catalogue.

What I think remarkable is the long time it took this man to achieve inner security and to ripen. Do pay special attention to what he did at different ages. I have seen things among his first works which were the result of years of study—and in the real sense of the term as pure as gold, thoroughly sound—but how people must have despised them! Corot's studies were a lesson for me when I saw them; I was already struck then by the difference between these studies and those of many other landscapists.

If I did not see more technique in your little "Village Churchyard" than in Corot's studies, I should draw a comparison between them. The sentiment is identical—an earnest endeavor to give only the intimate and the essential.

What I am saying in this letter amounts to this. Let us try to master the mysteries of technique to such an extent that people are deceived by it and will swear by all that is holy that we have *no* technique. Let our work be so savant that it seems naïve and does not stink of our sapience.

I do *not* believe that *I* have reached this point, which I so much desire, nor do I believe that even you, who are more advanced than I, have reached it yet. I hope you will see something more than trivial faultfinding in this letter.

I believe that the more one has intercourse with nature itself—the more deeply one penetrates her—the less one finds any attraction in the tricks of the studio, and yet I want to give them all the credit they deserve and to *see* others paint; actually I myself often feel the urge to visit studios.

> Niet in boeken heb ik het gevonden
> En van "geleerden"—och, weinig geleerd.
> [Not in books have I found it
> And of the "learned"—ah, learned but little.]

says De Genestet, as you know. We might make a variation of it by saying,

> Niet in 't atelier heb ik het gevonden
> En van de schilders ⎱ och, weinig geleerd.
>   de kenners ⎰
> [Not in the studio have I found it
> And of the painters ⎱ ah, learned but little.]
>   the connoisseurs ⎰

Perhaps you are shocked that I indiscriminately put in "painters" and "connoisseurs."

But to talk of something else—it is damned difficult not to feel anything, not to undergo some influence when those f—— fools say, "Does he paint for money?" I hear this drivel every blessed day, and one gets annoyed with oneself later for having been worried by it. This is how matters stand with me—and I imagine it must be pretty much the same with you. It's true one doesn't give a damn, but it makes one nervous all the same—just as if one heard someone sing out of tune, or *as if one were pursued by a malevolent barrel organ.* Don't you think that barrel organ mean, particularly as it seems to have singled you out especially?

Wherever you go you hear the same old tune.

Oh, as for me—I am going to do as I tell you now when people say such-and-such a thing to me—I am going to finish their sentence for them before they have had their say—the same way I treat a person who I know is in the habit of giving me a finger instead of frankly shaking hands (I played that trick on a venerable colleague of my father's yesterday), for then I myself also have a single finger ready with which to touch his very carefully, with a perfectly straight face, when we "shake hands"—in such a manner that the man can find nothing wrong with it, although he damn well feels that I'm making a fool of him in return.

The other day I put a fellow into a very nasty mood with a similar trick. Does one lose anything by that?—no, for by God such fellows hinder and do not help— and when I write you about certain expressions of yours, I do so only to ask you, Are you quite convinced of the good faith of those who are forever extolling technique to the skies?

I ask you this *exactly because I know it is your aim to avoid "studio elegance."*

361

Dear Theo,   Nuenen, 22-26 February 1884

I just received your letter. As your letter crossed one of mine, written in the same tone as the one you answered today, you will see that I am speaking in a different mood than the rash one which you suppose. Just because I say what I have to say quietly, be it not in the tone which is used every day (it is a serious question here), I cannot avail myself of your kindness in considering it said "in haste."

That very idea of yours (that I should have spoken in haste, and rashly) is sufficient proof to me that we have come to a point where more words won't do any good, and I think it better to let this question rest.

You say, you *must* speak about the financial side. So must I.

Brother, know it well, I repeat what I said before about your noble help without any alteration—and that "money *can* be repaid, but not kindness such as yours."

But this is what I want, and what you yourself will call reasonable. I must take such measures as are necessary to have freedom in disposing of what I receive.

I mean that I can only accept *such* money as I can spend as I like, without having to ask anybody's opinion.

I would rather have 100 francs a month and the free use of it, than 200 francs without that freedom.

If we were more of one mind in our way of looking at things, I should think an agreement like the one between you and me up to now by far the best.

But because of too great a difference in our ways of looking at things, because of our understanding each other too little, an agreement like the one between you and me is neither tenable nor sensible.

Supposing that your character *as well as* mine wants to avoid disorderliness or outbreaks of violence after all; we must part company quietly and collectedly—but decisively, in such a way that neither you nor I can be reproached with foolishness or recklessness.

I should like to receive the usual amount until March. That will enable me to pay everything I have to pay, and to lay up a supply of necessary things. This is the first measure to be taken.

Last year, the year '83, was a hard, sad year for me, and the end especially was bitterly, bitterly sad.

Well, we will not speak of that any more.

After March we shall both be free. But if you could pay Father some allowance for a time, as I do not want to be too great a burden to him, that will be wise and well, I think.

However, this must be between Father and you. If necessary, I shall then try and get a job. I do not even care what kind. But bear in mind that, realizing the fact that obviously we could not agree sufficiently if we continued together, I am absolutely serious about trying not to accept favors from you in the form of money any longer if they should not leave me quite free in my concept of life.

You will say that you leave me free, yes—but there is a certain restraint after all. And I prefer to have *less* from somebody else, when *after all I am not free in things that are nobody's business but my own.*

You must not infer from this that I want to have done with you, on the contrary—you are an art dealer, very well, when I make something which you think salable, I should prefer to sell it to you rather than to somebody else, but it must be an arrangement which does not put me in a false position; but in point of fact what I want is to *sell* in the literal sense.

I thank you for your letter, I appreciate many things in it. Good-by, and believe me,

Yours sincerely, Vincent

371

Dear Theo,   Nuenen, June 1884

I think I already told you in my last letter that I also wanted to start a large man's figure besides that woman spinning. Enclosed you will now find a sketch of it. Perhaps you remember two studies of the same nook, which I already had in the studio when you were here.

I have read *Les Maîtres d'Autrefois* [The Masters of the Past] by Fromentin with great pleasure. And that book frequently deals with the same questions which have greatly preoccupied me of late, and which, in fact, I am continually thinking of, especially because when I was last in The Hague I heard things Israëls had said about starting with a deep color scheme, thus making even relatively dark colors seem light. In short, to express light by opposing it to black. I already know what you're going to say about "too black," but at the same time I am not quite convinced yet that a gray sky, for instance, *must* always be painted in the local tone. Mauve does it, but Ruysdael does not, Dupré does not. Corot and Daubigny???

Well, it is the same with figure painting as it is with landscape. I mean Israëls paints a white wall quite differently from Regnault or Fortuny.

And consequently, the figure stands out quite differently against it.

When I hear you mention so many new names, it is not always easy for me to understand because I have seen absolutely *nothing* of them. And from what you told me about "impressionism," I have indeed concluded that it is different from what I thought, but it's not quite clear to me what it really is.

But for my part, I find Israëls, for instance, so enormously great that I am little curious about or desirous for other or newer things.

Fromentin says of Ruysdael that at present they are *much further* advanced in technique than he was, also much more advanced than Cabat, who sometimes greatly resembles Ruysdael in his stately simplicity, for instance in the picture at the Luxembourg.

But has what Ruysdael, what Cabat, said become untrue or superfluous for that reason? No, it's the same with Israëls, with De Groux too (De Groux was very simple).

But if one says what one has to say *clearly*, strictly speaking, isn't that enough? And it may become more pleasant to hear if it is said with more charm, something I do not disdain, yet it does not add very much to the beauty of what is true, because truth has a beauty of its own.

The measurements of the foregoing sketch are about 105 × 95 c.m., and that of the little woman spinning, 100 × 75. They are painted in a tone of bister and bitumen, which, in my opinion, are well suited to expressing the *warm* chiaroscuro of a close, dusty interior. Artz would certainly find it too dingy.

It has already annoyed me *for a long time*, Theo, that some of the present-day painters rob us of the bister and the bitumen, with which surely so many splendid things have been painted, and which, well applied, make the coloring ripe and mellow and generous, and at the same time are so distinguished and possess such very remarkable and peculiar qualities.

But at the same time they require some effort in learning to use them, for they must be used differently from the ordinary colors, and I think it quite possible that many are discouraged by the experiments one must make first and which, of course, do not succeed on the very first day one begins to use them. It is now just about a *year ago* that I began to use them, chiefly for interiors; at first I was awfully disappointed in them, but I could not forget the beautiful things I had seen made with them.

You have better opportunities than I to hear about art books. If you come across good books, such as that book of Fromentin's on the Dutch painters, for instance, or if you remember any, don't forget I should be *very glad* if you bought some—provided they treat *technical* matters—and if you deducted the money from my usual allowance. I certainly intend to study theory seriously, I do not think it at all useless, and I believe that what one feels by instinct or by intuition often becomes definite and clear if one is guided in one's efforts by some really practical words.

Even if there might be just *one* or *very few* things of that kind in a book, it is sometimes worth while not only to read it but even to buy it, particularly now.

And then in the time of Thoré and Blanc there were people who wrote things which, alas, are already being forgotten.

To give you an example.

Do you know what *"un ton entier"* and *"un ton rompu"* is? Of course you can *see* it in a picture, but can you also explain what you see? What is meant by *rompre*? Such things one ought to know theoretically also, either practically as a painter, or in discussing color as a connoisseur.

Most people give it *whatever meaning* they like, and yet these words, for instance, have a very definite significance.

The *laws* of the colors are unutterably beautiful, just because they are *not accidental*. In the same way that people nowadays no longer believe in fantastic *miracles*, no longer believe in a God who capriciously and despotically flies from one thing to another, but begin to feel more respect and admiration for and faith in nature—in the same way, and for the same reasons, I think that in art, the old-fashioned idea of innate genius, inspiration, etc., I do not say must be put aside, but thoroughly reconsidered, verified—and greatly modified. However, I do not deny the existence of genius, or even its being innate. But I certainly do deny the inference that theory and instruction should, as a matter of course, always be useless.

The same thing which I applied in the woman spinning and the old man spooling yarn, I hope, or rather I shall try, to do much *better* later on.

But in these two studies from life *I have been a little more myself* than I succeeded in being in most of the other studies—except perhaps in some of my drawings.

With regard to black—*accidentally* I did not use it in these studies, as I needed, among other things, some stronger effects than black; and indigo with terra sienna, Prussian blue with burnt sienna, really give much deeper tones than pure black itself. When I hear people say "there is no black in nature," I sometimes think, There is no real black in colors either.

However, you must beware of falling into the error of thinking that the colorists do not use black, for of course as soon as an element of blue, red, or yellow is mixed with black, it becomes a gray, namely, a dark, reddish, yellowish, or bluish gray. I found very interesting, for instance, what Ch. Blanc says about Velasquez' technique in *Les Artistes de mon temps;* his shadows and half-tones consist mostly of *colorless, cool grays,* the chief elements of which are black and a little white. In these neutral, colorless mediums, the least cloud or shade of red has an immediate effect.

Well, good-by, do write soon if you have anything to tell me.

It sometimes surprises me that you do not feel *as much* for Jules Dupré as I should like you to do.

I am firmly convinced that, if I again saw what I saw of his work in the past, far from thinking it less beautiful, I should think it *even more beautiful* than I always instinctively did. Dupré is *perhaps* even more of a colorist than Corot and Daubigny, though these two are that too, and Daubigny especially is very *daring* in this color. But in Dupré's color there is something of a splendid sym-

phony, *complete*, *studied*, *manly*. I imagine Beethoven must be something like that....
That symphony is *enormously* calculated, and yet simple, and infinitely deep as
nature itself. That is what I think of Dupré.

Well, good-by, with a handshake,

Yours sincerely, Vincent

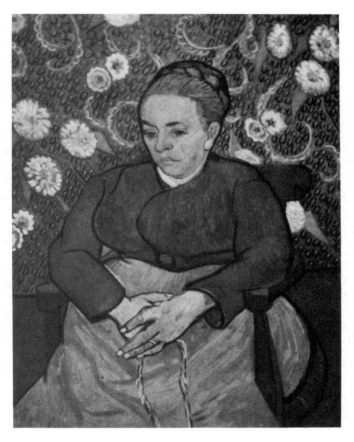

La Berceuse (Mme. Roulin), oil, 1888

378

Dear Theo, Nuenen, October 1884

Thanks for your letter, thanks for the enclosure. Now just listen. What you say
is all very well, and as to a scandal, I am now somewhat better prepared to meet
it than I used to be.

No fear of Father and Mother leaving, for instance.

Now there are people who say to me, "Why did you meddle with *her*," that's one fact. Now there are people who say to her, "Why did you meddle with *him*," that's another fact.

Both she and I have sorrow enough, and worries enough, but neither of us feels regret. Look here, I certainly believe, or know for sure, that she loves me. I certainly believe, or know for sure, that I love her, I have been sincere.

Was it foolish, etc.? Perhaps so, *if you like*, but aren't the *wise* people who never do a foolish thing more foolish in my eyes than I am in theirs?

That's my answer to your argument and to other people's arguments.

I say all this simply *to explain*, not in anger or in spite.

You say that you like *Octave Mouret*, you say, You are like him; since last year I have also read the second volume, in which he pleases me much better than in the first.

Recently I heard somebody say that *Au Bonheur des dames* would not greatly enhance Zola's reputation. I find the *greatest* and *best* things in it.

I have looked it up again, and I copy for you some sayings of Octave Mouret's.

You—*of late*, this past year and a half, haven't you developed in *Bourdoncle's direction?* You should have stuck to Mouret, that was and still is my opinion. But for the enormous difference in circumstances, yes, direct difference in circumstances, I incline, however, more toward Mouret's direction *than you may* think in the matter of my belief in women, and that one needs them, must love them. Mouret says, "*chez nous on aime la clientèle.*"

Please think this over, and remember my regret at your saying that you had "cooled down."

I repeat more emphatically than ever all that I said by way of bitter warning against the influence of what I called Guizot-esqueness. Why? Because it leads to mediocrity. And I do not want to see you among the mediocrities, because I loved you too much for that, and I still love you too much for that—I cannot endure to see you congeal. I know it is difficult. I am aware that I know too little about you—I know that perhaps I am mistaken. Never mind In any case just read your Mouret over again.

I spoke of the difference and *yet* the similarity between Mouret and what I should want. Look here, Mouret worships the modern Parisian woman, all right.

But Millet, Breton, worship the peasant woman *with the same passion.*

Those two passions are one and the same.

Read Zola's description of a room with women in the twilight, women often already over thirty, up to fifty, such a dim, mysterious corner.

I think it splendid, yes, *sublime.*

But to me, Millet's "Angelus" is just as sublime, *that* same twilight, that same infinite emotion, or that single figure of Breton's in the Luxembourg or his "Source."

You will say that I have no success—I don't care to conquer or to be conquered, in any case one has emotion and action, and that is more the same thing than it appears, or is said.

It remains a mystery to me how it must end with *this* woman in question, but neither she nor I will do *foolish* things.

I am afraid that the old bigotry will *again* benumb and freeze her with that damned icy coldness which *one already*, in the distant past, almost *killed* her, many years ago. Oh, I am no friend of the present Christianity, though its *Founder* was sublime; the present Christianity I know only too well. That icy coldness hypnotized even me in my youth, but I have taken my revenge since— how? by worshiping the love which they, the theologicans, call *sin*, by respecting a whore, etc., and *not* respecting many would-be respectable pious ladies.

For one group *woman* is always heresy and devilish. To me it is just the reverse. Good-by,

Yours sincerely, Vincent

This is from *Octave Mouret*:
Mouret says:
"Si tu te crois fort, parce que tu refuses d'être bête et de souffrir! Eh bien, alors tu n'es qu'une dupe, pas davantage."

"Tu t'amuses?"
Mouret ne parut pas comprendre tout de suite, mais lorsqu'il se fut rappelé leurs conversations anciennes sur la bêtise vide et l'inutile torture de la vie, il répondit:
"Sans doute, jamais je n'ai tant vécu... Ah! mon vieux, ne te moques pas! Ce sont les heures les plus courtes où l'on meurt de souffrance."

"Je la veux, je l'aurai... et, *si* elle m'échappe tu verras les choses que je ferai pour m'en guérir. Tu n'entends pas cette langue, mon vieux; autrement tu saurais que l'action contient en elle sa récompense; agir, créer, se battre contre les faits, les *vaincre* ou *être vaincu par eux*, toute la joie et toute la santé humaines sont *là*!" "Simple façon de s'étourdir," murmura l'autre. "Eh bien, j'aime mieux m'étourdir, crever pour crever, *je préfère crever de passion, que de crever d'ennui.*"

["If you think yourself strong, because you refuse to be stupid and to suffer! Well, then you are only a dupe, and nothing more."
"You amuse yourself?"
Mouret did not seem to understand at once, but when he remembered their earlier talks about the empty stupidity and the useless torture of life, he replied:
"Undoubtedly I have never lived so intensely... Ah! old fellow, don't scoff! The hours when one dies of suffering are shortest."

"I want her, I will have her... and, *if* she escapes me, you will see the things I'll do to cure myself of it. You don't understand this language, old fellow; otherwise you would know that action contains its own reward; to act, to create, to fight against facts, to *vanquish* them or *be vanquished by them*, the whole human joy and health are *there*!" "A simple way to stupefy oneself," muttered the other.

"Well, I prefer stupefying myself, to perish in order to perish, *I would rather die of passion than die of boredom.*"]

It is not only I who say this in spite of difficulties, but she also, that is why I saw something grand in her from the very beginning; but it is a confounded pity for her that in her youth she let herself be crushed by disappointments, crushed in the sense that the orthodox religious family *thought they had to suppress* the *active*, aye, *brilliant* quality in her, and have made her utterly passive.

If only they hadn't broken her *in her youth*! or if only they had stopped at that, and *five or six or more women, fighting against her alone*, had not driven her to distraction!

Just read in L'Evangéliste *by Daudet about those women's intrigues; they were different here*, yet of such a kind.

Oh, Theo, why should I change myself? I used to be very passive and very soft-hearted and quiet; I'm not any more, but it's true, I am no longer a child now that I sometimes feel my ego.

Take Mauve, why is he quick-tempered and *far from meek* at times? I have not got as far as he, but I too shall get further than I am now.

I tell you, if one wants to be active, one must not be afraid of failures, one must not be afraid of making some mistakes. Many people think that they will become good by *doing no harm*; that's a lie, and you yourself used to call it a lie.

It leads to stagnation, to mediocrity.

Just dash something down when you see a blank canvas staring you in the face with a certain imbecility.

You do not know how paralyzing that staring of a blank canvas is; it says to the painter, *You can't do anything.* The canvas stares at you like an idiot, and it hypnotizes some painters, so that they themselves become idiots. Many painters are afraid of the blank canvas, but the blank canvas is afraid of the really passionate painter who is daring—and who has once and for all broken that spell of "you cannot."

Life itself is also forever turning toward a man an infinitely vacant, discouraging, hopeless, blank side on which nothing is written, no more than on a blank canvas. But however vacant and vain and *dead* life may present itself, the man of faith, of energy, of warmth, and who knows something, does not let himself be led astray by it. He steps in and acts and builds up, in short he *breaks—ruins* they call it.

Let them talk, those cold theologians. Theo, I feel such damned pity for this woman, just because her age, and perhaps a disease of the liver and gallbladder menace her so terribly. And the emotions have aggravated this. But we shall see what can be done or what fatally cannot; however, I shall not do anything without a very good physician, so I shall do her no harm.

For the very reason that I foresee that, *if* our roads should lead us to one and the same spot, we might disagree to a rather large degree—for this reason I do not want you to be able to reproach me with anything, and at the same time be dependent on you.

I am still of two minds about what I shall try to do, but after all I shall most probably not stay here, but the question remains where I shall eventually go. I do not think you will appreciate my coming to Paris, but what can I do about that? You damn well refuse to look after my interests—all right, but on my part I cannot possibly leave things as they are. If you had written less positively that it was beneath you, it would never have occurred to me—but now, well, now I cannot pay attention to what you say any longer.

In short, I do not intend to exchange the *chance* (although it be no more than a *chance*) of pulling through on my own for the certainty of a protection that is a bit stifling after all.

Since I see that I am losing my chance of selling by continuing to take the money from you, we must separate.

Don't you think it quite understandable that, when I hear you say it will be impossible for you to do anything with my work during the next few years, I get a sort of feeling that if you persist in pretending to be so high and mighty in this respect, it is rather in contradiction with its invariably appearing to be impossible, when—because I cannot possibly sell anything, however hard I work—I am forced to say, Theo, I am 25 guilders short, can't you see your way to letting me have a little extra?

That is very inconsistent of you—for when one sends you anything, or begs, Do try and find an opening for me with one of the illustrated papers, so that I can earn something—one does not hear a single word in reply and *you do not lift a finger*.

But one is not allowed to say, I can't make both ends meet.

And as things have been up to now, don't let's talk about it—but it won't do to go on like this.

And I want to add that I am not going to ask you whether you approve or disapprove of anything I do or won't do, I shall not stand on ceremony. If I should feel like going to Paris, for instance, I should not ask you whether you like it or not.

381
Dear Theo,   Nuenen, October 1884
Here are two photographs of the weavers—next week I hope to send you two more sketches for Hermans' decorations.

You know well enough that your criticism of this past year and a half only seems like some kind of vitriol to me. But never suppose I don't know it is possible to protect oneself from such vitriol by a sort of leather which it cannot pierce so easily, and that as soon as one's hide is tanned so as to keep it out, it does not matter so much—so—what do I care?

Apart from this I believe you mean well. So what more do you want?

But I declare that it is not in the least *my* fault if the money you give me yields such a poor interest, not only to you, but also a poor interest to me. The former—that it yields a poor interest to you—grieves me more than the latter, its yielding a poor interest to me too.

Things may improve, you will say—yes, but in that case not only I but you too would have to change a good deal.

I just want to tell you that this winter, perhaps next month, I intend to leave here for a time; I have thought of Antwerp—I have thought of The Hague.

But during the last few days I have thought of something that is perhaps even better. In the first place I now want at all events some city life, some change of surroundings, having been either in Drenthe or in Nuenen for a full year or more. And I believe this will be a good distraction for me, for my spirits in general, which have not been and could not be as cheerful as I should like, especially recently.

Look here now, the sculptor Stracké lives in Bois-le-Duc; at the same time he is director of the drawing academy there. I saw a terre cuite by a pupil of his, and heard on that occasion that Stracké is not at all unkind or indifferent to anyone who practices art in this vicinity. That at Bois-le-Duc he has several models for the academy, and that there are people to whom he affords the opportunity to draw from the nude or to model in clay.

Probably, however, one would have to *pay the model* oneself, but that is not so very expensive, and then one has a spacious room for which one doesn't pay *anything*. I am going to see for myself how things are, and then it is not impossible that, just as Breitner, for instance, went to Cormon, I shall go to Stracké. It is in the neighborhood, and would be the cheapest thing too.

I have bought a very beautiful book on anatomy, *Anatomy for Artists* by John Marshall. It was in fact very expensive, but it will be of use to me all my life, for it is very good. I have also what they use at l'Ecole des Beaux-Arts, and what they use in Antwerp.

But such things make great holes in my pocket. I tell you this only to make you understand that my not paying Father and Mother for my board while I stay here is not because I do not *want* to pay, but because I have had many expenses which I for my part don't consider superfluous.

The key to *many* things is the thorough knowledge of the human body, but it costs money to learn it. Besides, I am quite sure that *color*, that *chiaroscuro*, that *perspective*, that *tone* and that *drawing*, in short, everything has fixed laws which one must and can study, like chemistry or algebra. This is *far from being* the easiest view of things, and one who says, "Oh, one must know it all instinctively," takes it very easy indeed. *If* that were enough! But it isn't enough, for even if one knows ever so much *by instinct*, that is just the reason to try ever so hard to pass from *instinct* to *reason*. That's what I think.

You must not imagine that I have earned anything by doing that work for Hermans; the first day I got two bills for the stretchers, canvases and a number of tubes, amounting to *more* than I had received from him to pay for them. I told him that I did not want these bills to remain unpaid, and asked him if he wanted to have them put in his name or if he would pay me something in advance. Oh no, he said, *let it wait, they need not be paid at once.*

I said, *Yes, they must be paid at once.* Then he gave me 25 guilders.

Then came all my other expenses for models, not counting my time, work, etc.; but since then I have not seen any of his money, *nor have I asked for it.* On the contrary, because my work pleased him from first to last, I consider myself already sufficiently paid, if need be. Besides, the pictures remain my property, and I must judge for myself what I am willing to lay out for them. But enough of this, since those stretchers, canvases, etc., I have had at least 20 guilders' worth of expenses, perhaps even more, and have not even got them back. But the man is satisfied and pleased with me. Is it then good policy to ask for money? One must be very careful in this, in my opinion, *just when people are satisfied, one must lower the price rather than raise it*. Especially when, after all, the sum is not so considerable that receiving it or not makes that much difference. If I succeed, it will perhaps be for the very reason that I work more cheaply than others, and make it easy for the art lovers.

As to Hermans, *he is very good*, and a man to remain on good terms with, and he is certainly rich, but—has always been stingy rather than generous. Quite different from a real miser, *but after all, I am earning less, much less than nothing*.

But notwithstanding this, I for my part have been very kind and obliging to him. I find in him a very pleasant, jovial *friend*, and it is really touching to see how a man of sixty tries hard to learn to paint with the same youthful enthusiasm as if he were twenty.

What he makes is not beautiful, but he works hard, and has already copied four of my six compositions, in quite a different sentiment, and it has something medieval, something like Peasant Breughel.

You once told me that I should always be isolated; I don't believe it, you are decidedly mistaken in my character there.

And I do not at all intend to think and live less passionately than I do. By no means—I may meet with rebuffs, I may often be mistaken—often be wrong—but that only as far as it goes—basically I am not wrong.

Neither the best pictures nor the best people have no faults or partis pris.

And I repeat, though these times may seem tame, they aren't really. I also positively deny that my assertion of certain parties still being as strongly opposed to each other in '84 as in '48 should be *exaggerated*. It is *something quite different* from that ditch of yours, I assure you—I am speaking of the parties now, rather than of you and me in particular, but you and I also belong *somewhere*, don't we? standing either on the right or on the left, whether we are *conscious* of it or not.

I for my part have at all events a parti pris if you like, and if you think you, for your part, can manage to stand neither on the right nor on the left, I take the liberty of doubting most strongly its feasibility. And especially the practical use.

I have had a fairly good letter from Utrecht, she has recovered enough to go to The Hague for a time. But I am still far from easy about her. The tone of her letters is much more self-confident, much more correct, and less prejudiced than when I first knew her. At the same time, something like the wail of a bird whose nest has been robbed; she is feeling perhaps less indignant than I toward society, but she too sees in it "the boys that rob the nests," who do it for fun and laugh about it.

But now there is a piece of news, that the pastor at Helvoirt has died, so that there is now a vacancy in that parish. I think it probable that they want to get

Father back there, at least that the family at Helvoirt is going to sound Father out on the subject. But seeing that it was only the day before yesterday that the dear reverend gentleman over yonder dropped dead, I do not know in the least whether they are going to call Father or not. However I think it highly probable.

Father is not going to accept the call, this much is certain.

As to what I call barricade and you call ditch, it can't be helped, but there is an old civilization that, in my opinion, is declining through its own fault—there is a new civilization that has been born, and is growing, and will grow more.

In short, there are *revolutionary* and *anti-revolutionary* principles.

Now I ask you whether you yourself have not often noticed that the policy of wavering between the old and the new isn't tenable? Just think this over. Sooner or later it ends with one's standing frankly either on the right or on the left.

It is no ditch. And I repeat, then it was '48, now it is '84; then there was a barricade of paving stones—now it is not of stones, but all the same a barricade as to the incompatibility of old and new—oh, it certainly is there in '84 as well as in '48. Good-by,

Yours sincerely, Vincent

386*a*

Dear Theo,   Nuenen, 9 December 1884

One cannot always find the right words to speak absolutely straightforwardly—but I am so firmly resolved to speak my mind to *you* without reserve—I don't give a damn whether you are suspicious or not—that after some consideration I have now perhaps found clearer words for the feelings I want to express.

I believe that it is in *our mutual interest* that we separate.

Your position—isn't this true?—does not admit of our associating with each other intimately, frequently, cordially. Your position—to mention only one thing by way of example—would not admit of my going to live at your house in Paris, let's say, either with the intention of studying or for financial reasons, however necessary and useful it might be, and might become more and more, if circumstances permitted. For—against my person, my manners, clothes, words, you, like so many others, seem to think it necessary to raise so many objections —weighty enough and at the same time obviously without redress—that they have caused our personal, brotherly intercourse to wither and die off gradually in the course of the years. To this must be added my past, and that at Goupil & Co.'s you are quite the plush gentleman, and I am a black sheep and an ill-natured fellow. Enough—this is how things are—aren't they?—and as here it is a question of analyzing, of manfully facing a situation, I suppose you are not going to contradict me in this matter.

Only—but I do not mention this by way of reproach—the moment is not opportune for this—it is past—I just mention it for clarity's sake—only I had thought that you had attached some value to our not drifting *too far* apart—that by your being on the qui vive in this field, by executing some adroit maneuvers, you might have been able to find a more satisfactory solution for this ticklish problem. For instance, in such a way that I could have got I don't say on friendly terms, but at least into touch with Tersteeg and Mauve again, and so on. But—a struggle is going on in your mind about this, which you prefer not to be reminded of. So as to the point in question, you don't even dream of doing it, and you don't think it nice of me to take the liberty of referring to it. In any case you think me foolish in these things, and you won't touch them with a barge pole.

This is the dark side of your character—I think you are mean in this respect—but the bright side of your character is your reliability in money matters.

Ergo conclusion—I acknowledge being under an obligation to you with the greatest pleasure. Only—lacking relations with you, with Tersteeg, or with whomever I knew in the past—I want *something else* by way of compensation.

For—personally I have to think of my future—I want to get on. If a hussy won't have me, it's all right with me; I can hardly take it ill of her—but nothing is more certain than that I shall try to find compensation elsewhere. And the same is true of other relations. I shall not obtrude myself upon *you*, neither shall I *force* you to be affectionate toward me—but—as a friend—let alone as a brother —you are too cool for my taste. Not as to money, old fellow; I am not speaking of that. But personally you aren't of the slightest use to me, nor am I to you. And it is possible, and it ought to be, that we should mean more to each other personally.

Well, we won't quarrel over it—things have their periods—the period of quarreling is over—the period of parting follows, I think. But remember that there are fellows who most certainly love you, and whom you *ought not* to be suspicious of, whose sympathy becomes *powerless* because of your distrusting them too much, whereas you would do better if you strengthened a man's self-confidence. So much for that.

I do not think it impossible that Marie—you know whom I mean, the one you helped when she was sick—notwithstanding full appreciation of your character and assistance, must have felt something of what I feel. Instinctively I dare suppose it.

Now I will take the liberty to say *one* thing—*we shall separate*—for me this is a precarious transition—and one coupled with financial difficulties that will certainly be a great worry to me. However, I shall try to see things through—but I most decidedly demand of you that at this moment, which is critical for me, you on your part will be very frank. *I know that you will agree to our separation*—for the very reason that it will be settled peacefully.

Tell me without reserve whether you approve of Antwerp—including my retaining my studio here in the country, which is too cheap to let go, and which for that matter I cannot do without as a storeroom and a refuge if necessary.

And, if it is not asking too much, help me to see things through—financial embarrassment in this period, toward the end of the year, is always worse for me. I should wish the period of the transition to be short if possible, because it is torture to feel that one thing is disappearing and you haven't got the other. I cannot help thinking of the reason for Marie and you parting company. I don't know any details, do I?—but you did not think she was a good woman. Maybe you are right, but it may also be that you did *not understand* her. And as for me, it is quite possible that similarly I am not a good man—this may well be—but in my case too, are you sure that you understand and feel the right way? I neither can nor will be the judge of this.

In Proudhon you may read "la femme est la désolation du juste"—but isn't it possible to answer this with, *The just is the desolation of woman?* Quite possible.

And ditto ditto one might say, "*The artist is the desolation of the financier,*" and *conversely,* "*The financier is the desolation of the artist.*"

You see—I do not know the *final solution* myself—but I see two sides to one and the same problem.

So you know my irrevocable intentions—for both our sakes I hope the time of transition will be short, and—*because I know you agree to a separation*—how can we act most quickly and satisfactorily?

With a handshake,

Ever yours, Vincent

388*b*

Dear Theo,   Nuenen, February 1885

I've a good deal to say about your calling my last letter "particularly unpleasant."

In the first place this—some time ago you wrote me quite a number of unpleasant things which I have been hearing from you and others for over fifteen years now—and that's a long time—about domestic relations here.

And especially added to this "that you are suspicious." If it had only been the former, it is probable that I should have paid no more attention to it.

But your additional remark about your suspiciousness was a bit too much for me, and I have repeatedly begged you to withdraw the word or to explain it, for I will not tolerate such a thing being said to me without my asking for an explanation.

In my last letter I compared suspiciousness in general to looking through black glasses.

And I said the ugliest misunderstandings were caused by it.

And this is true.

If you on your part *turn this inside out* now, and write me, "You make me think of old people who are always saying that in their young days everything was better, meanwhile forgetting that they themselves have changed," this does not stagger me in the least.

The thing we were discussing was suspiciousness, *which was not mentioned by me but by yourself,* i.e. on your part with regard to *me*; first apply what you say about old people to this, and after that see whether it may apply to me. If it *does* apply to me after that—then I shall have to reform.

As to what I wrote about a certain atmosphere at home, which I have more opportunity to observe than I care for, I am much afraid it is only too true.

As in your letter you ask me how it is that you no longer hear me say, "I should like to be like this or like that"—*the fact is* that in my opinion those who proclaim most loudly that they "want to be like this or like that" are the ones who try least to improve themselves.

As a rule those who say it don't do it.

If I should want to utter some such wish, I should hardly do it in the atmosphere of our present relations.

So *this* is the cause—and seeing that I strenuously exert myself to improve my work, there is no need for me to be forever lapsing into wishful exclamations. I am sorry you did not send *L'Illustration*, for I have followed Renouard's work pretty regularly, and for many years I have saved up what he did for *L'Illustration*. And this is one of the most splendid, which I think would delight you too.

When one orders the old *Illustrations* in the bookshops, at least here, one does not get them. I do wish you could get it for me. If it is too much trouble for you, then forget it, but heaven knows it is not so much trouble after all.

And—après tout—please note that with regard to that suspiciousness, and what I wrote you by way of rejoinder, this was not done so much because I won't suffer you and others to think whatever they like of me, but I cautioned you that it would give you little satisfaction if your character congealed in that mold.

Considering that you say repeatedly that you know me better than others do, and that it still all ends in suspicion, then it is serious enough for me to protest against it, to protest firstly against that "knowing me so well," and secondly against "being suspicious." I went through such an affair with Father—I decline to start all over again with Father No. II.

If I had resisted Father from the start instead of remaining silent, nothing much would have happened.

So don't resent my telling you unreservedly what I think of it. That is better for both of us. And for the rest, old fellow, I think I am working a bit too hard to doubt that it will not be long before I shall be able somewhat to lighten the financial burden I am imposing on you. Maybe it will take longer than I think agreeable, to you as well as to me, but plodding on is a way that will not lead to complete failure.

And if I insist on taking vigorous measures, it is to obviate the possibility of quarreling. For the *possibility* of a quarrel is gone at the very moment I find the means to cover my financial needs. Then my work will no longer be at issue, and now it is.

Therefore don't despair. But now it's wretched for both of us.*

Thanks for the remittance.

Good-by.

Ever yours, Vincent

* And to me my work is valuable; I must paint a lot, and therefore I am continually in want of models, which—at a time when my work is difficult and exhausting—is an additional reason for thinking it rather dismal to get suspicions in exchange. Never mind, it is a period I have to go through, and one does not paint in order to have an easy time of it.

393

Dear Theo,   Nuenen, January 1885

You would greatly oblige me by trying to get for me:

Illustration No. 2174, 24 October 1884.

It is already an old issue, but you will probably be able to get it at the office. There is a drawing by Paul Renouard in it, a strike of weavers at Lyons. Also one from a series of Opera sketches (of which he has also published etchings) —called "Le Harpiste," which I like very much.

Then just recently he also did "Le Monde Judiciaire," which I got from Rappard; you probably know it from the *Paris Illustré* by Damas.

But I think the drawing of the weavers the most beautiful of all; there is so much life and depth in it that I think this drawing might hold its own beside Millet, Daumier, Lepage.

When I think how he rose to such a height by working from nature from the very beginning, without imitating others, and yet is in harmony with the very clever people, even in technique, though from the very first he had his own style, I find him proof again that by truly following nature the work improves every year.

And every day I am more convinced that people who do not first wrestle with nature *never* succeed.

I think that if one has tried to follow the great masters attentively, one finds them all back at certain moments, deep in reality, I mean one will see their so-called *creations* in reality if one has similar eyes, a similar sentiment, as they had. And I do believe that if the critics and connoisseurs were better acquainted with nature, their judgment would be more correct than it is now, when the routine is to live only among pictures, and to compare them mutually. Which of course, as one side of the question, is good in itself, but lacks a solid foundation if one begins to forget nature and looks only superficially. Can't you understand that I am perhaps not wrong in this, and to say what I mean even more clearly, isn't it a pity that you, for instance, seldom or hardly ever go into those cottages, or associate with those people, or see that sentiment in the landscape, which is painted in the pictures you like best? I do not say that you *can* do this in your position, just because one must look much and long at nature before one becomes convinced that the most touching things the great masters have painted still originate in life and reality itself. A basis of sound poetry, which exists eternally as a fact, and can be found if one digs and seeks deeply enough.

"Ce qui ne passe pas dans ce qui passe," it exists.

And what Michelangelo said in a splendid metaphor, I think Millet has said without metaphor, and Millet can perhaps best teach us to see, and get "a faith." When I do better work later on, I certainly shall not work *differently* than now, I mean it will be the same apple, only riper; I shall not change my mind about what I have thought from the beginning. And that's the reason why I say for my part, If I am no good now, I won't be any good later on either; but if later on, then now too. For corn is corn, though city people may take it for grass at first, and also vice versa.

In any case, whether people approve or do not approve of what I do and how

I do it, I personally know no other way than to wrestle with nature long enough for her to tell me her secret.

I am working at various heads and hands all the time.

I have also drawn some again, perhaps you would find something in them, perhaps not, I can't help it. I repeat, I know no other way.

But I can't understand that you say, Perhaps later on we shall admire even the things done now.

If I were you, I should have so much self-confidence and independent opinion that I should know whether I could see *now* what there is in a thing or not.

Well, you must know those things for yourself.

Though the month is not quite over, my purse is quite empty. I am working on as hard as I can, and I for my part think that I shall keep a straight course by constantly studying the model.

I wish you could send me the money a few days before the first for the same reason that the end of the month is always hard, because the work brings such heavy expenses, and I don't sell any of it. But this will not go on forever, for I work too hard and too much not to succeed eventually at least in defraying my expenses without being in a dependent position. For the rest, nature outside and the interiors of the cottages are splendid in tone and sentiment just now; I try hard not to lose time.

Good-by,

Ever yours, Vincent

394

Dear Theo,   Nuenen, February 1885

Many thanks for the *Illustrations* you sent, I am much obliged to you. I think all the various drawings by Renouard beautiful and I did not know one of them.

However—this is not to give you extra trouble, but because I wrote things about them which perhaps cannot quite be applied to other drawings of his—the real Renouard composition I meant is not among them, perhaps that issue is sold out. The breadth of the figure in it was superb, it was an old man and some women and a child, I believe, sitting idle in a weaver's cottage where the looms stood still.

I had not yet seen *anything* in reproduction from the Salon of '84, and now I at least got some idea of a few interesting pictures from the Salon number. For instance of that composition by Puvis de Chavannes.

I imagine that the Harpignies with the setting sun must have been splendid. And the pictures by Feyen-Perrin which they give sketches of.

I was also struck by the figure of a girl by Emile Levy, "Japonaise," and the picture by Beyle, "Brûleuses de Varech" [Women burning seaweed], and the one by Cottin, "L'Eté," three figures of nude women.

I am very busy painting those heads. I paint in the daytime and draw in the evening. In this way I have already painted at least some thirty and drawn as many.

With the result that I see a chance of doing it even better before long, I hope.

I think that *it will help me for the figure in general.* Today I had one white and black against the flesh color.

And I am also looking for blue all the time. Here the peasants' figures are as a rule blue. That blue in the ripe corn or against the withered leaves of a beech hedge—so that the faded shades of darker and lighter blue are emphasized and made to speak by contrast with the golden tones of reddish-brown—is very beautiful and has struck me here from the very first. The people here instinctively wear the most beautiful blue that I have ever seen.

It is coarse linen which they weave themselves, warp black, woof blue, the result of which is a black and blue striped pattern. When this fades and becomes somewhat discolored by wind and weather, it is an infinitely quiet, delicate tone that particularly brings out the flesh colors.

Well, blue enough to react to all colors in which hidden orange elements are to be found, and discolored enough not to jar.

But this is a question of color, and what matters more to me at the point I'm at now is the question of form. I think the best way to express form is with an almost monochrome coloring, the tones of which differ principally in intensity and in value. For instance "La Source" by Jules Breton was painted almost in one color. But one really ought to study each color separately in connection with its contrast before one can be positively sure of being harmonious.

When there was snow, I also painted a few studies of our garden. The landscape has changed much since then; now we have splendid evening skies of lilac with gold over dark silhouettes of cottages between the masses of ruddy-colored brushwood—above which rise the spare black poplars, while the foregrounds are of a faded and bleached green, varied by strips of black earth and pale, withered rushes along the ditch edges.

I certainly see all this too—I think it just as superb as anybody else, but I am even more interested in the proportion of a figure, the division of the oval of the head, and I cannot master the rest before I have a better grip on the figure.

Well—first comes the figure; I personally cannot understand the rest without it, and it is the figure that creates the atmosphere. I can understand, however, that there are people, like Daubigny and Harpignies and Ruysdael and so many others, who are absolutely and irresistibly carried away by the landscape itself; their work satisfies us fully because they themselves were satisfied with sky and earth and a pool of water and a shrub.

But I think it a mighty clever saying of Israëls', when he remarked of a Dupré, It is just like "a picture of the figure."

Good-by and many thanks again for the *Illustrations.*

Ever yours, Vincent

399

Dear Theo, Nuenen, April 1885

I have wondered a little at not having heard from you yet. You will say that you have been too busy to think of it, and of course I understand this.

It is late in the evening, but I want to tell you once more how sincerely I hope that in the future our correspondence will become somewhat more animated than it has been of late.

Enclosed you will find two scratches of a few studies I made, while at the same time I am again working on those peasants around the dish of potatoes. I have just come home from this cottage and have been working at it by lamplight, though I began it by daylight this time.

This is what the composition looks like.

I painted it on a rather large canvas, and as the sketch is now, I think there is some life in it.

Yet I am sure C. M., for instance, would find fault with the drawing, etc. Do you know what a positive argument against that is? That the beautiful effects of light in nature demand a very quick hand in drawing.

Now I know quite well that the great masters, especially in the period of their ripest experience, knew both how to be elaborate in the finishing and at the same time to keep a thing full of life. But certainly that will be beyond my power for the present. At the point I am now, however, I see a chance of giving a true impression of what I see.

Not always literally exact, or rather never exact, for one sees nature through one's own temperament.

The advice I want to give, you know, is the following: Don't let the time slip by; help me to work as much as possible, and from now on keep all the studies together.

I do not like to sign any of them yet, for I do not want them to circulate as pictures, which one would have to buy up again later when one had some reputation. But it will be a good thing if you show them, for you will see that someday we shall find somebody who wants to do the same thing I propose to you now, namely make a collection of studies.

I intend to go out regularly every morning and to attack the very first thing I see people do, either in the field or at home, which in fact I am already doing now.

You are looking for new ideas for the art trade; the idea of being *kind* to the art lovers is not new, but it is one that *never gets old*.

Like that of guaranteeing a purchase. And I ask you, isn't it better for an art lover to possess from one painter, for instance, twenty quite different sketches at the same price which he in all fairness would have to pay for *one* finished picture which, as a salable article, had its value on the market? If I were in your place, as you know so many young painters who haven't a reputation yet, I would try to bring *painted studies* on the market, not as pictures, but mounted in some way on gilt Bristol, for instance, or black, or deep red.

Just now I mentioned giving a guarantee.

Not *all* painters make a lot of studies—but many do, and especially the young ones must do so as much as possible, mustn't they? He who possesses a painter's studies may always be sure (at least it seems that way to me) that there is a bond between the painter and himself which cannot easily be broken at a whim.

There are people, as you know, who support painters during the time when they do not yet earn anything, very well!

But how often doesn't it happen that it ends miserably, wretchedly, for both parties, partly because the protector is annoyed about the money, which is or at least seems quite thrown away, whereas, on the other hand, the painter feels entitled to more confidence, more patience and interest than is given him? But in most cases the misunderstandings arise from carelessness on both sides.

I hope this will not be the case between us.

And I hope that by and by my studies will give you some new courage. Neither you nor I are contemporaries of that race which Gigoux, in that book you sent me, rightly calls "Les vaillants."

But it seems to me right after all to keep the enthusiasm of those days in the present time, for it is often true that fortune favors the bold, and whatever may be true about fortune or "la joie(?) de vivre," as it is called, one must work and dare if one really wants to live.

I repeat, let us paint as much as we can and be productive, *and, with all our faults and qualities, be ourselves;* I say *us*, because the money from you, which I know costs you trouble enough to get for me, gives you the right, if there is some good in my work, to consider half of it your own creation.

Try to speak to somebody at *Le Chat Noir* and ask them if they want a sketch of those potato eaters, and if so, of what size, for it's all the same to me. Good-by, with a handshake,

Ever yours, Vincent

402

Dear Theo, Nuenen, April 1885

By the same mail you will receive a number of copies of the lithograph. Please give Mr. Portier as many as he wants. And I enclose a letter for him, which I am afraid you will think rather long, and consequently, unbusinesslike. But I thought that what I had to say couldn't be expressed more concisely and that the main thing is to give him arguments for his own instinctive feelings. And in fact, I also say to you what I write to him.

There is a school—I believe—of impressionists. But I know very little about it. But I do know who the original and most important masters are, around whom—as around an axis—the landscape and peasant painters will revolve. Delacroix, Corot, Millet and the rest. That is my own opinion, not properly formulated.

I mean there are (rather than persons) rules or principles or fundamental truths for *drawing* as well as for *color*, which *one proves to fall back on* when one finds out an actual truth.

In drawing, for instance—that question of drawing the figure starting with the circle—that is to say, using the elliptical planes as a foundation. A thing which the ancient Greeks already knew, and which will remain valid till the end of the world. As to color, those everlasting problems, for instance, that first question Corot addressed to Français when Français (who already had a reputation) asked Corot (who then had nothing but a negative or rather bad reputation) when he

(F.) came to Corot, to get some information: "Qu'est-ce que c'est un ton rompu? Qu'est-ce que c'est un ton neutre?"

Which can be shown better on the palette than expressed in words.

So what I want to tell Portier in this letter is my firm belief in Eugène Delacroix and the people of that time.

And at the same time, as the picture I am working on is different from lamplight scenes by Dou or Van Schendel, it is perhaps not superfluous to point out that one of the most beautiful things this country's painters have done is to paint *darkness* which nevertheless has *light* in it. Well, just read my letter and you will see that it is not unintelligible, and that it treats of a subject that just occurred to me while painting.

I hope to have some luck with that picture of the potato eaters.

I am also working on a red sunset.

One must be master of so many things to paint rural life. But on the other hand, I don't know anything at which one works with so much calmness, in the sense of serenity, however much one may be worried by material things.

I am rather worried just now about the moving; it's no easy job, on the contrary. But it had to happen sometime—if not now, then later—and the fact is that in the long run it is better to have a place of one's own.

To change the subject. How striking that saying about Millet's figures is: *"Son paysan semble peint avec la terre qu'il ensemence!"* [His peasant seems to be painted with the earth he is sowing!] How exact and how true. And how important it is to know how to mix on the palette those colors which have no name and yet are the real foundation of everything. Perhaps, I daresay *positively*, the questions of *color*, and more precisely of broken and neutral colors, will preoccupy you anew. Art dealers speak so vaguely and arbitrarily about it, I think. In fact, painters do too. Last week I saw at an acquaintance's a decidedly clever, realistic study of an old woman's head by somebody who is directly, or indirectly, a pupil of The Hague School. But in drawing, as well as in color, there was a certain hesitation, a certain narrow-mindedness—much greater, in my opinion, than one sees in an old Blommers or Mauve or Maris. And this symptom threatens to become more and more widespread. If one takes realism in the sense of *literal* truth, namely *exact* drawing and local color. There are other things than that. Well, good-by, with a handshake,

Ever yours, Vincent

404

Dear Theo,   Nuenen, 30 April '85

On your birthday I am sending you my best wishes for good health and serenity. I should have liked to send you the picture of the potato eaters on that day, but though it is getting on well, it is not quite finished yet.

Though the ultimate picture will have been painted in a relatively short time and for the greater part from memory, it has taken a whole winter of painting studies of heads and hands.

And as to those few days in which I have painted it now, it has been a real battle, but one for which I feel great enthusiasm. Although I was repeatedly afraid I should never pull it off. But painting is also "agir-créer."

When the weavers weave that cloth, which I think is called Cheviot, or also the peculiar Scottish plaids, then you know their aim is, for the Cheviot, to get special broken colors and grays, and for the multicolored checkered cloth, to make the most vivid colors balance each other so that, instead of the issue being crude, the *effet produit* of the pattern is harmonious at a distance.

A gray woven from red, blue, yellow, dirty white and black threads, a blue that is *broken* by a green, and orange-red, or yellow, thread, are quite different from *plain colors*, that is to say they are more iridescent, and primary colors become *hard*, cold and *dead* in comparison. But for the weaver, or rather the designer of the pattern or the combination of colors, it is not always easy to determine his estimation of the number of threads and their direction, no more than it is easy to blend the strokes of the brush into a harmonious whole.

If you could compare the first painted studies I made on my arrival here at Nuenen and the picture I'm now working on, I think you would see that things are getting a little more lively as to color.

I believe that the question of the analysis of colors will preoccupy you too someday, for as a connoisseur and expert, I think one must also have *a fixed opinion*, and possess certain *convictions*.

At least for one's own pleasure, and in order *to substantiate one's opinion*, and one must also be able to explain it in a few words to others who sometimes ask a person like you for information when they wish to know something more about art.

I have still something to say about Portier—of course I am not at all indifferent to his private opinion, and I highly appreciate his saying that he did not retract anything of what he had said.

Neither do I mind its appearing that he had not hung those first *studies*. But if I send a picture intended for him if he likes, *he can only get it on condition that he will show it.*

As to the potato eaters, it is a picture that will show well in gold, I am sure of that, but it would show as well on a wall, papered in the deep color of ripe corn.

It simply cannot be seen without such a setting.

It does not show up well against a dark background, and not at all against a dull background. That's because it gives a glimpse of a very gray interior. In reality too it stands in a gold frame, as it were, because the hearth and the glow of the fire on the white wall would be nearer to the spectator, now they are outside the picture, but in reality they throw the whole thing into perspective.

I repeat, it must be shut off by framing it in something of a deep gold or brass color.

If you yourself want to see it as it must be seen, don't forget this, please. This putting it next to a gold tone gives, at the same time, a brightness *to spots where you would not expect it*, and takes away the marbled aspect it gets when unfortunately placed against a dull or black background. The shadows are painted in blue, and a gold color puts life into this.

Yesterday I brought it to a friend of mine in Eindhoven who has taken up painting. After three days or so, I shall go and wash it there with the white of an egg, and finish some details.

The man, who himself is trying very hard to learn to paint, and to get a good palette, was very much pleased with it. He had already seen the study after which I had made the lithograph, and said he hadn't thought I could carry both the drawing and the color to such a pitch. As he paints from the model too, he also knows what is in a peasant's head or fist; and about the hands, he said that he himself had now got quite a different notion of how to paint them.

I have tried to emphasize that those people, eating their potatoes in the lamp-light, have dug the earth with those very hands they put in the dish, and so it speaks of *manual labor*, and how they have honestly earned their food.

I have wanted to give the impression of a way of life quite different from that of us civilized people. Therefore I am not at all anxious for everyone to like it or to admire it at once.

All winter long I have had the threads of this tissue in my hands, and have searched for the ultimate pattern; and though it has become a tissue of rough, coarse aspect, nevertheless the threads have been chosen carefully and according to certain rules. And it might prove to be a real *peasant picture*. *I know it is.* But he who prefers to see the peasants in their Sunday-best may do as he likes. I personally am convinced I get better results by painting them in their roughness than by giving them a conventional charm.

I think a peasant girl is more beautiful than a lady, in her dusty, patched blue skirt and bodice, which get the most delicate hues from weather, wind and sun. But if she puts on a lady's dress, she loses her peculiar charm. A peasant is more real in his fustian clothes in the fields than when he goes to church on Sunday in a kind of dress coat.

In the same way it would be wrong, I think, to give a peasant picture a certain conventional smoothness. If a peasant picture smells of bacon, smoke, potato steam—all right, that's not unhealthy; if a stable smells of dung—all right, that belongs to a stable; if the field has an odor of ripe corn or potatoes or of guano or manure—that's healthy, especially for city people.

Such pictures may *teach* them something. But to be perfumed is not what a peasant picture needs.

I wonder whether you will find something in it which pleases you? I hope so. I am glad that just now when Mr. Portier has said he is going to take up my work I, for my part, have something more important than just studies. As to Durand Ruel, though he did not think the drawings worth while, do show him this picture; he may sneer at it all right, but show it to him anyway, so that he may see there is some energy in our work. But you will hear: "*Quelle croûte.*" You may be sure of that; I am. Yet we must continue to give something *real* and *honest*.

Painting peasant life is a serious thing, and I should reproach myself if I did not try to make pictures which will rouse serious thoughts in those who think seriously about art and about life.

Millet, De Groux, so many others have given an example of character, and of not minding criticisms such as nasty, coarse, dirty, stinking, etc., etc., so it would be a shame to waver.

No, one must paint the peasants as being one of them, as feeling, thinking as they do.

Because one cannot help being the way one is.

I often think how the peasants form a world apart, in many respects so much better than the civilized world. Not in every respect, for what do they know about art and many other things?

I still have a few smaller studies, but you will understand that the large one has preoccupied me so much that I have been able to do very little else. As soon as it is quite finished and dry, I shall send you the picture in a box, and add a few smaller ones.

I think it will be well not to wait long before sending it, therefore I shall do so; probably the second lithograph will not be ready then, but I understand that, for instance, Mr. Portier must be somewhat strengthened in his opinion, so that we can firmly count on him as a friend. I sincerely hope this will succeed. I have been so absorbed in the picture that I literally almost forget my moving, which has to be looked to after all.

My cares will not become less, but the lives of all painters of that kind are so full of them that I should not wish to have an easier time of it than they. And seeing that they made their pictures in spite of everything, material difficulties will worry me, it is true, but, in short, they will not crush me or make me slacken.

I think the potato eaters will get finished after all; the last days are almost dangerous for a picture, as you know, because when it isn't quite dry, one cannot work on it with a large brush without a great risk of spoiling it. And the changes must be made quietly and calmly with a small brush. Therefore I have simply taken it to my friend and told him to take care that I do not spoil it in that way and that I come to his house to give those finishing touches. You will see it has originality.

Good-by, I'm sorry it was not ready by today; once more I wish you health and serenity. Believe me, with a handshake,

Ever yours, Vincent

Today I am still working on some smaller studies, which are to be sent at the same time.

Did you send that copy of the Salon edition?

413

Dear Theo,   Nuenen, June 1885
Thanks for your letter and the enclosure. It was just what I wanted, and helped me to work as hard at the end of the month as I did in the beginning.

I am very glad to hear that Serret is a painter, about whom you had already written things which I perfectly remember, but the name had escaped me. I should like to write you much more than I am going to in this letter, but lately when I come home, I don't feel like writing after I've been sitting in the sun all day.

As to what Serret says, I quite agree with him—I am just dropping him a line because I should like to be friends with him. As I already told you, recently I have been very busy drawing figures; I will send them especially for Serret's sake to show him that I am far from indifferent to the unity and the form of a figure.

Do you ever see Wallis, is that water color of the auction perhaps something for him? If it were something for Wisselingh, *he* would be the one to take it. I once gave a few heads to Wisselingh, and recently sent him that lithograph. But as he did not answer a single word, I think if I sent him something again, I should get nothing but an insult.

It just happened to me that Van Rappard, with whom I have been friends for years, after keeping silent for about three months, wrote me a letter, so haughty and so full of insults and so clearly written after he had been in The Hague that I am almost sure I have forever lost him as a friend.

Just because I tried it first at The Hague, *i.e.* in my own country, I have the full right and cause to forget all those worries and to try something outside my own country.

You know Wallis well; perhaps you can broach the subject apropos of that water color, but do what you think best. If I could earn something with my work, if we had some firm ground—no matter how little—under our feet for our daily existence, and if in your case then the desire to become an artist took the form of, let me say, Hennebeau in *Germinal*, apart from difference in age, etc.—what pictures you could make then! The future is always different from what one expects, so one never can be sure. The drawback to painting is that, even if one does not sell one's pictures, one still needs money for colors and models in order to make progress. And that drawback is a bad thing. But for the rest, painting and, in my opinion, especially painting rural life gives serenity, though one may have all kinds of superficial worries and miseries. I mean painting is a *home*, and one does not have that homesickness, that peculiar feeling Hennebeau had.

That passage I copied for you lately struck me particularly, because at the time I had almost literally the same longing to be something like a grassmower or a navvy. And I was sick of the *boredom* of civilization. It *is* better, one *is* happier, if one carries it out—literally though—at least one feels one is really alive. And it is a good thing to be deep in the snow in winter; in autumn, deep in the yellow leaves; in summer, amid the ripe corn; in spring, in the grass; it is a good thing to be always with the mowers and the peasant girls, with a big sky overhead in summer, by the fireside in winter, and to feel that it has always been so and always will be.

One may sleep on straw, eat black bread; well, one will only be the healthier for it.

I should like to write more, but I repeat, I am not in a mood for writing, and I also wanted to enclose a note for Serret, which you must read too, because in it I write about what I want to send before long, especially as I want to show Serret my finished figure studies. Good-by,

Ever yours, Vincent

Serret may agree with you that painting good pictures and selling them are two separate things. But it is not at all true. When the public at last saw Millet, all his work together, then the public was enthusiastic, both in Paris and London. And who were the persons who had kept him in the shade and refused Millet? The art dealers, the so-called *experts*.

418

Dear Theo,   Nuenen, July 1885

I wish the four pictures I wrote about were gone.

If I keep them here long, I might paint them over again, and I think it would be better if you got them just as they came from the heath.

The reason I do not send them is that I don't want to send them collect at a moment when you yourself are pinched perhaps, and yet I cannot pay the carriage myself.

I have never seen the little house in which Millet lived, but I imagine that those four little human nests are of the same kind.

One is the residence of a gentleman who is known by the name of the "mourning peasant"; the other is inhabited by a "good woman" who, when I came there, did nothing more mysterious than turn over her potato pit, but she must also be able to do witchcraft—at any rate she bears the name of "the witch's head."

You remember in Gigoux's book how it happened that 17 of Delacroix's pictures were refused at the same time. One sees from this—at least I do—that he and others of that period—placed before connoisseurs and non-connoisseurs, whom none of them either understood or would buy—one sees from this that those who in the book are rightly called "the valiant," did not call it a hopeless struggle, but went on painting. What I wanted to tell you once more is that if we take that story about Delacroix as a starting point, we still have to paint a lot.

I am forced to be the most disagreeable of all persons, namely I have to ask for money. And as I do not think that, as to selling, things will immediately take a turn for the better, this is bad enough. But I ask you, isn't it better after all for both of us to work hard, though it will bring difficulties, than to sit and philosophize at a time like this?

I do not know the future, Theo, but I do know the eternal law that everything changes; go back ten years, and things were different, the conditions, the mood of the people, well, everything. And ten years from now things will have changed again, I am sure.

But the thing one does remains, and one does not easily regret having done a thing. The more active one is, the better, and I would rather have a failure than sit and do nothing.

Whether Portier may or may not be the man to do something with my work, we want him now at any rate. And this is what I believe. After having worked for a year or so, we shall have a larger collection than now, and I know for sure that my work will show better the more I complete it. People who now have some sympathy for it, who speak of it as he does and show it, are useful because after my having worked, for instance, another year, they will have collected a few things that will speak for themselves, even if they were totally silent about them. If you happen to see Portier, tell him that, far from giving it up, I intend to send him much more. You must also continue to show the things if you meet likely people.

It won't be so very long before the things we can show will become more important. You will notice yourself, and it is a fact which pleases me enormously, that more and more they begin to arrange exhibitions of one person, or of a very few who belong together.

This is something in the art world which I am sure contains more promise for the future than any other undertaking. It is a good thing they begin to understand that a Bougereau does not show off well next to a Jacque, a figure by Beyle or Lhermitte does not do beside a Schelfhout or Koekkoek. Disperse the drawings of Raffaelli and judge for yourself whether it would be possible to get a good idea of that original artist.

He—Raffaelli—is different from Régamey, but I think he is as striking a personality.

If I kept my work here, I think I should go on repainting it.

When I send it to you and to Portier just as it comes out of the open air or out of the cottages, now and then there will be one among them which is no good; but things will be kept together which would not improve if they were often repainted.

Now if you have these four canvases and a few smaller studies of cottages besides, and somebody saw no other work of mine but these, he would of course think that I painted nothing but cottages. And it would be the same for the series of heads. But rural life includes so many different things that when Millet speaks of "travailler comme *plusieurs* nègres," this really must be the case if one wants to complete the thing.

One may laugh at Courbet's saying, "Peindre des anges, qui est-ce qui a vu des anges?" [Painting angels, whoever has seen angels?] But I should like to add, for instance, "Des justices au harem, qui est-ce qui a vu des justices au harem.[1] Des combats de taureaux, qui est-ce qui en a vu?" [Justice in the harem, who has seen justice in the harem? Who has seen bullfights?]. And so many other Moorish, Spanish things, Cardinals, and then all those historical paintings that they keep on painting and painting, by yards and yards. What is the use of it and why do they do it? After a few years it generally gets musty and dull, and becomes less and less interesting.

Well! Perhaps they are well painted, they may be; nowadays when critics stand before a picture, like the one by Benjamin Constant, like a reception at the Cardinal's by I don't know what Spaniard, it is the custom to speak with a philosophical air about "clever technique." But as soon as those very same critics would come before a picture of rural life, or before a drawing by, for instance, Raffaelli, they would criticize the technique with the selfsame air.

You think perhaps I am wrong in finding fault with this, but it strikes me that all those outlandish pictures are painted *in the studio.*

Picture by Benjamin Constant.

But just go and paint out-of-doors on the spot itself! then all kinds of things happen; for instance, I had to wipe off at least a hundred or more flies from the four paintings you will receive, not counting the dust and sand, not counting that when one carries them across the heath and through the hedges for several hours, some thorns will scratch them, etc. Not counting that when one arrives on the heath after some hours' walk in this weather, one is tired and exhausted from the heat. Not counting that the figures do not stand still like professional models, and that the effects one wants to catch change with the progressing day.

I don't know how it is with you, but as for myself, the more I work in it, the more I get absorbed in rural life. And I begin to care less and less either for those Cabanel-like things among which I also include Jacquet and the present-day Benjamin Constant, or the so highly praised but so inexpressibly dry technique of the Italians and Spaniards. Imagiers! I often think of that phrase of Jacque's. Yet I have no *parti pris*, I feel for Raffaelli who paints quite other things than peasants, I feel for Alfred Stevens, for Tissot, to mention something quite different from peasants; I feel for a beautiful portrait.

Though in my opinion he makes colossal blunders in his judgment of pictures, Zola says a beautiful thing about art in general in *Mes Haines*, "dans le tableau (l'œuvre d'art) je cherche, j'aime l'homme—l'artiste" [in the picture (work of art) I seek, I love the man—the artist].

Look here, I think this perfectly true; I ask you what kind of a man, what kind of a prophet, or philosopher, observer, what kind of a human character is there behind certain paintings, the technique of which is praised?—in fact, often *nothing*. But a Raffaelli is a personality, Lhermitte is a personality, and before many pictures by almost unknown artists, one feels that they are made with a *will*, with *feeling*, with passion and love. The technique of a painting from rural life or—like Raffaelli—from the heart of the city workmen—brings difficulties quite different from those of the smooth painting and pose of a Jacquet or Benjamin Constant. It means living in those cottages day by day, being in the fields like the peasants, in summer in the heat of the sun, in winter suffering from snow and frost; not indoors but outside, and not during a walk, but day after day like the peasants themselves.

And I ask you if one considers these things, am I then so far wrong when I find fault with the criticism of those critics who, these days more than ever, talk humbug about this so *often* misused word, technique (its significance is getting more and more conventional). Considering all the trouble and drudgery needed to paint the "rouwboerke"[1] and his cottage, I dare maintain that this is a longer and more tiring journey than many painters of exotic subjects (maybe "La Justice au Harem," or "Reception at a Cardinal's") make for their most exquisitely eccentric subjects. For in Paris any kind of Arabic or Spanish or Moorish models is to be had provided only that one pays for them. But he who paints, like Raffaelli, the ragpickers of Paris in their *own quarter* has far more difficulties, and his work is more serious.

[1] "Mourning peasant."

Nothing seems simpler than painting peasants, ragpickers and laborers of all kinds, but —no subjects in painting are so difficult as these commonplace figures!

As far as I know there isn't a single academy where one learns to draw and paint a digger, a sower, a woman putting the kettle over the fire or a seamstress. But in every city of some importance there is an academy with a choice of models for historical, Arabic, Louis XV, in short, *all really nonexistent figures.*

When I send you and Serret some studies of diggers or peasant women weeding, gleaning, etc., *as the beginning* of a whole series of all kinds of labor in the fields, then it may be that either you or Serret will discover faults in them which will be useful for me to know, and which I may even admit myself.

But I want to point out something which is perhaps worth while. All academic figures are put together in the same way and, let's say, *on ne peut mieux.* Irreproachable, *faultless.* You will guess what I am driving at, they do not reveal anything new.

This is not true of the figures of a Millet, a Lhermitte, a Régamey, a Daumier; they are also well put together, but after all in a different way than the academy teaches.

But I think that however correctly academic a figure may be, it will be superfluous in these days, though it were by Ingres himself (his "Source," however, excepted, because that really was, and is, and will always be, something new), when it lacks the essential modern note, the intimate character, the real *action.*

Perhaps you will ask: When will a figure *not* be superfluous, though there may be faults, great faults in it in my opinion?

When the digger digs, when the peasant is a peasant and the peasant woman, a peasant woman.

Is this something new?—yes—even the figures by Ostade, Terborch, are not in action like those painted nowadays.

I would like to say a lot more about this, and I would like to say how much I myself want to improve my work and how much I prefer the work of some other artists to my own.

I ask you, do you know a single digger, a single sower in the old Dutch school??? Did they ever try to paint "a laborer"? Did Velasquez try it in his water carrier or types from the people? No.

The figures in the pictures of the old masters do not *work.* I am drudging just now on the figure of a woman whom I saw digging for carrots in the snow last winter.

Look here, Millet has done it, Lhermitte, and in general the painters of rural life in this century—Israëls for instance—they think it more beautiful than anything else.

But *even* in this century, how relatively few among the innumerable painters want the figure—yes, above all—for the figure's sake, that is to say for the sake of line and modeling, *but cannot imagine* it otherwise than in action, and want to do what the old masters avoided—even the old Dutch masters who clung to many conventional actions—and I repeat—want *to paint the action for the action's sake.*

So that the picture or the drawing has to be a drawing of the figure for the sake of the figure and the inexpressibly harmonious form of the human body, but at the same time a digging of carrots in the snow. Do I express myself clearly? I hope so, and just tell this to Serret. I can say it in a few words: a nude by Cabanel, a lady by Jacquet and a peasant woman, *not by Bastien Lepage himself*, but a peasant woman by a Parisian who has learned his drawing at the academy, will always indicate the limbs and the structure of the body in one selfsame way, sometimes charming—correct in proportion and anatomy. But when Israëls, or when Daumier or Lhermitte, for instance, draws a figure, the shape of the figure will be felt much more, and yet—that's why I like to include Daumier—the proportions will sometimes be almost *arbitrary*, the anatomy and structure often quite wrong "in the eyes of the academician." But it will *live*. And especially Delacroix too.

It is not yet well expressed. Tell Serret that *I should be desperate if my figures were correct*, tell him that I do not want them to be academically correct, tell him that I mean: If one photographs a digger, *he certainly would not be digging then*. Tell him that I adore the figures by Michelangelo though the legs are undoubtedly too long, the hips and the backsides too large. Tell him that, for me, Millet and Lhermitte are the real artists for the very reason that they do not paint things as they are, traced in a dry analytical way, but as *they*—Millet, Lhermitte, Michelangelo—feel them. Tell him that my great longing is to learn to make those very incorrectnesses, those deviations, remodelings, changes in reality, so that they may become, yes, lies if you like—but truer than the literal truth.

And now I shall have to finish, but I wanted to say once more that those who paint rural life or the life of the people, though they may not belong to the men of the moment, may wear better in the long run than the painters of the exotic harems and Cardinal's receptions, painted in Paris.

I know that it is being very disagreeable to ask for money at inconvenient moments; my excuse, however, is that painting the apparently most ordinary things is sometimes most difficult and expensive.

The expenses I must make if I want to work are sometimes very high in proportion to what I have at my disposal. I assure you, if my constitution had not become, in all winds and weather, like that of a peasant, I should not be able to stand it, as absolutely nothing is left for my own comfort.

But I don't want comfort for myself, just as little as many peasants want to live differently than they do.

But the money I ask is for colors, and especially for models.

From what I write about drawings of the figure, you can perhaps judge sufficiently how passionately I want to carry them out.

You recently wrote me that Serret had spoken to you "with conviction" about certain faults in the structure of the figures of the potato eaters.

But you will have seen from my answer that my own criticism also disapproves of them on that score, but I pointed out that this was an impression after my having seen the cottage in the dim lamplight for many evenings, after having painted forty heads, so it is clear that I started from a different point of view.

But now that we begin to talk about figure drawing, I have a great deal more to say. In Raffaelli's words I find his opinion about "character"; what he says about this is good and to the point, and it is illustrated by the drawings themselves.

But people who move in artistic, literary circles, like Raffaelli in Paris, have, after all, ideas different from mine, for instance, here in the heart of peasant life.

I mean they want one word to sum up all their ideas; he uses the word "character" for the figures of the future. I agree with it, with the *meaning*, I think, but in the correctness of the word I believe as little as in the correctness of other words; as little as in the correctness, or appropriateness, of my own expressions.

Rather than say there must be character in a digger, I define it by saying, That peasant *must* be a peasant, that digger *must* dig, and then there will be something essentially modern in them. But I feel myself that from these very words conclusions may be drawn that I do not intend, even if I should add a whole oration.

Instead of lessening the expenses for models, now already so heavy for me, I should prefer, very much prefer, spending a little more on them, for what I aim at is quite different from being able to do a little figure drawing. To draw *a peasant's figure in action*, I repeat, that's what an essentially modern figure is, the very core of modern art, which neither the Greeks nor the Renaissance nor the old Dutch school have done.

This is a question which occupies me every day. But this difference between the great as well as the little masters of today (the great ones like, for instance, Millet, Lhermitte, Breton, Herkomer; the lesser ones such as Raffaelli and Régamey) and the old masters—I have not often found it openly expressed in the articles about art.

Just think over whether you don't find this true. They started a peasant's and a laborer's figure as a "genre," but at present, with Millet the great master as a leader, this is the very core of modern art, and will remain so.

People like Daumier—we must respect them, for they are among the pioneers. The simple *nude* but *modern* figure, as Henner and Lefèvre have renewed it, ranks high.

Baudry and especially the sculptors, as, for instance, Mercier, Dalou—theirs is also serious work.

But peasants and laborers are not nude, after all, and it is not necessary to imagine them in the nude. The more painters begin to paint workmen's and peasants' figures, the better I shall like it. And I myself know nothing I like so well. This is a long letter and I do not know whether I have expressed what I mean clearly enough. I shall perhaps write a little word to Serret; if I do, I shall send the letter to you so that you can read it, for I should like to make it very clear how much importance I attach to the question of figure drawing.

R 53

Amice Rappard,   Nuenen, before 21 July 1885

I just received your letter. It is drier and prosier than ever.

However, since you say in it, "I want to answer your esteemed letter at once in order not to encourage you in your opinion that there is any idea of a rupture, at least on my part," I feel impelled to repeat again that you should know once and for all that there is at your disposal, or at the disposal of any painter whatever who wants to come here to make studies, a spare bedroom in the house where I have my studio. And I for my part want to advise you, as well as Wenkebach, whom I shall probably see tomorrow, to come here once in a while, as there are enough beautiful things here. If you are inclined to appreciate this, very good; if not, very good just the same. But if you come, *each goes his separate way.*

Here is my explanation of the lithograph. I did it entirely from memory and in a single day; I thought a certain composition somewhat forced, and was using an altogether different process in an attempt to find a new idea to put it together. Besides, it was only an experiment and nothing more, and I used corrosives on the stone later on.

Originally—although the faulty drawing of an arm or a nose that made you fly into a rage remains—the chiaroscuro was much better, as it is in the composition that I painted later. And as for the latter, although there are faults in it too, there are still things in it that keep me from regretting that I painted it.

I cannot say that your letter of today was the least bit useful or necessary to me. Only I assure you that your saying your belief in me was shaken and all that leaves me pretty indifferent—you are no exception in this as far as certain others are concerned. I let people *say of me and think of me whatever they like and treat me just as they like*—that is their business; I am not obligated to listen to their everlasting drivel. My parents, my teachers, Messrs. Goupil & Co., and furthermore all kinds of friends and acquaintances have said *so* many unpleasant things to me for my own good and with the best intentions that in the end the burden has become a little too heavy for me; and since I let people talk without paying any attention to it, I have not fallen off, my friend—*this much I think I know for sure.*

In reply to your remarks, however, this. It is a fact that your work is good; but this does not mean, amice, that you are always right in thinking that there are no other ways and methods of arriving at something good and sound than yours; I should like very much to talk things over with you—but please don't gather from this that it would mean consulting you—but our discussions are becoming less and less successful. Speaking of self-knowledge—who has it? Here again it is a matter of *"la* science—*nul* ne l'a," only *de la* science—everyone greatly needs it for himself, as regards his good or bad propensities—and I started with myself. But don't think that you never deceive yourself because of a lack of it, don't think that you never hurt others horribly and undeservedly with superficial judgments ....

I know, *everyone* does this, and yet we must try to put up with each other. But for *you* to speak about self-knowledge—no, my friend, I am awfully sorry that *you* should touch upon the subject, as I am afraid it is the very weakest side of your character, from a human point of view. Oh well—but I will try to state clearly *what I think about when I think about you.*

As far as your work goes—here you are!—I think your present work is excellent —but here comes a thought exactly as it is in my mind, without concealing any-thing—I have known you for a pretty long time. There was a time—immediately *before* and immediately *after* your illness—when you were much *less* dry as a human being than you have been at other times—fuller, milder, broader, more generous —more straightforward and ingenuous.

Now you are speaking to me and behaving to me exactly as a certain *abominably* arrogant Rappard studying at a certain academy did at one time.

I am sorry that *this* acquaintance has come back to me, and I am still more sorry for the loss of you as a *friend*, which you were in the exceptional period when I found you changed and improved; and seeing that I have observed this, I can't help thinking, What about his work??—will that too be broader, fuller, nobler *for only a short time*?? Do you know the answer to that?

I have taken only half a sheet of paper to express this thought, but you will see from it that I am afraid at times that your work too may lose the nobler quality. I think I am stating this idea clearly and simply.

Whatever my faults of character may be, it is my sincere desire to do well in my efforts as a painter, and I also have the sincere desire to treat others well—I have too much heart to be *as* frivolous in my work as you are always reproaching me with being. I need not take what you wrote to heart, and I don't do so. And as for your saying that I am in need of someone who will tell me some home truths, that may be true, but it may also be true that I *myself* am the one to tell me some home truths, and that I can do without other people, especially if they are as prosy as you are.

Greetings. But your letter, as a whole, was unfair, even though there are details in it that are more or less accurate.

Vincent

You do not write me anything about your work, nor do I about mine.

423

Dear Theo,   Nuenen, 1 September 1885

Thanks for your letter and the enclosed 150 francs. I also received the two Lhermittes today. He is the absolute master of the figure, he does what he likes with it—proceeding neither from the color nor from the local tone but rather from the light—as Rembrandt did—there is an astonishing mastery in everything he does, above all excelling in modeling, he perfectly satisfies all that honesty demands.

People talk a great deal about Poussin. Bracquemond also speaks of him. The French call Poussin the very greatest painter among the old masters. Well, it is certainly true that what is said about Poussin, of whom I know so very little, is also true of Lhermitte and Millet. But with this difference, that Poussin seems to me the original grain; the others, the full ear. As for me, I think the modern ones *the most superior*.

These last two weeks I have been worried a lot by the Roman Catholic priests, who told me, evidently with the best intentions, and feeling obliged, like all the others, to meddle with it, that I ought not to get too familiar with people below my rank; expressing themselves to *me* in these terms but using quite a different tone toward "the people of lower rank," namely, threatening them about having themselves painted. I simply told the Burgomaster at once, and pointed out to him that it was a thing that did not concern the priests at all, who have to keep to their own territory of more abstract things. At all events, they stopped their opposition for the moment and I hope it will remain so.

A girl I had often painted was with child, and they suspected me, though I was innocent. But I had heard the real state of affairs from the girl herself, and as it was a case in which a member of the priest's congregation at Nuenen had played a very ugly part, they cannot, at least for this once, get at me.

But you see that it is not easy to paint or draw people in their own houses and at their work.

Well, they will not easily get the better of me in this case, and this winter I hope to keep the very same models, who are thoroughly typical of the old Brabant race.

I again have a few new drawings. But I could by no means get anybody to pose for me in the fields these days.

Happily for me, the priest is getting rather unpopular. But it is a bad thing, and if it continued, I should have to move. You will ask, What's the use of making yourself disagreeable?—but sometimes it cannot be avoided. If I had argued gently with them, they would undoubtedly have got the better of me. And when they hinder me in my work, I sometimes do not see any other way than an eye for an eye, and a tooth for a tooth. The priest even went so far as to promise the people money if they refused to be painted: but they answered quite spiritedly that they would rather earn money from me than beg some from him.

But you see they do it only for the sake of earning money, and they do *nothing* for *nothing* here.

You ask me if Rappard has ever sold anything. I know that at present he is better off than he used to be, that, for instance, for some time he took models for the nude every day, that now, for the picture of a brickyard, he rented a small house on the spot itself, and had it improved with a skylight; I know that he made another trip through Drenthe, and that he will also go to Terschelling. All these things are rather expensive, and the money for it must come from somewhere. Though he may possess some money of his own, he must certainly earn something too, otherwise he couldn't do what he does. Perhaps his family buys, or friends—that may be—but somebody must.

But tonight I am too much occupied with Lhermitte's drawings to go on writing about other things. When I think of Millet or of Lhermitte, I find modern art as great as Michelangelo and Rembrandt—ancient art is infinite, modern art infinite too—the ancient masters are *geniuses*—the modern ones are *geniuses* too. A person like Chenavard does not think so perhaps. But I, for my part, am convinced that in this respect one can have faith in modern art.

The fact that I have a definite belief about art makes me sure of what I want in my own work, and I shall try to reach it even at the risk of my own life.

Good-by,

Ever yours, Vincent

Dear Theo, Nuenen, October 1885

Today I received your letter with enclosure. I was very pleased with your letter, because I noticed a few things in it which I want to talk over. To begin at the beginning; what you write about a certain study of a basket with apples is very well observed, but does this observation come from yourself? ? ? because I fancy, I should almost say *I am sure*, that you used *not* to see that kind of thing: However this may be, here we are on our way to agreeing more about the colors.

Go more deeply into *those* questions, for that will be useful to you, and those are the things that Bürger and Mantz and Silvestre knew.

Just to explain how that study was painted—simply this: green and red are complementary colors. Now in the apples there is a red which is very vulgar in itself; further, next to it some greenish things. But there are also one or two apples of another color, of a certain pink which makes the whole thing right.

That pink is the broken color, got by mixing the above-mentioned red and the above-mentioned green.

That's why there is harmony between the colors.

Added to this is a second contrast, the background forms a contrast to the foreground, the one is a neutral color, got by mixing blue with orange; the other, the same neutral color simply changed by adding some yellow.

But I am awfully glad that you notice a combination of color, be it through direct or indirect personal perception.

Further, that one of the studies seemed to you a variation on the brown-gray theme, well, that certainly is the case, but all three potato studies are like that, with this difference, that one is a study in terre de Sienne, the second in terre de Sienne brûlée, the third in yellow ocher and red ocher.

The latter—that is the largest one—is in my opinion the best—notwithstanding the dull black background which I purposely left dull because the ochers are also naturally *non*-transparent colors. As to that study, the largest one of the potatoes, it is made by changing, by breaking, those untransparent ochers with a transparent blue. As red ocher with yellow ocher gives orange, their combination with blue is more neutral, and against that neutralized color, they become either more red or more yellow.

The highest light in that whole picture is simply some pure yellow ocher. The reason why this dull yellow stands out so is because it is put in a wide field of, be it neutral, violet; because ... red ocher with blue gives violet tones.

Well, the birds' nests were also purposely painted against a black background, because I want it to be obvious in these studies that the objects do not appear in their natural surroundings, but against a conventional background. A *living* nest in nature is quite different—one hardly sees the nest itself, one sees the birds.

But when one wants to paint nests from one's *collection of nests*, one cannot express strongly enough the fact that the background and the surroundings in nature are quite different, therefore I simply painted the background black. But it is a fact that in a still life a colored background can be beautiful—in Amsterdam I saw still lifes by Miss Vos that were *excellent*, much more beautiful than those by Blaisse Desgoffe[1]—really like Van Beyeren. I couldn't help thinking that those simple still lifes of hers had far more artistic value than many pretentious pictures by other Amsterdam painters.

They struck me as very well done. Especially one with a golden vase, a few empty oyster shells, a broken coconut shell and a crust of bread. I will send you the book by Blanc; I hope soon to get *L'Art au XVIIIme Siècle*; I am especially longing to hear something from de Goncourt about Chardin. Lacaze's Rembrandt is really also in the sentiment of Rembrandt's last period; it is about twelve years since I saw it, but I still remember it because it struck me, just like that head by Fabritius in Rotterdam. If I remember correctly, that nude woman in the Lacaze Collection is also very beautiful, also of a later period. The fragment, Rembrandt's "Lesson in Anatomy," yes, I was absolutely staggered by that too. Do you remember those flesh colors—it is—*de la terre*—especially the feet.

You know, Frans Hals's flesh colors are also earthy, used here in the sense that you know. Often at least. Sometimes, I almost dare say always, there is also a relation of contrast between the tone of the costume and the tone of the face.

Red and green are opposites; "The Singer" (Dupper Collection), who has tones of carmine in the flesh color, has tones of green in his black sleeves, and ribbons on those sleeves *of a red other* than that carmine. The orange-white-blue fellow I wrote about has a relatively neutral complexion, earthy-pink, violetish, in contrast with his Frans-Hals-yellow leather suit.

The *yellow* fellow, citron amorti, decidedly has dull violet in his mug. Well—the darker the costume, the lighter the face is sometimes—not accidentally—at least his portrait and that of his wife in the garden contain *two* blackish violets (blue-violet and reddish-violet) and a plain black (yellow-black?). I repeat, reddish-violet and blue-violet, black and black, the three gloomiest things, as it were; well, the faces are *very* fair, *extremely* fair, even for Hals.

Well, Frans Hals is a colorist *among colorists*, a colorist like Veronese, like Rubens, like Delacroix, like Velasquez.

Of Millet, Rembrandt and, for instance, Israëls, it has truly been said that they are more harmonists than colorists.

But tell me, *black* and *white*, may they be used or may they not, are they forbidden fruit?

I don't think so; Frans Hals has no less than twenty-seven blacks. White—but you know yourself what striking pictures some modern colorists make of white on white. What is the meaning of that phrase : *one must not?* Delacroix called them *rests*, used them as such. You must not have a prejudice against them, for if used only in their places, and in harmony with the rest, one may of course use all tones.

I can tell you that I often think the things by Apol, for instance, white on white, very well done.

His sunset in The Hague Wood, for instance, which is in Amsterdam. That thing is damn good indeed.

[1] A French still-life painter of the mid-nineteenth century.

No—black and white have their reason and significance, and when one tries to suppress them, it turns out wrong; to consider both *neutral* is certainly the most logical thing to do, white—the highest combination of the lightest red, blue, yellow; black—the highest combination of the darkest red, blue, yellow. I have nothing to say against that theory, I find it perfectly true. Well, *light* and *brown*, the *tone* in its *value* stands in direct relation to that 4th color scale from *white to black*. For one finds there:

Scale 1	from	yellow	to	violet,
" 2	"	red	"	green,
" 3	"	blue	"	orange,

Sum				
a fourth scale	from	white	to	black
(that of the neutral tones,		(red+blue+yellow,		(red+blue+yellow,
that of red+blue+yellow)		extreme light)		deepest black)

That is how I understand the blacks and the whites.

When I mix red with green to a red-green or green-red, by mixing it with white, I then get pink-green or green-pink. And if you like, by adding black, I get brown-green or green-brown. Isn't that clear? When I mix yellow with violet to a violet-yellow or yellow-violet, in other terms a neutralized yellow or a neutralized violet, by adding white and black, I get grays.

Well, *grays* and *browns*, there is especially question of them when one makes colors *lighter* or *darker*, whatever their nature and their gradation of red, yellow or blue may be.

It is quite correct to speak of light and dark grays and browns, I think. But how beautiful what Silvestre says about Delacroix is—that he put a fortuitous tone on his palette, *une nuance innommable violacée*, that he put that one tone down somewhere, *either for highest light or for deepest shadow*, but that of this *mud* he made something which either sparkled like light or was gloomily silent like a deep shadow.

So I have heard of an experiment with a sheet of neutral colored paper—which became greenish against a red background, reddish on a green one, bluish on orange, orange on blue, yellowish on violet, and violetish on yellow.

Just listen, suppose one wants such a *muddy tone* or *drab color* to become *light* in the picture, like Delacroix said of Veronese, that he could paint a blonde nude woman with a color like mud in such a way that she comes out fair and blonde in the picture—then the question arises—how is this possible, unless by contrast of great forces in bluish-blacks or violets, or reddish-browns?

You—who are looking for dark shadows somewhere, and think that when the shadows are dark, aye, black, that it is all wrong then, is this right? I don't think so. For then, for instance, the "Dante" by Delacroix, the "Fisherman of Zandvoort," for instance, would be wrong. For indeed, they contain the most vigorous blue-black or violet-black values. Rembrandt and Hals, didn't they use black? and Velasquez???

Not only one, but twenty-seven blacks, I assure you. So as to "one must not use black," are you yourself quite sure that you know what you mean by it?

and do you know what you want with it? Really, think it over carefully, for you might come to the conclusion—I think this very probable—that you have learned and understood that question of tones quite wrongly, or rather have learned it *vaguely* and understood it *vaguely*. Many people do, most of them do. But in the long run Delacroix and others of his time will teach you better.

Tell me—have you noticed that those studies of mine that have black backgrounds have their *highest light* put in *a low color scale???* And when in this way I put my study in a *lower color scale* than nature, I yet keep the harmony of tones because I become darker, not only in my shadows, but *also* in the same degree *in my lights.*

I painted my studies just as a kind of gymnastics, to rise and fall in tone, so —don't forget that I painted my white and gray moss literally with a mud color, and yet it looks light in the study.

Good-by,   Ever yours, Vincent

These things concerning complementary colors, simultaneous contrast, and the neutralizing of complementals, this question is the first and principal one; the second is the mutual influence of two *kindred colors*, for instance, carmine on a vermilion, a pink-violet on a blue-violet. The third question is a light blue against the same dark blue, a pink against a brown-red, a citron yellow against a chamois yellow, etc. But the first question is the most important.

If you come across some good book on color theories, mind you send it to me, for I too am far from knowing everything about it, and am searching for more every day.

429

Dear Theo,   Nuenen, 2 October 1885

I read your letter about black with great pleasure, and it convinces me that you have no prejudice against black.

Your description of Manet's study, "Le Toréador Mort," was well analyzed. And the whole letter proves the same thing that your sketch of Paris suggested to me at the time, namely that if you set yourself to it, you can paint a thing in words.

It is a fact that by studying the laws of the colors one can go from an instinctive belief in the great masters to the analysis of why one admires—what one admires —and that is indeed necessary nowadays when one realizes how terribly arbitrarily and superficially people criticize.

You just have to let me stick to my pessimism about the present-day art trade, for it does *not* at all include discouragement. This is my way of reasoning. Supposing I am right in considering that curious haggling about prices of pictures more and more like the bulb trade. I repeat, supposing that, like the bulb trade at the end of the last century, the art trade, together with other branches of speculation, will disappear at the end of this century the same way they came, namely rather quickly. The bulb trade may disappear—the *flower-growing* remains.

And I for myself am contented, for better or for worse, to be a small gardener who loves his plants.

Just now my palette is thawing and the barrenness of the first beginning has disappeared.

It is true, I still often blunder when I undertake a thing, but the colors follow of their own accord, and taking one color as a starting point, I have clearly in mind what must follow and how to get life into it.

Jules Dupré is in landscape, rather like Delacroix, for what enormous variety of mood did he express in symphonies of color.

Now a marine, with the most delicate blue-greens and broken blue and all kinds of pearly tones; then again an autumn landscape, with a foliage from deep wine-red to vivid green, from bright orange to dark havana, with other colors again in the sky, in grays, lilacs, blues, whites, forming a contrast with the yellow leaves.

Then again a sunset in black, in violet, in fiery red.

Then again more fantastic, as I once saw a corner of a garden by him which I have never forgotten: black in the shadow, white in the sun, vivid green, a fiery red and a dark blue besides, a bituminous greenish-brown, and a light brown-yellow. Colors that indeed have something to say for themselves.

I have always been very fond of Jules Dupré, and he will become even more appreciated than he is. For he is a real colorist, always interesting, and so powerful and dramatic.

Yes, he is indeed a brother of Delacroix's.

As I told you, I think your letter about black very good, and what you say about not painting local color is also quite correct. But it doesn't satisfy me. In my opinion there is much more behind that not painting local color.

"Les vrais peintres sont ceux qui ne font pas la couleur locale"—that was what Blanc and Delacroix discussed once.

Mightn't I presume to infer from it that a painter had better start from the colors on his palette than from the colors in nature? I mean, when one wants to paint, for instance, a head, and sharply observes the reality one has before one, then one may think: That head is a harmony of red-brown, violet, yellow, all of them broken—I will put a violet and a yellow and a red-brown on my palette and these will break each other.

Of nature I retain a certain sequence and a certain correctness in placing the tones, I study nature, so as not to do foolish things, to remain reasonable; however, I don't care so much whether my color is exactly the same, as long as it looks beautiful on my canvas, as beautiful as it looks in nature.

A portrait by Courbet is much truer—manly, free, painted in all kinds of beautiful deep tones of red-brown, of gold, of colder violet in the shadow with black as repoussoir, with a little bit of tinted white linen, as a rest for the eye— finer than a portrait by whomever you like, who has imitated the color of the face with horribly punctilious *precision*.

A man's head or a woman's head, well observed and at leisure, is divinely beautiful, isn't it? Well, one loses that *general harmony* of tones in nature by painfully exact imitation; one keeps it by recreating in a parallel color scale which may be not exactly, or even far from exactly, like the model.

Always intelligently making use of the beautiful tones which the colors form of their own accord when one breaks them on the palette, I repeat—starting from one's palette, from one's knowledge of the harmony of colors is quite different from following nature mechanically and servilely.

Here is another example: suppose I have to paint an autumn landscape, trees with yellow leaves. All right—when I conceive it as a symphony in yellow, what does it matter if the fundamental color of yellow is the same as that of the leaves or not? It matters *very little*.

Much, everything depends on my perception of the infinite variety of tones of one *same family*.

Do you call this a dangerous inclination toward romanticism, an infidelity to "realism," a "peindre du chic," a caring more for the colorist's palette than for nature? Well, que soit. Delacroix, Millet, Corot, Dupré, Daubigny, Breton, thirty names more, aren't they the heart and soul of the art of painting of this century, and aren't they all rooted in romanticism, though they *surpassed* romanticism?

Romance and romanticism are of our time, and painters must have imagination and sentiment. Fortunately realism and naturalism are not free from it. Zola creates, but does not hold up a *mirror* to things, he creates *wonderfully*, but *creates*, *poetizes*, that is why it is so beautiful. So much for naturalism and realism, which are still connected with romanticism.

And I repeat that I am touched when I see a picture of about the years '30–'48, a Paul Huet, an old Israëls like the "Fisherman of Zandvoort," a Cabat, an Isabey.

But I find so much truth in that saying, "Ne pas peindre le ton local," that I greatly prefer a picture in a lower key than nature to one which is exactly like nature.

Rather a water color that is somewhat vague and unfinished than one which is worked up to simulate reality.

That saying, "Ne pas peindre le ton local," has a broad meaning, and it leaves the painter free to seek colors which form a whole and harmonize, which stand out the more in contrast to another color scheme.

What do I care whether the portrait of an honorable citizen tells me exactly the milk-and-watery bluish, insipid color of that pious man's face—which I would never have looked at. But the citizens of the small town where the above-mentioned individual has rendered himself so meritorious that he thought himself obliged to impress his physiognomy on posterity are highly edified by the correct exactness.

Color expresses something in itself, one cannot do without this, one must use it; what is beautiful, really beautiful—is also correct. When Veronese had painted the portraits of his beau-monde in the "Noces de Cana," he had spent on it all the richness of his palette in somber violets, in splendid golden tones. Then—he still thought of a faint azure and pearly white—which does not appear in the foreground. He hurls it on in the background—and it was right, spontaneously it changes into the surrounding atmosphere of marble palaces and sky, which characteristically complete the cluster of figures.

That background is so beautiful that it arose spontaneously from a calculation of colors.

Am I wrong in this?

Isn't it painted *differently* than it would be by somebody who had thought at the same time of the palace *and* of the figures as one whole?

All that architecture and sky is conventional and subservient to the figures, it is calculated to make the figures stand out beautifully.

Surely *that is* real painting, and the result is more beautiful than the exact imitation of the things themselves. Thinking of one thing and letting the surroundings belong to it and result from it.

To study from nature, to wrestle with reality—I don't want to do away with it, for years and years I myself have done just that, almost fruitlessly and with all kinds of sad results.

I should not like to have missed that *error*.

I mean that it would be foolish and stupid to always go on in that same way, but *not* that all my pains should be absolutely lost.

"On commence par tuer, on finit par guérir," is a doctor's saying. One starts with a hopeless struggle to follow nature, and everything goes wrong; one ends by calmly creating from one's palette, and nature agrees with it, and follows. But these two opposites cannot be separated. The drudging, though it may seem futile, gives an intimacy with nature, a sounder knowledge of things. And a beautiful saying of Doré's (who sometimes is so clever!) is, *Je me souviens*. Though I believe that the best pictures are more or less freely painted by heart, I *can't* help adding that one can never study nature too much and too hard. The greatest, most powerful imaginations have at the same time made things directly from nature that strike one dumb.

In answer to your description of the study by Manet, I send you a still life of an open—so a broken white—Bible bound in leather, against a black background, with yellow-brown foreground, with a touch of citron yellow.

I painted that in *one rush*, on one day.

This to show you that when I say that I have perhaps not plodded entirely in vain, I dare say this because at present I find it quite easy to paint a given subject unhesitatingly, whatever its form or color may be. Recently I painted a few studies out-of-doors, autumn landscapes.

I'll write again soon, and I am sending this letter in haste to tell you that I was quite pleased with what you say about black.

Good-by,

Ever yours, Vincent

435c

Nuenen [Personal reminiscence of Van Gogh by Anton Kerssemakers]
It was some years after his stay in the Borinage—when, after having worked in The Hague and in Drenthe, he had come to stay in Nuenen, about the year 1884 —that I made the painter's acquaintance.

At the time I was engaged in painting a number of landscapes on the walls of my office, instead of having them covered with wallpaper, and in his peculiar way my house painter, who furnished me with colors, thought this so nice that one day he brought Van Gogh along to show him my work.

Van Gogh was of the opinion that I could draw, and kind-heartedly, as was his way, he at once showed himself willing to help me on with my painting. The consequence was our more intimate acquaintanceship and, on his friendly invitation, my visit to his studio at Nuenen, to which I shall revert later on.

My house painter had quite a lot of confidence in Van Gogh, and prepared for him the colors he most needed, such as the whites and the ochers and some others.

Seeing that the house painter was no expert at this job, these colors often left much to be desired in the matter of consistency, but Van Gogh had to content himself with them because of a lack of money.

I still have a little study as a souvenir of this unmanageable paint.

He painted it in a great hurry at my house, to instruct me; it was a view from my window in winter with melting snow, and the thin white color ran all over the landscape.

On the occasion of my first visit to his studio at Nuenen it was impossible for me to get the right insight into his work; it was so totally different from what I had imagined it would be up to then, so rough and unkempt, so harsh and unfinished, that with the best will in the world I was unable to think it good or beautiful; and, badly disappointed, I decided not to go and see him again, and go my own way.

However, shortly afterward I discovered that his work had made a certain impression on me after all, which it was impossible for me to dismiss from my mind; every now and then his studies rose up before my mind's eye again, so that I resolved to pay him another visit; it was as if I were drawn to it.

At my second visit the impression I got was considerably better, although in my ignorance I still thought that either he could not draw or that he carelessly neglected to draw his figures, and so on, and I took the liberty of telling him so straight out.

He was not at all cross at this, he only laughed a little and said quietly, Later on you will think differently. When I went away, he gave me some engravings from *The Graphic* and some by Adolf Menzel and others to take with me, saying that he advised me to look them over carefully and unhurriedly at home, and study them and draw copies of them. "You will learn a thing or two from this."

On another occasion I took along a number of small studies that I had painted in the meantime, so as to hear what he would have to say about them.

Probably in order not to discourage me he said:

"Well, after all there is some good in it. But now I advise you to try and make a few still lifes first instead of landscapes; you will learn a lot from that. After you have painted some fifty of them, you will see how much progress you have made. And I am willing to help you and to paint the same subjects along with you, for I myself still have a good deal to learn, and there is nothing to equal this for learning to put things in their right positions, and for learning to get them properly separated in space.

In this way, for days and even weeks on end, he tried to help me on with the utmost patience, in the meantime working on hard himself, doing innumerable drawings and water-color sketches and studies in oil, indoors and out.

Once, when I had pretty well lost courage, and said to him, "Oh, I don't think anything can be done with me, I am too old to turn myself into a painter," he mentioned a number of painters who had started late in life, and had become great masters for all that, including H. W. Mesdag.

Once, when we sat together in my studio painting the same still life, nothing more than a pair of wooden shoes and some pots taken at random, and I sat daubing away at it in my own manner, laying on the color and scratching it off again without being able to get any relief into it, he suddenly walked over to me: "Look here, now you put—no, you needn't be afraid I'll spoil your drawing—a vigorous dark transparent touch there and there"—and at the same time he was already assailing my tiny canvas with his big broad brush. "Do you see? Like that. Look, now the other part comes to the front. It is wrong to go brushing away on the same spot, you must set it all down at once and then leave it alone; don't be afraid, and don't try to make it pretty.

"We'll say we've done enough here for today, and now we must go and paint in the open air for a change; I'll come here, if you like, or else you might come to Nuenen again; I know enough nice interesting spots there."

So it came about that we made various painting excursions in the Nuenen district, as for instance to that little old medieval chapel that stood in the middle of a cornfield, and to the beautiful old windmill in the vicinity of Lieshout, of which I later saw in his house such a dashing, vigorous study with those small square sheep low down along the mill.

In those days he was starving like a true Bohemian, and more than once it happened that he did not see meat (for the purpose of eating) for six weeks on end, always just dry bread with a chunk of cheese. It won't go bad on the road, he would say. The following story may serve as proof that he was quite accustomed to this and would not have it otherwise. Once in Nuenen, when we were about to set out on a ramble—it was in the afternoon at the height of summer—I said, "To begin with we'll have a pot of coffee made in that inn over there, and eat a lot of bread and butter with trimmings, then we shall be able to keep going until late this evening."

No sooner said than done, for he invariably consented to whatever you proposed.

The table was well furnished with various kinds of bread, cheese, sliced ham and so on.

When I looked, I saw he was eating dry bread and cheese, and I said, "Come on, Vincent, do take some ham, and butter your bread, and put some sugar in your coffee; after all, it has to be paid for whether you eat it or not."

"No," he said, "that would be coddling myself too much: bread and cheese is what I am used to," and he calmly went on eating.

On the other hand he liked to have some brandy in his flask on his rambles, and he would not have liked to do without it; but as far as I know this was the only luxury he permitted himself. His studio too—he had rented a couple of rooms in the sexton's house—had quite a Bohemian look.

One was amazed at the way all the available hanging or standing room was filled with paintings, drawings in water color and in crayon, heads of men and women whose clownish turned-up noses, protruding cheekbones and large ears were strongly accentuated, the rough paws calloused and furrowed, weavers and weaving looms, women spooling yarn, potato planters, women weeding, innumerable still lifes, certainly as many as ten studies in oils of the little old chapel at Nuenen that I mentioned, which he was so enthusiastic about that he had painted it in all seasons and in all weathers. (Later this little chapel was pulled down by the Nuenen vandals, as he called them.)

A great heap of ashes around the stove, which had never known a brush or stove polish, a small number of chairs with frayed cane bottoms, a cupboard with at least thirty different bird's nests, all kinds of mosses and plants brought along from the moor, some stuffed birds, a spool, a spinning wheel, a complete set of farm tools, old caps and hats, coarse bonnets and hoods, wooden shoes, etc., etc.

Paintbox and palette he had had made in Nuenen according to his directions, as well as a perspective frame; this consisted of an iron bar with a long sharp point, on which he could mount, by means of screws, an empty frame like a small window. He said, The painters of old used a perspective frame at times, so why shouldn't we?

Some time later I visited a number of museums in his company, the National Museum at Amsterdam being the first.

As I was unable to spend the night away from home for domestic reasons, he went the day before and made an appointment to meet me the next day in the third-class waiting room of the Central Station at Amsterdam.

When I came into this waiting room I saw quite a crowd of people of all sorts, railway guards, workmen, travelers, and so on and so forth, gathered near the front windows of the waiting room, and there he was sitting, surrounded by this mob, in all tranquillity, dressed in his shaggy ulster and his inevitable fur cap, industriously making a few little city views (he had taken a small tin paintbox with him) without paying the slightest attention to the loud disrespectful observations and critical remarks of the esteemed (?) public. As soon as he caught sight of me, he packed up his things quite calmly, and we started for the museum. Seeing that the rain was coming down in torrents, and Van Gogh in his fur cap and shaggy ulster soon looked like a drowned tomcat, I took a cab, at which he grumbled considerably, saying, "What do I care about the opinion of all Amsterdam, I prefer walking; well, never mind, have it your own way."

In the museum he knew where to find what interested him most; he took me chiefly to the Van Goyens, the Bols and the Rembrandts; he spent the longest time in front of the "Jewish Bride"; I could not tear him away from the spot; he went and sat down there at his ease, while I myself went on to look at some other things. "You will find me here when you come back," he told me.

When I came back after a pretty long while and asked him whether we should not get a move on, he gave me a surprised look and said, "Would you believe it —and I honestly mean what I say—I should be happy to give ten years of my life if I could go on sitting here in front of this picture for a fortnight, with only a crust of dry bread for food?" At last he got up. "Well, never mind," he said, "we can't stay here forever, can we?"

After that we went to Van Gogh's Fine Art Establishment, where at his recommendation I bought two books, *Musées de Hollande* and *Trésors d'art en Angleterre* by W. Burger (Thoré); when I asked him if he would go inside with me, he replied, "No, I must not be seen on the premises of such a genteel, rich family." He still seemed to be on bad terms with his family; he remained standing in the street, waiting for me.

Some time later we visited the museums at Antwerp, and I still remember one characteristic incident vividly. It was when he caught sight of the fisherboy carrying a basket on his back (I think it is by Velásquez). Suddenly he disappeared from my side, and I saw him run to the picture; and of course I ran after him. When I reached him, he was standing in front of the picture with folded hands as if in devout prayer, and muttered, "God ... damn it, do you see that?" After a while he said, "That is what I call painting, look"—and, following with his thumb the direction of the broad brush strokes—"he was one to leave what he had once put down alone," and indicating the gallery with a wide, all-embracing gesture: "All the rest belongs to the periwig-and-pigtail period."

He felt a deep veneration for Corot, Daubigny, Diaz, Millet, and further the whole Barbizon school, he was always full of it, and in his disquisitions on his beloved art he invariably reverted to them.

However, he never spoke about art with totally uninitiated persons, and he was terribly annoyed when a so-called picture lover from his entourage told him that he thought a thing of his was beautiful; then he knew for certain, he was in the habit of saying, that it was bad, and as a rule such studies were destroyed or repainted. Only with a few chosen friends, to whom I also had the good fortune of belonging—although in those days these friends were also unable fully to agree with his manner of painting—did he like to talk about painting, drawing, etching and so on, and many a time I have reproached myself for not having understood him better at the time, for if I had, how much more might I have learned from him.

He was always drawing comparisons between the art of painting and music, and in order to get an even better understanding of the values and the various nuances of the tones, he started taking piano lessons with an old music teacher who was at the same time an organist in Eindhoven. This, however, did not last long, for seeing that during the lessons Van Gogh was continually comparing the notes of the piano with Prussian blue and dark green and dark ocher, and so on, all the way to bright cadmium-yellow, the good man thought that he had to do with a madman, in consequence of which he became so afraid of him that he discontinued the lessons.

I was also present at the painting of the water mill at Gestel, which picture

I later saw again at Oldenzeel's and in the Boymans Museum at Rotterdam.

At the time he thought he had found a means of preventing the, to him, so hateful, sinking in of the colors by using copaiba balsam, but seeing that he was rather lavish in the use of this ingredient, as he was of his colors too, he used too much of it, and the result was that the whole sky of the picture came floating down, so that he had to remove it with his palette knife, as may still be seen in the picture on close examination.

Only a few pieces were signed by him. When I once asked him why he did not sign his name in full, he replied: "Van Gogh is such an impossible name for many foreigners to pronounce; if it should happen that my pictures found their way to France or England, then the name would certainly be murdered, whereas the whole world can pronounce the name Vincent correctly."

He came to my house in Eindhoven very often. Once when I was sitting painting in my garden, I suddenly heard behind me: "Look here, yes, you are right to paint in the open air; you should do it often.... Yes, do you see the slant of that roof? It must be an angle of at least forty-five degrees; it's far too steep like that. And then I don't know how you are going to handle your colors, but all this is of no importance, just go ahead. There is nothing from which one learns so much as from painting in the open air. In particular you should compare the objects with each other, especially for the tone. Painting is like algebra: something is to this as that is to the other. And above all, study your perspective carefully; if you start by making things green in the background, how can you expect to get them green in the foreground?"

Whenever he saw a beautiful evening sky, he went into ecstasies, if one may use the expression. Once, when we were tramping from Nuenen to Eindhoven toward evening, he suddenly stood stock-still before a glorious sunset, and using his two hands as if to screen it off a little, and with his eyes half closed, he exclaimed, "God bless me, how does that fellow—or God, or whatever name you give him—how does he do it? We ought to be able to do that too. My God, my God, how beautiful that is! What a pity we haven't got a prepared palette ready, for it will be gone in a moment.

"Do let us sit down here for a minute. Take care you never forget to half-shut your eyes when you are painting in the open air. Once in a while those clodhoppers in Nuenen say that I am mad when they see me shuffling about over the moor, and stop, and crouch down in a half-sitting position, every now and then screwing my eyes half-shut, holding up my hands by my eyes, now in this way, now in that, in order to screen things off. But I don't give a damn about that, I just go my own way."

For weeks on end he would occupy himself exclusively with the drawing of hands, feet or wooden shoes. "That is something I must get a firm grip on," he used to say.

One of the female models whom he used for painting studies of heads was his Dulcinea, according to village gossip. One repeatedly encounters her in his paintings of heads. It had even happened that this was objected to by one of the guardians of the villagers' salvation, and moreover, he blamed the same person for his having been given notice to quit his studio. As he himself recounted, he had taken singular vengeance after that, something that we shall cover with the cloak of charity, as being less suitable to record here.

When he had finished his picture called "The Potato Eaters," a picture done in very dark colors, with a hanging lamp over the table, around which a peasant family is sitting and eating steaming potatoes out of a dish, he carried it with him to Eindhoven to show me.

Afterward he made a lithograph of this picture at a label factory; he made twenty prints of this lithograph, some of which may still be in existence. Mine, however, became hopelessly tattered later on, as it was printed on ordinary, inferior paper.

Another time he came to me with the study of a woman spooling yarn; he had painted no spokes in the spooling wheel, but one continuous, unicolored smear of transparent gray. This was such an extraordinary sight that I did not understand it at first, and I asked him why he had done it in this way.

"Don't you understand?" he asked me. "Once in a while the motion of the wheel is expressed this way."

He always spoke of Anton Mauve with the highest respect, although in the past he had been unable to get along with him, and had worked in his studio for only a short time. According to what he told me, Mauve once made a disapproving remark because he touched his canvas too often with his fingers while painting; this caused him to lose his temper, and he snapped at Mauve, "What the hell does it matter, even if I did it with my heels, as long as it is good and has the right effect!"

For that matter this was a favorite expression of his; accordingly he used to say, Those little sheep have the right effect, or, That little birch tree might have a better effect, or, What a fine effect it has against that evening sky, and so on.

He had already mentioned more than once that he wanted to go away, but I had never paid much attention to it, as I did not think he meant what he said, but at last he came to me and announced his departure for Antwerp, and after that to France.

Before he set off he visited me once more to say good-by, and as a souvenir he brought me a beautiful autumn study, not yet entirely dry, finished completely in the open air, and measuring 3 ft. 4 in. by 2 ft. 8 in., and took away with him a little canvas as a souvenir in return.

This autumn picture is still in my possession; it is painted in a very light range of colors, and the subject is very simple; in the foreground three gnarled oaks, still full of leaves, and one poor bare beggar of a pollard birch, in the background a tangled wilderness of various trees and shrubs, partly bare, shutting off the horizon, and in the center the little figure of a woman in a white cap, just dashed off in three strokes of the brush, but having a beautiful effect, as he would have said himself.

There is a striking atmosphere of autumn in this picture, it is painted in broad strokes, and the paint is richly laid on. When I remarked that he had not yet signed it, he said he might do so some time or other, "I suppose I shall come back someday, but actually it isn't necessary; they will surely recognize my work

later on, and write about me when I'm dead and gone. I shall take care of that, if I can keep alive for some little time."
[Reprinted from the Amsterdam weekly *De Groene* (The Green One) of April 14 and 21, 1912.]

437
Dear Theo,   Antwerp, November 1885-February 1886, Saturday evening
I want to write you a few more impressions of Antwerp.

This morning I took a most satisfactory walk in the pouring rain, the object of this excursion being to get my things at the customhouse; the various dock-yards and warehouses on the quays are splendid.

I have walked along the docks and the quays several times already, in all directions. Especially when one comes from the sand and the heath and the quiet of a peasant village, and has been in none but quiet surroundings for a long time, the contrast is curious. It is an unfathomable confusion. One of de Goncourt's sayings was: "Japonaiserie forever." Well, those docks are a famous Japonaiserie, fantastic, peculiar, unheard of—at least one can take this view of it.

I should like to walk there with you, just to know whether we see alike. One could make everything there, city views—figures of the most varied character —the ships as the principal things, with water and sky a delicate gray—but above all—Japonaiserie. I mean, the figures are always in action, one sees them in the queerest surroundings, everything fantastic, and at all moments interesting contrasts present themselves.

A white horse in the mud, in a corner where heaps of merchandise are lying covered with oilcloth—against the old smoky black walls of the warehouse. Quite simple, but an effect of Black and White.

Through the window of a very elegant English bar, one will look out on the dirtiest mud, and on a ship from which, for instance, attractive merchandise like hides and buffalo horns is being unloaded by hideous dock hands or exotic sailors; a very dainty, very fair young English girl is standing at the window looking at it, or at something else. The interior with the figure altogether in tone, and for light—the silvery sky above that mud, and the buffalo horns, again a series of rather sharp contrasts. There will be Flemish sailors, with almost exaggeratedly healthy faces, with broad shoulders, strong and plump, and thoroughly Antwerp folk, eating mussels, or drinking beer, and all this will happen with a lot of noise and bustle—by way of contrast—a tiny figure in black with her little hands pressed against her body comes stealing noiselessly along the gray walls. Framed by raven-black hair—a small oval face, brown? orange-yellow? I don't know. For a moment she lifts her eyelids, and looks with a slanting glance out of a pair of jet black eyes. It is a Chinese girl, mysterious, quiet like a mouse—small, bedbug-like in character. What a contrast to that group of Flem-ish mussel eaters.

Another contrast—one passes through a very narrow street, between tremen-dously high houses, warehouses, and sheds.

But down below in the street pubs for all nationalities with masculine and feminine individuals to match, shops selling eatables, seamen's clothes, glaringly colorful and crowded.

That street is long, every moment one sees something striking. Now and again there is a noise, intenser than anywhere else, when a quarrel is going on; for instance, there you are walking, looking about, and suddenly there is a loud cheering and all kinds of shouting. In broad daylight a sailor is being thrown out of a brothel by the girls, and pursued by a furious fellow and a string of prostitutes, of whom he seems rather afraid—at least I saw him scramble over a heap of sacks and disappear through a warehouse window.

Now, when one has had enough of all this tumult—at the end of the landing stages where the Harwich and Havre steamers are moored—with the city behind one, one sees nothing in front, absolutely nothing but an infinite expanse of flat, half-inundated fields, awfully dreary and wet, waving dry rushes, mud, the river with a single little black boat, the water in the foreground gray, the sky, foggy and cold, gray—still like a desert.

As to the general view of the harbor or a dock—at one moment it is more tangled and fantastic than a thorn hedge, so confused that one finds no rest for the eye, and gets giddy, is forced by the whirling of colors and lines to look first here, then there, without being able, even by looking for a long time at one point, to distinguish one thing from another. But when one stands on a spot where one has a vague plot as foreground, then one sees the most beautiful quiet lines, and the effects which Mols, for instance, often paints.

Now one sees a girl who is splendidly healthy, and who looks or seems to look loyal, simple and jolly; then again, a face so sly and false that it makes one afraid, like a hyena's. Not to forget the faces damaged by smallpox, having the color of boiled shrimps, with pale gray eyes, without eyebrows, and sparse sleek thin hair, the color of real pigs' bristles or somewhat yellower; Swedish or Danish types. It would be fine to work there, but how and where?

For one would very soon get into a scrape.

However, I have trudged through quite a number of streets and back streets without adventure, and I have sat and talked quite jovially with various girls who seemed to take me for a sailor.

I don't think it improbable that I shall get hold of good models by painting portraits.

Today I got my things and drawing materials, for which I was longing very much. And so my studio is all fixed up. If I could get good models for almost nothing, I should not be afraid of anything.

I do not think it so very bad either that I have not got so much money as to be able to force things by paying for them. Perhaps the idea of making portraits and having them paid for by posing is the safer way, because in a city it is not the same as it is with the peasants. Well, one thing is sure, Antwerp is very curious and fine for a painter.

My studio is not bad, especially as I have pinned a lot of little Japanese prints on the wall, which amuse me very much. You know those little women's figures in gardens, or on the beach, horsemen, flowers, knotty thorn branches.

I am glad I went, and hope not to sit still this winter. Well, I feel safe now that I have a little den where I can sit and work when the weather is bad.

But of course I shall not exactly live in immense luxury these days.

Try and send your letter off on the first, because I have provided myself with bread till then, but after that I should be in something of a fix.

My little room is better than I expected, and it certainly doesn't look dull. Now that I have the three studies I took with me here, I shall try to approach the picture dealers, who seem to live in private houses, however, with no show window on the street.

The park is nice too, I sat and drew there one morning.

Well, so far I have had no bad luck; as to my lodgings, I am well off, as by spending a few francs more I have got a stove and a lamp.

I shall not easily get bored, I assure you. I have also found the "October" by Lhermitte, women in a potato field in the evening, beautiful. But I have not seen "November," have you got it perhaps? I have also noticed that there is a *Figaro* illustrated with a fine drawing by Raffaelli.

My address you know is 194 Rue des Images, so please forward your letter there, and the second part of de Goncourt when you have finished it.

Good-by,

Ever yours, Vincent

It is curious that my painted studies seem darker in the city than in the country. Is that because the light is less bright everywhere in the city? I don't know, but it may make a greater difference than one would say offhand; it struck me, and I could understand that things you have look darker than I in the country thought they were. However, the ones I have with me now don't come out badly for all that, the mill, avenue with autumn trees and a still life and a few little ones.

439

Dear Theo,   Antwerp, November 1885-February 1886

I must write you again to tell you that I have succeeded in finding a model. I have made two fairly big heads, by way of trial for a portrait. First, that old man whom I wrote you about, a kind of head like Hugo's; then also a study of a woman. In the woman's portrait I have brought lighter tones into the flesh, white tinted with carmine, vermilion, yellow and a light background of gray-yellow, from which the face is separated only by the black hair. Lilac tones in the dress.

Rubens is certainly making a strong impression on me; I think his drawing tremendously good—I mean the drawing of heads and hands in themselves. I am quite carried away by his way of drawing the lines in a face with streaks of pure red, or of modeling the fingers of the hands by the same kind of streaks. I go to the museum fairly often, and then I look at little else but a few heads and hands of his and of Jordaens'. I know he is not as intimate as Hals and Rembrandt, but in themselves those heads are so alive.

Probably I don't look at those which are generally admired most. I look for fragments like, for instance, those blonde heads in "Ste Thérèse au Purgatoire." I am now looking for a blonde model just because of Rubens. But you must not be angry if I tell you that I cannot make both ends meet this month. I have bought some more colors and two new kinds of drawing brushes which suit me splendidly and with which I can work more accurately.

Then the canvases which I brought with me were too small for the heads, because by using other colors I need more space for the surroundings.

All that and the models are ruining me.

I tell you this as emphatically as possible, because when losing time one loses doubly.

In the last days of this month, after I have done some more heads, I hope to paint a view on the Scheldt, for which I have already bought a canvas. I can also go there in bad weather, to an inn at St. Anne's, that is on the other side, opposite the Lieve Vrouwekerk [Our Lady's Church]. Other painters have worked there before.

I am very glad I came here, for in many ways it is useful and necessary for me.

I made the acquaintance of Tyck, the best color manufacturer here, and he was very kind in giving me information about some colors. About green colors, for instance, that are fast. I also asked him things about Rubens's technique, which he answered in a way that proved to me how well he analyzes the material used, which not everybody does, although it is very useful.

What more shall I tell you? Oh yes, I have seen two collections of modern pictures, first, what was bought at the exhibition for the raffle, and then a collection of pictures that was for sale.

So I saw several fine things, two studies by Henri de Braekeleer; you know that he is absolutely different from the old De Braekeleer, I mean the one who is a famous colorist, and who analyzes rigorously. He is somewhat like Manet, that is to say as original as Manet.

One study was of a woman in a studio, or some such interior, with Japanese objects; the woman wore a costume of yellow and black. The flesh color, white with carmine. In the surroundings, all kinds of quaint little tones. The other one was a half-finished study of a landscape. Yellow, faded, flat fields à perte de vue [as far as the eye can see], crossed by a black cinderpath, with a ditch alongside; over it, a sky of lilac gray, with accents of carmined lilac. Far away the little red patch of vermilion of a roof, and two little black trees. Hardly anything, and yet for me a great deal, because of the peculiar sentiment in the juxtaposition of colors. I also saw an old study by De Groux, a woman beside a cradle, somewhat like an old Israëls.

Further, what shall I say about those modern pictures? I thought many of them *splendid*, and then I mean especially the work of the colorists, or of those who try to be so, who look everywhere for mother-of-pearl-like combinations in the light parts. But to me it is not always perfect by a long shot; it is too affected. I prefer to see a simple brush stroke and a less far-fetched, difficult color. More simplicity, in short that intelligent simplicity which is not afraid of frank technique.

I like Rubens just for his ingenuous way of painting, his working with the simplest means.

I don't count Henri de Braekeleer among those who look for mother-of-pearl effects everywhere, because his is a curious, very interesting endeavor to be literally true, and he stands quite apart. I also saw various gray paintings, including a printing shop by Mertens, a picture by Verhaert representing his own studio, where he himself is sitting etching and his wife standing behind him.

By La Rivière—an Amsterdam hired mourner after a funeral, *very fine* in the black tones, a Goya-like conception; that little picture was a masterpiece. In both collections I saw very beautiful landscapes and marines. But as to the portraits—those I remember best are the "Fisherboy" by Frans Hals, "Saskia" by Rembrandt, a number of smiling or weeping faces by Rubens.

Ah, a picture must be painted—and then why not simply? Now when I look into real life—I get the same kind of impressions. I see the people in the street very well, but I often think the servant girls so much more interesting and beautiful than the ladies, the workmen more interesting than the gentlemen; and in those common girls and fellows I find a power and vitality which, if one wants to express them in their peculiar character, ought to be painted with a firm brush stroke, with a simple technique.

Wauters understood this, used to at least, for so far I haven't seen any work of his here. What I admire so much in Delacroix, too, is that he makes us feel the life of things, and the expression, and the movement, that he *absolutely dominates his colors.*

And in a great many of the good things I saw, though I admire them, there is often far too much *paint*. At present I am getting more and more in the habit of talking to the models while painting, to keep their faces animated.

I have discovered a woman—she is old now—who used to live in Paris and provided the painters with models, for instance, Scheffer, Gigoux, Delacroix and another one who painted a Phryne.

Now she is a washerwoman and knows a lot of women, and could always supply some, she said.

It has been snowing, and the city was splendid early this morning in the snow, fine groups of street cleaners.

I am glad I came here, for I am already full of ideas, also for the time when I shall be in the country again.

It was in the *Etoile Belge*, I think, that I read an article by Eugène Bataille, reprinted from the *Figaro*, about conditions in Paris, an article which impressed me as being very well thought out; but according to him conditions in general are very bad. This Mr. Bataille has, contrary to the opinion of the Dutch journalists, expressed himself in Amsterdam pessimistically about the state of affairs in Holland.

As to art dealing—as I have already written you, the dealers here complain like misère ouverte. And yet I believe that so much might still be done. To mention one thing, for instance, one sees no pictures in the cafés, restaurants, café-chantants, at least hardly any. And how contrary this is to nature. Why don't they hang still lifes there, like the splendid decorations Fijt, Hondekoeter and so many others made in times of old? Why not women's portraits, if they want prostitutes? I know one must work cheaply for such purposes, but one can work relatively cheaply. Raising prices to such a height is the trade's ruin, and leads to no good after all.

Good-by, write again between times if you can. As to the money, do what you can, but remember that we must try our utmost to succeed. And I won't let that idea of painting portraits go, for it is a good thing to fight for, to show people that there is more in them than the photographer can possibly get out of them with his machine.

Good-by, with a handshake,

Ever yours, Vincent

I have noticed the great number of photographers here, who are just about the same as everywhere, and seem to be pretty busy.

But always those same conventional eyes, noses, mouths—waxlike and smooth and cold.

It cannot but always remain *lifeless*.

And the painted portraits have a life of their own, coming straight from the painter's soul, which the machine cannot reach. The more one looks at photographs, the more one feels this, I think.

442

Dear Theo,   Antwerp, 28 December 1885
It is high time I thanked you for the 50 fr. you sent, which helped me get through the month, though from today on it will be pretty much the same.

But—there are a few more studies made, and the more I paint, the more progress I think I make. As soon as I received the money, I took a beautiful model and painted her head life-size.

It is quite light except for the black, you know. Yet the head itself stands out simply against a background in which I tried to put a golden shimmer of light.

Here follows the color scheme—a well-toned flesh color, in the neck rather bronze-like, jet-black hair—black which I had to make with carmine and Prussian blue, dullish white for the little jacket, light yellow, much lighter than the white, for the background. A scarlet note in the jet-black hair and another scarlet ribbon in the dullish white.

She is a girl from a café-chantant, and yet the expression I sought was rather Ecce Homo-like.

But as I want to remain *true*, especially in the expression, though my own thoughts are in it too, this is what I wanted to express in it.

When the model came, she had apparently been very busy the last few nights, and she said something that was rather characteristic: "Pour moi le champagne ne m'égaye pas, il me rend tout triste" [As for me champagne does not cheer me up, it makes me quite sad].

Then I understood, and I tried to express something voluptuous and at the same time cruelly tormented.

I began a second study of the same model in profile.

Then I made that portrait which I mentioned, the one that was promised me, and I painted a study of that head for myself, and now these last days of the month I hope to paint another head of a man.

I feel quite cheerful, especially about the work, and it is good for me to be here.

I imagine that whatever those tarts may be, one can make money out of them, sooner than in any other way. There is no denying that they are sometimes damned beautiful and that it is the spirit of the time that this kind of picture is gaining more and more ground.

And even from the highest artistic point of view, nothing can be said against it; *to paint human beings*, that was the old Italian art, that is what Millet did and what Breton does.

The question is only whether one starts from the soul or from the clothes, and whether the form serves as a clothes peg for ribbons and bows or if one considers the form as the means of rendering impression and sentiment, or if one models for the sake of modeling, because it is so infinitely beautiful in itself.

Only the first is transitory, and the latter two are both high art.

What rather pleased me was that the girl who posed for me wanted me to paint a portrait for her to keep herself, exactly like the things I made for myself.

And she has promised to let me paint a study of her in her room, in a dancer's dress, as soon as possible. She cannot do this now, because the owner of the café where she is objects to her posing, but as she is going to take a room with another girl, both she and the other girl would like to have their portraits painted. And I fervently hope that she will come back, for she has a striking face and is witty.

But I must train myself, seeing that it all depends on skill and quickness; for they haven't much time or patience, though for that matter, the work need not be less well done for being done quickly, and one must be able to work even if the model does not sit rigidly still. Well, you see that I am at work with full vigor. If I sold something so that I earned a little more, I should work even more vigorously.

As to Portier, I do not lose courage yet, but poverty is hounding me, and at present all the dealers rather suffer from the same evil, that of being more or less "une nation retirée du monde," *i.e.* in hiding. They have too much spleen, and how can one be expected to feel inclined to grub in all that indifference and dullness? Besides, this complaint is catching.

For it is all nonsense that no business can be done, but in any case one must work with conviction and with enthusiasm, in short with a certain warmth.

As to Portier, you wrote me yourself that he was the first to exhibit the impressionists, and that he was completely crowded out by Durand Ruel. Well, one might conclude from this that he is a man of initiative, not just saying things but *doing* them. Perhaps it is the fault of his sixty years, and for the rest it may be one of the many cases in which at the time when pictures were the fashion and business prospered, a lot of intelligent persons were wantonly put aside, as if they were of no importance and without talent, only because they could not get themselves to believe in the stability of that sudden rage for pictures and the enormous rise of prices.

Now, as business is slack, one sees those very same dealers who were so very enterprising, let's say ten years ago, go more or less into hiding. And we are not yet at the end.

Personal initiative with little or no capital is perhaps the germ for the future. We'll see.

Yesterday I saw a large photograph of a Rembrandt which I did not know, and which struck me tremendously; it was a woman's head, the light fell on the bust, neck, chin and the tip of the nose—the lower jaw.

The forehead and eyes in the shadow of a large hat, with probably red feathers. Probably also red or yellow in the low-necked jacket. A dark background. The expression, a mysterious smile like that of Rembrandt himself in his self-portrait in which Saskia is sitting on his knee and he has a glass of wine in his hand.

These days my thoughts are full of Rembrandt and Hals all the time, not because I see so many of their pictures, but because among the people here I see so many types that remind me of that time.

I still go often to those popular balls, to see the heads of the women and the heads of the sailors and soldiers. One pays the entrance fee of 20 or 30 centimes, and drinks a glass of beer, for they drink very little spirits, and one can amuse oneself a whole evening, at least I do, by watching these people enjoy themselves.

To paint a great deal from the model—that is what I must do, and it is the only thing that seriously helps to make progress.

I notice that I have been underfed too long, and when I received your money, my stomach could not digest the food; but I will try to remedy that.

And it does not prevent my having all my energy and capacity when at work.

But when I am out-of-doors, working in the open air is too much for me, and I feel too faint.

Well, painting is a thing that wears one out. But when I went to see him shortly before I came here, Dr. Van der Loo told me that I am fairly strong after all. That I need not despair of reaching the age which is necessary for producing a life's work. I told him that I knew of several painters who, notwithstanding all their nervousness, etc., had reached the age of sixty or seventy even, fortunately for themselves, and that I should like to do the same.

Then I think that if one keeps one's serenity and good spirits, the mood in which one is helps a great deal. In that respect I have gained by coming here, for I have got new ideas and I have new means of expressing what I want, because better brushes will help me, and I am crazy about those two colors, carmine and cobalt.

Cobalt is a divine color, and there is nothing so beautiful for bringing atmosphere around things. Carmine is the red of wine, and it is warm and spirited like wine.

The same with emerald-green. It is bad economy not to use these colors, the same with cadmium.

Something about my constitution which made me very glad was what a doctor in Amsterdam told me, whom I consulted once about a few things which sometimes made me fear that I was not long for this world, and whose opinion I did not ask straight out, but just to know the first impression of somebody who absolutely did not know me. It was like this: making use of a small complaint I had then, in the course of the conversation I referred to my constitution in general—how glad I was when this doctor took me for an ordinary working-man and said, "I suppose you are an ironworker." That is just what I have tried to change in myself; when I was younger, I looked like one who was intellectually overwrought, and now I look like a bargeman or an ironworker.

And to change one's constitution so that one gets "a tough hide" is no easy matter.

But all the same I must be careful, and try to keep what I have, and gain in strength.

Above all I want you to write me if the idea seems so absurd to you that one should gain in courage if one planted the seed of a business of one's own?

As to my present work, I feel that I can do better; however, I need some more space and air, I mean—I ought to be able to spend a little more. Above all, above all I cannot take enough models. I could produce work of a better quality, but then my expenses would be heavier. But oughtn't one to aim at something lofty, something true, something distinguished?

The women's figures I see here among the people make a tremendous impression on me, much more to paint them than to possess them, though indeed, I should like both.

I reread the book by de Goncourt. It is excellent. The preface to *Chérie*, which you will read, tells the story of what the de Goncourts went through, and how at the end of their lives they were melancholy, yes, but felt sure of themselves, knowing that they had *accomplished* something, that their work would remain. What fellows they were! If we were more of one mind than we are now, if we could agree completely, why shouldn't we *do the same?*

By the way, because in any case I shall have four or five days of absolute fast in all respects at the end of this year, do send your letter on the first of January and not later. Perhaps you will not be able to understand, but it is true that when I receive the money my greatest appetite is not for food, though I have fasted, but the appetite for painting is even stronger, and I at once set out to hunt for models, and continue until all the money is gone. While all I have to live on is my breakfast served by the people I live with, and in the evening for supper a cup of coffee and some bread in the dairy, or else a loaf of rye bread that I have in my trunk.

As long as I am painting it is more than enough, but a feeling of weakness comes when the models have left.

I am attached to the models here because they are so different from the models in the country. And especially because the character is so entirely different, and the contrast gives me new ideas, especially for the flesh colors. And what I have now achieved in the last head I painted, though it is not yet so that I am satisfied with it, is different from the previous heads.

I know that you are sufficiently convinced of the importance of being *true* so that I can speak out freely to you.

If I paint peasant women, I want them to be peasant women; for the same reason, if I paint harlots I want a harlot-like expression.

That was why a certain harlot's head by Rembrandt struck me so enormously. Because he had caught so infinitely beautifully that mysterious smile, with a gravity such as only he possesses, the magician of magicians.

This is a new thing for me, and it is essentially what I want. Manet has done it, and Courbet, damn it, I have the same ambition; besides, I have felt too strongly in the very marrow of my bones the infinite beauty of the analyses of women by the very great men of literature, a Zola, Daudet, de Goncourt, Balzac.

Even Stevens does not satisfy me, because his women are not those I know personally. And those he selects are not the most interesting, I think. Well, however that may be—I want to get on à tout prix—and I want to be myself.

I feel quite obstinate, and I no longer care what people say about me or my work.

It seems very difficult to get models for the nude here, at least the girl I painted refused.

Of course that "refused" is perhaps only relative, but at least it would not be easy; but I must say she would be splendid. From a business point of view I can only say that we are already in what they are starting to call la fin d'un siècle—that women have a charm as in a time of revolution—in fact have as much influence —and one would be outside the world if one kept them outside one's work.

It is the same everywhere, in the country as well as in the city; one must take the women into account if one wants to be up-to-date.

Good-by, good wishes for the New Year. With a handshake,

Ever yours, Vincent

444

Dear Theo,   Antwerp, early in 1886

Last Sunday I saw for the first time the two large pictures by Rubens, and as I had looked at those in the museum repeatedly and at my ease, these two—"The Deposition from the Cross" and "The Elevation of the Cross"—were the more interesting. "The Elevation of the Cross" has a peculiarity that struck me at once, and that is—there is no female figure in it. Unless on the side panels of the triptych. Consequently, it is none the better for it. Let me tell you that I love "The Deposition from the Cross." But not because of any depth of feeling such as one would find in a Rembrandt or in a picture by Delacroix or in a drawing by Millet.

Nothing touches me less than Rubens expressing human sorrow.

To explain my meaning more clearly, let me begin by saying that even his most beautiful weeping Magdalenes or Mater Dolorosas always simply remind me of the tears of a beautiful prostitute who has caught a venereal disease or some such small misery of human life.

As such they are masterly, but one must not look for more in them.

Rubens is extraordinary in painting ordinary beautiful women. But he is not dramatic in the expression.

Compare him, for instance, to that head by Rembrandt in the Lacaze Collection; to the man's figure in "The Jewish Bride"—you will understand what I mean, as for instance, that his eight pompous figures of fellows performing a feat of strength with a heavy wooden cross in "The Elevation of the Cross" seem absurd to me from the standpoint of modern analysis of human passions and feelings. That Rubens's expressions, especially of the men (the real portraits always excepted), are superficial, hollow, pompous, yes—altogether conventional, like those of Jules Romain and even worse fellows of the decadence.

But I still love it because he, Rubens, is the very man who tries to express, and really succeeds in expressing, a mood of cheerfulness, of serenity, of sorrow, by the combination of colors—though sometimes his figures may be hollow, etc.

Thus in "The Elevation of the Cross" the pale spot of the corpse in a high accent of light—is dramatic in its contrast to the rest, which is kept in such a low color scale.

Of the same order, but in my opinion far more beautiful, is the charm of "The Deposition from the Cross," where the pale spot is repeated in the blonde hair, the fair face and neck of the female figures, whereas the somber surroundings are enormously rich because of the various low-toned harmonizing masses of red, dark green, black, gray and violet.

And once again Delacroix has tried to make people believe in the symphonies of the colors. And one would almost say in vain, if one remembers how almost everybody understands by good color the correctness of the local color, the narrow-minded exactness which neither Rembrandt nor Millet nor Delacroix nor whoever else, neither Manet nor Courbet, has aimed at, as little as Rubens or Veronese.

I have also seen several other pictures by Rubens in various churches.

And it is very interesting to study Rubens, because his technique is so very simple, or rather seems to be so. His means are so simple, and he paints, and particularly draws, with such a quick hand and without any hesitation. But portraits and heads and figures of women are his specialty. There he is deep and intimate too. And how fresh his pictures remain because of the very simplicity of his technique.

What more shall I say? That I feel increasingly inclined to do all my figure studies over again, very calmly and quietly, without any nervous hurry. I want to progress so far in the knowledge of the nude and the structure of the figure that I might be able to work from memory.

I should still like to work sometime either at Verlat's or in some other studio, besides working for myself as much as possible from the model.

For the moment I have deposited five pictures, two portraits, two landscapes, and one still life in Verlat's painting class at the academy. I have just been there again, but he was not there either time.

But I shall soon be able to tell you the result, and I hope that I shall be allowed to paint from the model all day at the academy, which will make things easier for me, as the models are so awfully expensive that my purse cannot stand the strain.

And I must find something to help me in that respect. At all events I think I shall remain in Antwerp for some time, instead of going back to the country; that would be much better than putting it off, and here there is so much more chance of finding people who would perhaps interest themselves in it. I feel that I dare undertake something, and can achieve something, and things have been dragging on far too long already.

You get angry whenever I expostulate with you, or rather you don't give a damn, and all the rest of it, which we know by now, and yet I believe a time will come when, of your own accord, you will come to the conclusion that you have been too weak to persevere in trying to help me regain some credit with people. But never mind, we are not faced by the past but by the future. And again I tell you—I am convinced that time will make you see that, if only there had been more cordiality and warmth between us, we might have built a business of our own together. Even if you had stayed with Goupil & Co.

Indeed, you said to me that you know perfectly well you will be rewarded with stinking ingratitude, but are you quite sure this isn't a misunderstanding of the type Father himself labored under? I for one shall not take it lying down, you can be sure of that. For there is still too much work to be done, even at present.

The other day I saw for the first time a fragment of Zola's new book *L'Œuvre*, which, as you know, appears as a serial in *Le Gil Blas*.

I think that this novel, if it penetrates the art world somewhat, may do some good. The fragment I read was very striking.

When you get right down to it, I'll admit that when one is working exclusively from nature, something more is needed: the facility of composing, the knowledge of the figure, but, after all, I do not believe I have been drudging absolutely in vain all these years. I feel a certain power within me, because wherever I may be, I shall always have an aim—painting people as I see and know them.

Whether impressionism has already had its last say or not—to stick to the term impressionism—I always imagine that many new artists in the figure may arise, and I begin to think it more and more desirable that, in a difficult time like the present, one seeks one's security in the deeper understanding of the highest art.

For there is, relatively speaking, higher and lower art; *people* are more important than anything else, and are in fact much more difficult to paint, too.

I will try hard to make acquaintances here, and I think that if I worked some time, for instance under Verlat, I would learn to know better what is going on here, and how to fit in with the rest.

So let me struggle along my own way, and for Heaven's sake do not lose courage, and do not slacken. I do not think you can reasonably expect me to go back to the country for the sake of perhaps 50 fr. a month less, seeing that the whole series of future years will depend so much on the relations I must establish in town, either here in Antwerp or later on in Paris.

And I wish I could make you understand how probable it is that there will be great changes in the art trade. And, consequently, many new chances will present themselves too if one has something original to show.

But *that* is certainly necessary if one wants to be of some use. It is no fault or crime of mine if I must sometimes tell you we must put more vigor into such and such a thing, and if we haven't got the money ourselves, we must find friends and new relations. I must earn a little more or have some more friends, preferably both. That is the way to success, but recently it has been too hard for me.

As for this month, I absolutely must insist on your sending me at least another 50 fr.

At present I am losing weight, and moreover my clothes are getting too shabby, etc. You know yourself that it isn't right as it is. Yet I feel sort of confident that we shall pull through.

But you wrote that if I fell ill, we should be worse off. I hope it will not come to that, but I should like to have a little more ease, just to prevent illness.

Just think how many people there are who exist without ever having the slightest idea what care is, and who always keep on thinking that everything will turn out for the best, as if there were no people starving or completely ruined! I begin to object more and more to your pretending to be a financier, and thinking me exactly the opposite. All people are not alike, and if one does not understand that in drawing up accounts some *time* must have passed over the account before one can be sure to have counted right, if one does not understand this, one *is no calculator*. And a broader insight into finances is exactly what characterizes many modern financiers. Namely not pinching, but allowing freedom of action.

I know, Theo, that you may also be rather hard up. But your life has never been so hard as mine has these last ten or twelve years. Can't you make allowances for me when I say, Perhaps it has been long enough now? Meanwhile I have learned something that I did not know before, that has renewed all my chances, and I protest against my always being neglected. And if I should like to live again in the city for some time, and afterward perhaps to work in a studio in Paris too, would you try to prevent this?

Be honest enough to let me go my own way, for I tell you that I do not want to quarrel, and I will not quarrel, but I will not be hampered in my career. And what can I do in the country, unless I go there with money for models and colors? There is no chance, absolutely none, of making money with my work in the country, and there is such a chance in the city. So I am not safe before I have made friends in the city—and that comes first. For the moment this may complicate things somewhat, but after all it is the only way, and going back to the country now would end in stagnation.

Well, good-by. De Goncourt's book is fine.   Ever yours, Vincent

453
Dear Theo,   Antwerp, January-February 1886
I write you often these days, and I often write the same thing, but let it prove to you that I have one thing especially in mind—the necessity of entering that period of figure drawing.

And then it may be egoistic if you like, I want my health restored. My impression of the time I have spent here does not change either; in a certain sense I am very much disappointed by what I have made here, but my ideas have been modified and refreshed, and that was the real object of my coming here. But as I have perceived that I relied too much on my health, and that, though the core is still all right, yet I am but a ruin compared to what I might have been, so it would not astonish me at all if you, too, were absolutely in need of that same more hygienic life that was prescribed for me.

If I am not mistaken in this, I think we cannot join each other soon enough, and I keep objecting to a stay in the country. For though the air is bracing, I should miss there the distraction and the pleasant company of the city, which we should enjoy so much more if we were together. And if we were together soon, I should disappoint you in many things, yes, to be sure, but not in everything, and not in my way of looking at things, I suppose.

Now that we are discussing things, I want to tell you to begin with that I wish both of us might find a wife in some way or other before long, for it is high time, and if we should wait too long, we should not be the better for it.

But I say this in all calmness. However, it is one of the first requisites for our more hygienic life. And I mention it because in that respect we may have to overcome an enormous difficulty, on which a great deal depends. And herewith I break the ice on the subject; we shall always have to return to it. And in the intercourse with women one especially learns so much about art.

It is a pity that, as one gradually gains experience, one gradually loses one's youth. If that were not so, life would be too good.

Have you already read that preface to *Chérie* by de Goncourt? The amount of work those fellows have achieved is enormous when one thinks of it.

It is such a splendid idea that working and thinking together. And every day I find new proof of the theory that the main reason for much misery among the artists lies in their discord, in their not co-operating, not being good but false to each other. And now, if we were more sensible in that respect, I do not doubt for a moment that within a year's time we should make headway, and be happier.

I am not getting on very well with my work, but I do not force things, because in fact I am almost completely forbidden to.

And I want to keep up my strength for that first time in Paris, if that is to follow first, without any other interval than that one month in the country. For I should like to go there in good condition.

It was Sunday today, almost a spring day. This morning I took a long walk alone all through the city, in the park, along the boulevards. The weather was such that I think in the country they will have heard the lark sing for the first time.

In short, there was something of resurrection in the atmosphere.

Yet what depression there is in business and among the people. I do not think it exaggerated to be pessimistic about the various strikes, etc., everywhere.

They will certainly prove not to have been useless for the following generations, for *then* they will have proved a success. But now it is of course hard enough for everybody who must earn his bread by his work, the more so because we can foresee that it will get worse and worse from year to year. The laborer against the bourgeois is as justifiable as was the tiers état against the other two a hundred years ago. And the best thing to do is to keep silent, for fate is not on the bourgeois side, and we shall live to see more of it; we are still far from the end. So although it's spring, how many thousands and thousands are wandering about, desolate.

I see the lark soaring in the spring air as well as the greatest optimist; but I also see the young girl of about twenty, who might have been in good health, a victim of consumption, and who will perhaps drown herself before she dies of any illness.

If one is always in respectable company among rather well-to-do bourgeois, one does not notice this so much perhaps, but if one has dined for years on la vache enragée, as I have, one cannot deny that great misery is a fact that weights the scale.

One may not be able to cure or to save, but one can sympathize with and pity them.

Corot, who after all had more serenity than anybody else, who felt the spring so deeply, was he not as simple as a workingman all his life, and so sensitive to all the miseries of others? And what struck me in his biography was that when he was already very old in 1870 and 1871, he certainly looked at the bright sky, but at the same time he visited the ambulances where the wounded lay dying.

Illusions may fade, but the sublime *remains*. One may doubt everything, but one does not doubt people like Corot and Millet and Delacroix. And I think that in moments when one does not care for nature any more, one still cares for humanity.

If you can, send me something extra this month, be it more or less, even if it's only 5 francs, do so. If you can't, then it can't be helped.

I am greatly longing to know your decision, if perhaps you would approve of my coming to Paris already about April 1. At all events write soon about it.

Good-by. With a handshake,

Ever yours, Vincent

458a

[Piérard, pp. 155–159] On the subject of Van Gogh's arrival at the academy in Antwerp, here are the reminiscences noted down from the lips of Mr. Victor Hageman (who died in October, 1938).

At the time I was a pupil in the drawing class. There were only a few weeks left until the end of the course. I remember quite well that weather-beaten, nervous, restless man who crashed like a bombshell into the Antwerp academy, upsetting the director, the drawing master and the pupils.

Van Gogh, who was then thirty-one years old, first went into the painting class taught by Verlat, the director of the academy, the perfect type of the official painter, whose duty it was to transmit to posterity, by means of the interpretative realizations of the art of painting, memories of great patriotic solemnities. One morning Van Gogh came into the class, in which there were about sixty pupils, more than a dozen of whom were German or English; he was dressed in a kind of blue blouse, of the type usually worn by the Flemish cattle dealers, and he wore a fur cap on his head. In place of a regular palette he used a board torn from a packing case that had contained sugar and yeast. On that day the pupils had to paint two wrestlers, who were posed on the platform, stripped to the waist.

Van Gogh started painting feverishly, furiously, with a rapidity that stupefied his fellow students. "He laid on his paint so thickly," Mr. Hageman told us, "that his colors literally dripped from his canvas on to the floor."

When Verlat saw this work and its extraordinary creator, he asked in Flemish, in a tone of voice that showed how dumfounded he was, "Who are you?"

Van Gogh replied quietly, "Well, I am Vincent, a Dutchman."

Then the very academic director proclaimed contemptuously, while pointing at the newcomer's canvas, "I won't correct such putrefied dogs. My boy, go to the drawing class quickly."

Van Gogh, whose cheeks had gone purple, restrained his anger, and fled to the course of good Mr. Sieber (sic), who was also frightened by the novel phenomenon, but who had a less irascible temperament than his director.

Vincent stayed there for some weeks, drawing zealously, taking great pains, and visibly suffering under his efforts to grasp the vigor of the subject, working rapidly, without making corrections, more often than not tearing up the drawing he had just finished, or else throwing it down behind him. He made sketches of everything that was to be found in the hall: of the students, of their clothes, of the furniture, while forgetting the plaster cast the professor had given him to copy. Already everybody marveled at the rapidity with which he worked, as he did the same drawing or painting over again ten or fifteen times.

One day, in the drawing class of the academy of Antwerp, they gave the students (as if by accident) a cast of the Venus de Milo to copy. Van Gogh, who evidently was struck by one of the essential characteristics of the model, strongly accentuated the breadth of the hips, and made Venus the victim of the same disfigurements he introduced into "The Sower" by Millet, or "The Good Samaritan" by Delacroix, other pictures that he was to copy in the course of his career. The beautiful Greek goddess had become a robust Flemish matron. When honest Mr. Sieber saw this, he tore Van Gogh's drawing sheet with the furious corrective strokes of his crayon, reminding his disciple of the inviolable canons of his art.

Then the young Dutchman, rustic (sic!) of the Danube (sic!) (or of the Lower Meuse) whose rudeness had terrified the fair clients of Goupil's at Paris, flew into a violent passion, and roared at his professor, who was scared out of his wits: "So you don't know what a young woman is like, God damn you! A woman must have hips and buttocks and a pelvis in which she can hold a child!"...

This was the last lesson Van Gogh took—or gave—at the Antwerp academy. He had made some stanch friends among the pupils there, especially among the English, such as Levens. (The latter was the man who painted the portrait of Vincent that was later published in the magazine *The Present and Presently.*)

With those who understood him, who had an inkling of his growing genius, he showed himself communicative, enthusiastic, fraternal. Very often he spoke to them about those rough and kind-hearted miners of the Borinage, whom he had catechized and cared for and helped and nursed with so much love. During the tragic strikes of 1886 he even wanted to go back to that Black Country.

The above was confirmed by Emanuel de Bom in an article published in the Rotterdam newspaper *Nieuwe Rotterdamse Courant* of November 3, 1938, in which he quotes a letter written by Victor Hageman. In this may be found (Tralbaut, p. 154):

"He was told to do a drawing of the Venus de Milo," De Bom writes. "He was of the opinion that 'that woman must have hips,' and he gave her very un-Grecian ones, they were *'comme ça'*! The drawing master (I will not mention his name—moreover, he is dead now) sent Van Gogh down to a lower class, and there Vincent, who scorned nothing, did drawings of 'noses and ears.' "

And Baseleer told Charles Bernard in the interview already quoted that Vincent was reported to have said of the Venus de Milo: "Fine female, nice hips." And he continues:

"I can still see before me that thickset Venus with an enormous pelvis, that extraordinary, fat-buttocked figure which had issued from Vincent's drawing pencil. Antiquity as seen by Rembrandt, Greece through the medium of a distorting windowpane on the Keizersgracht in Amsterdam."

Years of color and light

459*a*

[Letter written in English by Vincent van Gogh to the English painter Levens. The text is reproduced without alterations.][1]

My dear Mr. Levens,   Paris, Aug.–Oct. 1887

Since I am here in Paris I have very often thought of yourself and work. You will remember that I liked your colour, your ideas on art and literature and I add, most of all your personality. I have already before now thought that I ought to let you know what I was doing where I was. But what refrained me was that I find living in Paris is much dearer than in Antwerp and not knowing what your circumstances are I dare not say come over to Paris from Antwerp without warning you that it costs one dearer, and that if poor, one has to suffer many things—as you may imagine—. But on the other hand there is more chance of selling. There is also a good chance of exchanging pictures with other artists.

In one word, with much energy, with a sincere personal feeling of colour in nature I would say an artist can get on here notwithstanding the many obstructions. And I intend remaining here still longer.

There is much to be seen here—for instance Delacroix, to name only one master. In Antwerp I did not even know what the impressionists were, now I have seen them and though *not* being one of the club yet I have much admired certain impressionists' pictures—*Degas* nude figure—*Claude Monet* landscape.

And now for what regards what I myself have been doing, I have lacked money for paying models else I had entirely given myself to figure painting. But I have made a series of color studies in painting, simply flowers, red poppies, blue corn flowers and myosotys, white and rose roses, yellow chrysanthemums—seeking oppositions of blue with orange, red and green, yellow and violet seeking *les tons rompus et neutres* to harmonise brutal extremes. Trying to render intense colour and not a grey harmony.

Now after these gymnastics I lately did two heads which I dare say are better in light and colour than those I did before.

So as we said at the time : in *colour* seeking *life* the true drawing is modelling with colour.

I did a dozen landscapes too, frankly *green* frankly *blue*.

And so I am struggling for life and progress in art.

[1] According to John Rewald of New York, this letter was first published in *The Sunday Times*, London, February 17, 1929 (edited by E. V. Lucas). Levens painted mainly "farmyards." The letter was written in 1886 (not 1887).

Now I would very much like to know what you are doing and whether you ever think of going to Paris.

If ever you did come here, write to me before and I will, if you like, share my lodgings and studio with you so long as I have any. In spring—say February or even sooner I may be going to the South of France, the land of the *blue* tones and gay colors.

And look here, if I knew you had longings for the same we might combine.

I felt sure at the time that you are a thorough colourist and since I saw the impressionists I assure you that neither your colour nor mine as it is developping itself, is *exactly* the same as their theories. But so much dare I say we have a chance and a good one finding friends.—I hope your health is all-right. I was rather low down in health when in Antwerp but got better here.

Write to me in any case. Remember me to Allen, Briet, Rink, Durant but I have not often thought of them as I did think of you—almost daily.

Shaking hands cordially.

Yours truly Vincent

My present address is
Mr. Vincent van Gogh
54 Rue Lepic, Paris.

With regard my chances of sale look here, they are certainly not much but still *I do have* a beginning.

At the present moment I have found four dealers who have exhibited studies of mine. And I have exchanged studies with many artists.

Now the prices are 50 francs. Certainly not much—but—as far as I can see one must sell cheap to rise and even at costing price. And mind my dear fellow, Paris is Paris. There is but one Paris and however hard living may be here, and if it became worse and harder even—the french air clears up the brain and does good—a world of good.

I have been in Cormons studio for three or four months but I did not find that so useful as I had expected it to be. It may be my fault however, anyhow I left there too as I left Antwerp and since I worked alone, and fancy that since I feel my own self more.

Trade is slow here. The great dealers sell Millet, Delacroix, Corot, Daubigny, Dupré, a few other masters at exorbitant prices. They do little or nothing for young artists. The second class dealers contrariwise sell those at very low prices. If I asked more I would do nothing, I fancy. However I have faith in colour. Even with regards the price the public will pay for it in the long run. But for the present things are awfully hard. Therefore let anyone who risks to go over here consider there is no laying on roses at all.

What is to be gained is *progress* and what the deuce that is, it is to be found here. I dare say as certain anyone who has a solid position elsewhere let him stay where he is. But for adventurers as myself, I think they lose nothing in risking more. Especially as in my case I am not an adventurer by choice but by fate, and feeling nowhere so much myself a stranger as in my family and country.—Kindly remember me to your landlady Mrs. Roosmalen and say her that if she will exhibit something of my work I will send her a small picture of mine.

462

My dear friend,[1]   Paris, Summer 1887

Thank you for your letter and what it contained. It depresses me to think that even when it's a success, painting never pays back what it costs.

I was touched by what you wrote about home—"They are fairly well but still it is sad to see them." A dozen years ago you would have sworn that at any rate the family would always prosper and get on. It would be a great satisfaction to Mother if your marriage came off, and for the sake of your health and your work you ought not to remain single.

As for me—I feel I am losing the desire for marriage and children, and now and then it saddens me that I should be feeling like that at thirty-five, just when it should be the opposite. And sometimes I have a grudge against this rotten painting. It was Richepin who said somewhere:

> "The love of art makes one lose real love."
> [L'amour de l'art fait perdre l'amour vrai.]

I think that is terribly true, but on the other hand real love makes you disgusted with art.

And at times I already feel old and broken, and yet still enough of a lover not to be a real enthusiast for painting. One must have ambition in order to succeed, and ambition seems to me absurd. I don't know what will come of it; above all I should like to be less of a burden to you—and that is not impossible in the future—for I hope to make such progress that you will be able to show my stuff boldly without compromising yourself.

And then I will take myself off somewhere down south, to get away from the sight of so many painters that disgust me as men.

You can be sure of one thing, that I will not try to do any more work for the Tambourin. Besides, I think that it is going into other hands, and I certainly shall not try to stop it.

As for the Segatori, that's very different. I still have some affection for her, and I hope she still has some for me. But just now she is in a bad way; she is neither a free agent nor mistress in her own house, and worst of all she is ill and in pain. Although I would not say this openly, my own opinion is that she has had an abortion (unless, indeed, she has had a miscarriage), but anyway, in her position I do not blame her.

In two months' time she will be better, I hope, and then perhaps she will be grateful that I did not bother her. But bear in mind that if she refuses in cold blood to give me what belongs to me or does me any wrong once she is well, I shall not spare her—but that will not be necessary. I know her well enough to trust her still. And mind you, if she manages to keep her place going, from the

[1] Written in French. Theo was on a summer holiday in Holland.

point of view of business I should not blame her for choosing to be top dog, and not underdog. If she tramples on my toes a bit in order to get on, well, she has my leave. When I saw her again, she did not trample on my heart, which she would have done if she had been as bad as people said.

I saw Tanguy yesterday, and he has put a canvas I've just done in his window. I have done four since you left, and am working on a big one.

I know that these big long canvases are difficult to sell, but later on people will see that there is open air in them and good humor.

So now the whole lot would do for the decoration of a dining room or a country house.

And if you fall very much in love, and then get married, it doesn't seem impossible to me that you will rise to a country house yourself someday like so many other picture dealers. If you live well, you spend more, but you gain ground that way, and perhaps these days one gets on better by looking rich than by looking shabby. It's better to have a gay life of it than commit suicide. Remember me to all at home.

Ever yours, Vincent

469

My dear Theo,   Arles, 17 February 1888

Thank you very much for your letter, which I had not dared to expect so soon, as far as the 50-fr. note which you added was concerned.

I see that you have not yet had an answer from Tersteeg. I don't think that we need press him in another letter. However, if you have any official business to transact with B. V. & Co. in The Hague, you might mention in a P.S. that you are rather surprised that he has in no way acknowledged the receipt of the letter in question.

As for my work, I brought back a size 15 canvas today. It is a drawbridge with a little cart going over it, outlined against a blue sky—the river blue as well, the banks orange colored with green grass and a group of women washing linen in smocks and multicolored caps. And another landscape with a little country bridge and more women washing linen.

Also an avenue of plane trees near the station. Altogether twelve studies since I've been here.

The weather here is changeable, often windy with murky skies, but the almond trees are beginning to flower everywhere. I am very glad that the pictures should go to the Independents. You are right to go to see Signac at his house. I was very glad to see from your letter of today that he made a better impression on you than he did the first time. In any case I am glad to know that after today you will not be alone in the apartment.

Remember me kindly to Koning. Are you well? I am better myself, except that eating is a real ordeal, as I have a touch of fever and no appetite, but it's only a question of time and patience.

I have company in the evening, for the young Danish painter who is here is a decent soul: his work is dry, correct and timid, but I do not object to that when the painter is young and intelligent. He originally began studying medicine: he has read Zola, de Goncourt, and Guy de Maupassant, and he has enough money to do himself well. And with all this, a very genuine desire to do very different work from what he is actually producing now.

I think he would be wise to delay his return home for a year, or to come back here after a short visit to his friends.

But, old boy, you know, I feel as though I were in Japan—I say no more than that, and mind, I haven't seen anything in its usual splendor yet.

That's why—even although I'm vexed that just now expenses are heavy and the pictures worthless—that's why I don't despair of the future success of this idea of a long sojourn in the Midi.

Here I am seeing new things, I am learning, and if I take it easy, my body doesn't refuse to function.

For many reasons I should like to get some sort of little retreat, where the poor cab horses of Paris—that is, you and several of our friends, the poor impressionists—could go out to pasture when they get too beat up.

I was present at the inquiry into a crime committed at the door of a brothel here; two Italians killed two Zouaves. I seized the opportunity to go into one of the brothels in a small street called "des ricolettes."

That is the extent of my amorous adventures among the Arlésiennes. The mob *all but* (the Southerner, like Tartarin, being more energetic in good intentions than in action)—the mob, I repeat, all but lynched the murderers confined in the town hall, but in retaliation all the Italians—men and women, the Savoyard monkeys included—have been forced to leave town.

I should not have told you about this, except that it means I've seen the streets of this town full of excited crowds. And it was indeed a fine sight.

I made my last three studies with the perspective frame I told you about. I attach some importance to the use of the frame because it seems not unlikely to me that in the near future many artists will make use of it, just as the old German and Italian painters certainly did, and, as I am inclined to think, the Flemish too. The modern use of it may differ from the ancient practice, but in the same way isn't it true that in the process of painting in oils one gets very different effects today from those of the men who invented the process, Jan and Hubert van Eyck? And the moral of this is that it's my constant hope that I am not working for myself alone. I believe in the absolute necessity of a new art of color, of design, and—of the artistic life. And if we work in that faith, it seems to me there is a chance that we do not hope in vain.

You must know that I am actually ready to send some studies off to you, only I can't roll them yet. A handshake for you. On Sunday I shall write Bernard and de Lautrec, because I solemnly promised to, and shall send you those letters as well. I am deeply sorry for Gauguin's plight, especially because now his health is shaken: he hasn't the kind of temperament that profits from hardships—on the contrary, this will only exhaust him from here on, and that will spoil him for his work. Good-by for the present.

Ever yours, Vincent

283

B 4 [4]

My dear comrade Bernard,   Arles, About 20 April 1888

Many thanks for the sonnets you sent me; I very much like the form and the sonorous melody of the first one:

Sous les dômes dormeurs des arbres gigantesques.
[Beneath the somnolent domes of the gigantic trees.]

However, with regard to idea and sentiment it may be that I prefer the last one:

Car l'espoir dans mon sein a versé sa névrose.
[For hope has poured its neurosis into my bosom.]

But it seems to me that you do not say clearly enough what you want to make felt—the certainty that one seems to have, and which one can in any case prove, of the nothingness, the emptiness, the betrayal of the desirable good and beautiful things; and that, despite this knowledge, one lets oneself be eternally fooled by the charm which external life, the things outside ourselves, exercises on our six senses, as if one did not know anything, and especially not the difference between objectivity and subjectivity. Fortunately for us we remain stupid and hopeful in this way.

Now I also like:

L'hiver, n'avoir ni sou, ni fleurs—
[Winter, having neither a sou nor flowers—]

and *"Mépris"* [Contempt].

I think *"Coin de chapelle"* [Corner of a Chapel] and *"Dessin d'Albrecht Dürer"* less clear; for instance, which exactly is the drawing by Albrecht Dürer? But nevertheless there are excellent passages in it:

Venus des plaines bleues
Blémis par la longueur des lieues.
[Come from the blue plains,
Paled by the length of the leagues.]

renders very smartly the landscapes bristling with blue rocks, between which the roads meander, as in the backgrounds of Cranach and Van Eyck.

Tordu sur sa croix en spirale
[Twisted on his spiraled cross]

conveys very well the exaggerated leanness of the mystic Christs. But why not add that the anguished look of the martyr is, like the eye of a cab horse, infinitely sad; that would make it more Parisian of Paris, where one sees such looks in the eyes of the superannuated nags of the little carriages as well as in those of the poets, artists.

In short it is not as good as your painting yet; never mind, it will come; you must certainly continue your sonnets. There are so many people, especially among our comrades, who imagine that words are nothing—on the contrary, isn't it true that saying a thing well is as interesting and as difficult as painting it? There is the art of lines and colors, but the art of words is there nonetheless, and will remain.

Here is another orchard, rather simple as a composition: a white tree, a small green tree, a square patch of green, lilac soil, an orange roof, a large blue sky. I am working on nine orchards: one white; one pink, almost red; one white-blue; one grayish pink; one green and pink.

Yesterday I overdid one [canvas] of a cherry tree against a blue sky; the young leaf shoots were orange and gold, the clusters of flowers white, and that against the green-blue of the sky was wonderfully glorious. Unfortunately there is rain today which prevents my returning to the charge.

I saw a brothel here last Sunday—not counting the other days—a large room, the walls covered with blued whitewash—like a village school. Fifty or more military men in red and civilians in black, their faces a magnificent yellow or orange (what hues there are in the faces here), the women in sky blue, in vermilion, as unqualified and garish as possible. The whole in a yellow light. A good deal less lugubrious than the same kind of offices in Paris.

There is no "spleen" in the air here.

For the moment I am still lying low and keeping very quiet, for first of all I must recover from a stomach disorder of which I am the happy owner, but after that I shall have to make a lot of noise, as I aspire to share the glory of the immortal Tartarin de Tarascon.

I was enormously interested to hear that you intend to spend your time [as a soldier] in Algeria. That is perfect, and quite far from being a misfortune. Really, I congratulate you on it; at any rate we shall see each other in Marseilles.

You will see how delighted you will be with seeing the blue here and with feeling the sun.

At present I have a terrace for a studio.

I certainly intend to go do seascapes at Marseilles too; I don't yearn for the gray sea of the North. If you see Gauguin, remember me most kindly to him. I must write to him right now.

My dear comrade Bernard, don't despair and above all don't have *spleen*,[1] old fellow, for with your talent and with your stay in Algeria you will turn out a wonderfully good and true artist. You too will belong to the South. If I have any advice to give you it is to fortify yourself, to eat healthy things, yes, a full year in advance—from now on—for it won't do to come here with a damaged stomach and deteriorated blood.

This was the case with me, and although I am recovering, I am recovering slowly, and I regret not having been a bit more careful beforehand. But not such a damnable winter as the past one—what was there to be done?—for it was a superhuman winter.

[1] Vincent uses this word in the French sense, *i.e.* weariness of life coupled with eccentricity of behavior.

So get your blood in good condition in advance; here, with the bad food, it is difficult to pull through, but once one is in good health again it is less difficult to remain so than in Paris.

Write to me soon, always the same address: "Restaurant Carrel, Arles."

A handshake,

Sincerely yours, Vincent

481

My dear Theo,   Arles, 4 May 1888

Yesterday I went to the furniture dealer's to see if I could hire a bed, etc. Unfortunately they would *not* hire, and even refused to sell on a monthly installment plan. This is rather awkward.

I thought perhaps if Koning leaves after seeing the Salon, which I believe was his original intention, that you might send me the bed that he now occupies after his departure. One must take into account that if I sleep at the studio, it will make a difference of 300 frs. a year, which would otherwise have to be paid to the hotel. I know that it is impossible to say in advance that I shall stay here so long, but all the same I have many reasons for thinking that a long stay here is probable.

I was in Fontvieilles yesterday at McKnight's; he had a good pastel—a pink tree—and two water colors just started, and I found him working on the head of an old woman in charcoal. He has reached the stage where he is plagued by new color theories, and while they prevent him from working on the old system, he is not sufficiently master of his new palette to succeed in this one. He seemed very shy about showing me the things, I had to go there for that express purpose, and tell him that I was *absolutely* set on seeing his work.

It is not impossible that he may come to stay for some time with me here. I think we should both benefit by it.

I think very often of Renoir and that pure clean line of his. That's just how things and people look in this clear air.

We are having a tremendous lot of wind and mistral here, just now three days out of four, though the sun shines anyway: but it makes it difficult to work out-of-doors.

I think there would be something to do here in portraits. Although the people are blankly ignorant of painting in general, they are much more artistic than in the North in their own persons and their manner of life. I have seen figures here quite as beautiful as those of Goya or Velásquez. They will put a touch of pink on a black frock, or devise a garment of white, yellow and pink, or else green and pink, or else *blue and yellow*, in which there is nothing to be altered from the artistic point of view. Seurat would find some very picturesque men's figures here in spite of their modern clothes.

Now, as for portraits, I am pretty sure they'd take the bait.

But first before I dare start along that line, I want my nerves steadier, and also to be settled in so that I could have people in my studio. And if I must tell you roughly what I figure it would take to get me quite well and acclimatized for good, it will mean a year, and to set me up completely, a cool thousand francs. If during the first year—the present year—I spend 100 francs on food and 100 francs on this house per month, you see there won't be a cent left in the budget for painting.

But at the end of that year I should have a decent establishment and my own health to show for it—of that I am sure. And in the meantime I should spend my time drawing every day, with two or three pictures a month besides.

In figuring what it would cost to set me up, I am also counting in a complete new set of linen and clothes and shoes.

And at the end of the year I should be a different man.

I should have a home of my own and the peace to get back my health.

(Needless to say, if you have got canvases that take up too much room, you can send them here by goods service, and I will keep them in the studio here. If this is not yet the case, it will be later on, and I am keeping a good many studies which don't seem good enough to send to you.)

And then I can hope not to get exhausted before my time. Monticelli was physically stronger than I, I think, and if I had the strength for it, I'd live from hand to mouth as he did. But if even he was paralyzed, and that without being such a tremendous drinker, there'd be precious little hope for me.

I was certainly going the right way for a stroke when I left Paris. I paid for it nicely afterward! When I stopped drinking, when I stopped smoking so much, when I began to think again instead of trying not to think—Good Lord, the depression and the prostration of it! Work in these magnificent natural surroundings has restored my morale, but even now some efforts are too much for me: my strength fails me. And that was why, when I wrote you the other day, I said that if you left the Goupils, you would feel healthier in mind, but that the cure would be very painful. Whereas one does not feel the disease itself.

My poor boy, our neurosis, etc., comes, it's true, from our way of living, which is too purely the artist's life, but it is also a fatal inheritance, since in civilization the weakness increases from generation to generation. If we want to face the real truth about our constitution, we must acknowledge that we belong to the number of those who suffer from a neurosis which already has its roots in the past.

I think Gruby[1] is right about such cases—to eat well, to live well, to see little of women, in short to arrange one's life in advance exactly as if one were already suffering from a disease of the brain and spine, without counting the neurosis which is actually there. Certainly that is taking the bull by the horns, which is never a bad policy. And Degas did it, and succeeded. All the same, don't you feel, as I do, that it is frightfully hard? And after all, doesn't it do one all the good in the world to listen to the wise advice of Rivet and Pangloss, those excellent optimists of the pure and jovial Gallic race, who leave you your self-respect?

However, if we want to live and work, we must be very sensible and look after ourselves. Cold water, fresh air, simple good food, decent clothes, a decent

[1] An old physician in Paris, who in his time had treated Heine.

bed, and no women. And not to let oneself go with women, or with life that *is* life, as much as one would like to.

I am not set on sleeping at the studio, but *if* I went to sleep there, it would be because I saw a possibility of settling down pretty definitely for a long time.

Now that I need take up no more room in the hotel, seeing that I have the studio, I shall beat these people down to 3 francs a day, whether they like it or not. Consequently there is nothing urgent. But if it's all the same to you, send me 100 francs next time anyway, as I want to get some drawers made, just as I have had the shirts and shoes, and must send almost all my clothes to be cleaned and mended. Then they will be quite all right again. This is urgent in case I have to go to Marseilles or see people here. The more precautions we take now, the surer we are of being able to hold out in the long run, and of getting the work under control.

I have got ten canvases that I'm looking for a case for, and I'll send them one of these days.

A handshake for you, and Koning too. I got a postcard from Koning saying that he had had a letter telling him to take back the pictures from the Independents' show. Naturally it was the only thing to do, and what could I do about it?

Ever yours, Vincent

482

My dear Theo,   Arles, 5 May 1888

I write you a line to say that, on consideration, I think it would be best simply to get a rug and a mattress and make a bed on the studio floor. For during the summer it will be so hot that this will be more than enough.

In winter we can see whether we'll have to get a bed or not. As for the bed in your place, I think that the idea of having a painter stay with you is to the advantage of both the painter and yourself, from the point of view of having company and someone to talk to, so that when Koning goes, somebody might come in his place. And why shouldn't you keep the bed in any case?

It is really quite possible that as far as the house goes, I might find something even better either in Martignes on the coast or some other place. Only what is so delightful in this studio is the garden opposite.

But there, we'll put off doing any repairs or furnishing it better; it would be wiser, especially because, if we get cholera here in summer, I may pitch my camp in the country.

It is a filthy town this, with the old streets. As for the women of Arles that there's so much talk about—there is, isn't there?—do you want to know my real opinion of them? They are, no question about it, really charming, but no longer what they must have been. As things are now, they are more often like a Mignard than a Mantegna, for they are in their decadence. That doesn't prevent them from being beautiful—very beautiful, and I am talking now only of the type in the Roman style—rather boring and commonplace. But what exceptions there are!

There are women like a Fragonard and like a Renoir. And some that can't be labeled with anything that's been done yet in painting. The best thing to do would be to make portraits, all kinds of portraits of women and children. But I don't think that I am the man to do it. I'm not enough of a M. Bel Ami for that.

But I should be heartily glad if this Bel Ami of the Midi, which Monticelli was not—but was by way of being—whom I feel to be coming, though I know it isn't myself—I should be heartily glad, I say, if a kind of Guy de Maupassant in painting came along to paint the beautiful people and things here lightheartedly. As for me, I shall go on working and here and there among my work there will be things which will last, but who will be in figure painting what Claude Monet is in landscape? However, you must feel, as I do, that such a one will come. Rodin? He does not work in color, he's not the one. But the painter of the future will be *a colorist such as has never yet existed*. Manet was working toward it, but as you know the impressionists have already got a stronger color than Manet. But this painter who is to come—I can't imagine him living in little cafés, working away with a lot of false teeth, and going to the Zouaves' brothels, as I do.

But I think that I am right when I feel that in a later generation it will come, and that as for us we must work as we can toward that end, without doubting and without wavering.

Please will you tell Guillaumin that Russell wants to come and see him, and intends to buy another of his pictures. I am writing Russell today. I heard yesterday from McK. and the Dane that there is never anything good in the shop windows at Marseilles, and they think there is absolutely nothing doing there.

I should very much like to look around a little myself, but being in no way anxious to fly into a rage, I shall wait till my nerves are steadier.

In the very letter I had addressed wrongly I again said something about Bonger. It is probable that he dares to say so much because at the moment the Russians are having so much success at the Théâtre Libre, etc. But this is no reason, is it, to try and make use of this success in order to denigrate the French? I have just reread Zola's *Le [Au] Bonheur des Dames*, and it seems to me more beautiful than ever.

Now it is news indeed that Reid is back. I told Russell that as I was the one to introduce him, I felt it more or less my duty to explain the cause of the quarrel. That Reid was ambitious, and that, being short of money like all of us, he was beside himself when it was a question of earning money. That I looked upon these as involuntary acts (and consequently he was not responsible, but to be excused for them) committed by an overwrought nervous system.

But that in Reid's character the vulgar merchant predominates over the distinguished artist. This does not mean getting even with Reid, but isn't it right to tell the truth? I feel sure that now it isn't any better, but rather worse.

That friend of Russell's, MacKnight, is a dry sort of person and not too sympathetic either—so much the worse if I should have the two of them against me. Yet I have not said anything about MacKnight, though I suppose he has no more heart than Reid. If he could find his own painting, it would do him good, and it is not impossible that this will happen. He is still young, twenty-seven, I think.

Supposing you agree, we need be in no hurry to fix up the studio. It will do well enough as it is in the meantime, and if I sleep there, as I've said, it will cost me nothing, I save 30 francs at the hotel and I pay 15 for rent, so that there is clear profit.

With a handshake for you and Koning; I have another drawing.

Ever yours, Vincent

I saw a heap of boxes for my purpose in the market and am going back to take measurements. Was the subject of the De Groux which you mention the same as that in the Brussels gallery, the "Bénédicité"? It's true what you say of Braekeleer. Have you heard that he suffered from a disease of the brain which left him impotent??? I have heard this, but wasn't it only temporary? You talk of another one of his which I do not know.

B 5 [5]

My dear Bernard,   Arles, Second half of May 1888
I just received your last letter. You are quite right to see that those Negresses were heart-rending. You are quite right not to think such a thing innocent.

I have just read a book—not a beautiful one and not well written for that matter—about the Marquesas Islands, but sad enough when it tells of the extermination of a whole native tribe—cannibal in the sense that once a month, let us say, an individual got eaten—what does it matter!

The whites, very Christian and all that ... in order to put a stop to this barbarity(?), really not very cruel ... could find no better means than the extermination of the tribe of cannibal natives as well as the tribe against which the latter fought (in order to provide themselves from time to time with the necessary palatable prisoners of war).

After which they annexed the two isles, which then became unutterably lugubrious!!

Those tattooed races, Negroes, Indians, all of them, all, all are disappearing or degenerating. And the horrible white man with his bottle of alcohol, his money and his syphilis—when shall we see the end of him? The horrible white man with his hypocrisy, his greediness and his sterility.

And those savages were so gentle and so loving!

You are damned right to think of Gauguin. That is high poetry, those Negresses, and everything his hands make has a gentle, pitiful, astonishing character. People don't understand him yet, and it pains him so much that he does not sell anything, just like other true poets.

My dear comrade, I should have written you before, only I had a lot of things to attend to. I have sent a first batch of studies to my brother, that's number one. And I have been having trouble with my health, that's number two.

And number three is that I have rented a house, painted yellow outside, whitewashed within, in the full sun (four rooms).

On top of all that I am working on new studies. And in the evening I was often too beat to write. That's why my answer has been delayed.

Listen, that sonnet about the women of the boulevard has some good in it, but it isn't the real thing, the end is banal. A *"sublime* woman"... I don't know what you mean by that, neither do you when it comes right down to it.
Furthermore:

> *Dans le clan des vieux et des jeunes maraude*
> *Ceux qu'elle ammènera coucher le soir, très tard.*
> [Ensnaring among the tribe of the old and young ones
> Those whom she will take to bed with her that night, very late.]

Something like this is not characteristic at all, for the women of our boulevard —the little one—usually sleep alone by night, for they have five or six hauls during the day or in the evening, and très tard there is that honorable carnivore, their maquereau [pimp], who comes and takes them home, but he does not sleep with them (or rarely). The worn-out stupefied woman usually goes to bed alone and sleeps a leaden sleep.

But if you alter two or three lines, it will be all right.

What have you painted recently? As for me, I have done a still life of a blue-enameled iron coffeepot, a royal-blue cup and saucer, a milk jug with pale cobalt and white checks, a cup with orange and blue patterns on a white ground, a blue majolica jug decorated with green, brown and pink flowers and leaves. The whole on a blue tablecloth, against a yellow background, and among this crockery two oranges and three lemons.[1]

So it is a variation of blues, livened up by a series of yellows that go as far as orange.

Then I have another still life, lemons in a basket against a yellow background.

Further a view of Arles. Of the town itself one sees only some red roofs and a tower, the rest is hidden by the green foliage of fig trees, far away in the background, and a narrow strip of blue sky above it. The town is surrounded by immense meadows all abloom with countless buttercups—a sea of yellow—in the foreground these meadows are divided by a ditch full of violet irises. They were mowing the grass while I was painting, so it is only a study and not the finished picture that I had intended to do. But what a subject, hein! That sea of yellow with a band of violet irises, and in the background that coquettish little town of the pretty women! Then two studies of roadsides—later—done with the mistral raging.

If you were not expecting my prompt reply I should make you a sketch. Keep your courage up, good luck. A handshake. I am exhausted tonight. I shall write you again in the next few days, more at my ease.

Vincent

P.S. The portrait of a woman in your last letter but one is very pretty. My address: 2, Place Lamartine, Arles.

---

[1] *See* letter 489 to Theo.

489

My dear Theo, Arles, 20 May 1888

What you write about your visits to Gruby has distressed me, but all the same I am relieved that you went. Has it occurred to you that the dazedness—the feeling of extreme lassitude—may have been caused by this weakness of the heart, and that in this case the iodide of potassium would have nothing to do with the feeling of collapse? Remember how last winter I was stupefied to the point of being absolutely incapable of doing anything at all, except a little painting, although I was not taking any iodide of potassium. So if I were you, I should have it out with Rivet if Gruby tells you not to take any. I am sure that in any case you mean to keep on being friends with both.

I often think of Gruby *here* and *now*, and I am completely well, but it is having pure air and warmth that makes it possible. In all that racket and bad air of Paris, Rivet takes things as they are, without trying to create a paradise, and without in any way trying to make us perfect. But he forges a cuirass, or rather he hardens one against illness, and keeps up one's morale, I do believe, by making light of the disease one has got. If only you could have one year of life in the country and with nature just now, it would make Gruby's cure much easier. I expect he will make you promise to have nothing to do with women except in case of necessity, but anyhow as little as possible.

Now as for me, I am doing very well down here, but it is because I have my work here, and nature, and if I didn't have that, I should grow melancholy. If work had any attraction for you where you are, and if the impressionists were getting on, it would be a very good thing. For loneliness, worries, difficulties, the unsatisfied need for kindness and sympathy—that is what is hard to bear, the mental suffering of sadness or disappointment undermines us more than dissipation—us, I say, who find ourselves the happy possessors of disordered hearts.

I believe iodide of potassium purifies the blood and the whole system, doesn't it? And can you do without it? Anyway you must have it out frankly with Rivet; he oughtn't to be jealous.

I wish you had company more roughly, warmly alive than the Dutch. All the same, Koning with his caprices is an exception, better than most. And it is always a good thing to have someone. But I should like you to have had some friends among the French as well.

Will you do something which will give me great pleasure? My Danish friend who is leaving for Paris on Tuesday will give you two little pictures, nothing much, which I should like to give to Mme. la Contesse de la Boissière at Asnières. She lives in the Boulevard Voltaire, on the first floor of the first house, at the end of the Pont de Clichy. Old Perruchot's restaurant is on the ground floor.

Would you care to take them there for me in person, and say that I had hoped to see her again this spring, and that even here I have not forgotten her; I gave them two little ones last year, her and her daughter.

I hope that you will not regret making these ladies' acquaintance, for it is really *a family*. The countess is far from young, but she is countess first and then a *lady*, the daughter the same.

And it would be wiser for you to go, since I cannot be sure that the family will stay at the same place this year (though they have been coming there for several years, and Perruchot should know their address in town). Perhaps it is an illusion of mine, but I cannot help thinking of it, and perhaps it would give pleasure both to them and to you if you met them.

Look here, I will do my best to send you some new drawings for Dordrecht.[1] I have done two still lifes this week.

A blue enamel coffeepot, a cup (on the left), royal blue and gold, a milk jug in squares of pale blue and white, a cup—on the right—of white with a blue and orange pattern, on an earthen tray of grayish yellow, a jug in earthenware or majolica, blue with a pattern in reds, greens and browns, and lastly 2 oranges and 3 lemons; the table is covered with a blue cloth, the background is greenish-yellow, so that there are six different blues and four or five yellows and oranges.

The other still life is the majolica pot with wild flowers.

Thank you very much for your letter and the 50-fr. note. I hope the case will arrive soon. Next time I think I shall take the canvases off the stretchers, so as to send them rolled up by passenger train.

I think you will soon be friends with this Dane; he doesn't do anything much, but he has intelligence and feeling, and he probably didn't start painting such a long time ago. Take a Sunday sometime to get to know him.

As for me, I am feeling infinitely better, blood circulation good and my stomach digesting. I have found a place where the food is very, very good, and the result is immediately apparent.

Did you notice Gruby's face when he shuts his mouth tight and says—"No women!"? It would make a fine Degas, that. But there is no answering back, for when you have to work all day with your brain, calculating, considering, planning, you've had as much as your nerves can stand.

So go out now and meet women socially; you'll find that you'll get on swimmingly—artists and all that. That's how it will turn out, you'll see, and you won't miss much by doing it, you know.

I have not yet been able to do business with the furniture dealer. I have seen a bed, but it was dearer than I expected. I feel that I must polish off some more work before spending more on furnishing. I have my room for 1 fr. per night. I have bought some more linen, and some paints too. I took very strong linen.

Bit by bit as my blood quickens, the thought of success quickens too. I should not be greatly surprised if your illness were also a reaction from that terrible winter, which has lasted an eternity. And then it will be the same story as mine, get as much of the spring air as possible, go to bed *very early*, because you must have sleep, and as for food, plenty of fresh vegetables, and no *bad* wine or *bad* alcohol. And very little of women, and *lots of patience*.

It doesn't matter if you don't shake it off at once. Gruby will give you a strengthening diet of meat now, you being where you are. Here I could not take much, and it is not necessary here. It is precisely that sense of stupefaction that

---

[1] The committee of the Dutch Etchers Society had asked Theo to co-operate in their second annual exhibition, which was held in Amsterdam, not, as Vincent thought, at Dordrecht.

I'm getting rid of. I do not feel so much need of distraction, I am less harassed by my passions, and I can work more calmly, I could be alone without getting bored. I have come through rather older in the way I look at things, but no sadder.

I shall not believe you if in your next letter you tell me there's nothing wrong with you. It is perhaps a more serious change, and I should not be surprised if you were a trifle low during the time it will take you to recover. In the fullness of artistic life there is, and remains, and will always come back at times, that homesick longing for the truly ideal life that can never come true.

And sometimes you lack all desire to throw yourself heart and soul into art, and to get well for that. You know you are a cab horse and that it's the same old cab you'll be hitched up to again: that you'd rather live in a meadow with the sun, a river and other horses for company, likewise free, and the act of procreation.

And perhaps, to get to the bottom of it, the disease of the heart is caused by this; it would not surprise me. One does not rebel against things, nor is one resigned to them; one's ill because of them, and one does not get better, and it's hard to be precise about the cure.

I do not know who it was who called this condition—being struck by death and immortality. The cab you drag along must be of some use to people you do not know. And so, if we believe in the new art and in the artists of the future, our faith does not cheat us. When good old Corot said a few days before his death—"Last night in a dream I saw landscapes with skies all pink," well, haven't they come, those skies all pink, and yellow and green into the bargain, in the impressionist landscapes? All of which means that there are things one feels coming, and they are coming in very truth.

And as for us who are not, I am inclined to believe, nearly so close to death, we nevertheless feel that this thing is greater than we are, and that its life is of longer duration than ours.

We do not feel we are dying, but we do feel the truth that we are of small account, and that we are paying a hard price to be a link in the chain of artists, in health, in youth, in liberty, none of which we enjoy, any more than the cab horse that hauls a coachful of people out to enjoy the spring.

So what I wish for you, as for myself, is to succeed in getting back your health, because you must have that. That "Espérance" by Puvis de Chavannes is so true. There is an art of the future, and it is going to be so lovely and so young that even if we give up our youth for it, we must gain in serenity by it. Perhaps it is very silly to write all this, but I feel it so strongly; it seems to me that, like me, you have been suffering to see your youth pass away like a puff of smoke; but if it grows again, and comes to life in what you make, nothing has been lost, and the power to work is another youth. Take some pains then to get well, for we shall need your health.

A handshake for you and the same for Koning.

Ever yours, Vincent

497

My dear Theo,   Arles, 12 June 1888

I am writing you another line because I have not yet received your letter. But I suppose you said to yourself that I was probably at Stes.-Maries.

As the rent of the house and the painting of the doors and windows and the purchase of canvas came on me all at once and cleaned me out, you would do me a great kindness if you would send me some money a few days earlier.

I am working on a landscape with cornfields, which I think as well of as, say, the white orchard; it is in the style of the two landscapes of the Butte Montmartre which were at the Independents, but I think it has more firmness and rather more style. And I have another subject, a farm and some ricks, which will probably be a pendant.

I am very curious to know what Gauguin is going to do. I hope he will be able to come. You will tell me that it is no good thinking about the future, but painting goes slowly and in it you must reckon well in advance. It would not be Gauguin's salvation, any more than mine, to sell a few canvases. To be able to work, you must order your life, as much as possible, and it takes a fairly firm basis if existence is to be secure.

If he and I stay here long, our pictures will be more and more individual, just because we shall know our country through and through.

I do not find it easy to think of changing my direction now that I have begun on the South. It is better never to budge—but to get deeper and deeper into the scenery.

I think I have more chance of getting away with things, and of even bigger results, if I don't cramp myself by working on too small a scale. And for that very reason I think I am going to take a larger sized canvas and launch out boldly into the 30 square: they cost me 4 francs apiece here, and it isn't expensive considering the carriage.

The last canvas absolutely kills all the others; it is only a still life, with coffeepots and cups and plates in blue and yellow; it is something quite apart. It must be because of the drawing.

Instinctively these days I keep remembering what I have seen of Cézanne's, because he has rendered so forcibly—as in the "Harvest" we saw at Portier's—the harsh side of Provence. It has become very different from what it was in spring, and yet I have certainly no less love for this countryside, scorched as it begins to be from now on. Everywhere now there is old gold, bronze, copper, one might say, and this with the green azure of the sky blanched with heat: a delicious color, extraordinarily harmonious, with the blended tones of Delacroix.

If Gauguin were willing to join me, I think it would be a step forward for us. It would establish us squarely as the explorers of the South, and nobody could complain of that. I must manage to get the firmness of coloring that I got in the picture that kills the rest. I'm thinking of what Portier used to say, that seen by themselves the Cézannes he had didn't look like anything, but put near other pictures, they washed the color out of everything else. He also used to say that the Cézannes did well in gold, which means that the color scheme was pitched very high. So perhaps, perhaps I am on the right track, and I am getting an eye for this kind of country. We must wait and make sure.

This last picture can bear the surroundings of red brick, with which my studio is paved. When I put it on the ground, with this background of red, *very red* brick, the color of the picture does not become hollow or bleached. The country near Aix where Cézanne works is just the same as this, it is still the Crau. If coming home with my canvas, I say to myself, "Look! I've got the very tones of old Cézanne!" I only mean that Cézanne like Zola is so absolutely part of the countryside, and knows it so intimately, that you must make the same calculations in your head to arrive at the same tones. Of course, if you saw them side by side, mine would hold their own, but there would be no resemblance.

With a handshake, I hope that you will be able to write one of these days.

Ever yours, Vincent

506

My dear Theo,   Arles, 16 July 1888

I have come back from a day in Mont Majour, and my friend the second lieutenant was with me. We explored the old garden together, and stole some excellent figs. If it had been bigger, it would have made me think of Zola's Paradou, high reeds, and vines, ivy, fig trees, olives, pomegranates with lusty flowers of the brightest orange, hundred-year-old cypresses, ash trees, and willows, rock oaks, half-broken flights of steps, ogive windows in ruins, blocks of white rock covered with lichen, and scattered fragments of crumbling walls here and there among the green. I brought back another big drawing, but not of the garden. That makes three drawings. When I have half a dozen I shall send them along.

Yesterday I went to Fontvieilles to visit Bock and McKnight, only these gentlemen had gone on a little trip to Switzerland for a week.

I think the heat is still doing me good, in spite of the mosquitoes and flies.

The grasshoppers—not like ours at home, but like those you see in Japanese sketchbooks, and Spanish flies, gold and green in swarms on the olives. The grasshoppers (I think they are called cicadas) sing as loud as a frog.

I have been thinking too that when you remember that I painted old Tanguy's portrait, and that he also had the portrait of the old lady (which they have sold), and of their friend (it is true that I got 20 francs from him for this latter portrait), and that I have bought without discount 250 francs' worth of paints from Tanguy, on which he naturally made something, and finally that I have been his friend no less than he has been mine, I have good reason to doubt his right to claim money from me; and it really is squared by the study he still has of mine, all the more so because there was an express arrangement that he should pay himself by the sale of a picture.

By some queer freak of nature, Xantippe, Mother Tanguy, and some other good ladies have heads of silex or flint. Certainly these ladies are a good deal more dangerous in the civilized world they go about in than the poor souls bitten by mad dogs who live in the Pasteur Institute. And old Tanguy would be right a hundred times over if he killed his lady ... but he won't do it, any more than Socrates.

And for this reason old Tanguy has more in common—in resignation and long suffering anyhow—with the ancient Christians, martyrs and slaves than with the present day rotters of Paris.

That does not mean that there is any reason to pay him 80 francs, but it is a reason for never losing your temper with him, even if he loses his when, as you may do in this instance, you kick him out, or at least turn him away.

8 jours pour un petit voyage en Suisse.

Je crois que la chaleur me fait toujours du bien malgré les moustiques et les mouches.

Des cigales — non pas celles de chez nous mais des comme ceci on les voit sur les albums japonais Puis des Cantharides dorées et vertes en essaim dans les oliviers

Ces cigales (je crois que leur nom est cicada) chantent au moins aussi fort qu'une grenouille

I am writing Russell at the same time. I think we know, don't we, that the English, the Yankees, etc., have this much in common with the Dutch—that their charity ... is very Christian. Now, the rest of us not being very good Christians.... That's what I can't help thinking while writing again.

This Bock has a head rather like a Flemish gentleman of the time of the Compromise of the Nobles, William the Silent's time and Marnix's. I shouldn't wonder if he's a decent fellow.

I have written Russell that I would send my parcel in a roll direct to him, for our exchange, if I knew that he was in Paris.

That means he must in any case answer me soon. I shall soon need some more canvas and paints. But I have not got the address of that canvas at 40 francs per 20 meters.

I think it right to work especially at drawing just now, and to arrange to have paints and canvas in reserve for when Gauguin comes. I wish paint was as little trouble to work with as pen and paper. I often spoil a painted study for fear of wasting color.

With paper, whether it's a letter I'm writing or a drawing I'm doing, it doesn't make much difference—so many sheets of Whatman, so many drawings. I think that if I were rich, I'd spend less than I do now.

Well, old Martin would say, then it's up to you to get rich, and he is certainly right, just as he is about the masterpiece.

Do you remember in Guy de Maupassant the gentleman who hunted rabbits and other game, and who had hunted so hard for ten years, and was so exhausted by running after the game that when he wanted to get married he found he was impotent, which caused the greatest embarrassment and consternation. Without being in the same situation as this gentleman as far as its being either my duty or my desire to get married, I begin to resemble him physically. According to the worthy Ziem, man becomes ambitious as soon as he becomes impotent. Now though it's pretty much all the same to me whether I'm impotent or not, I'm damned if that's going to drive me to ambition. It's only the greatest philosopher of his place and time, and consequently of all places and all times, good old master Pangloss, who could—if he were here—give me advice and steady my soul.

There—the letter to Russell is in its envelope, and I have written as I intended. I asked him if he had any news of Reid, and I ask you the same question.

I told Russell I left him free to take what he likes, and from the first lot I sent as well. And that I was only waiting for his explicit answer, telling me whether he preferred to make his choice in your place or his; that in the first place if he wanted to see them at his own house, you would send him along some orchards, and fetch the lot back again when he had made his choice. So he cannot quarrel with that. If he takes nothing from Gauguin, it is because he cannot. If he can, I am inclined to expect that he will; I told him that if I ventured to press him to buy, it was *not* because nobody else would if he didn't, but because Gauguin having been ill, and with the further complication of his having been laid up and having to pay his doctor, the burden became rather heavy for us, and we were all the more anxious to find a purchaser for a picture.

I am thinking a lot about Gauguin, and I would have plenty of ideas for pictures, and about work in general.

I have a charwoman now for one franc, who sweeps and scrubs the house for me twice a week. I am counting heavily on her, expecting her to make our beds if we decide to sleep in the house. Otherwise we could make some arrangement with the fellow where I am staying now. Anyhow, we'll try to manage so that it would work out as an economy instead of an extra expense.

How are you now? Are you still going to Gruby? What you tell me of the conversation at the Nouvelle Athènes is interesting. You know the little portrait by Desboutin that Portier has?

It certainly is a strange phenomenon that all artists, poets, musicians, painters, are unfortunate in material things—the happy ones as well—what you said lately about Guy de Maupassant is fresh proof of it. That brings up again the eternal question: Is the whole of life visible to us, or isn't it rather that this side of death we see only one hemisphere?

Painters—to take them alone—dead and buried speak to the next generation or to several succeeding generations through their work.

Is that all, or is there more to come? Perhaps death is not the hardest thing in a painter's life.

For my own part, I declare I know nothing whatever about it, but looking at the stars always makes me dream, as simply as I dream over the black dots representing towns and villages on a map. Why, I ask myself, shouldn't the shining dots of the sky be as accessible as the black dots on the map of France? Just as we take the train to get to Tarascon or Rouen, we take death to reach a star. One thing undoubtedly true in this reasoning is that we *cannot* get to a star while we are *alive*, any more than we can take the train when we are dead.

So to me it seems possible that cholera, gravel, tuberculosis and cancer are the celestial means of locomotion, just as steamboats, buses and railways are the terrestrial means. To die quietly of old age would be to go there on foot.

Now I am going to bed because it is late, and I wish you good night and good luck.

A handshake,

Ever yours, Vincent

B 6 [6]

My dear comrade Bernard,   Arles, Second half of June 1888

More and more it seems to me that the pictures which must be made so that painting should be wholly itself, and should raise itself to a height equivalent to the serene summits which the Greek sculptors, the German musicians, the writers of French novels reached, are beyond the power of an isolated individual; so they will probably be created by groups of men combining to execute an idea held in common.

One may have a superb orchestration of colors and lack ideas. Another one is cram-full of new concepts, tragically sad or charming, but does not know how to express them in a sufficiently sonorous manner because of the timidity of a limited palette. All the more reason to regret the lack of corporative spirit among the artists, who criticize and persecute each other, fortunately without succeeding in annihilating each other.

You will say that this whole line of reasoning is banal—so be it! However, the thing itself—the existence of a renaissance—this fact is certainly no banality.

A technical question. Just give me your opinion on it in your next letter. I am going to put the *black* and the *white*, just as the color merchant sells them to us, boldly on my palette and use them just as they are. When—and observe that I am speaking of the simplification of color in the Japanese manner—when in a green park with pink paths I see a gentleman dressed in black and a justice of the peace by trade (the Arab Jew in Daudet's *Tartarin* calls this honorable functionary zouge de paix) who is reading *L'Intransigeant* ...

Over him and the park a sky of a simple cobalt.

... then why not paint the said zouge de paix with ordinary bone black and the *Intransigeant* with simple, quite raw white? For the Japanese artist ignores reflected colors, and puts the flat tones side by side, with characteristic lines marking off the movements and the forms.

In another category of ideas—when for instance one composes a motif of colors representing a yellow evening sky, then the fierce hard white of a white wall against this sky may be expressed if necessary—and this in a strange way— by raw white, softened by a neutral tone, for the sky itself colors it with a delicate lilac hue. Furthermore imagine in that landscape which is so naïve, and a good thing too, a cottage whitewashed all over (the roof too) standing in an orange field—certainly orange, for the southern sky and the blue Mediterranean provoke an orange tint that gets more intense as the scale of blue colors gets a more vigorous tone—then the black note of the door, the windows and the little cross on the ridge of the roof produce a simultaneous contrast of black and white just as pleasing to the eye as that of blue and orange.

Or let us take a more amusing motif: imagine a woman in a black-and-white-checked dress in the same primitive landscape with a blue sky and an orange soil—that would be a rather funny sight, I think. In Arles they often do wear black and white checks.

Suffice it to say that black and white are also colors, for in many cases they can be looked upon as colors, for their simultaneous contrast is as striking as that of green and red, for instance.

The Japanese make use of it for that matter. They express the mat and pale complexion of a young girl and the piquant contrast of the black hair marvelously well by means of white paper and four strokes of the pen. Not to mention their black thornbushes starred all over with a thousand white flowers.

At last I have seen the Mediterranean, which you will probably cross sooner than I shall.

I spent a week at Saintes-Maries, and to get there I drove in a diligence across the Camargue with its vineyards, moors and flat fields like Holland. There, at Saintes-Maries, were girls who reminded one of Cimabue and Giotto—thin, straight, somewhat sad and mystic. On the perfectly flat, sandy beach little green, red, blue boats, so pretty in shape and color that they made one think of flowers. A single man is their whole crew, for these boats hardly venture on the high seas. They are off when there is no wind, and make for the shore when there is too much of it.

Gauguin, it seems, is still sick.

I am very eager to know what you have been working at lately—I myself am still doing nothing but landscapes—enclosed a sketch [see the sketch of the boats]. I should also very much like to see Africa, but I hardly make any definite plans for the future, it will all depend on circumstances.

What I should like to find out is the effect of an intenser blue in the sky. Fromentin and Gérôme see the soil of the South as colorless, and a lot of people see it like that. My God, yes, if you take some sand in your hand, if you look at it closely, and also water, and also air, they are all colorless, looked at in this way. *There is no blue without yellow and without orange*, and if you put in blue, then you must put in yellow, and orange too, mustn't you? Oh well, you will tell me that what I write to you are only banalities.

A handshake in thought,

Sincerely yours, Vincent

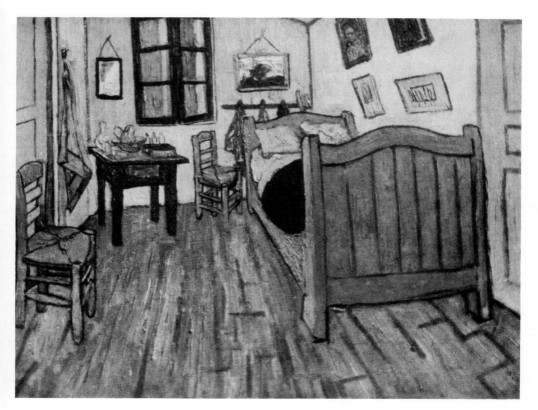

Vincent's Bedroom at Arles, oil, 1889

B 8 [*11*]

My dear Bernard,   Arles, End of June 1888

It is a very good thing that you read the Bible. I start with this because I have always refrained from recommending it to you. Whenever I read the numerous sayings of Moses, St. Luke, etc., I couldn't help thinking to myself, Look, that's the only thing he lacks, and now there it is in full force ... the artistic neurosis.

For the study of Christ inevitably calls it forth, especially in my case where it is complicated by the staining black of unnumerable pipes.

The Bible is Christ, for the Old Testament leads up to this culminating point. St. Paul and the evangelists dwell on the other slope of the sacred mountain.

How petty that story is! My God, only think. So there are only Jews in the world, who begin by declaring everything which is not themselves impure.

Why don't the other peoples under the great sun of those parts—the Egyptians, the Indians, the Ethiopians, Babylon, Nineveh—why don't they have their annals, written with the same care! The study of it is beautiful for all that, and being able to read everything would be tantamount to not being able to read at all.

But the consolation of that saddening Bible which arouses our despair and our indignation—which distresses us once and for all because we are outraged by its pettiness and contagious folly—the consolation which is contained in it, like a kernel in a hard shell, a bitter pulp, is Christ.

The figure of Christ, as I feel it, has been painted only by Delacroix and Rembrandt ... and later Millet painted ... the doctrine of Christ.

The rest makes me smile a little, all the rest of religious painting—from the religious point of view, not from the point of view of painting. And the Italian primitives—Botticelli; or say the Flemish primitives—Van Eyck; Germans—Cranach—they are nothing but heathens who interest me only in the same respect as the Greeks, as Velàzquez and so many other naturalists.

Christ alone—of all the philosophers, Magi, etc.—has affirmed, as a principal certainty, eternal life, the infinity of time, the nothingness of death, the necessity and the raison d'être of serenity and devotion. He lived serenely, *as a greater artist than all other artists*, despising marble and clay as well as color, working in living flesh. That is to say, this matchless artist, hardly to be conceived of by the obtuse instrument of our modern, nervous, stupefied brains, made neither statues nor pictures nor books; he loudly proclaimed that he made ... *living men*, immortals.

This is serious, especially because it is the truth.

This great artist did not write books either; surely Christian literature as a whole would have filled him with indignation, and very rare in it are literary products that would find favor in discerning eyes beside Luke's Gospel or Paul's Epistles—so simple in their hard, militant form. Though this great artist—Christ—disdained writing books on ideas (sensations), he surely disdained the spoken word much less—particularly the parable. (What a sower, what a harvest, what a fig tree! etc.)

And who would dare tell us that he lied on that day when, scornfully foretelling the collapse of the Roman edifice, he declared, Heaven and earth shall pass away, but my words shall not pass away.

These spoken words, which, like a prodigal *grand seigneur*, he did not even deign to write down, are one of the highest summits—the very highest summit—reached by art, which becomes a creative force there, a pure creative power.

These considerations, my dear comrade Bernard, lead us very far, very far afield; they raise us above art itself. They make us see the art of creating life, the art of being immortal and alive at the same time. They are connected with painting.

The patron saint of painters—St. Luke, physician, painter, evangelist—whose symbol is, alas, nothing but an ox, is there to give us hope.

Yet our real and true lives are rather humble, these lives of us painters, who drag out our existence under the stupefying yoke of the difficulties of a profession which can hardly be practiced on this thankless planet on whose surface "the love of art makes us lose the true love."

But seeing that nothing opposes it—supposing that there are also lines and forms as well as colors on the other innumerable planets and suns—it would remain praiseworthy of us to maintain a certain serenity with regard to the possibilities of painting under superior and changed conditions of existence, an existence changed by a phenomenon no queerer and no more surprising than the transformation of the caterpillar into a butterfly, or of the white grub into a cockchafer.

The existence of painter-butterfly would have for its field of action one of the innumerable heavenly bodies, which would perhaps be no more inaccessible to us, after death, than the black dots which symbolize towns and villages on geographical maps are in our terrestrial existence.

Science—scientific reasoning—seems to me an instrument that will lag far, far behind. For look here: the earth has been thought to be flat. It was true, so it still is today, for instance between Paris and Asnières. Which, however, does not prevent science from proving that the earth is principally round. Which no one contradicts nowadays.

But notwithstanding this they persist nowadays in believing that *life is flat* and runs from birth to death. However, life too is probably round, and very superior in expanse and capacity to the hemisphere we know at present.

Future generations will probably enlighten us on this so very interesting subject; and then maybe Science itself will arrive—willy-nilly—at conclusions more or less parallel to the sayings of Christ with reference to the other half of our existence.

However this may be, the fact is that we are painters in real life, and that the important thing is to breathe as hard as ever we can breathe.

Ah! that lovely picture by Eug. Delacroix: "Christ in the Boat on the Sea [*sic*] of Gennesaret." He—with his pale citron-colored aureole—luminously asleep against that patch of dramatic violet, somber blue, blood red, the group of mortally frightened disciples—on that terrible emerald sea, rising up, rising up to the very height of the frame. Oh! that sublimely brilliant conception. I should make some sketches of it for you if I were not so beat after drawing and painting from a model—a Zouave—for three or four days; but on the contrary, writing rests and distracts me.

What I have dashed off is very ugly: a drawing of a seated Zouave, a painted sketch of the Zouave against a completely white wall, and finally his portrait against a green door and some orange bricks of a wall. It is hard and utterly ugly and badly done. All the same, since it means attacking a real difficulty, it may pave the way for me in the future.

The figures I do are nearly always detestable in my own eyes, and all the more so in the eyes of others; yet it is the study of the figure that strengthens one's powers most, if one does it in a manner other than the one taught us, for instance, at Mr. Benjamin Constant's.

Your letter delighted me, the sketch is very, very interesting; many thanks for it. On my part I shall send you a drawing one of these days—tonight I am too exhausted; my eyes are tired even if my brain is not.

Just tell me, do you remember "John the Baptist" by Puvis [de Chavannes]? I myself think it amazing and as magical as Eugène Delacroix.

That passage you dug up in the Gospels about John the Baptist is absolutely what you have seen. People crowding around a man: "Are you the Christ? Are you Elias?" Just as it would be now, if one asked Impressionism or one of its seeking representatives: "Have you found it?" It's just like that.

At present my brother is having an exhibition of Claude Monet—10 pictures painted at Antibes from February to May—it is very beautiful, it seems.

Did you ever read a life of Luther? For Cranach, Dürer, Holbein belong to him. *He*—his personality—is the high light of the Middle Ages.

I don't like the Roi-Soleil any more than you do—to me he seems more of an extinguisher, this Louis XIV—my God, what a lousy bore in general, this sort of Methodist Solomon. I don't like Solomon either, just as I don't like the Methodists the least little bit—Solomon seems a hypocritical heathen to me; indeed, I have no respect for his architecture—an imitation of other styles—and still less for his writings, for the pagans have done better than that.

Just tell me, what about your military service? Do you want me to speak to that second lieutenant of the Zouaves, or don't you? Are you going to Africa or not? Do the years in your case count double in Africa or not? Above all, try to get blood; one makes no progress with anemia, painting goes slowly. You must try to cultivate a temperament which can stand a lot of wear and tear, a temperament which enables you to live to a great age; you ought to live like a monk who goes to a brothel once every two weeks—that's what I do myself; it's not very poetic, but I feel it my duty after all to subordinate my life to painting.

If I were in the Louvre with you, I should very much like to look at the primitives in your company.

As for me, when I'm in the Louvre, I still go, with a great love in my heart, to the Dutch, Rembrandt first of all. Rembrandt, whom I used to study so much—and then Potter, for instance, who ventures to paint a single white stallion on a size 4 or 6 panel—a stallion neighing and rutting—forlorn under a sky pregnant with a thunderstorm, tragically sad in the delicately green immensity of a damp meadow. In short, there are marvels in those old Dutchmen which have no connection with anything else whatever.

A handshake, and once again thanks for your letter and your sketch.

Sincerely yours, Vincent

P.S. The sonnets are doing well—that is to say, their color is fine; the drawing is less strong, or rather less sure, the drawing is still hesitant—I don't know how to express it—their moral purpose is not clear.

B 9 [*12*]   Arles, End of June 1888

P.S. As regards those sonnets, I add the explanation of what I mean by, their drawing is not very sure.

At the end you produce morality. You tell Society that it is infamous, because the whore reminds us of meat in the market place. That's all right, the whore is like meat in a butcher's shop. I, though, having become a mere brute; I understand, I feel it, I rediscover a sensation in my own life; I say, That is well spoken —for the sonorous rhythm of the colorful words evoke for me with great intensity the brutal reality of the slums, but on *me, the brute*, the reproaches directed against society, such hollow words as "le bon Dieu"—the good God—no longer make any impression. I say, That isn't the real thing—and I sink back into my brutish state; I forget poetry, which was powerful enough at first to dispel my stupefaction.

Is this true or not?

Establishing facts, as you do in the beginning, is cutting with the scalpel as the surgeon does when he explains anatomy. I listen, attentively and full of interest, but when the dissecting surgeon later starts moralizing at me like that, then I don't think his final tirade has the same value as his demonstration.

Studying, analyzing society means more than moralizing any time.

Nothing would seem queerer to me than saying, for instance, Here is that meat from the market place; now observe how, in spite of everything, it may be electrified for a moment by the stimulus of a more refined and unexpected love. Just like the sated caterpillar that doesn't eat any more, that crawls on a wall instead of crawling on a cabbage leaf, so this sated female can no longer love, even if she does her best. She is seeking, seeking, seeking—does she herself know what? She is conscious, alive, sensitive, galvanized, rejuvenated for a moment—but impotent.

Yet she can still love, so she is alive—here no prevarication is possible— although she may be finished and dying the death of a terrestrial beast. Where will this butterfly emerge from the chrysalis? This butterfly that was a sated caterpillar, this cockchafer that was a white grub?

Well, this is where I have got to in my study of old whores. I too should like to know approximatively what I am the larva of myself, perhaps.

B 12 [*10*]

My dear comrade Bernard,   Arles, End of July 1888

A thousand thanks for the drawings you sent me. I greatly like the avenue of plane trees on the seashore with two women chatting in the foreground and people strolling around. Likewise the woman under the apple-tree, the woman with the parasol; also the four drawings of nude women, particularly the one who is washing herself, a gray effect, pleasantly accented by black, white, yellow, brown. It is charming.

Ah! Rembrandt!... With all due admiration for Baudelaire, I venture to suppose, especially judging from those verses, that he knew almost nothing about Rembrandt—the other day I found and bought a little etching after Rembrandt, a study of a nude man, realistic and simple. He stands leaning against a door or a pillar, in a gloomy interior; a shaft of light from above fleetingly touches the face, which is bent forward, and the mass of reddish hair. One might call it a Degas on account of the true and deeply felt animality of that body. But look here, did you ever *really* look at the "Ox" or "The Interior of a Butcher's Shop" in the Louvre? You haven't really looked at it, and Baudelaire infinitely less. It would be a huge pleasure for me to spend a morning with you in the Gallery of the Dutch Painters. One can hardly describe all that, but with the pictures before us I could show you marvels and miracles, which are the reasons why the primitives don't have my admiration at all, that is to say primarily and most directly.

What do you expect?—I am not so very eccentric; a Greek statue, a peasant by Millet, a Dutch portrait, a nude woman by Courbet or Degas, those calm modeled perfections, are the reason why a lot of other things—the primitives like the Japanese—seem to me so much *penmanship*. It interests me enormously, but a complete thing, a perfection, renders the infinite tangible to us; and the enjoyment of a beautiful thing is like coitus, a moment of infinity.

For instance, do you know a painter called Vermeer who has painted, among other things, a very beautiful *pregnant* Dutch lady? The palette of this strange painter is blue, citron yellow, pearl gray, black, white. There are certainly, on close examination, all the riches of a complete palette in his rare pictures; but the combination of citron yellow, pale blue, pearl gray is as characteristic of him as black, white, gray and pink are of Velázquez.

Oh well, I know—Rembrandt and the Dutch painters are widely scattered over [public] museums and [private] collections, and it is not so easy to get an idea of them if one knows only the Louvre. And yet the fact is that Frenchmen—Charles Blanc, Thoré, Fromentin and certain others—have, better than the Dutch themselves, written about that special art.

Those Dutchmen had hardly any imagination or fantasy, but their good taste and their scientific knowledge of composition were enormous. They have not painted Jesus Christ, the Good God and so on—although Rembrandt *did* in fact —but he is the only one (and Biblical subjects are, relatively speaking, not numerous in his work). He is the only one, the exception, who has done Christs, etc. ... And in his case it is hardly like anything whatever done by the other religious painters; it is metaphysical magic.

Thus Rembrandt has painted angels. He paints a self-portrait, old, toothless, wrinkled, wearing a cotton cap, a picture from nature, in a mirror. He is dreaming, dreaming, and his brush resumes his self-portrait, but only the head, whose expression becomes more tragically sad, more tragically saddening. He is dreaming, still dreaming, and, I don't know why or how, but just as Socrates and Mohammed had their familiar spirits, Rembrandt paints behind this old man, who resembles himself, a supernatural angel with a da Vinci smile.

I am showing you a painter who dreams and paints from imagination, and I began by contending that the character of the Dutch painters is such that they do not invent anything, that they have neither imagination nor fantasy.

Am I illogical? No.

Rembrandt did not invent anything, that angel, that strange Christ, the fact is that he knew them; he felt them there.

Delacroix paints a Christ by means of the unexpected effect of a bright citron-yellow note, a colorful luminous note which possesses the same unspeakable strangeness and charm in the picture as a star does in a corner of the firmament; Rembrandt works with tonal values in the same way Delacroix works with colors.

Now there is a great distance between Delacroix's and Rembrandt's method and that of all the rest of religious painting.

I will write again soon. The present is to thank you for the drawings, which delight me enormously. I have just finished a portrait of a girl of twelve, brown eyes, black hair and eyebrows, gray-yellow flesh, the background heavily tinged with malachite green, the bodice blood red with violet stripes, the skirt blue with large orange polka dots, an oleander flower in the charming little hand.

It has exhausted me so much that I am hardly in a mood for writing. Till soon again, and once more many thanks.

Sincerely yours, Vincent

B 13 [8]

My dear comrade Bernard,   Arles, End of July 1888

I don't have the slightest doubt that you'll admit that neither you nor I can have a complete idea of Velázquez and Goya, of what they were as men and as painters, for neither of us has seen Spain, their country, and so many beautiful things which are still left in the South. But what one knows of them is already something nevertheless.

Of course as for the people of the North, Rembrandt first of all, it is highly desirable, when judging these painters, to know their work as a whole as well as their country, and also the somewhat intimate and concise history of the period and of the customs of the old country.

I emphatically repeat that neither Baudelaire nor you has a sufficiently clear idea of Rembrandt.

As for you, I cannot encourage you strongly enough to spend a long time looking at the great and minor Dutchmen before forming a fixed opinion. It is not merely a question of gems, but a question of selecting marvels among the marvels.

And then there is not a little paste among the diamonds.

So, as for me, who have been studying the school of my country for twenty years now, I shouldn't even answer if it were being discussed, because in general I hear too much talk which is beside the point, when the painters of the North are under discussion.

So that my only answer to you is, Bah! look a little closer than that; it will truly repay your trouble a thousandfold.

Look here, for instance, if I declare that the Ostade in the Louvre representing "The Painter's Family" (man, wife and a dozen children) is a picture infinitely worthy of study and reflection, as well as "The Peace of Munster" by Terborch —and then, when those pictures in the gallery of the Louvre which I personally prefer and think most astonishing are overlooked very often by artists, even by those who have come to see the Dutchmen, then I am not very surprised, as I know that my choice in that gallery is based on a knowledge of this subject which the majority of the French could not possibly share.

But if I disagreed with you, for instance, about these subjects, I should confidently expect you to grant that I was right later on. But what pains me so terribly in the Louvre is to see their Rembrandts going to ruin and the idiots of the administration letting so many beautiful pictures decay. So the annoying yellow tone of certain Rembrandts is the result of deterioration from moisture or some other causes; in some cases I could point it out to you with a wet finger.

It is as difficult to say what Rembrandt's color is as it is to give a name to Velázquez' gray. For want of a better name one might call it "Rembrandt gold." And this is what they have done, but it is pretty vague.

Coming to France as a foreigner, I, perhaps better than Frenchmen born and bred, have felt Delacroix and Zola, and my sincere and wholehearted admiration for them is boundless.

Since I had a somewhat complete notion of Rembrandt, one, Delacroix, got his results by colors, the other, Rembrandt, by tonal values, but they are on a par.[1]

In their quality as painters of a society, of a nature in its entirety, Zola and Balzac produce rare artistic emotions in those who love them, just because they embrace the whole of the epoch they depict.

When Delacroix paints humanity, life in general, instead of an epoch, he belongs no less to the same family of universal geniuses.

I very much like the last words of, I think, Silvestre, who ended a masterly article in this way: "Thus died—almost smiling—Delacroix, a painter of a noble race, who had a sun in his head and a thunderstorm in his heart, who turned from the warriors to the saints, from the saints to the lovers, from the lovers to the tigers, and from the tigers to the flowers."

Daumier is also a great genius.

And then Millet, the painter of a whole race and the environment it lives in.

It is possible that these great geniuses are only madmen, and that one must be mad oneself to have boundless faith in them and a boundless admiration for them. If this is true, I should prefer my insanity to the sanity of the others. Perhaps the most direct road is to approach Rembrandt indirectly. Let's talk about Frans Hals. He never painted Christs, annunciations to the shepherds, angels, crucifixions or resurrections; he never painted nude, voluptuous and bestial women.

He did portraits, and nothing, nothing else.

Portraits of soldiers, gatherings of officers, portraits of magistrates assembled to debate the affairs of the republic, portraits of matrons with pink or yellow skins, wearing white caps and dressed in wool and black satin, discussing the budget of an orphanage or an almshouse. He painted the portraits of middle-class men in their homes: the man, the woman, the child. He painted the drunken toper, an old fishwife in a mood of witchlike hilarity, the pretty gypsy whore, babies in their diapers, the dashing, self-indulgent nobleman with his mustache,

---

[1] In his haste Vincent must have left part of this sentence out, but his meaning is clear nonetheless.

top boots and spurs. He painted himself, together with his wife, young, deeply in love, on a bench on a lawn, after the first wedding night. He painted vagabonds and laughing urchins, he painted musicians and he painted a fat cook.

He does not know greater things than that; but it is certainly worth as much as Dante's Paradise and the Michelangelos and the Raphaels and even the Greeks. It is as beautiful as Zola, healthier as well as merrier, but as true to life, because his epoch was healthier and less dismal.

And now what is Rembrandt?

The same thing absolutely: a painter of portraits.

One must first of all have a healthy, broad, clear notion of these two brilliant Dutchmen, equal in value, before going any further into the subject. When we have understood this thoroughly—this whole glorious republic, depicted by these two prolific portraitists, reconstructed in bold outlines—then we still keep a very large margin for landscapes, domestic scenes, animals, philosophical subjects.

But I implore you, follow this straightforward reasoning carefully, for I am doing my best to present it to you in a very, very simple way.

Hammer into your head that master Frans Hals, that painter of all kinds of portraits, of a whole gallant, live, immortal republic. Hammer into your head the no less great and universal master painter of portraits of the Dutch republic: Rembrandt Harmensz [son of Harmen] van Rijn, that broad-minded naturalistic man, as healthy as Hals himself. And then we see issuing from this source, Rembrandt, a line of direct and true pupils: Vermeer of Delft, Fabritius, Nicholaes Maes, Pieter de Hooch, Bol, and those whom he influenced: Potter, Ruysdael, Ostade, Terborch. I mention Fabritius here although we know only two canvases of his, and I don't mention a lot of good painters, and especially not the paste among these diamonds, that paste so solidly crammed into the vulgar French noodles.

Am I very incomprehensible, my dear comrade Bernard? I am just trying to make you see the great simple thing: the painting of humanity, or rather of a whole republic, by the simple means of portraiture. This first and foremost. When later on—in the case of Rembrandt—we happen to meet with mysticism, with Christs, with nude women, then it is very interesting but it is not the main thing. Let Baudelaire hold his tongue in this domain; his words are sonorous but then infinitely shallow.

Let us take Baudelaire for what he is, a modern poet, just as Musset is another, but let him stop being a nuisance when we are speaking about painting.[1] I don't like your drawing "Lechery" as much as the others. I like "The Tree," however; it is very smart.

A handshake,

Sincerely yours, Vincent

[1] [Footnote by Bernard] All this was provoked by my quoting with admiration the quatrain from Charles Baudelaire's *Phares*:

> Rembrandt triste hôpital tout rempli de murmures
> Et d'un grand crucifix décoré seulement,
> D'où la prière en pleurs s'exhale des ordures
> Et d'un rayon d'hiver traversé brusquement.

[Rembrandt—sad hospital filled full of murmurs, and decorated only with a great crucifix, where the tearful prayer breathes out of the filth, and bruskly traversed by a wintry ray.]

My dear Theo,   Arles, 29 July 1888

Many thanks for your kind letter. If you remember, mine ended with "we are getting old, that is what it *is*, the rest is imagination and doesn't exist." Well, I said that more for myself than for you. And I said it because I felt the absolute necessity of behaving accordingly, of working, perhaps not more, but with a deeper understanding.

Now you talk of the emptiness you feel everywhere, it is just the very thing I feel myself.

Considering, if you like, the time in which we live a great and true renaissance of art, the worm-eaten official tradition still alive but really impotent and inactive, the new painters isolated, poor, treated like madmen, and because of this treatment actually becoming so, at least as far as their social life is concerned:

Then remember that you are doing exactly the same work as these primitive painters, since you provide them with money and sell their canvases for them, which enables them to produce others. If a painter ruins his character by working hard at painting, a thing which leaves him useless for many other things, for family life, etc., etc., if therefore he paints not only with colors, but with self-denial and self-renunciation and with a broken heart—as far as you are concerned, your own work is not only no better paid than his, but it costs you exactly what the painter's costs him, this sacrifice of the individuality, half voluntary, half accidental.

That is to say that if you paint *indirectly*, you are more productive than I am, for instance. The more irrevocably you become a dealer, the more you become an artist.

And in the same way I hope the same thing for myself. The more I am spent, ill, a broken pitcher, by so much more am I an artist—a creative artist—in this great renaissance of art of which we speak.

These things are surely so, but this eternally living art, and this renaissance, this green shoot springing from the roots of the old felled trunk, these are such abstract things that a kind of melancholy remains within us when we think that one could have created life at less cost than creating art.

If possible, you ought to make me feel that art is alive, you who love art perhaps more than I do. I tell myself that it depends not on art but on myself, that the only way to get back my confidence and peace of mind is to *improve my work*.

And there we are again, back at the end of my last letter—I am getting old, it's sheer imagination if I should think that art is old lumber too.

And now, if you know what a "mousmé" is (you will know when you have read Loti's *Madame Chrysanthème*), I have just painted one. It took me a whole week, I have not been able to do anything else, not having been very well either. That is what annoys me; if I had been well, I should have attacked some landscapes between times, but I had to reserve my mental energy to do the mousmé well. A mousmé is a Japanese girl—Provençal in this case—12 to 14 years old. That makes two portraits now, the Zouave and her.

Take care of your health, above all take baths *if Gruby recommends it*, for in the four years by which I am older than you, you will see how necessary comparatively good health is for being able to work. Now for us who work with our brains, our one and only hope of not breaking down too soon is this artificial eking-out by an up-to-date hygienic regimen rigorously applied, as much as we can stand. Because I for one do not do everything I ought. And a bit of cheerfulness is better than all the other remedies.

I have had a letter from Russell. He says that he would have written me before if he hadn't been busy moving to Belle Isle. He is there now, and says that he would be pleased if sooner or later I would go and spend some time there. He still wants to repaint my portrait. He says too—"I should have gone to Boussod's to see Gauguin's 'Negresses Talking' if the same thing had not prevented me from that too."

In short, he does not refuse to buy one, but makes it clear that he does not want anything inferior to the one we have. You see that at all events that is better than nothing.

I will write this to Gauguin and ask him for sketches of pictures. We must hurry things and give up R. for the moment, but regard it as a matter that will come off, but is in abeyance now.

And the same goes for Guillaumin.

I wish he [Russell] would buy a figure from G. He says that he has had a very beautiful bust of his wife done by Rodin, and that on this occasion he lunched with Claude Monet and saw the 10 pictures of Antibes. I am sending him Geffroy's article. He criticizes the Monets very ably, begins by liking them very much, the attack on the problem, the enfolding tinted air, the color. After that he shows what there is to find fault with—the total lack of construction, for instance one of his trees will have far too much foliage for the thickness of the trunk, and so always and everywhere from the standpoint of the reality of things, from the standpoint of lots of natural *laws*, he is exasperating enough. He ends by saying that this quality of attacking the difficulties is what everyone ought to have.

Bernard has sent me 10 sketches like his brothel; three of them were à la Redon; I do not altogether share the enthusiasm he has for that. But there is a woman washing herself, very Rembrandtesque, an effect like Goya, and a landscape with figures, very strange. He expressly forbade me to send them to you, but all the same you will get them by the same post.

I think that Russell will buy something more from Bernard.

Meanwhile I have seen this Bock's work; it is strictly impressionistic, but not powerful, it is the stage where this new technique still preoccupies him so much that he cannot be himself. He will gain in force and then his individuality will break free, I think. But McKnight does water colors of the quality of those by Destrée, you remember that Dutchman we used to know. However, he has washed some small still lifes; a yellow pot on a violet foreground, a red pot on a green, an orange pot on blue, better, but very poor.

The village where they are staying is *real Millet*, poor peasants and nothing else, absolutely *rustic* and homely. This quality completely escapes them. I think that McKnight has civilized and converted to civilized Christianity his brute of a landlord. Anyway the swine and his worthy spouse, when you go there, shake hands with you—it is in a café, of course—when you ask for drinks, they have a way of refusing money—"Oh! I could not take money from an artiss"—with two *ses*. Anyway, it is their own fault that it is so abominable, and this Bock must get pretty well stultified in McKnight's company.

I think that McKnight has some money but not much. So they contaminate the village; but for that, I'd go there to work often. What one ought to do there is not to talk to the civilized people; now they know the station master and a score of bores, and that is partly why they get nowhere. Naturally these simple and artless country folk laugh at them and despise them. But if they did their work without taking up with these village loungers with their starched collars, then they could go into the peasants' homes and let them earn a few pence. And then this blessed Fontvieilles would be a gold mine for them; but the natives are like Zola's poor peasants, innocent and gentle beings, as we know.

Probably McKnight will soon be making little landscapes with sheep for chocolate boxes.

Not only my pictures but I myself have become haggard of late, almost like Hugo van der Goes in the picture by Emil Wauters.

Only, having got my whole beard carefully shaved off, I think that I am as much like the very placid priest in the same picture as like the mad painter so intelligently portrayed therein.

And I do not mind being rather between the two, for one must live, especially because it is no use ignoring the fact that there may be a crisis some day or other if you were to change your relations with the Boussods. Another reason for keeping up this connection with artists, on my part as much as on yours.

Besides, I think I have spoken the truth, but if I should succeed in replacing in goods the money spent, I should only be doing my duty. And then, something practical I can do is portrait painting.

As for drinking too much ... if it is bad, I can't tell. But look at Bismarck, who is in any case very practical and very intelligent, his good doctor told him that he was drinking too much, and that all his life he had overtaxed his stomach and his brain. Bismarck immediately stopped drinking. After that he got run down and couldn't pick up. Secretly he must be laughing heartily at his doctor, because fortunately for him he did not consult him sooner.

So much for that, a good handshake.

Ever yours, Vincent

Mind, as to Gauguin we must not give up the idea of coming to his aid if the suggestion is acceptable as it stands, but *we do not need him*. So do not think that working alone bothers me, and do not push the affair on my account, *be very sure of that*.

The portrait of the girl is against a background of white strongly tinged with malachite green, her bodice is striped blood red and violet, the skirt is royal blue, with large yellow-orange dots. The mat flesh tones are yellowish-gray; the hair tinged with violet; the eyebrows and the eyelashes are black; the eyes, orange and Prussian blue. A branch of oleander in her fingers, for the two hands are showing.

520

My dear Theo,   Arles, 11 August 1888

You are shortly to make the acquaintance of Master Patience Escalier, a sort of "man with a hoe," formerly cowherd of the Camargue, now gardener at a house in the Crau. The coloring of this peasant portrait is not so black as in the "Potato Eaters" of Nuenen, but our highly civilized Parisian *Portier*—probably so called because he chucks pictures out—will be bothered by the same old problem. You have changed since then, but you will see that *he* has not, and it really is a pity that there are not more pictures *en sabots* in Paris. I do not think that my peasant would do any harm to the de Lautrec in your possession if they were hung side by side, and I am even bold enough to hope the de Lautrec would appear even more distinguished by the mutual contrast, and that on the other hand my picture would gain by the odd juxtaposition, because that sun-steeped, sunburned quality, tanned and air-swept, would show up still more effectively beside all that face powder and elegance.

What a mistake Parisians make in not having a palate for crude things, for Monticellis, for common earthenware. But there, one must not lose heart because Utopia is not coming true. It is only that what I learned in Paris is leaving me, and I am returning to the ideas I had in the country before I knew the impressionists. And I should not be surprised if the impressionists soon find fault with my way of working, for it has been fertilized by Delacroix's ideas rather than by theirs. Because instead of trying to reproduce exactly what I have before my eyes, I use color more arbitrarily, in order to express myself forcibly. Well, let that be, as far as theory goes, but I'm going to give you an example of what I mean.

I should like to paint the portrait of an artist friend, a man who dreams great dreams, who works as the nightingale sings, because it is his nature. He'll be a blond man. I want to put my appreciation, the love I have for him, into the picture. So I paint him as he is, as faithfully as I can, to begin with.

But the picture is not yet finished. To finish it I am now going to be the arbitrary colorist. I exaggerate the fairness of the hair, I even get to orange tones, chromes and pale citron-yellow.

Behind the head, instead of painting the ordinary wall of the mean room, I paint infinity, a plain background of the richest, intensest blue that I can contrive, and by this simple combination of the bright head against the rich blue background, I get a mysterious effect, like a star in the depths of an azure sky.

Again, in the portrait of the peasant I worked this way, but in this case without wishing to produce the mysterious brightness of a pale star in the infinite. Instead, I imagine the man I have to paint, terrible in the furnace of the height of harvesttime, as surrounded by the whole Midi. Hence the orange colors flashing like lightning, vivid as red-hot iron, and hence the luminous tones of old gold in the shadows.

Oh, my dear boy ... and the nice people will only see the exaggeration as a caricature.

But what has that to do with us? We've read *La Terre* and *Germinal*, and if we are painting a peasant, we want to show that in the end what we have read has come very near to being part of us.

I do not know if I can paint the postman *as I feel him;* this man is like old Tanguy in so far as he is a revolutionary, he is probably thought a good republican because he wholeheartedly detests the republic which we now enjoy, and because on the whole he is beginning to doubt, to be a little disillusioned, as to the republican principle itself.

But I once watched him sing the "Marseillaise," and I thought I was watching '89, not next year, but the one 99 years ago. It was a Delacroix, a Daumier, straight from the old Dutchmen.

Unfortunately he cannot pose, and yet to make a picture you must have an intelligent model.

And now I must tell you that these days, as far as material things go, are cruelly hard. Life, no matter what I do, is pretty expensive here, almost like Paris, where you can spend 5 or 6 francs a day and have very little to show for it.

If I have models, I suffer a good deal for it. But it doesn't matter, and I'm going to continue. And I can assure you that if you should happen to send me a little extra money sometimes, it would benefit the pictures, but not me. The only choice I have is between being a good painter and a bad one. I choose the first. But the needs of painting are like those of a wasteful mistress, you can do nothing without money, and you never have enough of it. That's why painting ought to be done at the public expense, instead of the artists being overburdened with it.

But there, we had better hold our tongues, because *no one is forcing us to work,* fate having ordained that indifference to painting be widespread and by way of being eternal.

Fortunately my digestion is so nearly all right again that I have lived for three weeks in the month on ship's biscuits with milk and eggs. It is the blessed warmth that is bringing back my strength, and I was certainly right in *going at once* to the South, instead of waiting until the evil was past remedy. Yes, really, I am as well as other men now, which I have never been except for a short while in Nuenen for instance, and it is rather pleasant. By other men I mean something like the navvies, old Tanguy, old Millet, the peasants. When you are well, you must be able to live on a piece of bread while you are working all day, and have enough strength to smoke and to drink your glass in the evening, that's necessary under the circumstances. And all the same to feel the stars and the infinite high and clear above you. Then life is almost enchanted after all. Oh! those who don't believe in this sun here are real infidels.

Unfortunately, along with the good god sun three quarters of the time there is the devil mistral.

Saturday's post has gone, damn it, and I never doubted but I should get your letter. However, you see I am not fretting about it.

With a handshake.

Ever yours, Vincent

My dear Theo,   Arles, 13 August 1888

I have to thank you for a lot of things, first for your letter and the 50-fr. note enclosed, but also just as much for the package of paints and canvas, which I have been to the station to get (the geranium lake has come too), and lastly for the Cassagne book, and for *La fin de Lucie Pellegrin*.

If Tasset divided his parcels better, it would make a difference in the cost of carriage; there were three parcels this time, two of them weighing more than 5 kilos. If he had kept back a few tubes, the whole would have cost about 5 francs. But I am very glad to have them all the same.

Lucie Pellegrin is very fine, it is quick with life and is still exquisite and moving, because it keeps the human touch. Why should it be forbidden to handle these subjects, unhealthy and overexcited sexual organs seek sensual delights such as da Vinci's. Not I, who have hardly seen anything but the kind of women at 2 francs, originally intended for the Zouaves. But the people who have leisure for love-making, they want the da Vinci mysteries. I realize that these loves are not for everyone's understanding. But from the point of view of what is allowed, one could write books treating worse aberrations of perversion than Lesbianism, just as it would be permissible to write medical documents on this sort of story, surgical disquisitions.

At all events, law and justice apart, a pretty woman is a living marvel, whereas the pictures by da Vinci and Correggio only exist for other reasons. Why am I so little an artist that I always regret that the statue and the picture are not alive? Why do I understand the musician better, why do I see the raison d'être of his abstractions better?

At the first opportunity I will send you an engraving after a drawing by Rowlandson, representing two women, as beautiful as a Fragonard or a Goya.

Just now we are having a glorious strong heat, with no wind, just what I want. There is a sun, a light that for want of a better word I can only call yellow, pale sulphur yellow, pale golden citron. How lovely yellow is! And how much better I shall see the North!

Oh! I keep wishing for the day when you will see and feel the sun of the South!

As to studies, I have two studies of thistles in a vague field, thistles white with the fine dust of the road. Then a little study of a roadside inn, with red and green carts; and also a little study of Paris-Lyons-Mediterranée carriages; these last two studies have been approved of as having "quite the modern touch" by the young rival of good old General Boulanger, the very resplendent 2nd lieutenant of Zouaves.

This valiant warrior has given up the art of drawing, into the mysteries of which I endeavored to initiate him, but it was for a plausible reason, namely that he had unexpectedly to take an examination, for which I am afraid he was anything but prepared.

Always supposing the aforesaid young Frenchman always speaks the truth, he has astonished his examiners by the confidence of his answers, a confidence he had reinforced by spending the eve of the examination in a brothel.

As François Coppée, I think, says in a sonnet, one might have "a despairing doubt" on the subject of "my lieutenant to be," for, Coppée goes on, "my thoughts are on our defeat." The fact remains that I have nothing to complain of in him, and if it is true that he will shortly be a full-fledged lieutenant, one must anyhow acknowledge his luck. He is literally like the good old general in that he has often frequented the pretty ladies of the so-called café-chantant type. It will be enough for me to write you, or rather he will send you a wire telling you by what train he will arrive on the 16th or 17th. Then he will hand over the painted studies, which will save us the cost of carriage. He owes me all that anyhow for my lessons. He will only stay in Paris one or two days, as he is going North, but on his return he will stop there longer.

After such coolness it is rather kind of Uncle to have left you a legacy, but I cannot easily get it into my head that C. M. and he did not actually condemn you to penal servitude for life that time they refused to lend you the capital necessary to set you up in business for yourself. This will always remain a grave error on their part. But I won't harp on that. All the more reason for trying to do the utmost in art, even if we shall always be in comparatively straitened circumstances as far as money is concerned. Well, my boy, at the time you were *ready for your part* to set up in business, and consequently you have a perfect right to feel that you are doing *your duty for your part*. Considered as a whole, you have taken up this business of the impressionists with their help. Without their help the thing can't go on; or will go on in some different way. If you have made no profit yet, you have deserved something, and if the Dutch confound these two very different things, having only their word "verdienen" for both meanings, so much the worse for them.

I am writing a line to Mourier too—you can read it—and I give you a hearty handshake.

Ever yours, Vincent

With regard to Gauguin, however much we appreciate him, I think that we must behave like the mother of a family and calculate the actual expenses. If one listened to him, one would go on hoping for something vague in the future, and meantime stay on at the inn, and go on living in a hell with no way out.

I would rather shut myself up in a cloister like the monks, free as the monks are to go to the brothel or the wine shop if the spirit moves us. But for our work we need a home. Altogether Gauguin leaves me quite in the dark about Pont-Aven; he tacitly accepts my suggestion of coming to him if necessary, but he writes nothing about any means of finding a studio of our own, or about what it would cost to furnish it. And I can't help feeling there's something queer about it.

So I have decided not to go to Pont-Aven, unless we could find a house there at a low rent like the one here (15 fr. per month is what mine costs) and could arrange it so that we could sleep in it.

I am going to write our sister this evening if I can find time.

A handshake.

Vincent

Have you got the drawings of the gardens, and the two figure drawings? I think that the picture of the old peasant's head is as strange in color as the Sower, but the Sower is a failure, and the peasant even more so. Oh, as to that—I will send it to you all by itself as soon as it is dry, and I am going to put a dedication to you on it.

525

My dear Theo, Arles, 15 August 1888

You will have got my wire telling you that 2nd lieutenant Milliet will arrive in Paris on Friday morning; he will arrive at the Gare de Lyon at 5:15 in the morning and go from there straight to the Cercle Militaire in the Avenue de l'Opéra. It would be simplest for both of you if you went to see him there at 7 o'clock sharp in the morning.

Of course you could also meet him at the Gare de Lyon itself, but to begin with that is farther off, and then you would have to get up very early. He has been very nice to me, particularly these last few days. He will return to Paris for a week, but he is spending the greater part of his leave in the North.

I am very glad to have these pictures sent off, and in this way our sister will see my studies, and that makes a difference to me, for by this she will share in something that is essentially part of our life in France, crude and casual as it may be. I mean, she will see painting in the raw. But to do me a great favor, show her one or two studies put on stretchers and framed in white. You can take some of the earlier ones out of their stretchers and frames. Don't let my stuff take up too much room, so don't get encumbered with stretchers and frames for my sake. For the comrades will see well enough what it is like just as it stands, and you even more. Later on—when the hundred are done—we will choose ten or fifteen of them to be framed. I have kept the big portrait of the postman, and the head which I included was done at a *single sitting*.

But that's what I'm good at, doing a fellow roughly in one sitting. If I wanted to show off, my boy, I'd always do it, drink with the first comer, paint him, and that not in water colors but in oils, on the spot in the manner of Daumier.

If I did a hundred like that, there would be some good ones among them. And I'd be more of a Frenchman and more myself, and more of a drinker. It does tempt me so—not drinking, but painting tramps. What I gained by it as an artist, should I lose that as a man? If I had the faith to do it, I'd be a notable madman; now I am an insignificant one, but you see I am not sufficiently ambitious for that fame to set a match to the powder. I would rather wait for the next generation, which will do in portraiture what Claude Monet does in landscape, the rich, daring landscape à la Guy de Maupassant.

But then I know that I am not—not their equal—but didn't the Flauberts and Balzacs make the Zolas and Maupassants? So here's to—not us, but to the generation to come. You are a good enough judge of painting to see and understand what I may have of originality, and also to see the uselessness of presenting what I am doing to the modern public, because the others surpass me in clearness of touch. That is more the fault of wind and circumstance, compared to what

I could do without the mistral and without the fatal conditions of vanished youth and comparative poverty. For my part I am in no way set on changing my condition, and I count myself only too happy to be able to go on as I do.

No answer from friend Russell, and Gauguin certainly deserved one.

I have put in this package a drawing after a picture which I am working on now—the boats with the man unloading sand. If some studies are not quite dry, so much the worse for them. They must be left to dry out, then washed with plenty of water, and retouched if necessary. But they cannot come to much harm, and it was a good opportunity for sending them.

A good handshake, and I do hope to hear from you by Friday or Saturday.

Ever yours, Vincent

531

My dear Theo,   Arles, 3 September 1888

I spent yesterday with the Belgian, who also has a sister among the "vingtistes." The weather was not fine, but a very good day for talking; we went for a walk and all the same saw some very fine things at the bullfight and outside of town. We talked more seriously about the idea that if I keep a place in the South, he ought to set up a sort of post among the coal mines. Then Gauguin and I and he, if the importance of a picture made it worth the journey, could change places —thus being sometimes in the North, but in familiar country with a friend in it, and sometimes in the South.

You will soon see him, this young man with the look of Dante, because he is going to Paris, and if you put him up—if the room is free—you will be doing him a good turn; he is very distinguished-looking, and will become so, I think, in his painting.

He likes Delacroix, and we talked a lot about Delacroix yesterday. He even knew the violent cartoon for the "Bark of Christ."

Well, thanks to him I at last have a first sketch of that picture which I have dreamed of for so long—the poet. He posed for me. His fine head with that keen gaze stands out in my portrait against a starry sky of deep ultramarine; for clothes, a short yellow coat, a collar of unbleached linen, and a spotted tie. He gave me two sittings in one day.

Yesterday I had a letter from our sister, who has seen a great deal. Ah, if she could marry an artist, it wouldn't be such a bad thing for her.

I have finished L'Immortel by Daudet. I rather like the sculptor Védrine's saying, that achieving fame is something like ramming the live end of your cigar into your mouth when you are smoking. But I certainly like L'Immortel less, far less than Tartarin.

You know, it seems to me that L'Immortel is not so fine in color as Tartarin, because with its mass of true and subtle observations it reminds me of the dreary pictures by Jean Bérend, which are so dry and cold. Now Tartarin is really great, with the greatness of a masterpiece, just like Candide.

I beg you to keep my studies of this place as well aired as possible, because they are not yet thoroughly dry. If they remain shut up or in the dark, the colors will lose their quality. So the portrait of "The Young Girl," "The Harvest" (a wide landscape with the ruin in the background and the line of the Alps), the "Little Seascape," the "Garden" with the weeping trees and clumps of conifers—it would be a good thing if you could put these on stretchers. I am rather keen on them. You will easily see from the drawing of the little seascape that it is the most thought-out piece.

I am having two oak frames made for my new peasant's head and for my Poet study. Oh, my dear brother, sometimes I know so well what I want. I can very well do without God both in my life and in my painting, but I cannot, ill as I am, do without something which is greater than I, which is my life—the power to create.

And if, frustrated in the physical power, a man tries to create thoughts instead of children, he is still part of humanity.

And in a picture I want to say something comforting, as music is comforting. I want to paint men and women with that something of the eternal which the halo used to symbolize, and which we seek to convey by the actual radiance and vibration of our coloring.

Portraiture so understood does not become like an Ary Scheffer just because there is a blue sky in the background, as in "St. Augustine." For Ary Scheffer is so little of a colorist.

But it would be more in harmony with what Eug. Delacroix attempted and brought off in his "Tasso in Prison," and many other pictures, representing a *real* man. Ah! portraiture, portraiture with the thoughts, the soul of the model in it, that is what I think must come.

The Belgian and I talked a lot yesterday about the advantages and disadvantages of this place. We quite agree about both. And on the great advantage it would be to us if we could *move* now North, now South.

He is going to stay with McKnight again so as to live more cheaply. That, however, has one disadvantage, I think, because living with a slacker makes one slack.

I think you would enjoy meeting him, he is still young. I think he will ask your advice about buying Japanese prints and Daumier lithographs. As to these —the Daumiers—it would be a good thing to get some more of them, because later on there won't be any more available.

The Belgian was saying that he paid 80 francs for board and lodging with McKnight. So what a difference living together makes, since I have to pay 45 a month for nothing but lodging. I always come back to the same calculation, that with Gauguin I should not spend more than I do alone, and be no worse off. But we must consider that they were very badly housed, not for sleeping, but for the possibility of working at home.

So I am always between two currents of thought, first the material difficulties, turning round and round to make a living; and second, the study of color. I am always in hope of making a discovery there, to express the love of two lovers by a wedding of two complementary colors, their mingling and their opposition, the mysterious vibrations of kindred tones. To express the thought of a brow by the radiance of a light tone against a somber background.

To express hope by some star, the eagerness of a soul by a sunset radiance. Certainly there is no delusive realism in that, but isn't it something that actually exists?

Good-by for now. I'll tell you another time when the Belgian may be leaving, because I'll see him again tomorrow.

With a handshake,

Ever yours, Vincent

The Belgian told me that they have a De Groux at home, the cartoon for the "Bénédicité" in the museum in Brussels.

The execution of the portrait of the Belgian is something like the portrait of Reid which you have.

533

My dear Theo,   Arles, 8 September 1888

Thank you a thousand times for your kind letter and the 300 francs it contained; after some worrying weeks I have just had one of the very best. And just as the worries do not come singly, neither do the joys. For just because I am always bowed under this difficulty of paying my landlord, I made up my mind to take it gaily. I swore at the said landlord, who after all isn't a bad fellow, and told him that to revenge myself for paying him so much money for nothing, I would paint the whole of his rotten joint so as to repay myself. Then to the great joy of the landlord, of the postman whom I had already painted, of the visiting night prowlers and of myself, for three nights running I sat up to paint and went to bed during the day. I often think that the night is more alive and more richly colored than the day.

Now, as for getting back the money I have paid to the landlord by means of my painting, I do not dwell on that, for the picture is one of the ugliest I have done. It is the equivalent, though different, of the "Potato Eaters."

I have tried to express the terrible passions of humanity by means of red and green.

The room is blood red and dark yellow with a green billiard table in the middle; there are four citron-yellow lamps with a glow of orange and green. Everywhere there is a clash and contrast of the most disparate reds and greens in the figures of little sleeping hooligans, in the empty, dreary room, in violet and blue. The blood-red and the yellow-green of the billiard table, for instance, contrast with the soft tender Louis XV green of the counter, on which there is a pink nosegay. The white coat of the landlord, awake in a corner of that furnace, turns citron-yellow, or pale luminous green.

I am making a drawing of it with the tones in water color to send to you tomorrow to give you some idea of it.

I wrote this week to Gauguin and Bernard, but I did not talk about anything but pictures, just so as not to quarrel when there is probably nothing to quarrel about.

But whether Gauguin comes or not, if I were to get some furniture, henceforth I should have, whether in a good spot or a bad one is another matter, a pied à terre, a home of my own, which frees the mind from the dismal feeling of being a homeless wanderer. That is nothing when you are an adventurer of twenty, but it is bad when you have turned thirty-five.

Today I read something about the suicide of Mr. Bing Levy in the *Intransigeant*. It can't be the Levy who is Bing's manager, can it? I think it must be someone else.

I am greatly pleased that Pissarro thought something of the "Young Girl." Has Pissarro said anything about the "Sower"? Afterward, when I have carried these experiments even further, the "Sower" will still be the first attempt in that style. The "Night Café" carries on the style of the "Sower," as do the head of the old peasant and of the poet also, if I manage to do this latter picture.

It is color not locally true from the point of view of the delusive realist, but color suggesting some emotion of an ardent temperament.

When Paul Mantz saw at the exhibition the violent and inspired sketch by Delacroix that we saw at the Champs Elysées—the "Bark of Christ"—he turned away from it, exclaiming, "I did not know that one could be so terrible with a little blue and green."

Hokusai wrings the same cry from you, but he does it by his *line*, his *drawing*, just as you say in your letter—"the waves are *claws* and the ship is caught in them, you feel it."

Well, if you make the color exact or the drawing exact, it won't give you sensations like that.

Anyhow, very soon, tomorrow or the day after, I'll write you again about this and answer your letter, and send you the sketch of the "Night Café."

Tasset's parcel has arrived. I'll write tomorrow on this question of the coarse-grain paints. Milliet is coming to see you and pay his respects to you one of these days, he writes me that he is coming back.

Thank you again for the money you sent. If I went first to look for another place, would it not very likely mean fresh expenses, equal at least to the cost of moving? And then should I find anything better all at once? I am so very glad to be able to furnish my house, and it can't but help me on. Many thanks then, and a good handshake, till tomorrow.

Ever yours, Vincent

537

My dear Theo,   Arles, 17 September 1888

Probably I shall hear from you tomorrow morning, but I have time to write you tonight, and the week has been rather eventful.

I expect to go to live in the house tomorrow, but as I have bought some more things and have still more to add to them, and I am speaking only of what is strictly necessary—you must again send me 100 francs instead of 50.

If I reckon 50 francs for myself for the past week and deduct them from the 300 francs you sent, all that is left, even with another extra 50 francs, is no more than the exact price of the two beds. So you will see that as in spite of that I have already bought many other things besides the beds and the bedding, I have already spent the greater part of the 50 francs for the week, and I have partly economized on both beds by having one of them somewhat plainer.

I am convinced that in the end we shall do well by furnishing the studio. And I already feel freer in my work, and less harried by unnecessary annoyances than I have been.

Only if, as I hope, I take more pains with the style and quality of my work, it will go a little more slowly, or rather I shall have to keep the pictures with me longer. That is, if they are subjects that are connected and complement each other. And also because there will be some pictures which I certainly do not want to send you till they are bone dry.

In this last category there is a square size 30 canvas, a corner of a garden with a weeping tree, grass, round clipped cedar shrubs and an oleander bush. The same corner of the garden, that is, which you have already had a study of in the last parcel. But as this one is bigger, there is a citron sky over everything, and also the colors have the richness and intensity of autumn. And besides it is in even heavier paint than the other one, plain and thick. That is picture number one this week.

The second represents the outside of a café, with the terrace lit up by a big gas lamp in the blue night, and a corner of a starry blue sky.

The third picture this week is a portrait of myself, *almost colorless*, in gray tones against a background of pale malachite.

I purposely bought a mirror good enough to enable me to work from my image in default of a model, because if I can manage to paint the coloring of my own head, which is not to be done without some difficulty, I shall likewise be able to paint the heads of other good souls, men and women.

The problem of painting night scenes and effects on the spot and actually by night interests me enormously. This week I have done absolutely nothing but paint and sleep and have my meals. That means sittings of twelve hours, of six hours and so on, and then a sleep of twelve hours at a stretch.

I read in the literary supplement of Saturday's *Figaro* (15 September) the description of an impressionist house. This house was built with bricks—as it were like the bottoms of bottles—of convex glass, violet glass. With the sunshine reflected in it, and the yellow refractions, the effect was incredible. To support these walls of glass bricks, shaped like violet-colored eggs, they had invented a support of black and gilt iron representing the weird branches of Virginia creeper and other climbing plants. This violet house was right in the middle of a garden where all the paths were of bright yellow sand. The ornamental flower borders were of course most unusual in coloring. The house is, if I remember correctly, in Auteuil.

Without changing anything in this house either now or afterward, I want all the same to make it an artist's house through the decorations. That will come. A good handshake. I went for a splendid walk by myself today among the vineyards.

Ever yours, Vincent

B 14 [9]

My dear comrade Bernard,   Arles, Beginning of August 1888

I see I forgot to answer your question as to whether Gauguin is still in Pont-Aven. Yes, he is still there, and if you should like to write to him, I am inclined to think he will be pleased. He has been staying there till now, but he will probably join me here before long, as soon as he himself or both of us can get the money for the journey.

I don't believe that this question of the Dutch painters, which we are discussing at the moment, is without interest. As soon as virility, originality, naturalism of whatever kind come into question, it is very interesting to consult them. But I must speak to you again first of all about yourself, the two still lifes you have done and the two portraits of your grandmother. Have you ever done anything better than that, and have you ever been more *yourself* and a personality? I think not. The profound study of the first thing which came to hand, of the first person who came along was enough to *create* really. Do you know why I like these three or four studies so much? Because of that unknown quality of deliberateness, of great wisdom, that inexpressible quality of being steady and firm and self-assured, of which they give evidence. You have never been closer to Rembrandt, old fellow, than in these studies.

In Rembrandt's studio that incomparable sphinx, Vermeer of Delft, found this extremely solid technique which has never been surpassed, which at present ... we are burning ... to find. Oh, I know we are working and reasoning with *colors*, just as they were with *chiaroscuro, tonal values.*

But what do these differences matter, when the great thing after all is to express oneself strongly?

At present you are studying the methods of the Italian and German primitives, the symbolic significance which the abstract mystical drawing of the Italians may contain. *Go ahead.* I myself rather like that anecdote about Giotto. There was a contest for painting some picture or other representing a Virgin. A lot of cartoons were submitted to the Administration of Fine Arts of the time. One of these cartoons, signed Giotto, was simply an oval, an egg shape. The Administration, perplexed—and confident—entrusted the Virgin in question to Giotto. I don't know whether it is true or not, but I like that anecdote quite a lot.

However, let us return to Daumier and your grandmother.

When are you going to show us studies of such vigorous soundness again? I urgently invite you to do it, although I most certainly do not despise your researches relating to the property of lines in opposite motion—as I am not at all indifferent, I hope, to the simultaneous contrasts of lines, forms. The trouble is —you see, my dear comrade Bernard—that Giotto and Cimabue, as well as Holbein and Van Dyck, lived in an obeliscal—excuse the word—solidly framed society, architecturally constructed, in which each individual was a stone, and all the stones clung together, forming a monumental society. When the socialists construct their logical social edifice—which they are still pretty far from doing— I am sure mankind will see a reincarnation of this society. But, you know, we are in the midst of downright laisser-aller and anarchy. We artists, who

323

love order and symmetry, isolate ourselves and are working to define *only one thing*.

Puvis [de Chavannes] knows this all right, and when he, so just and so wise—forgetting his Elysian Fields—was so good as to descend amiably into the intimacy of our time, he painted a fine portrait indeed: the serene old man in the clear light of his blue interior, reading a novel with a yellow cover—beside him a glass of water with a water-color brush and a rose in it. Also a fashionable lady, as the de Concourts have depicted them.

Now we see that the Dutch paint things just as they are, apparently without reasoning, just as Courbet painted his beautiful nude women. They painted portraits, landscapes, still lifes. Well, one can be stupider than that, and commit greater follies.

If we don't know what to do, my dear comrade Bernard, then let's do as they did, if only not to let our rare intellectual power evaporate in sterile metaphysical meditations which cannot possibly put the chaos into a goblet, as chaos is chaotic for the very reason that it contains no glass of our caliber.

We can—and this was done by these Dutchmen who are so desperately naughty in the eyes of people with a system—we can paint an atom of the chaos, a horse, a portrait, your grandmother, apples, a landscape.

Why do you say Degas is impotently flabby? Degas lives like a small lawyer and does not like women, for he knows that if he loved them and fucked them often, he, intellectually diseased, would become insipid as a painter.

Degas's painting is virile and impersonal for the very reason that he has resigned himself to be nothing personally but a small lawyer with a horror of going on a spree. He looks on while the human animals, stronger than himself, get excited and fuck, and he paints them well, exactly because he doesn't have the pretention to get excited himself.

Rubens! Ah, that one! he was a handsome man and a good fucker, Courbet too. Their health permitted them to drink, eat, fuck ... As for you, my poor dear comrade Bernard, I already told you in the spring: eat a lot, do your military excercises well, don't fuck too much; when you do this your painting will be all the more spermatic.

Ah! Balzac, that great and powerful artist, has rightly told us that relative chastity fortifies the modern artist. The Dutchmen were *married men and begot children*, a fine, very fine craftsmanship, and deeply rooted in nature.

One swallow does not make a summer. I don't say that among your new Breton studies there are none which are virile and sound; I have not seen them yet, so I could not possibly discuss them. But what I have seen were those virile things: the portrait of your grandmother, those still lifes. But judging from your drawings, I have vague misgivings that your new studies will not have the same vigor, exactly in point of virility.

Those studies, which I am speaking about first, are the first swallow of your artistic spring.

If we want to be really potent males in our work, we must sometimes resign ourselves to not fuck much, and for the rest be monks or soldiers, according to the needs of our temperament. The Dutch, once more, had peaceful habits and a peaceful life, calm, well regulated.

Delacroix—ah! that man!—"I found," he says, "my style of painting when I had neither teeth nor breath left!"—and those who saw this famous artist paint said, "When Delacroix paints, it is like a lion devouring his piece [of meat]."

He did not fuck much, and only had easy love affairs, so as not to curtail the time devoted to his work.

If you discover in this letter, which seems more incoherent than I should have liked it to be, considered by itself in relation to your correspondence and especially to the friendship which preceded it—if you discover in this letter some uneasiness—or at any rate solicitude—about your health, with a view to the severe trial you will have to undergo when you do your military service—obligatory, alas!—then you will read it correctly. I know that the study of the Dutch painters can only do you good, for their works are so virile, so full of male potency, so healthy. Personally I feel that continence is good for me, that it is enough for our weak, impressionable artists' brains to give their essence to the creation of our pictures. For when we reflect, calculate, exhaust ourselves, we spend cerebral energy.

Why exert ourselves to pour out all our creative sap where the well-fed professional pimps and ordinary fools do better in the matter of satisfying the genital organs of the whore, who is in this case more submissive than we are ourselves?

The whore in question has more of my sympathy than my compassion.

Being a creature exiled, outcast from society, like you and me who are artists, she is certainly our friend and sister.

And in this condition of being an outcast she finds—just as we ourselves do—an independence which is not without its advantages after all, when you come to think of it. So let's beware of assuming an erroneous attitude by believing that we can do her a service by means of a social rehabilitation which for that matter is hardly practicable and would be fatal to her.

I have just done a portrait of a postman, or rather even two portraits. A Socratic type, none the less Socratic for being somewhat addicted to liquor and having a high color as a result. His wife had just had a child, and the fellow was aglow with satisfaction. He is a terrible republican, like old Tanguy. God damn it! what a motif to paint in the manner of Daumier, eh!

He kept himself too stiff when posing, which is why I painted him twice, the second time at a single sitting. A blue, nearly white background on the white canvas, all the broken tones in the face—yellows, greens, violets, pinks, reds. The uniform Prussian blue, with yellow adornments.

Write me soon if you feel like it, am overburdened with work, and haven't found time yet for figure sketches. A handshake,

Yours sincerely, Vincent

P.S. Cézanne is a respectable married man just like the old Dutchmen; if there is plenty of male potency in his work it is because he does not let it evaporate in merrymaking.

B 17 [14]

My dear comrade Bernard,   Arles, Second half of September 1888
Just a word to thank you for your drawings; I think they were done a little too
hastily, and I like the drawings of the whores better; but for the rest there is an
idea in all of them. I have been overwhelmed with work lately, for the weather is
glorious, and I must make the most of the fine days, which are short.

I cannot withdraw what I said about the price: three francs, just for food, and
then the extras! But I have no doubt that all that Gauguin told you about the
prices here is correct. But all that I can see is that the moment of your departure to
do your military service is drawing near, and I very much wish to induce your
father to provide you with what's necessary to fortify yourself with good food,
without your work suffering under it. Let him do the handsome thing and give
you all that is reasonable in the interval between now and the time of your service.

I have written you insistently and repeatedly that, if you go to Africa, you will
work there, and you will see the very scenery which you ought to see to develop
your talent as a painter and a colorist to its full extent. But this can only be done
at the expense of your poor carcass, unless before your African hardships your
father enables you to avoid getting anemic or catching a debilitating dysentery as
a result of a lack of strengthening food.

It is hardly possible to fortify one's body over there; far be it from me to say
that when one is going into a hot climate one ought to fatten oneself up first,
but what I do say is that one should attend to one's nourishment some time in
advance; and I abide by this through thick and thin, as this regimen agrees with
me so well here, because there is some difference between the heat of Africa and
the heat of Arles.

You will either come out of this trial of your service much stronger, strong
enough for a whole artistic career—or a broken man.

However that may be, I should be enormously delighted if you came here,
and if Gauguin came too; and then the only thing to be regretted will be that it
is winter and not the season of fine weather. I am coming to believe more and
more that the cuisine has something to do with our ability to think and to make
pictures; as for me, when my stomach bothers me it is not conducive to the
success of my work.

In short, I think that, if your father made up his mind quietly to preserve your
pictures and grant you a somewhat generous credit, he would lose less in the end
than if he acted differently. In the South one's senses get keener, one's hand becomes more agile, one's eye more alert, one's brain clearer, however on condition:
that all this is not spoiled by dysentery or something else of a debilitating nature.

But apart from that I venture to believe most firmly that anyone who loves
artistic work will find his productive faculties develop in the South; but take care
of your blood and take care of everything else.

And now you will tell me perhaps that I am boring you with all this—that
you want to go to the brothel without giving a damn about all the rest. Good
heavens, it all depends, but I cannot speak differently than I do. Art is long and
life is short, and we must be patient, while trying to sell our lives dearly. How

I wish I were your age, and could go off, knowing what I know, to do my military service in Africa; but then I should get myself a better body than I have now, and no mistake!

If Gauguin and I are here together, which will probably happen, then we shall certainly do our utmost to save you expense; but then your father, on his part, ought to do his utmost too, and have confidence in us, and realize that we are not trying to do him out of more money than necessary. To do good work one must eat well, be well housed, have one's fling from time to time, smoke one's pipe and drink one's coffee in peace.

I do not say that all the other things are without value, I want to leave everybody free to do what he likes; but what I do say is that this system seems preferable to me to a good many others.

A hearty handshake.

Sincerely yours, Vincent

B 19*a*

My dear comrade Bernard,   Arles, End of October 1888

We have worked a lot these days, and in the meantime I read *Le rêve* [The Dream] by Zola, and because of this I had hardly any time to write. Gauguin interests me very much as a man—very much.

For a long time now it has seemed to me that in our nasty profession of painting we are most sorely in need of men with the hands and the stomachs of workmen. More natural tastes—more loving and more charitable temperaments—than the decadent dandies of the Parisian boulevards have.

Well, here we are without the slightest doubt in the presence of a virgin creature with savage instincts. With Gauguin blood and sex prevail over ambition.

But enough, you have seen him at close range for a longer time than I have; I only wanted to tell you in a few words what my first impressions are. Moreover, I do not think you will be greatly amazed if I tell you that our discussions tend to treat of the terrible subject of an association of certain painters. This association must or may have, yes or no, a commercial character. We haven't arrived at any conclusion yet, nor have we set foot on a new continent.

As for me, with my presentiment of a new world, I firmly believe in the possibility of an immense renaissance of art. Whoever believes in this new art will have the tropics for a home.

I have the impression that we ourselves serve as no more than intermediaries. And that only the next generation will succeed in living in peace. Apart from all this, our duties and the possibilities of action for us can become clearer to us only by experience and nothing else. I am a bit surprised at the fact that I have not yet received the studies you promised me in exchange for mine.

Now something that will interest you—we have made some excursions to the brothels, and it is probable that in the end we shall often go and work there.

At the moment Gauguin is working on a canvas of the same night café I painted too, but with figures seen in the brothels. It promises to turn out beautiful.

I myself have done two studies of the fall of leaves in an avenue of poplars, and a third study of this whole avenue, entirely yellow.

I must say I cannot understand why I don't do studies after the figure, seeing that it is often so difficult for me to imagine the painting of the future theoretically as otherwise than a new succession of powerful, simple portraitists, comprehensible to the general public. Well, perhaps I shall go do the brothels before long. I leave a page open for Gauguin, who will probably write to you too, and I heartily shake your hand in thought.

Sincerely yours, Vincent

Milliet, the second lieutenant of the Zouaves, has gone to Africa; he would like you to write him a letter one of these days.

[Underneath this letter there is a postscript by Gauguin, in which he says that he agrees with Vincent's idea of a new generation of painters in the tropics. He intends to go there as soon as he gets a chance. The two pictures by Vincent of the falling leaves are hanging in his room, and Bernard would think them fine.]

538

My dear Theo, Arles, 18 September 1888

Many thanks for your letter and the 50-franc note which it contained.

I also received Maurin's drawing, which is magnificent. That man is a great artist. Last night I slept in the house, and though there are some things still to be done, I feel very happy in it. Besides, I feel that I can make something lasting out of it, from which others can profit as well. Now money spent will not be money lost, and I think that you will soon see the difference. At present it reminds me of Bosboom's interiors, with the red tiles, the white walls, the furniture of white deal and walnut and the glimpses of an intense blue sky and greenery through the windows. Its surroundings, the public garden, the night cafés and the grocer's, are not Millet, but instead they are Daumier, absolute Zola.

And that is quite enough to supply one with ideas, isn't it?

Yesterday I had already written to you, saying that if I figure the two beds at 300 francs, the price will not allow of any further reduction. If I have already bought more than that anyway, it is because I put half of last week's money into it. Yesterday again I had to pay 10 francs to the innkeeper and 30 francs for a mattress.

At the moment I have 5 francs left, so I must beg you to send me what you can, or else—but do let it be by return mail—a louis to last me the week, or indeed 50 francs if it's possible.

In one way or another I'd like to be able to count on getting this month, meaning the whole month, another 100 instead of the 50, as I asked you in yesterday's letter.

If I myself save 50 francs during the month, and add the other 50 to that, I should have spent altogether 400 francs on furniture. My dear Theo, here we are on the right road at last. Certainly it does not matter being without hearth or home and living in cafés like a traveler so long as one is young, but it was becoming unbearable to me, and more than that, it did not fit in with thoughtful work. So my plan is all complete, I will try to paint up to the value of what you send me every month, and after that I want to paint to pay for the house. What I paint for the house will be to repay you for previous expenditure.

I am still a bit commercial, in the sense that I long to prove that I pay my debts, and that I know how much I want for the goods which this blasted poor painter's profession keeps me working at.

Altogether I think I can be almost sure of bringing off a set of decorations which will be worth 10,000 francs in time.

Listen to me. If we set up a studio and refuge here for some comrade who is hard up, no one will ever be able to reproach either you or me with living and spending for ourselves alone. Now to establish such a studio requires a floating capital, and I have eaten that up during my unproductive years, but now that I am beginning to produce something, I shall pay it back.

I assure you that I think it is essential for you as well as me, and no more than our right, too, to always have a louis or two in our pockets, and some stock of goods to do business with. But my idea is that in the end we shall have founded and left to posterity a studio where one's successor could live. I do not know if I explain myself clearly enough, but in other words we are working for an art and for a business method that will not only last our lifetime, but can still be carried on by others after us.

For your part you do this in your business, and it is certain that you will make good in the end, even though you have plenty to harry you at the moment. But for my part I foresee that other artists will want to see color under a stronger sun, and in a more Japanese clarity of light.

Now if I set up a studio and refuge right at the gates of the South, it's not such a crazy scheme. And it means that we can work on serenely. And if other people say that it is too far from Paris, etc., let them, so much the worse for them. Why did the greatest colorist of all, Eugène Delacroix, think it essential to go South and right to Africa? Obviously, because not only in Africa but from Arles onward you are bound to find beautiful contrasts of red and green, of blue and orange, of sulphur and lilac.

And all true colorists must come to this, must admit that there is another kind of color than that of the North. I am sure if Gauguin came, he would love this country; if he doesn't it's because he has already experienced more brightly colored countries, and he will always be a friend, and one with us in principle.

And someone else will come in his place.

If what one is doing looks out upon the infinite, and if one sees that one's work has its raison d'être and continuance in the future, then one works with more serenity.

Now you have a double right to that.

You are kind to painters, and I tell you, the more I think it over, the more I feel that there is nothing more truly artistic than to love people. You will say that then it would be a good thing to do without art and artists. That is true in the first instance, but then the Greeks and the French and the old Dutchmen accepted art, and we see how art always comes to life again after inevitable periods of decadence, and I do not think that anyone is the better for abhorring

329

artists and their art. At present I do not think my pictures worthy of the advantages I have received from you. But once they are worthy, I swear that you will have created them as much as I, and that we are making them together.

But I will not say more about that, because it will be as clear as daylight to you when I begin to do things more seriously. At the moment I am working on another square size 30 canvas, another garden or rather a walk under plane trees, with the green turf, and black clumps of pines.

You did well to order the paints and the canvas, because the weather is magnificent. We still have the mistral, but there are calm intervals and then it is wonderful.

If there were less mistral, this place would really be as lovely as Japan, and would lend itself as well to art.

As I was writing, a very kind letter arrived from Bernard; he is thinking of coming to Arles this winter, just a whim, but it is possible that Gauguin is sending him as a substitute, and would rather stay in the North himself. We shall soon know, because I am convinced that he will write you one way or the other.

In his letter Bernard speaks of Gauguin with great respect and sympathy, and I am sure that they understand one another.

And I really think that Gauguin has done Bernard good.

Whether Gauguin comes or not, he will remain friends with us, and if he does not come now, he will come another time.

I feel instinctively that Gauguin is a schemer who, seeing himself at the bottom of the social ladder, wants to regain a position by means which will certainly be honest, but at the same time, very politic.

Gauguin little knows that I am able to take all this into account. And perhaps he does not know that it is absolutely necessary for him to gain time, and that with us he will gain that, if he gains nothing else.

If someday he decamps from Pont-Aven with Laval or Maurin without paying his debts, I think in his case he would still be justified, exactly like any other creature at bay. I do not think it would be wise to offer Bernard straight off 150 francs for a picture every month, as you did Gauguin. And Bernard, who has evidently been over and over the whole business with Gauguin—isn't he rather counting on taking Gauguin's place?

I think it will be necessary to be very firm and very explicit about the whole thing.

And without giving any reasons, to speak very plainly.

I cannot blame Gauguin—speculator though he may be as soon as he wants to risk something in business, only I will have nothing to do with it. I would a thousand times rather go on with you, whether you are with the Goupils or not. And in my opinion, you know, the new dealers are exactly and in every way the same as the old.

In principle, and in theory, I am for an association of artists who guarantee each other's work and living, but in principle and in theory I am equally against attempts to destroy old, established businesses. Let them rot in peace, and die a natural death. It is pure presumption to hope to regenerate trade. Have nothing to do with it; let's guarantee a living among ourselves, live like a family, like brothers and friends, and this even if it should not succeed—I would like to be in this, but I will never have anything to do with an attack on other dealers.

With a handshake, and I hope that what I have been obliged to ask you will not be too terribly inconvenient. But I did not want to postpone sleeping at home. And in case you are short yourself, 20 francs more will get me through the week, but it is urgent.

Ever yours, Vincent

I am keeping all Bernard's letters, they are sometimes really interesting. You shall read them someday, there is quite a bundle already.

When I said that we must be firm with Gauguin, it is only because you had already given your opinion when he told you his plan of action in Paris. You made him a good answer then without committing yourself, but also without wounding his self-respect.

And the same thing may become necessary again.

I think I shall see Milliet today. Thank you in advance for the Japanese things.

542

My dear Theo,   Arles, 26 September 1888

The fine weather of the last few days has gone and we have mud and rain instead, but it will certainly come back again before winter.

Only the thing will be to make use of it, because the fine days are short. Especially for painting. This winter I intend to draw a great deal. If only I could manage to draw figures from memory, I should always have something to do. But if you take the cleverest figure done by all the artists who sketch on the spur of the moment, Hokusai, Daumier, in my opinion that figure will never come up to the figure painted from the model by those same masters, or other portrait painters.

And in the end, if models, especially intelligent models, are doomed to fail us too often, we must not despair for this reason or grow weary in the struggle.

In the studio I have arranged all the Japanese prints and the Daumiers, and the Delacroixs and the Géricaults. If you find the "Pietà" by Delacroix again or the Géricault, I strongly advise you to get as many of them as you can. What I should love to have in the studio too is Millet's "Travaux des Champs," and Lerat's etching of his "Sower," which Durand Ruel sells at 1.25 francs. And lastly the little etching by Jacquemart after Meissonier, the "Man Reading," a Meissonier that I have always admired. I cannot help liking Meissonier's things.

I am reading an article in the *Revue des deux Mondes* on Tolstoi. It appears that Tolstoi is enormously interested in the religion of his race, like George Eliot in England.

There must be a book by Tolstoi about religion. I think it is called *My Religion*, it must be very fine. In it he is trying to find, so I understand from this article, what remains eternally true in the religion of Christ, and what all religions have

331

in common. It appears that he does not admit the resurrection of the body, nor even of the soul, but says, like the nihilists, that after death there is nothing more, yet though the man dies, and dies thoroughly, humanity, living humanity, abides.

Anyway, not having read the book itself, I can't say what his concept is, but I think that his religion cannot be a cruel one which would increase our sufferings, but that on the contrary, it must be very comforting, and would inspire serenity and energy and courage to live and many other things.

I think the drawing of the blade of grass and the carnations and the Hokusai in Bing's reproductions are admirable.

But whatever they say, the most common prints colored with a flat wash are admirable to me for the same reason as Rubens and Veronese. I know perfectly well that they are not real primitive art. But even if the primitives are admirable, that's no reason whatever for me to say, as it is becoming the fashion to do, "When I go to the Louvre, I cannot get beyond the primitives."

If one said to a *serious* collector of Japanese prints, to Levy himself, "My dear sir, I cannot help admiring these prints at 5 sous," he would probably be rather shocked, and would pity one's ignorance and bad taste. Just as formerly it was considered bad taste to like Rubens, Jordaens and Veronese.

I think I shall end up not feeling lonesome in the house, and that during the bad days in the winter, for instance, and the long evenings, I shall find some occupation that will take all my attention. Weavers and basket makers often spend whole seasons alone or almost alone, with their handicraft their only distraction.

But what makes these people stay in one place is feeling at home, the *reassuring familiar look of things*. I'd certainly like company, but if I haven't got it, I shall not be unhappy because of it; and then too the time will come when I shall have someone with me. I have little doubt of it. I think that if you were willing to put people up in your house too, you would find plenty of artists for whom the question of lodgings is a very serious problem. For my part I think that it is absolutely my duty to try to make money by my work, and so I see my work before me very clearly.

Oh, if only every artist had something to live on, and to work on, but as that is not so, I want to produce, to produce a lot and with the utmost energy. And perhaps the time will come when we can extend our business and be more of a help to the others.

But that is a long way off, and there is a lot of work to get through first.

If you lived in time of war, you might possibly have to fight; you would regret it, you would lament that you weren't living in times of peace, but after all the necessity would be there, and you would fight.

And in the same way we certainly have the right to wish for a state of affairs in which money would not be necessary in order to live.

However, as everything is done by means of money now, one has to think about making it as long as one spends it, but I have more chance of making it by painting than by drawing. On the whole a good many more people can do clever sketches than paint readily and attack nature with color. That will always

332

be rarer, and whether the pictures take a long time to be appreciated or not, they will find a collector someday.

But about those pictures in rather thick impasto, I think they must be left *here* longer to dry. I have read that the Rubenses in Spain have remained infinitely richer in color than those in the North. Here ruins exposed to the open air remain white, whereas in the North they become gray, dirty, black, etc. You may be sure that if the Monticellis had dried in Paris, they would be much duller now.

I am now beginning to see the beauty of the women here better, and then again and again I must think of Monticelli. Color plays such a tremendous part in the beauty of the women here. I do not say that their shape is not beautiful, but that is not their special charm. That lies in the grand lines of the costume, vivid in color and admirably worn, in the *tone* of the flesh rather than the shape. But I shall have some trouble before I can do them as I begin to see them.

But what I am sure of is that staying here means making progress. And to make a picture that will really be of the South, it's not enough to have a certain dexterity. It's looking at things for a long time that ripens you and gives you deeper understanding. When I left Paris I did not think that I should once think Monticelli and Delacroix so *true*. It is only now, after months and months, that I begin to realize that they did not imagine it all. And I think that next year you are going to see the same subjects all over again, orchards, and harvest, but with a different coloring, and above all a change in the workmanship.

And these changes and variations will always go on.

I feel that while continuing to work, I must not hurry. After all, how would it be to put into practice the old saying, You must study for ten years, and then produce a few portraits. That's what Monticelli did, however, not counting some of his pictures as studies.

But then figures such as the woman in yellow, and the woman with the parasol —the little one you have, and the lovers that Reid had, those are complete figure studies in which as far as the drawing goes there is nothing left to do but to praise. For in them Monticelli achieves a sweeping, magnificent drawing like Daumier and Delacroix. Certainly considering the price Monticellis are at, it would be an excellent speculation to buy some. The time will come when his beautifully drawn figures will be considered very great art.

I think that the town of Arles has been infinitely more glorious once as to the beauty of its women and the beauty of its costumes. Now everything has a battered and sickly look about it.

But when you look at it for long, the old charm revives.

And that is why I see that I lose absolutely nothing by staying where I am and being content to watch things pass, as a spider waits for flies in its web. I cannot force anything, and now that I am settled, I can profit by all the fine days, and every opportunity for snatching a good picture from time to time.

Milliet is lucky, he has as many Arlésiennes as he wants; but then he cannot paint them, and if he were a painter he would not get them. I must bide my time without rushing things.

I have read another article on Wagner—"Love in Music"—I think by the same author who wrote the book on Wagner. How one needs the same thing in painting.

It seems that in the book *My Religion*, Tolstoi implies that whatever happens in the way of violent revolution, there will also be a private and secret revolution in men, from which a new religion will be born, or rather something altogether new, which will have no name, but which will have the same effect of comforting, of making life possible, which the Christian religion used to have. It seems to me that the book ought to be very interesting.

In the end we shall have had enough of cynicism and skepticism and humbug, and we shall want to live more musically. How will that come about, and what will we really find? It would be interesting to be able to prophesy, but it is even better to be able to feel that kind of foreshadowing, instead of seeing absolutely nothing in the future beyond the disasters that are all the same bound to strike the modern world and civilization like terrible lightning, through a revolution or a war, or the bankruptcy of worm-eaten states. If we study Japanese art, we see a man who is undoubtedly wise, philosophic and intelligent, who spends his time doing what? In studying the distance between the earth and the moon? No. In studying Bismarck's policy? No. He studies a single blade of grass.

But this blade of grass leads him to draw every plant and then the seasons, the wide aspects of the countryside, then animals, then the human figure. So he passes his life, and life is too short to do the whole.

Come now, isn't it almost a true religion which these simple Japanese teach us, who live in nature as though they themselves were flowers?

And you cannot study Japanese art, it seems to me, without becoming much gayer and happier, and we must return to nature in spite of our education and our work in a world of convention.

Isn't it sad that the Monticellis have never yet been reproduced in good lithographs or in etchings which vibrate with life? I should very much like to know what artists would say if an engraver like the man who engraved the Velásquez made a fine etching of them. Never mind, I think it is more our job to try to admire and know things for ourselves than to teach them to other people. But the two can go together.

I envy the Japanese the extreme clearness which everything has in their work. It is never tedious, and never seems to be done too hurriedly. Their work is as simple as breathing, and they do a figure in a few sure strokes with the same ease as if it were as simple as buttoning your coat.

Oh! someday I must manage to do a figure in a few strokes. That will keep me busy all winter. Once I can do that, I shall be able to do people strolling on the boulevards, in the street, and heaps of new subjects. While I have been writing this letter I have drawn about a dozen. I am on the track of it, but it is very complicated because what I am after is that in a few strokes the figure of a man, a woman, a child, a horse, a dog, shall have a head, a body, legs, all in the right proportion.

Good-by for the present and a good handshake from

Ever yours, Vincent

Mme. de Lareby Laroquette once said to me—"But Monticelli, Monticelli, why he was a man who ought to have been at the head of a great studio in the South."

I wrote to our sister and to you the other day, you remember, that sometimes I thought that I was continuing Monticelli's work here. Well, don't you see, that studio in question, we are founding it. What Gauguin does, what I do, will be in line with that fine work of Monticelli's, and we will try to prove to the good people that Monticelli did not die sprawled over the café tables of the Cannebière, but that the good old boy is still alive. And the thing won't end even with us, we shall set it going on a pretty solid basis.

544a

My dear Gauguin,   Arles, 29 September 1888

This morning I received your excellent letter, which I sent on to my brother; your concept of impressionism in general, of which your portrait is a symbol, is striking. I can't tell you how curious I am to see it—but this much I know in advance: this work is too important to allow me to make an exchange. But if you will keep it for us, my brother will take it at the first opportunity—which I asked him directly—if you agree, and let's hope that it will be soon.

For, once again, we are trying to hasten the possibility of your coming here. I must tell you that even while working I keep thinking incessantly of that plan to found a studio, which will have you and myself as permanent residents, but which the two of us would turn into a refuge and place of shelter for comrades at moments when they are encountering a setback in their struggle.

After you left Paris, my brother and I stayed together for a time, which will forever remain unforgettable to me! The discussions covered a wider field—with Guillaumin, with the Pissarros, father and son, with Seurat, whose acquaintance I had not made (I visited his studio only a few hours before my departure).

Often these discussions had to do with the problems that are so very near my brother's heart and mine, *i.e.* the measures to be taken to safeguard the material existence of painters and to safeguard the means of production (paints, canvases) and to safeguard, in their direct interest, their share in the price which, under the present circumstances, pictures only bring a long time after they leave the artists' possession.

When you are here, we are going to go over all these discussions.

However this may be, when I left Paris, seriously sick at heart and in body, and nearly an alcoholic because of my rising fury at my strength failing me—then I shut myself up within myself, without having the courage to hope!

Now, however, hope is breaking for me vaguely on the horizon; that hope in intermittent flashes, like a lighthouse, which has sometimes comforted me during my solitary life.

And now I am longing so much to give you a large share in that faith, namely that to a certain extent we shall succeed in laying the foundations of something that will endure.

When we are talking over those strange days of discussions in the poverty-stricken studios and the cafés of the "little boulevard," you will get a clear insight into that idea of my brother's and mine, which until now has not been realized at all, at least as far as starting a company is concerned. Nevertheless, you will see that this idea is such that all that will have to be done to end the terrible situation of the last few years is precisely what we said, or something along parallel lines. When you hear the whole explanation, you will see that we have put things on an unshakable basis. And you will admit that we have gone a long way beyond the plan we communicated to you. That we have gone beyond it is no more than our duty as picture dealers, for perhaps you know that in the past I was in the art-dealing business for years, and I do not despise the profession in which I once earned my bread.

Suffice it to say that, although apparently you have isolated yourself from Paris, yet you will not stop feeling in fairly direct contact with Paris.

These days I have an extraordinary feverish energy; at the moment I am struggling with a landscape that has a blue sky over an immense vine, green, purple, yellow, with black and orange branches. Little figures of ladies with red sunshades and of vintagers with their cart enliven it even more. In the foreground, gray sand. Yet another square size 30 canvas for the adornment of the house.

I have a portrait of myself, all ash-colored. The ashen-gray color that is the result of mixing malachite green with an orange hue, on pale malachite ground, all in harmony with the reddish-brown clothes. But as I also exaggerate my personality, I have in the first place aimed at the character of a simple bonze worshiping the Eternal Buddha. It has cost me a lot of trouble, yet I shall have to do it all over again if I want to succeed in expressing what I mean. It will even be necessary for me to recover somewhat more from the stultifying influence of our so-called state of civilization in order to have a better model for a better picture.

One thing gave me enormous pleasure: yesterday I received a letter from Bock (his sister belongs to the Belgian "Vingtistes"), who writes to tell me that he has settled down in the Borinage to paint the miners and coal mines there. Yet he intends to return to the South—in order to vary his impressions—and in that case it is certain that he will come to Arles.

I always think my artistic conceptions extremely ordinary when compared to yours.

I have always had the coarse lusts of a beast.

I forget everything in favor of the external beauty of things, which I cannot reproduce, for in my pictures I render it as something ugly and coarse, whereas nature seems perfect to me.

However, at present the élan of my bony carcass is such that it goes straight for its goal. The result of this is a sincerity, perhaps original at times, in what I feel, if only the subject can lend something to my rash and clumsy execution.

I think that if, from now on, you begin to feel like the head of the studio, which we shall try to turn into a refuge for many—little by little, as our strenuous work furnishes us with the means to complete the thing—I think that then you will feel more or less comforted after the present miseries of poverty and illness, taking into consideration that probably we shall be giving our lives for a generation of painters that will last a long while.

The part of the country where I live has already seen the cult of Venus—in Greece essentially artistic—and after that the poets and artists of the Renaissance. Where such things could flourish, impressionism will too.

I have expressly made a decoration for the room you will be staying in, a poet's garden (among the sketches Bernard has there is a first rough draft of it, later simplified). The ordinary public garden contains plants and shrubs that make one dream of landscapes in which one likes to imagine the presence of Botticelli, Giotto, Petrarch, Dante and Boccaccio. In the decoration I have tried to disentangle the essential from what constitutes the immutable character of the country

And what I wanted was to paint the garden in such a way that one would think of the old poet from here (or rather from Avignon), Petrarch, and at the same time of the new poet living here—Paul Gauguin....

However clumsy this attempt may be, yet it is possible you will see in it that I was thinking of you with a very strong emotion while preparing your studio.

Let's be full of courage with regard to the success of our enterprise, and you must go on considering this your home, for I am very much inclined to believe that it will last long.

A cordial handshake, and believe me

Ever yours, Vincent

However, I am afraid you will think Brittany more beautiful—even though here you will see nothing more beautiful than Daumier; for very often the figures here are absolutely Daumier. And, as for yourself, it will not take you long to discover antiquity and the Renaissance asleep beneath all this modernity. And as to this, you will be free to revive them.

Bernard tells me that he, Morel, Laval and somebody else are willing to exchange pictures with me. I am in fact a great advocate of the system of exchanges among artists, because I see that it used to be of considerable importance in the lives of the Japanese painters. Consequently, one of these days I am going to send you the studies I can spare that are dry, so that you will have first choice. But I refuse to make an exchange with you if on your part it would cost you such an important thing as your [self-]portrait, which would be too beautiful. Surely I should not dare, for my brother would be pleased to take it at the price of a whole month's money.

553

My dear Theo,   Arles, 15 October 1888

A letter from Gauguin telling me that he has sent you some pictures and studies. I'd be very glad if you could find time to write me some details of what they are. With his letter was one from Bernard, saying that they had received the canvases I sent, and that they are going to keep all seven. Bernard will send me another study in exchange, and the three others, Moret, Laval, and a young man will also send me portraits, I hope. Gauguin has my portrait and Bernard says that he would like to have one like it, though he already has one of me, which I exchanged with him some time ago for the portrait of his grandmother.

And I am pleased to hear that they did not dislike what I have done in figure painting.

I have been and still am nearly half dead from the past week's work. I cannot do any more yet, and besides, there is a very violent mistral that raises clouds of dust which whiten the trees on the plain from top to bottom. So I am forced to be quiet. I have just slept sixteen hours at a stretch, and it has restored me considerably.

And tomorrow I shall have recovered from this queer turn.

But I have done a good week's work, truly, with five canvases. If that somewhat takes it out on this one, well, it's natural. If I had worked more quietly, you can easily see that the mistral would have caught me again. If it is fine here, you must take advantage of it, otherwise you would never do anything.

Say, what is Seurat doing? If you see him, tell him once more from me that I am working on a scheme of decoration which has now got to 15 square size 30 canvases, and which will take at least 15 others to make a whole, and that in this work on a larger scale, it is often the memory of his personality and of the visit we made to his studio to see his beautiful great canvases that encourages me in this task.

I wish we had the self-portrait of Seurat. I told Gauguin that if I urged him to make an exchange of portraits it was because I thought that Bernard and he were sure to have made several studies of each other already. And since that was not so and he had done the portrait expressly for me, I did not want it as an exchange, as I thought it was too important for that. He wrote to say that he was determined I should have it in exchange, his letter is again very complimentary; as I don't deserve it, we will say no more.

I am sending you an article on Provence which seems well written to me. These *Félibres* are a literary and artistic society, Clovis Hugues, Mistral and others, who write fairly good, sometimes very good, sonnets in Provençal and sometimes in French.

If the *Félibres* stop being unaware of my existence someday, they will all come to the little house. I would rather this did not happen before I have finished my decorations. But since I love Provence as unreservedly as they do, I perhaps have a right to their attention. If I ever insist on that right, it will be so that my work may remain here or in Marseilles, where as you know I should so much like to work. Because I believe that the artists of Marseilles would do well to continue what Monticelli began.

If Gauguin and I were to write an article in one of the papers here, that would be enough to get in touch with them.

A handshake,

Ever yours, Vincent

"Calm even in the catastrophe."

574

My dear Theo,   Arles, 28 January 1889

Only a few words to tell you that my health and my work are not progressing so badly.

It astonishes me already when I compare my condition today with what it was a month ago. Before that I knew well enough that one could fracture one's legs and arms and recover afterward, but I did not know that you could fracture the brain in your head and recover from that too.

I still have a sort of "what is the good of getting better?" feeling about me, even in the astonishment aroused in me by my getting well, which I hadn't dared hope for.

During your visit I think you must have noticed the two size 30 canvases of sunflowers in Gauguin's room. I have just put the finishing touches to copies, absolutely identical replicas of them. I think I have already told you that besides these I have a canvas of "La Berceuse," the very one I was working on when my illness interrupted me. I now have two copies of this one too.

I have just said to Gauguin about this picture that when he and I were talking about the fishermen of Iceland and of their mournful isolation, exposed to all dangers, alone on the sad sea—I have just said to Gauguin that following those intimate talks of ours the idea came to me to paint a picture in such a way that sailors, who are at once children and martyrs, seeing it in the cabin of their Icelandic fishing boat, would feel the old sense of being rocked come over them and remember their own lullabys.

Now, it may be said that it is like a chromolithograph from a cheap shop. A woman in green with orange hair standing out against a background of green with pink flowers. Now these discordant sharps of crude pink, crude orange, and crude green are softened by flats of red and green.

I picture to myself these same canvases between those of the sunflowers, which would thus form torches or candelabra beside them, the same size, and so the whole would be composed of seven or nine canvases.

(I should like to make another duplicate for Holland if I could get hold of the model again.)

Since it is still winter, look here, let me go quietly on with my work; if it is that of a madman, well, so much the worse. I can't help it.

However, the unbearable hallucinations have ceased, and are now getting reduced to a simple nightmare, in consequence of my taking bromide of potassium, I think.

It is still beyond my powers to go into the details of this money question, and yet I want to do that very thing, and I am furiously at work from morning till night, to prove to you (unless my work is another hallucination), to prove to you that indeed and indeed we are following Monticelli's track, and what's more, that we have a light before our feet and a lamp upon our path in the powerful work of Brias of Montpellier, who did so much to create a school in the South.

Only don't be too amazed if during the next month I shall be obliged to ask you for the month's money in full and some extra money as well.

After all it is only right that during periods of productivity, on which I spend all my vital warmth, I should insist on what is necessary in order to take a few precautions.

Even in that case the difference in expenditure is certainly not excessive on my part.

And once again, either shut me up in a madhouse right away—I shan't oppose it, for I may be deceiving myself—or else let me work with all my strength, while taking the precautions I speak of. If I am not mad, the time will come when I shall send you what I have promised you from the beginning. Now perhaps the pictures are alas bound to be dispersed, but when you for one see the whole that is in my mind, I dare hope it will make a comforting impression on you.

You saw, as I did, part of the Faure collection being passed in review one by one in the little window of that picture framer's shop in the Rue Lafitte, didn't you? Like me, you saw that this slow succession of once despised canvases was strangely interesting.

Good. My great desire would be that sooner or later you should have a series of canvases of mine which might likewise march past in just that same window.

Now by continuing this furious work during next February and March, I shall hope to have finished the quietly composed repetitions of a number of studies I made last year. And these together with some canvases you have already had from me, such as the "Harvest" and the "White Orchard," will form a tolerably firm foundation. By that same time, not later than March, that is, we can arrange what there is to arrange on the occasion of your marriage.

But during February and March, though working, I shall go on considering myself an invalid, and I tell you beforehand that for those two months I shall perhaps have to take 250 a month from the year's allowance.

You will perhaps understand that what would reassure me in some fashion as to my illness and the possibility of a relapse would be to see that Gauguin and I had not exhausted our brains for nothing, but that some good canvases have come out of it.

And I dare to hope that someday you will see that by keeping steady and straight in this money business, in the long run it will prove to be impossible that you have acted against the interests of the Goupils.

But if I should have eaten their bread indirectly through you as an intermediary, in that case my integrity would be directly involved.

Then, however, far from going on feeling more or less embarrassed by each other because of it, we shall be able to feel even more like brothers after that has been arranged.

You will have gone on being poor all the time in order to support me, but I will give you back the money or give up the ghost. Meanwhile this tender-hearted wife of yours will have come, and will make us old fellows almost young again.

But this I believe, that you and I will have successors in our business, and that just as when the family, financially speaking, abandoned us to our own resources, once again it will be we who never flinched.

And after that, the deluge.... Am I wrong in this? Indeed, as long as this world lasts, so long will there be artists and picture dealers, especially those who, like you, are at the same time apostles.

What I am telling you is true. If it is not absolutely necessary to shut me up in a cell, then I am still good for paying, at least in goods, what I am considered to owe. In conclusion, I still have to tell you that the chief superintendent of police paid me a very friendly visit yesterday. He told me as he shook hands that if I ever needed him, I could consult him as *a friend*. I am far from refusing that, and I may soon be in just that position if they raise difficulties about the house.

I am waiting till the time comes for me to pay the month's rent to interview the agent or the proprietor face to face.

But if they try to kick me out, they will find themselves tripped up this time anyhow.

What would you? We have gone all out for the impressionists, and now as far as it's in my power I am trying to finish canvases which will undoubtedly secure me the little corner that I have claimed. Ah, the future of it all ... but since old Pangloss assures us that everything is always for the best in the best of worlds—can we doubt it?

My letter has grown longer than I intended, but it doesn't matter. The main thing is that I am asking categorically for two months' work before making the arrangements which will have to be made at the time of your marriage.

After that, in the spring, you and your wife will found a commercial house for several generations. It will not be too easy. And that settled, I only ask the position of a painting employee, at least as long as there is enough to pay one.

The work distracts my mind. And I *must* have some distraction. Yesterday I went to the Folies Arlésiennes, the budding theater here. It was the first time that I slept without a bad nightmare. They were giving (it was a Provençal literary society) what they called a *Noël* or *Pastorale*, reminiscent of the Christian theater of the Middle Ages. It was a very carefully studied performance, and must have cost them a lot of money.

It represented, of course, the birth of Christ, mixed up with the burlesque of a family of gaping Provençal peasants.

But the amazing thing about it, like a Rembrandt etching, was the old peasant woman, just such another as Mme. Tanguy, with a head of silex or flint, dishonest, treacherous, silly, all this very evident from the preceding scenes.

Now in the play that woman, led before the mystic crib, began to sing in her quavering voice, and then the voice changed, changed from the voice of a witch to that of an angel, and from an angel's voice to a child's, and then the answer came in another voice, strong and warm and vibrant, the voice of a woman behind the scenes.

It was amazing. I can tell you these so-called "Félibres" had certainly put themselves to expense.

As for me, being in this little country of mine, I have no need at all to go to the tropics. I believe and I shall always believe in the art that is to be created in the tropics, and I think it will be marvelous, but personally I am too old and (especially if I have a papier mâché ear put on) too jerry-built to go there.

Will Gauguin do it? It is not essential. For if this ought to be done, it will happen of itself.

We are nothing but links in a chain.

Old Gauguin and I understand each other basically, and if we are a bit mad, what of it? Aren't we also thoroughly artists enough to contradict suspicions on that score by what we say with the brush?

Perhaps someday everyone will have neurosis, St. Vitus' dance, or something else.

But doesn't the antidote exist? In Delacroix, in Berlioz, and Wagner? And really, as for the artist's madness of all the rest of us, I do not say that I especially am not infected through and through, but I say and will maintain that our antidotes and consolations may, with a little good will, be considered ample compensation.

Ever yours, Vincent

See "Hope" by Puvis de Chavannes.

577

My dear Theo,   Arles, 17 February 1889

I have been so completely out of sorts mentally that it would have been useless to try to write an answer to your kind letter. Today I have just come home provisionally, I hope for good. I feel quite normal so often, and really I should think that if what I am suffering from is only a disease peculiar to this place, I must wait here quietly till it is over, even if it returns again (and let's say that it won't).

But this is what I told M. Rey once and for all. If sooner or later it is desirable that I go to Aix, as has already been suggested, I consent beforehand and I will submit to it.

But in my character as a painter and a workman it is not permissible for anyone, not even you or a doctor, to take such a step without warning me and consulting *me* about it, also because since up till now I have always kept a comparative presence of mind in my work, I should have the right to say (or at least to have an opinion on) whether it would be better to keep my studio here or to move to Aix altogether. This so as to avoid the expenses and loss of moving as much as possible and not to do it except in case of absolute necessity.

It seems that people here have some superstition that makes them afraid of painting, and that they have been talking about it in the town. Very good, I know it is the same thing in Arabia, but nevertheless we have loads of painters in Africa, haven't we?

Which shows that with a little firmness you can modify these prejudices, at least as far as painting in spite of it is concerned.

The unfortunate thing is that I am rather inclined to be affected by the beliefs of others, and to feel them myself, and I cannot always laugh at whatever foundation of truth there may be in the absurdity.

As I have already been staying here for more than a year, and have heard almost all the ill that could be spoken of myself, Gauguin and painting in general —why shouldn't I take things as they come and wait for the upshot here? To what place worse could I go than where I have twice been: in the madhouse?

The advantages I have here are what Rivet used to say, "They are a sickly lot, all of them," so that at least I do not feel alone.

Then, as you well know, I am so fond of Arles, though Gauguin has uncommonly good reason to call it the dirtiest town in the whole South.

And I have already met with such friendliness from my neighbors, from M. Rey, and from everyone at the hospital besides, that really I would rather be always ill here than forget the kindness there is in the very people who have the most incredible prejudices against painters and painting, or at any rate have no clear, sane idea of it as we have.

Then they know me now at the hospital, and if it comes on again, nothing would be said, and they would know what to do at the hospital. I have no desire at all to be treated by other doctors, nor is there any necessity.

The only thing I should like to be able to do is to go on earning with my hands what I spend. Koning wrote me a very nice letter saying that he and a friend would probably be coming South to me for a long time. It was in reply to a letter I wrote him some days ago. I do not dare persuade painters to come here after what has happened to me, they run the risk of losing their wits like me; the same applies to De Haan and Isaäcson. Let them go to Antibes, Nice, or Mentone, it is perhaps healthier.

Mother and our sister have also written, the latter was terribly distressed about the patient she was nursing. At home they are very, very glad about your marriage.

Now mind, you must not think too much about me, nor fret yourself. It will probably have to take its course, and we cannot change much in our fate by taking precautions.

Once more let us try to resign ourselves to our fate whatever it is. Our sister wrote that your fiancée had just been staying some time at home. That is good. Well, I send my love with all my heart, and don't let's lose courage.

Believe me,

Ever yours, Vincent

Address next letter to Place Lamartine.

Kind regards to Gauguin. I hope he is going to write me. I shall write him too.

579

My dear brother,[1]   Arles, 19 March 1889

I seemed to see so much brotherly anxiety in your kind letter that I think it my duty to break my silence. I write to you in the full possession of my faculties and not as a madman, but as the brother you know. This is the truth. A certain number of people here (there were more than 80 signatures) addressed a petition to the Mayor (I think his name is M. Tardieu), describing me as a man not fit to be at liberty, or something like that.

The commissioner of police or the chief commissioner then gave the order to shut me up again.

Anyhow, here I am, shut up in a cell all the livelong day, under lock and key and with keepers, without my guilt being proved or even open to proof.

Needless to say, in the secret tribunal of my soul I have much to reply to all that. Needless to say, I cannot be angry, and it seems to me a case of qui s'excuse s'accuse.

Only to let you know that as for setting me free—mind, I do not ask it, being persuaded that the whole accusation will be reduced to nothing—but I do say that as for getting me freed, you would find it difficult. If I did not restrain my indignation, I should at once be thought a dangerous lunatic. Let us hope and have patience. Besides, strong emotion can only aggravate my case. That is why I beg you for the present to let things be without meddling.

Take it as a warning from me that it might only complicate and confuse things.

All the more because you will understand that, while I am absolutely calm at the present moment, I may easily relapse into a state of overexcitement on account of fresh mental emotion.

So you understand what a staggering blow between the eyes it was to find so many people here cowardly enough to join together against one man, and that man ill.

Very good—so much for your better guidance; as far as my mental state is concerned, I am greatly shaken, but I am recovering a sort of calm in spite of everything, so as not to get angry.

Besides, humility becomes me after the experience of the repeated attacks. So I am being patient.

The main thing, I cannot tell you this too often, is that you should keep calm too, and let nothing upset you in your business. After your marriage we can set ourselves to clearing all this up, and meanwhile I beg you to leave me quietly here. I am convinced that the Mayor as well as the commissioner is really rather friendly, and that they will do what they can to settle all this. Here, except for liberty, and except for many things that I could wish otherwise, I am not too badly off.

Besides, I told them that we were in no position to bear the expense. I cannot move without expense, and here are three months that I haven't been working, and mind, I could have worked if they had not vexed and worried me.

How are our mother and sister?

As I have nothing else to distract me—they even forbid me to smoke—though

[1] On Feb. 27, 1889, Theo wrote to his wife that Vincent had been taken to the hospital again.

344

the other patients are allowed to—I think about all the people I know all day and all night long.

It is a shame—and all, so to speak, for nothing.

I will not deny that I would rather have died than have caused and suffered such trouble.

Well, well, to suffer without complaining is the one lesson that has to be learned in this life.

Now with all this, if I am to take up my task of painting again, I naturally need my studio, and some furniture, and we certainly have nothing to replace them with in case of loss. You know my work would not permit being reduced to living in hotels again. I must have my own fixed niche.

If these fellows here protest against me, I protest against them, and all they have to do is to give me damages and interest by friendly arrangement, in short, only to pay me back what I have lost through their blunders and ignorance.

If—say—I should become definitely insane—I certainly don't say that this is impossible—in any case I must be treated differently, and given fresh air, and my work, etc.

Then—honestly—I will submit.

But we have not got to that, and if I had had peace I should have recovered long ago.

They pester me because of my smoking and eating, but what's the use? After all, with all their sobriety, they only cause me fresh misery. My dear boy, the best we can do perhaps is to make fun of our petty griefs and, in a way, of the great griefs of human life too. Take it like a man, go straight to your goal. In present-day society we artists are only the broken pitchers. I so wish I could send you my canvases, but all of them are under lock and key, guarded by police and keepers. Don't try to release me, that will settle itself, but warn Signac[1] not to meddle in it, for he would be putting his hand into a hornets' nest—not until I write again. I shake your hand in thought. Give my kind regards to your fiancée, and to our mother and sister.

Ever yours, Vincent

I will read this letter just as it stands to M. Rey, who is not responsible, as he was ill himself. Doubtless he will write to you himself as well. My house has been closed by the police.

If, however, you have not heard from me direct a month from now, then take action, but as long as I go on writing you, wait.

I have a vague recollection of a registered letter from you which they made me sign for, but which I did not want to take because they made such a fuss about the signature, and I have heard nothing about it since.

Explain to Bernard that I have not been able to answer him. It's quite a production to write a letter, there are as many formalities necessary now as if one were in prison. Tell him to ask Gauguin's advice, but give him a handshake for me.

[1] Theo had heard from Signac that he was going to the South, and had asked him to visit Vincent.

Once more kind regards to your fiancée and Bonger.

I would rather not have written to you yet for fear of dragging you into it and upsetting you in what is before you. Things will settle down, it is too idiotic to last.

I had hoped that M. Rey would have come to see me so that I could talk to him again before sending off this letter, but though I sent word that I am expecting him, no one has come. I beg you once more to be cautious. You know what it means to go to the civil authorities with a complaint. At least wait till after you've been to Holland.

I am myself rather afraid that, if I were at liberty outside, I should not always keep control of myself if I were provoked or insulted, and then they would be able to take advantage of that. The fact remains that a petition has been sent to the Mayor. I answered roundly that I was quite prepared, for instance, to chuck myself into the water if that would please these good folk once and for all, but that in any case if I had in fact inflicted a wound on myself, I had done nothing of the sort to them, etc.

So cheer up, though my heart fails me sometimes. For you to come just now, honestly, would precipitate everything. I shall move out, of course, as soon as I see how to manage it.

I hope this will reach you all right. Do not be afraid of anything, I am quite calm now. Let them alone. Perhaps it would be well if you wrote once more, but nothing else for the time being. If I have patience, it can only strengthen me so as to leave me in less danger of a relapse. Of course, since I really had done my best to be friendly with people, and had no suspicion of it, it was rather a bad blow.

Good-by, my dear boy, for a little while, I hope, and don't worry. Perhaps it is a sort of quarantine they are forcing on me, for all I know.

581

My dear Theo,   Arles, 24 March 1889

I am writing to tell you that I have seen Signac, and it has done me quite a lot of good. He was so good and straightforward and simple when the difficulty of opening the door by force or not presented itself—the police had closed up the house and destroyed the lock. They began by refusing to let us do it, but all the same we finally got in. I gave him as a keepsake a still life which had annoyed the good gendarmes of the town of Arles, because it represented two bloaters, and as you know they, the gendarmes, are called that. You remember that I did this same still life two or three times in Paris, and exchanged it once for a carpet in the old days. That is enough to show you how meddlesome and what idiots these people are.

I found Signac very quiet, though he is said to be so violent; he gave me the impression of someone who has balance and poise, that is all. Rarely or never have I had a conversation with an impressionist so free from discords or conflict on both sides. For instance he has been to see Jules Dupré, and he admires him. Doubtless you had a hand in his coming to stiffen my morale a bit, and thank you for it.

I took advantage of my outing to buy a book, *Ceux de la Glèbe*, by Camille

Lemonnier. I have devoured two chapters of it—it has such gravity, such depth! Wait till I send it to you. This is the first time in several months that I have had a book in my hands. That means a lot to me and does a good deal toward curing me.

Altogether there are several canvases to be sent to you, as Signac could see, he was not frightened by my painting as far as I saw. Signac thought, and it is perfectly true, that I looked healthy.

And with it I have the desire and the inclination for work. Still, of course, if I had to endure my work and my private life being interfered with every day by gendarmes and poisonous idlers of municipal electors petitioning the Mayor whom they have elected and who consequently depends on their votes, it would be no more than human of me to relapse all over again. I am inclined to think that Signac will tell you very much the same thing. In my opinion we must firmly oppose the loss of the furniture, etc. Then—my Lord—I must have liberty to carry on my handicraft.

M. Rey says that instead of eating enough and at regular times, I kept myself going on coffee and alcohol. I admit all that, but all the same it is true that to attain the high yellow note that I attained last summer, I really had to be pretty well keyed up. And that after all, an artist is a man with his work to do, and it is not for the first idler who comes along to crush him for good.

Am I to suffer imprisonment or the madhouse? Why not? Didn't Rochefort and Hugo, Quinet and others give an eternal example by submitting to exile, and the first even to a convict prison? But all I want to say is that this is a thing above the mere question of illness and health.

Naturally one is beside oneself in parallel cases. I do not say equivalent, being in a very inferior and secondary place to theirs, but I do say parallel.

And that is what the first and last cause of my aberration was. Do you know those words of a Dutch poet's—"Ik ben aan d'aard gehecht met meer dan aardse banden" [I am attached to the earth by more than earthly ties].

That is what I have experienced in the midst of much suffering—above all—in my so-called mental illness.

Unfortunately I have a handicraft which I do not know well enough to express myself as I should like.

I pull myself up short for fear of a relapse, and I pass on to something else. Before you leave, could you send me

3 tubes			zinc white
1 tube same size			cobalt
1	"	"	ultramarine
4	"	"	malachite green
1	"	"	emerald green
1	"	"	orange lead

This in case—probable enough if I find a way of resuming my work again—I should set to work shortly on the orchards again. Oh, if only nothing had happened to mess up my life!

347

Let's think well before going to another place. You see that I have no better luck in the South than in the North. It's pretty much the same everywhere.

I am thinking of frankly accepting my role of madman, the way Degas acted the part of a notary. But there it is, I do not feel that altogether I have strength enough for such a part.

You talk to me of what you call "the real South." The reason why I shall never go there is above. I rightly leave that to men who have a more well-balanced mind, more integrity than I. I am only good for something intermediate, and second rate, and self-effaced.

However intense my feelings may be, or whatever power of expression I may acquire at an age when physical passions have lessened, I could never build an imposing structure on such a moldy, shattered past.

So it is more or less all the same to me what happens to me—even my staying here—I think that in the end my fate will be evened up. So beware of sudden starts—since you are getting married and I am getting too old—that is the only policy to suit us.

Good-by for now, write me without much delay, and believe me, after asking you to give my kindest regards to Mother, our sister and your fiancée, your very affectionate brother,

Vincent

I will send the book by Camille Lemonnier pretty soon.

585

My dear Theo,   Arles, 22 April 1889

You will probably be back in Paris at the moment when this letter arrives. I wish you and your wife a great deal of happiness. Thank you very much for your kind letter and for the 100-franc note it contained.

Out of the 65 francs which I owe, I have paid only 25 francs to my landlord, having had to pay three months' rent in advance for a room which I shan't be living in, but where I have sent my furniture, and having besides had expenses of 10 francs or so for moving, etc.

Then as my clothes were not in too brilliant a condition and I had to have something new to go out in the street in, I got a suit for 35 francs and spent 4 francs on six pairs of socks. So out of the note I have only a few francs left, and at the end of the month I must pay the landlord again, though he might be kept waiting for a few days.

I settled my bill at the hospital today, and there is still almost enough for the rest of the month out of the money I still have on deposit. At the end of the month I should like to go to the hospital in St. Rémy, or another institution of this kind, of which M. Salles has told me. Forgive me if I don't go into details and argue the pros and cons of such a step.

Talking about it would be mental torture.

It will be enough, I hope, if I tell you that I feel quite unable to take a new studio and to stay there alone—here in Arles or elsewhere, for the moment it is all the same; I have tried to make up my mind to begin again, but at the moment it's not possible.

I should be afraid of losing the power to work, which is coming back to me now, by forcing myself and by having all the other responsibilities of a studio on my shoulders besides.

And temporarily I wish to remain shut up as much for my own peace of mind as for other people's.

What comforts me a little is that I am beginning to consider madness as a disease like any other and accept the thing as such, whereas during the crises themselves I thought that everything I imagined was real. Anyway, the fact is that I do not want to think or talk about it. You'll spare me any explanations, but I ask you and Messrs. Salles and Rey to arrange things so that I can go there as a resident boarder at the end of this month or the beginning of May.

Beginning again that painter's life I have been living, isolated in the studio so often, and without any other means of distraction than going to a café or a restaurant with all the neighbors criticizing, etc., *I can't face it*; going to live with another person, say another artist—difficult, very difficult—it's taking too much responsibility on oneself. I dare not even think of it.

So let's try it three months to begin with, and afterward we shall see. Now one's board ought to be about 80 francs, and I shall do a little painting and drawing without putting such frenzy into it as a year ago. Do not be grieved at all this. Certainly these last days were sad, with all the moving, taking away all my furniture, packing up the canvases that are going to you, but the thing I felt saddest about was that you had given me all these things with such brotherly love, and that for so many years you were always the one who supported me, and then to be obliged to come back and tell you this sorry tale—but it's difficult to express it as I felt it. The goodness you have shown me is not lost, because you had it and it remains for you; even if the material results should be nil, it remains for you all the more; but I can't say it as I felt it.

Meanwhile you do understand that if alcohol has undoubtedly been one of the great causes of my madness, then it came on very slowly and will go away slowly too, assuming it does go, of course. Or the same thing if it comes from smoking. But I should only hope that it—this recovery ——[1] the frightful superstition of some people on the subject of alcohol, so that they prevail upon themselves never to drink or smoke.

We are already ordered not to lie or steal, etc., and not to commit other crimes great or small, and it would become too complicated if it was absolutely indispensable to have nothing but virtues in the society in which we are very undeniably planted, whether it be good or bad.

I assure you that during those queer days when many things seem odd to me because my brain is agitated, through it all I don't dislike old Pangloss.

But you would do me a service by discussing the question frankly with M. Salles and M. Rey.

[1] Probably a word has been omitted here.

I should think that with an allowance of 75 francs or so a month there must be a way of interning me so that I should have everything I need.

Then, if it is possible, I'd very much like to be able to go out in the daytime and draw or paint outside.

Seeing that I go out every day now here, and I think that this could continue.

Paying more, I warn you, would make me less happy. The company of other patients, you understand, is not at all disagreeable to me; on the contrary, it distracts me.

Ordinary food suits me quite well, especially if they gave me a little more wine there, as they do here, usually a half-liter instead of a quarter, for instance.

But a private room—it remains to be seen what the arrangements of an institution like that would be. Mind you, Rey is overburdened with work, overburdened. If he writes to you, or M. Salles, better do exactly what they say. After all we must take our share, my boy, of the diseases of our time—in a way it is only fair after all that, having lived some years in comparatively good health, we should have our share sooner or later. As for me, you know well enough that I should not exactly have chosen madness if I had had a choice, but once you have an affliction of that sort, you can't catch it again. And there'll perhaps be the consolation of being able to go on working a bit at painting.

How will you manage not to speak too well or too ill of Paris and many other things to your wife? Do you feel in advance that you will be quite capable of keeping exactly the golden mean all the time and from all points of view?

I shake your hand in thought. I do not know if I shall write very, very often because not all my days are clear enough for me to write fairly logically.

All your kindness to me seemed greater than ever to me today. I can't put the way I feel it in words, but I assure you that this kindness has been pure gold, and if you do not see any results from it, my dear brother, don't fret about it; your own goodness abides. Only transfer this affection to your wife as much as possible. And if we correspond somewhat less, you will see that if she is what I think her, she will comfort you. That is what I hope.

Rey is a very nice fellow, a tremendous worker, always on the job. What men the modern doctors are!

If you see Gauguin or write to him, remember me to him.

I shall be very glad to hear any news you can give me of our mother and sister, and if they are well; tell them to look upon this affair of mine—I mean it—as nothing to be inordinately distressed about, because I may be comparatively unfortunate, but after all, in spite of that, I may still have some almost normal years before me. It is a disease like any other, and now almost everyone we know among our friends has something the matter with him. So is it worth talking about? I am sorry to give trouble to M. Salles, and Rey, and above all to you too, but what is one to do? My head isn't steady enough to begin again as before —then the important thing is not to cause any more scenes in public, and naturally, being a little calmer now, I distinctly feel that I was mentally and physically in an unhealthy condition. And then people have been kind, those I remember, and as for the others, after all I caused some uneasiness, and if I had been in a normal condition, things would never have happened the way they did.

Good-by, write when you can.

Ever yours, Vincent

588

My dear Theo,   Arles, 30 April 1889

Tomorrow being the first of May, I wish you a tolerable year, and above all health.

I should so like to be able to pass some physical strength on to you. At the moment I feel that I have more than enough. That doesn't mean that my head is still all that it ought to be.

How right Delacroix was, who lived on bread and wine only, and who succeeded in finding a manner of life in harmony with his profession. But the fatal question of money remains—Delacroix had property, Corot too. And Millet—Millet was a peasant and the son of a peasant. You will perhaps read with some interest the article which I have cut out of a Marseilles paper, because you will catch a glimpse of Monticelli in it, and I think the description of the picture representing a corner of the cemetery very interesting. But alas, that is still another lamentable story. How sad it is to think that a painter who succeeds, even only partially, involves in his turn half a dozen other artists who are worse failures than himself.

However, think of Pangloss, think of *Bouvard et Pécuchet*. I know it, then even that becomes clear, but perhaps these people do not know Pangloss or else forget all they know of him in the face of the fatal bite of actual despair and great grief.

And besides, under the name of optimism we are falling back once more into a religion which looks to me like the tail end of a kind of Buddhism. No harm in that; on the contrary, if you like.

I do not much like the article on Monet in the *Figaro*. How much superior that other article was in the *XIXme Siècle!* There you saw the pictures and this only contains commonplaces that depress me.

Today I am busy packing a case of pictures and studies. One of them is flaking off, and I have stuck some newspapers on it; it is one of the best, and I think that when you look at it you will see better what my now shipwrecked studio might have been.

This study, like some others, has got spoiled by moisture during my illness.

The flood water came to within a few feet of the house, and on top of that, the house itself had no fires in it during my absence, so when I came back, the walls were oozing water and saltpeter.

That touched me to the quick, not only the studio wrecked, but even the studies which would have been a souvenir of it ruined; it is so final, and my enthusiasm to found something very simple but lasting was so strong. It was a fight against the inevitable, or rather it was weakness of character on my part, for I am left with feelings of profound remorse, difficult to describe. I think that was the reason why I have cried out so much during the attacks, it was because I wanted to defend myself and could not do it. For it was not for myself, it was just for painters like the unfortunates the enclosed article speaks of that that studio would have been of some use.

Anyhow, we haven't been the only ones.

Brias at Montpellier gave a whole fortune, a whole life to it, and without the slightest apparent result.

Yes—a cold room in the municipal gallery, where you see a heartbroken face and many fine pictures, where you are certainly moved, but moved, alas, as in a graveyard.

Nevertheless it would be difficult to walk through a graveyard that showed more clearly the existence of that Hope which Puvis de Chavannes painted.

Pictures fade like flowers—even some of the Delacroixs have suffered in the same way, the magnificent "Daniel," the "Odalisques" (quite different from those in the Louvre, it was in a single scale of purple shades), but how they impressed me, those pictures fading there, little understood by most of the visitors, who look at Courbet and Cabanel and Victor Giraud, and so on. What are we worth, we painters? Well, I think Richepin is often right, for instance when he brutally bursts in and sends them all back to the madhouse with his blasphemies.

Now, however, I assure you that I know of no asylum where they would be willing to take me in for nothing, even supposing I took on myself all the expenses of my painting and left the whole of my work to the hospital. And perhaps this is, I do not say a great, but still a small injustice. I should be resigned if I found it. If I were without your friendship, they would remorselessly drive me to suicide, and however cowardly I am, I should end by doing it. There, as you too will see, I hope, is the juncture where it is permissible for us to protest against society and defend ourselves. You can be fairly sure that the Marseilles artist who committed suicide did not in any way do it as the result of absinthe, for the simple reason that no one would have offered it to him and he couldn't have had anything to buy it with. Besides, he would drink it, not solely for pleasure, but because, being ill already, he needed it to keep himself going.

M. Salles has been to St. Rémy—they are not willing to let me paint outside the institution, nor to take me for less than 100 francs.

This information is pretty bad. If I could get out of it by enlisting in the Foreign Legion for five years, I think I'd prefer that.

For on the one hand, if I am shut up and not working, I shall recover with difficulty, and on the other hand, they would make us pay 100 francs a month during the whole long life of an incurable madman.

It is serious, and what is one to think? But will they be willing to take me as a soldier? I feel very tired after the conversation with M. Salles and I do not quite know what to do.

I myself advised Bernard to do his service, so is it surprising that I think of going to Arabia as a soldier myself?

I say this to make sure that you will not blame me too much if I go. It's all so vague and strange. And you know how doubtful it is that we shall ever recover what it costs to go on painting. For that matter, I think that physically I am well.

352

If I cannot work unless under surveillance! and in an institution!—Good Lord, is it worth paying money for that! Certainly in that case I could work just as well in the barracks, even better. Anyway, I am thinking about it. You do the same. Let's remember that everything is always for the best in the best of worlds, which is not impossible.

A good handshake.

Ever yours, Vincent

590b

[From *Kunst und Künstler* (Art and Artists), 1928 (1926 Issue, p. 451).]

"With friends of Van Gogh's in Arles" (Memories of travels by Max Braumann).

As he told Serret, who was to be his friend afterward, he only wanted to interrupt his journey in Arles for a short time. But the luminous sky of Provence would not release its hold on him, and so he decided to stay there, and to tackle the manifold problems that came rushing at him in this region....

Serret (librarian of the Municipal Library) relates:

"Vincent lives in my memory as an extremely timid man, a child. I was not interested in him because of his art, because I attached much value to his peculiar manner of painting, nor even perhaps because I had a perception of the leadership which it indicated. To me he was an unhappy man, who suffered much; and sufferings like these are only borne by noble characters. The outward life he led was of the most modest description."

Serret drew a picture of the extremely primitive way in which he prepared his food, and which was also described later by Dr. Rey. "There can be no doubt that his body was perpetually undernourished, and this in conjunction with a productive energy intensified to a frenzy." Serret believes that the greater part of his mental perturbations were attributable to this excessive exploitation of his strength. "Only one thing was important to him, his painting. But occasionally, when the consignments of paints sent by his brother Theo were used up, and he had no means of procuring new materials, he had to give up painting. Then a general dealer by the name of Durand, moved by his misery, took pity on him and gave him the paints...."

One of Serret's colleagues joined us, and contributed the observation: "People did not like to associate with Van Gogh, as he was always hanging about in the brothels. I knew him too. He was my next-door neighbor, so to speak. Along with other young people I used to poke fun at this queer painter. Well, we were only children then. His appearance made a highly comical impression on us. His long smock, his gigantic hat, the man himself continually stopping and peering at things, excited our ridicule."

Serret continues: "At the time, after Doctor Rey had taken care of him and nursed him, he wanted to show his gratitude in his own way. He painted Doctor Rey's portrait, and made him a present of it. However, the doctor thought it so lacking in beauty that he put it in the garret. It is said that there it took the place of a broken windowpane, serving the purpose of keeping out the drafts. Afterward a friend who discovered it in the garret got hold of it...."

Serret can say nothing about the circumstances under which Vincent left Arles at firsthand. The fact is that before that time he had gone on a world tour which lasted several years, and of which he gave a description—Serret is a writer—in a several-volume work. When he came back, the star of the dead painter had risen gloriously. Then, at his own expense, he had a memorial tablet put up in the front of the house where Van Gogh had worked and suffered, which tablet contains the simple words: "The Dutch painter Vincent van Gogh lived in this house in 1887–1888 [sic!]" (*Le peintre hollandais V.v.G. habita cette maison en 1887–1888*)....

At the appointed hour we, Professor Julius Seyler and I, called on Dr. Felix Rey. As his daughter had already told him what kind of information we wanted from him, he started talking without any circumlocution:

"First and foremost Vincent was a miserable, pitiful man, small of stature (please get up for a moment! about your size), lean. He always wore a sort of overcoat, smeared all over with colors—he painted with his thumb and then wiped it on his coat—and an enormous straw hat without a hatband, of the type usually worn by the shepherds of the Camargue as a protection against the scorching sun. He often used to complain of being the only painter in the region, so that he could not talk to anybody about painting. In the absence of any colleague he used to converse with me on the nature of the complementary colors. But for the life of me I could not understand that red should not be red, and green not green!"...

In exactly the same way as Serret, Dr. Rey now described how Vincent used to take his food. "In the morning, before setting out to work with his easel and canvases, he would put a pot of chick peas on the coal fire. Then, when he came back, generally in the evening, dead tired and hungry, the fire had gone out, of course, and the mess of peas was usually only half done and in fact inedible. All the same, he consumed the hardly inviting food, unless he preferred to drink spirits to relieve his stomach."

591

My dear sister,   St. Rémy, 15 May 1889
Many thanks for your letter in which I especially looked for news of my brother. And I find it excellent. I see you have already noticed that he likes Paris, and this more or less surprises you, since you do not like it at all, or rather like mostly the flowers there, such as the wisterias, I suppose, which are probably coming into bloom.

Might it not be a fact that when you are fond of something, you see it better and more truly than when you are not fond of it? For him and me Paris is certainly already something like a graveyard where many artists have perished whom we once knew directly or indirectly.

Certainly Millet, whom you are learning to like so very much, and many others with him, tried to get out of Paris. But as for Eugène Delacroix, for instance, it is difficult to imagine him, as a man, otherwise than as a Parisian.

All this is to urge you—with all caution it is true—to believe in the *possibility* that there are *homes* in Paris and not just apartments.

Anyway—fortunately *you* are yourself his home.

It is rather queer perhaps that the result of this terrible attack is that there is hardly any very definite desire or hope left in my mind, and I wonder if this is the way one thinks when, with the passions lessened, one descends the hill instead of climbing it. And anyhow, my sister, if you can believe, or almost believe, that everything is always for the best in the best of worlds, then perhaps you will also be able to believe that Paris is the best of the cities in it.

Have you noticed that the old cab horses there have large beautiful eyes, as heartbroken as Christians sometimes have? However it may be, we are neither savages nor peasants, and it is perhaps *even a duty* to like civilization (so called). After all it would probably be hypocrisy to say or think that Paris is bad when one is living there. Besides, the first time one sees Paris, it may be that everything in it seems unnatural, foul and sad.

Anyway, if you do not like Paris, above all do not like painting nor those who are directly or indirectly concerned in it, for it is only too doubtful whether it is beautiful or useful.

But what is to be done?—there are people who love nature even though they are cracked or ill, those are the painters; then there are those who like what is made by men's hands, and these even go so far as to like pictures.

Though here there are some patients very seriously ill, the fear and horror of madness that I used to have has already lessened a great deal. And though here you continually hear terrible cries and howls like beasts in a menagerie, in spite of that people get to know each other very well and help each other when their attacks come on. When I am working in the garden, they all come to look, and I assure you they have the discretion and manners to leave me alone—more than the good people of the town of Arles, for instance.

It may well be that I shall stay here long enough—I have never been so peaceful as here and in the hospital in Arles—to be able to paint a little at last. Quite near here there are some little mountains, gray and blue, and at their foot some very, very green cornfields and pines.

I shall count myself very happy if I can manage to work enough to earn my living, for it worries me a lot when I think that I have done so many pictures and drawings without ever selling one. Do not be in too much of a hurry to think that this is an injustice. I myself don't know in the least.

Thanking you again for having written to me, I am so very glad to think that now my brother is not going home to an empty apartment when he goes back in the evening.

I shake your hand in thought, and believe me,

Your brother, Vincent

592

My dear Theo,   St. Rémy, 22 May 1889

The letter I have just received from you gives me great pleasure. You tell me that J. H. Weissenbruch has two pictures at the exhibition—but I imagined he was dead—am I wrong? Certainly he's a mighty good artist and a decent big-hearted fellow too.

What you say about "La Berceuse" pleases me; it is very true that the common people, who are content with chromos and melt when they hear a barrel organ, are in some vague way right, perhaps more sincere than certain men about town who go to the Salon.

If he will accept it, give Gauguin the copy of "La Berceuse" that was not mounted on a stretcher, and another to Bernard as a token of friendship. But if

Mais si Gauguin veut de la berceuse ce n'est qu'absolument comme je juge qu'il la [...] en échange quelque chose que [...] Gauguin lui-même et surtout avec les tournesols plus loin lorsqu'il les aurait vus longtemps. Il faut encore savoir que si tu les mets dans ce sens ci: soit la berceuse au milieu et les deux toiles des tournesols à droite et à gauche cela fait comme un triptyque. Et alors les tons jaunes et orangés de la tête prennent plus d'éclat par le voisinage des volets jaunes. Et alors tu comprendras ce que je t'en écrivais que mon idée avait été de faire une décoration comme je veux par exemple pour le fond d'un cabine dans un navire. Alors le format s'élargissant la facture prend sa raison d'être le cadre du milieu est alors le rouge. Et les deux tournesols qui vont avec sont ceux entourés de baguettes. Tu vois que cet encadrement de simples lattes

Gauguin wants the sunflowers, it is only fair that he should give you something you like equally well in exchange.

Gauguin himself liked the sunflowers better later on when he had been looking at them for a good while.

You must realize that if you arrange them this way, say "La Berceuse" in the middle and the two canvases of sunflowers to the right and left, it makes a sort of triptych.

And then the yellow and orange tones of the head will gain in brilliance by the proximity of the yellow wings.

And then you will understand what I wrote you, that my idea had been to make a sort of decoration, for instance for the end of a ship's cabin. Then, as the size increases, the concise composition is justified. The frame for the central piece

356

is the red one. And the two sunflowers which go with it are the ones framed in narrow strips.

You see that this frame of plain laths does quite well, and a frame like this costs only a very little. It would perhaps be a good idea to frame the green and red vineyards that way, the "Sower" and the "Furrows" and the bedroom interior as well.

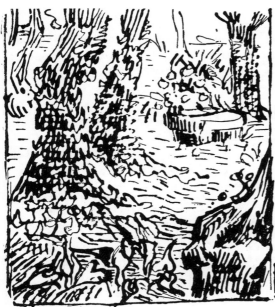

Here is a new size 30 canvas, once again as commonplace as a chromo in the little shops, which represents the eternal nests of greenery for lovers.

Some thick tree trunks covered with ivy, the ground also covered with ivy and periwinkle, a stone bench and a bush of pale roses in the cold shadow. In the foreground some plants with white calyxes. It is green, violet and pink.

The problem—which unfortunately is lacking in the chromos of the little shops and the barrel organs—is to get some style into it.

Since I have been here, the deserted garden, planted with large pines beneath which the grass grows tall and unkempt and mixed with various weeds, has sufficed for my work, and I have not yet gone outside. However, the country round St. Rémy is very beautiful and little by little I shall probably widen my field of endeavor.

But if I stay here, the doctor will naturally be better able to see what is wrong, and will, I hope, be more reassured as to my being allowed to paint.

I *assure* you that I am quite all right here and that for the time being I see no reason at all for going to a boardinghouse in or near Paris. I have a little room with greenish-gray paper with two curtains of sea-green with a design of very pale roses, brightened by slight touches of blood-red.

These curtains, probably the relics of some rich and ruined deceased, are very pretty in design. A very worn armchair probably comes from the same source; it is upholstered with tapestry splashed over like a Diaz or a Monticelli, with brown,

red, pink, white, cream, black, forget-me-not blue and bottle green. Through the iron-barred window I see a squarefield of wheat in an enclosure, a perspective like Van Goyen, above which I see the morning sun rising in all its glory. Besides this one—as there are more than thirty empty rooms—I have another one to work in.

The food is so-so. Naturally it tastes rather moldy, like in a cockroach-infested restaurant in Paris or in a boardinghouse. As these poor souls do absolutely nothing (not a book, nothing to distract them but a game of bowls and a game of checkers) they have no other daily distraction than to stuff themselves with chick peas, beans, lentils, and other groceries and merchandise from the colonies in fixed quantities and at regular hours.

As the digestion of these commodities offers certain difficulties, they fill their days in a way as inoffensive as it is cheap.

But all joking aside, the *fear* of madness is leaving me to a great extent, as I see at close quarters those who are affected by it in the same way as I may very easily be in the future.

Formerly I felt an aversion to these creatures, and it was a harrowing thought for me to reflect that so many of our profession, Troyon, Marchal, Méryon, Jundt, M. Maris, Monticelli and many more had ended like this. I could not even bring myself to picture them in that condition. Well, now I think of all this without fear, that is to say I find it no more frightful than if these people had been stricken with something else, phthisis or syphilis for instance. These artists, I see them take on their old serenity again, and is it a little thing, I ask you, thus to meet the old ones of our profession again? That, joking aside, is a thing I am profoundly thankful for.

For though there are some who howl or rave continually, there is much real friendship here among them; they say we must put up with others so that others will put up with us, and other very sound arguments, which they really put into practice. And among ourselves we understand each other very well. For instance I can sometimes chat with one of them who can only answer in incoherent sounds, because he is not afraid of me.

If someone has an attack, the others look after him and interfere so that he does not harm himself.

The same for those whose mania is to fly often into a rage. The old inhabitants of the menagerie come running and separate the combatants, if combat there is....

It is true there are some whose condition is more serious, who are either dirty or dangerous. These are in another ward.

I take a bath twice a week now, and stay in it for two hours; my stomach is infinitely better than it was a year ago; so as far as I know, I have only to go on. Besides, I shall spend less here, I think, considering that I have work in prospect again, for the scenery is lovely.

What I hope is that at the end of a year I shall know what I can do and what I want to do better than now. Then little by little the idea of a fresh start will come to me. Going back to Paris or anywhere at all in no way attracts me. I think my place is here. Extreme enervation is, in my opinion, what most of those who have been here for years suffer from. Now my work will preserve me from that to a certain extent.

The room where we stay on wet days is like a third-class waiting room in some stagnant village, the more so as there are some distinguished lunatics who always wear a hat, spectacles, and a cane, and traveling cloak, almost like at a watering place, and they represent the passengers.

I am forced to ask you again for some paints and especially for canvas. When I send you the four canvases of the garden I am working on, you will see that, considering my life is spent mostly in the garden, it is not so unhappy.

Yesterday I drew a very big, rather rare night moth, called the death's head, its coloring of amazing distinction, black, gray, cloudy white tinged with carmine or vaguely shading off into olive-green; it is very big. I had to kill it to paint it, and it was a pity, the beastie was so beautiful. I will send you the drawing along with some other drawings of plants.

When they are dry enough, you could take the canvases at Tanguy's or at your place off the stretchers, and then put any new ones that you think worth it on to them. Gauguin ought to be able to tell you the address of a man who could recanvas the canvas of "The Bedroom," and not too expensively. That, *I imagine*, ought to be repaired for 5 francs; if it is more, then don't have it done. I do not think that Gauguin paid more when he had his own canvases recanvased pretty often, or Cézanne's, or Pissarro's.

I am again—speaking of my condition—so grateful for another thing. I gather from others that during their attacks they have also heard strange sounds and voices as I did, and that in their eyes too things seemed to be changing. And that lessens the horror that I retained at first of the attack I have had, and which, when it comes on you unawares, cannot but frighten you beyond measure. Once you know that it is part of the disease, you take it like anything else. If I had not seen other lunatics close up, I should not have been able to free myself from dwelling on it constantly. For the anguish and suffering are no joke once you are caught by an attack. Most epileptics bite their tongue and injure themselves. Rey told me that he had seen a case where someone had mutilated his own ear, as I did, and I think I heard a doctor here say, when he came to see me with the director, that he also had seen it before. I really think that once you know what it is, once you are conscious of your condition and of being subject to attacks, then you can do something yourself to prevent your being taken unawares by the suffering or the terror. Now that it has gone on decreasing for five months, I have good hope of getting over it, or at least of not having such violent attacks. There is someone here who has been shouting and talking like me *all the time* for a fortnight, he thinks he hears voices and words in the echoes of the corridors, probably because the nerves of the ear are diseased and too sensitive, and in my case it was my sight as well as my hearing, which according to what Rey told me one day is usual in the beginning of epilepsy. Then the shock was such that it sickened me even to move, and nothing would have pleased me better than never to have woken up again. At present this *horror of life* is less strong already and the melancholy less acute. But I have no *will*, hardly any desires or none at all, and hardly any wish for anything belonging to ordinary life, for instance almost no desire to see my friends, although I keep thinking about them. That is why I have not yet reached the point where I ought to think of leaving here; I should have this depression anywhere.

And it is only during these very last days that my aversion to life is in any way being radically modified. There is still some way to go from that to will and action.

It is a pity that you are always condemned to stay in Paris and that you never see the country except the immediate environs of Paris. I think that it is not more unfortunate for me to be in the company I am in than for you to have always to do with the inevitable Goupil & Co. From this point of view we are pretty much even. For in your case you can only carry out your ideas partially. However, once we have got used to these annoyances, it becomes second nature.

I think that though the pictures cost canvas, paint, etc., nevertheless at the end of the month it is more profitable to spend a little more in this way and make use of what I have learned after all, than to abandon them, since anyhow you have to pay for my keep. And that is why I am doing it; so this month I have four size 30 canvases and two or three drawings.

But the money question, whatever we do, remains the chief enemy, and we cannot deny or forget it. In this respect I remember my obligation as much as anyone else could. And perhaps I shall be able even yet to pay back all I have spent, for what I have spent I consider as taken, if not from you, at least from the family, so consequently I have produced some pictures and shall do more. In this I am acting as you yourself are acting too. If I were a man of property, perhaps my mind would be more at liberty to work at art for art's sake; now I content myself with thinking that by working industriously, even without thinking about it, I may make some progress.

These are the colors I need:

3 emerald green
2 cobalt
1 ultramarine
1 orange lead   (big tubes)
6 zinc white
5 meters of canvas

Thanking you for your kind letter, I shake your hand, and your wife's too.

Ever yours, Vincent

594

My dear Theo,   St. Rémy, 9 June 1889
Many thanks for the package of canvases, brushes, tobacco and chocolate which reached me in good condition.

I was very glad of them, for I was feeling a little low after working. Also I have been out for several days, working in the neighborhood.

Your last letter, if I remember correctly, was dated May 21. I have had no more news of you since, except only that M. Peyron told me he had had a letter from you. I hope you are well, and your wife too.

M. Peyron intends to go to Paris to see the exhibition and he will pay you a visit then.

What news can I tell you?—not much. I am working on two landscapes (size 30 canvases), views taken in the hills, one is the country that I see from the window of my bedroom. In the foreground, a field of wheat ruined and hurled to the ground by a storm. A boundary wall and beyond the gray foliage of a few olive trees, some huts and the hills. Then at the top of the canvas a great white and gray cloud floating in the azure.

It is a landscape of extreme simplicity in coloring too. That will make a pendant to the study of the "Bedroom" which has got damaged. When the thing represented is, in point of character, absolutely in agreement and one with the manner of representing it, isn't it just that which gives a work of art its quality?

That is why, as far as painting goes, a household loaf is especially good when it is painted by Chardin.

Now what makes Egyptian art, for instance, extraordinary—isn't it that these serene, calm kings, wise and gentle, patient and kind, look as though they could never be other than what they are, eternal tillers of the soil, worshipers of the sun?

I should so have liked to have seen an Egyptian house at the exhibition constructed by Jules Garnier the architect—painted in red, yellow, and blue, with a garden regularly divided into beds by rows of bricks—the dwelling place of beings whom we know only as mummies or in granite.

But then to come back to the point, the Egyptian artists, having a *faith*, working by feeling and by instinct, express all these intangible things—kindness, infinite patience, wisdom, serenity—by a few knowing curves and by the marvelous proportions. That is to say once more, when the thing represented and the manner of representing it agree, the thing has style and quality.

So also the servant girl in Leys's great fresco, once she is engraved by Braquemond, becomes a new work of art—or the little "Reader" by Meissonier, when it is Jacquemart who engraves it—since the *manner of engraving* is one with the thing represented.

As I wish to preserve this study of the "Bedroom," if you would send it back to me, rolled up, when you send me the canvas, I will repaint it.

At first I had wished to have it recanvased because I did not think I could do it again. But as my brain has grown calmer since, I can quite well do it again now.

The thing is that among the number of things you make, there are always some that you felt more or put more into and that you want to keep in spite of everything. When I see a picture that interests me, I can never help asking myself, "In what house, room, corner of a room, in whose home would it do well, would it be in the right place?"

Thus the pictures of Hals, Rembrandt, Van der Meer [Vermeer], are only at home in an old Dutch house.

Now as to the impressionists—once again, if an interior is not complete without a work of art, neither is a picture complete if it is not in harmony with surroundings originating in and resulting from the period in which it was produced. And I do not know if the impressionists are better than their time or, on the contrary, are not yet so good. In a word, are there minds and interiors of homes more important than anything that has been expressed by painting? I am inclined to think so.

I have seen the announcement of a coming exhibition of impressionists called Gauguin, Bernard, Anquetin and other names. So I am inclined to think that a new sect has again been formed, no less infallible than those already existing. Was that the exhibition you spoke of? What storms in teacups.

My health is all right, considering; I feel happier here with my work than I could be outside. By staying here a good long time, I shall have learned regular habits and in the long run the result will be more order in my life and less susceptibility. That will be so much to the good. Besides, I should not have the courage to begin again outside. I went once, still accompanied, to the village; the mere sight of people and things had such an effect on me that I thought I was going to faint and I felt very ill. Face to face with nature it is the feeling for work that supports me. But anyway, this is to show you that there must have been within me some too powerful emotion to upset me like that, and I have no idea what can have caused it.

I get bored to death sometimes after working, and yet I have no desire to begin again. The doctor who has just called says that he is not going to Paris for several weeks, so do not expect his visit yet.

I hope you will write me soon.

During this month I shall really again be in need of

8 tubes flake white
6 " malachite green
2 " yellow ocher
1 " red ocher
2 " ultramarine
2 " cobalt
1 " raw sienna
1 " ivory black

It is queer that every time I try to reason with myself to get a clear idea of things, why I came here and that after all it is only an accident like any other, a terrible dismay and horror seizes me and prevents me from thinking. It is true that this is tending to diminish slightly, but it also seems to me to prove that there is quite definitely something or other deranged in my brain, it is astounding to be afraid of nothing like this, and to be unable to remember things. Only you may be sure I shall do all I can to become active again and perhaps useful, at least in the sense that I want to do better pictures than before.

In this country there are many things that often make you think of Ruysdael, but the figures of the laborers are absent.

Everywhere at home and at all times of the year you see men, women, children and animals at work, and here not a third of that, and besides, it is not the genuine worker of the North. They seem to work here with languid, clumsy hands, without energy. Perhaps this is a wrong idea I have got hold of, not belonging to the country, anyhow I hope so. But this makes things colder than one would think when reading *Tartarin*, but perhaps he had been exiled with his whole family for many long years.

Above all, write me soon, because your letter is very slow in coming; I hope you are well. It is a great consolation to me to know that you are not living alone any more.

If some month or other it should be too difficult to send me paint, canvas, etc., then do not send them, for believe me it is better to live than to work at art in the abstract.

And above all your home must not be sad or dull. That first and painting after.

Then I feel tempted to begin again with the simpler colors, the ochers for instance.

Is a Van Goyen ugly because it is painted entirely in oils with very little neutral color, or a Michel? The shrubbery with the ivy is completely finished. I very much want to send it to you as soon as it's dry enough to be rolled up.

With a right good handshake for you and your wife.

Ever yours, Vincent

596

My dear Theo,   St. Rémy, 25 June 1889

Enclosed you will find an order for paints to replace the one in my last letter. We have had some glorious days and I have set even more canvases going, so that there are twelve size 30 canvases in prospect. Two studies of cypresses of that difficult bottle-green hue; I have worked their foregrounds with thick layers of white lead, which gives firmness to the ground.

I think that very often the Monticellis were prepared like this. You put other colors on that. But I do not know if the canvases are strong enough for that sort of work.

Speaking of Gauguin and Bernard, and that they may well give us painting of greater consolation, I must however add what I have also said many a time to Gauguin himself, namely that we must not then forget that others have done it already. But however it may be, outside Paris you quickly forget Paris, when throwing yourself into the heart of the country, your ideas change; but I for one cannot forget all those lovely canvases of Barbizon, and it seems hardly probable that anyone will do better than that, and unnecessary besides.

What is André Bonger doing; you have not mentioned him in the last two or three letters.

As for me, my health remains very good and work distracts me. I have received —probably from one of our sisters—a book by Rod, which is not bad, but the title *Le Sens de la vie* is really a little pretentious for the contents, it seems to me.

It certainly is not very cheering. I think the author must be suffering a good deal from his lungs and consequently a little from everything.

Anyway, he admits that he finds consolation in the companionship of his wife, which is all to the good, but after all, for my own use he teaches me nothing about the meaning of life, whatever is meant by it. For my part I might well think him a little trite and be surprised that he has had a book like that published these days and gets it sold at 3.50 fr. Altogether I prefer Alphonse Karr, Souvestre and Droz because they are a bit more alive than this. It's true that I am perhaps ungrateful, not even appreciating Abbé Constantin and other literary works, which gave luster to the gentle reign of the naïve Carnot. It seems that this book has made a great impression on our good sisters. At least, Wil had mentioned it to me, but good women and books are two different things.

I have reread with much pleasure *Zadig ou la destinée* by Voltaire. It is like *Candide*. Here the mighty author gives at least a glimpse of the possibility that life may have some meaning, though it is agreed in conversation that things in this world do not always go as the wisest wish!

As for me, I do not know what to wish, to work here or elsewhere now seems to come to very much the same thing, and being here, staying here seems the simplest thing to do.

Only I have no news to tell you, for the days are all the same, I have no ideas, except to think that a field of wheat or a cypress is well worth the trouble of looking at close up, and so on.

I have a wheat field, very yellow and very light, perhaps the lightest canvas I have done.

The cypresses are always occupying my thoughts, I should like to make something of them like the canvases of the sunflowers, because it astonishes me that they have not yet been done as I see them.

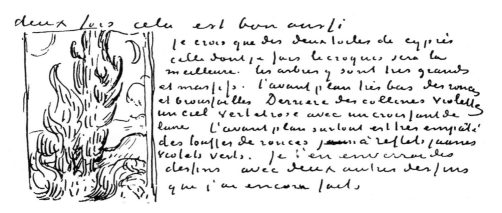

It is as beautiful of line and proportion as an Egyptian obelisk.

And the green has a quality of such distinction.

It is a splash of *black* in a sunny landscape, but it is one of the most interesting black notes, and the most difficult to hit off exactly that I can imagine.

But then you must see them against the blue, *in* the blue rather. To paint nature here, as everywhere, you must be in it a long time. Thus a Monthénard does not give me the true intimate note, for the light is mysterious, and Monticelli and Delacroix felt that. Then Pissarro used to talk very well about it in the old days, and I am still a long way from being able to do what he said would have to be done.

It would of course be a pleasure to me if you sent me the paints, if possible, soon, but above all do only what you can do without too much worry. So if you would rather send them to me at two different times, it will do just as well.

I think that of the two canvases of cypresses, the one I am making this sketch of will be the best. The trees in it are very big and massive. The foreground, very low with brambles and brushwood. Behind some violet hills, a green and pink sky with a crescent moon. The foreground especially is painted very thick, clumps of brambles with touches of yellow, violet and green.

I will send you the drawings of it with two other drawings that I have done too.

That will keep me busy these days. The great question here is to find occupation for the day.

What a pity one cannot shift this building here. It would be splendid to hold an exhibition in, all the empty rooms, the large windows.

I should have very much liked to see that picture by Rembrandt which you spoke of in your last letter.

Some time ago I saw in Braun's window a photo of a picture which must belong to the fine last period (probably in the Hermitage series). In this were great figures of angels, it was "Abraham's Meat," five figures, I think. That was extraordinary too. As moving as the "Men of Emmaus," for instance.

If later on there should ever be a question of giving something to M. Salles—for the trouble he has taken—we should give him Rembrandt's "Men of Emmaus."

Is your health good? A handshake for you and your wife, I hope to send you some new drawings next week.

Ever yours, Vincent

599

Dear brother and sister, St. Rémy, 6 July 1889

Jo's letter told me a very great piece of news this morning, I congratulate you on it and I am very glad to hear it. I was much touched by your thought when you said that neither of you being in such good health as seems desirable on such an occasion, you felt a sort of doubt, and in any case that a feeling of pity for the child who is to come passed through your heart.

Has the child in this case even before its birth been less loved than the child of very healthy parents, whose first movement must have been quick with joy? Certainly not. We know life so little that it is very little in our power to distinguish right from wrong, just from unjust, and to say that one is unfortunate because one suffers, which has not been proved. Remember that Roulin's child came to them smiling and very healthy when the parents were in straits. So take it as it comes, wait in confidence and possess your soul in great patience, as a very old saying has it, and with good will. Leave nature alone. As for what you say about Theo's health, although, my dear sister, I share your anxiety with all my heart, I must comfort you, just because I have realized that his health is, like mine too, more changeable and uneven than feeble.

I very much like to think that illness sometimes heals us, that is to say, when the discomfort comes to a crisis, it is necessary for the recovery of the body's normal condition. No, after he has been married for some time, he will recover his strength, as he still has a reserve of youth and power to restore him.

I am very glad that he is not alone, and truly I do not doubt but that after some time he will recover his old temperament. And then above all, when he is a father and the sense of his fatherhood has come to him, it will be so much gained.

In my life as a painter, and especially when I am in the country, it is less difficult for me to be alone, because in the country you feel more easily the ties that unite us all. But in town, as he has been for ten years on end with the Goupils in Paris, it is impossible to exist alone. So with patience it will all come back.

I am going to Arles tomorrow to get the canvases which are still there, and which I will send you soon. And I am going to send some of them as soon as possible to try to give you, even though you are in town, a peasant's thoughts.

This morning I talked a little with the doctor here—he told me exactly what I already thought—that I must wait a year before thinking myself cured, since the least little thing might bring on another attack.

Then he offered to store my furniture here, so that we should not be paying double. Tomorrow I am going to Arles to talk it over with M. Salles. When I came here, I left M. Salles 50 francs to pay the hospital in Arles; he is sure to have some of it left. But as I was still pretty often in need of various things here, the surplus which M. Peyron had is exhausted. I am rather surprised, myself, that while I have been living with the greatest possible frugality and regularity for six months, not counting having my studio free, I spend no less and produce no more than the previous year, which was comparatively less frugal, and inwardly I feel neither more nor less remorseful, as it is called. That is as much as to say that what is called good and bad is, however—as it seems to me—pretty relative.

I live soberly because I have a chance to, I drank in the past because I did not quite know how to do otherwise. Anyway, I don't care in the least!!! Very deliberate sobriety—it's true—leads nevertheless to a condition in which thoughts, if you have any, move more readily. In short, it is a difference like painting in gray or in colors. I am going to paint more in gray, in fact.

Only instead of paying money to a landlord, you give it to the asylum, I do not see the difference—and it is hardly any cheaper. The work is a thing apart and has always cost me a lot.

Thank you very much for the package of colors and canvas, which I am very glad to have. I hope to go and do the olives again. Unfortunately there are very few vineyards here.

I am well, however, and I have a feeling rather like I had when I was younger, when I was very sober, *too* sober they used to say then, I think. But it doesn't matter, I shall try to overcome my difficulties.

As for being godfather to a son of yours, when to begin with it may be a daughter, honestly, in the circumstances I would rather wait until I am away from here.

Then Mother would certainly rather set her heart on its being called after our father. I for one would think that more logical in the circumstances.

I enjoyed myself very much yesterday reading *Measure for Measure*. Then I read *Henry VIII*, in which there are such fine passages, such as that of Buckingham, and Wolsey's words after his fall.

I think that I am lucky to be able to read or reread this at leisure and then I very much hope to read Homer too at last.

Outside the cicadas are singing fit to burst, a harsh screeching, ten times stronger than that of the crickets, and the scorched grass takes on lovely tones of old gold. And the beautiful towns of the South are in the same state as our dead towns along the Zuyder Zee that once were so bustling. Yet in the decline and decadence of things, the cicadas dear to the good Socrates abide. And here certainly they still sing in ancient Greek. If our friend Isaäcson heard them, it would rejoice his heart.

What Jo writes about your having all your meals at home is splendid. Altogether I think it is all going very well, and once more, while sharing with all my heart all possible uneasiness about Theo's health, with me the hope predominates that in this case a more or less sickly condition is only the result of nature's efforts to right herself. Patience. Mauve always asserted that nature was good and even much more so than is generally believed; was there anything in his life that proves he was wrong? The fits of depression during his last days, do you think? I should be inclined to think otherwise.

Good-by for the present, but I wanted to write straight off and tell you how pleased I am with this morning's news.

A handshake from

Ever yours, Vincent

601[1]

My dear Theo,   St. Rémy, 18 August 1889

I thank Jo very much for having written, and knowing that you want me to drop you a line, I must let you know that it is very difficult for me to write, my head is so disordered. So I am taking advantage of an interval. Dr. Peyron is very kind to me and very patient. You can imagine that I am terribly distressed because the attacks have come back, when I was already beginning to hope that it would not return.

It would perhaps be a good thing if you wrote a few words to Dr. Peyron to tell him that working on my pictures is almost a necessity for my recovery, for these days without anything to do, and without being able to go to the room they had allotted me to do my painting in, are almost unbearable.

(My friend Roulin has written me too.)

I have received a catalogue of the Gauguin, Bernard, Schuffenecker, etc., exhibition, which I find interesting. Gauguin has also written a kind letter, though a little vague and obscure, but after all I must say that I think they are right to have an exhibition among themselves.

For many days *my mind has been absolutely wandering*, as in Arles, quite as much if not worse, and presumably the attacks will come back again in the future; it is *abominable*.

For four days I have been unable to eat because of a swollen throat.

I hope it is not complaining too much if I tell you these details, but I do it to show you that I am not yet in a condition to go to Paris or to Pont-Aven, unless it were to Charenton. I no longer see any possibility of having courage or hope, but

[1] Written in black crayon.

after all, it wasn't just yesterday that we found this job of ours wasn't a cheerful one.

All the same I am pleased that you have got the package from here: the landscapes. Thank you especially for that etching after Rembrandt.[1] It is amazing, and yet it reminds me of the man with the staff in the Lacaze Gallery.

If you want to give me great, great pleasure, then send a copy to Gauguin. Further, the pamphlet on Rodin and Claude Monet is very interesting.

This new attack, my boy, came on me in the fields, on a windy day, when I was busy painting. I will send you the canvas. I finished it in spite of it.

And truly it was a more sober attempt, mat in color without showing it, in broken greens, and reds and rusty yellow ocher, just as I told you that sometimes I felt a great desire to begin again with the same palette as in the North.

I'll send you this canvas as soon as I can. Good-by, thank you for all your kindness. A good handshake for you and Jo.

Vincent

Mother and Wil also wrote me a very nice letter.

While I have no extravagant liking for Rod's book, all the same I have made a canvas of the passage where he speaks of the mountains and the dark huts.

603

My dear Theo,   St. Rémy, 6 July 1889

The reason I am writing you a second time today is that I am enclosing a few words for our friend Gauguin; as I felt my calm returning these last days, it seemed to me sufficient so that my letter would not turn out to be absolutely ridiculous; besides, if you overrefine scruples of respect or sentiment, it is not certain that you gain in courtesy or common sense. That being so, it does one good to talk to the other fellows again even at a distance.

And you, old man, how are things going? Write me a few lines one of these days, for I think that the emotions which must seize the future father of a family, the emotions which our good father so liked to talk about, in your case as in his, must be great and fine, but are for the moment rather beyond your expressing in the rather incoherent medley of the petty vexations of Paris. After all, realities of this kind must be like a good mistral, not very caressing but purifying. I assure you it is a great pleasure to me too, and will contribute much to relieving me of my mental fatigue and, perhaps, of my indifference. After all, it is something to get back one's interest in life, when I think that I am about to pass into the state of an uncle to this boy planned by your wife. I find it very funny that she feels so sure it is a boy, but that remains to be seen.

Anyway, meanwhile the only thing I can do is plod a little at my pictures. I have one going of a moonrise over the same field as the sketch in Gauguin's letter, but in it some stacks take the place of the wheat. It is dull yellow-ocher and violet. Anyway, you will see it in a short time. I am also working on a new one with ivy.

Above all, old man, I beg you not to fret or be worried or unhappy about me;

[1] The figure of an angel.

the idea you might get into your head of this necessary and salutary quarantine would have little justification when we need a slow and patient recovery. If we can manage that, we will save our strength for next winter. Here I imagine the winter must be rather dismal. Anyway, I must try to occupy myself all the same. I often think that next winter I might retouch a lot of last year's studies from Arles. So just lately, having kept back a big study of an orchard which had given me great difficulty (it is the same orchard you will find a variant of, but very vague, in the package), I set myself to work it over again from memory, and I have found the way to express the harmony of the tones more strongly.

Tell me, have you received those drawings of mine? I sent you half a dozen once by parcel post and ten or so later on. If by chance you have not received them yet, they must have been lying at the station for weeks on end.

The doctor here said to me about Monticelli that he always thought him an eccentric, but that as for madness, he had only been a little that way toward the end. Considering all the misery of Monticelli's last years, is there any reason to be surprised that he gave way under too heavy a load, and has one any right to deduce from this that artistically speaking he fell short in his work?

I do not believe it, he had such a power of logical calculation and originality as a painter that it is still regrettable that he hadn't the stamina to make its flowering more complete.

I am sending you enclosed a sketch of the cicadas here.

Their song in the great heat here has the same charm for me as the cricket on the hearth for the peasants at home. Old man—don't let's forget that the little emotions are the great captains of our lives, and that we obey them without knowing it. If it is still hard for me to take courage again in spite of faults committed, and to be committed, which must be my cure, don't forget henceforth that neither our spleen nor our melancholy, nor yet our feelings of good nature or common sense, are our sole guides, and above all not our final protection, and that if you too find yourself faced with heavy responsibilities to be risked if not undertaken, honestly, don't let's be too much concerned about each other, since it so happens that the circumstances of living in a state so far removed from our youthful conceptions of an artist's life must make us brothers in spite of everything, as we are in so many ways companions in fate. Things are so closely connected that here you sometimes find cockroaches in the food as if you were really in Paris; on the other hand, it may be that in Paris you sometimes catch a real feeling of the fields. It certainly is not much, but after all it is reassuring. So take your fatherhood as a good soul on our old heaths would take it, those heaths which, through all the noise, tumult and fogginess of the cities, still remain with us, inexpressibly dear—however timid our tenderness may be. That is to say, let this be your notion of fatherhood, exile and stranger and poor man that you are, and henceforth, find strength, with the instinct of the poor, in the probability of a real, real life of one's fatherland, a life real at least in memory, even though we may forget it every day. Sooner or later, such as it is, we meet our destinies, but certainly it would be a sort of hypocrisy if I were to forget all the good humor, the happy-go-lucky carelessness of the poor devils that we were, coming and going in this Paris that has become so strange, and to let it weigh us down out of proportion to our real load of cares.

Indeed, I am so glad that if there are sometimes cockroaches in the food here, you have your wife and child at home.

Besides, it is cheering that Voltaire, for instance, has left us at liberty not to believe absolutely in everything we imagine.

Thus, while sharing your wife's anxiety about your health, I am not going so far as to believe what now and then for a moment I imagined—namely that worry on my account was the cause of your comparatively long silence—though that is so easily explained when one realizes how her condition must occupy your mind. But it is quite all right, and it is the road that everyone must take in our world.

Good-by for now and a good handshake for you and Jo.

Ever yours, Vincent

In haste, but I wanted not to delay sending the letter for old Gauguin, you surely have the address.

605

My dear Theo,   St. Rémy, 10 September 1889

I like your letter very much, what you say of Rousseau and artists such as Bodmer, that they are in any case *men*, and men such as you would like to see the world peopled with—yes, certainly that is what I feel too.

And that J. H. Weissenbruch knows and does the muddy towpaths, the stunted willows, the foreshortening, the strange and subtle perspective of the canals as Daumier does lawyers, I think that is perfect.

Tersteeg has done well to buy some of his work; I think the reason why people like that don't sell is because there are too many dealers trying to sell different stuff, with which they deceive the public and lead it astray.

Do you know that even now, if by chance I read an account of some energetic manufacturer or even more of a publisher, that then I feel the same indignation, the same wrath as I used to feel when I was with Goupil and Co.

Life passes like this, time does not return, but I am dead set on my work, for just this very reason, that I know the opportunities of working do not return.

Especially in my case, in which a more violent attack may forever destroy my power to paint.

During the attacks I feel a coward before the pain and suffering—more of a coward than I ought to be, and it is perhaps this very moral cowardice which, whereas I had no desire to get better before, makes me eat like two now, work hard, limit my relations with the other patients for fear of a relapse—altogether I am now trying to recover like a man who meant to commit suicide and, finding the water too cold, tries to regain the bank.

My dear brother, you know that I came to the South and threw myself into my work for a thousand reasons. Wishing to see a different light, thinking that looking at nature under a bright sky might give us a better idea of the Japanese way of feeling and drawing. Wishing also to see this stronger sun, because one feels that one could not understand Delacroix's pictures from the point of view of execution and technique without knowing it, and because one feels that the colors of the prism are veiled in the mist of the North.

All this is still pretty true. Then added to this is the natural inclination toward this South which Daudet described in *Tartarin*, and that occasionally I have also found friends and things here that I love.

Can you understand then that while finding this disease horrible, I feel that all the same I have formed ties to the place which are perhaps too strong—ties which may later induce me to long to work here again—and yet in spite of everything, it may be that in a comparatively short time I shall return to the North?

Yes, for I will not hide from you that in the same way that I now eat my food eagerly, I have a terrible desire coming over me to see my friends again and to see the northern countryside again.

My work is going very well, I am finding things that I have sought in vain for years, and feeling this, I am always thinking of that saying of Delacroix's that you know, namely that he discovered painting when he no longer had any breath or teeth left.

Well, I with my mental disease, I keep thinking of so many other artists suffering mentally, and I tell myself that this does not prevent one from exercising the painter's profession as if nothing were amiss.

When I realize that here the attacks tend to take an absurd religious turn, I should almost venture to think that this even *necessitates* a return to the North. Don't talk too much about this to the doctor when you see him—but I do not know if this is not caused by living in these old cloisters so many months, both in the Arles hospital and here. In fact, I really must not live in such an atmosphere, one would be better in the street. I am not indifferent, and even when suffering, sometimes religious thoughts bring me great consolation. So this last time during my illness an unfortunate accident happened to me—that lithograph of Delacroix's "Pietà," along with some other sheets, fell into some oil and paint and was ruined.

I was very distressed—then in the meantime I have been busy painting it, and you will see it someday. I made a copy of it on a size 5 or 6 canvas; I hope it has feeling.

Besides, having seen the "Daniel" and the "Odalisques" and the portrait of Brias and the "Mulatto Woman" at Montpellier not long ago, I still feel the impression they made on me.

That is what braces me, just like reading a fine book, like one by Beecher Stowe or Dickens; but what annoys me is continuing to see these good women who believe in the Virgin of Lourdes, and make up things like that, and thinking that I am a prisoner under an administration of that sort, which very willingly fosters these sickly religious aberrations, whereas the right thing would be to cure them. So I say again, better to go, if not to prison, at least into the army.

I reproach myself with my cowardice, I ought rather to have defended my studio, even if I had had to fight with the *gendarmes* and the neighbors. Others in my place would have used a revolver, and certainly if as an artist one had killed some rotters like that, one would have been acquitted. I'd have done better that way, and as it is I've been cowardly and drunk.

Ill as well, and I have not been brave. Then I also feel very frightened, faced with the sufferings of these attacks, and I do not know if my zeal is anything different from what I said, it is like someone who meant to commit suicide and, finding the water too cold, struggles to regain the bank.

But listen, to be locked up as I saw Braat in the past—fortunately that is long ago—no and again *no*. It would be different if old Pissarro or Vignon for instance would like to take me to live with them. Well, I'm a painter myself, that could be arranged, and it is better that the money should go to support painters than to the excellent sisters of charity.

Yesterday I asked M. Peyron point-blank—Since you are going to Paris, what would you say if I suggested that you should be kind enough to take me with you?

He replied evasively—it was too sudden, he must write you first. But he is very kind and very indulgent to me, and though he is not the absolute master here—far from it—I owe many liberties to him. After all, one must not only make pictures, but one must also see people, and from time to time recover one's balance and replenish oneself with ideas through the company of others. I have given up the hope that it will not come back—on the contrary, we must expect that from time to time I shall have an attack. But then at those times it would be possible to go to a nursing home or even into the town prison, where there is generally a cell.

In any case don't fret—my work goes well, and look here, I can't tell you how it warms my heart again to tell you sometimes that I am going to do this or that, the wheat fields, etc. I have done the portrait of the attendant, and I have a duplicate of it for you. This makes a rather curious contrast with the portrait I have done of myself, in which the look is vague and veiled, whereas he has something military in his small quick black eyes.

I have made him a present of it and I shall do his wife too if she wants to sit. She is a faded woman, an unhappy, resigned creature of small account, so insignificant that I have a great longing to paint that dusty blade of grass. I have talked to her sometimes when doing some olive trees behind their little house, and she told me then that she did not believe I was ill—and indeed, you would say the same thing yourself now if you could see me working, my brain so clear and my fingers so sure that I have drawn that "Pietà" by Delacroix without taking a single measurement, and yet there are those four hands and arms in the foreground in it—gestures and twisted postures not exactly easy or simple.

I beg you, send me the canvas soon if it is possible, and then I think that I shall need another ten tubes of zinc white. All the same, I know well that healing comes—if one is brave—from within through profound resignation to suffering and death, through the surrender of your own will and of your self-love. But that is no use to me, I love to paint, to see people and things and everything that makes our life—artificial—if you like. Yes, real life would be a different thing, but I do not think I belong to that category of souls who are ready to live and also at any moment ready to suffer.

What a queer thing the *touch* is, the stroke of the brush.

In the open air, exposed to the wind, to the sun, to the curiosity of people, you work as you can, you fill your canvas anyhow. Then, however, you catch the real and essential—that is the most difficult. But when after a time you again take up this study and arrange your brush strokes in the direction of the objects —certainly it is more harmonious and pleasant to look at, and you add whatever you have of serenity and cheerfulness.

Ah, I shall never be able to convey my impressions of some faces that I have seen here. Certainly this is the road on which there is something new, the road to the South, but men of the North find penetrating it difficult. And already I can see myself in the future when I shall have had some success, regretting my solitude and my wretchedness here, when I saw the reaper in the field below between the iron bars of the cell. Misfortune is good for something.

To succeed, to have lasting prosperity, you must have a temperament different from mine; I shall never do what I might have done and ought to have wished and pursued.

But I cannot live, since I have this dizziness so often, except in a fourth- or fifth-rate situation. When I realize the worth and originality and the superiority of Delacroix and Millet, for instance, then I am bold enough to say—yes, I am something, I can do something. But I must have a foundation in those artists, and then produce the little I am capable of in the same direction.

So old Pissarro is cruelly smitten by these two misfortunes at once.[1]

As soon as I read that, I thought of asking him if there would be any way of going to stay with him.

If you will pay the same as here, he will find it worth his while, for I do not need much—except work.

Ask him offhand, and if he does not wish it, I could quite well go to Vignon's. I am a little afraid of Pont-Aven, there are so many people there, but what you say about Gauguin interests me very much. And I still think that Gauguin and I will perhaps work together again.

I know that Gauguin is capable of better things than he has done, but to make that man comfortable!

I am still hoping to do his portrait.

Have you seen that portrait that he did of me, painting some sunflowers? Afterward my face got much brighter, but it was really me, very tired and charged with electricity as I was then.

And yet to see the country, you must live with the poor people and in the little cottages and public houses, etc.

And that was what I told Bock, who complained of seeing nothing that tempted him or impressed him. I went for walks with him for two days and I showed him how to make thirty pictures as different from the North as Morocco would be. I am curious to know what he is doing now.

[1] Pissarro had lost his mother and was having trouble with his eyes.

374

And then do you know why the pictures of Eug. Delacroix's—the religious and historical pictures, the "Bark of Christ," the "Pietà," the "Crusaders," have such a hold on one? Because when Eug. Delacroix did a "Gethsemane," he had first gone to see firsthand what an olive grove was, and the same for the sea whipped by a strong mistral, and because he must have said to himself—These people whom history tells us about, doges of Venice, Crusaders, apostles, holy women, were of the same character and lived in a manner analogous to that of their present descendants.

And I must tell you—and you will see it in "La Berceuse," however much of a failure and however feeble that attempt may be—if I had had the strength to continue, I should have made portraits of saints and holy women from life who would have seemed to belong to another age, and they would be middle-class women of the present day, and yet they would have had something in common with the very primitive Christians.

However, the emotions which that rouses are too strong, I shall stop at that, but later on, later on I do not say that I shall not return to the charge.

What a great man Fromentin was—for those who want to see the East—he will always remain the *guide*. He was the first to establish a link between Rembrandt and the Midi, between Potter and what he saw himself.

You are right a thousand times over—I must not think of all that—I must make things, even if it's only studies of cabbages and salad, to get calm, and after getting calm, then—whatever I am capable of. When I see them again, I shall make duplicates of that study of the "Tarascon Diligence," of the "Vineyard," the "Harvest," and especially of the "Red Cabaret," that night café which is the most characteristic of all in its color. But the white figure right in the middle must be done all over again as to color, and better composed. But that—I venture to say—is the real Midi, and a calculated combination of greens with reds.

My strength has been exhausted too quickly, but in the distance I see the possibility of others doing an infinite number of fine things. And again and again this idea remains true, that to make the journey easier for others, it would have been a good thing to found a studio somewhere in this vicinity. For instance, to make the journey from the North to Spain in one stage is not good, you will not see what you *should* see there—you must *get your eyes accustomed* first and gradually to the different light.

I haven't much need to see Titian and Velásquez in the galleries, I have seen some living types which have enabled me to know better what a Midi picture is now than before my poor journey.

Good Lord, Good Lord, the good people among the artists who say that Delacroix is not of the real East. Look here, is the real East the kind of thing that Parisians like Gérôme do?

Because you paint a bit of a sunny wall from nature and well and truly according to our way of seeing *in the North*, does that also prove that you have seen the people of the East? Now that is what Delacroix was seeking, but it in no way prevented him from painting walls in the "Jewish Wedding" and the "Odalisques." Isn't that true?—and then Degas says that drinking in the cabarets while you are painting pictures is paying too dearly for it; I don't deny it, but would he, like me, then go into cloisters or to church?—it is there that I am afraid. That is why I make an attempt to escape by writing this letter; with much love to you and Jo.

Ever yours, Vincent

I still have to congratulate you on the occasion of Mother's birthday. I wrote to them yesterday, but the letter has not yet gone off because I have not had the brains to finish it. It is queer that already, two or three times before, I had had the idea of going to Pissarro's; this time, after your telling me of his recent misfortunes, I do not hesitate to ask him.

Yes, we must be done with this place, I cannot do the two things at once, work and take no end of pains to live with these queer patients here—it is upsetting.

I tried in vain to force myself to go downstairs. And yet it is nearly two months since I have been in the open air.

In the long run I shall lose the faculty for work, and that is where I begin to call a halt, and then I shall send them—if you agree—about their business. And then to go on paying for it, no, then some artist who is hard up will agree to share a home with me.

It is fortunate that you can write that you are well, and Jo too, and that her sister is with you.

I very much wish that when your child comes, I should be back—not with *you*, certainly *not*, that is impossible, but in the vicinity of Paris with another painter. To mention a third possibility, I might go to the Jouves, who have a lot of children and quite a household.

You understand that I have tried to compare the second attack with the first, and I only tell you this, it seemed to me to be caused more by some outside influence than by something within myself. I may be mistaken, but however it may be, I think you will feel it quite right that I have rather a horror of all religious exaggeration. The good M. Peyron will tell you loads of things, probabilities and possibilities, and involuntary acts. Very good, but if he is more definite than that, I shall believe none of it. And we shall see then *what he will be definite about*, if it is definite.

The treatment of patients in this hospital is certainly easy, one could follow it even while traveling, for they do absolutely *nothing*; they leave them to vegetate in idleness and feed them with stale and slightly spoiled food. And I will tell you now that from the first day I refused to take this food, and until my attack I ate only bread and a little soup, and as long as I remain here I shall continue to do this. It is true that after this attack M. Peyron gave me some wine and meat, which I accepted willingly the first days, but he didn't want to make an exception to the rule for long, and he is right to respect the regular rules of the establishment. I must also say that M. Peyron does not give me much hope for the future, and I think this right, he makes me realize that *everything* is doubtful, that one can be sure of nothing beforehand. I myself rather expect it to return, however my work occupies my mind so thoroughly that I think that with the physique I have, things may continue this way for a long time.

The idleness in which these poor unfortunates vegetate is a pest, but there, it is a general evil in the towns and the country under this stronger sunshine, and having learned a different way of life, certainly it is my duty to resist it. I finish this letter by thanking you again for yours and begging you to write to me again soon and with many handshakes in thought.

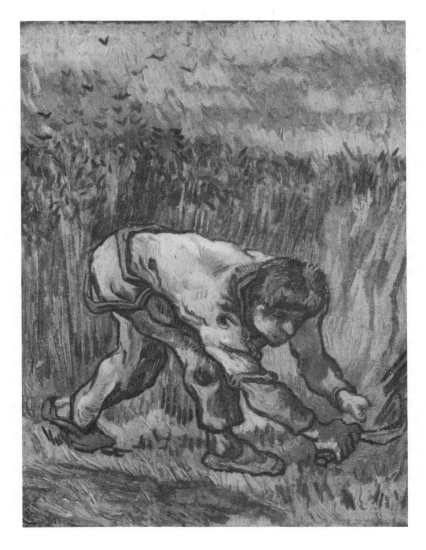

The Reaper, oil, 1889

My dear Theo, St. Rémy, 20 September 1889

Many thanks for your letter. First of all, I am very pleased to hear that you too had already thought of old Pissarro. You will see that there are still some chances, if not there, then elsewhere. Meanwhile business is business, and you ask me to answer you categorically—and you are right—about going into a home in Paris in case of an immediate departure this winter. I answer Yes to that, with the same calm and for the same reasons I had when I came to this place—even if this home in Paris should be a makeshift arrangement, which might easily be the case, for the opportunities to work are not bad here, and work is my only distraction.

But having said this, please note that in my letter I gave a very serious reason as a motive for wishing to make a change.

And I insist on repeating it. I am astonished that with the modern ideas that I have, and being so ardent an admirer of Zola and de Goncourt and caring for things of art as I do, that I have attacks such as a superstitious man might have and that I get perverted and frightful ideas about religion such as never came into my head in the North.

On the supposition that I am very sensitive to surroundings, the already prolonged stay in those old cloisters such as the Arles hospital and the house here would be enough in itself to explain these attacks. Then—even as a last resort—it might be necessary for the moment to go into a private asylum instead.

Nevertheless, to avoid doing, or having the appearance of doing, anything rash, I assure you, after having thus warned you of what I might wish at a given moment—that is, to go away—I assure you that I feel calm and confident enough to wait here another length of time to see if a new attack materializes this winter.

But if I write you *then*—"I want to go away from here"—you should not hesitate, and things should be arranged beforehand, for you would know then that I had a serious reason or even several for going into a home not run, as this one is, by nuns, however excellent they may be.

Now if by some arrangement or other, sooner or later, I should make a move, then let's begin as if practically nothing was wrong, being very cautious all the same and ready to listen to Rivet in the smallest matters, but don't let's begin by taking too formal measures straight off, as if it were a lost cause. As for eating a lot, I do—but if I were my doctor, I'd forbid it. I don't see any advantage for myself in enormous physical strength, because it would be more logical for me to get absorbed in the thought of doing good work and wishing to be an artist and nothing but that.

Both Mother and Wil have changed their surroundings after Cor's departure —they were damned right. Grief must not gather in our heart like water in a swamp. But it is sometimes both expensive and impossible to change. Wil wrote very nicely, it is a great grief to them, Cor's departure.

It is odd, just when I was making that copy of the "Pietà" by Delacroix, I found where that canvas has gone. It belongs to a queen of Hungary, or of some other country thereabouts, who has written poems under the name of

Carmen Sylva. The article mentioning her and the picture was by Pierre Loti, and he made you feel that this Carmen Sylva as a person was even more touching than what she wrote—and yet she wrote things like this: a childless woman is like a bell without a clapper—the sound of the bronze would perhaps be beautiful, but no one will ever hear it. I have now seven copies out of the ten of Millet's "Travaux des Champs."

I can assure you that making copies interests me enormously, and it means that I shall not lose sight of the figure, even though I have no models at the moment.

Besides, this will make a studio decoration for me or someone else.

I should also like to copy "The Sower" and "The Diggers."

There is a photograph of the drawing after "The Diggers."

And there is Larat's etching of "The Sower" at Durand Ruel's.

Among these same etchings is the snow-covered field with a harrow. Then the "Four Hours of the Day"; there are copies of them in the collection of wood engravings.

I should like to have all these, at least the etchings and the wood engravings. It is a kind of study that I need, for I want to learn. Although copying may be the *old* system, that makes absolutely no difference to me. I am going to copy the "Good Samaritan" by Delacroix too.

I have done a woman's portrait—the attendant's wife—which I think you would like. I have done a duplicate of it which is less good than the one from life.

And I am afraid they will take the latter; I should have liked you to have it. It is pink and black.

I am sending you my own portrait today, you must look at it for some time; you will see, I hope, that my face is much calmer, though it seems to me that my look is vaguer than before. I have another one which is an attempt made when I was ill, but I think this will please you more, and I have tried to make it simple. Show it to old Pissarro when you see him.

You will be surprised at the effect "Les Travaux des Champs" takes on in color, it is a very profound series of his. I am going to try to tell you what I am seeking in it and why it seems good to me to copy them. We painters are always asked to *compose* ourselves and *be nothing but composers*.

So be it—but it isn't like that in music—and if some person or other plays Beethoven, he adds his personal interpretation—in music and more especially in singing—the *interpretation* of a composer is something, and it is not a hard and fast rule that only the composer should play his own composition.

Very good—and I, mostly because I am ill at present, I am trying to do something to console myself, for my own pleasure.

I let the black and white by Delacroix or Millet or something made after their work pose for me as a subject.

And then I improvise color on it, not, you understand, altogether myself, but searching for memories of *their* pictures—but the memory, "the vague consonance of colors which are at least right in feeling"—that is my own interpretation.

Many people do not copy, many others do—I started on it accidentally, and I find that it teaches me things, and above all it sometimes gives me consolation. And then my brush goes between my fingers as a bow would on the violin, and absolutely for my own pleasure. Today I tried the "Woman Shearing Sheep" in a color scheme ranging from lilac to yellow. They are little canvases of about size 5.

Thank you very much for the package of canvas and paints. In return I am sending you with the portrait the following canvases:

> Moonrise (ricks)
> Study of Fields
> Study of Olives
> Study of Night
> The Mountain
> Field of Green Wheat
> Olives
> Orchard in Bloom
> Entrance to a Quarry

The first four canvases are studies without the effect of a whole that the others have.

I rather like the "Entrance to a Quarry"—I was doing it when I felt this attack coming on—because to my mind the somber greens go well with the ocher tones; there is something sad in it which is healthy, and that is why it does not bore me. Perhaps that is true of the "Mountain" too. They will tell me that mountains are not like that and that there are black outlines of a finger's width. But after all it seemed to me it expressed the passage in Rod's book—one of the very rare passages of his in which I found something good—about a desolate country of somber mountains, among which are some dark goatherds' huts where sunflowers are blooming.

The "Olives" with a white cloud and a background of mountains, as well as the "Moonrise" and the night effect, are exaggerations from the point of view of arrangement, their lines are warped as in old wood. The olives are more in character, as in the other study, and I tried to express the time of day when you see the green rose beetles and the cicadas flying about in the heat. The other canvases, the "Reaper," etc., are not dry.

And now in the bad weather I am going to make a lot of copies, for really I must do more figures. It is the study of the figure that teaches you to seize the essential and to simplify.

When you say in your letter that I have always only been working, no—I cannot agree—I am myself very, very dissatisfied with my work, and the only thing that comforts me is that people of experience say you must paint ten years for nothing. But what I have done is only those ten years of unfortunate studies that didn't come off. Now a better period may come, but I shall have to get the figure stronger and I must refresh my memory by a very close study of Delacroix and Millet. Then I shall try to get my drawing clearer. Yes, misfortune is good for something, you gain time for study. I am adding a study of flowers to the roll of canvases—nothing much, but after all I do not want to tear it up.

Altogether I think nothing in it *at all* good except the "Field of Wheat," the

"Mountain," the "Orchard," the "Olives" with the blue hills and the portrait and the "Entrance to the Quarry," and the rest tells me *nothing*, because it lacks individual intention and feeling in the lines. Where these lines are close and deliberate it begins to be a picture, even if it is exaggerated. That is a little what Gauguin and Bernard feel, they do not ask the correct shape of a tree at all, but they do insist that one can say if the shape is round or square—and honestly, they are right, exasperated as they are by certain people's photographic and empty perfection. They will not ask the correct tone of the mountains, but they will say: By God, the mountains were blue, were they? Then chuck on some blue and don't go telling me that it was a blue rather like this or that, it was blue, wasn't it? Good—make them blue and it's enough!

Gauguin is sometimes like a genius when he is explaining that, but as for the *genius* Gauguin has, he is very fearful of showing it, and it is touching the way he likes to say something that will really be of some use to the young ones.

What a queer creature he is all the same.

I am very pleased to hear that Jo is well, and I think that you will feel much more in your element thinking of her condition, and of course having worries too, than alone without these family worries. For you will feel more in nature.

When you think of Millet and Delacroix, what a contrast. Delacroix without a wife, Millet surrounded by a big family, more than anybody.

And yet what similarities there are in their work.

So Jouve has still kept his big studio and is working on decoration.

That man came very near to being an excellent painter.

It is money trouble with him, he is forced to do a hundred things besides painting for a living; if he does do something beautiful, it costs him more money than it brings in.

And he is quickly losing his knack of drawing with the brush. That is probably caused by the old way of education, which is the same as nowadays in the studios—they fill in outlines. And Daumier was always painting his face in the mirror to learn to draw.

Do you know what I think of pretty often, what I already said to you some time ago—that even if I did not succeed, all the same I thought that what I have worked at will be carried on. Not directly, but one isn't alone in believing in things that are true. And what does it matter personally then! I feel so strongly that it is the same with people as it is with wheat, if you are not sown in the earth to germinate there, what does it matter?—in the end you are ground between the millstones to become bread.

The difference between happiness and unhappiness! Both are necessary and useful, as well as death or disappearance ... it is so relative—and life is the same.

Even faced with an illness that breaks me up and frightens me, that belief is unshaken.

How I should have liked to see those Meuniers!

Well, let it be understood that if I were to write again expressly and briefly that I should like to go to Paris, I should have a reason for it, which I have explained above. That meanwhile there is no hurry, and that, having warned you, I have confidence enough to wait for the winter and the attack which will perhaps come back then. But if it is a fit of religious exaltation again, then no delay, I would like to leave *at once*, without giving reasons. Only we are not permitted, at least it would be indiscreet, to meddle with the sisters' management or even to criticize them. They have their own beliefs and their own ways of doing good to others, sometimes it does very well.

But I do not warn you lightly.

And it is not to recover more liberty or anything else that I don't have. So let's wait very calmly till an opportunity to settle things presents itself.

It is a great advantage that my stomach is behaving well, and then I do not think I am so sensitive to cold. And besides I know what to do when the weather is bad, having this project of copying several things that I like.

I should very much like to see Millet reproductions in the schools. I think there are children who would become painters if only they saw good things.

Regards to Jo and a handshake. Good-by for now.

Ever yours, Vincent

B 21 [27]

My dear friend Bernard,   Saint Rémy, Beginning of December 1889
Thanks for your letter and especially for the photographs, which give me an idea of your work.

My brother wrote to me about it the other day for that matter, and told me that he liked the harmony of the colors and a certain nobility in many of the figures very much.

Now look here, I am too charmed by the landscape in the "Adoration of the Magi" to venture to criticize, but it is nevertheless too much of an impossibility to imagine a confinement like that, right on the road, the mother starting to pray instead of giving suck; then there are those fat ecclesiastical frogs kneeling down as though in a fit of epilepsy, God knows how, and why!

No, I can't think such a thing sound, but personally, *if* I am capable of spiritual ecstasy, I adore Truth, the possible, and therefore I bow down before that study —powerful enough to make a Millet tremble—of peasants carrying home to the farm a calf which has been born in the fields. Now this, my friend, all people have felt from France to America; and after that are you going to revive medieval tapestries for us? Now honestly, is this a sincere conviction? No! you can do better than that, and you know you must seek after the possible, the logical, the true, even if you should have to forget the Parisian things à la Baudelaire a little. How much I prefer Daumier to that gentleman!

An "Annunciation," of what? I see figures of angels—dear me, quite elegant —a terrace with two cypresses which I like very much; there is an enormous amount of air, of brightness in it; but, once this first impression is past, I ask myself whether it is a mystification, and those secondary figures no longer mean anything to me.

But it will be enough if you will just understand that I am yearning to know such things of yours as that picture which Gauguin has, those Breton women strolling in a meadow, so beautifully ordered, so naïvely distinguished in color. And you will trade this for what is—must I say the word?—counterfeit, affected!

Last year you did a picture—according to what Gauguin told me—which I think was something like this: on a grassy foreground a figure of a young girl in a blue or whitish dress, lying stretched out full length; on the second plane the edge of a beech wood, the ground covered with fallen red leaves, the verdigris-colored tree trunks forming a vertical barrier.

I suppose the hair is an accent of a color tone which is necessary as a color complementary to the pale dress, black if the dress is white, orange if it is blue. But what I said to myself was, what a simple subject, and how well he knows how to create elegance with nothing.

Gauguin told me about another subject, nothing but three trees, an effect of orange foliage against a blue sky; but then very clearly designed, and very categorically divided into planes of contrasting and candid colors—bravo!

And when I compare such a thing with that nightmare of a "Christ in the Garden of Olives," good Lord, I mourn over it, and so with the present letter I ask you again, roaring my loudest, and calling you all kinds of names with the full power of my lungs—to be so kind as to become your own self again a little.

The "Christ Carrying His Cross" is appalling. Are those patches of color in it harmonious? I won't forgive you the *spuriousness*—yes, certainly, spuriousness—in the composition.

As you know, once or twice, while Gauguin was in Arles, I gave myself free rein with abstractions, for instance in the "Woman Rocking," in the "Woman Reading a Novel," black in a yellow library; and at the time abstraction seemed to me a charming path. But it is enchanted ground, old man, and one soon finds oneself up against a stone wall.

I won't say that one might not venture on it after a virile lifetime of research, of a hand-to-hand struggle with nature, but I personally don't want to bother my head with such things. I have been slaving away on nature the whole year, hardly thinking of impressionism or of this, that and the other. And yet, once again I let myself go reaching for stars that are too big—a new failure—and I have had enough of it.

So I am working at present among the olive trees, seeking after the various effects of a gray sky against a yellow soil, with a green-black note in the foliage; another time the soil and the foliage all of a violet hue against a yellow sky; then again a red-ocher soil and a pinkish green sky. Yes, certainly, this interests me far more than the above-mentioned abstractions.

If I have not written you for a long while, it is because, as I had to struggle against my illness, I hardly felt inclined to enter into discussions—and I found danger in these abstractions. If I work on very quietly, the beautiful subjects will come of their own accord; really, above all, the great thing is to gather new vigor in reality, without any preconceived plan or Parisian prejudice. Apart from that, I am very discontented with this year's work; but perhaps it will prove to be a solid foundation for next year. I have let myself be saturated with the air of the little mountains and the orchards; this much gained, I shall wait and see.

My ambition is limited to a few clods of earth, sprouting wheat, an olive grove, a cypress—the latter, for instance, by no means easy to do. I ask myself why you, who like the primitives, and study them, do not seem to know Giotto. Gauguin and I saw a tiny panel of his at Montpellier, the death of some good holy woman. The expression of pain and ecstasy in it is so utterly human that however nineteenth century one may be, one feels as though one were present —so strongly does one share the emotion.

If I saw the pictures themselves, I think it possible that I might be enraptured with the colors all the same; but you also speak of portraits you have done and which you have worked hard on; that's what will be good and where you will have been yourself.

Here is the description of a canvas which is in front of me at the moment. A view of the park of the asylum where I am staying; on the right a gray terrace and a side wall of the house. Some deflowered rose bushes, on the left a stretch of the park—red-ocher—the soil scorched by the sun, covered with fallen pine needles. This edge of the park is planted with large pine trees, whose trunks and branches are red-ocher, the foliage green gloomed over by an admixture of black. These high trees stand out against an evening sky with violet stripes on a yellow ground, which higher up turns into pink, into green. A wall—also red-ocher— shuts off the view, and is topped only by a violet and yellow-ocher hill. Now the nearest tree is an enormous trunk, struck by lightning and sawed off. But one side branch shoots up very high and lets fall an avalanche of dark green pine needles. This somber giant—like a defeated proud man—contrasts, when considered in the nature of a living creature, with the pale smile of a last rose on the fading bush in front of him. Underneath the trees, empty stone benches, sullen box trees; the sky is mirrored—yellow—in a puddle left by the rain. A sunbeam, the last ray of daylight, raises the somber ocher almost to orange. Here and there small black figures wander around among the tree trunks.

You will realize that this combination of red-ocher, of green gloomed over by gray, the black streaks surrounding the contours, produces something of the sensation of anguish, called "noir-rouge," from which certain of my companions in misfortune frequently suffer. Moreover the motif of the great tree struck by lightning, the sickly green-pink smile of the last flower of autumn serve to confirm this impression.

Another canvas shows the sun rising over a field of young wheat; lines fleeting away, furrows rising up high into the picture toward a wall and a row of lilac hills. The field is violet and yellow-green. The white sun is surrounded by a great yellow halo. Here, in contrast to the other canvas, I have tried to express calmness, a great peace.

I am telling you about these two canvases, especially about the first one, to remind you that one can try to give an impression of anguish without aiming straight at the historic Garden of Gethsemane; that it is not necessary to portray the characters of the Sermon on the Mount in order to produce a consoling and gentle motif.

Oh! undoubtedly it is wise and proper to be moved by the Bible, but modern reality has got such a hold on us that, even when we attempt to reconstruct the ancient days in our thoughts abstractly, the minor events of our lives tear us away from our meditations, and our own adventures thrust us back into our personal sensations—joy, boredom, suffering, anger, or a smile.

The Bible! The Bible! Millet, having been brought up on it from infancy, did nothing but read that book! And yet he never, or hardly ever, painted Biblical pictures. Corot has done a "Mount of Olives," with Christ and the evening star, sublime; in his works one feels Homer, Aeschylus, Sophocles, as well as the Gospel sometimes, yet how discreet it is, and how much all possible modern sensations, common to us all, predominate. But you will say, What of Delacroix? Yes!

Delacroix—but then you would have to study in quite a different way, yes, study history, before putting things in their places like that. So, old fellow, the Biblical pictures are a failure, but there are only a few who make such a mistake, and a mistake it is, but I dare think that the reversal will be magnificent!

Sometimes by erring one finds the right road. Go make up for it by painting your garden just as it is, or whatever you like. In any case it is a good thing to seek for distinction, nobility in the figures; and studies represent a real effort, and consequently something quite different from a waste of time. Being able to divide a canvas into great planes which intermingle, to find lines, forms which make contrasts, that is technique, tricks if you like, cuisine, but it is a sign all the same that you are studying your handicraft more deeply, and that is a good thing.

However hateful painting may be, and however cumbersome in the times we are living in, if anyone who has chosen this handicraft pursues it zealously, he is a man of duty, sound and faithful. Society makes our existence wretchedly difficult at times, hence our impotence and the imperfection of our work. I believe that even Gauguin himself suffers greatly under it too, and cannot develop his powers, although it is in him to do it. I myself am suffering under an absolute lack of models. But on the other hand there are beautiful spots here. I have just done five size 30 canvases, olive trees. And the reason I am staying on here is that my health is improving a great deal. What I am doing is hard, dry, but that is because I am trying to gather new strength by doing some rough work, and I'm afraid abstractions would make me soft.

Have you seen a study of mine with a little reaper, a yellow wheat field and a yellow sun? It isn't *it* yet, however, I have attacked that devilish problem of the yellows in it again. I am speaking of the one with the heavy impasto, done on the spot, and not of the replica with hatchings, in which the effect is weaker. I still have many things to say to you, but, although I am writing today now that my head has got a bit steadier, I was previously afraid to excite it before being cured. A very cordial handshake in thought, for you as well as for Anquetin and my other friends, if you see any of them, and believe me,

Sincerely yours, Vincent

P.S. I don't need to tell you how sorry I am for your sake, as well as for your father's, that he did not approve of your spending the season with Gauguin.

The latter wrote me that your military service has been postponed for a year because of your health. Thanks all the same for your description of the Egyptian house. I should have liked to know too whether it is larger or smaller than a rural cottage in this country—in short, its proportions in relation to the human figure. But it is above all about the coloration that I am asking for information.

615

My dear Theo,   St. Rémy, 16 November 1889

I have to thank you very much for a package of paints, which was accompanied by an excellent woolen waistcoat.

How kind you are to me, and how I wish I could do something good, so as to prove to you that I would like to be less ungrateful. The paints reached me at the right moment, because what I had brought back from Arles was almost exhausted. The thing is that this month I have been working in the olive groves, because their Christs in the Garden, with nothing really observed, have gotten on my nerves. Of course with me there is no question of doing anything from the Bible—and I have written to Bernard and Gauguin too that I considered that our duty is thinking, not dreaming, so that when looking at their work I was astonished at their letting themselves go like that. For Bernard has sent me photos of his canvases. The trouble with them is that they are a sort of dream or nightmare—that they are erudite enough—you can see that it is someone who is gone on the primitives—but frankly the English Pre-Raphaelites did it much better, and then again Puvis and Delacroix, much more healthily than the Pre-Raphaelites.

It is not that it leaves me cold, but it gives me a painful feeling of collapse instead of progress. Well, to shake that off, morning and evening these bright cold days, but with a very fine, clear sun, I have been knocking about in the orchards, and the result is five size 30 canvases, which along with the three studies of olives that you have, at least constitute an attack on the problem. The olive is as variable as our willow or pollard willow in the North, you know the willows are very striking, in spite of their seeming monotonous, they are the trees characteristic of the country. Now the olive and the cypress have exactly the significance here as the willow has at home. What I have done is a rather hard and coarse reality beside their abstractions, but it will have a rustic quality, and will smell of the earth. I should so like to see Gauguin's and Bernard's studies from nature, the latter talks to me of portraits—which doubtless would please me better.

I hope to get myself used to working in the cold—in the morning there are very interesting effects of white frost and fog; then I still have a great desire to do for the mountains and the cypresses what I have just done for the olives and have a good go at them.

The thing is that these have rarely been painted, the olive and the cypress, and from the point of view of disposing of the pictures, they *ought* to go in England, I know well enough what they look for there. However that may be, I am almost sure that in this way I'll do something tolerable from time to time. It is really my opinion more and more, as I said to Isaäcson, if you work diligently from nature without saying to yourself beforehand—"I want to do this or that," if you work as if you were making a pair of shoes, without artistic preoccupations, you will not always do well, but the days you least expect it, you find a subject which holds its own with the work of those who have gone before. You learn to know a country which is basically quite different from what it appears at first sight.

On the contrary, you say to yourself—"I want to finish my pictures better, I want to do them with care," lots of ideas like that, when one is confronted by the difficulties of weather and of changing effects, are reduced to impracticability, and finally I resign myself and say, It is the experience and the poor work *of every day* which alone will ripen in the long run and allow one to do something truer and more complete. So slow, long work is the only way, and all ambition and keenness to make a good thing of it, false. For you must spoil quite as many canvases, when you return to the charge every morning, as you succeed with. To paint, a regular tranquil existence would be absolutely necessary, and at the present time, what can you do, when you see that Bernard for instance is hurried, always hurried by his parents? He cannot do as he wishes, and many others are in the same fix.

Tell yourself, I will not paint any more, but then what is one to do? Oh, we must invent a more expeditious method of painting, less expensive than oil, and yet lasting. A picture ... that will end by becoming as commonplace as a sermon, and a painter will be like a creature left over from the last century. All the same, it is a pity it should be this way. Now if the painters had understood Millet better as a man, as some, *e.g.* Lhermitte and Roll, have now grasped him, things would not be like this. We *must* work as much and with as few pretensions as a peasant if we want to last.

And instead of grandiose exhibitions, it would have been better to address oneself to the people and work so that each one could have in his home some pictures or reproductions which would be lessons, like the work of Millet.

I am quite at the end of my canvas and I beg you to send me ten meters as soon as you can. Then I am going to attack the cypresses and the mountains. I think that this will be the core of the work that I have done here and there in Provence, and then we can conclude my stay here when it is convenient. It is not urgent, for after all Paris only distracts. I don't know, however—not always being a pessimist—I think that I still have it in my heart someday to paint a book shop with the front yellow and pink, in the evening, and the black passers-by—it is such an essentially modern subject. Because it seems to the imagination such a rich source of light—say, there would be a subject that would go well between an olive grove and a wheat field, the sowing season of books and prints. I have a great longing to do it like a light in the midst of darkness. Yes, there is a way of seeing Paris beautiful. But after all, book shops do not run away like hares, and there is no hurry, and I am quite willing to work here for another year, which will probably be the wisest thing to do.

Mother must have been in Leyden for a fortnight now. I have delayed sending you the canvases for her, because I will put them in with the picture of the "Wheat Field" for the Vingtistes.

Kindest regards to Jo, she is being very good to go on being well. Thank you again for the paints, and the woolen waistcoat, and a good handshake in thought.

Ever yours, Vincent

620

My dear brother,   St. Rémy, 31 December 1889

Many thanks for your letter of December 22, containing a 50-fr. note. First of all I wish you and Jo a happy New Year and regret that I have perhaps, though quite unwillingly, caused you worry, because M. Peyron must have informed you that my mind has once more been deranged.

At the moment of writing, I have not yet seen M. Peyron, so I do not know if he has written anything about my pictures. While I was ill, he came to tell me that he had heard from you and to ask whether or not I wanted to exhibit my pictures. I told him that I would rather not exhibit them. There was no justification for that and so I hope they were sent off anyway. But anyway I am sorry not to have been able to see M. Peyron today, to ask him what he has written you. Anyway, it doesn't seem very important on the whole, since you say that it starts as late as January 3, so that this will still reach you in time.

What a misfortune for Gauguin, that child falling out of the window and his not being able to be there. I often think of him, what misfortunes that man has in spite of his energy and so many unusual qualities. I think it is splendid that our sister is coming to help you when Jo has her confinement.

May that go well—I think about you two a great deal, I assure you.

Now what you say about my work certainly pleases me, but I keep thinking about this accursed trade in which one is caught as in a net, and in which one becomes less useful than other people. But there, it's no use, alas! fretting about that—and we must do what we can.

Odd that I had been working perfectly calmly on some canvases that you will soon see, and that suddenly, without any reason, the aberration seized me again.

I do not know what M. Peyron is going to advise, but while taking what he tells me into account, I think that he will dare less than ever to commit himself as to the possibility of my living as I used to. It is to be feared that the attacks will return. But that is no reason at all for not trying to distract oneself a little.

For cooping up all these lunatics in this old cloister becomes, I think, a dangerous thing, in which you risk losing the little good sense that you may still have kept. Not that I am set on this or that by preference. I am used to the life here, but one must not forget to make a little trial of the opposite.

However that may be, you see that I write comparatively calmly.

What you write about M. Lauzet's visit is very interesting. I think that when I send the canvases which are still here, he will certainly come back once more, and if I were there, I think I also should start lithographing.

Perhaps these canvases in question will be the very thing for Reid.

Above all, I must not waste my time, I am going to set to work again as soon as M. Peyron permits it; if he does not permit it, then I shall be through with this place. It is that which keeps me comparatively well balanced, and I have a lot of new ideas for new pictures.

Oh, while I was ill there was a fall of damp and melting snow. I got up in the night to look at the country. Never, never had nature seemed to me so touching and so full of feeling.

The rather superstitious ideas they have here about painting sometimes depress me more than I can tell you, because basically it is really fairly true that a painter as a man is too absorbed in what his eyes see, and is not sufficiently master of the rest of his life.

If you saw the last letter Gauguin wrote me, you would be touched to see how straight he thinks, and for so powerful a man to be almost helpless is unfortunate. And Pissarro too, and Guillaumin the same. What a business, what a business.

I have just received a letter from Mother and from Wil too.

Just now you and Jo will have many anxieties at times, and a bad time to get through, but these are the things without which life would not be life, and it makes one serious. It is a good idea to have Wil there.

As for me, don't worry too much. I fight calmly against my disease, and I think that I shall soon be able to take up my work again.

And this will be another lesson to me to work straightforwardly and without too many hidden meanings, which disturb one's consciousness. A picture, a book, must not be despised, and if it is my duty to do this, I must not hanker after something different.

It is time for this letter to go. Once more thanks for yours and a good handshake for you and Jo, believe me,

Ever yours, Vincent

622*a*

My dear friends, Mr. and Mrs. Ginoux,   St. Rémy, December 1889

I do not know whether you remember—I think it rather strange that it is nearly a year since Mrs. Ginoux was taken ill at the same time as myself; and that it remained the same until just before Christmas—for several days in the current year I had a rather bad attack, however it passed off very quickly; I have not had any for a week. So, my dear friends, as now and then we suffer together, this makes me think of what Mrs. Ginoux said—"When you are friends, you are friends for a long time...." Personally I believe that the adversities one meets with in the ordinary course of life do us as much good as harm. The very complaint that makes one ill today, overwhelming one with discouragement, that same thing—once the disease has passed off—gives us the energy to get up and to want to be completely recovered tomorrow.

I assure you that last year I almost hated the idea of regaining my health—of only feeling somewhat better for a shorter or longer time—always living in fear of relapses—I almost hated the idea, I tell you—so little did I feel inclined to begin again. Often I said to myself that I preferred that there be nothing further, that this be the end. Ah, well—it would seem that we are not the masters of this—of our existence—it seems that what matters is that one should learn to want to go on living, even when suffering. Oh, I feel so cowardly in this respect; even when my health has returned, I am still afraid. So who am I to encourage others, you will say, for actually this is hardly my style. Well, it is only to tell you, my dear friends, that I hope so ardently, and even dare believe, that Mrs. Ginoux's illness will be of very short duration, and that she will rise from her sickbed a much stronger fellow, but she knows only too well how fond we all are of her, and how much we wish to see her in good health. In my own case my disease has done me good—it would be ungrateful not to acknowledge it. It has made me easier in my mind, and is wholly different from what I expected and imagined; this year I have had better luck than I dared hope for.

But if I had not been so well cared for, if people had not been so good to me as they have been, I am convinced I should have dropped dead or lost my reason completely. Business is business, and in the same way duty is duty, and therefore it is only fair that I go back to see my brother soon, but I assure you that it will be hard for me to leave the South; I say this to all of you who have become my friends—my friends for a long time.

I have forgotten to thank you for the olives you sent me some time ago, they were excellent; I shall bring back the boxes in a little while....

So I write you this letter, my dear friends, in order to try and distract our dear patient for a moment, so that she may once again show us her habitual smile and give pleasure to all who know her. As I told you, within a fortnight I hope to visit you, wholly recovered.

Diseases exist to remind us that we are not made of wood, and it seems to me this is the bright side of it all.

And after that one dreams of taking up one's daily work again, being less afraid of obstacles, with a new stock of serenity; and even at parting one will tell oneself, "And when you are friends, you are friends for a long time"—for this is the way to leave each other.

Well, we shall be seeing each other soon, and my best wishes for Mrs. Ginoux's swift recovery.

Believe me

Ever yours, Vincent

626a

Dear Mr. Aurier, St. Rémy, 11 February 1890

Many thanks for your article in the *Mercure de France*, which greatly surprised me. I like it very much as a work of art in itself, in my opinion your words produce color, in short, I rediscover my canvases in your article, but better than they are, richer, more full of meaning. However, I feel uneasy in my mind when I reflect that what you say is due to others rather than to myself. For example, Monticelli in particular. Saying as you do: "As far as I know, he is the only painter to perceive the chromatism of things with such intensity, with such a metallic, gemlike luster," be so kind as to go and see a certain bouquet by Monticelli at my brother's —a bouquet in white, forget-me-not blue and orange—then you will feel what

I want to say. But the best, the most amazing Monticellis have long been in Scotland and England. In a museum in the North—the one in Lisle, I believe—there is said to be a very marvel, rich in another way and certainly no less French than Watteau's "Départ pour Cythère." At the moment Mr. Lauzet is engaged in reproducing some thirty works of Monticelli's.

Here you are; as far as I know, there is no colorist who is descended so straightly and directly from Delacroix, and yet I am of the opinion that Monticelli probably had Delacroix's color theories only at secondhand; that is to say, that he got them more particularly from Diaz and Ziem. It seems to me that Monticelli's personal artistic temperament is exactly the same as that of the author of the *Decameron*—Boccaccio—a melancholic, somewhat resigned, unhappy man, who saw the wedding party of the world pass by, painting and analyzing the lovers of his time—he, the one who had been left out of things. Oh! he no more imitated Boccaccio than Henri Leys imitated the primitives. You see, what I mean to say is that it seems there are things which have found their way to my name, which you could better say of Monticelli, to whom I owe so much. And further, I owe much to Paul Gauguin, with whom I worked in Arles for some months, and whom I already knew in Paris, for that matter.

Gauguin, that curious artist, that alien whose mien and the look in whose eyes vaguely remind one of Rembrandt's "Portrait of a Man" in the Galerie Lacaze —this friend of mine likes to make one feel that a good picture is equivalent to a good deed; not that he says so, but it is difficult to be on intimate terms with him without being aware of a certain moral responsibility. A few days before parting company, when my disease forced me to go into a lunatic asylum, I tried to paint "his empty seat."

It is a study of his armchair of somber reddish-brown wood, the seat of greenish straw, and in the absent one's place a lighted torch and modern novels.

If an opportunity presents itself, be so kind as to have a look at this study, by way of a memento of him; it is done entirely in broken tones of green and red. Then you will perceive that your article would have been fairer, and consequently more powerful, I think, if, when discussing the question of the future of "tropical painting" and of colors, you had done justice to Gauguin and Monticelli before speaking of me. *For the part which is allotted to me, or will be allotted to me, will remain, I assure you, very secondary.*

And then there is another question I want to ask you. Suppose that the two pictures of sunflowers, which are now at the *Vingtistes'* exhibition, have certain qualities of color, and that they also express an idea symbolizing "gratitude." Is this different from so many flower pieces, more skillfully painted, and which are not yet sufficiently appreciated, such as "Hollyhocks," "Yellow Irises" by Father Quost? The magnificent bouquets of peonies which Jeannin produces so abundantly? You see, it seems so difficult to me to make a distinction between impressionism and other things; I do not see the use of so much sectarian spirit as we have seen these last years, *but I am afraid of the preposterousness of it.*

And in conclusion, I declare that I do not understand why *you* should speak of Meissonier's "Infamies." It is possible that I have inherited from the excellent

Mauve an absolutely unlimited admiration for Meissonier; Mauve's eulogies on Troyon and Meissonier used to be inexhaustible—a strange pair.

I say this to draw your attention to the extent to which people in foreign countries admire the artists of France, without making the least fuss about what divides them, often enough so damnably. What Mauve repeated so often was something like this: "If one wants to paint colors, one should also be able to draw a chimney corner or an interior as Meissonier does."

In the next batch that I send my brother, I shall include a study of cypresses for you, if you will do me the favor of accepting it in remembrance of your article. I am still working on it at the moment, as I want to put in a little figure. The cypress is so characteristic of the scenery of Provence; you will feel it and say: "Even the color is black." Until now I have not been able to do them as I feel them; the emotions that grip me in front of nature can cause me to lose consciousness, and then follows a fortnight during which I cannot work. Nevertheless, before leaving here I feel sure I shall return to the charge and attack the cypresses. The study I have set aside for you represents a group of them in the corner of a wheat field during a summer mistral. So it is a note of a certain nameless black in the restless gusty blue of the wide sky, and the vermilion of the poppies contrasting with this dark note.

You will see that this constitutes something like the combination of tones in those pretty Scotch tartans of green, blue, red, yellow, black, which at the time seemed so charming to you as well as to me, and which, alas, one hardly sees any more nowadays.

Meanwhile, dear Sir, accept my gratitude for your article. When I go to Paris in the spring, I certainly shall not fail to call on you to thank you in person.

Vincent van Gogh

It will be a year before the study that I am going to send you will be thoroughly dry, also in the thick layers of paint; I think you will do well to lay on a goodly coat of varnish.

In the meantime it will be necessary to wash it a good many times with plenty of water in order to get the oil out. The study is painted with plain Prussian blue, the much-maligned color nevertheless used so often by Delacroix. I believe that as soon as the tones of this Prussian blue are quite dry, you will, by varnishing, get the black, the very black tones, necessary to bring out the various somber greens.

I am not quite sure how this study ought to be framed, but seeing that it makes one think of those nice Scotch materials, I mention that I have observed that a *very simple flat frame* in VIVID ORANGE LEAD would produce the desired effect in conjunction with the blues of the background and the dark greens of the trees. Without it there would not be enough red in the picture, and the upper part would seem a little cold.

My dear Theo,[1]   St. Rémy, 15 April 1890

Today I wanted to read the letters which had come for me, but I was not clear-headed enough yet to be able to understand them.

However, I am trying to answer you at once, and I hope that this will clear away in a few days. Above all I hope that you are well, and your wife and child too. Don't worry about me, even if this should last a bit longer, and write the same thing to those at home and give them kindest regards from me.

Remember me to Gauguin, who wrote me a letter for which I thank him very, very much; I am terribly dazed in the head, but must try to be patient. Once more kindest regards to Jo and her little boy and a handshake in thought,

                                                          Ever yours, Vincent

I take up this letter again to try to write, it will come little by little, the thing is that my head is so bad, without pain it is true, but altogether stupefied. I must tell you that there are, as far as I can judge, others who have the same thing wrong with them that I have, and who, after having worked part of their life, are reduced to helplessness now. It isn't easy to learn much good between four walls, that's natural, but all the same it is true that there are people who can no longer be left at liberty as though there were nothing wrong with them. And that means I am pretty well or altogether in despair about myself. Perhaps, perhaps I might really recover if I were in the country for a time.

My work was going well, the last canvas of branches in blossom—you will see that it was perhaps the best, the most patiently worked thing I had done, painted with calm and with a greater firmness of touch. And the next day, down like a brute. Difficult to understand, things like that, but alas! it's like that. I have a great desire, however, to start working again, but Gauguin also writes that he—and he is robust—also despairs of being able to go on. And isn't it true that we often hear the same story about artists? My poor boy, just take things as they come, don't be grieved over me, it will encourage and sustain me more than you think, to know that you are running your household well. Then after a time of affliction perhaps peaceful days will come again for me too. But all the same I will send you some canvases in a little while.

Russell wrote me too, and I think it is kind of him to have written, showing that he does not altogether forget us; on your part speak of him from time to time, so that people may know that though he works alone, he is a very sound man, and I think he will do good things like what one used to see in England, for instance. He is a thousand times right to barricade himself a bit.

Remember me to the Pissarros, very shortly I am going to read the letters more calmly, and I hope to write again tomorrow or the next day.

[1] On February 24 Dr. Peyron wrote Theo that Vincent had again had an attack after spending two days in Arles. He had been brought back to St. Rémy in a carriage, and it was not known where he had spent the night. The picture representing an Arlésienne which he had taken along with him to Arles was never found. On April 1 Dr. Peyron wrote again that the attack was lasting longer this time, and that it definitely proved that these trips were bad for him.

Dear Mother and sister, St. Rémy, 29 April 1890
After having been unwell for two months, it is only now that I am able to write you a letter.

Until today I have not been able either to bring myself to read your letter or to write one, and the doctor not being at home today, I cannot get the letters and the package you sent me, but in the meantime I don't want to postpone thanking you both most heartily. With all my heart I hope that all is well with you both, and also with Anna and Lies and their families.

Today I wrote Theo and sent him a number of pictures, some of which I expect him to send on to you. So you see I have not been able to work during the most favorable part of spring, consequently things aren't going too well. But what can a man do about it? Every change is not a change for the better, but I am longing to get away from here; what one has to endure here is hardly bearable.

These last few days I have been working on the picture of a lawn in the blazing sun with yellow dandelions. I continued painting even when my illness was at its height, among other things a memory of Brabant, hovels with moss-covered roofs and beech hedges on an autumn evening with a stormy sky, the sun setting amid ruddy clouds. Also a turnip field with women gathering green stuff in the snow.

I have asked Theo to let me have as many of my old drawings as he has kept.

Do you happen to have any of my old studies and drawings at home? Though they may not be good in themselves, they may serve to refresh my memory, and so be the subjects for new work, but I do not want those you have hanging on the walls, for instance. I should prefer quick sketches of peasant figures. But it is not important enough for you to rummage a long time to find them.

With all my heart I hope you are both well; and before long I shall write more. Believe me, I often think of you. I embrace you in thought.

Your loving Vincent

As soon as I heard that my work was having some success, and read the article in question, I feared at once that I should be punished for it; this is how things nearly always go in a painter's life: success is about the worst thing that can happen.

635
My dear Theo and dear Jo, Auvers-sur-Oise, 20 May 1890
Having made Jo's acquaintance, henceforth it will be difficult for me to write to Theo only, but Jo will allow me—I hope—to write in French; because after two years in the South, I really think that I shall say what I have to say more clearly by doing so.

Auvers is very beautiful, among other things a lot of old thatched roofs, which are getting rare. So I should hope that by settling down to do some canvases of this there would be a chance of recovering the expenses of my stay

—for really it is profoundly beautiful, it is the real country, characteristic and picturesque.

I have seen Dr. Gachet, who gives me the impression of being rather eccentric, but his experience as a doctor must keep him balanced enough to combat the nervous trouble from which he certainly seems to me to be suffering at least as seriously as I.

He piloted me to an inn where they ask 6 francs a day. All by myself I found one where I shall pay 3.50 fr. a day.

And I think I ought to stay there until a new arrangement is made. When I have done some studies, I shall see if it would be better to move, but it seems unfair to me, when you are willing and able to pay and work like any other laborer, to have to pay almost double because you work at painting. Anyway, I am going to the inn at 3.50 first.

Probably you will see Doctor Gachet this week—he has a *very* fine Pissarro, winter with a red house in the snow, and two fine flower pieces by Cézanne.

Also another Cézanne, of the village. And I in my turn will gladly, very gladly, do a bit of brushwork here.

I told Dr. Gachet that for 4 francs a day I should think the inn he had shown me preferable, but that 6 was 2 francs too much, considering the expenses I have. It was useless for him to say that I should be quieter there, enough is enough.

His house is full of black antiques, black, black, black, except for the impressionist pictures mentioned. The impression I got of him was not unfavorable. When he spoke of Belgium and the days of the old painters, his grief-hardened face grew smiling again, and I really think that I shall go on being friends with him and that I shall do his portrait.

Then he said that I must work boldly on, and not think at all of what went wrong with me.

In Paris I felt very strongly that all the noise there was not for me.

I am so glad to have seen Jo and the little one and your apartment, which is certainly better than the other one.

Wishing you good luck and good health and hoping to see you again soon, a good handshake,

Vincent

614*a*

Dear Mr. Isaäcson,   Auvers-sur-Oise, 3–8 June 1890
Back in Paris I read the continuation of your articles on impressionism.

Without wanting to enter into a discussion of the details of the subject that you have attacked, I wish to inform you that it seems to me that you are conscientiously trying to tell our fellow-countrymen how things are, basing yourself on facts. As it is possible that in your next article you will put in a few words about me, I will repeat my scruples, so that you will not go beyond a *few* words, because it is *absolutely certain* that I shall never do important things.

And this, although I believe in the possibility that a later generation will be, and will go on being, concerned with the interesting research on the subject of colors and modern sentiment along the same lines as, and of equal value to, those of Delacroix, of Puvis de Chavannes—and that impressionism will be their source, if you like, and future Dutchmen will likewise be engaged in the struggle —all this is within the realm of possibility and certainly your articles have their raison d'être.

But I was straying into vaguenesses: so here is the reason for this letter— I wanted to let you know that in the South I have been trying to paint some olive groves. You surely know the existing pictures of olive trees. It seems probable to me that there are such in Monet's and Renoir's work. But apart from this, I have not seen anything of the work I suppose to exist—apart from this, not much has been made of olive trees.

Well, probably the day is not far off when they will paint olive trees in all kinds of ways, just as they paint the Dutch willows and pollard willows, just as they have painted the Norman apple tree ever since Daubigny and César de Cock. The effect of daylight, of the sky, makes it possible to extract an infinity of subjects from the olive tree. Now, I on my part sought contrasting effects in the foliage, changing with the hues of the sky. At times the whole is a pure all-pervading blue, namely when the tree bears its pale flowers, and big blue flies, emerald rose beetles and cicadas in great numbers are hovering around it. Then, as the bronzed leaves are getting riper in tone, the sky is brilliant and radiant with green and orange, or, more often even, in autumn, when the leaves acquire something of the violet tinges of the ripe fig, the violet effect will manifest itself vividly through the contrasts, with the large sun taking on a white tint within a halo of clear and pale citron yellow. At times, after a shower, I have also seen the whole sky colored pink and bright orange, which gave an exquisite value and coloring to the silvery gray-green. And in the midst of that there were women, likewise pink, gathering fruits.

These canvases, together with a number of flower studies, are all that I have done since our last correspondence. These flowers are an avalanche of roses against a green background, and a very big bouquet of irises, violet against a yellow background, against a pink background.

I begin to feel more and more that one may look upon Puvis de Chavannes as having the same importance as Delacroix, at least that he is on a par with the fellows whose style constitutes a "hitherto, but no further," comforting for evermore.

Among other pictures his canvas, now at the Champ de Mars, seems to contain an allusion to an equivalence, a strange and providential meeting of *very* far-off antiquities and *crude* modernity. His canvases of the last few years are vaguer, more prophetic if possible than even Delacroix, before them one feels an emotion as if one were present at the continuation of all kinds of things, a benevolent renaissance ordained by fate. But it is better not to pursue the subject when one is standing gratefully enthralled before a finished painting like the "Sermon on the Mount." Ah, he would know how to do the olive trees of the South, he *the Seer*. As for me, I tell you as a friend, I feel impotent when confronted with such nature, for my Northern brains were oppressed by a nightmare in those peaceful spots, as I felt that one ought to do better things with the foliage. Yet